Mary
Summer Rain's
Guide
to
Dream Symbols

Judy

Doll

Books by Mary Summer Rain

Nonfiction
Spirit Song
Phoenix Rising
Dreamwalker
Phantoms Afoot
Earthway
Daybreak
Soul Sounds
Whispered Wisdom
Ancient Echoes
Bittersweet
Mary Summer Rain's Guide to Dream Symbols
The Visitation
Millennium Memories
Fireside
Eclipse
The Singing Web

Fiction
The Seventh Mesa

Children's
Mountains, Meadows and Moonbeams
Star Babies

Books on Audio Tape

Spirit Song
Phoenix Rising
Dreamwalker
Phantoms Afoot
The Visitation

Mary Summer Rain's Guide
to
Dream Symbols

Mary Summer Rain
and **Alex Greystone**

HAMPTON ROADS
PUBLISHING COMPANY, INC.

For information write:

Hampton Roads Publishing Company, Inc.
1125 Stoney Ridge Road
Charlottesville, VA 22902

Or call: (434) 296-2772
FAX: (434) 296-5096
e-mail: hrpc@hrpub.com
www.hrpub.com

If you are unable to order this book from your local
bookseller, you may order directly from the publisher.
Quantity discounts for organizations are available.
Call 1-800-766-8009, toll-free.

ISBN 1-57174-100-3

12 11 10 9 8 7 6 5

Printed on acid-free paper in Canada

*To slumbering memories awakened
through the power of dreams
and the wisdom of the watchful dreamer.*

MSR

NOTE: The multi-colored threads that intricately weave a dreamscape tapestry come from the creative subconscious of all unique individuals who, collectively, manifest a corresponding range of interpretive designs. A singular symbol will never mean the same for everyone; neither will it always mean the same for one person each time it is encountered. Therefore, this book does not presume to present definitive explanatory definitions, but rather it quietly invites the dreamer into the vast expanse of universal interpretations that remain . . . timeless.

Mary Summer Rain

Foreword

. . . from Alex Greystone

*D*uring my college years and through the ensuing decades of teaching and learning the skills of various professions, the seemingly endless search for spiritual fulfillment remained my highest priority. Purity of the Truths and locating the source of these took precedence over all my other endeavors. This primal quest led me along a multitude of diverse trails; yet, even after I gave close scrutiny to each of these varied philosophies, never did the truth finally ring clear until someone handed me a book entitled *Dreamwalker*.

This book was a piece of the spiritual treasure I'd long sought, and it was eagerly followed by everything Mary Summer Rain had written. Scrutinizing all the material within those subsequent volumes, I knew my long search had reached its conclusion. Ultimately, we became best of friends after I relocated to the Rocky Mountain region, where we conversed in a comfortable and open manner.

And so it was that on a sunny autumn afternoon I approached her on the subject of her dream material. I'd heard various readers comment that they'd wished that all her symbology were contained in a single volume for easier and quicker access. These same individuals frequently expressed the personal need for a wider range of symbols because many of their dreamscape fragments were not listed in Mary's *Earthway* or *Daybreak* interpretations.

Mary listened as I made some suggestions. Perhaps she could write a more comprehensive dream book—one that included a widely expanded listing of words and had much shorter definitions. I, for one, didn't especially like having to peruse a long explanation for a symbol I was looking up. My nature tends toward wanting the shortest answer as quickly as possible. Concise and to the point.

After hearing what I'd had to say, she frowned. "You mean something like a quick-reference guide. Something fast and as simple as possible." Then she grinned. "And you think I've got time to put this big volume of work together?"

That's when I grinned. "People say you're a prolific writer. This would be something that isn't out there. This would be a book for everyone, not just your readers. People everywhere want to know what their dreams mean. If they had some kind of quick-reference dictionary they could turn to, it'd mean a lot."

She agreed but was still somewhat reluctant. I remained silent as she thought on it.

Mary's eyes brightened. "I know," she beamed back at me, "*you* do the book!"

That response was the last I expected to hear from her. "Me? I'm not a writer."

Then she explained how it could be done without taking valuable time away from her other projects. She had little time left to accomplish all she had to do.

Mary Summer Rain was not one to expend time on the trivial aspects of the physical dimension. She existed on a higher plane, and her thought process was always "way up there." This I learned after spending much time with her and experiencing her thought patterns first hand.

So what she came up with was a way for people to have easy access to an extremely handy dream dictionary without her having to expend time on its production. Her proposal was for me to supply the entry words and do the technical part of putting the volume together. Her part would be providing short definitions to my entry words. All interpretations in this volume are Mary's. We put quotation marks around "key" words in some of the interpretations to pique your memory and help you make your own associations. Once we agreed on how it'd be done, she liked the project. All of her extensive background and technical explanations regarding dreams would remain for the reader to learn about in her previous *Earthway* and *Daybreak* books, making this new volume a one-of-its-kind tool for dreamers everywhere.

Alex Greystone

Foreword

...from Mary Summer Rain

*A*fter working six months on supplying interpretations to a listing of nearly 15,000 words, it became part of my routine to take breaks for the purpose of insuring that I remained focused and centered. For me, the only possible source for this grounding was to place myself within the comforting arms of the forest surrounding my cabin. And it was there, on one crisp and sun-dappled February afternoon, that Alex Greystone found me sitting among the snow-covered pines.

My friend quietly sat beside me and, for a measure of time, spoke not a word while we shared the sparkling beauty and magical essence of the deep, silent wood. And when the ember of my cedar incense had burned down to its last, my gaze came to rest on the face of my friend.

Alex smiled and respectfully whispered. "I have something to tell you."

My brow rose in question.

The smile broadened. "No-Eyes knew you were going to write this dream book. She predicted it."

My lack of any response encouraged Greystone to continue.

"She told you about this book way back in 1982."

I looked up at a pine bough where a plump chickadee had alighted and sent a gossamer veil of glitter cascading down through the sunrays. My eyes closed then slowly opened. "How is it you think you know something she said when you weren't even there? I don't remember any statement like that coming from her."

"She told you a lot. She gave you a lot of information and said volumes. Some of those things were cloaked in inference. Some of those things were mere suggestion."

The chickadee too was now joined by a friend. They appeared to take an interest in the two humans sitting on the fallen log.

"Alex," I softly said, "I'm really tired and I just don't recall anything about No-Eyes predicting that I'd write a whole dream book."

It was then that my friend pulled an old dog-eared copy of *Spirit Song* from a jacket pocket. The book was opened to a marked page and set in my hand. A gloved finger pointed to the print.

I read the words set down there. I read the words No-Eyes had spoken fourteen years ago. Over and over I read them. And when I looked to Alex, my friend was gone. I had been left alone to ponder the prediction my mentor had made so long ago. I had been left alone to relive that long-ago day. I had been left alone to . . . remember.

Mary Summer Rain

A

AARDVARK represents a tendency to hide from problems.

ABACUS denotes a need to "refigure" an old situation or condition.

ABALONE symbolizes inherent beauty of spiritual gifts, talents, or knowledge.

ABANDON connotes that which has been left unattended or shed.

ABBESS represents spiritual grace in leadership.

ABBEY symbolizes a need to regain one's spiritual sacredness toward beliefs.

ABBOT See abbess.

ABBREVIATIONS represent a need to cut short certain aspects in life.

ABDICATE denotes a need to finally leave something alone.

ABDOMEN means to take heed of one's inner prompting.

ABDUCTION denotes the "taking" of something the dreamer has not earned the right to own.

ABERRATION See abnormality.

ABEYANCE indicates a need to keep one's distance.

ABHOR means a hidden aversion.

ABIDANCE (compliance) represents a warning to follow the letter and spirit of the law.

ABIDING (enduring) connotes a lasting situation.

ABILITIES See talents.

ABJURE See forswear.

ABNORMALITY represents a diversion from the norm.

ABODE See house.

ABOLISH denotes a warning to "get rid" of something in one's life.

ABOMINABLE SNOWMAN represents spiritual truths that are not easily accepted.

ABORIGINE means a back-to-basics simplicity is required.

ABORTION symbolizes a "voluntary separation" from something.

ABORTIONIST denotes one who instigates a separation.

ABOUT-FACE represents a return to rightness.

ABOVE (direction) means a higher level.

ABOVEBOARD means following the law or rules.

ABOVE GROUND represents conventional standards in society.

ABRACADABRA See charm.

ABRASIONS (skin) mean aspects causing friction in life.

ABRIDGE symbolizes a need to curtail or shorten something.

ABSCESSES connote aspects leading to negative conditions.

ABSENT refers to a void in one's life.

ABSENTEE BALLOT signifies one's right to an opinion.

ABSENTMINDED reflects a lack of awareness.

ABSINTHE means a self-imposed bitterness in one's life.

ABSOLUTE PITCH represents something perfectly matched.

ABSOLUTION means dreamer must shed self-guilt.

ABSORBENT signifies a need to "take in" something.

ABSTINENCE warns of the need to "stop doing something" in life.

ABSTRACT (painting) symbolizes confusion.

ABSTRACT OF TITLE warns one to double-check facts.

ABSURDITY connotes an outrageous or ridiculous situation or belief.

ABUNDANCE is synonymous with enough or more than "enough" of something.

ABUSE means the serious misuse of something in one's life.

ABUT advises the need to "touch" or "get close."

ABYSS warns of a path to nowhere.

ACADEMY refers to unyielding and strict indoctrination.

ACCELERATOR symbolizes rate of one's action taken.

ACCENT means more emphasis is needed.

ACCEPTANCE SPEECH indicates one's need to acknowledge something.

ACCESS connotes the "way."

ACCESS CODE warns of a readiness needed before further advancement.

ACCESSORY represents useless aspects in one's life.

ACCESS ROAD points the way.

ACCESS TIME warns of the importance of being prepared for one's answers to questions asked.

ACCIDENT is a warning symbol that cautions one to be watchful.

ACCIDENT INSURANCE See insurance.

ACCIDENT PRONE represents a careless individual.

ACCLIMATIZE indicates the need to accept situations.

ACCOLADES come as praise for the dreamer.

ACCOMMODATION signifies the need to compromise.

ACCOMPANIMENT refers to the need for symmetry in one's life.

ACCOMPLICE warns of a negative relationship.

ACCORDION means alignment with the truth.

ACCOUNTANT symbolizes the need to make a personal accounting.

ACCOUNT represents the balance of payments (karma) in one's life.

ACCOUTERMENT connotes symbols of one's personal identity.

ACCREDITATION signifies one's level or standard of readiness.

ACCRUAL warns of the need for further knowledge gained.

ACCUMULATION indicates excesses.

ACCURSED (under a curse) denotes one's tendency toward suggestibility.

ACCUSATION signifies possible wrongdoing.

ACE means a winning situation.

ACE IN A HOLE symbolizes a secret advantage.

ACERBIC warns the dreamer of a "bitterness" in one's life.

ACETYLENE TANK advises of a good situation that could turn explosive.

ACHES represent life pains the dreamer allows self to feel.

ACHIEVEMENT TEST means personal advancement.

ACHILLES (Greek mythology) warns one of weak points.

ACID signifies a "burning" situation or relationship.

ACID ON HEAD represents a drug user.

ACIDOPHILUS MILK signifies the need to better digest information.

ACID RAIN warns of dangerous spiritual concepts.

ACID ROCK connotes negative influences.

ACID TEST symbolizes ultimate verification.

ACID WASHING refers to a "lightening up" needed.

ACKNOWLEDGMENT means some type of response is required.

ACME See summit.

ACNE signifies the need to remove negative aspects from one's life.

ACOLYTE warns of misplaced adoration of spiritual personalities.

ACORNS signify beginning traits of an unyielding personality.

ACOUSTICIAN means one who insists on being accurately heard.

ACQUAINTANCE refers to people in one's life who will affect changes.

ACQUIESCE connotes a "giv-ing-in" situation.

ACQUISITION signifies some-thing needed in the dreamer's life.

ACQUITTAL denotes inno-cence.

ACRE symbolizes the extent of one's spiritual talents.

ACRIMONY See acerbic.

ACROBAT represents the "con-tortions" one goes through to gain a goal.

ACRONYM advises one to give greater attention to one's path.

ACROPHOBIA (fear of high places) denotes a reluctance to gain higher attainment or knowledge.

ACROSS A BOARD refers to "everyone."

ACTIVATED CHARCOAL de-notes the need to "filter" informa-tion.

ACT OF GOD represents unpre-ventable situations.

ACTIVE LIST symbolizes one's readiness for action.

ACTIVIST signifies one who fights for one's beliefs.

ACTIVITIES AND POSI-TIONS of people in dreams are extremely important to take note of and recall. They shed invalu-able light on the overall intent and serve to clarify other questionable symbols. See specific activities.

ACTOR/ACTRESS warns of the need to stop "acting."

ACUPRESSURE See shiatsu.

ACUPUNCTURE denotes the need to give closer attention to specific aspects of a situation.

ADAGIO (dance) reflects the need for trust.

ADAM (biblical) characterizes a weak personality; lack of self-control.

ADAMANT See stubborn.

ADAM'S APPLE symbolizes difficulty in "swallowing" for-eign ideas.

ADAPTERS signify an ability to adapt to changing situations.

ADDENDUM means something additional must be included in a situation or relationship.

ADDER refers to a venomous na-ture.

ADDICT symbolizes one who is not in control of one's life.

ADDING MACHINE represents the need to more accurately cal-culate one's situations and rela-tionships. Closer attention needed.

ADDITION (symbol) means something more is needed in one's life.

ADDITIVE designates some-thing not of pure form.

ADDLE See confusion.

ADDRESS represents an important place for the dreamer.

ADDRESS BOOK refers to quality of friends. Check its condition.

ADENOID symbolizes difficulty in speaking.

ADEPT denotes a proficiency.

ADHESION signifies a strong attachment to something.

ADHESIVE represents the need to "connect" with someone or bring a situation together.

ADHESIVE TAPE denotes the need for the dreamer to bring a connectedness into life. He or she is too scattered.

AD HOC symbolizes an active one-mindedness.

ADJOURN means a time-out needed.

ADJUDICATE warns to make a legal settlement.

ADJUSTING designates the need to make alterations, usually acceptance.

AD LIBS signify the need to stop making excuses in life.

ADMINISTRATOR refers to the need to oversee a situation.

ADMIRAL signifies one who is in command, not necessarily properly so.

ADMIRATION cautions the dreamer against excesses in this area.

ADMISSION TICKET connotes one's right to participate in something.

ADMONISHMENT is always a strong warning symbol.

ADOBE means a "down-to-earth" attitude or relationship.

ADOLESCENT denotes a juvenile outlook or belief.

ADONIS (Greek mythology) warns against self-love.

ADOPTING connotes a "taking-in" of something.

ADORATION is a warning symbol. Only God is allowed to be adored.

ADORNMENT represents one's outward presentation of self.

ADRENAL GLANDS signify aspects affecting one's emotions.

ADRENALINE/EPINEPHRINE refers to situations or individuals who bring about high emotion in the dreamer's life.

ADRIFT means spiritual "drifting."

ADULT denotes a mature aspect.

ADULTERY warns against the taking of something that cannot be yours.

ADVANCE (payment) symbolizes responsibility.

ADVANCE GUARD refers to the need to be watchful.

ADVANCE PERSON signifies preparedness.

ADVENTUROUS warns the dreamer to be more cautious.

ADVERSARY signifies an opposition aspect in one's life.

ADVERTISEMENT cautions one to look closer at a situation.

ADVERTISER is one who attempts to get people's attention.

ADVISING symbolizes action the dreamer should take.

ADVISOR suggests the dreamer needs to be counseled.

ADVOCATE designates an action one should take.

ADZ represents personal work required.

AERATOR connotes a need for breathing room or less intense mental concentration.

AERIALIST cautions against compulsiveness in thought or convoluted thought patterns.

AERIAL LADDER refers to the reaching for higher thought or deeper meanings to life.

AERIAL RAILWAY See cable car.

AERIE signifies high philosophical thought.

AEROBIC EXERCISE represents a caution against being over-emotional.

AERODYNAMIC (shape) means streamlined thought.

AERONAUTICS refer to one's energy applied to thought.

AERONEUROSIS warns of excessive thought given to an issue.

AEROPHOBIA signifies one's fear of expressing one's own opinion or thoughts.

AEROSOL CANS warn the dreamer of being "under pressure" too much.

AEROSPACE refers to how one processes one's thoughts.

AESOP will be one who speaks truth in a simplistic manner.

AESTHETICIAN is one who has mesmerizing speech, yet may not always speak the truth.

AFFAIR symbolizes lack of loyalty.

AFFECTATIONS represent a false sense of self or the need to impress others.

AFFIDAVIT refers to proof.

AFFINITY GROUP denotes one's lack of individuality and ability to stand alone for one's beliefs.

AFFIRMATION means confidence in one's belief system.

AFFIRMATIVE ACTION connotes equality.

AFFLICTION represents aspects in one's life that the dreamer allows to cause negative effects.

AFFLUENT signifies earthly wealth.

AFGHAN See blanket.

AFGHAN (dog breed) infers an interfering friend or associate.

A-FRAME (house design) symbolizes one's lifestyle striving toward spiritual alignment.

AFRICA represents uncluttered thoughts and ideas.

AFRICANIZED BEE See killer bee.

AFRICAN VIOLET denotes purity of manner and thought.

AFRO (hair style) alludes to confused thoughts.

AFTERBIRTH refers to aspects leading up to the "birth" of an idea.

AFTERBURNER denotes more physical or mental energy required to avoid quitting before something is accomplished.

AFTERGLOW signifies inner light.

AFTER-HOURS represents the need for additional work applied to an aspect of the dreamer's life.

AFTERIMAGE symbolizes impressions one is left with.

AFTERLIFE connotes a reassurance that no situation is hopeless.

AFTERMATH usually means the consequences of something and comes as a premonition type of symbol.

AFTERNOON designates a more relaxed time to accomplish something.

AFTERPAINS symbolize the need to let go of a hurtful aspect.

AFTERSHAVE represents the need to soothe an abrasive situation or relationship.

AFTERSHOCK signifies negative effects remaining after an event in the dreamer's life.

AFTERTASTE denotes secondary thoughts on an issue.

AFTERTHOUGHT symbolizes the need to thoroughly discuss something and think it through before leaving the issue.

AFTERWORD See epilogue.

AGATE designates multiple talents.

AGAVE signifies one's diversity.

AGENCY denotes a controlling center of operation.

AGENDA cautions one to give more serious attention to responsibility.

AGENT refers to a "middleman" who is not necessary.

AGENT ORANGE represents an extremely negative aspect in one's life. This being one that may appear beneficial at first.

AGE OF AQUARIUS means a time of great change and major shifts in societal thought.

AGE OF CONSENT warns of being old enough to know better or take responsibility for one's actions.

AGE OF REASON means old enough to understand.

AGGRANDIZE is a serious caution against boastfulness.

AGGRAVATE warns of one's habit of making situations worse.

AGGREGATE defines a need to consider the "whole" rather than focusing on the parts.

AGGRESSOR designates individuals who may turn on one.

AGILITY signifies one's talent to persevere.

AGING denotes the passing of time in the dreamer's life.

AGITATION symbolizes aspects in the dreamer's life that cause mental or emotional disturbances.

AGONY signifies the need to stop dwelling on the past.

AGNOSTIC warns of the tendency to demand proof of everything.

AGOUTI connotes an introverted personality.

AGREEMENT represents an aspect in the dreamer's life that must be resolved.

AGRICIDE represents an intentionally destructive nature.

AGRICULTURE symbolizes one's interest in seeing things come to fruition.

AGROCHEMICAL denotes as-pects in one's life that appear to improve situations, yet may prove to be detrimental in the end.

AGROUND designates an off-course spiritual situation.

AID signifies a need with which the dreamer can assist.

AIDE denotes the requirement for an assistant or helper.

AIDE-DE-CAMP symbolizes one's need to be more regimented and efficient.

AIDS (disease) represents fear of expressing intimate feelings.

AIKIDO See martial arts.

AILMENT signifies aspects in one's life that could be detrimental.

AIM reflects a personal goal, purpose, or chosen course in life.

AIMLESS warns against having no ambition or direction in life.

AIR always symbolizes one's mental/emotional state.

AIR BAG denotes the need to protect one's thoughts.

AIR BASE connotes the mind and its condition in respect to one's thought patterns and process.

AIRBORNE refers to the act of thinking.

AIRBRUSH warns against "touching up," changing one's basic ideas to please others.

AIR CASTLE means daydreaming.

AIR CONDITIONER represents "cool" or cold attitudes. Insensitivity.

AIRCRAFT See airplane.

AIRCRAFT CARRIER symbolizes a caution for the dreamer to cease letting one's thoughts and opinions ride on those of others.

AIRDROP connotes the "dropping" of new ideas. A mental laziness.

AIRFIELDS represent how an individual "takes off" with new ideas and plans.

AIR FILTER refers to the need to "filter" new ideas instead of letting them flood in and overwhelm.

AIRFLOW signifies free-flowing thought patterns.

AIR FORCE represents forced thought or opinions on another.

AIRFREIGHT means excessive thought, "bulk" mental weight.

AIR GUN signifies explosive thoughts, ideas.

AIRHEAD denotes one who cannot discern incoming information, an individual who fails to recognize the varying values of thoughts and ideas.

AIR LANE symbolizes one's lack of thought diversity and individuality.

AIR LAYERING means to intermix the application of various thoughts.

AIRLESS represents a thought-less personality. No creativity; no ingenuity.

AIRLIFT connotes renewed spark to old thoughts and ideas.

AIRLINER See airplane.

AIR LOCK signifies thoughts one shuts off from self. Self-imposed ignorance.

AIRMAIL refers to one's acceptance of another's idea.

AIRMAN represents one who is a concentrated thinker.

AIR MATTRESS denotes the need to "sleep on it."

AIRPLANE represents highest ideals, attitudes, and belief systems.

AIR PLANT typifies an intellectual; learning is a priority in life.

AIR POCKET symbolizes a temporary loss of ideas or new thoughts on an issue.

AIRPORT TERMINAL denotes one's ability to sort out thoughts and ideas.

AIR PUMP refers to the ability to expand on thoughts. Take ideas further.

AIR RAID signifies a warning to stop allowing others to change your mind, attitudes, or thoughts on an issue.

AIR RIFLE See air gun.

AIRSICKNESS symbolizes a fear of having or expressing one's unique or different ideas.

AIR SOCK See windsock.

AIRSPACE denotes the need to make time to think. Contemplate.

AIR SPEED refers to rate of thought and how ideas are processed.

AIR STRIKE connotes a warning for the dreamer to protect self from harmful ideas or belief systems.

AIRSTRIP represents the manner in which one's ideas are expressed.

AIR TAXI (commuter plane) signifies short-term ideas that are quickly exchanged for others.

AIR TERRORISM warns against forced ideas or allowing others to change your mind.

AIRTIGHT signifies solid ideals or thoughts on an issue.

AIRTIME symbolizes one's tendency to "broadcast" personal thoughts, ideas, or beliefs.

AIR TRAFFIC CONTROLLER indicates the need to keep one's thoughts from crossing or mixing, creating confusion.

AIR WALK signifies "connecting" thoughts. The ability to put ideas and concepts together.

AIRWAVES connote various levels of thought.

AIRWAY most often refers to inspiration. New life breathed into an idea or old thought.

AIRWORTHY means "worthy" ideas or thoughts.

AISLE represents a passageway for the dreamer.

AJAR indicates an "out" or "opening" left for the dreamer.

ALABASTER refers to a "hard coldness" in attitude.

À LA CARTE symbolizes a caution to look at aspects separately instead of as a conglomerate whole.

ALADDIN symbolizes one's wishes for easy access to desires.

ALAMO indicates a final confrontation.

ALARMS represent a severe warning for the dreamer. Take notice.

ALARM CLOCK signifies that it's "time to wake up!" Change ways.

ALARMIST is one who exaggerates in the negative. One who incites worry or fear.

ALARM SYSTEM denotes a need for higher awareness of one's environment or immediate surroundings.

ALBATROSS denotes one's burdens, sometimes self-inflicted.

ALBACORE See tuna.

ALBINO represents a lack of individuality.

ALBUM (photo) indicates the value of family and friends.

ALCATRAZ See prison.

ALCHEMIST is one who attempts to force impossible results.

ALCOHOLIC BEVERAGE symbolizes a need to relax. **Abuse** denotes a need to face problems.

ALCOHOLIC is one who attempts to escape life's problems or past.

ALCOTT (Louisa May) portrays a desire to reform repressive attitudes and perceptions.

ALCOVE represents places of respite.

ALDERMAN See councilman.

ALERT (signal) represents a warning for the dreamer to be more aware.

ALFALFA denotes a need for nourishment.

ALGAE indicate life aspects that are spiritually nourishing.

ALGEBRA signifies one's beginning calculations and process of analyzation.

ALIAS indicates identification with more than one personality of self.

ALI BABA represents one who holds the key or answers.

ALIBI signifies guiltlessness.

ALIEN connotes that which is foreign.

ALIENATION designates a separateness imposed. May be self-induced.

ALICE IN WONDERLAND symbolizes a stage of discovery.

ALIGNMENT denotes the need to return to the course.

ALIMENTARY CANAL signifies a need to focus on one's priorities.

ALIMONY represents payments due.

ALKALI indicates dangerous situations or relationships.

ALKALOID refers to the duality of possessing positive and negative aspects.

ALLAY refers to the dreamer's need to be rid of fears of problematical aspects to life.

ALLEGATION signifies unproven claims made.

ALLEGIANCE connotes "support" needed.

ALLERGIST is one who finds the root cause of people's problems.

ALLEGORY reflects the parable-like message; deeper meaning.

ALLERGY indicates negative aspects directly associated with the dreamer's relationships or belief system.

ALLEVIATE constitutes a life element that serves to lessen intensity or severity.

ALLEY means the "back way" in or out of a situation.

ALLEY CAT signifies a degenerate lifestyle or a hardscrabble existence.

ALLIANCE represents the need for a partner or associate.

ALLIGATOR connotes spiritual aspects that are self-serving.

ALL-NIGHTER infers greater effort or attention given to a particular issue.

ALLOTMENT See ration.

ALLOWANCE refers to the need to make allowances in life.

ALLOY connotes an aspect of one's life where an inferior element has been added.

ALL-STAR reflects an idea composed of the "best" elements.

ALL TERRAIN VEHICLE (ATV) symbolizes one's versatility.

ALLUDE See inference.

ALLURING symbolizes temptations.

ALLIES refer to friendships that are true.

ALMANAC cautions one to check facts.

ALMOND represents the need to avoid stress and/or give more attention to one's physical condition.

ALMS See donation.

ALOE warns one to soothe a burning situation or desire.

ALONE signifies a situation that may be needed for the dreamer.

ALOOF connotes an arrogant personality.

ALPACA See llama.

ALPENGLOW indicates one's gentle nature.

ALPENHORN means a "call" to tranquillity. This indicates one is experiencing a hectic lifestyle.

ALPHA AND OMEGA define "the most important aspect" of an issue or concept.

ALPINE See mountain.

ALPHABETICAL signifies order and priorities needed.

ALTAR denotes adoration. Watch this.

ALTAR RAIL represents respect for one's spiritual beliefs.

ALTERATIONS refer to changes required.

ALTER EGO symbolizes a need to know the completeness of self.

ALTERNATING CURRENT (AC) connotes indecision.

ALTERNATIVE SCHOOL symbolizes free thinking.

ALTERNATOR denotes the source of one's indecision.

ALTIMETER cautions against one's changing emotions. May indicate a manic-depressive.

ALTITUDE SICKNESS symbolizes a "high attitude, stance, or position" that isn't yet deserved.

ALTRUISM corresponds with empathy; selflessness.

ALUM warns of the need to "stop" something in one's life.

ALUMINUM signifies the need to "reflect" on something.

ALUMINUM FOIL connotes a warning regarding food one ingests.

ALYSSUM typifies inner balance and peace.

ALZHEIMER'S DISEASE cautions one to be more focused.

AMANITA symbolizes a dangerous situation or relationship.

AMARANTH indicates perseverance and inner strength.

AMARYLLIS constitutes a focused personality; well grounded.

AMATEUR NIGHT represents one's ability to "hear out" others.

AMAZEMENT refers to a revelation in one's life.

AMAZON (jungle) symbolizes confusion.

AMAZON RIVER indicates spiritual confusion.

AMBASSADOR refers to one's goodwill and helpfulness.

AMBER connotes resiliency and loyalty.

AMBIANCE indicates the type of one's surroundings.

AMBIDEXTROUS denotes one's ability to see all aspects of a situation.

AMBIGUITY symbolizes doubts.

AMBISEXUAL means a total lack of prejudice in one's life.

AMBITION represents the level of one's energy applied to goals.

AMBIVALENCE signifies a contrary personality.

AMBLING means nonchalance or loss of clear direction or purpose.

AMBROSIA warns that quick solutions are not always the right ones.

AMBULANCE warns of the need for immediate medical attention.

AMBULANCE CHASER means one who takes advantage of another's ill-fortune.

AMBUSH connotes a deceitful situation or relationship.

AMENABLE designates an agreeable personality.

AMENDMENT means additions or changes are required in one's life.

AMENDS cautions one to make reparation.

AMENITIES denote positive benefits to a situation or relationship.

AMETHYST means spiritual inner beauty that shines without.

AMIABLE defines an agreeable personality.

AMICABLE represents a good-natured individual. This may have a negative meaning in that one could be easily taken advantage of.

AMINO ACID symbolizes aspects in life that are needed but may be lacking.

AMISH signifies simplicity.

AMMONIA warns of dangerous thoughts.

AMMONITE reflects an ability for intricate thought; high intelligence and great wisdom.

AMMUNITION signifies validations.

AMNESIA indicates forgetfulness.

AMNESTY symbolizes absolute forgiveness.

AMNIOCENTESIS represents an "inner" knowing or precognition.

AMOEBA refers to the beginning formation of an idea or plan.

AMORPHOUS indicates an inability to bring thoughts together.

AMORTIZATION connotes a need to pace oneself.

AMPERE denotes a one-minded personality.

AMPHETAMINE warns of one's lack of energy and/or awareness.

AMPHIBIAN denotes one who is spiritually grounded.

AMPLIFIER cautions the dreamer to listen better.

AMPHITHEATER indicates a "clear view" of events. A good understanding.

AMPUTATION strongly suggests the need to "cut off" something in the dreamer's life.

AMUCK warns of a violent personality or relationship.

AMULET See charm.

AMUSEMENT PARK refers to a thrill-seeking personality.

AMALOGIST warns against making false relationships.

ANABIOTIC cautions the dreamer to start being more aware.

ANACONDA reveals an "uptight" personality.

ANAGRAM signifies solutions available within the problem itself.

ANALGESIC symbolizes that painless resolutions are possible.

ANALOGY refers to type of one's relationships.

ANALYSIS suggests the need for the dreamer to carefully analyze something important.

ANARCHY warns of lack of purpose or direction.

ANASAZI PEOPLE represent "beginnings" and a return to the Way.

ANATHEMA reveals an issue or individual to avoid.

ANATOMY (study of) signifies a need to look at "all parts" of a problem or situation.

ANCESTOR refers to past relationships.

ANCHOR warns one to get spiritually "grounded."

ANCHOVY typifies a spiritual aspect that is not readily accepted.

ANCIENT connotes old and wise.

ANDIRON symbolizes that which "fires" one into action.

ANDROID signifies a mindless personality or one incapable of thinking for self.

ANECDOTE denotes the need for the dreamer to learn more of an issue.

ANEMIA indicate one's lack of basics (nutrients).

ANESTHESIA warns of apathy.

ANESTHETIC (general) signifies one's total apathy.

ANESTHETIC (local) symbolizes one's "selective" apathy.

ANESTHETIST is one who incites apathy in others.

ANEURYSM warns one to stop dwelling on emotional pain.

ANGEL represents spiritual messages.

ANGEL DUST symbolizes dangerous practices.

ANGELFISH denotes the finer aspects of spiritual truths.

ANGEL FOOD CAKE signifies the "ingestion" of spiritual "fluff."

ANGELICA corresponds to insights.

ANGEL OF DEATH is most often a death premonition.

ANGINA warns of overdoing and voluntarily placing self in stressful situations.

ANGLE IRON refers to "support" required.

ANGLER connotes one who "fishes" around instead of being direct.

ANGLEWORM refers to "bait."

ANGLING denotes a spiritual nonchalance.

ANGORA represents a gentle and thoughtful personality.

ANGUISH warns of immersing self in painful memories.

ANIMA pertains to feminine aspects; the gentle elements of one's inner being; the positive aspects.

ANIMAL CARETAKER refers to one's level of compassion.

ANIMAL CRACKER indicates a respect for life.

ANIMAL HUSBANDRY connotes a nurturing nature.

ANIMALISM symbolizes a lack of spirituality.

ANIMAL MAGNETISM denotes one who inherently possesses a powerful personality that attracts the attention of others.

ANIMAL SHELTER refers to respect and care given to friends and close associates.

ANIMAL TRAINER signifies a manipulation of friends and relationships with others.

ANIMATION signifies one's immature outlook on life.

ANIMISM reflects the life force in all things; the fundamental essence.

ANIMUS infers the male aspects; harsher elements to one's character; the more aggressive elements.

ANISE corresponds to a strong personality trait that affects one's behavior.

ANKHS represent peace and spiritual knowledge.

ANKLE denotes "support" of one's burdens in life.

ANKLET shows the condition or state of one's own self-support system.

ANNALS (historic) refer to lessons learned from the past.

ANNEX signifies the need to "join" something. Could be thoughts, relationships, etc.

ANNIE OAKLEY is one who is independent.

ANNIHILATE represents a need to "get rid" of an aspect in one's life.

ANNIVERSARY signifies important dates in the dreamer's life.

ANNOTATION constitutes an explanation.

ANNOUNCEMENT connotes one's need to tell others of something.

ANNOUNCER is someone who has a message. The words are usually for the dreamer alone. Listen to what was said.

ANNOY See irritate.

ANNUAL (yearly) refers to one's tendency to repeat actions.

ANNUAL RING symbolizes a warning to stop continually "going in circles."

ANNUITY represents good karma returning.

ANNULMENT signifies the breaking of a relationship.

ANNUNCIATION See announcement.

ANODE denotes one's level of energy, impetus, drive.

ANOINTING denotes a blessing. Higher recognition.

ANOMALY refers to a deviation of one's path or belief system.

ANONYMOUS represents "hidden" intentions.

ANORAK emphasizes one's personal methods of overall protection; shielding measures.

ANOREXIA refers to one's lack of motivation, direction, or purpose.

ANOREXIA NERVOSA warns of an obsessive nature.

ANSWERING MACHINE symbolizes one's lack of communication.

ANT denotes cooperation with others.

ANTACID warns of stressful situations or relationships.

ANTE means "putting in" your share of time or energy into something.

ANTEATER signifies one who disrupts order.

ANTECHAMBER See foyer.

ANTELOPE connotes a free-spirited personality.

ANTENNA suggests the need for clarity of thought and ideas.

ANTEROOM See foyer.

ANTHEM denotes loyalties and the expression of same.

ANTHILL represents order and/or group cooperation.

ANTHOLOGY indicates the variety of philosophies in which one believes.

ANTHONY (Susan B.) characterizes one who fights for one's rights, especially against gender-repressive abuses.

ANTHRAX signifies the often-fatal effects of being a follower rather than an original thinker.

ANTHROPOLOGIST is one who sparks past-life memories within the dreamer.

ANTHROPOLOGY denotes the importance of learning from past lives.

ANTIAIRCRAFT symbolizes the "shooting down" of one's thoughts or ideas.

ANTI-ANTIBODY warns of highly dangerous persons or relationships.

ANTIBALLISTIC MISSILE represents one's immunity to the destructive ideas and thoughts of others.

ANTIBIOTIC signifies one's need for increased defenses, protection.

ANTIBODY signifies one's personal defense mechanisms.

ANTICHRIST connotes an embodiment of negativity or evil.

ANTICIPATION reveals one's level of anxiety over future events.

ANTICOAGULANT warns the dreamer to "keep things fluid" and moving.

ANTIDOTE signifies a solution.

ANTIFREEZE cautions against allowing spiritual interest to "freeze up."

ANTIGEN denotes destructive aspects in the dreamer's life.

ANTIGRAVITY refers to personal freedoms and rights.

ANTIHISTAMINE symbolizes aspects in one's life that allow "breathing" room and times of respite.

ANTI-INFLAMMATORY portrays a need to reduce stress in one's life.

ANTIPASTO represents variety, choices, and opportunities.

ANTIQUE DEALER is one who places a high value on self or services of self.

ANTIQUE SHOP symbolizes antiquated thoughts or beliefs that are being "sold" and represented as highly valuable.

ANTISEPTIC reveals a need to protect self against a negative situation or relationship.

ANTISOCIAL refers to an introverted personality.

ANTITANK symbolizes one's need for major defense or protection against an aspect in life.

ANTITOXIN warns one to increase personal defenses against a specific danger in the dreamer's life.

ANTLER alludes to one's personal defense mechanisms; a method of body language.

ANTONYM signifies opposition.

ANTSY typifies a restlessness; lacking acceptance.

ANUBIS warns one to pay more attention to the ramifications of actions.

ANVIL indicates a need to "reshape" something in the dreamer's life.

ANXIETY represents worry. This is a caution to be more within the attitude of acceptance.

AORTA refers to aspects closest to the heart. Highly emotional aspects.

APARTHEID denotes racial prejudice.

APARTMENT indicates a personal need to be around others.

APATHY warns of being emotionally neutral and without compassion.

APE cautions against loss of individuality.

APERITIFS refer to the lack of good nutrition.

APERTURE symbolizes "sight" or "awareness" of one's perceptions.

APEX See summit.

APHID refers to a mentally or emotionally draining personality.

APHRODISIAC indicates ill-attained love.

APHRODITE (Greek mythology) means one who "uses" love for various ends.

APIARY refers to an industrious nature.

APOCALYPSE connotes a personal "revelation."

APOLLO (Greek mythology) refers to male inner beauty, which is often self-denied.

APOLOGY symbolizes an admission of guilt.

APOPLEXY warns of a self-induced inability.

APOSTLE means one who follows a true spiritual path.

APOSTROPHE indicates an omission.

APOTHECARY See pharmacy.

APPALACHIAN TRAIL refers to a concerted effort to follow the natural way. Simplicity.

APPARATUS See equipment.

APPARITION means an important message for the dreamer.

APPEAL refers to a difference of opinion.

APPEASE suggests a compromise needed.

APPENDECTOMY indicates the need to "remove" an unnecessary aspect in one's life.

APPENDIX (listing) signifies the need to do further research.

APPETITE represents one's motivational state.

APPETIZER signifies one's sources of personal motivation.

APPLAUSE means a personal commendation for the dreamer.

APPLE symbolizes good health.

APPLEJACK See alcoholic beverage.

APPLE PIE signifies aspects one most closely identifies with as representing the home hearth.

APPLESAUCE denotes a pleasant blending of ideals.

APPLIANCE indicates helpful aspects in life.

APPLICATIONS refer to one's need to "apply" self.

APPLIQUÉ connotes a tendency to "add to" or "decorate" that which can stand on its own.

APPOINT represents arrogance.

APPOINTMENT signifies a need to communicate with another.

APPRAISAL represents an understanding of true value.

APPREHEND denotes a "catching" or "taking hold" of something important.

APPRENTICE symbolizes a need to learn from the bottom up.

APPRISE See inform.

APPROVAL warns against one requiring this in order to feel self-worth.

APRIL denotes a time to begin expanding renewal efforts on one's path.

APRIL FOOL'S DAY implies a day when the dreamer will experience the possibility of being made a fool of or doing something foolish.

APRON alludes to self-protection of some type.

APRON STRING refers to not wanting to let go of a protective situation or relationship.

APSE connotes the need to make more time for meditation and/or contemplation.

APTITUDE TEST refers to one's personal understanding of something.

AQUAMARINE pertains to the healing benefits of spiritual truths.

AQUANAUT is one who totally immerses self in a spiritual life; a cloistered nun, monk, or reclusive visionary.

AQUARIUM means spiritual arrogance.

AQUEDUCT represents a specific spiritual "course."

ARABESQUE denotes balance.

ARACHNID See spider.

ARACHNOPHOBIA portrays paranoia.

ARBITRATOR characterizes the need for some type of mediation.

ARBOR applies to the perceptible aura of highly spiritual people.

ARBOR DAY calls for an outward display of spiritual attitudes.

ARBORETUM cautions the dreamer to surround self with more spiritual aspects.

ARCADE alludes to games people play in life.

ARCANE pertains to the ability to understand complex concepts.

ARCH portrays a gentle passing through "openings" in one's life.

ARCHAEOLOGIST is one who ill-uses the past, such as exposing past transgressions of others.

ARCHAEOLOGY (study of) represents a fascination with the past to the extent of ignoring the present.

ARCHAIC exposes an outdated idea or perspective.

ARCHANGEL portrays critical spiritual messages from the highest source.

ARCHER is a messenger.

ARCHETYPE characterizes a model individual or represents a person one wishes to emulate.

ARCHFIEND reveals a person in one's life who has great potential to cause harm or negativity.

ARCHIPELAGO signifies resting points along one's spiritual path.

ARCHITECT characterizes individuals who attempt to plan out their lives in great detail.

ARCHIVE exemplifies the spirit and letter of God's laws.

AREA CODE denotes a specific region important to the dreamer.

ARENA symbolizes one's "circle" of relationships.

ARGONAUT (Greek mythology) reflects one on an adventurous quest.

ARGUING See fight.

ARGYLE (pattern) infers well-defined perspectives.

ARID implies a low level of spirituality.

ARISTOCRACY stands for arrogance.

ARITHMETIC See mathematics.

ARK is synonymous with compassion and generosity.

ARK OF THE COVENANT exemplifies our connective bond to God.

ARLINGTON NATIONAL CEMETERY represents honor.

ARM signifies personal work/efforts applied to one's purpose.

ARMADA pertains to an overbearing and manipulative personality.

ARMADILLO stands for one's personal defense mechanisms.

ARMAGEDDON alludes to a major conflict forthcoming in one's life.

ARMBAND represents an outward show of emotions or attitudes.

ARMCHAIR indicates a rest period.

ARMISTICE DAY constitutes a conflict resolution.

ARMOIRE alludes to hidden aspects of self.

ARMOR illustrates the dreamer's personal level of protection.

ARMORED CAR/TRUCK signifies one's emotional "shield" or untouchability.

ARMORY applies to perseverance and inner strength.

ARM-TWISTING characterizes a manipulative individual.

ARM WRESTLING indicates that someone loves a challenge.

ARMY pertains to one's personal capability to be assertive.

ARMY ANT exposes a strong opposition or force.

AROMATHERAPY alludes to one's receptivity to surroundings.

ARRAIGNMENT is a call to explain one's actions.

ARREARS reflects an "overdue" communication.

ARREST refers to "being caught" for something negative done.

ARRHYTHMIA denotes an irregularity in one's emotional foundation.

ARROGANCE alludes to egotism.

ARROW pertains to a swiftly traveled course.

ARROWHEAD illustrates the beginning of one's course.

ARROWROOT defines an aspect that counters a harmful element in one's life.

ARROYO denotes dangerous probabilities that are currently present along one's path.

ARSENAL See armory.

ARSENIC applies to "poisonous" aspects one voluntarily accepts in life.

ARSON stands for willful destruction done in one's life.

ARSONIST is one who enjoys destroying others.

ARTEMIS (Greek mythology) characterizes cleverness and resourcefulness.

ARTERY refers to aspects in life that emotionally affect us.

ART GALLERY symbolizes what one admires in life.

ARTHRITIS reveals a hidden fear.

ARTICHOKE is a warning against accepting half-truths or "immature" concepts that are not complete.

ARTICLE (written) signifies the need for further in depth study.

ARTICULATE cautions one to fully express self.

ARTIFACT denotes validating aspects in one's life.

ARTIFICIAL signifies a lack of genuineness or credibility.

ARTIFICIAL INSEMINA-TION alludes to a "way around" things that produce the same goal.

ARTIFICIAL INTELLI-GENCE warns of giving another too much power or control of one's life.

ARTIFICIAL RESPIRATION See respirator.

ARTILLERY indicates one's level of mental quickness.

ARTISAN represents personal expression; sense of freedom and individuality.

ARTIST signifies creativity.

ASBESTOS represents the duality of one's spiritual gifts depending on how they are personally used.

ASCENDING always indicates one's advancement.

ASCETICISM symbolizes a life of self-denial, deferring to others.

ASCORBIC ACID relates to inner strength.

ASCOT suggests airs, outward affectations one puts on.

ASEXUAL applies to physical and emotional independence.

ASH signifies a de-emphasis of the physical aspects in deference to the higher spiritual ones.

ASHAMED calls for a personal examination of one's actions.

ASHCAN implies getting rid of one's materialistic trappings.

ASHEN warns of ill health or discovery of one's negative action.

ASHRAM cautions against spiritual reclusiveness.

ASHTRAY represents reminders. To leave the past behind.

ASH WEDNESDAY applies to penance; a reminder of our physical mortality.

ASKANCE (look) means disapproval.

ASKEW refers to confusion in one's life.

ASPARAGUS comes as a reminder of our current physical beginnings; youth.

ASPHALT denotes a serious separation from "grounding" aspects in life.

ASPHYXIA means something is "smothering" the dreamer.

ASPIRANT applies to one seeking the highest level.

ASPIRATOR warns of a need to clear out a "congested" mind.

ASPIRIN signifies the need for respite.

ASSAILANT is one who can do harm in some way to the dreamer.

ASSASSIN pertains to an individual who could ruin one's life.

ASSAY OFFICE depicts a need to "reassess" one's priorities.

ASSEMBLY LINE cautions against routine conformity in life.

ASSENT See agreement.

ASSERTIVENESS TRAINING implies the dreamer needs to be more assertive.

ASSESSMENT stands for "taking stock" of various life aspects.

ASSET represents all that has value in the dreamer's life.

ASSIGNMENT pertains to a message to "be about one's work" or path.

ASSIMILATE refers to the dreamer's need to "take in" that which is important; to understand.

ASSISTANT is one who helps. Does the dreamer need help with something?

ASSOCIATE characterizes partnerships; a working together.

ASSUMPTION cautions to stick with the facts.

ASTERISK stands for high importance; getting the dreamer's attention.

ASTEROID signifies minor events in one's life.

ASTHMA connotes "more breathing room" is required.

ASTIGMATISM symbolizes the lack of clear understanding.

ASTRAL PLANE indicates a call to stay in the "here and now."

ASTRINGENT signifies a severe personality.

ASTRODOME denotes hidden activities.

ASTROLOGER alludes to one who can pull many aspects together.

ASTROLOGY (study of) denotes an attempt to better understand self.

ASTRONAUT characterizes our ability to expand ourselves and traverse finer dimensions.

ASTRONOMER is one who intellectually focuses on humankind's ancient heritage as a basis for other life aspects.

ASTRONOMY (study of) signifies one's interest in humankind's ancient ancestry.

ASYLUM warns of "craziness" going on in one's life.

ASYMMETRICAL suggests a "balance" is required.

A-TEAM represents the Power of spiritual forces.

ATHEIST connotes those who would destroy spiritual beliefs.

ATHENAEUM refers to further study, specifically extensive reading.

ATHLETE signifies physical accomplishments.

ATHLETE'S FOOT cautions against giving priority to physical accomplishments rather than focusing on spiritual aspects.

ATHLETIC SUPPORTER symbolizes one's weak points.

ATLANTIS cautions against negative or wrong use of high knowledge and intelligence.

ATLAS indicates expanded world knowledge required.

ATMOSPHERIC PRESSURE reveals the amount of stress currently present within one's immediate surroundings.

ATOLLS signify spiritual serenity through protection.

ATOM BOMB exemplifies lack of compassion and a disregard for life.

ATOMIZER means a "cover-up."

ATONEMENT infers reparation; reconciliation.

ATRIUM depicts an openness of outwardly displayed attitudes and/or emotions.

A

ATROCITIES illustrate an absolute disregard for life.

ATROPHY warns of letting talents go unused.

ATTACHÉ is the front person for another's mission or purpose.

ATTACHÉ CASE stands for priority material regarding one's mission.

ATTENDANT implies a personal helper.

ATTENTION DEFICIT DISORDER (ADD) symbolizes inattention and cautions one to begin focusing and concentrating more on an issue in one's life.

ATTIC pertains to the conscious mind.

ATTORNEY emphasizes a need for complete honesty.

ATTORNEY GENERAL relates to one's need to do a reassessment of major moves planned in their life.

AUCTION warns one of always attempting to "get the most" out of relationships and situations.

AUCTIONEER is one who exaggerates value.

AUDIENCE exemplifies the ever-present "watchers" in one's life; the "eyes" on us.

AUDIO BOOK refers to bringing the written word "to life." Giving fuller and expanded meaning to what is written.

AUDIO CASSETTE represents alternative means of receiving messages.

AUDIO VISUALS signify the need to "look" at differing aspects of a situation or relationship.

AUDITION cautions against trying to always be what others want you to be.

AUDIT denotes "suspected transgressions" committed.

AUDITOR represents someone who "checks up" on another.

AUDITORIUM signifies a need for an audience.

AUGER cautions the dreamer to "dig down" for more information.

AUGMENTATION means an exaggeration.

AUGUST denotes a time to repair relationships; address closures.

AULD LANG SYNE connotes an overly reminiscent nature.

AU NATUREL implies a tendency toward aspects that are natural; without trappings, decoration, or dressing.

AUNT relates to a maternal alternative.

AURA portrays one's spiritual condition.

AURORA BOREALIS comes as a spiritual comfort or acknowledgment.

AUSPICIOUS stands for an upcoming situation or relationship being a favorable one.

AUSTERITY alludes to a disassociating type of personality; one who voluntarily withdraws from society and its trappings.

AUTHENTICATE means verification.

AUTHOR denotes "originator."

AUTHORITY FIGURE most often directly refers to higher spiritual forces.

AUTHORIZE symbolizes permission granted.

AUTISM indicates willful suppression of one's inner light and/or spiritual knowledge.

AUTOBIOGRAPHY represents shared experiences; an opening up of oneself.

AUTOCLAVE See sterile.

AUTOCRAT indicates a warning against manipulating the lives of others.

AUTOGRAPH relates to someone important to the dreamer.

AUTOHYPNOSIS denotes the need to "go within," to learn more of self.

AUTOMAT signifies "quick fixes."

AUTOMATED TELLER MACHINE (ATM) symbolizes "fast cash." A source of solving short-term cash-flow situations.

AUTOMATIC PILOT cautions against letting others lead your way.

AUTOMATION represents a loss of personal input.

AUTO MECHANIC implies a need to seek a medical evaluation.

AUTOMOBILE corresponds to the physical body.

AUTOPSY signifies a need to analyze a past action, relationship, or belief system; pick it apart piece by piece.

AUTOSUGGESTION stands for self-taught acceptance.

AUTUMN (season) means a time to reflect.

AVALANCHE denotes spiritual smothering; an overload of conceptual intake.

AVALON cautions one against the tendency to have utopian dreams and life goals.

AVATAR is synonymous with spiritual arrogance.

AVENGER symbolizes an activist on the side of spiritual or humanitarian justice.

AVENUE represents a wide path ahead; possibly many distractions along the way.

AVERSION signifies one's distaste for one or more aspects entering or interfering in life.

AVIARY warns against "confining" one's spiritual talents or knowledge.

AVIATOR is one who holds to one's own ideals, beliefs, and attitudes.

AVIATOR GLASSES denote single-vision; only one's personal view.

AVOCADO implies a soft-hearted personality with a tough skin.

AVOIDANCE warns against running away from situations or relationships.

AWARD most often exemplifies commendations from higher sources.

AWL pertains to the presence of deceit; situations or relationships that are full of "holes."

AWNING symbolizes temporary shelter.

AX warns of trouble ahead along the dreamer's path.

AXIS connotes a central focus; that around which other aspects revolve.

AXLE exemplifies a motivating force that supports one's actions.

AYERS ROCK alludes to the spiritually obvious; an aspect or even an individual who "stands out."

AZALEA signifies hidden talents.

AZTECS portray ancient belief systems.

AZURITE denotes high spiritual capabilities.

B

BABBLING (talk) warns of meaningless dialogue.

BABOON See monkey.

BABUSHKA implies a caution against keeping one's thoughts confined or tied down instead of expressing them.

BABY relates to false innocence; immaturity.

BABY BONNET applies to a juvenile thought process.

BABY BOOMER characterizes societal changes.

BABY CARRIAGE represents undeveloped ideas and concepts carried around.

BABY'S BREATH (flower) connotes the "breath of new life" breathed into an aspect of a dreamer's life.

BABY SHOES signify "baby steps" one is taking along a path.

BABYSITTER refers to nurturing and a "mothering" condition.

BABY TOOTH See milk tooth.

BACHELOR portrays a reluctance to make commitments.

BACK (anatomy) refers to unseen or unanticipated events.

BACK (directional placement) symbolizes "background" position; may caution the dreamer to come forward or else stay in the background.

BACKACHE refers to burdens carried, possibly in a silent manner which can frequently internalize emotional pain.

BACKBITE implies a vindictive personality.

BACKBOARD warns against a reluctance to seek emotional support or counsel.

BACKBONE pertains to strength of character. Check condition and alignment of these.

BACK BURNER means something being kept "on hold."

BACKCOUNTRY alludes to simplicity.

BACKDOOR denotes a "way out."

BACKDRAFT symbolizes a combustible situation, nearing flashpoint.

BACKDROP warns against redesigning one's past.

BACKFIELD relates to a secondary position of support.

BACKFIRE indicates repercussions; not working out according to plan.

BACKGAMMON applies to a noncommittal relationship.

BACKGROUND illustrates underlying aspects in one's life.

BACKHAND represents a versatility in handling problems.

BACKHOE denotes a need to "dig back" for more information.

BACKLASH indicates a negative reaction.

BACKLIGHT signifies a false aura; one manufactured and presented as authentic.

BACKLIST applies to something that endures.

BACKLOG relates to an aspect in the dreamer's life that's unfinished; something requires attention.

BACKPACK implies the necessities pertinent to one's life.

BACKPEDAL symbolizes a retreat; a going backward.

BACKPRESSURE denotes a restrained condition.

BACKREST depicts the necessary pauses along one's path.

BACKROAD represents in-depth study.

BACKROOM connotes hidden aspects.

BACK RUB represents "care" of one's burdens; an ability to take burdens on while pacing oneself.

BACK SEAT denotes one's rightly designated position.

BACKSEAT DRIVER is one who gives orders and opinions without a right to them.

BACKSLIDING warns of a "slipping back" action.

BACKSPACING suggests the need to "go back" and discover something that was missed. Oftentimes, more frequently than realized, the spaces between events are full of lessons needed to be learned.

BACKSPIN applies to a shock or revelation.

BACKSTAB portrays a vindictive personality.

BACKSTAGE stands for one's private life, attitude, or that which one does not publicly display.

BACKSTAIRS denotes hidden or secret movements; alternative agendas.

BACKSTITCH cautions of the need to make amends from the past.

BACKSTOP symbolizes safeguards one creates for self.

BACKSTRETCH suggests a "halfway point."

BACKSTROKE warns of a need to review; go back over spiritual concepts.

BACKTRACK stresses the need to return to the right path.

BACKUP denotes one's reserves.

BACKWARD (direction) connotes a reverse in one's direction.

BACKWASH refers to an aftermath in turmoil; spiritual truths coming back at a reluctant individual.

BACKWATER warns of stagnant spiritual belief systems.

BACKWOODS portray pure spiritual talents.

BACKYARD alludes to one's rightful territory, perhaps cautioning one against sticking one's nose into other people's business.

BACON symbolizes one's job; working.

BACTERIA denotes "infectious" situations or relationships. A warning symbol.

BAD BLOOD denotes animosities; bad relationships; grudges.

BADGE signifies identity; a need to be identified. Sometimes will also mean a commendation of some type.

BADGER stands for a "nagging" personality, usually one who interferes in another's life.

BADLANDS pertain to places one should not be. This may refer to geography, life situations, belief systems, or personal relationships.

BADMINTON denotes a "back-and-forth" situation or relationship. May also refer to one's own thought process; indecision.

BAFFLES signify a thwarted aspect in the dreamer's life. It cautions of the probability that something will not succeed.

BAG represents some type of interference in one's life.

BAGEL implies the "ingestion" or acceptance of a diversity of multicultural aspects.

BAGGAGE means excesses in one's life; a carrying of unnecessary aspects, possibly referring to attitudes, beliefs, material possessions, etc.

BAG LADY characterizes priorities; giving attention to only those life aspects that are necessary.

BAGMAN portrays debts.

BAGPIPE symbolizes an individual who consistently talks about nothing important; a gossip; one who talks to gain attention.

BAGUETTE (gem shape) depicts a "supporting" aspect in one's life. This could refer to an individual, situation or belief.

BAGUETTE (bread) pertains to life's necessities.

BAIL (bond) means a temporary reprieve.

BAIL (eject) warns against staying in a situation; it's literally time to "bail out."

BAIL (water) cautions one to "empty" one's mind of damaging spiritual concepts.

BAILIFF characterizes one who maintains order.

BAILSMAN See bondsman.

BAIT denotes enticements. This is a warning dream symbol.

BAIT AND SWITCH cautions

against being "taken in" through deceit.

BAKE relates to something "finished."

BAKE-OFF represents the "best possible outcome."

BAKER signifies an expanding scope of one's spiritual understanding and personal application.

BAKER'S DOZEN means personal generosity; giving more than required; going the extra mile for another.

BAKERY most frequently stands for the ingestion of sweet and/or high-caloric foodstuffs. This is usually a warning symbol.

BAKING POWDER signifies aspects in one's life that need to be blended or "mixed" with others.

BAKING SODA symbolizes a cleansing aspect in one's life.

BAKLAVA depicts those sweeter life aspects that come quite naturally.

BALANCE BEAM reminds us to "walk a balanced" path.

BALANCE OF POWER implies a need to share responsibility and control; each individual requires his or her own portion which is answerable for.

BALANCE OF TRADE pertains to our daily "give-and-take" equilibrium.

BALANCE SHEET refers to one's karmic record.

BALANCE WHEEL denotes a "stabilizing" aspect or influence.

BALCONY portrays perceptual clarity.

BALD (head) characterizes a thoughtless individual; one who rarely thinks for self.

BALE stands for a need to open up. This may refer to one's thoughts, emotions, or finances.

BALEEN See whalebone.

BALL suggests simplicity, ease of communicating ideas.

BALLAD relates to lessons learned.

BALLAST warns of a need to "unload." This means one is carrying excessive weight in relation to emotions, mental, or spiritual aspects.

BALL BEARING connotes an easier, smoother method of operation.

BALL COCK cautions against not taking personal responsibility in the regulation of one's spiritual quest for the truth.

BALLERINA portrays a woman who is a true lady; genteel thoughts, actions, and graceful manner (within and without).

BALLET represents a situation that has been engineered; players dancing through their parts.

BALLET SLIPPERS indicate a lack of seriousness; dancing through life.

BALL GAME See specific game.

BALL LIGHTNING illustrates a concentrated effort to gain one's attention. This is directed toward the dreamer and comes as a warning signal.

BALL OF LIGHT exemplifies high spiritual illumination.

BALL OF WAX refers to a complete aspect or issue encompassing all related elements.

BALLOON means an exaggeration.

BALLOON MORTGAGE depicts the ultimate payment of karmic debts.

BALLOT stands for freedom of speech; one's right to have a say.

BALLPARK symbolizes one's recognition of limits; bounds.

BALLROOM represents the "place" or life arena in which we do our dancing. We shouldn't be doing "fancy footwork" anywhere in life.

BALM indicates that which soothes in life.

BALMY reflects an enjoyable atmosphere that is free of difficulty; uplifting.

BALSA WOOD applies to our innate personal talents or thoughts that "make light" of our burdens.

BAMBI characterizes true innocence; a naiveté.

BAMBOO connotes developing talents.

BAN pertains to lack of freedom and/or rights in one's life.

BANANA symbolizes inner goodness. Sometimes seen only after other aspects have been "peeled" away.

BANANA SPLIT denotes one's inner goodness that is frequently enhanced by other expressions of one's talents.

BAND (musical) depicts the beginning stage of being able to work together with others; cooperation.

BANDAGE indicates that a healing is needed. It's time for an emotional wound to heal.

BANDANNA means unclear speech or thought; a tendency to "cover" same.

BANDBOX signifies the care one gives to important life aspects.

BANDICOOT implies small blessings.

BANDIT characterizes one who possesses that which has been ill-gotten.

BANDLEADER portrays an individual who instigates a mood of cooperation among people.

BANDOLEER illustrates a "warrior" type of personal preparedness.

BAND SAW alludes to "cutting" remarks or deeds in a relationship.

BANDSTAND refers to a tendency to be the center of attention.

BANDWAGON warns against the inclination to follow others or fad ideas.

BANISH symbolizes an exile type of situation or attitude. What does the dreamer want to "get rid of" for good?

BANISTER See handrail.

BANJO stands for gaiety.

BANK (build up) implies a situation, concept, or relationship that requires additional supportive aspects applied.

BANK (money) pertains to that which one "saves" as being highly meaningful to self; personal riches.

BANK See riverbank.

BANKBOOK suggests one's personal wealth. Is all the money hoarded or withdrawn to help others?

BANKCARD means an individual's right to aspects in life that would be considered personal assets.

BANKROLL (moneyroll) portrays a generous personality.

BANKRUPT denotes one who is wealthy yet remains spiritually devoid of assets; a miser.

BANK TRANSACTIONS indicate how well riches (talents) are managed.

BANNER denotes a means of getting attention.

BANNS reveal an intent; announcement.

BANQUET indicates a generous situation; sharing.

BANSHEE warns of death. This may forewarn of a spiritual, mental, or actual physical death.

BANTER infers playful teasing yet usually exposes some type of hidden message.

BAPTISM connotes a spiritual birth; rebirth.

BAR See tavern.

BAR (exclude) infers denial. Who was barred from what?

BARB implies hurting, "sharp" aspects in life.

BARBARIAN characterizes a severely unmannered or uncultured person; crude thought patterns; primitive behavior.

BARBECUE represents a burning thought or attitude that "cooks" and "sizzles" inside a person.

BARBED WIRE connotes an individual's harmful attitude (tendency) to angrily cut self off from another; animosity.

BARBELL alludes to those life aspects that build strength; endurance-builders.

BARBER See beautician.

BARBERSHOP implies a need to "trim" or "restyle" one's thoughts, attitudes, or belief systems.

BAR CODE relates to systematically hidden information.

BARD See storyteller.

BAREBACK (riding) exemplifies a free spirit; one going forward unrestrained; unfettered.

BARE BONES apply to "essentials"; bottom-line facts.

BAREFOOT characterizes an individual who walks a path with full knowledge of what each step means.

BAREHEADED signifies an expressive individual; honest; forthright.

BARE-KNUCKLE implies one who is vulnerable.

BARGAIN will emphasize a good plan or course.

BARGE pertains to a spiritually lethargic rate of progress.

BARHOPPING indicates a restlessness.

BARK (dog) represents a warning or greeting from a friend. Refer to dream details for clarity.

BARK (tree) applies to one's external show of strength.

BARKEEPER See bartender.

BARKER symbolizes a loudmouth; one who has much to say about nothing.

BARLEY applies to essential aspects.

BAR MITZVAH/BAT MITZVAH denotes the point of responsibility for self.

BARN connotes those life aspects that one shelters from others.

BARNACLE pertains to extraneous aspects that one allows to weigh down or impede progress.

BARNYARD stands for down-home attitudes and/or relationships; an unaffected personality.

BAROMETER portrays the amount of pressure one is under.

BARRACKS suggest a lack of individuality; self-repression.

BARRACUDA characterizes a lack of moral or ethical value; a vicious personality.

BARREL connotes a great amount of something.

BARREL CHAIR applies to personal mass. This warns of the tendency to "carry around" more weight than necessary. May refer to various aspects in life, not merely body weight.

BARREN implies a lack of new life; new growth.

BARRETTE represents thoughts that are "caught up" or restrained.

BARRICADE means self-imposed blocks one places in the way of progress.

BARRIER exemplifies a "temporary" pause for the dreamer. This may refer to various aspects.

BARRIER REEF stands for a time of rest during one's spiritual quest.

BARROOM depicts a tendency to need sympathy.

BARSTOOL See high chair.

BARTENDER is one who frequently "serves" potential negatives to others.

BARTER implies give and take; a sharing of talents.

BARTON (Clara) characterizes a great desire to provide others with basic comforts.

BASALT applies to an individual who has become hardened after a highly emotional life stage; verging on apathetic.

BASE refers to foundational elements or a "secure" position.

BASEBALL relates to winning through skill and speed. Not a totally commendable symbol.

BASEBOARD alludes to "finished" ideas that conclude previous lines of thought and brought them together.

BASE LEVEL cautions one to research spiritual concepts back to their beginnings.

BASEMENT stands for the subconscious mind.

BASE PAY exemplifies required time and work; a tendency to avoid doing more than necessary.

BASIC TRAINING implies having the "basics" regarding something. This would infer further learning is required.

BASIL corresponds to a light flavoring or hint; a suggestion.

BASILICA warns against spiritual arrogance, believing one is more spiritually special than others.

BASIN See sink.

BASK connotes voluntary absorption of something; a pleasurable time of rejoicing in happiness.

BASKET alludes to a need to "gather" more information.

BASKET CASE characterizes an emotionally confused individual.

BASS (tone) refers to depth of meaning or emotion.

BASS DRUM represents that which affects us most deeply on an emotional level.

BASSET HOUND (dog breed) symbolizes melancholy; sadness.

BASSINET means spiritual respite; a need to rest along one's newly-begun spiritual search.

BASSOON reflects deep thoughts; high philosophic contemplation.

BASTE (cook) cautions against allowing spiritual beliefs to "dry" up.

BASTE (sew) refers to a temporary "pulling together" of some aspect in the dreamer's life.

BAT (animal) means the use of spiritual intuition in all aspects of life.

BAT (sport) illustrates the condition and quality of one's progression.

BATBOY/-GIRL is one who can supply another with the abilities (tools) to further progress in life.

BATHHOUSE represents a serious need to "cleanse" some aspect in the dreamer's life.

BATHING signifies a lack of negatives in the dreamer's life.

BATHING CAP warns against a reluctance to approach spiritual concepts.

BATHING SUIT signifies a tendency to submerge self into spiritual concepts but "not let it touch" one; a spiritual distancing.

BATH MAT refers to spiritual protection; personal safeguards one uses against "slipping" spiritually.

BATHOLITH applies to wisdom of the ancients.

BATHOMETER signifies an aspect that determines the "depth" of spiritual belief and/or application.

BATHOPHOBIA warns against being afraid to delve deeper into spiritual concepts.

BATHROBE symbolizes how relaxed or comfortable one is with one's personal spiritual beliefs.

BATHROOM means a spiritual cleansing is needed.

BATH SALTS bring a message to "soften" one's spiritual attitude.

BATHTUB suggests a spiritual "submersion" is required. This would imply an individual who is fearful or has a reluctance to really get into their beliefs.

BATH WATER pertains to the quality of one's spiritual beliefs. Check the condition of this water—its color, etc.

BATHYSPHERE alludes to a journey into the deeper aspects of spiritual concepts.

BATIK cautions against a tendency toward "selective" beliefs.

BATON characterizes an arrogant or egotistical personality.

BATTALION denotes a great amount of force, people, support, or opposition. Other dreamscape aspects will clarify this.

BATTER (cooking) means condition and quality of something before it is ready to be finalized; preparations.

BATTER (sports) alludes to the "one who scores" or a main player.

BATTERING RAM connotes "force" applied. This is most often a warning against the necessity of applying force.

BATTERY depicts "reserve energy" needed. This cautions against using up most of one's energy before something is accomplished.

BATTING AVERAGE reveals the state of one's progress.

BATTLE indicates a tough time ahead; a real struggle to reach a goal.

BATTLE-AX characterizes a stern and frequently angry personality.

BATTLE CRUISER denotes an ability to easily maneuver through spiritual conflict.

BATTLE CRY exemplifies a need to generate greater courage.

BATTLE FATIGUE seriously warns against continual struggles without taking the needed time to reflect, meditate, gain inner peace.

BATTLEMENT denotes the logic, reason, and foresight given when considering the possibility of a forthcoming conflict.

BATTLESHIP stands for a well-armed but cumbersome approach to a conflict.

BAUBLE reflects an unimportant element; insignificant.

BAWDRY exposes crudeness.

BAY reveals a sheltered spirituality.

BAYBERRY pertains to the reminiscing of times past.

BAY LEAF applies to a life aspect that enhances one's life.

BAYONET illustrates a threatening position or situation.

BAYOU portrays a spiritual situation where one has become complacent or sluggish in advancing or has allowed aspects to become stagnant.

BAY WINDOW denotes a "greater view" or perspective may be required.

BAZAAR alludes to the vast array of learning sources and opportunities available to us.

BAZOOKA signifies one's inner power; personal resources in respect to defending self against various threatening aspects in life.

BEACH denotes the transition stage of how well spiritual beliefs are applied to the physical (the "living" of them). Is the beach rocky? Smooth? Is the sand white or black?

BEACH BUGGY See dune buggy.

BEACH BUM characterizes one who lives one's spiritual beliefs at all times.

BEACHCOMBER exemplifies "looking for" spiritual rarities that one can treasure.

BEACHFRONT portrays "an eye toward spirituality." This indicates a condition of spiritual priority.

BEACON means a source of enlightenment that will further spiritual development or understanding.

BEAD signifies a small matter of importance. Although small, it's still important for the dreamer.

BEADWORK stands for taking deserved pride in one's work.

BEAGLE (dog breed) refers to a sympathy-seeking friend.

BEAKER applies to some aspect in the dreamer's life that needs precision blending.

BEAM (facial expression) stands for inner joy; happiness.

BEAM (ray) symbolizes higher knowledge or intelligence.

BEAM (timber) indicates inner strength.

BEAN represents one of many connecting aspects; a portion.

BEANBAG pertains to the "whole" made up of many parts.

BEAN COUNTER characterizes someone who looks at all aspects of a relationship or situation.

BEANIE See skullcap.

BEAN SPROUTS caution against ignoring the importance of each part or aspect of a situation.

BEANSTALK refers to the unique aspects of individuality, strength, and potential that touch our lives.

BEAR (animal) characterizes an overbearing personality or situation.

BEARD symbolizes hidden physical aspects in one's life.

BEAR HUG connotes the potential for a smothering type of affection.

BEARNAISE SAUCE relates to a beneficial added element in one's life.

BEARSKIN alludes to emotional warmth and security.

BEAST corresponds to crude or unacceptable behavior.

BEAUTICIAN signifies individuals with a tendency or talent to alter the thoughts of others; persuasiveness.

BEAUTY MARK portrays the "distinctive" qualities one has.

BEAUTY PAGEANT pertains to an over-emphasis placed on the physical.

BEAUTY SHOP illustrates an attempt to enhance appearances.

BEAVER stands for the ability to recognize one's spiritual aspects at "home" while balancing and utilizing life's opportunities.

BECKON almost always applies to a "draw" or inclination toward something.

BED cautions against overdoing; a need for rest.

BED AND BREAKFAST stands for an "easy" or comfortable personality or situation; an individual who is "at home" anywhere.

BEDBUG warns of a negative aspect related to sleeping arrangements or sleep patterns.

BED CHECK indicates a need to make sure you're where you need to be; doing what you know you're supposed to be doing.

BEDDING (clothes or linen) portrays our condition or state of rest.

BEDDING PLANTS depict good and/or well-developed beginnings of something.

BEDLAM means complete confusion. This may refer to a relationship, a situation, or a mental/emotional state.

BEDOUIN denotes spiritual separatism; keeping one's beliefs apart from the possibility of other concepts infiltrating them.

BEDPAN cautions against an inability to rest well; a tendency to bring work into times designated for rest.

BEDPOST symbolizes those aspects that support or lead to a resting period.

BEDRIDDEN is a state of "forced" rest. This comes as a warning against working too hard.

BEDROCK stands for strong and enduring foundations.

BEDROLL represents an easygoing personality.

BEDROOM signifies one's personal atmosphere or surrounding that induces rest.

BEDROOM COMMUNITY denotes a separation of rest and work.

BEDROOM EYES exemplify a magnetic personality.

BEDSIDE MANNER illustrates one's sensitivity to others.

BEDSORE warns against not being motivated to work.

BEDSPREAD portrays the type of rest one is receiving.

BEDSPRING indicates the quality and/or variety of restful activities one utilizes.

BEDSTEAD symbolizes aspects that support one's state of rest; the qualitative value of such rest.

BEDTIME STORY pertains to restful and peaceful thoughts.

BED-WETTING illustrates a tendency for self-induced rest interruption; an individual who can't allow time for rest.

BEE characterizes industrious and cooperative teamwork.

BEEF cautions one to "ingest" well-defined and developed concepts; a warning against the acceptance of "raw" aspects.

BEEHIVE means the "center" or focus of activity; main interest or point of attention.

BEEKEEPER characterizes hidden agendas; an individual who wants something in return; one who takes and takes.

BEELINE means a straight course; shortest and most direct route.

BEELZEBUB See devil.

BEEPER advises to "stay in contact" or keep communication links open.

BEER See alcoholic beverage.

BEESWAX refers to an industrious nature.

BEET reflects intensity, frequently indicates anger.

BEETLE signifies negative interference's in one's life.

BEGGING stands for desperation.

BEGINNER implies lack of experience or knowledge.

BEGONIA stands for balance.

BEHAVIORAL THERAPY suggests an attitude adjustment is needed; a change in how one behaves because of incorrect thought.

BEHEAD infers that someone needs to bring one's thinking back in line because of "losing one's head" over something; or it means one is in serious trouble and is getting closer to the chopping block.

BEHEMOTH symbolizes an aspect in one's life that is mammoth; perhaps overwhelming; too big to handle alone.

BEHIND (direction) relates to a lower level; slower; or it may point to the proper position one should take.

BEHIND THE SCENES alludes to hidden aspects of what is seen or manifested in the open.

BEIGE (color) defines a neutral position; possible indecision.

BEJEWELED means self-aggrandizement; seeing self as brilliant and full of worth.

BELATED reflects inefficiency; lacking attention to one's awareness level.

BELCH signifies a need to "bring up" negative attitudes that could eventually be harmful.

BELFRY warns of alarming relationships or situations.

BELL is a call to duty or responsibility.

BELLADONNA implies an emotional settling is needed; a calming.

BELLBOY represents personal assistance; possible servitude.

BELL BUOY serves as a spiritual marker that guides one through a safe passing.

BELL JAR alludes to narrow-mindedness.

BELLOWS indicate a requirement for more air; a need to remove self from some aspect in life that's suffocating.

BELLY See abdomen.

BELLY DANCE connotes a tendency to brag; to show off.

BELLY FLOP applies to unexpected or disappointing spiritual results.

BELLY LAUGH means great joy.

BELLY-UP portrays failure.

BELOW (direction) stands for "under" or may indicate a positioned placement.

BELOW THE BELT indicates retaliation and vindictiveness; unethical retribution.

BELT symbolizes self-created restraints.

BELTANE exemplifies a "spring-like" timeframe in one's life; a time of purification and renewal.

BELT BUCKLE defines the excuse for one's self-restraint.

BELT-TIGHTENING represents severe self-restraint; self-denial.

BELTWAY stands for a way around something.

BELVEDERE See gazebo.

BENCH indicates a need to take a pause; a short rest; time to consider or contemplate.

BENCHMARK depicts an ultimate example or sample of something.

BENCH PRESS refers to aspects in life that serve as strengtheners.

BENCHWARMER characterizes inaction, yet preparedness for action.

BENCH WARRANT seriously warns against wrongdoing.

BEND See bent.

BEND (in road) connotes a slight veering away from something; a change of direction.

BENDER exposes a desire to escape reality.

BENEATH usually reveals a hidden element.

BENEDICTION means a spiritually-sanctioned individual or deed.

BENEFACTOR symbolizes the source or impetus that serves to provide ways to advance or succeed.

BENEFICIARY means recipient of something. Perhaps good luck coming.

BENEFIT (event) alludes to being of help through the aid of others.

BENEFIT OF THE DOUBT connotes trust.

BENEVOLENCE defines generosity, yet may also indicate an ulterior motive.

BENIGN alludes to innocence; harmless; neutral.

BENT refers to an aspect in life that isn't straight (true or honest).

BENTWOOD implies a natural inclination.

BENZENE symbolizes one's control over highly-flammable situations or relationships.

BEQUEST represents the act of giving.

BEREAVEMENT reveals a personal sorrow.

BERET pertains to a carefree, often eccentric personality.

BERG See iceberg.

BERGAMOT refers to the duality of personality. That which is sour can also be fragrant.

BERIBERI characterizes a highly repulsive or extremely distasteful aspect that one tries to avoid getting close to.

BERM represents support; protective aspects.

BERMUDA TRIANGLE means spiritual fluctuations; vacillations.

BERNHARDT (Sarah) exposes an overdramatized emotion.

BERRY relates to those life aspects that are fruitful.

BERTH (anchorage) indicates a comfortable spiritual position.

BERYL alludes to pure intentions; true life offerings that come our way.

BESIDE (directional placement) connotes an equal aspect.

BESIEGED reflects an overwhelming situation.

BESTIAL means lack of reason and or intelligence; behaving like an animal.

BESTIARY denotes a high interest in animals and what can be learned from them.

BEST MAN characterizes male support in life.

BESTSELLER means that which is most popular; aspects having the greatest draw.

BET signifies chances taken; a willingness to second-guess outcomes; a tendency to dismiss or give weight to facts.

BETA BLOCKER stands for a need to be calm.

BETEL NUT implies a mesmerized state of mind.

BETHLEHEM illustrates spiritual beginnings.

BETONY cautions one to take care of some type of wound. This may be an emotional injury.

BETRAYAL applies to untrustworthy relationships.

BETROTHAL refers to personal commitments made.

BETWEEN stands for the middle position.

BEVELED signifies "angles" to an issue or situation that should be seen.

BEVERAGE reflects a life element that has the potential of fulfillment; quenching a thirst; satisfying an emptiness.

BEVERLY HILLS corresponds with those who have the greatest responsibility and potential to help others.

BEWITCHED warns against allowing anyone to capture one's free will; a lack of individuality or thought.

BIANNUAL applies to something happening twice.

BIAS means "slanted"; prejudice.

BIB warns against sloppy talk from sloppy thought; a call to halt gossip; caution against thoughtless speech.

BIBLE portrays "revised" or altered words.

BIBLIOGRAPHY symbolizes literary works one should peruse; additional research needed.

BICARBONATE OF SODA See baking soda.

BICYCLE depicts mental, physical, or spiritual balance.

BIDET warns against incomplete hygiene.

BIER See coffin.

BIFOCAL indicates more than one perspective to any aspect; an ability to see the surface and deeper levels.

BIGAMY illustrates a lack of commitment; a disregard for others; a tendency toward self-importance.

BIG BANG THEORY denotes explosive beginnings.

BIG BROTHER characterizes an overseer in one's life.

BIG ENCHILADA implies one who is most important or holds the most power, a possible inflated self-image.

BIGFOOT connotes aspects of reality that are not accepted.

BIGHEAD stands for arrogance; egotism.

BIG LEAGUE pertains to highest level; aspects holding the power.

BIGMOUTH warns against gossiping, telling more than is necessary.

BIGOTRY means intolerance.

BIG SHOT characterizes someone of importance; influential.

BIG STICK denotes threats.

BIKE See bicycle.

BIKER pertains to independence; a "free-wheeling" personality.

BIKINI symbolizes a lack of inhibitions.

BILE portrays aspects in one's life that are considered bitter.

BI-LEVEL indicates balance.

BILGE suggests a personal transitional spiritual stage.

BILGE WATER means negative aspects infiltrating one's spiritual transition.

BILINGUAL connotes a talent for conceptual interpretation.

BILL stands for karma that comes due.

BILLBOARD means a warning or reminder; an attention-getter.

BILLET cautions one to make "accommodations" for those who would provide protection or help.

BILLFOLD See purse.

BILLIARD BALL pertains to an aspect of skill and/or ability to pre-plan.

BILLIONAIRE exemplifies great monetary wealth.

BILL OF GOODS refers to dishonesty; a bad transaction.

BILL OF HEALTH characterizes one's state of health.

BILL OF LADING pertains to the manner in which one holds to promises.

BILL OF RIGHTS means one's right to have rights. This is an important dream fragment. Everyone has rights.

BILL OF SALE represents a completed transaction.

BILLOW implies "expansion" of something related to the dreamer's life.

BILLY CLUB exemplifies force; a forceful nature; ill-used power.

BIMBO portrays misplaced priorities; having little interest in intellectual aspects.

BINARY means double purpose; two-fold.

BINARY STAR denotes wisdom shining forth from knowledge and reason.

BINDER (legal) stands for warranted promises or agreements.

BINDER (notebook) cautions one to "retain" that which has been learned or recorded.

BINDERY depicts a need to keep records, thoughts, concepts, or beliefs "together." This would come as a warning against letting these aspects become scattered.

BINGE signifies an overindulgence; an excessive personality.

BINGO cautions against a steady tendency toward expectation.

BINOCULARS imply a need for closer inspection; get focused.

BIOFEEDBACK cautions one to listen to one's inner prompting more; emphasizes the strength of our inner power; the power of thought.

BIOGRAPHY implies depth of

B

personality; more to an individual than on the surface.

BIOHAZARD warns of a high risk factor connected with an aspect of the dreamer's life.

BIOLOGICAL CLOCK always denotes physical age and the passing of time. This means one is getting older so it'd be wise to attend to priorities.

BIOLOGICAL WARFARE warns of an aggressively dangerous situation or individual in the dreamer's life.

BIOLOGY (study of) connotes a personal interest in all living aspects of one's world. This would indicate a high respect for life.

BIONICS refer to the integration of conceptual and technical aspects; may relate to one who has the talent of visualizing great advances through inventive means.

BIOPSY symbolizes a questionable aspect in one's life.

BIORHYTHM characterizes our vibratory and cyclical connectedness to earth and all life upon it.

BIOSPHERE signifies synergetic relationships; self-supporting.

BIOTELEMETRY portrays self-awareness; a heightened awareness of all aspects of self.

BIPLANE implies the tendency to double-check one's thoughts; a habit of caring about the possibility of wrong thinking.

BIPOLAR denotes balance.

BIRCH exemplifies an open and honest situation or atmosphere.

BIRD reflects personality characteristics. See specific type.

BIRDBATH suggests the need for emotional cleansing.

BIRDBRAIN connotes a lack of intelligence, reason, or logic; may refer to silliness or flightiness.

BIRDCAGE stands for restrained thoughts; fear of extending one's thought process or doing further research.

BIRDCALL represents a "call" to think more deeply and follow ideas and concepts as far as they can go.

BIRD DOG warns of a "hounding" being done.

BIRD FEEDER implies deeper understandings. A thought process that relates to the interconnectedness of all life.

BIRDHOUSE signifies noble and high ideals that are held to.

BIRD OF PARADISE illustrates extravagant and elaborate thoughts.

BIRDSEED refers to research; the feeding of one's thoughts; a thought process that is nourished.

BIRD'S-EYE characterizes broad understanding; comprehensive overview.

BIRD WATCHER stands for "watching" one's thoughts; analyzing self and how conclusions are reached.

BIRTH symbolizes new life.

BIRTH CANAL means the path to some type of rebirth or a new life.

BIRTH CERTIFICATE denotes past life identity which represents one's spiritual heritage.

BIRTH CONTROL (methods) warn of a reluctance to change one's life or make new beginnings.

BIRTHDAY suggests a special reason to recall one's heritage (usually spiritual).

BIRTH DEFECT cautions one to watch out for some type of "defect" presenting itself along a new path taken.

BIRTHING CENTER reveals the atmosphere or surroundings that will provide opportunities for new beginnings.

BIRTHMARK advises one to accept imperfections.

BIRTH PANG signifies adjustments required along one's new path.

BIRTHRIGHT underscores everyone's right to choose new beginnings.

BIRTHSTONE depicts a vibrationally-aligned set of aspects that will best serve an individual.

BISCUIT See cracker.

BISECT suggest an importance to a middle position or path.

BISEXUAL See hermaphrodite.

BISHOP applies to spiritual arrogance.

BISON See buffalo.

BISQUE (color) reflects a lack of ambition; loss of direction.

BISQUE (soup) connotes a hearty constitution; a strong, earthy personality.

BISTRO represents an informal relationship or atmosphere.

BIT (tool) corresponds to an effective aid in accomplishing a goal.

BITEWING (x-ray) suggests a need to check one's language for negativity or harmful words.

BIT PART reveals a small role one is playing or needs to play in a relationship or some type of situation.

BITTER denotes something that's distasteful; something painful or hard to take in life.

BITTERNUT pertains to the unavoidable, naturally-occurring events in life that are irritating yet not lasting.

BITTERROOT relates to continual blessings in life that may, at first, appear as negatives.

BITTERSWEET (plant) reminds

us that beauty frequently follows our pains in life.

BIVOUAC applies to keeping oneself free and unencumbered while walking a new path.

BLACK (color) stands for mystery or negativity. Black will always accompany a premonition of death.

BLACK-AND-BLUE alludes to relationships or situations that will end up harming the dreamer.

BLACK-AND-WHITE stands for clarity; clear perception; the facts.

BLACKBALL denotes negative choices or a shutting-out of something.

BLACK BEAR characterizes an extremely dangerous person closely associated with the dreamer.

BLACK BELT symbolizes self-confidence in one's personal quality and strength of protection.

BLACKBERRY represents fruitful aspects of life that manifest through one's personal nature; the fruits of a spiritual life.

BLACKBIRD signifies an omen.

BLACKBOARD brings messages. What was written?

BLACK BOOK denotes secrecy.

BLACK BOX (flight recorder) indicates a record of events; the recording of one's life; karmic record.

BLACK CLOTHING is a forewarning of death; may be physical, emotional or spiritual.

BLACK DEATH means a fatal situation or relationship.

BLACK DIAMOND stands for ill-use of material wealth.

BLACK EYE (bruise) implies interfering actions.

BLACK EYES (color) suggest dark perceptions; a pessimistic view.

BLACK-EYED SUSAN connotes favorable results forthcoming.

BLACK FLAG See Jolly Roger.

BLACK FOREST symbolizes an attitude of mystery behind spiritual gifts.

BLACK FROST warns of a destructive freezing of one's spiritual beliefs or the cessation of spiritual application.

BLACK GOLD See oil field.

BLACKGUARD alludes to an unprincipled individual; one who exhibits a vile, abusive nature.

BLACKHEAD indicates negative aspects that "clog" understandings; obstructions to clarity.

BLACK HILLS denote sacred aspects that need protection and reverence.

BLACK HILLS GOLD stands for a defilement of sacredness.

BLACK HOLE pertains to depression; futileness; a place of no return.

BLACK HUMOR reveals poor taste or an intent to shock.

BLACK ICE warns against spiritual concepts that are dangerous and difficult to perceive.

BLACKJACK (game) suggests a tendency toward playing the odds; taking chances in life.

BLACKJACK WEAPON See billy club.

BLACK LIGHT alludes to lessons learned from negative experiences.

BLACKLIST means prejudice.

BLACK LUNG corresponds to the acceptance of dark thoughts and ideas.

BLACK MAGIC warns against obtaining personal goals through the use of negativity.

BLACKMAIL portrays a gross negative use of knowledge.

BLACK MARKET applies to underhandedness in obtaining goals.

BLACK MASS denotes spiritual negativity; a destructive spiritual force.

BLACK MONEY represents hidden assets; secret wealth.

BLACK NIGHTSHADE illustrates the duality of nature. This may apply to human nature as well.

BLACK OAK denotes a strong negative aspect in one's life.

BLACKOUT (consciousness) exemplifies selective memory.

BLACKOUT (electrical) warns against sporadic or selective perception.

BLACK PEPPER refers to aspects to which the dreamer has a strong reaction.

BLACK SHEEP characterizes a personalized or unique path; one who dares to be different.

BLACKSMITH illustrates reformations or rejuvenations that will be solid and strong.

BLACKSTRAP See molasses.

BLACK TEA pertains to negative effects of an overingestion of a few selective foodstuffs. This would indicate one who eats only a small variety of food lacking any protein value.

BLACK TIE alludes to an extremely formal personality.

BLACKTOP See asphalt.

BLACK WIDOW symbolizes an extremely dangerous individual or relationship in one's life.

BLADDER stands for an aspect in one's life that "holds negatives" within; warns of a need to release negatives.

BLADE See knife.

BLAME reminds us to double-check our thoughts and actions.

This may not apply to the dreamer but to another person associated with the dreamer.

BLANCH denotes shocking information.

BLAND alludes to neutrality or uninteresting aspects.

BLANK refers to lack of thought or ideas.

BLANK CARTRIDGE suggests a lack of power or effectiveness.

BLANK CHECK stands for unlimited resources or opportunities.

BLANKET signifies a compassionate personality.

BLANKET STITCH reflects an intent to "finish" or complete a project or goal.

BLANK EYES characterize apathy.

BLARNEY STONE denotes a desire to be eloquent or persuasive.

BLASPHEMY pertains to contempt.

BLAST FURNACE warns of internalized negatives such as anger, hate, jealousy, guilt.

BLAZE See fire.

BLEACH cautions against a tendency to "whitewash" things; a habit of being overly optimistic.

BLEACHER warns of complacency; a tendency to sit back and "watch" others do the work.

BLEARY-EYED connotes a need to pace one's intake of information; a need to rest; overwork.

BLEEDER See hemophilia.

BLEEDING indicates a loss of essential life elements; waning energy and motivation; a lessening of one's inner strength and power.

BLEEDING HEART (plant) characterizes a sympathetic personality.

BLEMISH illustrates an imperfection connected to an aspect of the dreamer's life.

BLENDER suggests mixing; cautions against a separatist attitude toward various life aspects.

BLESS portrays a recognition of sacredness.

BLESSED THISTLE denotes aspects pertaining to female assistance or support.

BLIGHT applies to that which impedes growth or advancement.

BLIMP illustrates cumbersome thoughts and ideas; overblown concepts; a cluttered thought process.

BLIND (hunting) warns against the tendency to "hide" self from others.

BLIND (sightless) connotes self-induced lack of understanding; purposeful ignorance.

BLIND (Venetian) indicates a habit of altering one's scope of perception; self-controlled views of life; choosing how much to see and understand.

BLIND ALLEY stands for futile efforts.

BLIND DATE exemplifies questionable relationships.

BLINDER warns of apathy; self-generated ignorance; disinterest.

BLINDFOLD represents confusion; being misled.

BLINDMAN'S BLUFF (game) reflects "grasping in the dark"—attempting to proceed without adequate information or clear perception.

BLINDSIDED cautions one to be more perceptive, more aware; the need to look at all angles.

BLIND SPOT advises of an obstructed view or perception.

BLINK implies inattention; a temporary loss of awareness.

BLINKER (light) attempts to bring one to attention; a warning.

BLIP means a shift from the norm.

BLISTER stands for the effects of one's actions.

BLITZ illustrates an "overwhelming" aspect in one's life.

BLIZZARD warns of a spiritual suffocation; the intake of too many spiritual concepts too fast.

BLOATED warns against excesses.

BLOB stands for something that's undefined; nebulous; vague.

BLOCK (shape) represents an insensitive personality; unforgiving; opinionated.

BLOCK (toys) signify crude planning; uncreative activity.

BLOCKADE exemplifies those "blocks" in our life that are put in our path by others. These can be overcome.

BLOCK AND TACKLE stands for aspects that allow us to overcome obstacles in life.

BLOCKHEAD characterizes a narrow-minded individual.

BLOCKHOUSE applies to one's defenses.

BLOND (hair) refers to a "sunny" disposition; an optimist.

BLOOD pertains to those aspects that equate to one's "life force" or driving motivation.

BLOOD BANK refers to a need to be motivated.

BLOOD BROTHER portrays a bonded relationship.

BLOOD CLOT depicts a negative aspect that's blocking one's motivation.

BLOOD COUNT alludes to the need to review those aspects that motivate the dreamer. Perhaps some of these are not all positive ones.

BLOODHOUND (dog breed) suggests a friend with acute deduction and perceptual abilities.

BLOODLESS warns against a lack of motivation; self-apathy.

BLOODLETTING means misconceptions that lessen one's motivation.

BLOOD MONEY warns of goals gained at the cost of another; ill-gotten gains; the destruction of another.

BLOOD POISONING denotes dangerously negative motivations.

BLOOD PRESSURE alludes to one's motivational energy and interest.

BLOOD RELATION refers to individuals who are motivated by the same aspects as the dreamer.

BLOODROOT connotes negative motivations.

BLOODSHOT (eyes) represents one who is confused regarding motivations.

BLOODSTAIN pertains to the effects of one's motivation; what one's actions leave behind due to their specific motivation.

BLOODSTONE See heliotrope.

BLOODSTREAM portrays the motivating "current" that flows through one's life.

BLOODSUCKER characterizes one who diminishes the motivation of another.

BLOOD TEST suggests one's motivation is in question.

BLOODTHIRSTY stands for vengeful motivation.

BLOOD TYPING relates to a desire to stay true to one's motivational aspects.

BLOOPER suggests that we laugh at our mistakes.

BLOSSOM represents the "beautiful effect" of right living.

BLOTTER refers to a need to "clean up" mistakes; admit to blame; make amends.

BLOW-DRYER cautions against letting viable thoughts and ideas "dry up."

BLOW GUN See blowpipe.

BLOWHARD characterizes a gossip; a braggart.

BLOWHOLE denotes breathing room; aspects in life that give us a breather.

BLOWING A WHISTLE warns of an informer.

BLOWOUT illustrates an aspect that will cause temporary delays.

BLOWPIPE cautions against a dangerous individual or situation.

BLOWTORCH relates to a need for the dreamer to make either "connections" or "separations" in life.

BLOWUP depicts emotional explosions or a failed endeavor.

BLUBBER (cry and mutter) cautions against self-pity.

BLUBBER (fat) symbolizes one's excesses.

BLUE represents spirituality and spiritual aspects in life.

BLUE BABY connotes a new beginning that lacks spirituality.

BLUEBEARD characterizes spiritual indecision and lack of faith.

BLUEBELL illustrates spiritual joy.

BLUEBERRY corresponds to the fruits of one's personal spirituality.

BLUEBIRD refers to spiritual joy and contentedness.

BLUE BOOK symbolizes the value of various spiritual concepts.

BLUE CHEESE stands for spiritual nourishment.

BLUE CHIP portrays "preferred" spiritual beliefs. This may be a negative if connected to fads or current popularity.

BLUE-COLLAR signifies one who applies spiritual beliefs to daily life.

BLUEGRASS (music) signifies a "down-home" type of spirituality.

BLUE JAY See bluebird.

BLUE JEANS depict one who is comfortable and relaxed with one's spiritual beliefs.

BLUE MOON implies rare and extremely valuable spiritual wisdom.

BLUENOSE characterizes spiritual arrogance.

BLUE-PLATE refers to one's specific spiritual foundation.

BLUEPRINT signifies spiritual planning.

BLUE RIBBON pertains to praise from the highest source.

BLUES (music) cautions against spiritual melancholy; a need for balance between the lightness and beauty of spirituality and the heaviness of physical life.

BLUE SPRUCE connotes one's connectedness to spirituality through nature.

BLUESTOCKING refers to a woman with spiritual wisdom.

BLUE STREAK symbolizes spiritual swiftness; some spiritual aspect has come as a bolt of lightning.

BLUE WHALE signifies spiritual generosity; one who has a spiritually magnanimous nature.

BLUFF (promontory) connotes a "front" depicting a bluffing situation or aspect.

BLUING warns against spiritual arrogance; pretending more spirituality than owning.

BLUR denotes a need for more clear understanding.

BLURB reflects one person's opinion.

BLUSH illustrates embarrassment.

BOA CONSTRICTOR characterizes a smothering or constricting situation or relationship.

BOAR indicates a haughty personality; a bore to others.

BOARDER (renter) refers to opportunities; temporary and short-term openings to utilize karma-balancing situations.

BOARDING SCHOOL is synonymous with the reality of life. We eat, sleep, and learn as we go.

BOARDROOM portrays decision-making; the knowing of our higher self.

BOARDWALK cautions against a voluntary separation from one's spiritual aspects.

BOAST See brag.

BOAT represents a spiritual path and its quality.

BOAT CAPTAIN stands for the one who spiritually leads. This should be none other than self following inner guidance.

BOATHOUSE corresponds with a spiritual home; the living of spiritual beliefs.

BOATLIFT portrays spiritual compassion; a spiritual rescue endeavor.

BOAT PEOPLE characterize those wanting to be spiritually saved.

BOBBIN pertains to order of one's priorities; maintaining a smooth and untangled manner of operating; a first-things-first attitude.

BOBBY PIN refers to keeping one's thoughts or attitudes in place instead of letting them become tangled or go wild.

BOBBY SOCKS imply an informal attitude; a casual personality.

BOBCAT See lion.

BOBLSED denotes a spiritual path that's quickly sped over; a rush to a spiritual goal without gaining the riches and depth along the way.

BOCK BEER symbolizes a strong constitution; strong beginnings.

BODHISATTVA characterizes absolute selflessness.

BODY (unidentified) exemplifies outstanding aspects that require attention in one's life.

BODY BAG depicts a failure to attend to important aspects in one's life.

BODYBUILDING applies to an attention to one's weaknesses; a building-up of them.

BODYGUARD connotes an awareness of one's protective aspects (tools) and the utilization of same.

BODY LANGUAGE indicates the nonverbal messages we send out; unspoken communications.

BODY SEARCH indicates a suspicion of concealment; possible dishonesty.

BODY SHOP suggests "repair" work needed. This will refer directly to some physical aspect in your life.

BODY STOCKING pertains to a "second skin" one wears; thick-skinned; possibly represents a fear of being hurt.

BODYSURFING symbolizes a willingness to get close to spiritual issues; an adventuresome spiritual attitude.

BOG illustrates something that "bogs" one down, keeps one from going forward in an unfettered manner.

BOGEYMAN characterizes those we fear in life.

BOHEMIAN depicts a free-thinking personality; one who is not afraid to live an unconventional lifestyle or have differing attitudes.

BOIL (hot liquid) stands for an agitated or "heated" situation or attitude.

BOIL (skin) warns of suppressed emotions.

BOILER exemplifies "hot" situations or relationships in one's life.

BOILER ROOM pertains to one's surroundings that could lead to explosive encounters or outcomes.

BOILING POINT connotes the point at which a condition or relationship becomes explosive.

BOLDFACE (type) means emphasis. This is a call to pay attention.

BOLOGNA alludes to a belief system derived from a variety of sources.

BOLO TIE relates to attitudes that are not consistent; a changeable personality.

BOLSTER signifies a need for support; to be "bolstered" up.

BOLT denotes strength of connections. This may relate to relationships or ideas.

BOLT CUTTER alludes to cutting strong ties.

BOMB represents explosive situations or relationships; also disappointments; failures.

BOMB BAY means aspects in one's life that are on the verge of exploding unless they are calmed or altered.

BOMBER (aircraft) characterizes an unpredictable individual.

BOMBSHELL depicts great disappointments; shocking news.

BOMB SHELTER illustrates fear of disappointments; a lack of faith.

BOMBSIGHT portrays destructive intentions.

BONANZA suggests a great find of some type; coming across something that has been searched for.

BONBON See candy.

BOND (fastener) signifies a connection in one's life.

BOND (monetary) applies to a need for security.

BONDSMAN characterizes a trusted individual; one who provides security.

BONE represents aspects in one's life that signify foundations. This could be attitudes, relationships, or belief systems.

BONE MARROW pertains to the "life" of one's foundational beliefs.

BONE MARROW TRANSPLANT refers to a need for "new life" brought into one's foundational beliefs or attitudes.

BONFIRE portrays one's inner fire; motivation.

BONGO DRUMS stand for dual operations; the working together of two individuals.

BONING KNIFE warns of a threatening aspect directed toward one's foundational attitudes or beliefs.

BONNET characterizes old-fashioned ideas; often a prudish attitude.

BONSAI stands for forced attitudes; thoughts or ideas that are not naturally come by; mental manipulation.

BONUS pertains to actions or decisions that will lead to the manifestation of greater benefits than realized.

BONUS POINTS imply the accumulation of good karma.

BOOBY PRIZE refers to "some" benefit or reward forthcoming.

BOOBY TRAP symbolizes a "rigged" situation or relationship.

BOOK signifies knowledge and the need for same; further study needed.

BOOKCASE denotes broad-scope knowledge and suggests a need to study a variety of volumes.

BOOK CLUB pertains to a wide variety of writings on one subject.

BOOKEND cautions one to stop studying a subject until deeper comprehension has been attained.

BOOKING See appointment.

BOOKKEEPER characterizes the Book of Life; one's karmic record.

BOOKMAKER (bookie) indicates one who is seen as an instigator.

BOOKMARK suggests a "pause" in studying or learning is needed. This would usually indicate a need for contemplation and assimilation of that already learned.

BOOKMOBILE connotes the learning of healing methods; physiological research; the reading of medical books.

BOOKPLATE warns against an arrogance of knowledge; an intellectual possessiveness.

BOOK REVIEW pertains to a message from one's higher self in respect to the quality of material and personal relevance of a book title.

BOOKSHELF See bookcase.

BOOKSTORE signifies research and knowledge.

BOOK VALUE denotes the true value of something.

BOOKWORM warns against a tendency to accumulate knowledge without applying it.

BOOM (flourish) portrays a productive path.

BOOM (sound) signifies a "call" for the dreamer to be more aware or to listen and pay more attention to life.

BOOM BOX symbolizes arrogance; a need for personal attention.

BOOMERANG cautions one to watch for aspects that will "come back" at or turn on self.

BOOMTOWN characterizes a productive life.

BOONDOCK represents spiritual remoteness; spiritual apathy.

BOOSTER CABLE advises that helpful or supportive "connections" be made in one's life.

BOOSTER SEAT alludes to a need to "see better" on an issue; better perspective is required.

BOOSTER SHOT warns against not following through with something; a need to be mindful of one's continual progress.

BOOT symbolizes the outward quality and style of one's pathwalk.

BOOT CAMP applies to getting the "basics" of something.

BOOTH connotes privacy; individuality.

BOOTJACK relates to a time to pause along one's path.

BOOTLEG warns against attempting to accomplish or gain something through unethical or immoral means.

BOOTSTRAP refers to a path walked with determination.

BOOTY illustrates that which has been obtained or gained through stealth or manipulation.

BOOZE See alcoholic beverage.

BOOZEHOUND See alcoholic.

BORAX denotes a lack of quality.

BORDELLO See house of ill repute.

B

BORDER marks some aspect in one's life that represents a dividing line.

BORDERLAND exemplifies a "fringe" area in one's life or beliefs.

BORDERLINE represents a "questionable" aspect in one's life.

BORE (drill) implies perseverance; pushing forward.

BORE (dull) cautions against a lack of motivation; suggests the need to expand interests.

BOREAL (north) signifies a higher direction to one's path; elevated levels of study; higher attitudes and perspectives.

BOREHOLE alludes to a "testing" aspect in one's life that should be followed though with.

BOROUGH refers to a specific area of concern in one's life.

BORROW implies a "temporary" solution.

BORROWED TIME warns against overdoing; trying to accomplish too much too fast.

BOSS characterizes a higher authority, perhaps one's higher self.

BOTANICAL symbolizes the quality and quantity of how well one applies spirituality to life.

BOTANICAL GARDEN represents an ideal spiritual life; a life of applying beliefs in all aspects.

BOTANIST illustrates one who works hard at applying spirituality to daily life.

BOTANY (study of) portrays an individual who looks for ways to apply spiritual concepts to everyday living situations and relationships.

BOTTLE warns against keeping something "bottled-up" inside.

BOTTLEBRUSH advises one to keep clarity within self; a caution to "clean out" imperfect attitudes.

BOTTLED GAS See propane.

BOTTLE-FEED means "forced" ideas, thoughts, or concepts.

BOTTLENECK denotes complications; congested aspects; backed-up thoughts or plans.

BOTTOM denotes foundation or beginning point.

BOTTOMLESS signifies great depth to something or someone.

BOTTOM LINE signifies the "point" of something; the bare facts.

BOTULISM cautions against the severely damaging effects of negative thought and action.

BOUCLE pertains to a gentle, down-home individual who takes life in stride.

BOUDOIR See bedroom.

BOUFFANT (hair style) characterizes an egotistical personality; one whose ideas are blown up to

57

present a more impressive perception.

BOUGAINVILLEA portrays a bright spiritual life.

BOUGH connotes an opportunity to utilize one's spirituality.

BOUILLABAISSE illustrates spiritual diversity; a broad base of spiritual concepts from which one can learn.

BOUILLON stands for clarity in understanding.

BOUILLON CUBE pertains to aspects in one's life that bring clarity.

BOULDER represents major problematical aspects in one's life.

BOULEVARD pertains to a wide and well-used path. This may not be the best traveled by the dreamer.

BOUNCE indicates a suggestion to be more resilient.

BOUNCER characterizes one who keeps order and maintains a peaceful atmosphere.

BOUNTY means a reward for something accomplished.

BOUNTY HUNTER symbolizes misplaced priorities; wrong motives; being in expectation of rewards for good deeds done.

BOUQUET (flower) illustrates a commendation from higher spiritual sources.

BOUQUET (scent) implies quality; positive or negative indications.

BOURBON See alcoholic beverage.

BOURBON STREET pertains to a person's tendency to not take life seriously; a somewhat hedonistic perspective.

BOURGEOIS exemplifies middle-class conventions and attitudes.

BOUT signifies a confrontation between rivals; a needed meeting to settle differences.

BOUTIQUE relates to specialty; specific aspects in life.

BOUTONNIERE marks distinction; one singled out for a specific reason.

BOW (archery) stands for an aspect that helps to target a problem.

BOW (bend) illustrates an act of respect; concession.

BOW (boat) denotes the leading aspect of one's spiritual search; that which is the forerunner of such a path.

BOW (ribbon) connotes finality; a finished aspect in one's life.

BOWED (shape) signifies a "rounded" aspect; gentleness.

BOWER See arbor.

BOWIE KNIFE See knife.

BOWL (sport) refers to obtaining goals through unethical means.

BOWL (utensil) indicates a need for containment regarding an aspect in the dreamer's life.

BOWLEGGED illustrates perseverance throughout one's life.

BOWLING ALLEY denotes a condition or situation where one will have opportunities to act in unethical manners.

BOWLING BALL symbolizes specific unethical acts.

BOWSTRING connotes that which "connects" aspects pointing to a specific problem.

BOW TIE alludes to a constrained personality; an individual who is frequently considered stuffy or straight-laced.

BOX (container) warns of a "boxed-in" condition, situation, or relationship. Individuals can also box themselves in.

BOX (shape) represents a "square" thought process; not open-minded.

BOX (sport) portrays an argumentative personality.

BOX CAMERA suggests old-fashioned attitudes; out-of-date perspectives.

BOXCAR refers to extra aspects we carry around in life that are heavily weighted; negative memories; bad feelings retained.

BOXER SHORTS exemplify sexist perspectives; a sexually domineering attitude.

BOXING GLOVE connotes a combative nature.

BOX LUNCH applies to conservative attitudes; frugal.

BOX OFFICE implies that which attracts attention; a draw; popularity.

BOX SEAT means a high position; benefit of wealth or position.

BOX SPRING relates to quality of rest times; quality of relaxation and pause from the daily grind.

BOX TOP represents something that needs "opening" in one's life. What kind of box is the dream presenting? Are there words on it?

BOY characterizes beginning or foundational male perspectives.

BOYCOTT means a demonstrative protest; an active coercion.

BOYFRIEND symbolizes male relationships.

BOY SCOUT represents good deeds and the formation of ethical life perspectives.

BOYSENBERRY portrays the fruits of enduring life struggles.

BOY WONDER depicts high accomplishments gained from an early recognition of opportunities.

BRACE means support. What is braced? This answer will clearly define what needs support in the dreamer's life.

BRACELET connotes a subjugated situation or relationship.

BRACKEN stands for a tangled and prickly path due to one's lack of spiritual application.

BRACKET represents an aspect that assists in supporting the personal weight of life problems and adversity.

BRAG exemplifies a lack of peace within self.

BRAID (hair) pertains to "twisted" thought patterns; confusion; convoluted thinking process; twisted perspectives.

BRAILLE advises of opportunities to "see" clearly; warns against a tendency to claim ignorance.

BRAIN pertains to one's thought process and quality of same.

BRAINCHILD characterizes a brilliant idea.

BRAIN CORAL connotes spiritual intelligence and/or high knowledge.

BRAIN DAMAGE applies to thought patterns or perspectives that are not correct; inability to correctly reason or perceive logically.

BRAIN DEATH portrays total apathy; may also come as a premonition of someone's physical death.

BRAIN FEVER denotes a condition that "inflames" one's thoughts.

BRAINLESS means irrationality; unreasonable; illogical.

BRAIN-PICKING relates to in-depth contemplation and analysis.

BRAIN SCAN advises one to self-examine thought processes and paths of logic; a self-check of one's reasoning abilities.

BRAINSTORMING means deep thought applied to problem-solving or inventiveness.

BRAINTEASER signifies a problematical aspect in one's life that's extremely difficult to solve or resolve.

BRAINWASHING stands for a willful destruction of another's ideals, attitudes, or perspectives.

BRAIN WAVE connotes mental impulses; inspiration; sudden ideas.

BRAKE warns of the need to halt something in the dreamer's life.

BRAKE FLUID pertains to a life element utilized to control the pace of one's progression.

BRAKE LIGHT symbolizes the intention to slow down.

BRAKE LINE pertains to the ability to control one's life pace.

BRAKE PEDAL refers to aspects in one's life that allows a slower pace; that which brings about a slowing.

BRAMBLE See bracken.

BRANCH See bough.

BRAND denotes possession; the exclusive owner of something.

BRANDING IRON stands for possessiveness.

BRAND NAME pertains to general knowledge; that which is recognizable.

BRANDY See alcoholic beverage.

BRASS characterizes a harsh boisterous personality; unrefined.

BRASS KNUCKLES stand for a severely aggressive nature with intent to cause harm.

BRASS RING symbolizes an aspect that suggests a strong possibility to have the ability to realize goals; something that may manifest one's dreams.

BRASS TACKS apply to the basic facts of an issue or situation.

BRAT signifies an ill-mannered, juvenile attitude.

BRAWL cautions against loss of temper; inability to settle differences in an intelligent and reasonable manner.

BREAD represents aspects that sustain us; the necessities.

BREAD AND BUTTER means one's livelihood; that which provides basic needs.

BREADBASKET denotes those life aspects that contribute to the quality and dependability of our livelihood.

BREADBOARD refers to life aspects that "support" one's livelihood.

BREAD BOX portrays "quantity" of energy put into one's livelihood.

BREAD LINE denotes a lack of necessities. This may indicate one's "basic" moral, emotional, or spiritual aspects.

BREAD MOLD suggests a possible need to change jobs or breathe freshness into the present one.

BREADWINNER characterizes one who supplies necessities; one who does the work.

BREAKDOWN implies a "falling-apart" situation or condition.

BREAKFAST connotes the quality of a new beginning.

BREAKFRONT signifies a "crack" in one's presented veneer; a "break" in one's affected presentation.

BREAK-IN (dispel newness) advises one to reach a comfortable point or position.

BREAK-IN (robbery) pertains to inadequate or ineffective defenses.

BREAKING POINT connotes a critical point where one either breaks away or is overstressed by conditions.

BREAKOUT signifies a form of escape.

BREAKTHROUGH means a great advancement or realization has been accomplished.

BREAKUP illustrates the separation of a specific life aspect. This may be a promising dream fragment.

BREAKWATER stands for a major spiritual barrier. This may be a temporary necessity.

BREAST relates to emotions, usually unexpressed sensitivity.

BREAST-BEATING denotes sorrow. This action may represent a desire to elicit sympathy from others.

BREAST FEEDING usually refers to a nurturing nature; may also indicate immaturity and/or a fear to be independent.

BREASTPLATE warns of a fear of being hurt; indicates a lack of confidence in self or one's own defenses.

BREASTSTROKE suggests spirituality taken to heart.

BREATH exemplifies the quality of one's inner life-force.

BREATHLESS cautions the dreamer to slow down. One or more aspects in life are being rushed through.

BREECH DELIVERY warns of a possible "backward" outcome to a developing relationship or situation.

BREEDER connotes an individual who maintains interest in something for the prime purpose of "getting something back" out of it.

BREEDING GROUND means a "fertile" condition or atmosphere; an atmosphere conducive to productivity.

BREEZE implies low mental activity. This may not be a negative dream fragment.

BREEZEWAY denotes thoughts that "connect" main ideas to form more complex concepts.

BREW (concoct) symbolizes a "mix" of various thoughts or ideas; long contemplation on innovative concepts; inventiveness.

BREWER'S YEAST represents the "source" of innovative thought; brilliant thought and ideas.

BRIAR See bracken.

BRIBE means ill-gotten favors, benefits, or goals.

BRIC-A-BRAC stands for the unnecessary aspects with which one clutters life.

BRICK signifies life's building blocks; one's personal foundational aspects that should be solid and strong.

BRICKLAYER characterizes one who works hard and diligently at insuring strong foundational values.

BRIDE portrays a desire or need for male influence.

BRIDEGROOM represents a desire or need for female influences in life.

BRIDESMAID/BEST MAN characterizes a need for support in decision-making or support while walking one's path.

BRIDE PRICE pertains to an unnecessary "payment" extended for a personal relationship; a "forced" or bribe-generated relationship.

BRIDGE always denotes some type of connection.

BRIDLE denotes a means of control.

BRIDLE PATH relates to a controlled life path; a path that is traveled at an easy pace.

BRIEF (legal) pertains to facts presented in a concise manner.

BRIEFCASE cautions one to have all facts together before making decisions or judgments.

BRIM depicts a full capacity; a life aspect that has been fully developed or explored.

BRIMSTONE relates to a passionately demonstrative attitude connected to a specific cause or issue.

BRINE portrays the preservation of spiritual concepts or truths.

BRINE SHRIMP represent individual spiritual concepts.

BRINK symbolizes the point at which a major decision or action must be taken.

BRIQUETTE stands for that which serves as an impetus; life aspects that light a fire and serve as motivation.

BRISKET denotes emotionally warming feelings.

BRITTLE portrays something that's dry, unyielding; a lack of nourishment which may be mental, emotional, or spiritual.

BRITTLE STAR characterizes spiritual "reaching"; one's research that extends as far as it can be taken.

BROADCAST connotes the spreading of information.

BROAD JUMP See long jump.

BROADSIDE indicates unexpected events; surprises in life that deeply affect us.

BROADSWORD See sword.

BROADWAY (NYC) cautions against a tendency toward theatrics; a habit of overdramatizing; exaggerations.

BROCADE (fabric) illustrates a way of life that's rich in compassion and possesses an emotional depth; a life of living spiritual beliefs.

BROCCOLI signifies multi-level talents and the utilization of same.

BROCHURE portrays a "hyped" aspect; something that's portrayed in a glossy presentation.

BROIL refers to "heat from above"; pressure from one's boss or higher self.

BROILER characterizes the aspect in one's life that has the capability of bringing pressure or heat.

BROKER See agent.

BROKERAGE stands for a precarious aspect in one's life.

BRONCHITIS alludes to an inability to clearly process thoughts and ideas.

BRONCO represents individuality and the freedom to express same.

BRONZE is suggestive of the beauty that comes from the blending of specific life aspects.

BRONZE CAST exemplifies the resulting product of blending specific life aspects; the touchable goal or creation.

BRONZE STAR portrays recognition for perseverance.

BROOCH (jewelry) connotes an attention-getting aspect or one who enjoys getting the attention of others.

BROOD (deep in thought) cautions against a tendency to dwell on specific aspects without productive results.

BROOD (many young) characterizes many new opportunities in the offing.

BROOK See stream.

BROOM cautions one to look past the surface; sweep away surface debris to get a clearer perception of what's beneath.

BROOMSTICK refers to an aspect that allows one to see past the surface.

BROTHEL See house of ill repute.

BROTHER characterizes a close male associate in life; a male who is a close friend.

BROTHERHOOD signifies male camaraderie that has a deeply connecting aspect.

BROUGHAM See carriage.

BROW See forehead.

BROWN symbolizes one's "earthy" aspects; life, attitude, and emotional side rather than anything spiritual.

BROWN BAGGING portrays a frugal nature.

BROWN BREAD typifies a down-home nature.

BROWNIE (fairy) characterizes the assistance we receive at night through our higher self and dreams.

BROWNIE (sweet) pertains to those life aspects one views as personal treats.

BROWNIE (young Girl Scout) denotes the beginning development of ethics and feminine perspectives.

BROWNIE POINT cautions against the expectation of praise; doing good for the purpose of gaining praise or reward.

BROWN-OUT warns against overwork; loss of energy.

BROWN RICE relates to "wholeness"; acceptance of the whole rather than choosing easier, softer aspects.

BROWNSTONE commends one's tendency to give others space; an acceptance of another's totality.

BROWN SUGAR connotes a genuinely sweet personality; one whose true nature is without negative qualities.

BROWSE pertains to selectiveness; looking for specifics.

BRUISE characterizes minor emotional or psychological injuries.

BRUNCH depicts a starting point that begins in the middle; suggests one goes back to the beginning.

BRUNT denotes one's main burden or responsibility.

BRUSH warns of a tendency to "brush" things aside; a habit of avoiding priorities or serious aspects.

BRUSHFIRE stands for a willful neglect or destruction of one's talents; a voluntary cessation of spiritual acts.

BRUSSELS SPROUTS indicate the little acts of goodness we do that nourish or encourage others.

BRUTUS (Marcus Junius) warns of the self-destructing power that vindictiveness has.

BUBBLE connotes negative aspects in one's life.

BUBBLE BATH warns against "submerging" self in negative situations, relationships, or beliefs.

BUBBLE GUM illustrates an arrogance in the face of negatives; a foolish attitude.

BUBBLE TOP signifies a fear of being injured; lack of confidence in one's protective abilities.

BUBONIC PLAGUE pertains to highly contagious negative attitudes; demonstrates the speed and destructive force of following the crowd when the crowd is in serious error.

BUCCANEER characterizes those who harm another's spiritual beliefs.

BUCKBOARD signifies a "rough" ride along one's path, yet the rider persists without complaint.

BUCKET denotes the retention of important spiritual truths.

BUCKET BRIGADE characterizes the "sharing" of spiritual truths.

BUCKET SEAT means self-confidence; individualism; or separatism.

BUCK FEVER reveals a predatory nature.

BUCKING denotes reluctance; a hesitancy to carry through.

BUCKLE portrays determination.

BUCKSHOT pertains to solid facts or "ammunition" that back up one's goal or claim.

BUCKSKIN refers to a "soft-touch" aspect of one's nature.

BUCKTEETH typifies an outspoken individual; often one who speaks before thinking.

BUCOLIC alludes to an extremely peaceful situation or relationship.

BUD indicates new beginnings.

BUDDHA means highest spiritual attainment; enlightenment and the true wisdom that accompanies it.

BUDDY portrays a reluctance to be on one's own; a fear of solitude.

BUDDY SYSTEM symbolizes a companion need.

BUDGERIGAR See parakeet.

BUDGET cautions against the practice of disproportionate activities; suggests a need to prioritize.

BUD VASE signifies a personal pride and feeling of rightness in respect to one's new beginnings.

BUDWORM is an extremely negative aspect that damages new beginnings.

BUFF (polish) represents the act of "finishing" something to the best of one's ability.

BUFFALO symbolizes gullibility. May also indicate perseverance.

BUFFALOHEART represents great inner strength; endurance through intense adversity.

BUFFALO ROBE denotes one's shield of inner strength.

BUFFALO WINGS relate to attempts to intermix specific aspects that do not blend or will not coalesce.

BUFFER ZONE represents one's social distance or "space" separating self from others.

BUFFET See sideboard.

BUFFET (meal) symbolizes the wide variety of opportunities open to us.

BUFFING WHEEL stands for that which allows one to finalize goals.

BUFFOON See clown.

BUG portrays irritations in life. May have positive meaning when specific insects are shown. See specific name.

BUGABOO implies the subject of one's worst fear; a continual problem or irritation.

BUG-EYED connotes ignorant perception; amazement due to a lack of knowledge or understanding.

BUGLE is a call to action or attention.

BUILDINGS See specific kind.

BUILDING SOMETHING depicts the act of creating; active efforts.

BUILT-IN denotes instinctual behavior; inherent qualities or talents.

BUILT-UP signifies development, may pertain to self by way of implying one's boastfulness or egotistical nature.

BULB (flower) refers to an upcoming budding of talent or other aspect in one's life.

BULB (light) applies to a new awareness; solutions; bright ideas.

BULGE pertains to a need to "release" something, usually pressure. May refer to emotions that are building up inside.

BULGUR signifies strength of character; a strong constitution.

BULIMAREXIA illustrates a lack of self-control; a love/hate attitude toward self.

BULKHEAD symbolizes an as-

pect in life that serves as one's main support system.

BULK PURCHASE typifies a personal need for security; expresses a need to be well-provisioned.

BULL characterizes a tendency toward narrow-mindedness.

BULLBOAT refers to the avoidance of spiritual concepts due to primitive attitudes.

BULLDOG (dog breed) denotes a bullish associate or friend.

BULLDOZER illustrates a need for clear understanding; to clear away the rubble that covers the ground-level facts.

BULLET pertains to the negative aspects of self that could injure others.

BULLETIN draws attention to something that should be known; news that affects the dreamer.

BULLETIN BOARD pertains to messages; news; communications.

BULLETPROOF VEST exemplifies an emotionally-devoid personality; a fear of being affected or affecting others.

BULLET TRAIN infers high-speed travel; advises one to slow down in order to absorb that which is presented along the way.

BULLFIGHT means hard-headedness; an inability to compromise.

BULLFROG connotes a need to give serious attention to spiritual matters.

BULLHEADED characterizes a stubborn nature; one rarely given to compromise.

BULLHORN advises one to voice personal attitudes or opinions; a need to express feelings.

BULLION See gold or silver.

BULLPEN points to a situation where several individuals share a narrow-minded group attitude or opinion.

BULLPEN (baseball) represents one's "backup" resources; a source of reserve energy.

BULLRING stands for a manipulative situation or condition.

BULL SESSION advises of the need to casually discuss something; air opinions; express attitudes and perspectives.

BULL'S-EYE confirms one's right course; on target.

BULLWHIP implies an aggressively bullish nature; unyielding; demanding.

BUMBLEBEE characterizes one-mindedness; a focused mind; industrious.

BUMPER pertains to one's tenacity; an ability to "bounce back" from problems or emotional injury.

BUMPER CAR alludes to a personal enjoyment of "the game." A tendency toward conflict for the thrill of winning.

BUMPER STICKER connotes one who is openly opinionated.

BUMPER-TO-BUMPER means little movement; a condition or situation that isn't going anywhere.

BUNDLE See package.

BUNDT CAKE signifies the little rewards in life that come in many forms and from various sources.

BUNGALOW See cottage.

BUNGEE CORD denotes secured defenses; backup safeguards applied when taking life chances.

BUNION refers to the "bumps" and pains received during one's walk through life.

BUNK BED relates to multilevel dreams; dreamscape fragments often have dual meanings for the dreamer.

BUNKER identifies one's lack of faith and/or self-confidence; a fear of one's life path.

BUNKHOUSE typifies the nature of one's casual relationships.

BUNNY See rabbit.

BUNSEN BURNER calls for a need for self-analysis or serious introspection.

BUOY is a directional marker for one's spiritual path.

BUOYANCY portrays spiritual resiliency.

BUREAU See dresser.

BUREAUCRAT means narrow-mindedness; focused on self-serving issues; centered on own agendas.

BURGER symbolizes the tendency to embellish facts or add to foundational aspects.

BURGLAR characterizes an untrustworthy individual; underhandedness; ulterior motives.

BURIAL GROUND See graveyard.

BURL (wood) is the inherent beauty of individuality; the creativity of each individual's unique talents.

BURLAP symbolizes strength of character and an enduring constitution.

BURLESQUE means that something or someone is being mocked; a travesty.

BURN (incinerate) denotes a total destruction of something.

BURN (skin) stands for one being defeated; cheated; outsmarted.

BURNED-OUT pertains to a state of exhaustion; being worn out.

BURNOOSE represents an ability to control stress.

BURNT OFFERING signifies subjugation; attempts to appease or plead.

BURP infers some irregularity with an aspect in one's life.

BURR portrays a slight or temporary problem; minor irritation.

BURRO See donkey.

BURROW indicates trepidation; escapism; attempts to hide from something.

BURROWING OWL characterizes an ability to see through others; acute perception into other's psychological maneuvers.

BURSITIS represents a reluctance to act or go forward.

BURYING SOMETHING stands for cover-ups; secrets; hiding something.

BUS pertains to an aspect in one's life that serves to benefit many. May also refer to an overblown situation or even obesity.

BUSBOY connotes one who is capable of repairing wrongs done; one who has the ability to "clean up" a situation.

BUS DRIVER exemplifies a caring and giving personality.

BUSH denotes "fullness" of spiritual/humanitarian acts.

BUSHEL indicates a large quantity of something.

BUSH JACKET characterizes an adventurous nature.

BUSH LEAGUE See minor league.

BUSHMAN is one who immerses self in a spiritually humanitarian lifestyle.

BUSH PILOT typifies one who guides others to a spiritually interactive life.

BUSHWACKER connotes an individual who is capable of making one's way through life's difficulties; also can denote one who ambushes others.

BUSINESS CARD represents an egotistical personality; a desire to be known and recognized.

BUSING means a "forced" integration of ideas by another.

BUS STATION suggests a need to be helpful at a different location; implies assistance is needed somewhere else.

BUST (sculpture) represents an individual or ideal that's important for the dreamer.

BUSTED See arrest.

BUSTLE (rush) cautions against too fast a pace.

BUSTLE (skirt attachment) means social haughtiness; status conscious.

BUSYBODY stands for an interfering personality.

BUSY SIGNAL denotes a wrong time to communicate with someone. This indicates a communication that wouldn't go well and suggests a later time to attempt the connection.

BUTANE represents thoughts that could be damaging depending how they are acted upon.

BUTCHER characterizes a scathing personality; one who focuses on the negative aspects of others.

BUTCHER BLOCK denotes negative aspects of one's life that others can gossip about or use negatively.

BUTCHER KNIFE connotes a "cutting-up" or "chopping-at" situation; an aspect used to "cut down" someone or something.

BUTLER portrays an individual who is submissive to another; giving deference to another; subservient.

BUTLER'S PANTRY refers to the comfort and convenience of being well-prepared.

BUTTER signifies the richness of a simple life and the unaffected perspectives that accompany it.

BUTTERBALL portrays excessiveness; an extraneous aspect; overblown or "fattened" to extreme.

BUTTER CHURN connotes those aspects that create life's true riches.

BUTTERCUP means life's real joys; inner happiness; laughter.

BUTTERFINGERS caution against letting things slip through your fingers; denotes a need to "get a grasp" on self, life, or some important aspect.

BUTTERFLY exemplifies renewal and rejuvenation. May refer to an ability to bounce back after specific setbacks or disappointments.

BUTTERMILK alludes to life's spiritually-rich rewards.

BUTTERSCOTCH implies something that has a "rich flavor" to it, rich as in spiritually or heartily wholesome.

BUTTON advises of the need for some kind of physical connection or "link-up" needed.

BUTTON-DOWN refers to a need to "secure" something in one's life.

BUTTONHOLE represents the "openings" that life presents to us for opportunities.

BUYER'S MARKET pertains to "the best time" to take advantage of opportunities.

BUY OUT connotes an acquisition of the whole; obtaining something in its entirety; having it all.

BUZZARD characterizes a gloating nature; one who stands in wait to pick over what's left.

BUZZER advises of a need to make communications in a discreet manner. This will directly refer to a specific aspect in the dreamer's life.

BUZZ SAW See circular saw.

BUZZWORD warns against a desire to impress others; a need to bolster self-esteem and worth.

BYLINE denotes an acknowledgment; giving credit where credit is due.

BYPASS pertains to the avoidance of unnecessary aspects; a "going-around" something.

BYPRODUCT illustrates that which all thoughts, words, and actions may cause. We don't always see the widespread effects of what we say and do in life.

BYSTANDER is synonymous with apathy; one who watches yet does not act.

CAB See taxi.

CAB (of truck) indicates the "controlling" aspects of one's life.

CABAL refers to schemers that in some way affect the dreamer's life.

CABANA symbolizes a need for temporary shelter; to remove oneself from heated situations.

CABARET See bistro.

CABBAGE pertains to the rougher aspects directly affecting one's life.

CAB DRIVER characterizes individuals who serve as motivational factors in life.

CABERNET See wine.

CABIN denotes a life aligned with nature; an inner connection or inherent bond with nature.

CABIN CRUISER alludes to a spiritual "cruising along"; a lack of spiritual seriousness.

CABINET portrays that which is kept from the public eye.

CABIN FEVER signifies a desire to be close to nature without being vibrationally aligned; a forcing action applied to one's wants or goals.

CABLE stands for an aspect in life that serves as a strong support.

CABLE CAR connotes advancement generated by a strong supporting aspect in one's life. Can also refer to threatening thoughts.

CABLE TELEVISION implies information obtained through the assistance of others.

CABOOSE means a finalization; the end of something.

CABSTAND exemplifies a "waiting" time. This usually refers to one's inability to advance on one's own.

CACHE symbolizes the high value of one's hidden talents. This is most often a warning to stop "stashing away" one's abilities.

CACTUS applies to spiritual beliefs that are protected.

CADAVER most often denotes learning opportunities.

CADDY represents a "follower" and implies indecision or an inability to think for self.

CADET characterizes the beginning stages of developing combative perspectives; one who can be perceived as a fledgling headed for a draw toward the "military-machine" attitude.

CAFETERIA represents a lack of choice; not realizing the wide scope of opportunities available.

CAFFEINE denotes motivational

factors that serve as an impetus in life.

CAFTAN See burnoose.

CAGE pertains to an aspect that prevents the exercise of one's freedoms or rights. This may even refer to self.

CAGED BIRDS refer to suppressed emotions.

CAIMAN See alligator.

CAIRN illustrates "markers" along life's path. This serves as a guiding aspect.

CAKE portrays a goal or that which is strived for.

CAKE PAN refers to that which assists in achieving goals.

CALAMARI warns against the mental intake of too many differing spiritual concepts at once.

CALCIFICATION suggests an "unyielding" viewpoint, grown "hard" through lack of a giving nature or experience.

CALCIUM symbolizes those aspects in life that serve to strengthen us. A caution is indicated for dream symbols that portray an excess of calcium.

CALCULATOR pertains to complex thought patterns; intricate planning; detailed and analytic contemplation.

CALDERA represents a formerly "hot" issue or situation and the possibility of it reactivating.

CALENDAR signifies time; a specific date. This dream fragment is usually presented as being important for the dreamer.

CALF (bovine) characterizes the beginnings of an end; a fatalistic aspect; something that will not manifest as planned.

CALIBRATE connotes an attempt to make perfect.

CALICO means a natural gentleness; lack of affectation.

CALIPER signifies a desire for perfection; accuracy.

CALISTHENICS mean preparedness; one's level of experience.

CALK See caulk.

CALL pertains to communication.

CALL BOX suggests an immediate need to communicate something. The dreamer will know what this is.

CALL GIRL implies a lack of self-respect; poor self-image; one who lacks individuality and requires the guidance and/or attention of others.

CALLIGRAPHY refers to important messages.

CALLING CARD connotes one's intention or outward presentation to the public.

CALLIOPE indicates a whimsical personality; one who fails to take life seriously; optimism taken to the far extreme.

CALL SIGN pertains to one's "chosen" identity; that which one wants to be known by.

CALLUS characterizes a "hardened" attitude or nature.

CALORIE alludes to an aspect that helps keep a "balance" for the dreamer.

CALORIE CHART illustrates opportunity options for balance in life.

CALUMET See peace pipe.

CALVARY exemplifies personal sacrifices that may not be needed.

CAMBRIDGE (Mass.) typifies the frequent negativity that may result from intelligence wrongly utilized.

CAMCORDER is a sign to "remember" some event in one's life. This infers important lessons to be learned.

CAMEL connotes tenacity and perseverance.

CAMELLIA stands for affected beauty and innocence. This is a caution dream fragment that warns against a tendency toward pretense.

CAMELOT characterizes a Paradise-like society; earthly utopia.

CAMEO signifies prominence; an aspect in one's life that's uniquely treasured or featured.

CAMERA represents that which preserves the truth; the facts. This would be a caution for the dreamer to recall things factually.

CAMERA PERSON characterizes one who is focused on the truth or facts.

CAMERA SHOP portrays the many and various methods of preserving the truth or collecting facts.

CAMISOLE depicts innocence.

CAMOUFLAGE means hidden aspects; pretense.

CAMPING signifies a "temporary" life situation.

CAMPAIGN illustrates an "activist" aspect.

CAMP DAVID suggests a required pause needed in one's intellectual pursuits.

CAMPFIRE denotes an inner tranquility; inner peacefulness with one's current place in life or along the path.

CAMPGROUND pertains to an understanding of life's frequent temporary conditions and/or situations.

CAMPHOR OIL pertains to a "relief" of some type. This will usually refer to something that provides "breathing" room or eases some type of pain for the dreamer.

CAMPSTOOL implies situational ease; one is comfortable in most situations; adaptability.

CAMPUS connotes an attitude of camaraderie toward learning. May also indicate a caution against an attraction to learning *because* of the socializing.

CAN is a container. What the can contains determines the dream interpretation. See specific dream symbol entry words for this meaning.

CANAL denotes spiritual connections.

CANAPÉ signifies "attempts" made; a time period of trying out varied aspects; exploration; expanding one's experience.

CANARY exemplifies "singing" and may refer to a joyful emotion or a gossip situation.

CANCELLATION advises against going through with something.

CANCER is a grave warning to watch for an extremely dangerous negative in one's life.

CANDELABRA signifies an enlightening source that reaches out to illumine multiple life aspects.

CANDIDATE implies chosen or self-desired leadership.

CANDID CAMERA advises to remember that we're never alone; never unwatched.

CANDLE typifies that which can ignite our spiritual talents or abilities.

CANDLE HOLDER See candlestick.

CANDLE MAKING represents those activities that bring light and compassion to others.

CANDLE SNUFFER illustrates an individual with a tendency to reverse the effects of spiritual acts or "smother" the enlightening effects of another's spiritual deeds.

CANDLESTICK connotes quality of one's spiritual perception and manner of reception; condition of an individual's inner state toward spiritual acceptance.

CANDLEWICK portrays the basis for one's moral, ethical, and spiritual motivation.

CANDY pertains to the "sweet" aspects of life.

CANDY CANE illustrates the quality of familial relationships.

CANDY SHOP indicates the varied ways and methods that are available for experiencing life's small but meaningful joys.

CANDY STRIPER alludes to the attainment of inner joy through doing for others.

CANE See walking stick.

CANISTER (food) represents basic necessities; the main ingredients that can be built on.

CANKER SORE implies speech "infected" with a slant toward personal attitudes.

CANKERWORM characterizes a destructive force in one's life which damages perspective and attitudes.

CANNABIS See marijuana.

CANNERY means preservation. Usually advises the dreamer of a need to recall or retain the memory of an event for the purpose of learning from it.

CANNIBAL is a fatally destructive individual; one who has no ethics, morals, or spiritual beliefs.

CANNON represents explosive aspects to one's life. May even mean the dreamer's own personality.

CANNONBALL denotes the act of outraged explosions; acting in an uncontrollable manner.

CANOE symbolizes a well-paced and tranquil spiritual path.

CAN OF WORMS means troubling aspects; problems.

CANOLA indicates proper and well-prepared plans; the right atmosphere for advancement.

CANONIZE signifies spiritual conclusions based on personally-devised criteria.

CANON LAW stands for religion, not necessarily spiritual truths; pseudo-spirituality; spiritual laws set down by humans.

CAN OPENER portrays the act of remembering or utilizing important life aspects.

CANOPIC JAR See cannery.

CANOPY See awning.

CANTALOUPE pertains to good beginnings.

CANTEEN means spiritual reserves; spiritual beliefs that one can always fall back on and gain encouragement from.

CANTICLE denotes inner spiritual joy; a full heart.

CANTILEVER portrays an unrecognizable balance; a seemingly unlikely solution.

CANVAS (fabric) relates to a coarse yet strong personality.

CANVASS See survey.

CANYON symbolizes the more troublesome times of one's life walk; the deeper, more shadowed paths we're forced to travel.

CAPACITOR See condenser.

CAPE (clothing) denotes temporary protective measures taken or required.

CAPE (land point) signifies a projection of the way one delves into spiritual aspects; living a spiritual life.

CAPER refers to those unnecessary aspects that an individual believes are important to life; a self-generated need for more and more interesting and exciting aspects.

CAPILLARY is a finely-defined aspect to one's life.

CAPITAL GAIN represents an increase in return for good works done.

CAPITALIST is one who does good deeds for the sole purpose of personal gain.

CAPITAL LETTER marks an emphasis on something.

CAPITAL PUNISHMENT portrays an excessive retaliation; unjust judgment; vindictiveness.

CAPITOL defines the "source" or seat of something with which the dreamer will identify.

CAPITOL HILL (Congress) signifies one's individualized set of governing principles.

CAPITULATE means giving in; a surrender.

CAPOTE See serape.

CAP PISTOL pertains to the tendency to "make noise" without having any supporting strength; baseless verbiage; idle threats.

CAPPUCCINO connotes personal motivations enriched by generosity.

CAPSIZE means a spiritual reversal; an overturn.

CAPSTONE symbolizes the completion of one's purpose; finalization.

CAPSULE See pill.

CAPSULE (space) represents an exploration of the unknown with the intention of not being touched by it; a reserved interest.

CAPTAIN characterizes one who leads others. This may advise the dreamer to be captain of self.

CAPTAIN HOOK portrays a devious personality.

CAPTAIN'S CHAIR refers to a leadership position. Who was sitting in this chair?

CAPTION defines something for the dreamer; an explanation.

CAPTIVE connotes unwillingness; a forced situation.

CAPUCHIN See monkey.

CAR illustrates quality of physical condition. This most often refers to one's personal physiological system.

CARAFE represents spiritual quality. What is the condition of the carafe?

CARAMEL denotes the little joys in life that are worked for and savored for a time.

CARAPACE signifies one's defenses; an ability to remain sensitive within a hardened society.

CARAVAN connotes a protected life path through a tight association with others of like mind. This may not be a positive symbol.

CARBINE See gun.

CAR BOMB describes a self-destructive aspect in one's life.

CARBON denotes the harmful effects of negative actions.

CARBON-14 DATING indicates a need for verification.

CARBON COPY suggests duplication; a veering away from one's individuality.

CARBON MONOXIDE warns of a dangerous condition, situation, or relationship that appears innocent.

CARBON PAPER stands for an aspect that allows for the duplication of something in the dreamer's life.

CARBUNCLE denotes a negative aspect that causes personal harm.

CARCASS represents lack of life; a death. The carcass of a dog means the death of a friendship.

CARD (greeting) reveals emotions and/or attitudes.

CARD (playing) signifies insecurities.

CARDBOARD exemplifies insubstantial aspects in one's life; a superficial personality or relationship.

CARD CATALOG alludes to order.

CAR DEALERSHIP pertains to the physical aspects in one's life.

CARDHOLDER connotes special treatment; a membership; belonging to a specific group.

CARDIAC ARREST warns of over-exertion or over-stressing self. May precede an unexpected event or bit of news.

CARDIAC MASSAGE illustrates a need to externalize emotions.

CARDIGAN refers to an easy-going nature; maturity through experience.

CARDINAL (bird) portrays an aspect of high importance; a need to give one's attention to.

CARDINAL See religious figure.

CARDINAL POINT indicates one's directional priority.

CARDIOPULMONARY RE-SUSCITATION (CPR) advises to reactivate an aspect in one's life that the dreamer has left behind or abandoned.

CARD SHARP/SHARK characterizes one with ulterior motives; having a hidden agenda; deviousness.

CARD SHOP cautions one to carefully choose how something is said; advises to search for the right words.

CAREER DAY relates to the wide choices one has in life.

CARE GIVER stands for one who cares for another. This may not always indicate a compassion or loving personality.

CARESS typifies feelings of affection.

CARETAKER denotes a custodial position.

CARFARE implies a "price" for advancement.

CARGO suggests aspects one views as personally important.

CARHOP connotes those who make life a little easier or more convenient.

CARIBOU See reindeer.

CARICATURE warns of one's tendency to perceive others in a distorted manner; an exaggerated view of others.

CAR-JACKER characterizes one who has no personal direction or motivation for same.

CARLSBAD CAVERNS depict the inherent beauty of natural talents and abilities when shared.

CARNAGE denotes dangerously negative aspects in one's life that have the capability of causing far-reaching destruction.

CARNATION applies to one who is socially correct; an individual who is overly concerned about social mores.

CARNEGIE HALL pertains to high attainment and the recognition of same.

CARNIVAL defines a whimsical atmosphere or condition; a situation lacking seriousness; verging on the ridiculous.

CARNIVORE implies a predatory nature.

CARNY (person) characterizes one who is out of touch with reality; unrealistic perceptions of life.

CAROB identifies the "substitutes" that are available for us to utilize. This applies to being innovative in respect to "making do" when first choices are not available.

CAROUSEL exemplifies a path that's "going in circles" and will prove to be unproductive.

CARP represents the act of nagging; nit-picking; belittling.

CARPENTER characterizes one who has the ability to "build on" knowledge and talents to make use of knowledge.

CARPENTER ANT indicates a destructive personality, one who "tears down" that which is being created or built upon.

CARPET pertains to "underlying" characteristics of an individual.

CARPETBAG means self-interest; self-gain.

CARPETBAGGER typifies one who takes advantage of another's misfortune.

CAR POOL denotes attempts to conserve one's energy and resources. This doesn't mean to hold them back, just not expend them in unproductive manners.

CARPORT implies temporary shelter. This meaning will be clarified by surrounding dream symbols.

CAR RENTAL signifies an advancement along one's path through the assistance of another.

CARRIAGE means antiquated health practices; also may refer to a physiological system that's low on energy.

CARRIAGE TRADE portrays "selective" relationships; a catering to wealthy, powerful, or influential individuals.

CARRIER PIGEON See messenger.

CARRION illustrates the "remains" of a situation or relationship.

CARRION CROW typifies the feeding on remains. This is not necessarily a negative aspect depending on surrounding dream aspects. It could infer a "cleaning up" or "utilization" of what remains.

CARROT represents enticements; inducements.

CARRYING CHARGE relates to aspects in life that have a price; an extra price paid for what one wants or does.

CARRY OUT connotes shortcuts.

CAR SEAT (child's) symbolizes an immature perspective; a path taken with juvenile attitudes.

CARSICK indicates an inner recognition of a wrong path taken.

CART See wheelbarrow.

CARTE BLANCHE stands for a "no limit" situation; ability or freedom to take things as far as one can.

CARTEL signifies a controlling group.

CARTILAGE implies tenacity; resilient personality.

CARTOGRAPHER illustrates far-sightedness; an ability to "map out" one's own path.

CARTON refers to dual aspects; an aspect that "contains" some other aspect.

CARTOON can advise the utilization of humor in life or it may warn of a tendency to avoid reality.

CARTOUCHE connotes an important individual in one's life.

CARTRIDGE stands for the convenience of easy replacement; the ease by which something is utilized or replaced.

CARTRIDGE CLIP (ammo) signifies one's preparedness to back up facts or means of defense.

CARTWHEEL refers to feelings of joy.

CARVE suggests the need to make one's own way; express greater individuality.

CARVINGS stand for fine details to which the dreamer needs to give attention.

CAR WASH denotes a need to clean up one's act.

CASANOVA (Giovanni Jacopo) characterizes a philanderer; a user.

CASCADE See waterfall.

CASCARA SAGRADA warns of a serious need to get "rid of" wasteful aspects in one's life. These may refer to beliefs, attitudes, or situations.

CASE HISTORY advises one to look into and know the background information on something important.

CASELOAD implies an excessive backlog of work or information being processed.

CASEWORKER characterizes one who attempts to assist many others.

CASH pertains to genuineness; having the resources one claims.

CASH CROP signifies one's personal efforts to support self.

CASH DISCOUNT stands for benefits gained by one's resources.

CASHIER See clerk.

CASHIER'S CHECK alludes to guarantees; a secured aspect.

CASH MACHINE See automated teller machine.

CASHMERE connotes a gentle nature.

CASH REGISTER symbolizes materialism.

CASINO See gambling.

CASKET exemplifies life's precariousness.

CASPER (ghost) characterizes the demystification of reality.

CASSANDRA (Greek mythology) pertains to skepticism; one whom others don't believe.

CASSEROLE typifies a situation or condition created by several aspects in one's life.

CASSETTE represents something that the dreamer needs to hear.

CAST (bone) stands for a "caution" message; warns against going too fast; a headlong pace without looking.

CAST (fishing) refers to spiritual fishing; a "reaching" for some type of spiritual information.

CAST (of play) cautions one to take a better look at those involved in relationships or those with whom one is associated; people may not be the same as they present themselves.

CASTANET applies to inner delight after proving one right; personal gloating.

CASTAWAY denotes spiritual individuality and independence.

CASTE pertains to segregation; a separatist; tendency to classify others according to personal perceptions.

CASTER denotes a desire to protect.

CAST IRON indicates strength; a strong constitution.

CASTLE exemplifies one's perspective that lacks reality or clear vision.

CASTOFF (boat) means a beginning spiritual journey.

CASTOFF (discard) refers to that which one disregards; shedding one's relationships or beliefs.

CASTOR OIL advises of the need for a personal purification; a cleansing. This may refer to emotional, mental, or situational aspects.

CAT pertains to one's quality or type of independence. See specific type such as cheetah, Cheshire, etc.

CATACOMB represents buried or hidden information.

CATALEPSY signifies deep-seated fears.

CATALOG illustrates the vast array of choices in life.

CATALYST alludes to those individuals or situations that serve as motivational surges in life.

CATALYTIC CONVERTER advises us to make the most out of every situation or opportunity given us.

CATAMARAN portrays spiritual freedom; an unencumbered spiritual journey.

CATAMOUNT See lion.

CAT-AND-MOUSE implies "games" being played in one's life.

CATAPULT refers to highly motivational aspects that serve to speed one forward or into action.

CATARACT (of eye) denotes impaired perception; a clouded viewpoint.

CATARACT See waterfall.

CATASTROPHE denotes major events that end in a devastating manner.

CATATONIA characterizes an autistic-type of perception; extreme apathy.

CAT BURGLAR portrays a devious personality; sneaky; activity behind one's back.

CATCALL means disrespect; uncouth expressions.

CATCH 22 typifies a situation that appears to have no outlet for advancement; an appearance of having no means of movement; a boxed-in situation.

CATCHWORD denotes ideas that are widely known.

CATECHISM represents spiritual indoctrination.

CATEGORY denotes separatism; attitudes based on "class" or position.

CATER means the act of waiting on or serving another; subservience.

CATERCORNER See diagonal.

CATERPILLAR characterizes the transitional phases in life.

CATFIGHT means vicious disputes; uncontrolled disagreement.

CATFISH denotes a "cattiness" to one's spiritual belief; a pretentious or arrogant spiritual attitude.

CATHARSIS advises of the need to release emotions; a closure needed.

CATHEDRAL connotes spiritual excesses; a grandiose spiritual attitude.

CATHETER applies to a need to "empty" out that which one is retaining; the need for routine self-analysis.

CATHOUSE See house of ill repute.

CATNAP advises one to take a break; pause; short rest.

CATNIP signifies a mesmerized state; warns of a need to awaken self to reality.

CAT SCAN advises one to look at all angles. This dream symbol would suggest that the dreamer is not seeing something in its totality.

CAT'S-EYE (gem) symbolizes a "watcher" in one's midst.

CATTAIL denotes the need to recognize life's little benefits that come our way; to appreciate the things we have.

CATTLE represent a lack of individuality and self-confidence.

CATTLE CALL illustrates a desire to alter self according to how others wish you to be.

CATTLE GUARD connotes the self-created limits and barriers one devises to prevent decision-making or exercising individuality.

CATTLE PROD signifies an aspect that one willingly accepts regarding the prevention of individualized expression.

CATWALK exemplifies ways to get around things; alternate routes.

CAUCUS stands for a specialized meeting of selected people.

CAULDRON warns of a "brewing" situation, condition, or relationship.

CAULIFLOWER alludes to "bigness" or generosity.

CAULIFLOWER EAR suggests the habit of listening to gossip.

CAULK denotes the need to "seal" something in one's life; a promise; a conclusion.

CAUSEWAY signifies feeble or noncommitted attempts to delve into spiritual concepts.

CAUTERIZE advises of the need to heal a wound; a closure is required.

CAVALRY characterizes "following orders" and charging ahead with the crowd; a lack of individualized thought and reason.

CAVE signifies natural defenses; inherent knowledge.

CAVEAT EMPTOR advises one to know one's issues; do one's homework and be knowledgeable regarding a specific aspect.

CAVE DWELLER stands for one who lives by one's instincts.

CAVE-IN symbolizes a loss of instinctual reactions or knowledge; some aspect in life will not turn out as planned.

CAVERN alludes to nature's hidden aspects of the extended realities.

CAVIAR means spiritual arrogance; a spiritually egotistical individual.

CAVITY (tooth) warns against the speaking of "infected" words. This would indicate gossip, slander, or crass speech.

CAYENNE PEPPER See red pepper.

CB RADIO advises to keep communications open.

C-CLAMP applies to a need to "hold" something together until it can maintain its position. This usually refers to a relationship.

CEASE FIRE obviously means to stop fighting or maintaining an on-going disagreement.

CEDAR illustrates a need for spiritual cleansing or energized protection of one's spiritual beliefs.

CEDAR CHEST reflects care given to the preservation of one's cherished memories.

CEILING portrays the "top" of something; one's limit.

CELEBRATION means a reason for rejoicing.

CELEBRITY relates to one who stands out for some reason. Surrounding dreamscape aspects will clarify why this is important for the dreamer.

CELERY denotes difficulties that require acceptance.

CELESTIAL OBJECTS symbolize pure spiritual aspects. See specific terms.

CELIBACY calls for some type of abstinence required.

CELL (biological) relates to an inclusion of reality; an overall scope of reality; the wholeness of one's life experience.

CELL (enclosure) represents one's quantitative quality of experience. Recall how the cell was designed and/or decorated.

CELLAR indicates the deeper aspects of the subconscious where fears, bad memories, etc. are kept hidden away.

CELLMATE characterizes one of like mind.

C

CELLULAR TELEPHONE symbolizes preparedness and/or efficiency.

CELLULITE cautions against the acceptance of extraneous aspects in life; excesses.

CELTIC (atmosphere) denotes a need to delve into the spirituality that relates to this ancient culture.

CELTIC CROSS signifies an esoteric spiritual aspect.

CEMENT portrays unresolved or inconclusive aspects in one's life and advises to get these settled; a need to finalize something.

CEMENT MIXER means that aspect in life that will manifest a needed resolution or conclusion.

CEMENT SHOES stand for something one needs to answer for; an extremely negative deed needs to be repaired or made amends for.

CEMETERY See graveyard.

CENSER (incense vessel) stands for that which creates an affected atmosphere.

CENSOR characterizes a manipulative personality; one who would have others view life according to the perspectives and attitudes of self.

CENSUS cautions of one's inability to exist anonymously.

CENTAUR (Greek mythology) depicts a balance of physical strength and intellectual capability.

CENTER defines a position that offers the widest variety of choices.

CENTER FIELD indicates a position where one is able to maintain balance through an awareness of one's proper position in life.

CENTERFOLD depicts a position of prominence for the purpose of gaining the most attention.

CENTERPIECE signifies decorative appeal; attractiveness; that which creates an appealing atmosphere.

CENTIPEDE suggests an ability or need to overcome life's little irritations.

CENTRAL PARK (NY) portrays a means of respite within one's workday; may also refer to the positive and negative duality of life.

CENTRIFUGE cautions one against mixing separate life aspects; a need to keep ideas or concepts separate.

CENTURION characterizes one who is perpetually on guard.

CERAMIC connotes the aspects in life that have a tendency to be more fragile, such as one's emotional sensitivity.

CEREAL stands for the basic, foundational beginnings.

CEREBRAL PALSY illustrates

85

intellectual clarity accompanied by aspects that hamper physical action; an understanding of one's direction and path with some trouble with carrying it out.

CEREBRUM See brain.

CEREMONY implies a ritual; societal custom; specialized observance.

CERTIFICATE suggests a commendation for accomplishments.

CERTIFIED CHECK means solid facts; guaranteed aspect.

CERTIFIED MAIL represents a need to make sure something is done or carried out; certain delivery or communication.

CERTIFIED PUBLIC ACCOUNTANT (CPA) See accountant.

CESAREAN SECTION warns of immediate action needed to save a new beginning.

CESSPOOL connotes humanity's most base aspects.

CHABLIS See wine.

CHACO CANYON portrays ancient wisdom; hidden human heritage.

CHAFF illustrates leftover, unusable aspects.

CHAFING DISH exemplifies an aspect that requires constant attention; a need to prevent some aspect from getting cold.

CHAIN means "interconnected" aspects.

CHAIN GANG stands for individuals who are strongly connected by a shared negativity.

CHAIN LETTER symbolizes the strong possibility and probability of failure.

CHAINLINK FENCE is a dream fragment that refers to one's inner need to define ownership; possessiveness; marking personal perimeters.

CHAIN MAIL denotes a lack of confidence in one's own protection; personal fear of not being able to defend self.

CHAIN REACTION exemplifies the vast effects caused by what we think, do, and say.

CHAIN SAW represents the utilization of natural aspects to "cut through" problematical aspects in life.

CHAIN-SMOKING means an internalization of problems; high anxiety.

CHAIR signifies a short or temporary rest period may be needed.

CHAIR LIFT connotes a "rising" on the thoughts of others; unearned advancements through resting on laurels.

CHAIRPERSON characterizes organized leadership of a specialized aspect in one's life.

CHAISE LOUNGE implies an attitude of nonchalance; indifference.

CHAKRA symbolizes inner resources; reserves of energy.

CHALET pertains to a gentle personality; natural lifestyle.

CHALICE applies to one's spiritual aspects. This may not be a positive dream fragment, depending on the chalice's condition or color.

CHALK portrays subliminal or peripheral knowledge that may or may not be remembered.

CHALKBOARD defines temporary thoughts; subliminal messages that may be given.

CHALLENGER alludes to one-upmanship; one who strives to outdo others.

CHAMBER portrays a special room or place unique to the dreamer.

CHAMBERMAID See housekeeper.

CHAMBER MUSIC represents a specialized audio unique to the dreamer; personalized sound that soothes or motivates.

CHAMBER OF COMMERCE alludes to business associates and manner of group operation.

CHAMBER POT connotes an aspect that is out of character; out of place.

CHAMELEON may refer to indecision; a vacillation; or aspects that keep reversing direction.

CHAMOIS (cloth) implies a "soft" nature.

CHAMOMILE stands for an easygoing personality.

CHAMP See champion.

CHAMPAGNE See alcoholic beverage.

CHAMPION characterizes proven abilities or talents.

CHANCE denotes the unexpected; that which comes our way.

CHANCELLOR portrays a ranking position; authoritarian aspect.

CHANDELIER exemplifies specialized "light" of ideas or thoughts that are outwardly displayed in a focused or attention-getting manner.

CHANGELING illustrates a state of evolution; a metamorphosis; transition.

CHANGE OF LIFE See menopause.

CHANGEOVER represents a state of conversion; change of thought or attitude.

CHANNEL (trench) pertains to a "directed" flow or worn path; a direction traveled by many in the past.

CHANNEL (TV/radio) represents choices.

CHANNELER characterizes one who listens for the guidance of others instead of self.

CHANNEL LOCKS refer to an aspect that contains several opportunities or useable outlets.

CHANT denotes a means to inner light and/or knowing.

CHAOS represents disorder of some kind; confusion.

CHAOS THEORY attempts an explanation of true reality; the interconnectedness of all things.

CHAP (skin) implies an inability to accept differing ideas or attitudes of others.

CHAPARRAL refers to an aspect that's capable of bringing about an emotional healing.

CHAPEL illustrates a temporary time of spiritual respite or peace.

CHAPERON characterizes one's higher self; higher guidance; one's conscience.

CHAPLAIN signifies someone who will listen; a nonjudgmental individual.

CHAPS symbolize a need for temporary or short-term protection.

CHAPTER (book) indicates a stage in life; a special period of time.

CHAR denotes emotional sensitivity.

CHARADES stand for an inability to verbalize thoughts or adequately express self.

CHARBROIL See barbecue.

CHARCOAL represents positive outcomes from negative aspects; the event of good effects generated from bad happenings.

CHARGE (accuse) implies a placing of blame; to implicate.

CHARGE (care) refers to an aspect one needs to take special care of; protective wardship; safekeeping.

CHARGE (debit) pertains to the realization that payment for something will come due; a deferment of reciprocation for a time.

CHARGE (energize) illustrates a strong motivation; excitement.

CHARGE (race forward) means a committed intention backed by an urgency to carry it out.

CHARGE CARD alludes to impatience; lack of priorities.

CHARIOT cautions one to slow down; a need to utilize reason before taking action.

CHARITY stands for opportunities.

CHARLATAN characterizes pretenses.

CHARLIE CHAPLIN illustrates the importance of humor in life.

CHARM exemplifies a lack of faith.

CHARMED LIFE indicates an "appearance" of good fortune.

CHART defines specific course perceptions. These may show what the dreamer has planned out or may clarify what *should* be drawn up.

CHARTER (document) depicts a statement or record of one's purpose.

CHARTER See lease.

CHARTER MEMBER denotes one who participated in an aspect's beginning stage.

CHARTREUSE portrays an inner joy through healing.

CHASE symbolizes "going after" something; pursuit.

CHASM illustrates perceived difficulties.

CHASTE refers to a "modest" personality; may mean humility.

CHASTISE signifies some type of criticism.

CHASTITY BELT implies "forced" modesty or false humility.

CHAT suggests passing conversation; surface communication.

CHATEAU portrays extravagant goals.

CHATELAINE indicates one who is attracted to grandeur.

CHATTERBOX characterizes one who does little in-depth thinking; a gossip or someone who incessantly speaks of issues that are unimportant.

CHAUFFEUR infers a lack of self-motivation; taking a back seat.

CHAUVINIST denotes an attitude of superiority.

CHEAP designates something of low value; obtaining something without putting much effort or personal expense out.

CHEAPSKATE warns of a tendency to hoard abilities, knowledge, or one's personal humanitarian assets.

CHECK (bill) refers to one's valid debts.

CHECK (examine) connotes a need to substantiate something.

CHECK (mark) connotes aspects that need attending to.

CHECK (stop) cautions one to get something "in check" and under control; put a stop to something.

CHECKBOOK represents one's personal distribution of assets; where one utilizes abilities.

CHECKER See clerk.

CHECKER (game piece) is one aspect of one's planned direction.

CHECKED (pattern) means continual duality expressed; an ability to see both sides of a situation.

CHECKERBOARD typifies the many decisions in life; planning; the wisdom of analyzing situations.

CHECKLIST advises increased awareness; attention to detail.

CHECKMATE signifies an unavoidable aspect in one's life; may indicate a defeat or a personal conquest, depending on the surrounding dream symbols.

CHECKPOINT advises self-analysis or introspection.

CHECKROOM pertains to trust.

CHECKUP stands for some aspect in the dreamer's life that requires examining.

CHEEK implies audacity; impudence.

CHEER connotes encouragement; that which spurs one on.

CHEERLEADER characterizes those who encourage us in life.

CHEESE signifies those life aspects that are complete, full.

CHEESECAKE (food) suggests a rich reward; well-deserved outcomes.

CHEESECAKE (photo) connotes misplaced priorities.

CHEESECLOTH (fabric) represents an aspect that contributes to and serves to maintain wholesome attitudes.

CHEETAH signifies swiftness; quick action.

CHEF characterizes the method and quality of food preparation. This may infer food for the mind or emotional fulfillment.

CHEF'S HAT applies to the action of "cooking up" something.

CHEF'S SALAD indicates a balanced blend; the combining of several aspects in the dreamer's life.

CHEMICALS symbolize compound aspects, usually negative.

CHEMICAL ABUSE See substance abuse.

CHEMICAL WARFARE applies to a manner of conflict resolution that causes debilitating or fatal effects.

CHEMISE See camisole.

CHEMIST stands for one who utilizes a wide variety of aspects to create desired responses or goals.

CHEMISTRY (study of) portrays an interest in many life aspects and how they may or may not interrelate.

CHEMOTHERAPY pertains to the utilization of negatives to attempt positive outcomes.

CHENILLE (fabric) depicts old-fashioned ideas that remain valid throughout time.

CHERNOBYL emphasizes the dangers of too little knowledge.

CHEROOT See cigar.

CHERRY typifies a "sweet" situation; prime aspects.

CHERRY BOMB indicates something or someone in life with the capability of making a lot of noise with little or no damage.

CHERRY PICKER (truck) signifies high-minded work; high-level work to be done.

CHERRY TOMATO connotes those little often-overlooked aspects in life that present us with a convenience or ease.

CHERUB denotes young innocence; an angelic youth.

CHESAPEAKE BAY refers to deeper spiritual conceptual connections.

CHESHIRE CAT characterizes cleverness; a sly watchfulness.

CHESS illustrates the intricacies of life; the many moves.

CHESSBOARD exemplifies the options which life presents to us.

CHESS PIECE alludes to which direction is open to us.

CHEST connotes retained emotions.

CHEST (of drawers) See dresser.

CHESTNUT stands for heartfelt feelings; warm emotions.

CHEVAL (glass) typifies the need to "see" the totality of self. This would infer aspects that are being denied.

CHEVRON (pattern) implies strong goals.

CHEW (masticate) connotes a need to deeply think something over.

CHEW (tobacco) symbolizes a habit of mentally dwelling on something too long.

CHIC represents an over-emphasis placed on appearances.

CHICKEN denotes fear; a reluctance to face life.

CHICKEN (game) denotes ultimate irresponsibility and disregard for others, not to mention self.

CHICKEN COOP signifies the self-confining aspects of insecurities.

CHICKEN FEED means an aspect of little value.

CHICKEN-HEARTED pertains to lack of courage.

CHICKEN LITTLE characterizes paranoia; unnecessary fear.

CHICKENPOX warns of the negative effects caused by a lack of courage or faith.

CHICKEN WIRE portrays how we "fence" self in when there is a lack of courage, faith, or perseverance.

CHICORY alludes to an aspect that serves as a "substitute" for the ones we believe will strengthen and motivate us.

CHIEF defines a "prime" aspect in one's life.

CHIFFON (fabric) signifies those aspects that are easily seen through.

CHIFFOROBE See dresser.

CHIGGER typifies aspects in life that are irritating; those aspects that get under the skin.

CHIGNON implies "knotted" thoughts; a need to sort things out.

CHIHUAHUA (dog breed) advises to never underestimate the abilities or power of another.

CHILDPROOF reminds us to attend to each advancing stage in life and not attempt things we're not well-prepared to take on.

CHILDREN connote a stage of acceptance and innocence.

CHILD RESTRAINT alludes to the importance of preserving certain child-like qualities such as trust.

CHILD'S PLAY defines an activity that's easy; simplistic.

CHILI denotes situations or relationships that could develop into "hot" ones for the dreamer.

CHILI CON CARNE reminds us that we have the ability to control the "heat" of a situation.

CHILI BEANS indicate aspects we add to already-heated situations in life.

CHILI DOG pertains to one's preference for involvement in "spiced-up" or heated situations.

CHILI POWDER illustrates one's personal ability to maintain control of situations.

CHILL connotes a "cooling-down" aspect to a situation or relationship.

CHILL FACTOR cautions one to be aware of "additional" cooling factors that may seriously affect a situation or relationship.

CHILLY refers to cool or unfriendly attitudes.

CHIME denotes a "call" to listen; a calling to something in one's life.

CHIMERA characterizes self-delusion.

CHIMNEY pertains to emotional control.

CHIMNEY POT portrays an aspect that improves the outward flow of one's emotions; that which "draws" out feelings and emotional expression.

CHIMNEY SWEEP relates to the need to maintain a state of untainted attitudes.

CHIMPANZEE See monkey.

CHINA See ceramic.

CHINA SYNDROME is a symbol that seriously warns of the fatal effects caused by overheated and uncontrolled emotions; self-destruction.

CHINATOWN refers to the synergetic absorption of seemingly foreign aspects into one's belief system.

CHINCHILLA defines egotism; apathy toward others; a dangerous focus on self.

CHINESE PUZZLE denotes confusion; difficulty in finding resolutions.

CHINK (opening) typifies faulty conclusions; a "hole" in one's perception or thought process.

CHINKING applies to aspects that serve to "fill in" the empty or missing spaces in one's life; answers; those factors that make something solid or whole.

CHINOOK WIND represents a factor that "heartens" one; encouragement; uplifting aspects.

CHINTZ (fabric) defines an emotional or perceptual cover-up.

CHIPMUNK portrays hoarding; emotional reserves; the withholding of communication or expression.

CHIPPED BEEF stands for a tendency to criticize; a nagging personality.

CHIPPENDALE (furniture style) cautions one against forcing beliefs and perceptions upon others.

CHIPPENDALE (dancer) exposes those who entice others toward negative or at the least less-than-positive elements.

CHIPPER (wood) advises to utilize aspects to their fullest.

CHIROPRACTIC ADJUSTMENT emphasizes a desire for inner balance and alignment to one's current path.

CHIROPRACTOR characterizes integrity; perseverance; advancement through one's own efforts.

CHISEL refers to advancement by way of self-discovery.

CHIVALROUS denotes a high respect for others; respect for life; selfless.

CHIVE indicates positive factors we intentionally add to our life.

CHLORINE advises of a need to clean or "purify" specific aspects in one's life.

CHLOROFORM warns of a dangerous lack of awareness or attention to vitally important aspects in one's life.

CHLOROPHYLL stands for the quality and level of one's personal healing ability.

CHOCK BLOCK defines an aspect that prevents one from backsliding or rushing headlong.

CHOCOLATE indicates questionable pleasures; temporary enjoyments that may bring negative effects.

CHOIR signifies a group expression; shared joys.

CHOIR LOFT depicts spiritual joy.

CHOKE CHAIN See choke collar.

CHOKECHERRY exemplifies life aspects that bring sorrow.

CHOKE COLLAR warns of life factors that we allow to control us.

CHOKE HOLD refers to dangerous situations or individuals in life that threaten advancement. These can be self-generated.

CHOKER (necklace) represents voluntary self-restraint; the act of holding self back.

CHOKING warns against attempting to "swallow" ideas one knows are wrong or one is not prepared to absorb.

CHOLERA means a lack of intestinal fortitude.

CHOLESTEROL stands for the positive/negative duality of many life aspects.

CHOPHOUSE portrays an emotionally upsetting atmosphere in one's life.

CHOPPER See helicopter.

CHOPPER See motorcycle.

CHOPPING BLOCK represents a dangerous path or result.

CHOP SHOP emphasizes incorrect analyzation; improper "dismantling" of conceptual ideas; fragmented conclusions.

CHOPSTICKS imply the utilization of incorrect means to reach a specific end.

CHOP SUEY warns of one's tendency to "mix" concepts.

CHORD (music) refers to an aspect that has a specialized meaning for the dreamer.

CHORE denotes something needed to be accomplished.

CHOREOGRAPHER characterizes an individual who does the planning.

CHORUS symbolizes an idea or perception shared by many.

CHOW (dog breed) stands for "strength" within self.

CHOWDER exemplifies "heavy" spiritual concepts.

CHOWHOUND denotes an insatiable appetite. May refer to a seeker of knowledge or other desires.

CHRISTENING See baptism.

CHRISTMAS defines a major spiritual awakening.

CHRISTMAS CARD portrays spiritual greetings and messages.

CHRISTMAS CAROL indicates sharing of spiritual joys.

CHRISTMAS CLUB cautions against the "saving-up" of spirituality for a special occasion.

CHRISTMAS FERN stands for spiritual growth.

CHRISTMAS STOCKING represents expectation of spiritual rewards.

CHRISTMAS TREE denotes extraneous, unrelated aspects attached to spiritual truths.

CHROME denotes an attraction to the "shiny" aspects in life; a draw toward outwardly affected aspects.

CHROMOSOME advises one to know self.

CHRONICLE pertains to developmental stages leading up to the present; a need to research how something came about.

CHRYSALIS stands for developing spirituality.

CHRYSANTHEMUM pertains to the golden time of life; a time of respite and reflection; a restful time of introspection.

CHRYSOTHERAPY represents an understanding of the healing qualities of natural aspects.

CHUCKHOLE See pothole.

CHUCK WAGON signifies an aspect that serves to nourish us along our path.

CHUGALUG warns against an impulsive intake of information without adequately understanding it.

CHUM See friend.

CHUMP means a foolish person or one with a habit of being disinterested in things; someone never having an opinion.

CHURCH indicates type of spiritual connection and quality of same.

CHURCH MOUSE character-izes a quiet spirituality; cherished spiritual beliefs.

CHURCHYARD defines spiritual inactivity; dormant spirituality.

CHURN (butter) applies to personal efforts applied to one's path.

CHUTE (passageway) refers to a quick exit or end of something.

CHUTE See parachute.

CHUTZPAH portrays a disinterest in others' opinions; one who displays great nerve.

C.I.A. AGENT characterizes suspicion; distrust; hidden agendas.

CIBORIUM connotes a high respect for one's spiritual beliefs.

CICADA denotes an obsession with self.

CIDER represents an aspect that contributes to one's time of respite or reflection.

CIDER PRESS reflects quality rest time; tranquility.

CIGAR connotes an absorption of specialized ideas or concepts.

CIGAR BOX alludes to the manner by which one "holds" specific ideas or concepts.

CIGARETTE pertains to an absorption of well-defined ideas.

CINCH advises one to obtain a better understanding of something or "get a grip" on some life aspect.

CINDER See ash.

CINDER BLOCK characterizes a rebuilding; the capability of good coming out of a seemly bad situation; the utilization of "what's left" to build on.

CINDERELLA represents acceptance of one's situation; perseverance.

CINEMATOGRAPHER typifies one who is interested in recording life in its reality; one with an eye on reality.

CINNABAR refers to emotional expressiveness; a zest for life.

CINNAMON signifies an aspect that the dreamer perceives as being especially "homey" and companionable.

CIPHER suggests a need to solve or resolve something in the dreamer's life; represents a "key" or solution.

CIRCLE implies completion.

CIRCLE (ceremonial) may expose the "putting on" or "wearing" of another's path through fantasized, self-created means for the purpose of self-aggrandizement.

CIRCUIT stands for a designated path; making the rounds.

CIRCUIT BOARD portrays an individualized thought process; how one perceives life, forms ideas, deduces and resolves problems.

CIRCUIT BREAKER warns of a situation of mental or emotional overload.

CIRCUIT RIDER (traveling cleric) advises one to utilize spirituality wherever one is.

CIRCUIT TESTER suggests a need for self-analysis; introspection.

CIRCULAR SAW expresses a need to "quickly" and "cleanly" cut through an aspect in one's life.

CIRCUMCISION calls for a need to "excise" an aspect in one's life.

CIRCUMNAVIGATE advises one to "go around" something in life.

CIRCUMSTANTIAL EVIDENCE means a lack of solid proof.

CIRCUS indicates a laughable or ridiculous situation.

CIRRHOSIS warns of a situation filled with negatives; a negatively congested aspect.

CIST See coffin.

CISTERN refers to the spiritual aspects one holds within self.

CITADEL symbolizes the "high point" of one's life; the goal or purpose for which one strives.

CITATION stands for a communication from a higher authority.

CITIZEN implies a group or location with which one is connected.

CITIZEN'S ARREST indicates one's responsibility to take action against negative aspects.

CITRINE represents joyful spirituality.

CITRONELLA pertains to the act of conflict resolution by way of positive means.

CITY stands for group density; concentrated area saturated with multiple perspectives.

CITY DESK connotes a need to be informed of aspects surrounding one.

CITY EDITOR characterizes one who is kept abreast of aspects surrounding self.

CITY HALL represents a need to conduct self appropriately.

CITY MANAGER advises one to handle personal business instead of depending on others to manage it.

CITY SLICKER indicates an individual who expertly utilizes societal aspects.

CIVICS (study of) connotes a desire to understand the workings of surrounding authoritative systems.

CIVIL DEFENSE portrays the protection of one's surrounding aspects.

CIVIL DISOBEDIENCE symbolizes one's right to disagree with authority.

CIVIL ENGINEER denotes an individual who plans and creates amenities for others.

CIVILIAN exemplifies an individual who is not subject to the demands or wiles of others.

CIVIL RIGHTS reminds us of our personal freedoms; the positive aspects of personal perspectives and private directional planning.

CIVIL SERVICE alludes to serving others; a selfless nature.

CIVIL WAR connotes an internal conflict within self regarding one's immediate surroundings.

CLAIM stands for possessiveness; a declaration of ownership.

CLAIRAUDIENCE represents an intensified hearing ability; understanding what others leave unsaid.

CLAIRVOYANCE depicts an acute ability to "see beyond" that which is presented; great insight.

CLAM characterizes a state of silence.

CLAMBAKE alludes to possible negative aspects to keeping silent about something.

CLAM CHOWDER signifies "rich" and valued spiritual concepts that are utilized.

CLAMMY cautions of unpleasant aspects in life; an uneasiness; apprehensiveness; nervousness.

CLAMP advises of a need to restrain or secure something.

CLAMSHELL warns of broken promises or secrets told.

CLAN characterizes a tightly related group of people bonded by shared beliefs or perspectives.

CLAP See applause.

CLAPBOARD implies an "overlapping" of issues in one's life. This would suggest a need to separate out different aspects instead of creating a confusing situation.

CLARET See wine.

CLARINET symbolizes lyrical verbiage; enhanced statements.

CLASH indicates a conflict.

CLASP signifies a "holding on" to something.

CLASS See category.

CLASS (learning) refers to issues or subjects one requires better understanding of.

CLASS ACT alludes to high quality; distinction.

CLASS ACTION means action taken on behalf of others; someone ready to fight for the rights of others.

CLASSIC pertains to a distinctive aspect that has endured through time.

CLASSIFICATION See category.

CLASSIFIED ADVERTISE- MENT serves as a guide for the dreamer. This specific dream symbol will lead one to that which is sought or else will indicate that which one needs to give to others.

CLASSMATE characterizes those who walk the same path as the dreamer; those with like interests.

CLASSROOM indicates a learning atmosphere or source.

CLATTER represents a great disturbance. Usually this will refer to one's vibrational field or personal aura.

CLAUSE (in document) comes to bring your attention to something important; a reminder.

CLAUSTROPHOBIA warns of being in a "closed-in" situation or relationship. This may also be self-generated.

CLAW (animal) cautions of an attitude that goes against nature.

CLAW (fetish) indicates a desire to perspectively emulate or be protected by a specific characteristic.

CLAW HAMMER indicates the duality of one's ability to secure something in life or take it apart.

CLAY portrays a necessity to be resilient as one walks life's path.

CLAYMORE See sword.

CLAY PIGEON exemplifies a life aspect that serves to sharpen our responses and instincts.

CLEANSER connotes some type of "cleansing" is needed.

CLEAN-SHAVEN illustrates a desire to keep things out in the open; honesty; an aversion to hidden aspects.

CLEARANCE (height) denotes the amount of "room" one has. This will be clarified by surrounding dream presentations.

CLEARANCE (sale) cautions of a "last chance" to accomplish something.

CLEAR-EYED symbolizes one who sees clearly; a lack of distortion.

CLEAR-HEADED represents an individual who reasons calmly without letting personal perspectives or extraneous factors interfere.

CLEARINGHOUSE indicates a need to "sort out" issues or feelings.

CLEAT advises of a need to get a better "grip" on one's path.

CLEAVAGE (a split) indicates a separation; a division.

CLEAVER symbolizes a life aspect that has the capability of severing something. The dreamer will know what this refers to.

CLEFT PALATE stands for untruths; unbalanced statements; the addition of personal input into alleged statements of fact.

CLEMATIS exemplifies the beautiful and prolific effects of spiritual acts that endure or "cling" to others.

CLEMENCY alludes to unconditional forgiveness.

CLENCH depicts a need to grasp something; the act of holding on.

CLENCHED TEETH indicate controlled anger or the rising of anger.

CLEOPATRA warns against the utilization of one's physical attributes as a means of manipulation.

CLERIC See religious figure.

CLERICAL COLLAR portrays a tendency to present self in a spiritual light.

CLERK pertains to the selling of something; may infer the selling of self or one's personal perspectives.

CLICHÉ has a dual meaning. It may infer that one is too nonchalant or it may indicate that one has acceptance. Surrounding dreamscape factors will clarify this meaning for the dreamer.

CLICK means that something has finally been understood. This specific type of sound also accompanies actual psychic experiences, therefore it may relate to this factor for the dreamer.

CLIENT characterizes an individual for whom one does a service; those one assists.

CLIFF signifies a situation that is "on the edge" in life; living on the edge.

CLIFF DWELLER denotes one who finds security by living on the edge; self-confidence; reliance on one's "carved out" position in life.

CLIFFHANGER exemplifies high anxiety; suspense; left "on the edge" while waiting for results or conclusions.

CLIMATE gives clues to the general attitude or feeling of a dream. See specific climate types.

CLIMATOLOGY (study of) represents an interest in understanding how surroundings affect events or people's reactions in life.

CLIMAX stands for the manifestation of long-sought goals; a dramatic or intense conclusion to something.

CLIMBING symbolizes an upward or forward striving.

CLINGING cautions of a need to "let go" of something in one's life.

CLINIC (instructional) advises of the need to gain further information or knowledge about something in the dreamer's life.

CLINIC (medical) refers to a factor in life that has the capability of providing assistance for minor problems.

CLINICIAN is one who has specific knowledge; a specialized teacher.

CLIP (clasp) infers the act of holding something together.

CLIP (cut off) pertains to a separation; severing; shortening.

CLIP (swindle) means the act of taking advantage of another.

CLIPBOARD portrays an orderly individual; efficiency; one who attends to details.

CLIPPER See ship.

CLIPPERS (hair) symbolize life factors that affect one's attitude and perspective; aspects that alter thought.

CLIPPERS (nail) indicate an attempt to control one's negative aspects such as anger, aggressiveness, etc.

CLIQUE cautions against social arrogance or selectiveness.

CLOAK See serape; burnoose. May also have the additional interpretation of inferring secretiveness.

CLOAK AND DAGGER signifies the act of "leading on" or may indicate intriguing aspects to a situation or relationship; successive surprises.

CLOAKROOM stands for a specific life factor that is not what it seems; an aspect full of cover-ups or misrepresentations.

CLOCK always calls the dreamer's attention to a warning of time.

CLOCK MAKER characterizes an individual who sets limits; one who is highly efficient; one who motivates others.

CLOCK RADIO indicates an acceptance of one's responsibility.

CLOCK TOWER portrays a major sign that indicates the "right time" for major events to happen in one's life.

CLOCK-WATCHER connotes the wasting of time; one who ill-uses time.

CLOCKWISE pertains to advancements.

CLOCKWORK advises of the proper "workings" of one's life; things are unfolding as they are meant to; in a "regular" and normally expected manner.

CLOG (obstruction) warns of a life factor that needs immediate attention (clearing) before further advancement can occur.

CLOG (shoe) means that one's path is being traversed in a clumsy or difficult manner. This situation is correctable.

CLOISONNE represents heavily layered and elaborately designed identity presentations; false appearances; a major problem with the acceptance of self.

CLOISTER exemplifies the ability to obtain inner tranquility through one's spiritual beliefs.

CLONE cautions of the tendency toward imitation of others.

CLOSE CALL implies a need to give closer attention to one's actions.

CLOSED suggests an attempt to approach a path or obtain knowledge for which one is not yet prepared.

CLOSED BOOK suggests a person, situation, or concept that cannot be understood; puzzling; too convoluted to analyze at this point.

CLOSED-CAPTIONED advises of one's options open for further understanding.

CLOSED CIRCUIT connotes one's free-flowing energies; energies that have no blockages; free-flowing current through the chakras.

CLOSED DOOR advises against attempting to enter regions one is not advanced enough to travel.

CLOSED-MINDED warns against being opinionated or lacking the desire to intellectually seek an understanding of new theories.

CLOSED SHOP See union.

CLOSE ENCOUNTER illustrates personal experience.

CLOSE-FISTED warns against being greedy; stingy.

CLOSE-KNIT indicates strong bonds; solid ties with another.

CLOSE-MOUTHED relates to trustworthiness; integrity.

CLOSE SHAVE See close call.

CLOSET stands for aspects of self that one keeps hidden. These may be kept hidden from self—denied.

CLOSE-UP (photograph) portrays close inspection.

CLOT may indicate the beginnings of a healing or it may refer to a life factor that prevents advancement.

CLOTH See specific type.

CLOTHESHORSE characterizes an individual obsessed with appearances.

CLOTHESLINE emphasizes the need for increased awareness.

CLOTHESPIN suggests an opportunity to "air" grievances or something kept hidden.

CLOTHING gives indications into one's personality, spirituality, or physical condition.

CLOUDS connote thought patterns; ability to analyze and reason.

CLOUDBURST pertains to sudden realizations; a "pouring" out of new ideas.

CLOUD NINE signifies a state of elation.

CLOUD SEEDING represents "forced" or "planted" ideas.

CLOVE (multi-sectioned bulb) stands for beginnings that have more than one generating aspect.

CLOVE (spice) connotes a life aspect that one utilizes to make specific factors more appealing.

CLOVE OIL stands for something that temporarily relieves pain.

CLOVER represents spiritual abundance.

CLOVERLEAF (four leaves) See charm; **(three leaves)** See shamrock.

CLOWN characterizes one's "foolish" aspects.

CLOWN FISH portrays foolish factors connected to one's spiritual beliefs.

CLOWN SUIT illustrates immaturity; false happiness.

CLUB (bat) indicates a "bullish" personality; manipulative.

CLUB (group) exemplifies those with a like perspective or interest.

CLUB CAR pertains to an expectation for preferential treatment.

CLUBFOOT connotes personalized difficulties traversing one's path. These will be meant for the dreamer to overcome.

CLUBHOUSE symbolizes a desire to belong; a personal need for acceptance.

CLUB SANDWICH refers to "multilayered" or "multifaceted" aspects to a concept, situation, or perception one holds.

CLUB SODA See soda water.

CLUE comes as hints from one's higher self or inner knowing.

CLUNKER implies inefficient or inoperable life factors such as outdated and primitive beliefs.

CLUSTER connotes multiples of the same aspect, such as more than a couple adversaries or friends.

CLUSTER BOMB portrays a major outcome or effect that will create devastating effects on a wide variety of life aspects.

CLUTCH See clench.

CLUTCH (vehicle) denotes that which causes one to "gear" up or down; a motivational factor in life.

CLUTCH BAG refers to aspects one holds close or dear.

CLUTTER defines a disorderly state.

COACH (tutor) cautions us to use discernment when being advised or taught by another.

COACH See carriage.

COAGULATE See clot.

COAL portrays deep-seated negativity; undesirable attitudes.

COALITION See alliance.

COAL MINE advises one to dig down and bring out negative attitudes for the purpose of neutralizing them.

COAL OIL See kerosene.

COAL TAR illustrates that which we utilize for the purpose of insulating self from hurtful aspects.

CO-ANCHOR signifies a dual responsibility.

COAST See shore.

COASTER signifies protective influences or aspects.

COAST GUARD characterizes those who work to provide spiritual safety for others; one's advisors or spiritual guardians.

COASTING warns of a downward path; sliding downward.

COASTLINE represents a position approaching spiritual involvement; the precursor stage to spiritual searching.

COAT represents one's exterior presentation to the world; how we want to be seen or what we use to conceal the real self.

COAT OF ARMS infers ancestral arrogance.

COATROOM See cloakroom.

COATTAIL warns of the desire to let others lead; cautions of the tendency to let others do the work in advance of self; advancing through the efforts of others instead of self.

COB See corncob.

COBBLER See shoemaker.

COBBLER (dessert) symbolizes will-deserved rewards.

COBBLESTONE portrays a rough road that one chooses to take.

COBRA illustrates a threatened or dismayed individual. See snake.

COBWEB indicates "sticky" situations or relationships in which one gets caught because of not applying adequate reasoning.

COCAINE warns of an inability to cope with reality; a lack of taking self-responsibility; escapism.

COCCYX BONE signifies one's "base" or foundational attitudes.

COCK See rooster.

COCK (firearm hammer) warns of one's tendency toward conflict.

COCKATIEL See parrot.

COCKATOO See parrot.

COCKCROW connotes beginnings; a new day; a "dawning" aspect.

COCKED (position) indicates imbalance; a "slanted" aspect or perspective.

COCKER SPANIEL (dog breed) characterizes companionship; gentle associations. May have communication troubles.

COCKEYED alludes to foolishness; absurdity.

COCKFIGHT warns of a tendency to use others to resolve one's conflicts.

COCKLE symbolizes one's innermost feelings.

COCKLEBUR depicts emotional pain.

COCKLESHELL signifies the "remains" of one's emotional feelings; leftover feelings following an emotionally-charged event.

COCKPIT pertains to mental or emotional control.

COCKROACH refers to major disruptions in one's emotional, spiritual, or physical life.

COCKSCOMB warns of egotistical attitudes.

COCKTAIL See alcoholic beverage.

COCKTAIL TABLE See coffee table.

COCOA portrays a life aspect that soothes.

COCOA BUTTER pertains to emotional healing.

COCONUT expresses the fact that strength and nourishment can result from life's harder lessons.

COCONUT MILK characterizes a life aspect that provides rich lessons or rewards.

COCONUT OIL signifies those factors in one's life that serve to soothe and soften the hurtful or difficult aspects of one's path.

COCOON connotes a stage of respite where one "absorbs" what has been learned before advancing to the next spiritual stage of gaining wisdom from that knowledge.

CODDLE warns of overindulgence; a lack of discipline.

CODE stands for specialized communication; hidden messages understood by a select group.

CODE BLUE warns of an extremely dangerous situation approaching.

CODEBOOK symbolizes an aspect that serves as the "key" to understanding something.

CODEINE represents those life factors that we believe help us get through the more difficult times.

CODE NAME signifies a secret identity.

CODE WORD See password.

CODEX suggests highly valuable information or knowledge.

CODGER portrays a disinterested or irascible elder.

CODICIL See addendum.

COD-LIVER OIL advises of a deficiency in one's life.

COEDUCATION symbolizes information that will benefit everyone associated with the dreamer.

COFFEE stands for persevering energy; that which enriches one's motivations.

COFFEE BEANS depict the "freshness" of renewed energy; sparked motivation.

COFFEE BREAK symbolizes a need to pause for the purpose of restoring one's energy.

COFFEECAKE denotes nourishment through energizing pauses of respite.

COFFEE GROUNDS signify the negative aspects left behind after being reenergized.

COFFEE KLATCH pertains to the emotional uplift brought by sharing restful energizing times.

COFFEE MILL refers to an aspect that has the capability of energizing one.

COFFEEPOT illustrates a "brewing" situation and may indicate a "percolating" condition within self that advises of a period of rest.

COFFEE SHOP exemplifies a rest period and the need to choose a specific manner for same.

COFFEE TABLE typifies an offering of comfort left out for others.

COFFEE-TABLE BOOK applies to something we openly share with others.

COFFER See cache.

COFFIN may mean an emotionally comatose state of being or it may actually be a forewarning of death.

COFFIN NAIL stands for any negative aspect in one's life that is serving as a detriment.

COG portrays a vitally important part of an aspect.

COG RAILWAY denotes that which provides "movement" for specific aspects of one's life.

COGWHEEL symbolizes an important aspect of one's life.

COHORT See partner.

COIL may refer to the act of "going in circles" or it may warn of the dangerous situation of "coiling" up as an internal spring, indicating inner tension and stress.

COIN signifies the little rarely-recognized opportunities that come our way.

COINCIDENCE connotes destined connections.

COIN COUNTER is a symbol that advises us to count our blessings.

COIN PURSE denotes a recognition and appreciation of one's gifts.

COIN WRAPPER represents the act of "saving" one's opportunities. This indicates appreciation of their value.

COKEHEAD characterizes total irresponsibility and a lack of interest in dealing with reality.

COLANDER applies to the ability to "drain" off excess or waste aspects from self.

COLD (illness) See head cold.

COLD means a lack of warmth.

Specific surrounding dreamscape symbols will clarify this reference.

COLD-BLOODED signifies a lack of emotional response; an individual having absolutely no sensitivity.

COLD CASH refers to immediately-available assets. These may be in the form of money, emotional support, virtues, means of assisting others, etc.

COLD CREAM denotes a need for emotional softening.

COLD CUTS represent aspects that provide immediate nourishment.

COLD DUCK See alcoholic beverage.

COLD-EYED implies a lack of personal opinion or involvement.

COLD FEET portrays a lack of faith or courage; a giving in to one's fears.

COLD FISH characterizes one in the habit of not showing emotions.

COLD FRAME stands for tough love; holding back on emotional warmth or compassion for the purpose of strengthening another.

COLD FRONT means the approach of an unresponsive attitude.

COLD-HEARTED refers to a lack of warm emotional expressiveness.

C

COLD PACK (canning) represents unbiased information gathering followed by proper emotional expressiveness.

COLD PACK (compress) denotes a need to cool down emotions.

COLD SHOULDER warns against judging others; calls for forgiveness and a resulting response of at least neutrality.

COLD SHOWER advises of a "cooling-off" period.

COLD SORE See canker sore.

COLD STORAGE portrays a protection of what one values.

COLD SWEAT indicates nervousness, fear, or anxiety.

COLD TURKEY stands for immediate and absolute withdrawal of something in one's life; complete abstinence.

COLD WAR warns against maintaining deep animosities.

COLD WATER represents a diminishing of value; disagreement.

COLD WAVE typifies a time period of unemotional responses.

COLESLAW implies several factors contributing to the reason for one receiving neutral responses from others.

COLEUS refers to an acceptance of "varied" personalities of those with whom one is associated.

COLIC signifies life aspects that are not well accepted.

COLITIS warns of intolerance.

COLLAGE reminds us of life's diversity and the beauty of same. This dreamscape symbol usually calls for more acceptance on the dreamer's part.

COLLAGEN stands for the revitalizing and binding aspects in one's life.

COLLAPSE indicates failure; lack of support or strength.

COLLAR symbolizes an aspect that one considers burdensome; possible guilt.

COLLARD GREENS See kale.

COLLATE advises one to give detailed attention to the orderly integration of facts.

COLLEAGUE See associate.

COLLECT stresses the need for "gathering" something of importance for the dreamer. This may refer to information, emotions, or even the collecting of self, indicating "scattered" emotions, thoughts, or beliefs.

COLLECTIBLE represents highly valued aspects as viewed by the dreamer.

COLLECTION denotes a personal possessiveness.

COLLECTION BOX See poor box.

COLLECTIVE UNCONSCIOUS reminds us of our interrelatedness to all living things.

COLLECTOR connotes a specific interest and one's strong attraction for aspects of same.

COLLEGE implies higher learning.

COLLIE (dog breed) characterizes a faithful friend.

COLLISION pertains to a harmful or negative result.

COLLISION COURSE warns of a destructive relationship or dangerous perspective, emotional basis, or path.

COLLOQUIALISM in dreams helps to narrow down meanings in the spoken language of other dream characters presented.

COLLUSION warns of deceitfulness or secretiveness.

COLOGNE See perfume.

COLON (mark) is an indication that something will follow, usually an explanation.

COLON stands for preparations or timeframe preceding the act of shedding some excesses in one's life.

COLONEL characterizes a highly regimented individual.

COLONIAL portrays self-sufficiency.

COLONIST characterizes perseverance; self-reliance; one who isn't hesitant to experience new ideas or adventures.

COLONNADE defines the way leading to something important for the dreamer.

COLONY connotes a group of like-minded individuals who desire to establish a location of camaraderie in relation to ideals.

COLOR aspects of dreams are extremely revealing. See specific color for interpretation.

COLORBLINDNESS emphasizes the fact that one views all aspects of life according to personal perspectives; opinionated.

COLOR-CODED indicates a need for proper identification or classification. This would imply that there is a problem with sorting out feelings or situations.

COLORFAST represents no chance for change; immutability.

COLOR FILTER means an altered or "colored" perspective.

COLOR GUARD signifies pride of heritage.

COLORING pertains to the desire to change reality.

COLORIZATION (old films) stands for enhancement; enrichment without altering anything.

COLORLESS stands for neutral; having no personal animation or unique expressiveness.

COLOSSUS portrays something of great size.

COLOSTOMY denotes the utilization of alternate means of shedding one's excesses or extraneous aspects; bypassing the normal means.

COLOSTRUM defines an aspect that richly nourishes and protects.

COLUMBINE relates to inner peacefulness.

COLUMBUS (Christopher) characterizes misinterpretations; confusion; perceptual problems; possessiveness.

COLUMN See pile.

COMA means an unresponsive state. This does not infer a lack of awareness.

COMB pertains to a need to straighten out one's thoughts.

COMBAT warns against the wrong type of conflict resolution.

COMBAT FATIGUE exemplifies the self-destructive effects of conflict.

COMBAT FATIGUES indicate preparedness for conflict, ready for a fight.

COMBINATION LOCK denotes the various methods of "opening" something up or solving problems.

COMBINE connotes a blending or mixing of something in the dreamer's life.

COMBINE (machine) stands for several tasks being handled by a single aspect or solution.

COMBUSTION See flashpoint.

COMEDIAN characterizes an unrealistic perspective; one who makes a joke of everything.

COMET defines spiritual awakenings; enlightening insights.

COMFORTER See quilt.

COMFORT STATION signifies the resting points along our path.

COMFREY defines self-healing capabilities.

COMIC BOOK connotes a manner of escape from life; unrealistic perceptions; a hesitancy to face reality.

COMIC RELIEF advises of a need to maintain a sense of humor throughout life.

COMMA (mark) symbolizes a separation of ideas and comes as a caution for the dreamer to avoid running concepts together.

COMMAND is an authoritative directive. The clue here will be whether or not the authority figure is a positive or negative one as discerned by the dreamer.

COMMANDER IN CHIEF pertains to an authority figure of the highest rank. For the dreamer, this may be in reference to an individual that is highly respected.

COMMANDO represents impulsiveness; knee-jerk reactions; a short-tempered personality; destructive resolutions.

COMMENCEMENT means the

beginning stage of applying what has been learned.

COMMENDATION portrays approval.

COMMENTARY defines the opinion or perspective of another.

COMMERCIAL signifies an offered aspect; something being shown.

COMMISSARY See grocery market.

COMMISSION depicts having the authority to do something; one's right to act or proceed.

COMMITMENT emphasizes a promise; a responsibility.

COMMITTEE symbolizes a group chosen to perform a function. This would indicate a tone of authority or confirm rightness for the dreamer.

COMMON DENOMINATOR pertains to an aspect that is shared by others.

COMMON GROUND refers to a unifying factor.

COMMON-LAW MARRIAGE underscores the concept of living by the "spirit" of the law; arrangements agreed to without contractual formalities; having a mutual "understanding" of something.

COMMOTION denotes disruption.

COMMUNE (group) represents a living arrangement based on the utilization of talents and supplies that are provided by and for all participants; unconditional sharing.

COMMUNITY CENTER applies to the enjoyment of social contacts.

COMMUNITY CHEST symbolizes one's reserves of generosity; one's ability to share or give to others.

COMMUTER pertains to a vacillating period in one's life.

COMPACT (makeup) designates the act of smoothing over or covering up one's perceived faults.

COMPACT (size) signifies something that's condensed; efficient; convenient.

COMPACT DISC (CD) symbolizes condensed information; acquiring a large block of knowledge in a short span of time.

COMPACTOR advises of a need to diminish the amount of one's wastefulness.

COMPANION characterizes one with whom the dreamer closely associates.

COMPANION PLANTING denotes a mutually beneficial relationship.

COMPANY TOWN portrays group dependency.

COMPARISON-SHOPPING advises of a need to research something; don't accept the first presentation of an aspect.

COMPASS connotes direction. This usually will point to a path different from the one the dreamer is walking.

COMPENSATION depicts a "return" for something; amends; balance or counterbalance.

COMPETITION denotes a situation of rivalry; a need to prove something.

COMPLACENT defines a lack of motivation yet may also indicate acceptance. Surrounding dreamscape symbols will clarify this intent.

COMPLAINT indicates an active objection to something.

COMPLICATION means entanglement. This may even refer to one's own thought process.

COMPLIMENT means praise or encouragement from one's higher self.

COMPOSITE PHOTOGRAPH illustrates one's multifaceted aspects.

COMPOST See mulch.

COMPRESSED AIR advises one to get more breathing room; move away from some life aspect that feels suffocating.

COMPRESSOR characterizes an individual or situation that brings about better understanding.

COMPROMISE stands for the need to make some concessions in life.

COMPULSION cautions one to gain better control over impulsiveness.

COMPUTER connotes a need for analyzation or better understanding.

COMPUTER PROGRAM indicates a life aspect that greatly shortens one's research time and provides extensive information.

COMPUTER PROGRAMMER characterizes an individual who believes in the ability to make reality coincide with personal perspectives, desires, or plans.

COMPUTER VIRUS pertains to "disinformation" willfully given.

CONCEALMENT warns of a cover-up or the hiding of something.

CONCERT (performance) represents a display of talent or knowledge.

CONCERT (synergy) advises of the benefits of a collaboration.

CONCESSIONAIRE characterizes one who associates with another for self-serving purposes.

CONCH (shell) represents spiritual aspects that are cherished.

CONCH BELT implies a desire to surround self with the more natural aspects of life.

CONCIERGE portrays an individual who serves to make life easier.

CONCLUSION directly relates to an ending.

CONCOCTION connotes a mix of personal perceptions.

CONCOURSE alludes to a "passing stage" or life situation.

CONCRETE See cement.

CONCUBINE implies feminine inferiority; chauvinism; subservience.

CONCUSSION defines a personally shocking event; mentally or emotionally shocking.

CONDEMNATION signifies absolute rejection of something.

CONDENSATION symbolizes life aspects that naturally generate spiritual effects or benefits.

CONDENSED MILK pertains to rich nourishment.

CONDENSER suggests a need to be more concise or look at the "basic" issue rather than its extraneous elements.

CONDIMENT connotes an additional aspect one interjects to life; a "dressing" or spicing of something.

CONDOM connotes the level of one's protective concerns.

CONDOMINIUM illustrates self-confidence and independence realized through the support of others.

CONDOR See vulture.

CONDUCTOR (music) connotes an individual who has the ability to bring harmony to a situation.

CONDUCTOR (physics) denotes an individual, situation, or other life factor that insures continuance; serves as a "connecting" force.

CONDUCTOR (transit) characterizes those who offer helpful guidance along one's path.

CONDUIT denotes that which conveys in a supporting, protective manner.

CONE (shape) suggests a need to "pinpoint" something; bring to a defined point or conclusion.

CONE (traffic) signifies a "cautionary" advisement; cautionary guidelines.

CONEHEAD portrays unrealistic perspectives.

CONESTOGA WAGON See covered wagon.

CONEY ISLAND See amusement park. See hot dog.

CONFECTION exemplifies an aspect perceived as "sweet" or desirable; little life aspects to which we "treat" ourselves.

CONFERENCE indicates a situation that requires further discussion.

CONFERENCE CALL advises of a need to communicate with several other individuals on something important to the dreamer.

CONFERENCE TABLE applies to a life factor that has the capability of bringing about resolutions or productive communications.

CONFESSIONAL signals a need for honesty; suggests an untruth is preventing advancement.

CONFETTI represents joyful celebration.

CONFIDANTE characterizes someone to whom you can openly talk; one who can be trusted with personal information.

CONFIDENCE GAME See swindler.

CONFIDENTIAL FILE illustrates multiple secrets or hidden aspects.

CONFIGURATION (shape) applies to a wide variety of life factors and has an even greater scope of interpretation. See specific shape.

CONFINEMENT advises of an inability to proceed; marks a timeframe when a pause or delay is required. There is also another meaning for this symbol and that is a warning that the dreamer is confining "self" in some way.

CONFIRMATION represents verification.

CONFISCATE implies a need to retrieve or seize something.

CONFLUENCE stands for the act of joining or coming together. This usually indicates a need for an agreement to take place.

CONFORMIST warns of a lack of individuality or thought.

CONFRONTATION may be giving advice to get something out in the open.

CONFUSION usually indicates mental turmoil.

CONGEAL means a "coming together" or nearing solidification.

CONGESTION suggests a need to "untangle" or sort things out.

CONGLOMERATE means the joining of several factors. The dreamer will understand what this means by including surrounding dream symbols.

CONGREGATION connotes a large group. This does not specifically infer a spiritual connection.

CONGRESS represents a meeting of several people or groups for the purpose of a specific communication. This typifies a need for resolving differences between more than two or three people.

CONIFER denotes "everlasting" beauty and benefits of spiritual acts.

CONJUNCTIVITIS warns of a major error in perception; strongly advises to "clear up" one's way of seeing things.

CONJURER characterizes an individual who has the capability to make things happen; someone who gets things done.

CONNOISSEUR portrays an individual who has spent a great deal of time gaining full knowledge of something; an expert.

CONQUISTADOR connotes one who enjoys winning; having control over others.

CONSCIENTIOUS OBJECTOR pertains to an individual who stands up for personal beliefs.

CONSECRATION defines a recognition of sacredness or spirituality.

CONSEQUENCE doesn't always infer negativity; it may only indicate the result of something else.

CONSERVATIONIST relates to one who places a high priority on the preservation of positive life aspects.

CONSERVATISM marks a tendency to avoid change; fear of something new or innovative.

CONSERVATORY See greenhouse. See college.

CONSIGNMENT SHOP indicates a mutually beneficial relationship or situation.

CONSOLATION PRIZE portrays the fact that benefits are derived from the act of participation.

CONSOMMÉ exemplifies the rewards and benefits of clear perspectives.

CONSPIRACY warns of dangerous planning.

CONSTELLATION comes in dreams to give recognition for spiritual acts.

CONSTIPATION denotes an inability to express self.

CONSTITUTION refers to the "foundation" of something.

CONSTRUCTION PAPER illustrates a need to formulate a plan of agreement to build on.

CONSTRUCTION SITE signifies a time of building; constructive advancements.

CONSULATE represents a place of safety; where protection is provided.

CONSULTATION infers the need for advice.

CONTACT DERMATITIS advises one to avoid a life aspect that causes extreme irritation or anxiety.

CONTACT LENS See glasses.

CONTAGION warns of an extremely harmful influence.

CONTAGIOUS connotes a perception, belief, or attitude that will quickly be accepted by others.

CONTAINER suggests a need for "containment." What was in the container?

CONTAINMENT denotes a completely controlled situation; something that has no ability to spread or affect others.

CONTAMINATION warns of the infiltration of an extremely corrupt or deadly facet into one's life.

CONTEMPLATION advises one to give deeper thought to something.

CONTEST represents a competitive nature.

CONTINENT will point the dreamer to an important aspect that's pertinent to him or her. Clarity will come when the specific continent name or country is shown.

CONTINENTAL BREAKFAST suggests a physiological need to "lighten" up one's routinely stressful mornings.

CONTINENTAL DIVIDE advises of a major division in one's life. This may be a serious disagreement in a relationship or it may even relate to a division within self.

CONTINENTAL DRIFT suggests the possibility of a firm decision, perspective or attitude shifting position.

CONTINENTAL SHELF pertains to "underlying" facets to something that create supporting extensions; something backed by additional facts that have not yet surfaced.

CONTINGENCY means a possibility.

CONTINGENCY FEE symbolizes a reward or benefit resulting from a successful outcome.

CONTINUITY denotes a state of absolute coherence; a perceptual manner that contains no distortable aspects.

CONTORTIONIST characterizes a manipulative personality.

CONTRABAND means the utilization or possession of negative aspects such as selfish motives, apathetic attitudes, etc.

CONTRACEPTIVE See birth control methods.

CONTRACT portrays a bonafide agreement one must honor.

CONTRACT (on a life) portrays an agreement about which one must make a choice. Whose life was the contract on? Yours? And who put the contract out?

CONTRACTOR defines an individual who gains by doing your work.

CONTRADICTION alludes to discrepancies in one's life. This symbol cautions the dreamer to examine self and associates.

CONTRAIL represents a spiritual effect generated by positive perspectives or attitudes.

CONTRIBUTION means one's personal input.

CONTROL TOWER connotes a defined source of manipulation for the dreamer.

CONTROVERSY applies to a difference of opinion. This may even imply a self-generated factor whereby an individual's actions don't match his or her expressed attitudes.

CONVALESCENT HOME illustrates a situation or life aspect that will serve as a "healing" factor.

CONVENIENCE STORE exemplifies a tendency to take shortcuts.

CONVENT pertains to voluntary spiritual isolation.

CONVENTION CENTER relates to the meeting of like-minded individuals for the purpose of sharing information and learning.

CONVERSATION PIECE symbolizes an aspect that draws attention or curiosity.

CONVERT denotes a complete belief reversal.

CONVERTIBLE implies a means of exchange; a life aspect that can be utilized in different ways or forms.

CONVEYOR BELT signifies a means of communication or delivery.

CONVICT relates to an individual who has done wrong in the past. However, this does not infer that this person is still doing so.

CONVOLUTED (shape) symbolizes a twisted aspect that curls back on itself. This could refer to a thought process or an actual situation or relationship.

CONVULSION portrays a violently uncontrolled response.

COOK (food preparation) connotes the act of planning; in the process of completing something.

COOK (person) usually indicates a hyperactive mental state; continual thinking; always planning or analyzing.

COOKBOOK denotes the many opportunities and ways that serve to provide the formula to reach goals.

COOKIE pertains to life's small rewards.

COOKIE JAR connotes that which one "reaches" for; goals; aspirations.

COOKING UTENSIL See specific tool.

COOL (temperature) signifies self-control.

COOLANT will represent an aspect that serves as a "settling-down" or calming source for the dreamer.

COOLER is any factor that maintains a state of control or calm.

COONSKIN CAP represents a backward perspective or way of thinking.

COOPERATIVE depicts a mutually beneficial relationship or situation.

COOTIE See lice.

COPIES connote multiples of the some thing. This usually denotes an advisement to "repeat" some positive aspect.

COPILOT characterizes confidence; the "reserves" one can utilize.

COPING SAW stands for the "tools" used to plan and carve out one's personally-designed path.

COPPER (color) represents intellectual brilliance coupled with an outgoing personality.

COPPER (metal) denotes a choice aspect for one to utilize for the purpose of communicating something.

COPPERHEAD See snake.

COPPERSMITH characterizes an individual who inherently brings positive influences into the lives of others.

COPPER TUBING denotes a questionable life aspect.

COPPERWARE is a dream symbol that means a warning. The dreamer will understand this by combining surrounding dream fragments.

COPPER WIRE portrays clear communications.

COPSE stands for one's personally-inherent attributes that serve to benefit others.

COPULATION implies a temporary joint effort.

COPY relates to a duplicate or imitation.

COPYCAT cautions against imitating others. We can aspire to acquire virtuous qualities but we are each uniquely different and distinctly defined.

COPY MACHINE denotes an opportunity to emulate another or obtain a personal imitation of something. All opportunities are not positive aspects.

COPYREADER See editor.

COPYRIGHT points to the "originator" of something.

CORAL symbolizes one's spiritual attributes and/or talents.

CORAL (jewelry) indicates the visibility of one's spirituality.

CORAL REEF represents the fragile balance of maintaining a spiritual balance within a physical plane of existence.

CORAL SNAKE See snake.

CORD (electrical) connotes that which conducts energies; gives power to.

CORD See rope.

CORDLESS pertains to one's inner reserves.

CORDONED alludes to an attempt at protective measures.

CORDUROY (fabric) implies a

rugged personality; accepting of life's tougher experiences.

CORDWOOD defines one's level of preparedness.

CORE signifies a center point; beginnings; most emotionally sensitive or vulnerable aspect.

CORRESPONDENT refers to an individual who communicates with and for others.

CORIANDER signifies aspects unique to one's personality.

CORK (bark) stands for one's multilevel abilities.

CORK (float) pertains to a resilient nature.

CORK (stopper) represents control; restraint.

CORKBOARD connotes acceptance.

CORKSCREW portrays deep involvement; may infer a "twisted" situation.

CORM illustrates storage; preservation.

CORMORANT denotes spiritual nourishment.

CORN typifies a nourishing aspect that comes from within self; a self-generated power source.

CORN (on foot) reflects an irritating factor in walking one's life path.

CORNBRAID See cornrow.

CORN BREAD represents nourishment through personal efforts.

CORNCOB portrays personal effort.

CORNCOB PIPE connotes the reaping of benefits generated through one's personal efforts.

CORNCRIB symbolizes life aspects that serve to preserve the benefits of personal efforts.

CORNDOG pertains to the multiple benefits of one's efforts.

CORNER means a turning point in one's life; a different direction.

CORNERSTONE stands for concepts or beliefs that serve as one's foundation.

CORN-FED relates to inner strength; healthy perspectives.

CORNFIELD signifies an abundance of inner strength.

CORN FLAKES represent strongly-motivated beginnings.

CORNFLOWER portrays the beauty of one's inner strength that results from self-reliance.

CORNHUSKING denotes the actual work of one's personal efforts.

CORNICE symbolizes an elaborate concealment.

CORN KERNEL applies to the great significance of each small effort one makes.

CORNMEAL typifies the versatile benefits of personal effort.

CORN OIL defines the promise of beginning efforts.

CORNROW (hairstyle) characterizes the beauty of mental efforts applied to organized planning.

CORN SILK connotes the inner healing aspects of personal efforts.

CORNSTALK exemplifies the "strengthening" effects of hard work.

CORNSTARCH pertains to the personal "enrichment" one gains through personal efforts.

CORN SYRUP See sugar.

CORN TASSEL refers to the multiple energies associated with spiritual nourishment.

CORNUCOPIA symbolizes one's inherent spiritual aspects and the wide variety of benefits resulting from the utilization of same.

CORN WHISKEY See alcoholic beverage.

CORONA See aura.

CORONATION defines recognition from higher sources.

CORONER See medical examiner.

CORONET See crown.

CORPORATION signifies an organized group of individuals associated with the dreamer in some capacity.

CORPSE signifies an aspect in the dreamer's life that has no more viability; a dead issue.

CORRAL denotes personally controlled or confined aspects.

CORRELATION symbolizes interconnecting aspects; a relationship between ideas.

CORRESPONDENCE SCHOOL emphasizes learning opportunities.

CORRIDOR indicates a passageway; the way between stages of life.

CORROSION stands for the deterioration of something in one's life.

CORRUGATED portrays a timeframe consisting of rough roads.

CORSAGE pertains to one's inner beauty that others perceive and admire.

CORSET See girdle.

CORTEGE alludes to an individual's personal surround of associates or assistants.

CORTISONE typifies one's inherent aspects that have the capability to heal and restore.

COSMETICS denote those superficial aspects one utilizes to improve appearances.

COSMETIC SURGERY represents an "altered" appearance; improved self-image.

COSMIC DUST represents the constant presence of spiritual forces.

COSMIC NOISE pertains to the sounds within the silence; eternal vibratory frequency activity.

COSMIC RAY signifies the intellectual "dawning" of a profound spiritual truth.

COSMOLOGY (study of) connotes an emersion into spiritual aspects.

COSMOPOLITAN signifies intellectual sophistication pertaining to worldwide cultures; an extensive intellectual base.

COSMOS means the higher spiritual realm.

COSPONSOR characterizes an associate supporter or provider.

COSSACK illustrates one who charges forth to action without having complete information.

CO-STAR pertains to a second individual in the limelight or in a position of centered attention.

COST OF LIVING will relate to that of the dreamer and usually refers to the personal "cost" of actions, thoughts, and motivations.

COSTUME represents characterization. This may indicate one's alter-ego or complete opposite personality.

COT portrays short periods of rest or pauses.

COTILLION (formal ball) cautions against the need to be accepted or recognized in some way.

COTTAGE signifies acceptance of self; one who is comfortable with just having basic needs met.

COTTAGE CHEESE implies wholesome perspectives and attitudes.

COTTAGE INDUSTRY means self-sufficiency; an inner contentedness through personal efforts applied.

COTTER PIN symbolizes simple solutions.

COTTON connotes unsophisticated self-image; a lack of expressive ego; a comfortable perspective of self.

COTTON CANDY refers to simple pleasures derived from life.

COTTON GIN pertains to unadulterated attitudes; pure thought.

COTTONMOUTH See snake.

COTTON PICKING applies to the wholesomeness of honest, hard work.

COTTONSEED stands for foundational ideals that generate a positive self-image later in life.

COTTONSEED OIL typifies the richness of a wholesome life coupled with an accepting self-image.

COTTON SWAB denotes a cautious attitude.

COTTONTAIL See rabbit.

COTTONWOOD (tree) exemplifies the beauty of combining wholesome living with spirituality.

COUCH represents physical comfort.

COUCH GRASS See quack grass.

COUCH POTATO cautions against laziness, physical and mental.

COUGAR characterizes the strength of quiet wisdom.

COUGH portrays a fear of disclosure; fear of the truth.

COUGH DROP/SYRUP indicates an aspect that soothes one's fears.

COUNCIL advises of the need to deliberate. This may even infer self-examination.

COUNCILMAN/WOMAN exemplifies one who researches and decides something.

COUNSELOR stands for one who advises another.

COUNT (ING) advises of a need to "take stock" of something; there is imperative reason to count blessings or opportunities.

COUNTDOWN cautions of a need to keep an eye on the time; warns of a situation where time may be running out.

COUNTENANCE relates to facial expressions and what can be read from same. See specific expressions.

COUNTER (response) usually refers to a compromise.

COUNTERATTACK indicates a retaliatory response.

COUNTERBALANCE connotes an action or response that offsets another or serves as a balancing factor.

COUNTERCLOCKWISE illustrates an aspect that goes against the grain; an unexpected event; a reversal; going backward.

COUNTERCULTURE defines something that is considered a turn from the norm; visible expressions of individuality that veer away from those shared by the majority.

COUNTERFEIT defines something misrepresented.

COUNTERPART characterizes a clone-like aspect of something or someone; a complementing factor.

COUNTER PERSON See clerk.

COUNTER TOP denotes work convenience.

COUNTRY (foreign) will have a uniquely specific meaning for each dreamer.

COUNTRY (decor) alludes to "relaxed" attitudes.

COUNTRY CLUB represents social and recreational opportunities.

COUNTRY COUSIN advises of the many benefits and strengths that come from being honest and unsophisticated.

COUNTRY DANCE represents the joys of being unaffected by negative worldly aspects.

COUNTRY MILE connotes a very long way to go; a long life path.

COUNTRY MUSIC symbolizes one's specific manner of expressing emotions.

COUNTRYSIDE stands for the beautiful aspects of innocence; unsophisticated attitudes; an honest, down-home personality.

COUNTY pinpoints a specific message for each dreamer.

COUNTY FAIR connotes wholesome pride in one's hard work and the sharing of the resulting products.

COUNTY SEAT will refer to an aspect of legal offices and a specific connection the dreamer has for one of these.

COUP stands for a clever move; a strategic move that has been successfully executed; results from a masterful plan.

COUP DE GRACE signifies an aspect that brings about a finality.

COUP D'ÉTAT denotes an overthrow of authority.

COUPE (car type) implies a questionable situation; a situation with few exit possibilities.

COUPLING stands for "connecting" aspects.

COUPON illustrates life aspects that "save" time, energy, or money.

COUPSTICK stands for the resulting benefits of bravery and courage.

COURIER characterizes those who serve as messengers.

COURSE (route) typifies a visual of one's personal path. This most often will refer to that which one is headed for.

COURTESY CARD signifies "little" amenities in life; small conveniences.

COURTHOUSE refers to legal aspects.

COURT-MARTIAL alludes to an infraction of the set of rules by which one agreed to live.

COURT ORDER symbolizes an imperative aspect in one's life; a "must comply" directive.

COURT REPORTER warns against repeating falsehoods; cautions one to get the facts right.

COURTROOM connotes an analytic atmosphere; a situation where one attempts to get at the truth.

COURTSHIP stands for persuasion.

COURTYARD exemplifies temporary pauses or times of relaxation.

COUSIN characterizes trace association.

C

COUSTEAU (Jacques) signifies an in-depth spiritual search.

COUTURE See fashion designer.

COVE portrays spiritual security; one's sense of one's spiritual belief's protective qualities.

COVEN pertains to a spiritually related group of people.

COVENANT See agreement.

COVENANT (property) connotes restrictions devised and upheld by another.

COVERALLS denote protective measures.

COVER CHARGE implies a "price" for certain benefits enjoyed.

COVERED BRIDGE represents a connecting path that will be safe to travel upon.

COVERED WAGON stands for a path traveled with courage and self-reliance.

COVER GIRL indicates the tendency to believe one needs dramatic attention-getting aspects to be noticed.

COVERING LETTER denotes an introduction or "synopsis" of a more detailed aspect.

COVER STORY pertains to major news or information.

COVER-UP portrays an attempt to hide something.

COW alludes to compassion and the expression of same.

COWARD applies to one's inner fears.

COWBELL calls for the expression of compassion.

COWBIRD implies a tendency to take advantage of others.

COWBOY characterizes the sense of freedom in following one's personal path.

COWBOY BOOTS represent precautionary measures applied to insuring a reasonably safe course.

COWBOY HAT refers to independent thoughts.

COWCATCHER illustrates an attempt to "clear" one's way as one's path is traveled.

COW COLLEGE connotes a learning stage that provides for personal growth.

COWHAND See cowboy.

COWHIDE applies to the power of compassion.

COWL pertains to protected thoughts; an enigmatic personality.

COWLICK portrays a perspective that is not in line with others one has.

COWORKER characterizes those associated with one's work. This "work" may be one's spiritual work or a personal situational relationship.

COW TOWN defines an unsophisticated setting or situation.

COYOTE signifies a preference for solitude.

CRAB denotes a negative personality or situation.

CRAB APPLE alludes to a "tart" personality; a cantankerous disposition.

CRABGRASS exemplifies a negative aspect that has infiltrated and spread through one's life.

CRABS See sexual disease.

CRACK (attempt) advises one to proceed in spite of doubts.

CRACK (drug) See cocaine.

CRACK (expert) See expert.

CRACK (fissure) indicates an aspect in one's life that has an imperfection; may refer to one's belief system or personal perspectives.

CRACK (mental breakdown) See breakdown.

CRACK (sound) is a means of drawing attention to something the dreamer needs to be aware of.

CRACK (to solve) means a resolution is forthcoming.

CRACKER (food) denotes small benefits or considerations.

CRACKER (party favor) signifies inconsequential noise-making; an aspect that may appear serious yet proves to be innocuous.

CRACKER BARREL connotes informal discussions and the need to continue these.

CRACKER JACK portrays one who has great ability.

CRACK HOUSE stands for a highly dangerous situation or condition.

CRADLE represents immaturity, often a preferred state for the purpose of avoiding responsibility.

CRADLE BOARD illustrates a dependence on others.

CRAFTSPEOPLE See artisan.

CRAG exemplifies major chances taken in life.

CRAM warns against a tendency to take in too much information too fast.

CRAMP is a dream symbol that means restrictions.

CRANBERRY symbolizes one's natural talents.

CRANBERRY BOG connotes a nourishment of one's talents.

CRANE (bird) indicates inquisitiveness.

CRANE (machine) portrays a penchant for learning; continual "reaching"; extending of self.

CRANK refers to a life aspect that has the capability of providing a beginning.

CRANK (drug) See cocaine.

CRANKSHAFT denotes one aspect of several that generate new starts.

CRANKY stands for bad-tempered; unpredictability.

CRANNY reminds us of "space" left in our lives for something; having an ability to accommodate.

CRAPS (dice game) warns against taking slim chances.

CRASH refers to a destructive aspect in one's life; serious consequences.

CRASH CART connotes last minute efforts to save some failing aspect in the dreamer's life.

CRASH HELMET advises of a great need to protect one's thoughts. This may indicate the necessity of keeping thoughts to self.

CRASH LANDING depicts a sudden and unexpected conclusion to something that may or may not end up in total devastation.

CRASH PAD exemplifies preparations for the unexpected.

CRASH TRUCK pertains to the immediate action taken after an unexpected failure or great disappointment.

CRATE refers to one's desire to hide specific aspects of self.

CRATER See caldera.

CRAVAT applies to a desire to distinguish self from others.

CRAVE implies an inner weakness of some type.

CRAVEN See coward.

CRAWLING means a slow pace and may not infer a negative interpretation.

CRAWLSPACE denotes access to something.

CRAYFISH applies to a voluntary withdrawal from an agreed-upon event or responsibility.

CRAYON indicates an immaturity; undeveloped ideas.

CRAZY See insanity.

CRAZY QUILT indicates confusion or may mean that something is comprised of an odd mixture of aspects.

CREAKY stands for something that's outmoded or has been ignored for too long.

CREAM (color) represents gentle joy; an inner peacefulness and acceptance of life.

CREAM (dairy) portrays the quality of "richness" to one's life. This, of course, does not refer to monetary aspects.

CREAM CHEESE illustrates a smoothly consistent and wholesome life aspect.

CREAMER represents a life aspect that has the capability of providing deeper elements to one's life.

CREAMERY symbolizes the dreamer's wholesome aspects

that blend to create a richly rewarding life.

CREAM PUFF advises of something in the dreamer's life that's still in excellent condition.

CREAM SODA illustrates a rewarding or beneficial aspect in one's life.

CREASE denotes level of perfection. Is the crease ironed-in or was it caused by wrinkles?

CRÈCHE serves as a reminder of spiritual responsibilities.

CREDENTIALS connotes experiential documentation; level of one's knowledge. This is usually a warning dream symbol that advises the dreamer to check someone's qualifications—even those of self.

CREDENZA symbolizes a superstitious nature; paranoia; a lack of trust.

CREDIT implies an assumption of one's good character; a certain level of confidence.

CREDIT BUREAU represents a "record" of one's life activities; frequently refers to the Book of Life or one's personal karmic record.

CREDIT CARD relates to a life aspect that is capable of obtaining something in advance of one's readiness.

CREDIT HOUR indicates learning or knowledge acquired.

CREDIT LINE (of article) See byline.

CREDIT LINE (monetary) indicates the amount of leeway one has before its time to answer for one's actions. This dream symbol can refer to a life span.

CREDITOR usually pertains to those to whom one owes a karmic debt.

CREDIT RATING signifies one's level of trustworthiness.

CREDIT UNION illustrates an opportunity.

CREDITWORTHY underscores one's high trust and confidence.

CREED defines one's basic spiritual beliefs.

CREEK See stream.

CREEL signifies one's personal "tools" for a spiritual search or involvement.

CREMATORIUM connotes a finality; an aspect conclusion; an absolute closure.

CRÈME DE LA CRÈME stands for the "best" manifestation of something; highest standard; most desired perfection.

CREOSOTE signifies a buildup of negative attitudes or perspectives.

CREPE (fabric) suggests a personality whose mental aberrations are easily perceived.

CREPE (pancake) pertains to fragile beginnings.

CREPE PAPER refers to temporary celebrations; short-lived joys.

CRESCENT (shape) portrays bright beginnings or endings, depending on surrounding dream factors.

CREST See ridge.

CREVICE applies to unexpected situations that make one's life path more difficult.

CRIB exemplifies immaturity; an inability (or refusal) to face reality.

CRIBBAGE pertains to some aspect in one's life that's been exposed.

CRIB DEATH (SIDS) represents a voluntary withdrawal from reality.

CRICKETS indicate certain emotionally soothing aspects in life.

CRIMINAL characterizes a lawbreaker. This will usually refer to someone the dreamer knows in life.

CRIMP symbolizes an attempt to shorten or "pinch" something into a smaller timeframe.

CRINGE denotes a personal reaction that may indicate revulsion, fear, disappointment, or dismay.

CRIOSPHINX characterizes inner strength through belief in one's convictions.

CRIPPLED defines an impairment that will not halt advancement.

CRISIS means an unexpected disturbing event that one must face and overcome.

CRISP connotes an aspect that's fresh yet fragile at the same time.

CRISPER implies an attempt to preserve something; a desire to keep something new and fresh.

CRISSCROSS relates to a "return" to some aspect in one's life.

CRITIC characterizes one who has the habit of looking for another's faults.

CRITIQUE stands for personal assessment; judging through one's personal perspectives.

CROAKING typifies a fear to speak. This usually refers to the voicing of truths that are preferably kept to oneself.

CROCHET depicts personal acts done for others.

CROCKERY See earthenware.

CROCODILE connotes underlying negative spiritual aspects or forces.

CROCODILE TEARS characterize the expression of false emotions for the sake of obtaining sympathy or attention; insecurity.

CROCUS marks a change in one's direction or situation.

CROISSANT defines beginnings rich in spiritual factors.

CRONE See hag.

CROOKED (shape) denotes distortion which may indicate one's manner of thought process.

CROP (food) symbolizes an aspect of nourishment.

CROP (riding whip) represents impatience.

CROP (trim) portrays an aspect that has been "shortened" prematurely or one that should never have been touched.

CROP CIRCLE characterizes skepticism in the face of facts.

CROP-DUSTING connotes wrong beginnings.

CROP ROTATION indicates a concern for another's welfare.

CROQUET exemplifies vindictiveness that is hidden behind sophistication.

CROSS (shape) portrays burdens.

CROSS (sign of the cross) exposes religious rather than spiritual faith.

CROSSBEAM illustrates a "supporting" aspect.

CROSSBONES denote severe consequences.

CROSSBOW alludes to that which leads straight to one's goals.

CROSSBREED See hybrid.

CROSS-COUNTRY symbolizes a long journey traversed along untraveled paths.

CROSSCURRENT connotes conflicting perspectives, usually within self.

CROSS-DRESSING pertains to a desire to share or understand the condition or experiential aspects of another.

CROSS-EXAMINE indicates a need to double-check something.

CROSS-EYED infers a distorted perception.

CROSSFIRE warns of being caught in the middle of a situation or relationship.

CROSS HAIR advises of a need to readjust or alter one's "sights" on something.

CROSSING GUARD characterizes protective elements in one's life.

CROSS-LEGGED stands for insecurities; a reluctance to share aspects of self.

CROSS MATCHING implies an attempt to seek compatibility. This may not refer to the obvious aspect of one's relationship with another but could be indicating the search for belief systems that feel right for self.

CROSSOVER pertains to appropriate "crossing" points along one's life path.

CROSS-REFERENCE advises of a need to check out some aspects to determine the facts.

CROSSROAD pertains to the

time for making a major decision in life. This most often has to do with a change in direction.

CROSS SECTION advises of the wisdom of "looking within" something, usually self.

CROSS-STITCH alludes to precision and the need to give it attention.

CROSSWALK defines the most safe route to take in life.

CROSSWIND signifies life's unexpected aspects that can "blow" us off balance.

CROSSWORD PUZZLE denotes miscommunications; trouble communicating.

CROTCH infers a junction in one's path; a fork in the road.

CROUCHING symbolizes insecurities; poor self-image.

CROUPIER characterizes someone who urges another to take chances or an individual who will benefit or lose by the chances you take.

CROUTON refers to hard choices.

CROW represents clear messages; straight talk.

CROWBAR indicates a "forced" aspect.

CROWD illustrates wide appeal; an attention-getting aspect.

CROWN warns against egotism or goals of grandeur.

CROWN JEWEL defines one's greatest desire.

CROWN OF THORNS connotes self-sacrifice.

CROW'S NEST cautions one of the need for a "better view" of something; wider perspective required; greater vision.

CRUCIFIX is an outward sign that marks one's self-sacrifices; a desire to display one's personal pains.

CRUDE OIL characterizes an unrefined and often rude personality.

CRUET represents specialized knowledge.

CRUISE cautions against displaying spiritual affectations.

CRUISE CONTROL advises one to alter the speed by which one's path is taken. This usually refers to the need to slow down.

CRUISE MISSILE warns of the destructive power of uncontrolled thoughts.

CRUISER (cabin) denotes a spiritual journey that lacks seriousness.

CRUISER (warship) denotes the long-range effects of a nonchalant spiritual search.

CRULLER portrays an inflated and twisted perspective.

CRUMB pertains to aspects one isn't satisfied with.

CRUSADES imply negative spiritual activism.

CRUST alludes to the harder aspects of life that precede one's smoother and more palatable path.

CRUTCH warns against the use of others as excuses for not taking personal responsibility; a message to stand on your own feet and utilize inner strength.

CRYING pertains to the grief of regret or remorse.

CRYONICS is a strong warning against one's love of self and one's physical essence.

CRYPT connotes hidden aspects; secrets.

CRYPTOGRAM defines secret communications.

CRYPTOGRAPHY (study of) indicates a desire to understand esoteric matters and comprehend life's enigmatic aspects.

CRYSTAL (glassware) implies displayed sophistication; a touch of social arrogance.

CRYSTAL BALL cautions one against impatience to know the future and/or the utilization of unnecessary perceptive tools.

CRYSTALS (natural) relate to the clarity and depth of one's personal spiritual attunement.

CUBBYHOLE stands for the tendency to segregate people according to personal attitudes and judgments.

CUBE (shape) See square.

CUBIC ZIRCONIA denotes a lack of genuineness; an attempt at grandeur through imitation; misrepresentation.

CUCKOO CLOCK characterizes an extremely regimented personality.

CUCUMBER pertains to possible difficulties forthcoming.

CUE BALL refers to a beginning move.

CUE CARD defines an individual who rarely speaks for self.

CUE STICK alludes to the level of precision; a beginning move is made.

CUFF LINK represents an arrogance toward one's work.

CUFF (shirt) refers to that which protects one's mobility and tenacity.

CUL-DE-SAC connotes a need to backtrack; reverse one's path.

CULL warns against a tendency to choose only the best of something.

CULT exemplifies a group of individuals who have specific beliefs that are considered aberrant or dangerous. This symbol usually comes as a warning message regarding some associates of the dreamer.

CULTIVATE defines a "nurturing" personality or life aspect.

C

CULVERT denotes the direction and manner one utilizes his or her personal spiritual gifts.

CUNEIFORM (shape) alludes to an "opening up" aspect or result.

CUP symbolizes one's personal perspective on the quality and quantity of his or her life situation.

CUPBOARD represents personal life aspects that nourish one.

CUPCAKE signifies the generous giving of self.

CUPID characterizes love.

CUPOLA denotes mental "extensions" of thought that typify the activity of an analytic mind.

CURARE warns against continual states of stress; a need to relax.

CURATOR defines an individual who is devoted to the protection and preservation of intellectual pursuits and values.

CURB advises of a need to "curb" some aspect in the dreamer's life; a caution against excesses.

CURB SERVICE denotes convenience.

CURD connotes rich rewards and nourishment through self-effort.

CURDLE implies changes that may go bad.

CURE alludes to some type of healing or it may refer to the preservation of something.

CURETTE signifies a life aspect that has the capability to "remove" a negative factor from one's life.

CURFEW cautions against a prolonged activity; a time for everything; time management.

CURIE (Marie) characterizes the application of intelligence.

CURIO exemplifies a life aspect that is of high interest to the dreamer.

CURL (hair) pertains to an analytic thought process.

CURLER connotes one's attempt to figure something out.

CURLING IRON cautions against "forcing" conclusions; making attempts to understand complicated or high-minded concepts.

CURRANT refers to the little nourishing aspects that are abundant in our lives.

CURRENCY See money.

CURRENT (electrical flow) relates directly to one's personal energy circuitry and may be referring to physical, emotional, or mental energy.

CURRENT (time) indicates the present and most often is an advisory message given for the purpose of "bringing" the dreamer back to the here-and-now.

CURRENT (water flow) portrays the rate of speed one travels

131

along the spiritual path. This will clarify if it is too fast and dangerous or if there is a "drag" factor.

CURRICULUM will most often identify specific learning areas on which the dreamer should be focusing.

CURRYCOMB connotes the attention and control given to one's wilder aspects.

CURSE (spell) See spell.

CURSE (swear) See swear.

CURSOR stands for a reminder for one to keep focused; stay aware and mentally attentive.

CURTAIN means privacy; the time separating daily activities; may refer to denials or secrecy.

CURTAIN CALL denotes appreciation for one's shared talents.

CURTSY See bow.

CURVE (shape) connotes a gentle veering of course.

CURVE BALL warns against having expectations; events or happenings that don't turn out as expected.

CUSHION denotes an aspect that softens or eases.

CUSP symbolizes crossroads or turning points in one's life.

CUSPIDOR See spittoon.

CUSS See swear.

CUSTARD alludes to the richly nourishing inner rewards of applying one's spirituality.

CUSTER (George) characterizes the karmic results of bigotry and racism.

CUSTODIAN pertains to individuals who are designated with the authority to be the Keepers, the Preservers of spiritual truths.

CUSTOM connotes traditionally accepted practices.

CUSTOM-BUILT indicates personalized attitudes; perception based on one's specialized database of knowledge.

CUSTOMER denotes one who has a right to receive service.

CUSTOMER SERVICE DESK implies a life aspect from which one can receive assistance or information.

CUSTOMS exemplifies a "check" time in one's life; a point in time when one needs to "inspect" paths and the manner they are traveled.

CUT illustrates the act of severing something.

CUT-AND-DRIED means having no questions about; an aspect that is clear and factual.

CUTBACK advises one to "ease up" on something; lessen the amount of energy spent on something.

CUT FLOWER See bouquet.

CUT GLASS signifies a finely faceted aspect in one's life.

CUTLASS See sword.

CUTOFF (limit) denotes the need to detach self from a harmful element.

CUTOFF (clothing) refers to the preservation of a partially worn but still useable aspect.

CUTOUT (paper) represents an element in one's life that needs to be "cut out" or stopped.

CUTTHROAT warns of a vicious personality; having no scruples.

CUTTLEBONE advises of a need to "sharpen" one's speech for the purpose of bringing clarity.

CYANIDE stands for the dangerous ramifications of making financial gain a priority.

CYBORG characterizes the natural blend of spirituality and physics that create Reality.

CYCLONE See tornado.

CYCLOPS (Greek mythology) pertains to the lost aspects of Reality.

CYLINDRICAL (shape) connotes a message for the dreamer. What color was it? Did it contain any writings?

CYMBALS are attention-getters; a call to listen; an advisement to be watchful and aware.

CYNIC defines a distrustful personality.

CYPRESS (tree) stands for grief; a mourning time.

CYST denotes the presence of a destructive negative aspect that has taken hold of the dreamer. This may be a negative spiritual concept, a negative idea or attitude, or a harmful emotion.

D

DABBLE represents a lack of seriousness.

DACHSHUND (dog breed) implies a caution against the tendency to make the physical aspects a priority; a high interest in materialism.

DADDY See father.

DADDY LONGLEGS refer to fears that are overcome.

DAFFODIL portrays the bright prospects of new beginnings.

DAGGER signifies harmful aspects in one's life. Frequently this symbol indicates an associate or someone the dreamer knows.

DAGGER FERN See Christmas fern.

DAGUERREOTYPE advises of a special current meaning for past relationships; importance of old friends.

DAHLIA connotes opportunity.

DAILY DOUBLE represents a situation that has the capability of bringing multiple rewards or disappointments.

DAIQUIRI See alcoholic beverage.

DAIRY alludes to nourishment.

DAIRY FARM refers to a major aspect of one's life that nourishes the perspectives of self and others.

DAISY illustrates happiness; a joyous attitude toward life.

DAISY CHAIN symbolizes exuberance.

DALMATIAN (dog breed) signifies a traveling companion.

DAM always means some type of spiritual block.

DAMASK (fabric) exemplifies a rich and full experience.

DAMP indicates the presence of an additional aspect to something in the dreamer's life.

DAMPER stands for a life factor that can be utilized to increase or decrease one's understanding, depending on how it is used.

DANCE refers to a personal manner of expressing emotions.

DANCE HALL pertains to an emotional outlet.

DANCE INSTRUCTOR characterizes those who have the capability to bring out another's emotions or self-expression.

DANCEWEAR connotes an outward desire to express one's emotions.

DANDELION means benefits that are not readily seen or realized.

DANDER pertains to irritations that bring about mental or physical reactions.

DANDRUFF implies a need to shed misconceptions.

DANDY warns against a preoccupation with one's appearance.

DANGER of any kind clearly means just that. The surrounding dream symbols will help to narrow down the source.

DAPPLED (pattern) signifies an attitude or perspective that is not consistent.

DARE refers to intimidations; challenges.

DAREDEVIL portrays an attitude of over-confidence; a disregard for obvious high risks; a tempt of fate.

DARK suggests something that is difficult to perceive; may refer to negativity; obscure or enigmatic.

DARK HORSE alludes to an individual or situation that surprisingly overcame low expectations.

DARKROOM denotes a life aspect that has the capability of reversing negative factors in one's life.

DARNING NEEDLE symbolizes an opportunity to repair or make amends.

DART signifies events that we allow to impede our progress.

DART BOARD advises to con-tinually vent negative emotions in a positive and nonharmful manner.

DARTH VADER characterizes an individual who misuses spirituality; may clearly refer to a spiritually "dark" individual.

DARWIN (Charles) alludes to evolution. This does not refer to biological aspects but rather emotional, perceptual, mental, or spiritual.

DASHBOARD pertains to protective measures.

DATA relates to information the dreamer needs.

DATABASE stands for one's personal scope of attained knowledge or information. This will not refer to the "comprehension" of same.

DATA PROCESSOR connotes the utilization of information; how one uses what he or she knows.

DATE (food) denotes versatility.

DATE (point in time) comes in dreams to pinpoint an important timeframe for the dreamer.

DATE (time reservation) marks a need to give attention to an activity or meeting.

DATE BOOK represents a reminder for important scheduled events in one's life.

DATELINE pertains to time or place of origination; the source of something.

DATURA illustrates a life aspect that alters one's perspectives, reactions, or comprehension.

DAUGHTER characterizes a younger, female individual toward whom one has a protective and nurturing relationship in life.

DAVENPORT See couch.

DAVY JONES' LOCKER warns of a spiritual fatality.

DAWN indicates the "light" of new beginnings.

DAY (time) implies the time of light, activity, or progression.

DAY BED suggests the importance of pause times during one's day.

DAYBOOK See diary.

DAYBREAK See dawn.

DAY CAMP refers to the reservation of a portion of one's day for relaxation and mental rests.

DAY CARE alludes to the manner in which our routine responsibilities are managed.

DAYDREAM pertains to personal, private thoughts, often expresses unrealistic scenarios or desires. To daydream is to veer from reality.

DAYLIGHT-SAVING TIME denotes an attempt to alter reality.

DAY LILY denotes emotional sensitivity.

DAY ROOM signifies a pause from one's routine or regimentation.

DAYSTAR See morning star.

DAZED connotes a nonreceptive state of mind; unclear thought.

DAZZLED warns against being blinded by amazement; cautions against perceptual abnormalities; affected by seemingly spectacular aspects.

DEACON characterizes an individual who has been spiritually helpful in one's life.

DEAD means lifeless; an absolute conclusion; a final closing.

DEAD AIR indicates an interruption in communication or thought.

DEAD-AIR SPACE exemplifies a lack of "fresh" ideas; stale concepts or a stage of intellectual neutrality.

DEADBEAT warns against personal apathy; emotionally unaffected.

DEAD BOLT implies attention to security. This may infer protection from others in respect to the exposure of one's hidden activities, thoughts, or perceptions. A desire to keep an aspect of one's life secure.

DEAD DUCK pertains to certain failure; death.

DEAD END represent fruitless paths or relationships.

DEAD EYE denotes an "expert" level of attainment; one who always knows exactly what he or she is doing.

DEAD FALL stands for unappreciated or unrecognized life aspects that serve to nourish.

DEAD HEAT warns against obsessive competition.

DEAD LETTER advises of failed communication attempts.

DEADLINE cautions one of the passing of time; may warn that time is running out. Often this symbol refers to the time restrictions one places on self.

DEADLOCK means an impasse; a no-win situation or relationship.

DEADLY NIGHTSHADE See belladonna.

DEADPAN portrays an individual who is expressionless; one who does not show emotion.

DEAD SPOT connotes a mental block or lack of communication.

DEAD WEIGHT cautions of a need to unload the negative aspects one carries around that slows down or prevents advancement or growth.

DEADWOOD warns of a tendency to hold onto the negatively emotional effects of past events; a need for closure.

DEAF usually refers to self-denial or a willful avoidance of the truth.

DEAL (distribute) means active sharing of something.

DEAL (situation) refers to a specific condition or event in the dreamer's life.

DEALER characterizes one who is the "source" of something; one who can supply something to others.

DEALERSHIP connotes a specialized source; an outlet supplying the individualized needs of others.

DEAN characterizes intellectual authority or counsel.

DEAN'S LIST denotes intellectual accomplishments.

DEATH stands for termination; finality.

DEATHBED alludes to an approaching end or conclusion.

DEATH BENEFIT relates to life aspects associated with a finalization of something; aspects that result from a conclusion.

DEATHBLOW signifies a devastating event in one's life.

DEATH DUTY See inheritance tax.

DEATH HOUSE See death row.

DEATH MASK may forewarn of an actual physical death but most often it relates to an extremely dangerous situation or relationship that has the strong potential to have devastating ramifications or conclusions.

DEATH PENALTY means no opportunity for a second chance; no way out.

DEATH RATTLE forewarns one of approaching finality; a need to prepare for the worst.

DEATH ROW relates to the realization that one cannot hide or run from making retribution.

DEATHTRAP warns of an extremely dangerous life situation for the dreamer.

DEATH VALLEY pertains to a long-suffering stage in one's life.

DEATH WARRANT applies to a life aspect that will seal one's fate in an extremely negative manner. Who is signing the death warrant? Is it yourself?

DEATHWATCH symbolizes an irreversible situation that is heading toward devastation.

DEATH WISH warns against fatalism; self-destructive perspectives or actions.

DEBATE advises one to listen to the perspectives of others.

DEBAUCHERY warns against a tendency to focus on the physical aspects of life, especially the sensual pleasures.

DEBONING connotes an attitude or action that removes one's support.

DEBRIDEMENT advises of a need to go "into" something and clean it up. This would relate to a situation left unattended too long.

DEBRIEFING alludes to the wisdom of conducting frequent mental self-examinations. We learn from ourselves when we spend time double-checking our motives, perspectives, and actions.

DEBRIS signifies a need to clean up the remaining aspects of past conclusions.

DEBT stands for something we owe and need to pay.

DEBUT indicates the time to introduce something; time to bring something out into the open.

DEBUTANTE warns against the need for attention or to be recognized. Also warns against making one's class or station in life or society a priority.

DECAFFEINATED implies a lessening of one's motivation or energy.

DECAL may advise the dreamer to pay attention to what the dream decal represented as a personal message or it may indicate the dreamer's personal attitude about something. A decal symbol signifies the public "expression" of an attitude.

DECAPITATION warns of a situation where one figuratively "loses one's head" over something. This symbol calls for an immediate return to logic and reason.

DECATHLON represents the "extent" to which one goes for the purpose of accomplishing something.

DECAY illustrates a "decomposing" situation, relationship, or perspective.

DECELERATION refers to a "slowing-down" of something; may be actually "advising" the action.

DECEMBER stands for a time of renewal and reflection.

DECENTRALIZATION calls for an admonition to stop being too focused, causing a myopic perspective. This dream symbol advises one to view things with a more opened eye, bringing a wider scope of information.

DECEPTION is a warning symbol. The word is self-explanatory. There is some type of deceiving going on in your life. The real clue here is: "Who" is doing it? Self?

DECIDUOUS defines an atmosphere of change, the inevitability of such.

DECIMAL POINT symbolizes value or the end of something.

DECISION denotes the need to give serious thought to something; time to stop vacillating.

DECK (boat) connotes deeper spiritual perspectives.

DECK (of cards) implies game-playing in connection with one's interaction with others.

DECK (pack of drugs) cautions

against the utilization of negative or altering aspects to accomplish something.

DECK (platform) represents improved perspectives.

DECK CHAIR alludes to an acceptance of improved perspectives.

DECK HAND characterizes one who assists in bringing about one's spiritually enlightened perceptions.

DECK SHOES denote a self-styled spiritual insulation; a voluntary separation from spiritual issues or concepts.

DECODE means comprehension; clarity of understanding.

DECOMPOSITION See decay.

DECOMPRESSION CHAMBER warns against the tendency to speed through high spiritual concepts without taking the time to thoroughly comprehend them; a fast spiritual retreat.

DECONGESTANT pertains to a need to "clear" emotional congestion within self.

DECORATE relates to special preparations. What is being decorated? How is it being done? With what type of items?

DECORATION DAY See Memorial Day.

DECOUPAGE exemplifies the "addition" of specialized aspects to something.

DECOY connotes imitation or diversion in one's life.

DECREE signifies an authoritative statement; an order or advisement.

DECREPIT alludes to time-worn and will most often refer to the mental state of defeat or lost motivation.

DEED will underscore one's "right" to something.

DEEP implies a "considerable" distance and will be associated with surrounding dreamscape aspects.

DEEP-DISH illustrates an aspect in one's life that took some doing to create.

DEEP FREEZER stands for a life aspect that has been set aside for further time.

DEEP FRYER connotes serious trouble.

DEEP POCKETS represent a current status of "considerable" wealth.

DEEP-ROOTED refers to an attitude or perspective that has been held for a long time.

DEEP-SEA portrays higher spiritual philosophy.

DEEP SIX exemplifies a total rejection of something due to spiritual beliefs.

DEEP SPACE stands for great extensions of thought; contemplation of philosophical possibilities; the serious consideration of the far reaches of physics.

DEEP WATER implies an in-depth spiritual search or path.

DEER applies to a tendency to be cautious; watchful; aware.

DEER FLY refers to the "biting" aspects in life that can cause temporary irritations if one isn't watchful and aware.

DEERSKIN connotes some type of attachment to nature.

DEFACE warns against vindictiveness; uncontrolled anger or retaliation.

DEFAME warns against gossip or maliciousness; advises forgiveness and closure.

DEFAULT stands for some life aspect with which one has failed to follow through.

DEFEAT may apply to a winning situation or a losing one, depending on other aspects of the dream. Either way, it reminds one to act the same way—accepting without the expression of pride or jealousy.

DEFECTIVE illustrates a "flawed" aspect in one's life. Surrounding dream factors will usually clarify this for the dreamer.

DEFENDANT most often characterizes an individual who has need to explain self.

DEFENSE MECHANISM stands for psychological methods

D

utilized to protect oneself from guilt, low self-esteem, conflict, shame, or other personally-injurious feelings.

DEFERMENT suggests a postponement or permanent release from responsibility.

DEFIBRILLATOR warns against stress and refers to a positive life aspect that will help one to accomplish this.

DEFICIENCY DISEASE See specific disease.

DEFICIT indicates an inadequate aspect in one's life. The dreamer will usually know what this aspect is.

DEFINITION spelled out in a dream will clearly come as an important personal message for the dreamer. Pay attention to these.

DEFLATION relates to a loss of motivation or a need to go back and begin something over again.

DEFLECTOR corresponds with one's protective measures.

DEFOGGER advises of a need to improve perspectives.

DEFOLIANT See Agent Orange.

DEFROCK cautions against doing something that isn't aligned with one's high ideals.

DEFORMITY denotes an opportunity for growth.

DEFROST advises of a need to be

less rigid; attain or express more understanding and compassion.

DEFUSE depicts a need to halt further progression toward an "explosive" situation, relationship, or belief.

DEGREASE exemplifies an action that causes friction.

DEHUMIDIFIER signifies a life aspect that is devoid of any associated spirituality; the act of removing spiritual aspects from a selected portion of one's life.

DÉJÀ VU pertains to the manifestation of past precognitive or dream experiences.

DELEGATE characterizes a representative individual.

DELETION suggests a "missing" or "removed" aspect in one's life.

DELFT (pottery) stands for a fragile yet cherished attitude toward one's heritage.

DELICATESSEN portrays ethnic karmic connections.

DELIRIUM suggests a loss of all control.

DELIVERY PEOPLE pertain to one's "delivery" or presentation to others in life; may also indicate a forthcoming conveyance.

DELIVERY ROOM See birthing center.

DELPHINIUM See larkspur.

DELTA (shape) See triangle.

141

DELTA relates to the "discards" of one's spiritual search.

DELUGE See flood.

DEMENTIA See insanity.

DEMERIT connotes a negative aspect or karmic debt.

DEMITASSE (cup) pertains to the need for a small portion of motivation or energy to get one back on track.

DEMOCRACY implies a relationship, situation, or condition that benefits all people.

DEMOGRAPHICS advise of the wisdom of "knowing" those with whom one associates.

DEMOLITION denotes the absolute destruction of something in the dreamer's life.

DEMOLITION CREW characterizes the life aspect or those associated with it that brings about a destruction of something in the dreamer's life.

DEMOLITION DERBY connotes a clash of conflicting forces. This could even refer to opposing attitudes or inner conflicts within self.

DEMON characterizes any negative aspects that plague one's life or mind.

DEMONSTRATION is a symbol that usually brings a visually explanatory message for the dreamer. It may show "how" to accomplish something.

DEMOTION advises of a need to watch one's arrogance or "heightened" perception of self-worth.

DEMULCENT will portray a "soothing" aspect that may be needed in one's life.

DEN symbolizes the quality and frequency of the dreamer's personal enrichment or restorative time.

DENALI (mountain) represents strength and power of the spirit.

DENIAL infers a refusal to accept or acknowledge something. This symbol most often comes when the dreamer is not acknowledging this denial.

DENIM (fabric) alludes to long-lasting; an aspect that endures.

DENIZEN See inhabitant.

DEN MOTHER characterizes a woman in one's life who is nurturing of many others.

DENOUNCE corresponds to an open condemnation, denial, or accusation.

DENSE exemplifies "thick" or compact. This is usually meant to advise one to "clear out" or "give air" to some life aspect.

DENT connotes a life aspect or action that has made a "small" difference or effect on something.

DENTAL FLOSS warns against making innuendos or voicing assumptions.

DENTAL HYGIENIST characterizes an individual in one's life who continues to remind or guide others away from making assumptions.

DENTAL TECHNICIAN portrays one who helps others to express themselves appropriately.

DENTIFRICE See toothpaste.

DENTIST represents one who works to help others articulate their thoughts.

DENTISTRY (study of) indicates a desire to help others express themselves.

DENTURE denotes a new manner of beautiful speech. This would also include the voicing of new, enlightening perspectives.

DEODORANT implies a cover-up; or an attempt to avoid offending another.

DEPARTMENT STORE connotes an aspect that offers a variety of opportunities.

DEPENDENT pertains to anyone who looks to you for support.

DEPILATORY alludes to an aspect or agent that has the capability of drastically negating another's thoughts or perspectives.

DEPORTATION refers to the permanent physical removal of someone or something from one's life.

DEPOSIT (initial payment) marks firm intentions.

DEPOSIT (money account) portrays asset accumulation. This will refer to finances unless silver was deposited.

DEPOSIT (security) pertains to some type of assurance given; a promise; an insuring factor.

DEPOT reflects a directional or course change.

DEPRECIATION advises of something that has reached a state of lessening value.

DEPRESSION (economic) forewarns of a need to watch finances.

DEPRESSION (mental) warns against a perception of hopelessness.

DEPRESSION (recess) indicates a low point or an aspect that has sunk below the normal level.

DEPRESSURIZE advises of a need to reduce personal pressures.

DEPRIVATION may indicate a need to live without something or it may refer to something the dreamer is willfully leaving out of life.

DEPROGRAMMING is a strong advisement to counteract some negative aspect in one's life.

DEPTH CHARGE stands for a negative life aspect that will destroy one's spiritual foundation.

DEPTH FINDER indicates the "depth" of one's spirituality.

143

DEPTH PERCEPTION denotes analytic ability; capable of extensive reasoning and logical thought.

DEPTH SOUNDER See depth finder.

DEPUTY characterizes one's chosen assistant or associate.

DERAILMENT pertains to going "off track" in life.

DERBY (hat) suggests out-dated ideas; old fashioned.

DERBY (race) denotes a competitive personality or aspect.

DERELICT (person) characterizes a need to be motivated, usually through a new perspective of self-worth.

DERELICT (remiss) warns against neglecting responsibilities.

DERMATITIS stands for life's irritating aspects; annoyances that get under the skin.

DERMATOLOGY (study of) characterizes those who are interested in understanding the hows, whys, and cure of other peoples reaction to certain life factors. This could also indicate a psychologist, psychiatrist, or some type of counselor.

DERRICK represents valuable resources, particularly material ones.

DERRINGER exemplifies a source of hidden power.

DESCENDING implies a downward or lowering move and could refer to several aspects in one's life, depending on surrounding symbols.

DESCRAMBLER (electronic device) symbolizes an inherent ability to understand others; a natural capacity for seeing psychological ploys of others.

DESECRATION signifies spiritual disrespect or apathy.

DESEGREGATION represents an integration of perceptions, attitudes, or concepts; usually this is an advisory message.

DESENSITIZED warns of apathy or emotional indifference.

DESERT (forsake) See abandon.

DESERT (hot, sandy region) connotes a life stage or condition whereby one needs a reserve of strength and perseverance.

DESERTED (devoid of human habitation) stands for a call for self-reliance and ingenuity.

DESIGNS portray an array of specific meanings for each dreamer. For generalized interpretations, please refer to the name of specific pattern types.

DESIGNER characterizes an individual who creates specific situations or conditions in one's life.

DESIGNER DRUG warns against using self-styled "crutches" in life.

144

DESIGNER SHOES caution against walking a path "designed" or initiated by another.

DESK denotes type, quantity, and quality of work being done. This usually applies to individualized efforts given to a life path or advancement.

DESKTOP PUBLISHING portrays personalized construction of one's precisely-delivered communications.

DESPAIR illustrates nonacceptance.

DESPERADO specifically refers to one reacting to a "desperate" condition or situation.

DESSERT means the ingestion of something sweet "after" a meal. This is different than eating a sweet anytime. In this context, dessert refers to the "rewards" received in life for one's efforts applied to one's path.

DESSERT SPOON relates to "special" rewards.

DESTINY exemplifies life aspects that cannot be altered.

DESTITUTION indicates a complete lack of basic foundations.

DESTROYER (ship) warns of a life aspect that has the capability of destroying spirituality.

DESTRUCTION typifies any life aspect that causes great harm.

DETAIL PERSON (pharmaceutical) warns of an individual who would attempt to convince others of utilizing "their specific" resource of help. There are *many* options.

DETAINEE defines one held against one's will. This may refer to any number of aspects, even self-confinement.

DETECTIVE characterizes one who has a high interest in understanding the facts and the sequential process of development.

DETENTION CENTER/HOME signifies a situational condition that is confining.

DETERGENT advises of a need to "clean" something in one's life. This will usually refer to one's outward presentation to others.

DETERRENT points the way to avoid an undesirable situation.

DETONATE comes as an extreme warning that some aspect in one's life has reached an "explosive" stage.

DETOXIFY advises of a great need to get rid of personally damaging or harmful aspects that are associated with one's life.

DEUCE (evil, bad) pertains to a situation that characterizes a perfect example of something bad; epitomizes the worst of something.

DEUCE (game) refers to the number two and will be clarified by surrounding dream aspects.

DEVELOPER (chemical) represents a life aspect that has the ability to bring something to completion; capable of bringing through the sequential stages leading to conclusion; turning a negative into a positive.

DEVELOPER (of land) typifies misuse of one's resources.

DEVIL characterizes an individual or life aspect that is extremely negative and personally harmful.

DEVIL'S ADVOCATE illustrates self-examination. This means that there is a reason in one's life to examine motives or attitudes.

DEVIL'S FOOD CAKE connotes rewards or joys one feels unworthy of receiving or enjoying; unjustified guilt.

DEVOTEE characterizes an unrealistic and fanatical attraction to something. This is a warning message.

DEW symbolizes a light spiritual touch.

DEWCLAW connotes an extraneous aspect. This may refer to an attitude, belief, or emotion that is unnecessary for one to hold onto.

DEW POINT refers to the stage in one's life where spiritual factors begin to be integrated into daily living.

DIABETES alludes to an imbalance in one's life.

DIABLO See devil.

DIADEM See crown.

DIAGNOSIS points to the specific "cause" of something.

DIAGNOSTICIAN refers to an individual who has the capability and knowledge to help others pinpoint the source of their problems.

DIAGONAL (direction) connotes an attitude, perspective, or path that is slanted.

DIAGRAM advises of the need for clarification before comprehension is attained.

DIAL portrays an indication of level or quantity. This may refer to several aspects and will be clarified by surrounding dream facets.

DIAL TONE advises of non-responsiveness from another; one's attempts at communication falling on deaf ears.

DIALYSIS implies a need for certain aspects of one's life to be separated from others.

DIAMOND exemplifies perfection.

DIAMONDBACK RATTLE-SNAKE See snake.

DIAMOND IN THE ROUGH alludes to quality in need of refinement.

DIAMOND MINE depicts a source of wealth, usually not in reference to monetary aspects.

146

DIAPER exemplifies an effort to control something in one's life.

DIAPHANOUS suggests a delicate life aspect.

DIARRHEA defines an aspect in one's life that is difficult to control.

DIARY connotes personal life accounts; importance of remembering.

DIATRIBE implies the act of routine complaining.

DICE (cut into small cubes) denotes a need to "break down" ideas so the components can be easily "digested" or understood.

DICE (game pieces) pertain to changeability; the many probabilities for each outcome.

DICHOTOMY signifies opposing attitudes regarding one idea.

DICKENS (Charles) portrays old-fashioned morals that are still viable.

DICKINSON (Emily) characterizes the beauty of heartfelt expressions.

DICTATOR pinpoints a manipulative personality.

DICTIONARY illustrates a need to clarify misunderstandings or misconceptions.

DIE See death.

DIE (model) stands for "the original" from which replicas are formed. This symbol warns against a desire or tendency to imitate others. A die may also indicate a situation that cannot be altered.

DIENER characterizes an individual who has the capability and knowledge to properly "clean up" the remaining aspects of a concluded situation or condition.

DIET usually advises of a need to "shed" excessive aspects in one's life. This may refer to attitudes, beliefs, negative emotions, etc.

DIETETIC (foods and drinks) represent aspects that assist one in getting rid of the excessive or harmful facets of self.

DIETICIAN characterizes a person in one's life who has the knowledge to assist in bringing about a healthful state. This may also include mental health.

DIFFUSER connotes a lessening of intensity; an aspect that serves to disperse effects rather than condense them.

DIGGING denotes a search; a deeper search.

DIGIT See toe; specific finger.

DIGITALIS refers to an aspect that will ease heart trouble; usually implies "emotional" pain.

DIGNITARY is associated with individuals specific to the dreamer who are perceived as highly respected.

DIGRESSION warns of not staying mentally focused; a tendency to easily get off track.

DIKE depicts the use of a life aspect to separate self or shield self from personally distasteful facets.

DILAPIDATED portrays a well-worn aspect that may still be viable.

DILEMMA illustrates the presence of a problematical situation that is difficult to resolve; extremely difficult decision.

DILL implies an "added" aspect to something.

DILL PICKLE connotes a slight problem entering one's life.

DILUTE means a "softened" or "lessened" situation.

DIM advises of a situation that lacks clarity or sharp definition.

DIME represents basic needs; life necessities.

DIME NOVEL alludes to unnecessary information; intellectual waste of time.

DIME STORE See variety store.

DIMMER SWITCH may advise one to "tone down" an attitude of anxiety or excitement or it may suggest adding energy and light to something in the dreamer's life.

DIMPLE (other surface) stands for a flaw; imperfection.

DIMPLE (skin) indicates individuality.

DINER (person) characterizes one who is in the process of nourishing self. This will usually refer to some type of personal nourishment other than physical.

DINER (place) represents commonly-used aspects of nourishment that are recognized and utilized by many.

DINETTE SET connotes informal or common aspects that are used to nourish one.

DINGBAT (symbol) portrays an opportunity for self-expression.

DINGHY applies to small spiritual securities; the spiritual comforts we fall back on in life.

DINGO See wild dog.

DINGY indicates a condition, situation, or relationship that is negatively affected in some manner; a need to clean up.

DINING CAR corresponds with a need to attend to inner nourishment while attending to one's life journey; a reminder to not be so centered on purpose that energizing aspects are ignored.

DINING ROOM usually typifies a more concentrated and enjoyable manner of being nourished. Surrounding details will clarify which life aspect is being fed.

DINNER connotes one's main source of nourishment.

DINNER JACKET See tuxedo.

DINNERWARE portrays one's

personal perspective toward nourishing self.

DINOSAUR exemplifies outdated concepts; primitive thought.

DIORAMA pertains to a visual example of something; a touchable and completely comprehensible presentation.

DIP (depression) suggests a temporary diversion from the norm.

DIP (food) connotes a personal choice.

DIP (immerse) signifies an aspect that has been changed or altered by adding something to it.

DIPHTHERIA symbolizes the potential vulnerability of one's emotional state.

DIPLOMA alludes to presumed knowledge or an acquired stage of same.

DIPLOMAT characterizes an individual who is tactful.

DIPLOMATIC IMMUNITY pertains to special benefits for those who use tactful methods of communication.

DIPSTICK stands for inquisitiveness; the act of searching for answers.

DIRECT CURRENT (DC) warns against perceiving only one option or opportunity.

DIRECT MAIL connotes a sales pitch from someone. This may

not refer to a "purchase" but could pertain to a situation where "convincing" will be attempted.

DIRECTOR characterizes the act of controlling; manipulating.

DIRECTORY advises of a need to contact someone or get specific assistance from another.

DIRGE portrays the possibility of a great sorrow coming; precedes the "end" of something.

DIRNDL connotes simplicity.

DIRT may indicate hard work or it might refer to an unclean or marred aspect; surrounding details will clarify this intent.

DIRT BIKE implies an attempt to speed over life's rougher roads.

DIRT FARMER stands for perseverance; great efforts.

DIRT POOR may not refer to a monetary connotation, but rather emotional and spiritual riches that are somehow lacking.

DIRT ROAD applies to personally chosen paths in life.

DIRTY LINEN denotes misdeeds and the hidden facts of same.

DIRTY OLD MAN warns against growth that never makes a priority of spirituality; a life immersed in physical gratifications.

DIRTY POOL exemplifies a lack of scruples; underhandedness.

DIRTY VEHICLE advises of a

need to cleanse an aspect of self. Dream aspects will clarify this.

DIRTY WORD See obscenity.

DISABLED means something that's impaired or not functional.

DISADVANTAGED applies to a lack of a basic need.

DISAGREEMENT connotes conflict. May even be within self.

DISAPPEARANCE illustrates an unexpected loss or departure.

DISAPPOINTMENT warns against having expectations.

DISARM refers to an action that neutralizes a negative aspect.

DISASSEMBLE usually signifies a need to look at the "parts" of an issue, idea, or situation. It may also refer to a confused state of mind that is scattered.

DISASTER implies a devastating event or great emotional distress.

DISBAND means a separation from associates.

DISCARD connotes the act of getting rid of an unusable aspect; a rejection.

DISCARNATE refers to a hidden life aspect or something the dreamer isn't seeing.

DISC BRAKE illustrates "pressure" applied for the purpose of slowing or halting further progression.

DISCIPLE characterizes an advocate; a devoted supporter.

DISC JOCKEY represents the spreading or acceptance of selected ideas.

DISCLAIMER pertains to denial; a repudiation.

DISCOLORED signifies an emotion altered by being affected by an outside factor.

DISCONNECTED (electrical plug) warns of mental aberrations or scattered thought process.

DISCONNECTED (phone) refers to a severance of communication; no flow of communication.

DISCONTINUED denotes a termination; no longer participating in an action.

DISCOUNT (disregard) means a choice to not believe or accept something.

DISCOUNT (reduce) represents an opportunity to chose a different path leading to the same end.

DISCOVERY signifies a perceptual discernment.

DISCREPANCY connotes an inconsistency; a question of credibility.

DISCUS THROWER characterizes a competitive nature.

DISEASE exemplifies a state lacking well-being. This may indicate a mental, physical, or spiritual aspect.

DISEMBARK portrays a "grounded" condition or state.

DISEMBODY See discarnate.

DISENGAGE alludes to an act of releasing something; a break from some life aspect.

DISFIGURED pertains to a specialized purpose.

DISGUISE warns of hypocrisy.

DISH connotes a presentation of something.

DISH ANTENNA See satellite dish.

DISHARMONIOUS (sounds) portray a vibrationary misalignment.

DISHCLOTH implies the clarity quality of something presented.

DISHEVELED stands for priorities placed on higher aspects, such as intellectual pursuit or spirituality.

DISHONORABLE DISCHARGE advises of grave admonishments from one's higher self.

DISHPAN pertains to one's habit of communicating clearly.

DISHPAN HANDS indicate concerned efforts to communicate well.

DISHWASHER denotes helpful aspects one utilizes to ensure clear communication.

DISINFECTANT advises of a need to maintain efforts toward countering negative aspects that could contaminate one's mental, emotional, or spiritual well-being.

DISINFORMATION connotes the act of willfully misleading others.

DISINHERIT warns against the voluntary decision to leave nothing behind. We should all make some difference through our existence.

DISINTEGRATION defines absolute finality.

DISJOINTED stands for a lack of continuity.

DISLOCATION connotes a conceptual or emotional lack of alignment.

DISMAL SWAMP warns of a mental or emotional state of self-generated hopelessness.

DISMOUNT refers to a return to congeniality; warns against arrogance.

DISNEYLAND warns against unrealistic perceptions or goals.

DISORIENTATION advises of one's lack of direction or place; confusion.

DISPATCHER characterizes one's higher self.

DISPENSARY See pharmacy.

DISPENSATION comes as a grave warning for those who believe they are above the law.

DISPENSER indicates a life aspect that provides opportunities.

DISPLAY applies to the act of visual communication; showing something to others.

DISPOSAL (garbage) advises of the wisdom of completely letting go of a closure's residual aspects.

DISPROPORTIONATE means unbalanced; perceptual irregularity.

DISQUALIFY means an aspect eliminated from one's life; ejected; excluded.

DISROBE alludes to a removal of all extraneous aspects of self; honesty; the real self.

DISSECT signifies the act of or need to thoroughly analyze or examine something in one's life.

DISSERTATION See thesis.

DISSIDENT characterizes a disagreeing activist; one who strongly opposes an idea or perception.

DISSOLVE denotes a changed or terminated life aspect.

DISTEMPER refers to excessive irritability.

DISTILLERY is in reference to condensing conceptual ideas down to the basic facts; simplification.

DISTORTION depicts a perspective made unclear by slanted personal attitudes.

DISTRACTION emphasizes the fact that the dreamer is allowing diversions to interfere with advancement or focusing attention on his or her purpose.

DISTRESS SIGNAL is always a call for help. The dreamer may be calling for this help or one's higher self may be attempting to awaken the dreamer to this end.

DISTRIBUTOR (engine) represents proportionate utilization of one's energies.

DISTRIBUTOR (person or outlet) symbolizes a specialized source.

DISTRICT ATTORNEY characterizes one's higher self.

DITCH warns of an "off-course" direction and marks a potential danger.

DITTY BAG denotes emergency measures of preparedness.

DIURETIC implies a life aspect that will aid one in ridding self of negatives.

DIVE signifies a "head-long" plunge into something.

DIVE-BOMB portrays an obsession with a goal or target.

DIVER connotes spiritual impulsiveness.

DIVERGENCE means a veer from one's normal or customary character or path.

DIVERSION cautions one to remain focused.

DIVIDEND pertains to benefits.

DIVIDER See partition.

DIVING BELL alludes to a fear of losing one's grounded aspects during a spiritual search.

DIVING BOARD relates to a spiritual search that needs a motivational impetus.

DIVING SUIT implies spiritual insulation.

DIVINING ROD See dowsing rod.

DIVISION (sign) indicates a reduction of something. Surrounding dream symbols will clarify this for the dreamer.

DIVORCE applies to a clear separation of self from some formerly associative factor in life.

DIZZY stands for confusion; lack of balance or comprehension.

DNA indicates individualism; a one-of-a-kind uniqueness.

DOBERMAN PINSCHER (dog breed) connotes a friend or associate who represents a law-abiding factor in one's life.

DOCENT See tour guide.

DOCK See pier.

DOCKET See date book.

DOCTOR characterizes those in one's life who are capable of bringing about healing aspects.

DOCTOR JEKYLL characterizes an individual's hidden aspects.

DOCTRINE represents a principle; a belief system.

DOCUMENT (paper) signifies something recorded or official.

DOCUMENT (support) pertains to proof of something.

DOCUMENTARY denotes a factual presentation or explanation.

DODGE 'M CARS See bumper car.

DODO (bird) connotes ignorance; a fear of knowledge and the responsibility that attends it.

DOG alludes to one's friends and close associates. See specific breed.

DOG BISCUIT signifies the joys of friendships.

DOG BONE indicates a conflict with a friend or associate.

DOG CATCHER cautions against the manipulations of one's friends.

DOG CHEW exemplifies a trusting friend; being able to have someone to talk to; loyalty.

DOG COLLAR warns against "forced" friendships.

DOG DAYS symbolize a lack of motivation; inaction.

DOG-EARED (page) relates to information one should take note of.

DOGFIGHT portrays a serious conflict between friends.

DOGGIE BAG denotes the nourishing benefits of friends.

DOGHOUSE represents personal trouble with a friend.

DOG PADDLE (swim style) alludes to a spiritual search accompanied by friends.

DOGSLED signifies a spiritual path that follows that of a friend.

DOG TAG usually advises of a need to "identify" one's friends. This is a cautionary message and reveals the existence of a necessity for the dreamer to check loyalties.

DOGWOOD typifies "beautiful" beginnings.

DO-IT-YOURSELF (projects) connote self-reliance.

DOLDRUMS warn of a lack of motivation; a slump period; a call to draw on reserves.

DOLL characterizes a message to re-evaluate relationship motives.

DOLLAR See money.

DOLLAR DAYS (sale) indicates opportunities.

DOLLAR SIGN defines some type of beneficial effect. May also indicate a "cost" or expense for the dreamer. Surrounding dream factors will clarify this.

DOLLHOUSE is a message to return to reality.

DOLLY (wheeled tool) represents a life aspect that serves as a support or help; a life factor that eases our way.

DOLPHIN reflects spiritual companionship.

DOME (shape) denotes balance.

DOMINO stands for one aspect of a questionable situation.

DONATION signifies an offering; thoughtfulness; generosity.

DONKEY emphasizes independence.

DONOR (blood) typifies a compassionate individual who freely gives of self.

DONOR CARD (organ) signifies an understanding and acceptance of life realities.

DON QUIXOTE characterizes an unrealistic optimism; a fear of facing negatives or accepting bad endings.

DONUT See doughnut.

DOODLE may be representative of unconscious thoughts or may indicate a warning against idleness.

DOOMSAYER stands for pessimism. Depending on surrounding dream symbols, a doomsayer may also be bringing truths home to a skeptical dreamer.

DOOR indicates a life factor that one must experience or "pass through" to achieve advancement or progress along one's path.

DOORBELL comes as an attention-getting symbol that "calls" one to an important experience or opportunity.

DOORKEEPER characterizes an individual who must be communicated with before an opportunity can be taken advantage of.

DOORKNOB refers to "access" to advancement or opportunity.

DOORMAN characterizes one who is ready to "open doors" for the dreamer as long as the dreamer is deserving or well-prepared.

DOORMAT may indicate a respect for and appreciation of opportunities or it may warn against a poor self-image. Surrounding details will clarify this meaning.

DOOR PRIZE indicates extra benefits gained by taking opportunities.

DOORSTEP points to "steps" or aspects leading to new opportunities.

DOORSTOP stands for "open" opportunities.

DOPE See narcotic.

DOPPELGANGER warns against imaginary or self-created fears.

DORMER signifies an acute conscious awareness.

DORMITORY pertains to a subconscious fear of being alone.

DOSAGE points to a proper amount of something.

DOSSIER typifies extensive "background" information.

DOT (pattern) represents a fragmented aspect that could refer to a mental state, a belief, or a situation.

DOT See decimal point.

DOTING warns against an overbearing or smothering nature.

DOUBLE AGENT characterizes hypocrisy or willful deception.

DOUBLE BOILER indicates increased mental activity. Depending on surrounding dream factors, this may refer to "boiling" emotions or situation.

DOUBLE CHIN signifies melancholia; self-pity.

DOUBLE-CROSS warns of a betrayal.

DOUBLE-DECKER means twice the amount of something.

DOUBLE DIPPED denotes two benefits generated by the same source.

DOUBLE-EDGED signifies an aspect which has two interpretations or purposes.

DOUBLE-FACED (two-faced) pinpoints a betrayer or hypocrite.

DOUBLE FEATURE advises of two important facets to one aspect.

DOUBLE-HEADER connotes an event, relationship, or situation that will generate two major benefits.

DOUBLE HELIX defines the living components of reality.

DOUBLE-JOINTED illustrates ingenuity.

DOUBLE-PARKED advises against being impulsive or hasty.

DOUBLE-SPACED is a call to slow down and understand more; clarity needed.

DOUBLE STAR See binary star.

DOUBLE TAKE advises of the need for a second look at something.

DOUBLE TALK warns against making excuses.

DOUBLE-TIME indicates a need to make up for lost time.

DOUBLE VISION usually defines heightened perception.

DOUBLOON will refer to something of extreme value.

DOUBTING THOMAS signifies skepticism.

DOUGH emphasizes the beginnings of specific aspects coming together; a period that precedes ultimate physical manifestation.

DOUGHNUT pertains to idle time.

DOVE defines a peaceful nature or condition.

DOVECOTE typifies a contentment with self and surroundings.

DOVETAIL stands for a harmonious relationship.

DOWAGER implies "riches" gained through wisdom. These riches are not necessarily financial.

DOWAGER'S HUMP portrays a life filled with extensive intellectual pursuits and great personal efforts applied to obtaining wisdom.

DOWN (direction) represents a "return" to the basics; a fundamental level.

DOWN (feathers) refers to an "insulating" or softening quality.

DOWN DRAFT applies to a decline in one's mental or emotional state.

DOWNGRADE pertains to a lowering of value or condition.

DOWNHILL may refer to a worsening condition or it may mean that a time of easier, swifter progress is approaching. Surrounding dream facets will clarify this.

DOWNLOAD implies a transfer of information.

DOWN PAYMENT denotes proof of intent; good intentions.

DOWNSHIFT advises of a need to slow one's pace.

DOWNSIZE cautions one to lessen the scope of something. This could refer to goals, expectations, impressions, area of study, etc.

DOWNSPOUT reminds us to utilize all aspects of spirituality in our daily lives.

DOWNSTREAM suggests we review our spiritual beliefs. This usually comes because of a need to thoroughly understand our spiritual foundations before searching deeper or further.

DOWNTIME usually is a call to rest. This is a cautionary message for one who is working or searching too intently.

DOWNTOWN indicates the "center" or foundational basis of something. This symbol may be advising of a need to return to one's center.

DOWNWIND connotes a tendency to follow the crowd or general attitude.

DOWRY designates "bought" aspects. This could refer to friendships, benefits, favors, employment, etc.

DOWSER characterizes one who utilizes spiritual gifts.

DOWSING ROD applies to a spiritual talent or opportunity.

DOZE illustrates a restful pause, often needed to refresh self.

DRACULA characterizes an infatuation with the overdramatized negative aspects of power.

DRACULA CAPE warns of delving into the dark side of esoteric aspects.

DRAFT (air) represents an interference in one's life.

DRAFT (conscription) warns of a "forced" attendance or attitude.

DRAFT (drawn liquid) implies one's act of "drawing" on inner reserves of energy; fortitude.

DRAFT (outline) connotes beginning plans.

DRAFT (pulling) signifies hard work; great efforts.

DRAFTING BOARD advises one to "sketch" out plans. This would represent a certain need to do this before action is taken.

DRAG (pull along) may refer to perseverance or it may warn against a tendency to brood or complain about one's problems.

DRAG (pulling force) pertains to hampering factors that impede one's progress.

DRAG (race) connotes dangerous competition.

DRAG (weighted implement) signifies the act of smoothing out; passing through life and leaving a smoother trail for those who follow the same path.

DRAGNET warns against spiritual gullibility; the act of "collecting" and absorbing *every* aspect found in the spiritual pool.

DRAGON characterizes one's self-generated fears.

DRAGONFLY denotes a strong, positive spiritual force or aspect.

DRAG STRIP indicates a "fast lane" or a detrimental path.

DRAIN (empty) warns of an energy or emotionally-depleting aspect.

DRAINPIPE symbolizes a need to discard spiritual excesses or unnecessary aspects from one's life.

DRAMATIZATION is usually a message for the dreamer. Take note of any symbolism acted out.

DRAPE See curtain.

DRAW See sketch.

DRAW (select) pertains to choices in life.

DRAWBRIDGE alludes to self-generated barriers and their selective use.

DRAWER stands for organization.

DRAWING connotes creative expression of inner aspects.

DRAWKNIFE represents personal efforts applied to something.

DRAWL alludes to a communication hesitancy.

DRAWSTRING typifies personal choices and the presence of leeway in respect to how one follows up on those choices.

DREADLOCKS indicate intellectual analyzation. The "quality" and accuracy of that analyzation depends on the condition of the locks.

DREAM (hope) implies strong aspirations or optimism.

DREAM (imagine) connotes wishful thinking.

DREAMY (atmosphere) represents a reality shift.

DREARY (atmosphere) suggests a downcast emotional state.

DREDGE applies to the act of "scraping the bottom" of some issue. This usually is a warning to leave well enough alone. Depending on surrounding dreamscape facets, this dream symbol may actually be "advising" you to scrape the bottom.

DRENCH indicates a saturation point. This will infer an issue that holds no more new information.

DRESSAGE pertains to the ability to manage one's life.

DRESS CODE denotes controlling others; placing restrictions.

DRESSER signifies compartmentalized aspects of self.

DRESSING ROOM relates to the intentional affectations people display for others.

DRESSING TABLE See vanity table.

DRESSMAKER See seamstress.

DRESS REHEARSAL connotes a need to take life seriously.

DRESS SHOES come as a warning to stop trying to impress others—be yourself.

DRIBBLE (ball) implies a "marking-time" stage in life; an interim.

DRIBBLE (trickle) indicates a state of consistency; a slow-paced advancement allowing full absorption of lessons.

DRIED FLOWERS exemplify a need to preserve one's natural talents through continual utilization.

DRIFTER characterizes a search for self.

DRIFTWOOD denotes a state of spiritual indecision and uncertainty.

DRILL (practice) illustrates the importance of routine practice of one's talents (utilization); learning through repetition.

DRILL (tool) denotes thoroughness in learning.

DRILL BIT exemplifies the wide variety of learning tools available.

DRILL INSTRUCTOR characterizes unavoidable learning experiences.

DRILL PRESS typifies those life aspects that improve the accuracy of the learning process.

DRINKING FOUNTAIN indicates a source of basic nourishment. Check condition.

DRIP represents a saturation point; overflow; a need for some type of containment.

DRIP PAN connotes a life facet that serves as a safeguard; a containment factor.

DRIPPINGS relate to "leftover" aspects of something that could be useful in other ways.

DRIVE-IN See fast food.

DRIVE-IN (movie) represents an extra effort applied to some aspect in the dreamer's life.

DRIVEWAY pertains to a region of approach; specific approachability.

DRIVING BACKWARD warns of reversals; going backward.

DRIZZLE signifies a state of gentle spirituality; a peaceful and accepting manner of spiritual intake.

DROOLING reflects a lack of control for one's desires.

DROP (fall) symbolizes the need to "get a handle" or grip on something.

DROP (liquid measure) means a minute amount.

DROP (location) relates to a specific locale associated in some way with the dreamer.

DROP CLOTH indicates preparedness; a safeguard; protective measure.

DROP-OFF stands for an abrupt decline or decrease in something.

DROPOUT exemplifies the act of withdrawing from something.

DROPPER portrays a life aspect that serves to regulate the controlled measurement or quantity of something; a controlling aspect.

DROUGHT warns of self-generated spiritual starvation.

DROWNING is a strong advisement to "come up for spiritual air" instead of over-saturating self with a flood of spiritual research.

DROWSY is a call to awareness.

DRUDGERY is a dream aspect that comes to remind us that all our efforts are worthwhile, no matter how tedious or boring.

DRUG DEALER characterizes an extremely negative individual in one's life who has the ability to manipulate, control, and make one a dependent.

DRUGGIST See pharmacist.

DRUGS stand for a lack of self-confidence; dependency.

DRUGSTORE See pharmacy.

DRUID represents esoteric spiritual aspects.

DRUM See barrel.

DRUM (sound) pertains to the heart center.

DRUMBEAT is a call to the way of nature; natural inner aspects.

DRUM MAJORETTE relates to boastfulness.

DRUMMER characterizes self-confidence and contentedness.

DRUMSTICK (food) refers to

personal efforts leading to nourishment.

DRUMSTICK (music) represents an aid for soul expression and journeying within.

DRUNK (state) warns of overindulgence; an escape from reality and one's responsibility to same.

DRY CLEANER comes as a strong advisement to give more care to the removal of negative factors from one's life.

DRY DOCK suggests a temporary rest from one's spiritual search or learning. This would indicate an overload or a need to absorb more.

DRYER (clothes or hair) infers a need for more seriousness and maturity.

DRY HOLE indicates a situation or personal attempt that came up empty.

DRY ICE represents a stage of spiritual cooling; a decline in interest.

DRY KILN advises of a need to absorb and fully comprehend that which one has attempted to learn; a "seasoning" time.

DRY MOP See dust mop.

DRY ROT warns of the danger of prolonging a "dry" period in one's life; motivation is urged.

DRY RUN refers to practice. A need to test something out.

DRY SOCKET indicates a negative effect resulting from one's verbiage.

DRYWALL symbolizes hidden personality aspects.

DUCK (bird) pertains to spiritual vulnerability; questionable inner strength.

DUCK (evade) is a sign of awareness; watchfulness.

DUCK (fabric) portrays a self-absorbed personality.

DUCKBILL See platypus.

DUCK BLIND warns of deception.

DUCKING STOOL advises of unjust and unwarranted conclusions.

DUCK SOUP means something easily accomplished.

DUCT represents a connection or passageway that serves as some type of conveyance.

DUCT TAPE calls for a need to attend to the condition of one's relationships.

DUDE characterizes an over-concern for outward appearances.

DUDE RANCH connotes an attempt to soften and round out one's stern and sharp personality aspects.

DUEL advises of the strong possibility that an outcome or effect will be fatal.

DUET typifies a situation that involves two individuals.

DUFFLE BAG suggests a transition stage.

DUGOUT implies a temporary withdrawal from some aspect in the dreamer's life.

DULCIMER stands for inner contentedness.

DULL (finish) is a call to awareness and motivation; as lack of clarity.

DUMBBELLS apply to self-strengthening aspects.

DUMBWAITER portrays personal resources; self-reliance.

DUMDUM BULLET defines powerful defenses; an awareness of one's protective preparedness and strength of same.

DUMMY characterizes voluntary ignorance; a willful state devoid of personal responsibility or independence.

DUMP See landfill.

DUMPLING signifies a nourishing aspect or one that relates to a sweet reward or benefit.

DUMP TRUCK portrays the act of actually "dumping" something from your life.

DUNCE CAP connotes foolish thinking; a need to reason and apply a greater amount of intelligence.

DUNE comes as a warning to stop "shifting" thoughts or attitudes.

DUNE BUGGY symbolizes an attempt to override and obtain control over one's shifting thoughts or attitudes.

DUNG BEETLE reminds us that everything in life has meaning and purpose.

DUNGEON pertains to self-induced states of negativity.

DUPLEX indicates a double aspect to something.

DUSK represents a "calming" period; a time of inner ease.

DUST symbolizes unnecessary aspects of one's life that intrude.

DUST BOWL warns of an extremely unproductive stage in one's life.

DUST COVER signifies measures that protect against an intrusion from negative or unnecessary aspects.

DUST DEVIL cautions against mental vacillations and confusion.

DUSTER refers to actions taken to prevent extraneous factors from taking one's attention from the important aspects.

DUSTING POWDER symbolizes the utilization of small opportunities that help us personally feel better.

DUST JACKET See dust cover.

DUST MOP stands for one's active efforts to keep his or her path and purpose free of distractions.

DUST MOTE defines an existing distraction.

DUSTPAN connotes the "collecting" and willful disposal of one's distracting factors. This means that one is focused on his or her life path or purpose and refuses to be sidetracked.

DUST STORM warns of an inundation of distractions.

DUTCH DOOR emphasizes the variety of ways one can access opportunities.

DUTCH OVEN denotes solid and sure methods of obtaining nourishment. This nourishment can be emotional, physical, mental, or spiritual.

DUTCH TREAT reminds us of individual responsibility.

DUTY-FREE pertains to life aspects that bring extra benefits.

DWARF characterizes the existence of power regardless of size.

DYE signifies misrepresentations; alterations.

DYED-IN-THE-WOOL advises of an unyielding personality.

DYING forewarns of the death of one's high ideals or an actual physical demise.

DYNAMITE indicates an "explosive" aspect to something. May refer to a sudden revelation.

DYNAMO See generator.

DYSENTERY indicates a mental

state that lacks the ability to ab-sorb or "retain" information.

DYSLEXIA represents an inabil-ity to comprehend, yet reminds us of the wide variety of other effec-tive learning methods available.

DYSPNEA cautions of a need to slow one's pace for the purpose of breathing more deeply and more freely; a need for breathing room.

E

EAGLE defines the self confidence of intellectual freedom to pursue unconventional concepts or issues.

EAGLE SCOUT characterizes a highly ethical and moral nature.

EAR symbolizes the quality of auditory reception; how well one listens and, consequently, processes and responds.

EARACHE represents the result of listening to too much verbiage that is unnecessary or extraneous.

EARDROPS advise of measures needed to repair some damage caused by what one has heard or listened to.

EARDRUM connotes how well one listens in respect to comprehending with the application of logic and reason.

EARLOBE indicates the quality and quantity of one's receptiveness to verbal communication.

EARLY WARNING SYSTEM stands for an individual's inner awareness; their perceptual watchfulness.

EARMARK emphasizes a distinctive characteristic or something that has been set aside for a specific purpose; allocated.

EAR MUFF refers to a closed mind; hearing only what one wants to.

EARPHONE portrays increased perception and/or attention given.

EARPLUG warns of a closed mind, not even hearing what one wants to.

EARRING pertains to embellished or exaggerated statements.

EARSPLITTING (sounds) apply to that which causes a strongly disruptive response within one's being.

EARTH symbolizes humankind's physical side; the three-dimensional touchable aspects of our world.

EARTHENWARE (pottery) illustrates an awareness of reality; a down-to-earth state of being.

EARTH MOTHER signifies the warm and glowing essence of love within all living things; absolute compassion and innocence.

EARTHMOVER denotes overcoming obstacles.

EARTHQUAKE exemplifies dangerously shaky foundations or beliefs.

EARTH STATION pertains to inner awareness; intuition; a cognizant link to one's higher self.

EARTHWORM indicates life aspects that serve to enrich one's foundations.

EARWAX warns of self-generated misconceptions due to personal selectiveness.

EASEL alludes to a life aspect that is capable of "supporting" one's future goals or plans.

EASEMENT exemplifies a "passage" opportunity; a "way" to something.

EAST (direction) marks beginnings.

EASTER signifies victory; ascendancy over life's problems.

EASTER BASKET connotes optimism; hope for a positive outcome.

EASTER BUNNY characterizes an individual or specific life aspect that one believes will resolve difficulties.

EASTER EGG portrays a "colored" or decorated perception.

EASTER EGG HUNT marks a search for a more pleasing or acceptable reality.

EASTER ISLAND typifies those solid, worldly aspects that stand to point the way to reality.

EASTER LILY See lily.

EASY CHAIR implies a "relaxed" attitude.

EASY STREET defines a desire for an easier life.

EATING portrays the "consumption" or absorption of something, usually perceptions or ideas.

EAVES symbolize protective aspects.

EAVESDROP denotes information of which others are cognizant.

EAVES TROUGH illustrates a directed flow of something away from self.

EBB TIDE portrays a time of lessening spiritual involvement or interest.

EBONY (color) See black.

EBONY (wood) implies an enduring puzzlement.

ECCENTRIC alludes to the freedom that comes with separating the "I" from self, whereby one exercises intellectual pursuits and special interests without regard to public opinion.

ECHO pertains to a "repeated" message for the dreamer.

ECLAIR relates to a lack of self-control.

ECLAMPSIA warns of a hazardous path chosen.

ECLECTIC applies to the utilization of many varied aspects; using any available resource; the expression of one's unique totality.

ECLIPSE (lunar) pertains to an awareness of true existential Reality.

ECLIPSE (solar) advises of a need to reaffirm spiritual beliefs.

ECOLOGY (study of) calls attention to one's environmental responsibility.

ECONOMICS (study of) usually comes as a personal message to reassess one's current distribution of talents.

ECTOPIC PREGNANCY warns of the danger of "forcing" new beginnings before one has reached the appropriate time and place along one's path.

ECTOPLASM denotes a misplaced focus on spiritualism.

ECZEMA connotes an attitude that needs to be overcome.

EDDY warns of an off-course spiritual situation where one is "caught" in a distracting current.

EDELWEISS represents courage; tenacity.

EDEMA warns of too much focus being done on a specific spiritual aspect.

EDEN connotes an unrealistic life perspective.

EDGER (lawn) cautions against attempting to control the natural order of things.

EDITING signifies a need to choose appropriate words or phrasing when attempting to define one's thoughts and ideas.

EDITOR characterizes one who gets to the point.

EDITORIAL denotes an expression of opinion.

EEL alludes to spiritual vacillation.

EFFERVESCENT suggests high excitement over something in the dreamer's life.

EFFICIENCY APARTMENT emphasizes a prioritized personality.

EFFICIENCY EXPERT characterizes one who defines priorities for others. This is not always a positive dream symbol because people need to define their own priorities.

EFFIGY warns of energies being misdirected in a negative manner.

EGG implies beginning perceptions; the formation of new ideas.

EGGBEATER (utensil) warns of attempting to form concepts from "scrambled" idea fragments.

EGGCUP refers to an organized concept.

EGGNOG symbolizes a rich or "nourishing" concept, plan, or idea.

EGGPLANT implies ideas that incorporate spiritual aspects.

EGG ROLL stands for several individual aspects that are enveloped by a larger, all-encompassing one.

EGGSHELL warns of a fragile or precarious belief. This may not be a negative situation, but rather one that necessitates close attention.

EGG TIMER advises of the wisdom to closely monitor a specific concept or situation.

EGG TOOTH alludes to one's level of developed preparedness to begin a new path or direction.

EGG WHITE defines the extraneous aspects of a situation, belief, or perception.

EGG YOLK defines the basic foundation of an idea or perception.

EGOCENTRICITY marks a self-absorbed individual or situation.

EGRET typifies a spiritual sign; a spiritually-related message.

EGYPTOLOGY (study of) exemplifies a high interest in enigmatic aspects of life; a subconscious yearning to discover human beginnings.

EIDERDOWN See down.

EIGHT pertains to balanced thought. This most often comes to warn the dreamer of unclear or distorted thinking.

EIGHT BALL signifies a problematic situation or relationship. This may even refer to one's own thought process.

EIGHTEEN-WHEELER See semi trailer.

EIGHTY-SIX (86) comes as a strong suggestion to "reject" some personally harmful aspect in one's life.

EINSTEIN (Albert) characterizes the high responsibility of directing one's knowledge in appropriate manners; positive use of intelligence.

EJECTION SEAT implies the preparedness of planning with precautionary measures in place.

ELAND represents innocence and gentleness associated with strength.

ELASTIC denotes a "giving" or flexible relationship or situation.

ELBOW signifies personal space affording comfortable distance from others.

ELBOW GREASE illustrates personal effort applied to something.

ELBOWROOM implies a need for greater personal space from others; more distance required.

ELDER pertains to one possessing experience and wisdom.

ELDERBERRY symbolizes naturally-occurring opportunities that are too frequently overlooked.

ELECTION connotes a firm decision.

ELECTRIC BLANKET See heating blanket.

ELECTRIC CHAIR warns of the finality of one's actions; unavoidable retribution.

ELECTRIC EYE See photoelectric cell.

ELECTRIC FIELD represents a surrounding vibrational space that emits perceptual impulses; one's intuitive perception.

ELECTRIC GUITAR cautions of a self-serving need to gain attention.

ELECTRICIAN characterizes one's personal thought process.

ELECTRIC OUTLET See outlet.

ELECTRIC RAZOR connotes a personal urgency to shed certain thoughts or concepts.

ELECTROCARDIOGRAPH advises of an immediate need for self-analyzation in respect to the expression of one's emotions; implies misdirected attitudes.

ELECTROCUTION warns against the desire for power. This can infer many types of power such as knowledge, wealth, leadership, etc.

ELECTROENCEPHALO-GRAPH advises of an immediate need for self-analyzation in respect to one's process of thought; implies the use of disassociative or aberrant thinking.

ELECTROLYSIS signifies the destruction of personally-rejected ideas.

ELECTRONIC FETAL MONITOR advises of a serious need to closely watch the developing aspects leading to one's new path or beginning.

ELECTRONIC MAIL (e-mail) signifies perceptual impressions; readily available information within one's personal surround.

ELECTROPLATING symbolizes a determined effort to insure the protection or concealment of something.

ELEMENT (of nature) denotes the four facets of life: physical, mental, emotional, and spiritual. See the specific elements of air, earth, fire, and water.

ELEMENTARY SCHOOL illustrates the specific developmental stage that one is at in life.

ELEPHANT stands for a generous and gregarious nature.

ELEVATOR connotes an "easy" way up; advancing with little effort applied.

ELEVATOR SHOES allude to poor self-image; an attempt to present self in a brighter light or higher station.

ELEVEN signifies misplaced values.

ELEVENTH HOUR comes as a message of "fair warning" that one's time is running out in respect to accomplishing something.

168

E

ELF characterizes proof of something one is skeptical of or doubts. This symbol eradicates doubt with proof.

ELF SHOES signify a path traveled with an intellectual awareness of reality's true nature.

ELIXIR represents an imagined "cure-all" to life's problems.

ELOPING connotes strong individuality.

EMBALM advises of a need to "preserve" something in one's life.

EMBARGO implies the act of disassociation; a refusal to deal with or communicate with another.

EMBARRASSMENT typifies an ill-at-ease state. This can be a telling symbol when combined with surrounding dreamscape facets.

EMBASSY portrays some type of help or assistance for the dreamer.

EMBER emphasizes the present existence of some "life" left of something in the dreamer's life. This could be an attitude, emotion, perception, relationship tie, etc.

EMBEZZLE warns against taking or claiming something that belongs to another.

EMBLEM comes as a message for the dreamer. It usually attempts to call attention to whatever the emblem represents, for this will have a specific meaning to each dreamer.

EMBOLISM indicates a self-induced path obstruction.

EMBOSSED is a symbol of emphasis on something. It comes to draw attention.

EMBRACE implies a closeness; a special connection.

EMBROIDERY depicts exaggerations; a tendency to embellish.

EMBRYO illustrates the beginning stage of a new direction or belief.

EMBRYOLOGY (study of) represents an interest in the many methods of generating new beginnings and the development of same.

EMERALD signifies the presence and quality of one's specialized talent to heal others.

EMERGENCY BRAKE advises of a critical need to "stop" something the dreamer is doing.

EMERGENCY MEDICAL TECHNICIAN (EMT) characterizes someone in the dreamer's life who has the ability to give immediate help or some type of needed assistance.

EMERGENCY ROOM comes as a strong warning. Surrounding dreamscape facets will clarify this for the dreamer.

EMERY BOARD See nail file.

EMISSARY cautions against having others speak for you or do your work.

EMMY is a warning message. No one in life should receive an award for acting. This is an advisement to start being yourself.

EMOLLIENT (lanolin, etc.) represents an element one uses to soften or smooth life's rough aspects.

EMPATHY usually is an advisement to better understand another's situation or response.

EMPHYSEMA warns of dishonesty.

EMPIRE usually refers to a specific individual's extent of power or control.

EMPLOYMENT AGENCY directly suggests a change in the manner one works. This may not relate to one's type of "employment" but could pertain to how one goes about laboring along one's path.

EMPRESS/EMPEROR denotes a domineering personality.

EMPTY connotes a lack or void.

EMPTY-HANDED brings the message of "nothing given, nothing received."

EMPTY NEST underscores the timeframe allotted for self. This is not a self-serving message, but rather comes as a sign of encouragement and motivation to redis-

cover the beautiful individuality of one's own inner essence.

EMULSION portrays the reinforcing message that, although some life aspects cannot completely blend together, they can co-exist in a peaceful and pleasing manner.

ENAMEL represents a condition of "heavy" coating; a thick veneer to one's outward presentation.

ENCAMPMENT See campground.

ENCAPSULATE portrays self-devised enclosure of self; emotional distancing.

ENCEPHALITIS warns of distorted thoughts due to unchecked anger.

ENCHANTED emphasizes acute vibrational perception.

ENCHANTRESS characterizes one who has the talent to communicate the beauty of multi-frequency perceptions to others.

ENCHILADA typifies life aspects that serve to provide one or more of an individual's preferred methods of relaxation; manner of experiencing enjoyment.

ENCORE represents a need to repeat something. Surrounding dreamscape facets will clarify what this is.

ENCOUNTER GROUP advises of a need to talk something through with others.

ENCROACHMENT alludes to some type of infringement being done.

ENCYCLOPEDIA emphasizes a need to gain a greater depth of knowledge on some aspect in the dreamer's life.

END (of something) clearly means just that. As simple as this interpretation is, it can relate to just about anything in the dreamer's life and the surrounding details will clarify this.

ENDANGER warns of the current timeframe that is approaching, some type of hazardous or personally-compromising situation.

ENDEARMENTS come to make one aware of another's personal perception of a relationship.

ENDIVE connotes learning experiences that are somewhat bittersweet.

ENDLESS defines a condition or aspect that has no limit; immortal; boundless.

ENDNOTE refers to concluding explanation; afterthought.

ENDOCRINOLOGY (study of) alludes to a deep interest in understanding the powerful functions and applications of our energy centers.

ENDORSE applies to one's personal approval of something.

ENDOWMENT stands for an un-expected opportunity that has been freely presented or gifted.

ENDPAPER portrays the final stage of an issue; a concluding symbol.

END TABLE suggests convenience; something close at hand.

END ZONE relates to a point of rest beyond the goal; the place in one's path where personal efforts are rewarded.

ENEMA advises of a situation that requires assistance in helping one shed extraneous life aspects.

ENEMY informs the dreamer of negative aspects or associations in his or her life.

ENERGY AUDIT is a call to assess one's use of personal energy. This infers a change in disbursement is required.

ENGAGEMENT (wedding) See betrothal.

ENGINE denotes aspects of the heart (physical or emotional).

ENGINEER characterizes one who is adept at complex planning.

ENGLISH MUFFIN infers a beginning to a two-fold purpose.

ENGLISH SADDLE typifies control of one's path.

ENGLISH SETTER (dog breed) symbolizes loyalty.

ENGLISH SHEEPDOG (dog breed) portrays devotion; protective nature.

ENGLISH WALNUT represents a richly nourishing life aspect in one's life.

ENGORGED See gorge.

ENGRAVE denotes something that's unalterable.

ENIGMA defines confoundments. These may be solvable, depending on the extent of efforts applied to contemplating them.

ENLARGEMENT calls attention to something the dreamer needs to be made more aware of.

ENLIST suggests a need to join something, perhaps be an activist for a specific issue or to openly express a belief or perspective.

ENROLL See register.

ENTERPRISE ZONE points to choices that benefit others instead of solely self.

ENTERTAINMENT usually comes as a specific message for each dreamer. Perhaps one needs more relaxation time, perhaps less. What form of entertainment was being shown?

ENTITLEMENT PROGRAM corresponds with "additional assistance" needed or given to a specific group or issue.

ENTRAILS See viscera.

ENTRANCEWAY represents choices. We all have a choice whether or not to pass through any entrance.

ENTRÉE symbolizes the "main" issue or concept.

ENTREPRENEUR characterizes an enterprising individual.

ENTRY-LEVEL denotes a "beginning" stage. This usually points out the real level one is at.

ENVELOPE signifies a communication. What color is it? Who is it from? To? Is it empty?

ENVIRONMENTALIST exemplifies one who possesses inner balance and harmony.

ENVOY See messenger.

ENZYME relates to an aspect in one's life that acts as a motivating catalyst.

EPAULET implies a haughty personality; pomposity; presumptuousness.

EPIC denotes an issue that is vastly detailed or complex.

EPIDEMIC cautions of a concept or attitude that is widely held.

EPIGRAM usually comes as an important message for the dreamer and is unique to his or her individual life situation.

EPILEPSY typifies dream symbols that represent one's involuntary perceptions, the experience and response to same.

EPILOGUE indicates the "final" words on something; concluding statement.

EPIPHANY pertains to a sudden

enlightening event; a shuddering revelation.

EPITAPH comes as a message that summarizes one's life.

EPOCH symbolizes a specific span of time. This will be unique to each dreamer.

EPOXY warns of a need to "secure" some type of connection in the dreamer's life.

EPSOM SALTS pertains to an aspect in one's life that produces a calming effect.

EQUAL OPPORTUNITY applies to a nondiscriminatory situation or relationship; may advise this attitude.

EQUATION relates to a "relative" balance; a comparable aspect.

EQUATOR denotes a "central" point; basic premise.

EQUILIBRIUM alludes to balance. This may refer to mental, emotional, physical, or spiritual aspects for the dreamer.

EQUINE See horse.

EQUIPMENT stands for life aspects that serve as "tools" or even opportunities one can utilize.

ERASER portrays "chances" to reverse or eradicate something.

ERMINE cautions against altering self for others; advises of the wisdom of being yourself.

EROSION cautions of a need to give more supportive efforts to some aspect in one's life; something is being worn away.

EROTICA exemplifies the baser aspects of life; may warn of a situation where one is too engrossed in physical aspects, especially pleasures.

ERRAND reminds us of the importance of attending to responsibilities no matter how small.

ERUPTION forewarns of a serious confrontation or exposure of something.

ESCALATOR cautions against laziness.

ESCAPE advises of a way out of something.

ESCAPE ARTIST characterizes one who has a tendency to always cover one's options; never being manipulated or controlled. This may also refer to one who refuses to face or accept responsibilities.

ESCARPMENT signifies a resulting condition or situation caused by a lack of foresight or planning.

ESCORT characterizes a close associate in one's life.

ESCROW represent safeguards; protected or guaranteed aspects.

ESOPHAGUS denotes level of gullibility. Check surrounding dream facets and health or condition of the esophagus shown.

ESOTERICA represents conceptual aspects in one's life that require deeper contemplation.

ESPIONAGE advises of some type of pretension existing in one's life.

ESPRESSO illustrates "rich" and nourishing spiritual concepts; conceptual depth.

ESSAY alludes to an expression of one's opinion. This usually advises one to be more open.

ESSENE characterizes a true visionary messenger who is quietly cognizant of the true aspects comprising Reality, including All-Life interrelationships.

ESSENTIAL OIL will point to that which is a priority in one's life; that which is essential.

ESTATE connotes the whole of one's assets. This may be all-inclusive of the four aspects of life: emotional, mental, physical, and spiritual.

ESTATE TAX refers to the right use of one's talents.

ESTIMATE represents approximations; that which cannot be pinpointed or predicted as an absolute.

ESTUARY pertains to the point in time where several spiritual concepts converge; the stage when the dreamer relates several spiritual ideas in an interconnective manner.

ETCH suggests firm opinions and attitudes.

ETHER (anesthetic) warns of total apathy or a stage in one's life where selective awareness is utilized. This is a warning message.

ETHER (space) stands for higher dimensional aspects to Reality.

ETHEREAL denotes spiritual or true Reality aspects that are associated with one's life.

ETHNOLOGY (study of) indicates a high interest in those different from the dreamer.

ETHOLOGY (study of) alludes to a high personal interest in the interrelatedness of all life.

ETIOLOGY (study of) illustrates a high interest in origins; a desire to understand how things began.

ETIQUETTE signifies a concern for social attitudes; politeness. This could also advise against an "over-concern" regarding what others think.

ETYMOLOGY (study of) denotes a high interest in language, specifically how a certain communication was passed from one to another.

EUCALYPTUS illustrates a life aspect that has the capability of nourishing through healing.

EUCHARIST See Holy Communion.

EULOGY reminds us to focus on the good points of another instead of any negative characteristics.

EUNUCH alludes to one uninterested in the physical aspects of life.

EUPHORIA typifies a state of absolute joy and serenity. Depending on surrounding dreamscape facets, this may or may not be a positive sign.

EUTHANASIA signifies deep compassion.

EVACUATION warns of a situation or relationship from which the dreamer should withdraw.

EVALUATION suggests a need for self-examination in respect to one's actions, beliefs, or motives.

EVANGELIST characterizes a zealous personality; one who is strongly impassioned.

EVAPORATION represents the absorption of spiritual ideals.

EVAPORATED MILK signifies a life aspect that is capable of providing the dreamer with a highly concentrated dose of nourishment. This may be emotional, mental, physical, or spiritual.

EVASIVENESS cautions against avoiding reality or responsibilities.

EVE defines a counter to the theory of evolution.

EVENING denotes a rest period; a call from one's labors.

EVENING GOWN refers to extravagance; a tendency to maintain efforts even in respect to relaxation methods.

EVENING STAR signifies a guiding aspect in one's life; a light in the dark.

EVENSONG symbolizes an appreciation for life's beauty and joys experienced each day; an expression of gratefulness; prayer.

EVERGLADES connote spiritual sluggishness; mired or tangled spiritual aspects in one's life.

EVERGREENS emphasize the "eternal" spiritual aspects in one's life. Check condition and quality of these.

EVICTION NOTICE comes as a serious advisement to "get out" of some situation.

EVIDENCE denotes validation or proof.

EVIL may not bring "certain" negative aspects; it could be saying only that one *thinks* a person, concept, or thing is evil.

EVIL EYE makes one's personal fears known to the conscious mind.

EVOLUTIONISM cautions one to take a closer look at the periodic consistency of a concept, situation, or idea.

EXAGGERATION warns against embellishments or advises of a situation in one's life where this is present.

EXALT is a message to remember that all people are equal and nobody should be exalted. Only God.

EXAMINATION usually calls for one to analyze self. This could be one's emotions, mental processes, spiritual beliefs, or physical condition. Surrounding dream aspects will clarify this.

EXAMPLE most often comes from one's higher self as a communication to the conscious aspect of the dreamer.

EXASPERATION advises one to "accept" more; be more accepting instead of getting so annoyed.

EXCALIBUR symbolizes something one has a singular "right" to.

EXCAVATION suggests a need for the dreamer to "dig deeper" into something that requires further understanding.

EXCELSIOR exemplifies a protective aspect in one's life; a need to protect something important to the dreamer.

EXCHANGE RATE implies karmic balance.

EXCLAMATION POINT indicates a clear message of great importance attached to something in the dreamer's life; an attempt to get the dreamer's clear attention.

EXCLUSIONIST characterizes a separatist; bigot.

EXCOMMUNICATION represents judgment; spiritual judgment through arrogance; spiritual judgment is God's alone.

EXCREMENT alludes to extra-

neous life aspects that one has successfully shed.

EXCUSE cautions against not taking personal responsibility for self.

EXECUTIONER may come as a warning against paranoia or it may actually refer to an individual or event in one's life who is capable of bringing personal disaster. Lastly, is the executioner you? This would warn against a tendency toward self-persecution.

EXERCISE EQUIPMENT advises of a need to apply more personal energy to something. This may refer to one's thought process, the expression of emotions or opinions, spiritual practice, or actual physical exercise.

EXHAUST (vehicle) refers to a lack of energy; a run-down condition. This may also indicate some type of "finality" experienced in one's life.

EXHAUST PIPE refers to withheld emotions, opinions, or energy. This is an advisement to release pent-up aspects of self.

EXHIBITION emphasizes one's overall general perceptions; what one is aware of looking at.

EXHIBITIONIST warns against a need to focus attention on self.

EXHUMATION comes as a call to re-examine something in one's life; go back and take another look at something that was missed.

EXILE most often refers to a self-induced state of aloneness.

EXIT POLL cautions against a desire to know what others think of something.

EXORCISM characterizes a personally-concerted effort to rid self of certain life aspects that don't necessarily have to be negatives.

EXPANSION signifies growth.

EXPECTATION warns against being impatient and calls for acceptance.

EXPECTORANT denotes a life aspect that helps one to release negative emotions or energies.

EXPEDITION typifies a dream symbol that defines a "search" or quest.

EXPENSE ACCOUNT pertains to the amount of one's personal talents, opportunities, or tools available for a goal's utilization.

EXPERIMENT stands for personal attempts made; trials; first-starts.

EXPERT characterizes an adept; one who has specific knowledge and the corresponding experience.

EXPIRATION DATE will usually be a personal indicator for the dreamer that reminds him or her of how much time is left to accomplish a certain thing.

EXPLANATIONS come to clarify a specific aspect for the dreamer.

EXPLETIVE denotes emphasis placed on something to which the dreamer will personally relate.

EXPLOITATION warns of deception or manipulation being done.

EXPLORER characterizes a freethinker; one who follows his or her interests or curiosity; a seeker of knowledge.

EXPLOSION forewarns of an emotional event.

EXPLOSIVE refers to a life aspect that has the potential of creating a devastating event in one's life.

EXPORTS refer to those personal talents we give to others; the sharing of one's abilities.

EXPOSÉ forewarns of some type of public "exposure" being done in one's future.

EXPOSURE METER denotes one's tendency to monitor self.

EXPRESSWAY exemplifies a fast lane; quickest way to a destination.

EXPULSION forewarns of disastrous results coming if one doesn't alter current ways.

EXTENDED FAMILY refers to close relationships.

EXTENSION suggests a need for

one to "reach" further; express self more often; don't accept short explanations.

EXTENSION CORD suggests a greater use of one's personal energies and/or efforts; the dreamer could be doing more.

EXTERMINATOR (vermin) characterizes an individual in the dreamer's life who is capable of helping to rid one's life of unwanted aspects.

EXTINCT indicates a life aspect that no longer exists. This symbol usually comes as a warning to those who are attempting to "hold onto" something that has gone from their lives.

EXTINGUISHER most often comes as a negative sign that indicates one is attempting to cut one's emotional responses off.

EXTORTION is a negative symbol referring to the wrong use of information.

EXTRACT (concentration) illustrates "basic" aspects of an issue or idea.

EXTRAPOLATE cautions of attempts to "extend" one's knowledge for the sake of others.

EXTRASENSORY PERCEPTION (ESP) is a misnomer because there is nothing "extra" about it; however, if one has this event in a dreamscape it usually will be an attempt to "normalize" this talent for the dreamer.

EXTRAVAGANCE comes as a warning against same.

EXTREME UNCTION is a forewarning of someone's death probability.

EXTREMIST characterizes one who easily loses self-control; one who takes things too far.

EXTRICATION advises of a need to remove self from some harmful situation, relationship, or belief system.

EYE defines one's personal perceptual characteristics.

Bleeding eyes indicate an empathetic nature.

Blinking eyes refer to a lack of seriousness.

Cloudy eyes denote a lack of clarity.

Colored eyes have unique meanings. Refer to specific color.

Crossed eyes denote an inability to keep concepts separate.

Darting eyes signify a vacillating perspective.

Dull eyes stand for a lack of interest.

Feline eyes portray an acute awareness; watchfulness.

Glass eyes refer to a heightened ability to perceive vibrational images through an extended awareness of true Reality.

Hawk eyes connote a far-reaching perceptive ability.

Hooded eyes represent a calculating approach to perceptions.

Large eyes pertain to a broad-scope perceptual ability.

Misty eyes characterize perceptions affected by compassion.

Owl eyes relate to an ability to perceive what others overlook.

Slanted eyes warn of perceptions affected by personal opinions.

Small eyes define a "small" perceptual scope; short-ranged.

Squinty eyes represent self-imposed perceptual selectiveness.

Staring eyes indicate judgmental perceptions.

Starry eyes symbolize unrealistic perceptions; too optimistic.

Unfocused eyes allude to undefined perceptions; disinterest.

EYEBALL (out of head) advises of "watchers" around one.

EYE BANK suggests a need for one to view something through the "eyes of another" and suggests a current state of misinterpretation.

EYE BATH See eyecup.

EYEBROW reveals the manner in which one's personal perceptions are shielded from others.

EYEBROW PENCIL applies to aspects used to hide personal perceptions.

EYE CHART suggests a need to check one's personal perceptions for clarity and accuracy.

EYE CONTACT represents a personal perceptual connection with another.

EYECUP indicates a negative aspect has infiltrated one's perception.

EYEDROPPER connotes a need to add another factor to one's perceptual viewpoint.

EYE GLASSES See glasses.

EYEHOOK infers "secured" perceptions; those that one is unwilling to alter.

EYELASH signifies protection of one's opinions or perceptions.

EYELID relates to aspects utilized during the perceptual process. What condition are the dream eyelids? Are they infected? Clean? Closed?

EYELINER defines a tendency to "emphasize" perceptions by outlining them to others.

EYE SHADOW pertains to "colored" perceptions; enhanced.

EYE SOCKET See socket.

EYESORE warns of "hurtful" personal perceptions; slanted by paranoia.

EYESTRAIN represents a habit of "straining" one's perceptions. This indicates a tendency to make more of something than there is.

EYEWASH exemplifies a life aspect that clarifies one's perceptual ability.

EYEWITNESS indicates verification of one's perception of something.

F

FABLE symbolizes truths clothed in a story line or experience.

FABRIC/SEWING SHOP denotes a specific type of personality. What kind of fabric was being looked at? See specific fabric names.

FACADE represents a false front; phoniness; possibly hypocritical.

FACE (characteristics) exemplify one's true personality.

> **Distorted face** indicates some mental aberrations.
>
> **Flushed face** warns of an explosive personality or it may refer to "withheld" emotions.
>
> **Heavy makeup** denotes hypocrisy.
>
> **No face** stands for a conformist.
>
> **Oversized face** represents egotism.
>
> **Pale face** characterizes an introvert.
>
> **Protruding nose** refers to an interfering nature.
>
> **Red face** depicts a shy personality.
>
> **Round face** suggests avarice.
>
> **Scarred face** indicates perseverance.
>
> **Square face** denotes an adamantly opinionated nature.
>
> **Thin face** implies a reserved personality.
>
> **Two faces** allude to a hypocritical nature.
>
> **Undersized face** represents an introvert or one who thinks small.
>
> **Unremarkable face** applies to a conformist.

FACE CARD indicates a personal message revealing how one is currently acting in life.

FACE CLOTH See washcloth.

FACEDOWN (position) represents "hidden" aspects.

FACE-LIFT symbolizes a focus on the self; possible hypocrisy.

FACEMASK See mask.

FACE-OFF indicates a confrontation.

FACET (gem) stands for one of the many concurrently-existing aspects of self.

FACE VALUE implies true value of something.

FACT-FINDING suggests a need to do some in-depth research or gather more information on something. This indicates a lack of full facts.

FACT OF LIFE connotes an

event or life aspect one cannot avoid facing.

FACTORY represents the manner in which one arranges or assembles path aspects that lead to goals.

FACULTY (natural ability) defines those talents or intellectual factors that are available for one's constant use in life.

FACULTY See teacher.

FADE illustrates a "lessening" of something in the dreamer's life. This could be a positive or negative dreamscape sign depending on the surrounding aspects.

FADE-IN forewarns of a specific event or personal attitude beginning to enter one's life.

FADE-OUT pertains to something in one's life that is losing strength or interest.

FAERIE See fairy.

FAIL-SAFE illustrates one's self-preservation aspects. This may refer to the emotions, mental faculties, spiritual factors, or one's physical immune system.

FAILURE signifies a call for acceptance and perseverance; a message to make further attempts.

FAINT denotes a lack of inner strength.

FAIRGROUND stands for a "fair ground" to work within; a good atmosphere that is conducive to success.

FAIR-HAIRED indicates an even temper.

FAIR WEATHER alludes to a time without any problems; a span of time when one's life appears to be going well.

FAIRY represents the intellect's far conceptual reach through reality.

FAIRY GODMOTHER characterizes the reward of a brilliant spiritual revelation through one's personal efforts of reaching and stretching intellectual reason out past the imaginary limits of reality.

FAIRY RING symbolizes concepts of the true Reality that cannot yet be proven through currently known laws of physics.

FAIRY TALE represents hidden lessons.

FAITH HEALER is a warning to "go within" for one's strength and inner healing.

FAKE NAILS denotes a false sense of security.

FAKIR symbolizes the power within each of us.

FALCON defines our personal relationship with the higher spiritual forces.

FALCONER is one who recognizes, understands, and quietly accepts a connection with higher spiritual forces.

FALLACY comes as a caution to

check the facts of something in one's life.

FALL GUY characterizes one who is falsely blamed.

FALLING exemplifies one's fear of failure or the unknown; a lack of self-confidence.

FALLING STAR applies to personal disappointments.

FALLOPIAN TUBE indicates the initial aspect that could lead to a new beginning.

FALLOUT advises of forthcoming repercussions.

FALL-OUT connotes a possible future disassociation from someone in the dreamer's life.

FALLOW symbolizes an "unproductive" condition or state.

FALSE ALARM alludes to one's false fears; imagined fears.

FALSE ARREST refers to a situation indicating false blame. This is a revealing dream fragment.

FALSE BOTTOM indicates incomplete conclusions; more to be discovered.

FALSE EYELASHES warn of misplaced confidence placed in one's belief that his or her attitudes and opinions are remaining private.

FALSE IMPRISONMENT warns of a serious error in judgment.

FALSE PRETENSE advises of a deception or manipulation.

FAME usually comes as a precognitive symbol.

FAMILY connotes close associations that are supposed to be unified.

FAMILY NAME calls attention to one's heritage or family core.

FAMILY PLANNING pertains to personal responsibility for one's future.

FAMILY ROOM symbolizes congeniality.

FAMILY TREE will most often reveal one's true spiritual heritage, that is, a record of one's past lives.

FAMISHED cautions of some aspect in the dreamer's life that is being starved. Surrounding details usually clarify what this means.

FAN indicates a need for a "cooling-off" period. This implies a rest period or a need to pull back; ease up.

FANATIC warns of a lack of applying wisdom to one's perceptions.

FAN BELT signifies an important life aspect that keeps other life factors going.

FANFARE comes in a dream to emphasize something important.

FANG represents vicious and cutting speech.

FAN MAIL most often reveals how one is behaving, the condition of one's spiritual life. This symbol may also represent how others perceive the dreamer.

FANTASIA portrays the diversity of one's options for expressing spirituality.

FANTASY LAND cautions of a need to return to reality.

FARAWAY (perspective) indicates a life stage that is approaching a personal attitude of losing faith and motivation.

FARCE indicates exaggerated perceptions.

FARM denotes an atmosphere rich in spiritual or ethical nourishment.

FARMER characterizes one who cultivates spiritual or ethical aspects.

FARMERS' MARKET illustrates a nourishing opportunity. This nourishment is usually related to spiritual or corporal factors.

FARMHOUSE pertains to home and family life. The condition of this house will be revealing.

FARRIER applies to a serene personality.

FASHION DESIGNER warns against dictating another's lifestyle or manner of path progression.

FASHION SHOW signifies "popular" perspectives; what others are buying.

FASHION PLATE warns against latching onto the latest popular beliefs.

FAST BALL advises of a need to sharpen one's personal awareness. This symbol may forewarn of something coming into the dreamer's life that wasn't foreseen.

FAST FOOD suggests nourishment. This doesn't necessarily indicate unhealthy types of nourishment as much as an indication that one requires "quick" nourishment of some type.

FAST LANE is a call to personal responsibility.

FAST-TALK warns against making excuses.

FAST TRACK is an advisement that the fastest way is not always the most productive means of achievement.

FAT See grease.

FAT (shape) connotes a fullness; usually overabundance in reference to excesses.

FATALISM is a direct call to use one's free will and assume the responsibilities resulting from same.

FAT CAT characterizes one who has abundant resources. This may not be a negative symbol as the term often can imply.

FATHER doesn't necessarily

refer to one's biological relation, for this symbol usually represents a "fatherly" individual to whom the dreamer personally relates in life.

FATHER'S DAY alludes to the importance of openly giving recognition to the individual in the dreamer's life who is closely associated with "fatherly" confidence and advice.

FATHOM connotes puzzlement in one's life.

FATHOMLESS advises of concepts that are over one's head.

FATIGUE is a call to re-energize oneself and usually indicates energy ill-spent due to a weakened condition.

FATIGUES See combat fatigues.

FAUCET implies the control one has.

FAULT LINE advises of negatives generated by self; one's own faults.

FAUST comes as a reminder that power and knowledge are nothing unless accompanied by the wisdom of the soul.

FAVOR represents generosity of spirit.

FAWN characterizes an emotionally sensitive nature; innocence.

FAX (machine) pertains to a need for a speedy communication. This would indicate a situation or relationship that could be saved by immediate communication.

FBI AGENT represents one who has an analytic nature; one who has a tendency to check background details.

FEAR signifies one's personal insecurities; a lack of self-confidence.

FEARLESS may allude to carelessness; a lack of giving due respect to dangerous life aspects.

FEAST connotes great satisfaction or personal pleasure.

FEAT designates a great step that is forthcoming and will be successfully achieved. This symbol comes as encouragement for one who is anxious about accomplishing this deed.

FEATHER stands for a free-spirit thinker; applies to an open and expanding intellect; deep wisdom.

FEATHER BED suggests a down-to-earth perspective regarding one's personal attainment of wisdom.

FEATHER DUSTER denotes the use of wisdom to make determining decisions; discerning intellect.

FEATHERWEIGHT signifies the presence of intellect and wisdom regardless of size.

FEATURE (characteristics) See specific types.

FEATURE (main item) draws attention to an important life aspect that one may be overlooking or ignoring.

FEBRUARY usually connotes a time to begin the formulation of new plans.

FEDERAL BUILDINGS represent major issues in one's life.

FEDERAL CASE warns of serious ramifications.

FEDERAL RESERVE SYSTEM cautions of a situation that is slipping out of one's personal control.

FEDERATION portrays a unified group of individuals.

FEDORA relates to underhandedness.

FEE alludes to some type of "cost" attached to something in the dreamer's life. Surrounding aspects will clarify what this specifically refers to.

FEEBLENESS warns of a dependency.

FEEBLE-MINDED advises of a self-generated condition of psychological escapism for the purpose of avoiding personal responsibility.

FEEDBACK suggests a need to "listen" to one's own words.

FEEDBAG illustrates a need for motivation.

FEEDER (any type) applies to a "supportive" life factor.

FEEDLOT indicates a situation or relationship that is being deceptively nurtured; congeniality for the sake of self-motivations.

FEELER See antenna.

FEELING (tactile motion) connotes a cautious approach.

FEET indicate how one travels his or her path. Check condition.

FELINE See cat.

FELINE DISTEMPER See distemper.

FELT (fabric) implies a softened attitude through the compression of comprehensive factors; acceptance by way of overlooking the more personally-viewed negatives.

FEMALE represents intellect coupled with compassion.

FEMINIST characterizes equality regardless of separatist characteristics.

FEMME FATALE pertains to alluring life aspects.

FENCE denotes self-generated barriers; one's personal distance.

FENCE-SITTING implies indecision.

FENCING (material) denotes that which one utilizes to create personal barriers, perhaps even from self.

FENCING (sporting art) refers to the act of being evasive.

FENDER portrays one's personal guard; protective factors.

FENNEL connotes a need for emotional calming.

FENUGREEK defines an attitude that serves to aid acceptance.

FERAL (characteristic) will most often refer to an expression of deep passion. This is not a sexual reference, but rather one that reaches to the core of one's beingness. An example would be a feral love of nature.

FERMENTATION usually refers to a state of in-depth analyzation; contemplation; extensive research.

FERN defines fruitful corporal acts. Check condition of the dreamscape fern to determine the precise quality of these acts.

FEROCIOUS (behavior) will most often imply a deeply passionate attitude attached to a specific life aspect. An example would be a mother's protective response toward a defenseless child.

FERRET typifies attitudes or responses tempered with a sense of humor.

FERRIS WHEEL emphasizes a circling in place; lack of advancement or development.

FERRY represents opportunities to utilize spirituality in life.

FERTILIZER exemplifies a need to rejuvenate or nourish a life aspect that could refer to one's mental, emotional, physical, or spiritual facet.

FERVOR See passion.

FESTER advises one to release pent-up emotions.

FESTIVAL represents a cause for celebration.

FESTOON defines a joyous state of being.

FETAL DISTRESS warns of dangerous aspects related to new beginnings.

FETAL POSITION means a severe lack of self-confidence; fear of facing reality or one's personal responsibilities.

FETISH See charm.

FETUS characterizes a new life; new beginning.

FEUD indicates a state of altercation.

FEUDALISM warns of a domineering personality or situation.

FEVER usually refers to fanaticism. This dreamscape symbol may also indicate a self-generated negative state that one must internally fight to overcome.

FEVER BLISTER See canker sore.

FEVERFEW indicates a means to overcome one's psychological negatives.

FEZ connotes a thought process that is affected by specific perspectives or belief systems.

FIASCO advises of a situation or relationship that will have so many negative aspects that it will go wrong from the time of its inception.

FIBERBOARD represents the coming together of diverse aspects for the purpose of blending into a new creation; the result of utilizing one's diversified talents and knowledge.

FIBERFILL applies to "padding" being done; exaggerations.

FIBERGLASS connotes "dual" aspects to something in the dreamer's life. Surrounding dreamscape facets will clarify this.

FIBER OPTICS characterize the subtle sensory facets of one's perceptive reception.

FIBRILLATION pertains to instinctual responses.

FICKLE stands for an undisciplined personality; unpredictability.

FICTION implies an imaginative scenario; perhaps inventiveness.

FIDDLE See fidget.

FIDDLE See violin.

FIDDLER CRAB cautions against spiritual gullibility.

FIDGET denotes restlessness; impatience; anxiety.

FIELD suggests openness; opportunities.

FIELD DAY signifies a state of great enjoyment or opportunity.

FIELD GLASSES See binoculars.

FIELD GOAL exemplifies achievements or levels of success that are less than the expected goal.

FIELD HOSPITAL cautions one to monitor self throughout the process of traveling life's more difficult path stages.

FIELD MOUSE portrays the "observers" we seldom become aware of.

FIELDSTONE connotes that which provides "building" aspects as opportunities are taken advantage of.

FIELD STRIP (disassemble) implies preparedness.

FIELD STRIP (leaving no trace) advises to be thorough; leave no trace or loose ends.

FIELD TEST suggests the need for a "dry run" of something the dreamer is planning. This could indicate a need for further planning.

FIELD TRIP relates to the possible need for "hands-on" learning experiences. This may indicate a need for one to personally experience what another is going through in order to adequately understand it.

FIELDWORK symbolizes knowledge gained through actual experience.

FIEND is a warning sign that most often will relate to someone with whom the dreamer is associated.

FIERY usually connotes an emotionally impetuous personality; often experiencing emotional outbursts.

FIESTA alludes to a joyous inner celebration of one's spirituality.

FIFTH AMENDMENT represents a decision to keep personal matters a private affair.

FIFTH AVENUE defines the manner by which one presents self to others.

FIFTH WHEEL indicates an unnecessary aspect.

FIFTH WHEEL See recreational vehicle.

FIFTH WHEEL See spare tire.

FIG refers to a triviality.

FIGHT warns of aggressive opposition.

FIGHTER (sport) See box.

FIG LEAF pertains to a "concern" over trivialities.

FIGURINE comes as a warning message for the dreamer. The "character" of the symbolic figurine will clarify the precise meaning.

FILAMENT advises of fragile relationships.

FILE (claim) implies an act of exposing or making something public.

FILE (line) signifies a need to recognize one's "place" in life. This could indicate an arrogant personality.

FILE (sort) is a call to put one's life or priorities in order.

FILE (tool) suggests a need to smooth over some type of roughness. Could refer to one's manner of expression or severity of opinion.

FILE CABINET defines "stored" information. This is usually within self.

FILE CLERK characterizes efficiency.

FILET MIGNON portrays some type of life aspect that is "choice" for the dreamer; a highly desirable aspect.

FILIBUSTER warns of an obstruction to one's goals.

FILIGREE means entanglements; complexities that were not foreseen.

FILLING (food) depicts a "main" idea or issue.

FILLING (tooth) portrays an active effort to remove negative aspects from one's speech. This does not single out obscenities, but is most often meant to relate to one's expression of over-opinionated attitudes.

FILM (photo) advises of a need to be sharply aware of a specific life aspect and remember it. Surrounding details will clarify this.

FILM See translucent.

FILTER denotes a need for personal discernment.

FIN (any type) represents a life factor that serves as a directional or motivational force.

FINALE means a conclusion; a dramatic ending.

FINALIST denotes success.

FINANCE COMPANY illustrates a life factor that serves to provide a "means" to a goal.

FINDER'S FEE represents the "price" for having others uncover or provide opportunities for you.

FINE ART refers to talented skill. This could pertain to any type of skill such as communication, analyzation, discernment, etc.

FINE PRINT advises one to be aware of details.

FINE-SPUN refers to intricate and delicate details.

FINE-TOOTHED COMB is a call to triple-check facts and conduct in-depth research.

FINGER See specific digit.

FINGER (pointing) denotes an accusation or guilt.

FINGER BOWL suggests an attempt to disassociate self from something in the dreamer's life; washing one's hands.

FINGERNAIL connotes the quality of one's personal efforts. The condition will clarify this.

FINGER PAINTING indicates an immature manner of expressing self.

FINGERPRINT pertains to one's uniquely distinguishing characteristics or qualities; may refer to the "mark" we leave behind.

FINISHING SCHOOL doesn't normally stand for fine social mores, but rather the spiritually-based attributes such as kindness, compassion, understanding, forgiveness, unconditional love, etc.

FINISH LINE marks the stage when one's goals are attained. What was the dreamscape distance to this line?

FIORD defines the narrow and often dangerous rites of passage through one's spiritual life.

FIRE means extreme emotional intensity.

FIRE ALARM warn of dangers stemming from intense emotions.

FIRE ANT cautions of a relationship, situation, or personal attitude that could end up "stinging" you.

FIREARM See gun.

FIREBALL means an uncontrollable, unstoppable ramification of one's explosive emotional expressions.

FIREBIRD stands for the proper utilization of emotional intensity.

FIREBOAT denotes personal safeguards against spiritual fanaticism.

FIREBOMB stands for emotional explosions directed at another.

FIREBRAND characterizes an individual who has tendencies toward stirring emotions that are directed toward revolt.

FIRE BREAK stands for stopgap methods one utilizes to control over-emotional states.

FIREBRICK represents an individual or situation that remains unaffected by another's emotional outbursts or tirades.

FIREBUG See arsonist.

FIRECRACKER indicates a means of channeling one's intense emotions in a controlled manner.

FIRE DOOR portrays personal efforts utilized to protect self from the intense emotionalism of others.

FIRE DRILL signifies the importance of practicing emotional control.

FIRE-EATER pertains to one who effectively absorbs intense emotional expressions; being unaffected while dealing with another's emotionalism.

FIRE ENGINE alludes to life aspects that have the capability to control another's emotional explosiveness.

FIRE ESCAPE indicates one's personal methods of avoiding or escaping from intense emotional situations or events.

FIRE EXTINGUISHER suggests the existence of a specific method to calm another's emotionalism.

FIREFIGHTER represents emotional self-control.

FIREFLY defines times of intensely emotional spiritual illumination.

FIRE HYDRANT applies to an aid in calming emotionally distraught individuals.

FIRE IRONS See andiron.

FIRELIGHT symbolizes emotionalism that has the ability to affect many others.

FIREPLACE denotes emotional warmth; heart warmth.

FIREPOWER represents one's level of emotional effectiveness on others.

FIREPROOF exemplifies a state or condition of being totally unaffected by another's intense emotional displays.

FIRE SCREEN connotes means of emotional protection; methods whereby one guards self from personally displaying emotional

191

outbursts or guards self from the tirades of others.

FIRESIDE most often refers to a feeling of emotional warmth and comfort.

FIRE STATION refers to an emotional emergency; an immediate motivational need.

FIRESTONE denotes a life aspect that can emotionally motivate one.

FIRESTORM warns of an extended state or time of intensive emotional outbursts or displays.

FIRE TOWER emphasizes a state of personal awareness regarding one's emotions and the expression of same.

FIRETRAP connotes an atmosphere which easily generates emotional explosiveness.

FIREWALL indicates an emotional barrier.

FIREWOOD See cordwood.

FIREWORKS forewarn of an explosive situation or relationship.

FIRING LINE illustrates a position of personal responsibility for one's emotional reactive control.

FIRING SQUAD characterizes devastating ramifications; may refer to a call to openly admit personal responsibility.

FIRMAMENT represents the unimagined expanse of true Reality.

FIRST AID KIT advises of an urgent need to "patch up" or heal the harmful effects one's actions have caused. This may even refer to a quick-fix healing of self.

FIRST-BORN characterizes one's initial achievement of a new beginning that lead to additional ones.

FIRST CLASS defines optimum quality or mode of operation.

FIRST-DEGREE BURN indicates a lesson learned through a lack of awareness.

FIRST DOWN (football) denotes a first chance or opportunity.

FIRST EDITION denotes the initial dissemination of specific information.

FIRST LADY characterizes a woman who epitomizes something specific.

FIRST NAME usually has a unique meaning for each dreamer. Most often the surrounding dreamscape details will clarify this.

FISH/MARINE LIFE symbolizes spiritual aspects in one's life. See specific types of marine life.

FISH (card game) connotes intermittent cooperation from others.

FISHBOWL stands for transparencies of character; a lack of privacy or confidentiality.

FISHEYE means spiritual perceptiveness.

FISH HATCHERY denotes a spiritual birthing; developing spiritual beliefs.

FISHHOOK warns of a lazy or faulty spiritual search. We mustn't attempt to "snag" any spiritual concept that happens by.

FISHING represents an unorganized or undisciplined spiritual search.

FISHING LURE warns of an arrogantly lazy approach to one's spiritual search.

FISHING ROD signifies a life aspect that has the capability of assisting in one's personal search.

FISH MARKET defines the quality and extent of one's personal spiritual belief system. Check the amount of fish available and the condition of same.

FISHNET cautions of a personal lack of spiritual discernment; a tendency to "gather" in all spiritual concepts without being discriminating in respect to the truths.

FISHPOND illustrates spiritual opportunities.

FISH STORY alludes to elaborations; exaggerations.

FISHTAIL usually refers to a "backlash" reaction to some facet in the dreamer's life.

FISSION portrays the multi-faceted individualities of the self soul.

FISSURE warns of a "crack" or deep separation beginning to form within a specific aspect in one's life. Surrounding details will serve to clarify this intent.

FIST cautions of building internal emotions.

FISTFIGHT warns against the utilization of negative resolutions.

FIVE signifies change.

FIVE-STAR (rated) defines the highest quality.

FIX (drug) stands for dependency; lack of responsibility; fear of facing reality.

FIX (mend) reflects a desire to correct or repair a situation or relationship.

FIXATION warns against an obsessive nature.

FIXATIVE See preservative.

FLACCID means a loss of resilience; lack of motivation or energy.

FLAG symbolizes loyalty.

FLAG BEARER represents one's outward expression of loyalty.

FLAG PERSON comes as a warning message. What type of flag is this dream person waving? Is it a traffic caution to slow down? Stop?

FLAGPOLE alludes to opportunities to prove one's loyalties.

FLAGSHIP advises of precedent-setting individuals or events.

FLAGSTONE denotes specific life aspects that serve to "pave" one's way along his or her path.

FLAIL reflects a tendency to blame others; strikeout.

FLAK JACKET See bulletproof vest.

FLAMBÉ connotes an intensely nutritional aspect. This will not infer dietary nutrition but rather an emotional factor for the dreamer.

FLAMBOYANT refers to an elaborately shown personality; one who must outdo others; a need to stand out in a crowd.

FLAME signifies great intensity, usually connected to the emotions.

FLAMENCO represents an outward expression of intense emotions.

FLAMETHROWER warns against directing uncontrolled emotions at others.

FLAMINGO is an advisement to keep both feet on the ground. This may indicate a perspective that lacks reality and needs grounding.

FLAMMABLE (objects) imply a life aspect that has the potential to become explosive.

FLANNEL (fabric) relates to level-headedness; down to earth.

FLAPJACK See pancake.

FLAPPER denotes a frivolous nature.

FLARE See torch.

FLASH (of light) most often comes as an attention-getting message and may accompany some type of powerful words of wisdom.

FLASHBACK always reveals an important event or fact for the dreamer to remember.

FLASH CARD indicates that which must be remembered or utilized on a consistent basis.

FLASHER (light) comes as some type of warning that will be clarified by surrounding dreamscape details.

FLASHER portrays negative motivations and attention-getting methods.

FLASH FLOOD warns of an overload of spiritual intake.

FLASHLIGHT advises of a need to better "illumine" a specific aspect in one's life; more light (knowledge) needs to be gained.

FLASHPOINT forewarns of the approaching stage where a situation or relationship will come into serious trouble.

FLASK implies convenience. This would refer to a condition whereby an important factor to the dreamer is readily available; close at hand.

FLAT (bland) represents a lack of emotional expression.

FLAT (level ground) means a span of obstacle-free pathway.

FLAT (living quarters) See apartment.

FLAT (shape) denotes little substance.

FLAT (tire) connotes a setback along one's path.

FLATBED pertains to a life factor that constitutes a "heavy load" for the dreamer to carry.

FLATBOAT cautions against carrying too heavy a spiritual load; spread out one's conceptual spiritual intake over time.

FLATBREAD See unleavened.

FLATCAR advises of the danger of taking on philosophical perspectives of others that are "narrow-minded" or one-track.

FLAT-FOOTED illustrates an uncompromising nature.

FLATIRON See iron.

FLATLAND See flat.

FLATLANDER characterizes one who is fearful of taking risks or encountering difficulties in life.

FLATTERY warns of ulterior motives.

FLATTOP (hair style) alludes to surface thinking; having no interest in deeper thought.

FLATULENCE relates to a pretentious nature; tediously verbose.

FLATWARE See specific utensils.

FLAVORING represents the addition of personal perspectives to facts; making something more palatable to self.

FLAW refers to shortcomings.

FLAWLESS symbolizes a "sound" aspect.

FLAX signifies a life aspect that offers multiple benefits.

FLEA portrays an interference of some type.

FLEABAG (lodging) cautions against misplaced trust.

FLEABANE pertains to a defense or counter aspect to interfering life factors.

FLEABITE alludes to a temporary inconvenience or annoyance.

FLEA COLLAR implies one's personal immunity to slight setbacks; strength of character.

FLEA MARKET alludes to opportunities, especially unexpected ones.

FLECK comes as an attention-seeking message for one to notice something "outstanding" in one's life.

FLECKED (pattern) See speckled.

FLEDGLING stands for a beginner; a novice.

FLEECE means fraudulence.

FLESH pertains to one's overall character. Check condition.

FLESH WOUND marks a temporary setback.

FLEUR-DE-LIS (design) connotes aloofness.

FLEX (connector) implies adaptability.

FLEX (muscles) denotes a challenge.

FLIGHT (airline) exemplifies a "departure" from the norm.

FLIGHT ATTENDANT characterizes someone in the dreamer's life who makes one's life journey easier.

FLIGHT BAG signifies a planned departure from the norm.

FLIMFLAM MAN depicts fraudulence; deception; delusions. Who was this symbolic person? Yourself?

FLIMSY indicates superficiality.

FLINCH relates to a failure to control responses or reactions.

FLINT signifies a quick response or reaction.

FLINTLOCK See gun.

FLIPPANT relates to disrespect; arrogance.

FLIPPER See fin.

FLIRT connotes an attempt to approach in a testing manner.

FLOAT See meander.

FLOATPLANE denotes vacillating thought patterns.

FLOCK cautions against a lack of individualized thought.

FLOE (ice) See ice floe.

FLOOD warns of spiritual inundation; drowning in unprocessed spiritual information.

FLOODGATE pertains to personal controls that appropriately regulate one's spiritual intake.

FLOODLIGHT applies to an acute awareness.

FLOODPLAIN warns of potentially dangerous ground. This usually refers to one's thought process or a specific situation.

FLOOD WALL portrays personal safeguards that shield one from being overcome by too much information; an awareness of one's intellectual capabilities; personal informational-intake regulation.

FLOOR pertains to one's moral, ethical, or spiritual foundations.

FLOOR MANAGER See floorwalker.

FLOOR PLAN constitutes thoughtful planning.

FLOOR SAMPLE connotes multiple opportunities.

F

FLOORSHOW cautions of misplaced priorities.

FLOORWALKER signifies the wisdom of frequently checking one's personal foundational ethics against current actions.

FLOPHOUSE See fleabag.

FLOPPY means indecision; a lack of firm attitudes or strong ideals.

FLOPPY DISK relates to one's stored information; personal knowledge; memory bank.

FLORAL See flower.

FLORIST characterizes one with a multitude of natural talents. What was the condition of the flowers?

FLOSS See dental floss.

FLOTSAM denotes erroneous spiritual concepts.

FLOUNDER warns of spiritual faltering or vacillation.

FLOUR advises of a need to increase one's efforts.

FLOW CHART details one's best method of progression along his or her path.

FLOWER pertains to one's natural and inherent talents that should beautifully blossom as they are utilized.

FLOWER CHILD characterizes a return to ethical and spiritual values.

FLOWER GIRL represents the utilization of one's natural talents.

FLOWERPOT signifies the conscious caring and personal cultivation of one's natural abilities and talents.

FLOW METER advises one to better regulate energies or emotions.

FLU See virus.

FLUE See vent.

FLUFF refers to a lack of substance.

FLUME denotes a quick way to spiritual resources.

FLUNK means a failure of some type.

FLUORESCENT LAMP symbolizes one's inner light.

FLUORIDE relates to misconceptions.

FLUOROCARBONS connote life aspects that are dangerous.

FLUSHED (complexion) implies embarrassment or guilt; may indicate repressed emotions.

FLUTE applies to personal power.

FLUTIST refers to a balanced and centered individual.

FLUTTER implies perplexity.

FLUX symbolizes instability.

FLY illustrates a life aspect that

has the capability of becoming a harmful interference.

FLYBLOWN signifies corruption.

FLYBY pertains to a need for close observance of something in the dreamer's life.

FLY-BY-NIGHT constitutes something in the dreamer's life that is unscrupulous and deceptive.

FLY-CASTING warns of intermittent spiritual "fishing" done.

FLYING pertains to awareness; may indicate spiritual aspects.

FLYING DUTCHMAN warns of spiritual imaginings.

FLYING SAUCER See Unidentified Flying Object.

FLYING SQUIRREL connotes the hidden aspects of self.

FLYPAPER portrays personal awareness.

FLYSHEET See handbill.

FLY SWATTER indicates an opportunity to personally deal with some of life's irritations or interferences.

FOAL characterizes new beginnings.

FOAM (rubber) pertains to exaggerations; something that's being "padded" for extra importance or weight.

FOAM (sea) symbolizes spiritual confusion.

FOAMY (consistency) refers to a life aspect that serves to soften or insulate.

FODDER typifies useless information; lacking substance or quality.

FOE See enemy.

FOG warns of spiritual obscurity; unclear spiritual perception.

FOGHORN is always a spiritual warning. Surrounding details should clarify this for the dreamer.

FOLIAGE connotes natural abilities.

FOLK ART suggests an honest, open expression of self.

FOLK DANCE defines a healthy, comfortable perspective of self.

FOLKLORE constitutes the preservation of truths.

FOLK MEDICINE pertains to a natural, inner healing capability.

FOLKSINGER characterizes one who keeps tradition alive.

FOLKTALE See folklore.

FOLLOWING warns of a lack of self-confidence or individual thought.

FOLLOW-UP advises of a need to recheck something or make a second communication with another individual.

FOLLY indicates a lack of reasoning and logic; impulsiveness; recklessness.

FONDUE signifies warm emotional responses; congeniality.

FONT (receptacle) means abundance.

FONT (type style) emphasizes one's individual character.

FOOD always connotes some type of nourishment.

FOOD BANK represents inner strength; stored nourishment, energy.

FOOD CHAIN advises one to do deeper thinking.

FOOD POISONING warns of nourishment obtained from contaminated sources. This would indicate a situation where one is absorbing false concepts, misconceptions, delusions, slanted perceptions, etc.

FOOD PROCESSOR indicates one's personal manner of processing information.

FOOD SERVICE cautions against being "handed" any type of nourishment offered rather than personally "choosing" for self.

FOOD STAMPS emphasize the fact that everyone is entitled to emotional, mental, and spiritual nourishment.

FOOL warns against willfully avoiding knowledge and the intellectual processing of same.

FOOLPROOF defines solidness; no possibility of error.

FOOL'S CAP relates to foolhardiness and associated ramifications.

FOOL'S GOLD warns against jumping to conclusions; not thinking things out; lacking appropriate knowledge.

FOOT See feet.

FOOTAGE (film) denotes solid proof; verification.

FOOTBALL relates to winning through force and deception. Who were the players?

FOOTBALL PLAYER alludes to aggressiveness.

FOOTBATH symbolizes care taken along one's traveled path.

FOOTBRIDGE connotes the "connective" aspects to one's life path.

FOOT-DRAGGING warns against a reluctance to continue along one's life path; a possible inner fear causing this.

FOOTGEAR See shoe.

FOOTHILL points out a life aspect that presents a slight upward climb; a time when more energies are needed.

FOOTHOLD defines a "grip" on something; the attainment of a secure position.

FOOTLIGHTS warn against willfully "highlighting" one's individual path for the arrogant purpose of leadership.

FOOTLOCKER will reveal one's personal priorities in life.

FOOTLOOSE signifies acceptance.

FOOTNOTE advises of the wisdom to check informational sources.

FOOTPATH represents one's individualized and unique life path that, when walked, presents specialized opportunities for one's particular advancement.

FOOTPRINTS denote trace markings of those who have gone before us or those marks in life we leave behind.

FOOTRACE warns against a competing attitude as one walks her or his life path.

FOOTREST advises of a need for a pause time; a resting period from walking one's path; a need to re-energize self.

FOOT SOLDIER characterizes one who walks his or her path as a warrior.

FOOTSORE is a warning. Your walk along your life path has been too full of attempts to "force" goals. You need to ease up and allow events to unfold naturally.

FOOTSTOOL is another dream symbol that comes as a message to slow down as your life path is traveled. Perhaps you need to assimilate deeper meanings of lessons being presented.

FOOTWEAR signifies the manner in which one's path is traveled. See specific footwear terms for more in-depth explanations.

FOOTWORK connotes how one reacts to events and opportunities encountered along her or his life path.

FORAGE pertains to efforts actively applied to taking advantage of every benefit, trial, and opportunity presented along one's life path.

FORBIDDEN CITY portrays a fear of knowledge and the attending responsibility of same.

FORBIDDEN FRUIT stands for those truths of Reality that exist for our discovery, but we're fearful of admitting knowledge of them.

FORCED MARCH illustrates a life situation that needs focused attention, yet shouldn't be "forced" into a conclusion.

FORCE-FEED warns against forcing opinions or concepts on others. Who was being fed? Who was doing the feeding?

FORCE FIELD means a barrier. This could be a self-created psychological barrier, a barrier caused by fear, a personal field of one's energy or protection. Surrounding details will clarify this intent.

FORCEPS warns against forcing a spiritual rebirth.

FOREARM alludes to defense attitudes or preparations.

FOREBODING comes as a warning sign and advises one to be acutely aware of surroundings and developing events.

FORECAST (weather) applies to the utilization of one's senses to perceive developing aspects to a relationship, event, or condition.

FORECLOSURE forewarns of an upcoming failure or some aspect in the dreamer's life that will not be fulfilled.

FOREFATHER See ancestor.

FOREFINGER See index finger.

FOREFRONT (of dreamscape) represents the most pressing or important aspects. Most often denotes the present time frame.

FOREGONE CONCLUSION alludes to conclusions believed to be inevitable; however, this belief may not prove to be an actuality.

FOREGROUND See forefront.

FOREHEAD indicates a clue to how one perceives life aspects

  Broad forehead applies to an open mind.

  Narrow forehead denotes narrow thinking.

  Pitted forehead relates to "ingrained" opinions; one-mindedness.

  Scarred forehead stands for lessons learned through previous misconceptions.

  Slanted forehead depicts biased or prejudiced perceptual handicap.

  Wrinkled forehead would mean one who worries or is skeptical.

FOREIGN connotes new and different ideas.

FOREIGN AID signifies assistance coming from an unexpected source.

FOREIGN CORRESPONDENT characterizes a "connective" line to different ideas; one's personal receptivity to such.

FOREIGN EXCHANGE pertains to the sharing of new ideas.

FOREIGN MINISTER characterizes an individual who presents new and innovative concepts to another.

FOREIGN MISSION typifies spiritual work one does outside the scope of their own specific path.

FOREIGN POLICY will be unique to each reader in that it represents one's own personal perspective toward innovative or foreign ideas.

FOREMAN characterizes one who has the knowledge and experience to guide another.

FORENSIC MEDICINE emphasizes a need to "examine" all aspects of a situation, relationship, or event before forming an intelligent conclusion.

FOREPLAY alludes to preparations made for something; getting into the right frame of mind.

FORERUNNER represents prerequisite research.

FORESIGHT usually advises of a need to increase one's personal awareness and perceptive abilities.

FOREST signifies one's individualized attitudes in relation to natural talents; may also refer to how one utilizes corporal deeds. Check condition of this forest.

FOREST RANGER characterizes one's conscience, specifically related to spiritual aspects.

FORESTRY (study of) represents a concentrated effort to uncover ways to utilize one's talents for the purpose of helping others.

FORETELL See prediction.

FORFEIT pertains to some life aspect that needs to be abandoned or given up.

FORGE (mold) connotes a "standard" of something which may not be right for everyone.

FORGE warns against impersonation or fraudulent activities.

FORGET-ME-NOTS advise of a very specific need to remember something. Usually surrounding details will clarify this.

FORK (in road) defines a choice in one's direction.

FORK (utensil) denotes a repressed personality.

FORKLIFT connotes life aspects that have the capability to ease one's burdens or path.

FORMALDEHYDE represents a need to preserve some facet of the dreamer's life.

FORMALWEAR stands for high-minded attitudes.

FORMLESS (shape) constitutes a lack of definition to one's opinions, attitudes, and perspectives; an unclear or vacillating viewpoint.

FORM LETTER signifies a group of people or a situation of considerable size; a situation common to many.

FORMULA comes in dreams to offer solutions.

FORNICATION warns of dangerous relationships; misdeeds in relation to another.

FOR-PROFIT cautions against a tendency toward self-interest as one's prime motivational force.

FORSAKEN refers to some life aspect that must be given up. This may also indicate a self-generated psychological ploy for sympathy or attention if it refers directly to the dreamer's beingness.

FORSWEAR connotes denials.

FORT symbolizes one's personal

F

quality and strength of defense. Depending on surrounding dreamscape details, this symbol can mean one who is an "introvert," who desires to remain safe within self, or it can refer to a "need" for self-protective measures.

FORTHRIGHT pertains to honesty.

FORTITUDE applies to perseverance. Perhaps the dreamer needs this or the word may denote a commendation.

FORT KNOX defines a situation, relationship, or opportunity that has the possibility of bringing great rewards or benefits.

FORTNIGHT comes as a unique "time" message for the dreamer.

FORTRESS See fort.

FORTUNA (Roman mythology) characterizes a priority placed on material goods; a love of and a striving for riches.

FORTUNE COOKIE illustrates a desire for knowing one's future; anxiety over being the beneficiary of only good aspects in life.

FORTUNE HUNTER implies one who is extremely materialistic.

FORTUNETELLER characterizes one who lives for the future instead of the moment; a fear of seeking within self.

FORTY-NINER connotes expectations.

FORWARD (direction) advises one to refrain from stopping one's path walk; a need to continue going forward.

FOSSEY (Dian) defines one who strongly believes in convictions and has the fortitude and strength to fight for them.

FOSSIL relates to preserved, immutable truths.

FOSTER CARE reminds us that we must have sisterly love and take personal responsibility to care for anyone needing it.

FOUL LINE represents the boundaries that encompass the atmosphere of rightness. To cross this warns of misdeeds done.

FOUL-MOUTHED denotes arrogance and a lack of respect for others.

FOUL PLAY warns of serious misdeeds. Who was doing this foul play?

FOUNDATION (building) connotes the moral, ethical, and spiritual tenets by which one lives.

FOUNDLING comes as a message to consciously admit to personal responsibilities.

FOUNDRY alludes to the beginning stage when one is forming ideals and perspectives.

FOUNTAIN means spiritual abundance. Check its dreamscape condition. Was the water colored? Lighted? How was it constructed, decorated?

FOUNTAIN (drinking) signifies spiritual refreshment.

FOUNTAIN PEN suggests quality of writing. What was or about to be written with the pen? Who was picking it up or using it?

FOUR exemplifies reference to the physical body.

FOUR-H CLUB connotes good values instilled in youth.

FOUR HUNDRED stands for love of self; conceited; egotistic; arbitrarily haughty.

FOUR-LEAF CLOVER denotes an attitude of expectation without factoring in any probabilities for failure or disappointment.

FOUR-POSTER (bed) depicts night fears.

FOURSCORE comes to indicate that the number eighty has some unique meaning specific to the dreamer.

FOURSQUARE See square.

FOUR-STAR represents excellence.

FOURTH DIMENSION alludes to "higher" knowledge or levels of experience.

FOURTH ESTATE See journalist.

FOURTH OF JULY denotes questionable independence; selective freedoms.

FOUR-WHEEL DRIVE signifies the need for greater strength and extra efforts forthcoming.

FOWL See specific type.

FOX connotes cunning; shrewdness.

FOXFIRE portrays an aspect of true Reality.

FOXGLOVE exemplifies the powerful healing abilities of natural talents.

FOXHOLE (dugout) advises one to stop hiding and fight his or her own battles.

FOXHOUND signifies a tendency to gravitate to shrewd and cunning personalities rather than thinking for self.

FOYER connotes an entrance to something to which the dreamer will personally relate.

FRACAS applies to a conflict.

FRACTAL pertains to one small aspect of the true Reality.

FRACTION denotes one part of something greater; one needs to realize that what he or she sees or understands is not the whole of it.

FRACTURE implies a defect; a crack in one's personality or plan; something amiss. Surrounding details will clarify this specific meaning to the dreamer.

FRAGILE is a caution to tread lightly; handle something carefully.

FRAGMENT See fraction.

F

FRAGMENTATION BOMB forewarns of approaching fallout ramifications to some aspect in the dreamer's life.

FRAGRANCE comes with unique interpretations associated with specific scents. See individual terms.

FRAIL pertains to a weakened state.

FRAME (picture) reveals individual perception of what is framed in the dream. Check condition and color of frame.

FRAME-UP warns of deception; possibility of scapegoat meant here.

FRAMEWORK (construction) denotes one's preparations for beginning a new project or endeavor.

FRANCHISE pertains to the right or granted authority that frees one to pursue a specific endeavor; within one's right.

FRANGIPANI (flower) signifies a sensitive nature.

FRANK (Anne) characterizes strength of character in the face of adversity.

FRANKENSTEIN stands for self-created monsters in one's life; those out-of-control emotions or attitudes that require containment.

FRANKINCENSE alludes to a biblical age past life.

FRANKLIN (Benjamin) illustrates diversified talents.

FRANTIC warns of a lack of acceptance; lack of faith.

FRATERNITY emphasizes male camaraderie; friends sharing a specific interest or attitude.

FRAUD advises of a relationship, situation, or specific aspect that is not what it seems; not authentic.

FREAK SHOW comes to remind us that compassion and intellectual understanding brings acceptance for that which is different.

FREE (cost) represents blessings; opportunities.

FREE AGENT reminds us that we are our own mind; the decisions are ours to be responsible for.

FREEBASING See cocaine.

FREEBOOTER See pirate.

FREEDMAN stands for the right to express one's unique individuality without fear of reprisal. This, of course, is confined to moral, ethical, and spiritual bounds.

FREEDOM FIGHTER characterizes active responses to unjust or oppressive authoritarianism. American history created Freedom Fighters of the Native Americans, did it not?

FREEDOM MARCH connotes organized protests against injustice or oppression.

205

FREEDOM OF THE SEAS defines one's right to explore all spiritual ideologies; spiritual freedom.

FREE FALL denotes confidence.

FREE-FLOATING cautions of spiritual indecision.

FREEHAND indicates independence and the following of one's own ideals and perceptions.

FREEHEARTED relates to compassion and emotional generosity.

FREELANCE portrays the utilization of various opportunities.

FREELOADER characterizes a lack of self-responsibility and self-image.

FREE LOVE applies to indiscriminate behavior; irresponsibility.

FREE LUNCH connotes an unexpected benefit that presents itself in one's life; a positive aspect that comes without thought or personal effort applied to its manifestation.

FREE REIN relates to a boundless opportunity; a limitless aspect.

FREE RIDE cautions one against depending on others to carry one along the path.

FREE SPEECH reminds us not to be reticent or fearful of expressing self.

FREE SPIRIT characterizes an unconcern for conventional aspects; the ability to wholly express one's unique individuality.

FREESTANDING indicates independence; not needing supportive aspects.

FREESTYLE symbolizes freedom of personal expression.

FREETHINKER characterizes one who stretches his or her mind to explore far-reaching possibilities rather than confining perceptions to conventional concepts boxed within established popular boundaries.

FREE TRADE represents open relationships and communications that are not restricted by any taboo issues.

FREE UNIVERSITY suggests a need to look into unconventional concepts.

FREE VERSE expresses the freedom to speak one's mind regardless of unconventionality.

FREEWAY See expressway.

FREEWHEELING indicates a carefree personality or situation.

FREE WILL comes to remind us of our right to make our own choices in life.

FREEZE-DRIED is one of many dream symbols that imply a need to preserve something in the dreamer's life.

FREEZE-FRAME emphasizes a

scene, object, or individual that is important to the dreamer. The surrounding details will clarify this.

FREEZER suggests that something in the dreamer's life needs to be "put on ice" for a time; a postponement or preservation needed.

FREIGHT denotes that which we carry around with us, usually mentally or psychologically.

FREIGHTER pertains to one's individualized spiritual baggage.

FREIGHT TRAIN cautions of the negativity and detriment of carrying the excessive beliefs or perspectives of others instead of being more of an independent life traveler.

FRENCH BERET See beret.

FRENCH DOOR represents a life passageway that offers many opportunities for different perspectives.

FRENCH FRY connotes short-cuts; life aspects that have time-saving qualities.

FRENCH HORN implies verbosity; an elaborated way of saying something.

FRENCH KNOT portrays a socially delicate situation.

FRENCH TOAST relates to a life aspect that carries some added benefit.

FRENCH WINDOW signifies an opportunity to have a broader view or perspective.

FREQUENT FLIER applies to one who routinely has thoughts that are a departure from the norm; inquisitiveness.

FRESCO denotes ingrained attitudes.

FRESHET pertains to a sudden influx of "fresh" spiritual ideas.

FREUD (Sigmund) comes as a caution when conducting a self-examination of one's motivational factors.

FRIAR See religious figure.

FRICTION TAPE advises to smooth over a situation or relationship; a need to protect a life aspect from "sparking" or causing a "shocking" incident.

FRIDAY is the day to address closures; attend to loose ends.

FRIEND usually characterizes loyalty and trust.

FRIGATE warns of a personal spiritual conflict within self.

FRIGHT (sudden) advises one to maintain awareness; realize that the unexpected is part of reality.

FRIGID indicates a stiff and unemotional personality; a rigid and straitlaced nature.

FRINGE denotes border; an aspect that is not well defined or encompassed within a specific conceptual realm.

FRINGE BENEFIT connotes an extra benefit to something; additional rewards or unexpected benefits.

FRISBEE is one of many dreamscape symbols that refer to a good "intent" at communicating.

FRISK (body search) cautions to be aware of possible concealments.

FRISKINESS reveals lightheartedness; joyful expressions.

FRITTER (food) connotes a breaking-down process; a fragmenting.

FRIVOLOUS means inconsequential; lacking any importance or relevance.

FROCK See smock.

FROG/TOAD represents an impaired mental or physical condition.

FROGMAN characterizes an unhealthy spiritual attitude or belief system.

FROLIC See friskiness.

FRONT (position) denotes priority.

FRONTAGE ROAD See service road.

FRONT BURNER signifies a current situation that takes priority over others of less importance.

FRONT-END LOADER alludes to a need for intensive clarification. The surrounding dreamscape details will clarify this for the dreamer.

FRONTIER characterizes a new and exciting path that holds multiple discovery opportunities.

FRONTIERSWOMAN connotes one who is traveling a path of self-discovery.

FRONTLINE represents the position of action or exposure.

FRONT MONEY emphasizes one's intent; a life aspect that reinforces a greater measure of confidence.

FRONT OFFICE depicts responsibility or authority.

FRONT PAGE stands for priority; a place of importance; something to take note of.

FRONT RUNNER constitutes the option most likely to succeed; an option that appears to have the highest probability of being chosen.

FRONT-WHEEL DRIVE advises of a path traveled half-heartedly.

FROST alludes to a temporary "chilled" attitude.

FROSTBITE comes when one reacts in a willfully unresponsive manner; karmic effects of refusing to respond or communicate.

FROST-FREE signifies open communication or emotions.

FROSTING may indicate a cov-

F

erup or it may refer to an aspect that constitutes a final action that makes matters better or worse.

FROST LINE applies to an individual's point of abiding acceptance; the point where one gives up or stops being responsive.

FROTHY refers to mental, emotional, or spiritual confusion.

FROWN implies displeasure or sorrow.

FROZEN FOOD defines nourishing life aspects that are not being utilized or benefited from.

FROZEN LAKE warns of spiritual aspects that are not being utilized.

FRUGAL may commend thrift or advise against it. Thrift in this context refers to the utilization of one's talents or expressions of emotions. Surrounding dream details will clarify this intent.

FRUIT most often refers to the nourishing and beneficial effects of using one's talents for the benefit of others. Check the condition of the dreamscape fruit for further clarification.

FRUIT BASKET represents a "gift" of one's talents; a bountiful benefit received or given.

FRUITCAKE denotes a lack of logic and reason.

FRUIT COCKTAIL constitutes a multitude of benefits.

FRUIT FLY pertain to destructive spiritual aspects.

FRUIT GROWER characterizes one who has a high interest in cultivating talents, abilities, and means of helping others.

FRUITLESS warns of unexercised spirituality.

FRUIT TREE exemplifies spiritual talents and humanitarian expressions.

FRUSTRATION is a message of acceptance and perseverance.

FRY pertains to quick conclusions.

FRYING PAN denotes increased activity; a quickening of action.

F-STOP (setting) suggests a need to "adjust" one's perspective for better clarity.

FUCHSIA (flower & color) represents compassion, love, and humanistic expressions.

FUDGE (food) applies to hedging; grey areas.

FUEL corresponds to one's energy and/or that which nourishes.

FUEL TANK comes as an aid in determining the amount of energy one is running on. Is the tank empty? Full?

FUGITIVE advises to stop running from one's problems or fears. This may even refer to an attempt to escape self.

FUGUE denotes a state of un-

209

awareness, possibly a self-willed one.

FULL (capacity) represents a condition that has reached its ultimate state.

FULL-BLOODED will not necessarily refer to heritage, as it usually implies "purity" as in a belief system or an individual's intentions.

FULL-BLOWN defines something in the dreamer's life that cannot be developed or advanced beyond its present state.

FULL-BODIED applies to intensity or richness.

FULL-BORE denotes thoroughness.

FULL CIRCLE signifies completeness; a return to the beginning.

FULL DRESS relates to appropriateness in action and one's presentation.

FULL MOON indicates a period of strong magnetic draw; a time of heightened interest in something.

FULL-SCALE exemplifies total effort applied; strong determination.

FULL-SERVICE denotes the act of giving one's all to something.

FULL-SIZE reveals accurate proportions. This may indicate that the dreamer is either exaggerating or belittling something.

FULL-TIME advises of a need to devote attention or energy to a specific aspect more than part-time.

FUMBLE represents a temporary setback; a small glitch.

FUMES indicate harmful situations generated from one's lack of controlled response.

FUNDRAISING pertains to the act of helping another.

FUNERAL underscores a state of loss; relates to an acceptance of losing something in one's life.

FUNERAL DIRECTOR characterizes one who helps another to gain acceptance.

FUNERAL HOME connotes a dying condition.

FUNGUS warns against inactivity. This suggests a need for the dreamer to "get going" regarding a specific life aspect.

FUN HOUSE is an advisement to face one's fears and see them for what they are.

FUNNEL suggests a need to slow one's intake of knowledge in order to assimilate more; indicates a need for better comprehension.

FUNNY BONE corresponds to the "funny" feelings we get; perceptual sensations and insights.

FUNNY MONEY See counterfeit.

FUNNY PAPERS See comic book.

FURS denote a selfish personality.

FURL suggests a need to "open" or uncover something in one's life.

FURLOUGH See vacation.

FURNACE connotes emotional intensity. Was the furnace blasting? Was it cold?

FURNISHINGS reveal atmosphere. How was a room furnished? Did it have a warm or cold feeling to it? Were there any period or ethnic decorations?

FURNITURE alludes to one's character. Is it elaborate? Sparse? Spotless? Lived in?

FURRIER characterizes a self-serving nature.

FURROW See groove, trench.

FUSE (electrical) represents energy level. Was it new? Burned out?

FUSE (explosive) stands for amount of patience or acceptance. Check length of fuse line for more clarity.

FUSE BOX defines one's level of comprehension and readiness for higher knowledge. The number of good fuses clarifies this message.

FUSELAGE most often symbolizes an individual's capacity for understanding new concepts. Check size and condition.

FUSION emphasizes a need to incorporate several different aspects into a centrally focused issue. This will be specific to each dreamer.

FUSSY defines impatience or anxiety.

FUTILE reveals an unproductive situation, relationship, or effort.

FUTURE is usually a precognitive revelation.

FUTURE SHOCK defines a fear or lack of acceptance for one's path direction.

FUTURISTIC (scene) most often corresponds with an individual's personally unique vision or conceived idea of same.

FUZZ represents a "coating" of some type being done; misrepresentation.

FUZZY advises of an unclear perception or attitude.

GAB See chatterbox.

GABARDINE (fabric) signifies diligent work effort.

GABLE denotes a differential facet to one's thought process; thought affected by a unique quirk.

GADFLY alludes to a life irritation.

GADGET represents personal aids utilized to "implement" goals.

GAFF See hook.

GAFFER characterizes one who sheds light on an issue or situation.

GAG See practical joke.

GAG (over mouth) is a warning against talking too much; gossip; revealing more than one should.

GAG (reflex) pertains to an inability to "swallow" something; a lack of acceptance; having to deal with a distasteful issue.

GAG ORDER is a message to keep silent about something. Surrounding dreamscape details will clarify this.

GAIETY suggests a lighthearted atmosphere or situation.

GAITERS refer to protective measures taken as one walks her or his path.

GALA denotes a celebration; a joyous event or situation.

GALAPAGOS ISLANDS portray perseverance; a long-lasting condition or situation.

GALAXY typifies higher aspects to knowledge; deeper meanings.

GALE cautions against overexerting one's mental facilities.

GALL stands for audacity; a provocation.

GALLBLADDER relates to accumulation of life trials. Check condition.

GALLEON connotes an esoteric spiritual journey.

GALLERY (art) represents qualities and life aspects one admires.

GALLERY (audience) illustrates those who watch you and listen.

GALLERY (balcony) signifies a clarity of perception.

GALLEY (large rowboat) cautions of a spiritual journey propelled by others rather than self.

GALLEY (narrow kitchen) refers to a "narrow" assortment of nourishing benefits one chooses to utilize.

GALLEY PROOF advises of a need to check for errors that lead to misconceptions.

GALLOP connotes a "bounding" speed; a fast-paced advancement.

GALLOWS exemplify a need to complete something, finish it up.

GALLSTONE characterizes an accepted tribulation.

GALVANIZED stands for motivation; an electrifying spur forward or into awareness.

GAMBLER characterizes those who attempt to beat the odds; taking chances.

GAMBLING denotes a lack of personal responsibility.

GAMBLING CASINO advises of risks taken.

GAMBREL (roof) corresponds with a thought process that is seriously affected by two differing perspectives.

GAME (amusement) depicts mental stimulation.

GAME (hunting) See prey.

GAME BOARD reveals "moves" made in life.

GAMEKEEPER advises of self-serving motives.

GAME LAWS denote the "limits" of one's predatory nature.

GAME ROOM symbolizes a concerted effort applied to one's mental stimulation.

GAME SHOW cautions against a boastful intelligence; a desire to be intellectually superior.

GAMUT connotes an entire scope of something; all-encompassing.

GANDER implies self-imposed ignorance.

GANDHI (Mohandas Karamchand) characterizes living spirituality; fighting for spiritual principles.

GANG applies to a group of people. Recall surrounding details to determine if this symbol is a positive or negative one.

GANGLAND (style) represents a harmful, negative method of achieving something.

GANGPLANK indicates a "way" or path to self-destruction.

GANGRENE denotes a self-destructive aspect in one's life.

GAP may indicate an "opening" opportunity or it may refer to a "missing" aspect in one's life.

GAPE (stare) corresponds to a reaction of awe or astonishment.

GARAGE represents a place of rest or stored energy.

GARAGE SALE typifies the act of ridding self of extraneous aspects; getting down to basics; making priorities.

GARB See specific clothing types.

GARBAGE defines the useless aspects in one's life.

GARBAGE CAN connotes what is thrown away and not considered useful in one's life. What was in the garbage can? Was it something that should not have been tossed away?

GARBAGE COLLECTOR characterizes one's willful accumulation of useless aspects such as negative attitudes, erroneous perceptions or beliefs, or materialistic factors.

GARBLED (speech) denotes perplexity; mental bewilderment; talking about issues one has no clear understanding of.

GARBO (Greta) characterizes solitude and a need for same.

GARDEN constitutes spiritual blessings and talents. What condition was this dream garden in?

GARDENER characterizes one who nurtures humanitarian acts and spiritual attitudes.

GARDENIA implies purity.

GARDEN PARTY indicates personal joy taken in one's rewarding benefits brought through humanitarian and spiritual acts.

GARFIELD (comic cat) pertains to self-absorption.

GARGANTUAN (size) illustrates an "overwhelming" aspect to one's life.

GARGLE indicates an effort to clarify one's communication skills.

GARGOYLE usually represents an attempt to protect one's spiri-

tuality. It also may refer to some type of distortion being done in one's life.

GARISH See gaudy.

GARLAND (botanical) symbolizes bountiful spiritual acts; continual utilization of one's humanitarian and/or spiritual gifts.

GARLIC/ONION pertains to personal defenses against negative aspects or forces.

GARMENT See specific type.

GARMENT BAG relates to "protected" characteristics or attitudes; a part of us that is kept protected and hidden.

GARNET (color & stone) refers to intense emotions. (Garnet can be a variety of colors; this interpretation corresponds to the more commonly-known color of deep, dark red.)

GARNISH stands for "enhancing" aspects applied to a basic one; adornment; embellishment.

GARRISON See military post.

GARTER symbolizes the act of "upholding" something.

GARTER SNAKE denotes harmless qualities or aspects that many fear.

GAS constitutes duality; the positive and negative aspects of something.

GAS BURNER pertains to personal responsibility regarding how potentially harmful aspects are utilized in a positive way.

GAS CHAMBER advises to use discernment; suggests increased awareness.

GAS FITTER See pipe fitter.

GAS-GUZZLER (vehicle) warns of utilizing methods of advancement that consume more personal energy than necessary.

GASH denotes a temporary setback; a hurtful incident from which one quickly recovers.

GASKET alludes to a need to "seal" something; a finalization; a need to stop the "leakage" of something in the dreamer's life.

GASLIGHT signifies a perpetual illumination maintained by one's personal awareness.

GAS LOGS refer to imitations in life; second-best options.

GAS MAIN exemplifies a potential hazard in one's life.

GAS MASK cautions one to protect self from potentially harmful situations or relationships.

GASOLINE applies to physical energy.

GASP advises against being caught unaware or off-guard.

GAS STATION signifies the "source" of one's energy or motivational force.

GAS STATION ATTENDANT represents one who "attends" to another's needs, especially for the purpose of conserving another's energy level.

GAS TANK connotes an individual's personal energy level. Recall if the tank was empty or full.

GATE pertains to that which must be passed through (experienced) for one to further advance along his or her path.

GATECRASHER warns against "forcing" advancement.

GATEHOUSE symbolizes one's "right" to experience an event or passage.

GATEKEEPER characterizes one's higher self; conscience.

GATEPOST connotes a supporting factor that helps to mark specific events one must experience.

GATHERING indicates the act of seeking out and obtaining required information or other aspects vital to one's path advancement.

GATLING GUN stands for an immediate response.

GATOR See alligator.

GAUCHE implies a lack of tact or sensitivity.

GAUCHO See cowboy.

GAUDY connotes a state of extremes; over-emphasis done.

GAUGE depicts quantity. Recall

what the dreamscape gauge was measuring.

GAUNTLET (armored glove) relates to one's personal protective methods of not being touched or affected by the negative or hazardous factors that we have to come in contact with in life.

GAUNTLET (ordeal) illustrates life's tribulations; these are frequently generated from self.

GAUZE (fabric) warns of an ineffective coverup being done.

GAVEL defines finality; a message from a higher authority.

GAWK connotes rude attention given.

GAZEBO represents a place or time of respite; a needed rest.

GAZELLE characterizes an innocent characteristic; naiveté.

GAZPACHO suggests mental and emotional nourishment.

GEAR connotes mechanisms utilized to effect movement; motivational factors, instigators; personally forceful aspects.

GEARBOX See transmission.

GEARSHIFT corresponds with control of pace and level of energy. We each must appropriately regulate our energies and pace through life.

GECKO See lizard.

GEESE defines instincts; inherent characteristics. Depending on surrounding dreamscape details, geese may also warn of one's personal desire to escape problematic issues.

GEIGER COUNTER pertains to an individual's intuitive perceptions.

GEISHA characterizes servitude; a tendency to react or behave in response to the anticipated desires of others. This is usually a warning symbol.

GELATIN denotes cohesiveness; aspects that serve to bind.

GELDING characterizes a need to control the expression of emotional extremes.

GEMOLOGY (study of) portrays an interest in understanding natural spiritual talents and the varied methodologies of same.

GEMSTONE alludes to personality characteristics and behavioral responses. See specific gem types.

GENERAL DELIVERY suggests an "unsettled" situation.

GENERAL PRACTITIONER See physician.

GENERAL STORE connotes a variety of opportunities.

GENERATION GAP stands for differences in attitudes.

GENERATOR connotes inner energies; strength of character.

GENERIC means all-inclusive;

common; nonspecific. This would usually be a message to express one's individuality more often.

GENESIS defines a new beginning.

GENE-SPLICING warns against mixing concepts; a loss of purity in respect to identity.

GENETIC ENGINEERING represents a control over one's behavior; personal responsibility to alter negative behavior generated by psychologically manipulative conduct.

GENETICS (study of) indicates an interest in the historical trail of another's behavior or characteristic expression.

GENIE characterizes false promises and hopes; empty visions of goals or desires quickly obtained; unrealistic perspective.

GENITALIA may suggest a need to be more productive in life or it may warn of some type of negative aspect specific to a physical condition.

GENIUS symbolizes high intelligence. This dream detail may be a warning to use "wisdom" in connection with mental brilliance.

GENOCIDE may not relate to racial or ethnic aspects, as it most often refers to a willful destruction of some facet of self.

GENRE implies a specific category of something. This will pinpoint an important factor in the dreamer's life and will be unique to each dreamer.

GENTEEL doesn't necessarily refer to a prudish attitude; it may indicate simple refinement.

GENTIAN denotes simplicity; innocence.

GENTIAN VIOLET applies to the healing benefits of inner spiritual convictions.

GENTLEMAN'S AGREEMENT depicts trust; dependability.

GENTLEWOMAN characterizes decency.

GENUFLECTING indicates respect; giving honor; a recognition of worth.

GEODE emphasizes the inherent beauty of the living spirit within everyone.

GEODESIC DOME represents the interlocking aspects of life.

GEOGRAPHY (study of) connotes an interest in physical characteristics. This may or may not be a positive dream symbol depending on the surrounding aspects.

GEOLOGY (study of) indicates a high interest in understanding humankind's genetic relationship with earth.

GEOMAGNETIC STORM See magnetic storm.

GEOMETRIC (patterns) See specific type.

GEOMETRY (study of) refers to a high interest in comprehending the interconnectedness of life.

GEOPHYSICS (study of) signifies an awareness of the true Reality.

GEOTHERMAL (activity) most often warns of inner turmoil.

GERANIUM alludes to optimism.

GERBIL (as pet) depicts life aspects that serve as small comforts.

GERMS represent negative aspects with which the dreamer could contaminate self.

GERMAN SHEPHERD (dog breed) characterizes a helpful friend or associate.

GERMICIDE See disinfectant.

GERMINATING applies to a life aspect that has "taken hold" within the dreamer. This could relate to an attitude, belief, emotion, etc.

GERM WARFARE defines vicious and unconscionable retaliative responses.

GERONIMO characterizes one's familial protective qualities.

GERONTOLOGY (study of) represents a high interest in elders. This will be specific for each dreamer in respect to which quality or characteristic is focused on.

GESTAPO characterizes restraints; factors that severely hamper one's choices, individuality, or ability to advance.

GETHSEMANE implies abandonment; betrayal.

GEYSER symbolizes one's active outpouring of spiritual and humanitarian talents.

GHETTO exemplifies tribulations to be overcome.

GHOST indicates a fear of spiritual matters. Also may refer to recurring episodes of guilt.

GHOST DANCER characterizes a strong spiritual belief; faith in the power of spiritual strength.

GHOST DANCE SHIRT denotes spiritual protection.

GHOST STORY implies a possibility; a subject to contemplate.

GHOST TOWN corresponds to a tendency to live in the past; pining over what once was.

GHOSTWRITER cautions against doing another's thinking for him or her.

GIANT pertains to one who is idolized or looked-up to.

GIANT SEQUOIA relates to ancient truths comprising Reality that remain immutable.

GIANT SLALOM comes as a warning message to slow down in order to avoid a collision course.

GIBBET usually warns against an

action or personal course that could result in self-destruction; a path toward one hanging self.

GIBBON See ape.

GIBLETS connote utilization; a message to make use of the whole aspect of something. This carries a specific interpretation for each dreamer.

GIFT indicates an offering; perhaps an unexpected opportunity.

GIFT CERTIFICATE denotes unconditional assistance from another.

GIFT OF TONGUES See glossolalia.

GIFT SHOP illustrates opportunities for kindness.

GIFT WRAP denotes personal joy taken when helping others or from expressing acts of kindness.

GIGGLING exemplifies inner joy. What is revealing here is "what" one is giggling over.

GIGOLO characterizes one who takes advantage of others for the purpose of avoiding personal responsibility.

GILD warns against a personal need to enhance self; represents a poor self-image.

GILL stands for spiritual breathing; the "intake" of spiritual aspects as one's very breath.

GILT-EDGED (pages) connotes an advisement to note the high quality of value of something. Surrounding dreamscape factors will clarify this.

GIMLET (drink) See alcoholic beverage.

GIMLET (tool) indicates a personal need to "bore" into or penetrate something in one's life; research for deeper understanding.

GIMMICK warns against utilizing trickery or manipulation methods.

GIN (drink) See alcoholic beverage.

GIN (machine) represents a personal aid that assists in advancing toward goals.

GINGER depicts a life aspect that can be utilized or "internalized" to aid in obtaining personal acceptance.

GINGER ALE exemplifies a soothing factor; a calming aspect.

GINGERBREAD constitutes a nourishing factor that serves to settle temporary emotional upsets.

GINGERBREAD HOUSE warns of a self-induced perspective on one's personal life as being the epitome of sweet perfection.

GINGERSNAP typifies a calm that nourishes and restores one's emotional strength.

GINGIVITIS See gum disease.

GINSENG corresponds with one's overall health; an aspect that has the capability to bring general wellness.

GIRAFFE warns against the habit of meddling in the affairs of others.

GIRDER portrays main support; a life aspect that serves as one's main source of strength.

GIRDLE usually refers to that which "surrounds" self. This will indicate a separate aspect for each dreamer. What did the dream say about this girdle that you surround self with?

GIRL SCOUT characterizes a female who strives to live according to her moral and spiritual beliefs.

GIVEAWAY defines generosity; materialistic unconcern.

GIVEN NAME most often comes as an important message that indicates a personal importance for the name. Recall what the name was and watch for it to show up during your waking state.

GIZMO See gadget.

GIZZARD corresponds with an aid to acceptance.

GLACIER denotes "frozen" spirituality; a call to "thaw" and utilize one's talents.

GLACIOLOGY (study of) indicates a high interest in understanding people's lack of humanitarian and spiritual responsiveness.

GLADIATOR advises of illogical reasoning for negative actions performed.

GLADIOLUS represents an upcoming span of peacefulness in one's life.

GLAMORIZED warns against "downplaying" negative aspects to something.

GLARING (brightness) is an advisement against jumping to conclusions.

GLARING (eyes) indicates hostility.

GLASS pertains to a state or condition of fragility.

GLASSBLOWER characterizes subtle, delicate creativity.

GLASS CUTTER connotes something done with precision.

GLASSES (eye) refer to added aspects to one's sight (perceptual ability).

Bifocal glasses See bifocal.

Broken glasses denote an inability to adjust perspectives.

Cracked glasses indicate a "fractured" viewpoint.

Dirty glasses imply a perspective altered by negative attitudes.

Foggy glasses refer to an unclear perspective.

Granny glasses allude to a narrow view of things.

Heavily framed glasses denote a seriously obstructed perspective.

Oversized glasses indicate a wide, comprehensive perspective.

Pitted glasses connote a perspective altered by hardships.

Rimless glasses define an unobstructed view of things.

Rose-colored glasses apply to an overly-optimistic perspective.

Scratched glasses suggest a perspective marred by personally damaging aspects.

Scratch-resistant glasses indicate unaffected perspectives.

Shattered glasses pertain to "fragmented" perspectives.

Smeared glasses pertain to negative attitudes affecting the ability to clearly perceive.

Sunglasses denote a perspective resistant to popular opinion.

Thick glasses represent major adjustments made to clearly perceive.

Tinted glasses portray a "colored" or slated perspective.

GLASS EYE refers to a heightened ability to perceive vibrational images through an extended awareness of true Reality.

GLASSHOUSE reminds us that we are always being observed.

GLASS JAW warns of one's state of vulnerability.

GLASS WOOL is a "cautionary" symbol; an advisement for one to be more aware; stay watchful.

GLAUCOMA represents a deteriorating perspective; losing one's perspective.

GLAZE connotes a coverup of some type. Surrounding details will usually clarify this for the dreamer.

GLEE CLUB typifies short periods of contentedness.

GLIDER (plane) implies a lack of mental focus.

GLIDER (swing) suggests a time of contemplation; restful thought times. In a few instances, a glider may warn against self-generated unawareness.

GLITCH indicates a temporary setback or problem.

GLITTER denotes a fascination.

GLOBE portrays "earthly" matters that need attention. Frequently this will infer a more "broadscope" view of something.

GLOCKENSPIEL refers to accuracy. In the dream, were the notes struck right?

GLOOMY (atmosphere) most often is caused by a psychological source. Who was within this atmosphere? Just yourself?

GLORY See fame.

GLOSSARY advises of a need to correct the usage of one's specific terminology that is in error.

GLOSSOLALIA warns of unintelligible speech; a personal need to be noticed.

GLOSSY symbolizes insincerity.

GLOVES represent personal service to others. Depending on the style and condition of these gloves, the dreamer can determine if this "service" is for self, begrudging or purely humanitarian.

GLOVE COMPARTMENT indicates readiness to assist others.

GLOW (inner) implies inspiration or emotional warmth.

GLOW (light) suggests a radiance of some type; resplendence.

GLOWWORM indicates a light in the darkness.

GLOXINIA exemplifies deep joy; bright happiness.

GLUE pertains to a "sticky" situation, condition, or relationship.

GLUTTON characterizes a greedy personality; insatiability.

GLYPH depicts some kind of symbology specific to the dreamer. This "glyph" will reveal a unique symbolism for the dreamer.

GNARLED warns of a strongly-held negative attitude; a twisted idea.

GNAT relates to mental or emotional irritations.

GNAW is an advisement message to get focused and get to the bottom of something in one's life.

GNOME comes in a dream to warn of a need to guard one's beliefs or attitudes.

GNU See antelope.

GOAL signifies aspirations.

GOALKEEPER characterizes an individual who keeps one motivated.

GOAL LINE is an advisement to keep one's eye on her or his goals.

GOALPOST is another symbol for one's aspirations or goals. What's important to recall from the dream is the condition of the goalpost. Was it upright? Falling down? In disrepair? Shiny?

GOAT warns against a voracious intake. This could refer to information, self-consumption, etc.

GOATEE indicates a pretentious personality.

GOBBLE implies a ravenous appetite, usually for information.

GOBLET typifies quiet sophistication.

GOBLIN connotes a spiritual fear.

GO-CART advises of a need to reassess direction.

GOD represents the highest authority; ultimate goal.

GODDESS signifies God's feminine aspect personified.

GODFATHER warns us to achieve goals through personal efforts.

GODLESS stands for a lack of life or spirituality.

GODMOTHER characterizes comforting warmth; welcoming hearth.

GODSEND represents a blessing; windfall or a manifested need.

GODZILLA corresponds to fears; the fearsome events one is afraid to experience.

GOGGLE-EYED relates to astonishment; stunned.

GOGGLES are an attempt to better understand something.

GOITER warns of a current state of perceptual aberration.

GOLD (color) denotes goodness.

GOLD (metal) means financial aspects; facets of one's physical life.

GOLDBRICKER characterizes one who shirks responsibility.

GOLD DIGGER represents the willful manipulation of others for personal gain; a tendency to use another.

GOLD DUST usually refers to material benefits gained from one's deeds.

GOLDEN AGE constitutes peace and/or prosperity.

GOLDEN CALF warns of negative goals and misplaced priorities.

GOLDEN HANDCUFFS define bribery; manipulation; an attempt to snag one in a Catch-22 situation.

GOLDENROD illustrates a natural talent.

GOLDEN RULER signifies ethical and moral behavior.

GOLDENSEAL refers to a healing aspect in one's life.

GOLDFIELD indicates an opportunity.

GOLDFISH warns of a spiritually confining situation, belief, or condition.

GOLDILOCKS (character) connotes irresponsibility; a dependence on others.

GOLD LEAF See gild.

GOLD MINE denotes a great material benefit; a highly beneficial source.

GOLD RUSH alludes to material desires; financial priorities.

GOLDSMITH characterizes a fascination with manipulating specific aspects of life.

GOLEM pertains to misused spiritual abilities.

GOLF applies to the easiest path chosen.

GOLF CAP warns against lazy thought; a lack of seriousness.

GOLF CLUB emphasizes a life aspect that one utilizes to lessen personal efforts needed to achieve a goal.

GOLF COURSE typifies a tract of one's path that is not taken seriously.

GOLF SHOES imply a path traveled in leisure; excessive complacency.

GOLIATH characterizes an individual or situation that must be overcome in order for advancement to proceed.

GONDOLA (boat) cautions of a lack of spiritual seriousness; a lazy spiritual journey.

GONDOLIER characterizes an individual who "carries" others along a spiritual path. This is not a good symbol, for it means that people are depending on a leader for their spiritual guidance rather than following their own inner guidance.

GONG is a call to attention. The higher self is attempting to bring the dreamer's attention to something important.

GOOD OLD BOY warns of negative camaraderie.

GOOD SAMARITAN defines humanitarian acts.

GOOSE advises of a need for more seriousness in life.

GOOSE BUMPS connote one's immediate reaction to fear.

GOOSE EGG represents some type of mistake made; an unfruitful result.

GOOSE NECK cautions against excessive curiosity taken to the extent of becoming intrusive.

GOPHER represents multiple starts; a simultaneous "digging" around.

GORGE (eating) warns against periods of excessive ingestion, usually refers to intake of specific information.

GORGE (ravine) denotes the narrow and oftentimes rocky stretches of one's unique path.

GORGON characterizes those who are negative or make unproductive relationships.

GORILLA may indicate mental or emotional dysfunctions, but it usually refers to gregariousness. Surrounding dreamscape details will clarify this dual meaning.

GOSLING implies fledgling instincts; the beginnings of newly formed responses.

GOSPEL applies to a "truth" as perceived by a specific individual.

GOSPEL MUSIC alludes to spiritual joy.

GOSSAMER See fine-spun.

GOSSIP MONGER advises to "hold one's tongue" and stop spreading hearsay. Recall "who" was doing the gossiping in the dream.

GOTHIC (setting) pertains to mystery; esoteric aspects.

GOUGE See chisel.

GOULASH implies full-bodied nourishment of some type, usually not in reference to food.

GOURD exemplifies a spiritual opportunity.

GOURMAND characterizes a gluttonous nature.

GOURMET illustrates high-quality nourishment of some type; mental, emotional, or spiritual sustenance.

GOVERNESS corresponds to the quality of care one gives to his or her developing humanitarian aspects.

GRAB warns against impulsiveness.

GRAB BAG advises one to be more discerning.

GRACE PERIOD stands for a time extension given.

GRADER connotes a life aspect that has the capability of smoothing something out in one's life.

GRADUATION implies a completion of learning not yet rounded out by experience.

GRADUATION CAP emphasizes information gained through study rather than life experiences; learned perspectives vs. those gained through developed wisdom.

GRAFFITI usually comes as a warning specific to the dreamer. Recall what the graffiti said or depicted.

GRAFT (botany) connotes an attempt to join forces.

GRAFT (gain) warns against self-gain through unscrupulous methods.

GRAHAM CRACKER implies a positive experience bringing personal satisfaction.

GRAIL See Holy Grail.

GRAIN connotes life aspects that have the capability of bringing emotional, mental, or spiritual nourishment.

GRAIN ELEVATOR symbolizes reserve talents; the capacity for great stores of humanitarian deeds. The hint is to recall what this dreamscape grain elevator looked like. Was it in good shape? Full or empty?

GRAMMAR SCHOOL See elementary school.

GRAMMY AWARDS relates to receiving recognition.

GRAMOPHONE signifies "old tunes" used as excuses; cautions against falling back on the "same old tunes" for one's actions.

GRANARY See grain elevator.

GRAND CANYON exemplifies solid evidence; time-tested, visible effects.

GRANDCHILD characterizes a personal responsibility for nurturing those who follow us.

GRANDEUR represents arrogance; a tendency to be showy.

GRANDFATHER CLAUSE pertains to an exemption of some type given.

GRANDFATHER CLOCK is a message that applies a serious connotation of "time" for the dreamer.

GRAND JURY comes as a severe warning. Surrounding details will clarify the precise meaning.

GRAND LAMA characterizes high spiritual attainment.

GRAND MAL (seizure) indicates serious repercussions forthcoming.

GRAND MARCH implies self-importance.

GRANDPARENT characterizes an individual who has the capability of sharing great wisdom.

GRAND PIANO corresponds with the great potential of one's personal talents. The key here is the condition of the dreamscape piano. Was it highly polished? Were the ivory keys yellowed? Broken?

GRAND SLAM defines the best possible outcome.

GRANDSTAND warns against having a self-absorbed tendency to always want to impress others.

GRAND TOUR signifies a recognition of one's limits.

GRANGE illustrates an interest in nurturing the talents of others.

GRANITE depicts a solid foundation.

GRANOLA is another dreamscape symbol that applies to inner nourishment of one's emotional, mental, or spiritual aspects.

GRANT applies to some type of life aspect or event that serves to "clear one's way" toward achieving a goal.

GRANULE illustrates a "fragment" of a whole; a part of something greater.

GRAPE refers to multiple aspects, the fact that an issue holds many varying facets.

GRAPEFRUIT advises one to shed certain excesses in life.

GRAPEVINE typifies a life of rumor; the sequential and progressive alteration of facts.

GRAPH See diagram.

GRAPHICS connote a need for further explanation; a visual required for complete comprehension.

GRAPHOLOGY (study of) denotes an interest in obtaining insights into others.

GRAPH PAPER usually is a call to "figure" something out on paper before acting on it.

GRAPPLE (tool) indicates a struggle to hold onto something.

GRASS corresponds to spiritual foundations.

GRASSHOPPER signifies a destructive force of some type.

GRASSROOTS defines people power; activism generated by common folk.

GRASS SEED pertains to a life aspect that has the capability of taking hold and developing into a spiritual foundation or perspective.

GRATUITY implies thankfulness; a reciprocal response denoting gratitude.

GRAVE symbolizes finality.

GRAVE DIGGER characterizes one on a fatal course; the act of digging one's own grave.

GRAVEL represents loose footing; a need to pay attention to one's pathwalk.

GRAVEN IMAGE See idol.

GRAVE ROBBER is one who enjoys gaining from the downfall of others.

GRAVESTONE usually reveals one's fatal course; may forewarn of a death date.

GRAVEYARD has ominous connotations. Most often advises of a condition or situation where the dreamer is treading on dangerous ground in life.

GRAVEYARD SHIFT reveals a "darkness" surrounding one's life and advises of the wisdom of bringing some light into her or his life.

GRAVITY defines self-imagined limitations.

GRAVY represents an easy access to something.

GRAVY BOAT signifies a life aspect that has the capability of providing an easier course.

GRAY corresponds with the physical brain and the mind contained within.

GRAZE portrays nonchalance; a skimming of the surface.

GREASE warns of bribes and ulterior motives.

GREASE MONKEY See mechanic.

GREASEPAINT warns of hypocrisy; a "false face" presented to others.

GREASY SPOON implies questionable aspects in one's life; factors that "should" be questioned. The surrounding details will assist the dreamer in pinpointing these.

GREAT BARRIER REEF signifies spiritual concepts that are highly cherished and perceived as "fragile" treasures.

GREATCOAT warns against distancing self from others.

GREAT DIVIDE indicates solid strength.

GREAT LAKES emphasize multiple spiritual reserves.

GREAT PLAINS allude to a span of time when one journeys through an unproductive period; a time of neutrality lacking advancement.

GREAT SALT LAKE exemplifies an unexpected event.

GREAT SERPENT EARTH MOUND connotes personal verification. The dreamer will understand what this proof relates to. It will be different for everyone.

GREAT SPHINX corresponds to skepticism.

GREAT PYRAMID applies to historical ignorance; lacking a true and clear comprehension of Reality.

GREAT WALL OF CHINA warns of a deep rift in a relationship.

GREED warns against a tendency toward self-interest and self-centeredness.

GREEN represents health and growth.

GREENBELT pertains to preservation; realizing something's worth.

GREEN CARD gives reassurance regarding one's current project or course of effort.

GREEN DRAGON comes to reveal self-denied envy.

GREEN EYES depending on brilliance vs. dullness and depth of color intensity, can refer to healing abilities or jealousy.

GREENHORN indicates inexperience.

GREENHOUSE reveals one's current state of spirituality. Recall what condition the greenhouse was in. Was it full of bountiful and healthy botanicals? Empty?

GREEN LIGHT naturally means permission granted; the "go-ahead" signal.

GREENROOM constitutes a "waiting" period.

GREEN SOAP connotes a healing factor, usually emotionally.

GREEN THUMB corresponds with a nurturing nature.

GREETING CARD will portray a specific sentiment depending on the type of card it was. This message will be different for everyone.

GREGORIAN CHANTS relate to prayer.

GREMLIN pertains to a temporary problem or "catch" in one's plans.

GRENADE signifies an aspect that has the capability of exploding if not carefully handled; a potentially explosive situation or relationship.

GRENADINE typifies a personality smothered in false sweetness.

GREYHOUND (dog breed) refers to a "fast" friend or associate.

GRIDDLE defines a "hot" situation or relationship. This advises of a need to take a neutral position in order to effect a cooling-down status.

GRIDDLECAKE See pancake.

GRIDLOCK constitutes a deadlock condition or a Catch-22 situation.

GRIEF depicts a needed release of emotions.

GRIFFIN characterizes strength and intelligence.

GRILL (cooking) alludes to a more productive way to accomplish something. This will be defined by surrounding dreamscape details and will mean something different for each dreamer.

GRILLWORK symbolizes effective defenses; protective measures that are strong without being able to be detected by others.

GRIMACE connotes displeasure.

GRIME reveals depression.

GRIM REAPER warns of a potentially dangerous associate, situation, or course.

GRINDER/GRINDSTONE advises of a need to apply greater effort.

GRISTLE constitutes a disbelief; skepticism; something hard to believe.

GRISTMILL corresponds to spiritual talents and the utilization of same.

GRIT (granules) illustrates irritations in life.

GRIT (teeth) pertains to negative emotions.

GRITS connote unwilling acceptance.

GROCERY MARKET represents diet. Recall what was purchased for a better understanding of what this symbol is attempting to convey.

GROGGY warns against a lack of awareness.

GROOVE denotes an old routine; old tendencies or methods.

GROPE alludes to a lack of direction.

GROSGRAIN (fabric) signifies a "rough" personality.

GROSS ANATOMY (study of) suggests a high interest in understanding technicalities.

GROTESQUE reveals a distorted perspective out of touch with reality.

GROTTO reveals a need to take spiritual respite time.

GROUCH implies a need to talk to someone.

GROUND denotes a generally-defined beginning point, yet it's really what is underneath (unseen) that must be discovered.

GROUND BREAKING portrays an effort to discover hidden aspects. For some dreamers this may indicate a beginning.

GROUND CLOTH suggests a protective measure taken.

GROUND COVER defines prolific spiritual or humanitarian qualities that are fruitfully utilized.

GROUND CREW represents one's emotional support group.

GROUND FLOOR connotes the beginning stage of a project or course.

GROUNDHOG reflects a fear of responsibility; hiding from reality or problems.

GROUNDHOG DAY reveals superstition.

GROUND RULES allude to moral, ethical, and spiritual guidelines.

GROUNDSKEEPER See gardener.

GROUND SQUIRREL See prairie dog.

GROUNDSWELL portrays a growing perspective or movement; quickly gaining in popularity or belief.

GROUND WATER See spring.

GROUNDWORK denotes preliminary preparations.

GROUND ZERO signifies a target for destruction. This is usually a serious message for one to cease "zeroing" in on someone or something with a destructive intent.

GROUPER is a caution against following others instead of listening to the inner voice that leads self.

GROUP THERAPY advises of the wisdom of talking through one's problems.

GROUSE connotes a troublesome factor in one's life; a cause for complaint.

GROVE pertains to the need to pause and contemplate.

GROVEL alludes to a lack of self-respect and inner strength.

GROWING PAINS are an advisement to slow down; indicates a "forcing" of development or advancement.

GROWL warns of adversity; a potentially threatening situation or relationship.

GROW LIGHT signifies any aspect that is capable of providing "light" upon one's path.

GROWTH RING stands for a specific age; references time that is meaningful to each dreamer.

GRUBS characterize a destructive force present in an early stage of development.

GRUBSTAKE denotes "assistance" provided for self-interest.

GRUEL reveals an unproductive factor; a false nourishment.

GRUESOME connotes a repulsive reaction; a loathsome and unacceptable aspect in one's life.

GRUMBLE advises one to accept those life aspects that cannot be altered.

GUARANTEE marks verification; reassurance.

GUARD denotes a protective measure or factor.

GUARD HAIR indicates one's personal first defenses.

GUARDIAN characterizes an individual who watches out for another. In actuality, we are all guardians of someone.

GUARDIAN ANGEL portrays one's Higher Self; the Inner Voice heeded.

GUARDRAIL refers to a life aspect that keeps one on course; protective measures applied to keeping one from overextending self or overstepping bounds.

GUAVA connotes bountiful spiritual talents.

GUERRILLA reveals a forceful activist; one who aggressively fights a resistant force.

GUESS reveals a lack of knowledge or information; an assumption.

GUEST characterizes a temporary association.

GUESTHOUSE represents a personal receptivity to others.

GUIDE suggests a person who is capable of showing the way.

GUIDEBOOK symbolizes a life aspect that serves to keep one on course.

GUIDED MISSILE reveals a destructive intent.

GUIDE DOG emphasizes a knowledgeable friend who is capable of assisting another along his or her life path.

GUIDEPOST serves to "mark" one's way.

GUILD denotes a group that shares the same interest. This usually advises the dreamer of the existence of such a group.

GUILE reveals deceit.

GUILLOTINE warns against sticking one's neck out; interference.

GUILT comes to reveal culpability and many times it's the dreamer.

GUINEA PIG reveals a lack of self-confidence; fear of experience.

GUITAR suggests self-expression.

GULAG connotes a situation or relationship that "forces" another in some manner.

GULCH stands for a temporary situation when extra efforts are required.

GULF advises of a spiritual gap.

GULL See seagull.

GULLET See esophagus.

GULLIVER characterizes one who has trouble dealing with personal adversity or trials.

GULLY See gulch.

GUM indicates a need to "chew" something over; a lack of understanding.

GUMBALL exemplifies a difficult concept or idea to understand.

GUM DISEASE infers infected (negative) speech.

GUMDROP advises of a need to ponder something over for a time.

GUMSHOE characterizes a stealthy individual or personality.

GUN warns of mental or emotional dysfunctions; erroneous attitudes or perceptions.

GUNBOAT pertains to dangerous spiritual attitudes or beliefs.

GUN CONTROL warns of attempts to gain power supreme.

GUNFIGHT portrays negative resolutions.

GUNFIRE (hearing of) advises of a potentially dangerous situation close to the dreamer.

GUN MOLL signifies an attraction to power.

GUNNY (fabric) denotes an unsophisticated personality; warm but a little coarse.

GUNNYSACK alludes to one's personal down-to-earth qualities.

GUNPOINT (held at) warns of a "forced" situation; against one's will.

GUNPOWDER reveals a highly-explosive aspect in one's life. This could refer to a relationship, situation, belief, or psychological state.

GUN ROOM defines a personal supply of defensive methods.

GUNRUNNER indicates one who is capable of privately supplying others with protective means. This is not a negative dream aspect.

GUNSMITH characterizes an individual who creates protective aspects for others to utilize.

GUPPY represents a spiritual neophyte.

GURNEY advises of a serious physical condition.

GURU connotes spiritual arrogance; current spiritual fads.

GUST pertains to a sudden emotional outburst; advises control.

GUTTER may indicate the preservation of spiritual aspects or it may warn of a lack of spirituality depending on the surrounding dream details.

GUZZLE warns against impatience; "inhaling" information instead of digesting it with comprehension.

GYMNASIUM denotes an atmosphere that provides exercise, usually indicating "mental" exercise.

GYMNAST warns of a conniving personality; one who contorts and twists the truth.

GYPSY characterizes a free spirit. Depending on surrounding dream details, this may or may not be a positive sign.

GYPSY MOTH reveals a destructive force.

GYROSCOPE stands for steadfastness; remaining true to one's course.

H

HABERDASHERY relates to the manner in which thoughts are displayed or covered up. Refer to specific hat types for more specific information.

HABIT signifies repetitiveness; action without thought.

HACIENDA portrays a relaxed lifestyle where individuals are afforded personal space and privacy.

HACKAMORE denotes control.

HACKLES indicate one's position of defensiveness.

HACKSAW alludes to difficult solutions.

HADES (Greek mythology) characterizes the dark forces and also may connote hell.

HAG signifies old grudges.

HAGGARD portrays a long struggle; exhaustion; tired of continually putting forth the effort.

HAGGLE See bargain.

HAIGHT-ASHBURY characterizes an atmosphere that is conducive to free thinking.

HAIL warns of an inundation of spiritual concepts.

HAIR symbolizes thoughts. Refer to specific hair types, conditions, and colors for specific interpretations.

HAIRBALL connotes a misconception that must be gotten rid of — regurgitated.

HAIRBRUSH advises of a need to clean out and untangle confused thoughts or ideas.

HAIRCLOTH See horsehair.

HAIRDRESSER represents one who affects the thoughts of others.

HAIRDRESSING signifies controlled thoughts.

HAIR NET warns of a need to contain one's uncontrollable thoughts.

HAIRPIECE warns of a thought process that is partially in error.

HAIRPIN applies to a method of controlling the "odd" thought.

HAIRPIN CURVE (in road) indicates a tendency to do a lot of backtracking as one travels his or her life path.

HAIR SHIRT denotes self-reproach; guilt.

HAIRSPLITTING means faultfinding; pettiness.

HAIR SPRAY pertains to "stiff" thinking; unyielding attitudes.

HAIRSTYLE See specific type.

HAIR TRIGGER stands for an explosive temperament.

HALCYON illustrates a peaceful atmosphere.

HALF (of something) implies more to be obtained; one doesn't have the all of it yet.

HALF-AND-HALF connotes a "tempered" situation or attitude.

HALF-BAKED signifies a premature aspect; an undeveloped idea.

HALF BLOOD constitutes a rightful identity or authority.

HALF COCKED (gun) means ill-prepared.

HALF-DOLLAR depicts a starting point; all is not lost.

HALFHEARTED represents a lack of interest.

HALF-LIGHT See dusk.

HALF-MAST reveals sorrow.

HALF-MOON exemplifies partial illumination of one's path; underscores "enough" light to be guided by. This would indicate an individual who believes he or she has no guidance.

HALF NOTE implies a quickened pace.

HALF-PINT defines a smaller aspect that may be as important as a larger one for the dreamer; something not to be overlooked or viewed an insignificant.

HALF-SLIP pertains to something that's partially shielded, usually refers to an aspect of one's personality.

HALFTIME advises of a time of respite; a "break" to re-energize and regroup.

HALFTONE suggests subtlety; a need to soften harshness.

HALF-TRACK reveals a need to venture into untraveled regions; enter new territory. This refers to knowledge.

HALFWAY HOUSE is an advisement to remove self from an undesirable situation or relationship.

HALIBUT pertains to spiritual nourishment.

HALITOSIS applies to offending language.

HALL (large room) indicates an important gathering.

HALL (way) suggests a transition.

HALLEY'S COMET relates to the continual fluctuations of true Reality.

HALLMARK exemplifies a sign of approval.

HALL OF FAME represents narrowly-perceived greatness.

HALLOWEEN illustrates personal revelations; insights into another's hidden character.

HALLUCINATING may, in reality, be insights into true Reality or it may warn against conscious imaginings that one believes as truth.

HALO portrays spiritual enlightenment.

HAM applies to theatrics; over-emotionalism; dramatics.

HAMBURGER signifies questionable nourishment; an aspect one depends on for support that may not be a positive factor.

HAMLET implies a surround of close associates; one's circle of friends.

HAMMER warns of "forced" attitudes or beliefs.

HAMMER AND SICKLE relate to a common bond.

HAMMERTOES indicate difficulty walking one's path.

HAMMOCK cautions against laziness.

HAMPER suggests that which needs cleaning up in one's life.

HAMSTER See gerbil.

HAND connotes service done for others. Recall condition of same.

HANDBAG See purse.

HANDBALL depicts personal efforts expended.

HANDBILL signifies broadcasted information.

HANDBOOK warns against following a stilted lifestyle; regimentation.

HANDCAR cautions against fanaticism related to following another's life or spiritual path.

HANDCART stands for the carrying of one's personal burdens.

HANDCLASP represents a unifying force.

HAND COVERING See specific type.

HANDCUFFS reveal self-imposed restraints.

HANDICAPPED indicates subconscious fears that hold one back.

HANDICRAFTS denote creativity generated from personal efforts.

HAND IN GLOVE cautions against forming relationships that are too close, too revealing of self.

HANDKERCHIEF implies preparedness.

HANDLE (object) relates to comprehension.

HANDLE (touch) means getting a "feel" for something in life.

HANDLEBAR pertains to personal control.

HANDLEBAR MUSTACHE reveals pretentiousness.

HAND-ME-DOWN refers to a highly useful aspect in one's life.

HANDOFF applies to an "exchange" being done; passing of information or benefits.

HANDOUT exemplifies sharing.

HAND OVER FIST suggests a fast pace.

HANDPICKING means personal choice or decision.

HANDPRINT denotes that which we leave behind; a mark of our identity.

HANDRAIL portrays one's personal means of support along his or her path.

HANDS DOWN stands for complete agreement; a reinforcing sign.

HANDSHAKE portrays good intentions.

HANDSOME (appearance) suggests an "attractive" aspect. Recall surrounding details to see if this is true.

HANDSPRING relates to a sudden burst of joy or excitement.

HANDSTAND depicts happiness.

HAND-TO-MOUTH connotes a time of great tribulation and personal struggle.

HAND WRINGING defines worry; lack of acceptance.

HANDWRITING emphasizes one's inner character. What qualities did it have?

HANDWRITING ON WALL reveals a message; forewarning.

HANGAR (plane) advises of the need for a time of contemplation; a rest period from research.

HANGER is an advisement to "let go" of something one is clinging to or hanging on to; hang it up.

HANG-GLIDE corresponds with effortless thought; ideas or concepts that come easily.

HANGMAN characterizes one who is capable of posing a dangerous threat to another; someone who could hang you; a betrayer.

HANGNAIL denotes a lack of acceptance; worries or anxieties we "pick" over; fretting.

HANGOVER represents the negative results of irresponsibility.

HANSEL AND GRETEL characterize a loss of direction and mistrust.

HANSOM See carriage.

HAPHAZARD advises of a fragmented mind; a lack of orderly thought.

HAPPY HOUR typifies a short period of time when troubles can be set aside.

HARANGUE cautions against sermonizing to others.

HARASSMENT denotes a lack of acceptance; hanging on to irritations; a refusal to let go and let things be.

HARBINGER connotes forerunner; something that comes first.

HARBOR pertains to a spiritual comfort; a spiritually safe place to be; a secure spiritual belief system.

HARBOR MASTER characterizes an individual who has the

capability to guide others to a spiritually safe place.

HARD (consistency) usually implies a difficult aspect; unyielding; harsh or insensitive.

HARDBALL symbolizes a tough situation to deal with.

HARD-BOILED defines an insensitive personality.

HARD COPY means a visible, touchable aspect.

HARD-CORE signifies a strong opinion or perspective; one that cannot be changed.

HARDCOVER (book) relates to an enduring quality; lasting.

HARD DISK implies the capability of containing a great amount of information.

HARDHAT portrays strong opinions; a thought process that resists new ideas.

HARD-HANDED indicates an overbearing personality; tyrannical.

HARD-HEADED applies to a realistic perspective; shrewdness.

HARDHEARTED reveals an aloof personality; unemotional and insensitive.

HARD LABOR (maternity) signifies great personal efforts applied to changing one's life.

HARD LANDING portrays a difficult ending; hard work applied to a conclusion or closure.

HARD LINE denotes a firm position or belief; uncompromising.

HARD-NOSED applies to a firm position; a difficult-to-change attitude.

HARD ROCK MINER characterizes one who expends great personal efforts to advance along her or his path.

HARDSCRABBLE reveals perseverance in the face of adversity.

HARD SELL corresponds with the "pressure" one feels.

HARDTACK exemplifies something that's hard to swallow; difficult to accept.

HARDTOP implies thought given to protective methods or aspects.

HARDWARE STORE refers to hard work. May indicate a need for hard work applied to "fixing up" some aspect in one's life.

HARELIP illustrates impaired speech relating to errors in perception or attitude.

HAREM denotes separatism; an attitude based on class or position.

HARLEM represents adversities to be overcome.

HARLEQUIN characterizes one who avoids responsibility; lacks a true view of reality and takes life too lightly.

HARLOT See prostitute.

HARMONICA corresponds with relaxation; a time for self.

HARMONIZING pertains to efforts applied to obtaining balance.

HARNESS represents control and/or containment.

HARP (musical) implies spiritual peace.

HARP (nag) indicates a lack of acceptance; a tendency to interfere.

HARPOON stands for spiritual selectivity.

HARP SEAL defines innocence; spiritual vulnerability.

HARPSICHORD represents outdated ideas.

HARRIER See hawk.

HARROW implies a greatly disturbing incident.

HARVEST portrays the fruits of one's shared gifts.

HARVEST HOME signifies the inner joy felt when one helps others.

HARVEST MOON alludes to a bountiful time in one's life.

HASH relates to something comprised of multiple factors.

HASH BROWNS represent an important, basic factor in one's life.

HASHISH See marijuana.

HASSOCK See footstool.

HAT corresponds with one's way of thinking; personal inner thoughts. See specific type of hat for further information.

HATBAND reveals added aspects to one's character.

HATBOX signifies altered or changeable perspectives; a tendency to switch attitudes.

HATCH (emerge) refers to personal expression of self; coming out of one's shell.

HATCHBACK pertains to an open-ended situation or relationship.

HATCH COVER alludes to a "way out" of something.

HATCHECK connotes the "holding back" of expressing personal opinions or attitudes.

HATCHERY connotes multiple ideas or theories; one who is full of new ideas.

HATCHET pertains to a resentment; a desire to get even; retaliation.

HATCHLING denotes a new beginning; a fresh start or brand new plan for one's personal direction.

HATE MAIL reveals a lack of acceptance; intolerance; negativity.

HATPIN indicates a need to hold on to one's thoughts or attitudes; easily persuaded or manipulated.

HAULING TRAILER warns of excessive weight carried around. This could refer to physical body weight or voluntarily-held burdens.

HAUNTING corresponds to self-generated fear.

HAUTE COUTURE warns against letting others dictate your personal style or method of expression; a loss of individuality.

HAUTE CUISINE implies extravagant methods of nourishment; reaching for nourishment that is highly regarded without realizing that the most beneficial nourishment comes from the simplest and most basic source.

HAVELOCK pertains to a lack of trust; an attempt to protect one's back.

HAVEN illustrates a life aspect within which one believes he or she is well-protected; may refer to a place within self; a retreat within.

HAVE-NOT characterizes an individual who refuses to recognize his or her own gifts; a lack of acceptance; ignoring one's real riches in deference to materialism.

HAVERSACK portrays a light traveler; one who recognizes the basics as opposed to excessive baggage.

HAVOC pertains to total confusion, usually one's thought process.

HAWK characterizes acute perceptions; an ability for quick discernment.

HAWK-EYED stands for heightened awareness.

HAWSER represents a life aspect that keeps one spiritually bound to a specific belief system; spiritual constriction.

HAWTHORN exemplifies unrecognized benefits.

HAWTHORNE (Nathaniel) characterizes ethical and spiritual living.

HAY implies active efforts; work time.

HAY FEVER warns against a reluctance to work; laziness.

HAYFORK connotes a tool that helps us accomplish a goal.

HAYLOFT pertains to the resulting evidence of one's efforts.

HAYRIDE reveals an inner joy taken from hard work.

HAYSTACK signifies the completion of one's specific work.

HAYWIRE means the final work to be done before completing something; may also infer something gone completely wrong.

HAZARD LIGHT refers to one's personal ability to sense dangerous situations; forewarning insights.

HAZARDOUS WASTE warns of harmful aspects surrounding

the dreamer. This will be different for everyone.

HAZE (atmospheric) alludes to an unclear aspect, usually a lack of clear thought or understanding.

HAZE (harass) stands for a ridiculing personality or situation.

HAZEL (color) means a cheery, down-to-earth personality or attitude.

HAZELNUT implies common sense.

HEAD pertains to the thought process.

HEADACHE exemplifies difficulty in processing one's thoughts.

HEADBAND warns against confining one's thoughts; advises expanding and exploring new concepts; a need to express oneself.

HEAD COLD signifies a "clogged" mind; a need to "clear" one's thoughts.

HEAD COVERING See specific type.

HEADDRESS reveals a uniquely specific and individualistic attachment; corresponds with a certain attitude or association.

HEADHUNTING connotes one's search for a specific individual or type of personality; a quest for knowledge.

HEADLESS warns of a thought-less person; one who has no intellectual pursuits or interests; a lack of personal opinion.

HEADLIGHT represents logic and reason; a "light" on a subject.

HEADLINES correspond with important messages for the dreamer. These will carry different meanings for each individual.

HEADMISTRESS characterizes an individual who helps to guide another's learning process.

HEADPHONES illustrate focused thought; the blocking out of unimportant audibles.

HEADQUARTERS portray a central source regarding a specific idea.

HEADREST indicates intellectual respite; a time to pause from one's pursuit of knowledge.

HEADROOM pertains to time and space to think.

HEAD SHOP corresponds with a "source" that provides one with tools to escape from problems.

HEAD START represents an opportunity.

HEADSTONE See gravestone.

HEADSTRONG warns against being obstinate.

HEAD-TO-HEAD denotes an intellectual conflict.

HEADWATERS stand for a spiritual source.

HEADWIND constitutes a counterforce to be overcome along one's path.

HEALER characterizes an individual who is capable of restoring the well-being of others. Was this dreamscape healer you?

HEALTH CLUB/SPA advises of a need to shape up or restore some specific aspect of self.

HEALTH FOOD STORE represents a choice of multiple tools to maintain personal health. This may refer to mental or emotional health, depending on surrounding dreamscape details.

HEALTH INSURANCE denotes self-doubt; a lack of faith in one's own healing abilities.

HEARING AID indicates a lack of attention and awareness; implies one does not "listen" well.

HEARSAY implies questionable information.

HEARSE corresponds with death. This could refer to the death of a relationship, situation, condition, or some aspect within self. Sometimes this symbol may forewarn of an actual physical demise.

HEART applies to the emotions and health of same.

HEART ATTACK portrays an emotional shock.

HEARTBEATS signify emotional stability. Recall if the beats were steady or irregular.

HEARTBURN connotes emotional pain that can easily be alleviated if one so desired.

HEARTH symbolizes homey aspects; warmth and comfort.

HEARTHRUG implies protective measures utilized to protect one's personal feelings of comfort and privacy.

HEARTLESS relates to complete insensitivity; sternness.

HEART-OF-HEARTS signifies that which one cherishes most.

HEARTS (card game) suggest a manipulation of another's emotions.

HEART-TO-HEART implies confidentiality; open expression of sincerity.

HEARTWORM warns of an emotionally destructive force in one's life. This may even indicate a self-generated source.

HEAT connotes one's energy.

HEAT EXCHANGER pertains to the act of helping to re-energize another or rejuvenate them in some manner.

HEAT EXHAUSTION warns of a depletion of one's energy; a time to rest and recoup.

HEATHEN characterizes spirituality versus organized religious dogma.

HEATHER represents a bountiful stage in life.

HEATING BLANKET stands for emotional comfort.

HEATING PAD advises of a need to re-energize self.

HEAT LIGHTNING exemplifies a sudden depletion of one's energy.

HEAT RASH portrays the utilization of one's energy for self-defeating purposes; an unproductive effort.

HEAT SHIELD signifies a specific method one utilizes to conserve personal energy; efficient use of one's time and energy.

HEAT STROKE connotes overwork; unregulated energy utilization.

HEAT WAVE defines a span of time during one's path walk when extra efforts are required for advancement.

HEAVEN characterizes the ultimate state of being.

HEAVY implies an intense or profound burden. Surrounding details will clarify which meaning is intended.

HEAVY HAND represents a harsh and tyrannical personality.

HEAVY-HEARTED denotes melancholia.

HEAVY METAL (music or metal) warns of an extremely negative aspect.

HEAVYWEIGHT characterizes an intellectual.

HECKLE warns against a tendency to irritate another; taunting.

HEDGE exemplifies a habit of circumventing; evading issues or responsibility.

HEDGEHOG See porcupine.

HEDGEROW implies a guiding facet in one's life.

HEDGE TRIMMERS denote an attempt to "reshape" one's path.

HEDONISM warns against excessive self-indulgence; a preoccupation with self.

HEEL symbolizes exhaustion.

HEIMLICH MANEUVER advises of a need to get something out of one's system; get an "internalized" emotion or attitude out in the open.

HEIRESS characterizes one's "right" to something. This could be a multifaceted symbol in that it may refer to factors such as knowledge, material goods, an employment position, etc. Surrounding dreamscape details will clarify this specific meaning.

HEIRLOOM signifies great personal value.

HELEN OF TROY represents the factor that has caused great strife in one's life.

HELICOPTER reveals a vacillating mental state; frequent indecision.

HELIOTHERAPY advises of a dark, depressive condition that needs brightening with a recognition of one's blessings.

HELIOTROPE signifies inherent spiritual talents.

HELIPORT corresponds with a "grounding" aspect in one's life.

HELIUM indicates a life aspect that has the capability of "uplifting" attitudes, emotions, or situations.

HELL may illustrate various conditions such as a great tribulation, extremely difficult situation, a dark and depressive state of mind, etc.

HELLEBORE exemplifies a state of duality.

HELM represents control.

HELMET connotes "protected" or hidden thoughts.

HELPER characterizes one who has the capability to aid another.

HELPER T CELL portrays an agent that has the ability to destroy specific negative aspects in one's life.

HEM stands for something that surrounds; encircled; something one is surrounded by.

HEMATITE pertains to the power and strength of one's life force.

HEMATOLOGY (study of) illustrates a high interest in understanding esoteric concepts.

HEMATOMA warns of a need to release a blockage of one's continuously circulating energy flow within the body.

HEMISPHERE illustrates "half" of something. Surrounding dreamscape details will clarify this intention.

HEMLOCK advises of a dangerous factor in one's life.

HEMOPHILIA warns of a dangerously low energy level; some aspect in one's life is draining energy.

HEMOPHOBIA pertains to a fear of personal responsibility; a lack of self-confidence.

HEMORRHAGE represents a sudden outpouring of one's energy. This may indicate a needed course of action for the dreamer.

HEMORRHOID corresponds with a harmful situation in one's life. Each dreamer will recognize what this situation is for him or her.

HEMOSTAT connotes a "stanching" factor of one's energy outflow. This may be required or warned against, depending on other dream details.

HEMP refers to a strong or powerful factor in one's life.

HEMSTITCH applies to the act of "finishing" something; a conclusion or closure.

HEN characterizes productivity.

H

HEN AND CHICKENS apply to a fruitful life factor; bountiful.

HENBANE alludes to something in one's life that possesses duality.

HENCHMAN portrays an individual who is content being an underling; one who gains self-esteem by pleasing another.

HENNA pertains to repressed emotions.

HEPATICA connotes inner strength.

HEPATITIS A advises of a harmful effect caused by something to which one has *innocently* exposed self.

HEPATITIS B reveals a harmful effect caused by something to which one has *willfully* exposed self.

HERALD See messenger.

HERALDRY signifies extreme self-absorption; arrogance.

HERBS pertain to a variety of meanings. Non-specific herbs relate to natural talents. See specific type for further information.

HERBALIST denotes natural methods and techniques.

HERBARIUM represents a "study of" the many productive uses of botanicals. This dreamscape symbol would indicate a call for one to utilize personal talents more extensively.

HERB GARDEN connotes a "cultivation" of one's abilities.

HERBICIDE warns of a destructive force that has the potential of hampering the utilization and growth of one's natural abilities.

HERBIVORE will emphasize a more "natural" lifestyle; a return to the rejuvenating benefits of nature.

HERCULES (Greek/Roman mythology) alludes to great strength. This could be strength of character and the important revealing factor here is "how" this strength was utilized.

HERD most always indicates a warning to follow one's own path.

HERDER may not mean one who keeps others in line; it may pertain to a personal need to keep "self" in line.

HEREAFTER (time) connotes the future.

HEREDITARY depicts an "inherent" personal aspect that *can* be altered through understanding and will. This would refer to a negative personality characteristic.

HERETIC characterizes a diversion from popular belief systems. This may be a positive symbol in that it represents individuality; a free-thinker.

HERMAPHRODITE symbolizes balance; a wholeness of being and thought.

HERMIT may advise one to

"open up" more and be communicative or it might be indicating a need to retreat and contemplate for a time. Surrounding dreamscape details will clarify which meaning this had for the dreamer.

HERMIT CRAB denotes spiritual reclusiveness.

HERNIA reveals a "forced" action taken in one's life.

HERO/HEROINE represents courage and perseverance.

HERO (Greek mythology) defines great devotion and love.

HEROD THE GREAT characterizes a fear of being bested; refers to an obsession with self; a fear of someone else perceived as being better or more admired than self.

HERON defines the beauty of spiritual wisdom.

HERO WORSHIP warns against an obsessive admiration of another; advises of a need to follow one's personal path.

HERPES SIMPLEX signifies dormant inherent negative qualities of one's personality that can be activated through a lack of control.

HERRING portray spiritual bounty.

HERRINGBONE (pattern) represents order.

HESPERIDES (Greek mythology) applies to the protection of one's spiritual values.

HESTIA (Greek mythology) characterizes one who places a high priority on home and family life.

HETEROSEXISM warns against discriminating against those who are different from self.

HEW refers to personal efforts put forth.

HEX (sign) typifies a method one uses to maintain spiritual protection.

HEXAGON applies to mental, emotional, or spiritual protection.

HEXAGRAM (star) signifies wisdom, particularly spiritual wisdom.

HIATUS constitutes a break in one's work; a rest period.

HIBACHI represents the utilization of the right tool or method for accomplishing specific jobs.

HIBERNATING indicates escapism; a desire to avoid facing reality.

HIBISCUS denotes spirituality.

HICCUP stands for an interruption of some type. Surrounding dream details will relate this to a situation in the dreamer's life.

HICKORY emphasizes the "strength" and enduring characteristics of one's natural abilities as they are used and developed.

HIDE-AND-SEEK typifies the "games" people play in life; manipulation; ulterior motives; hidden agendas.

HIDEOUT may infer a need for sanctuary or it may indicate the act of running away from one's problems. Surrounding dreamscape details will clarify which meaning it has for the dreamer.

HIERARCHY represents "stages" of development or attainment.

HIEROGLYPH symbolizes spiritual truths that are beyond one's current stage of understanding.

HIEROPHANT characterizes an enlightened individual; one who has the advanced development of knowledge coupled with wisdom.

HIGH pertains to an advanced level or position of prominence.

HIGHBALL See alcoholic beverage.

HIGH BEAM (light) suggests more "light" be given to an issue in the dreamer's life that she or he is having trouble understanding.

HIGH BLOOD PRESSURE warns of a need to slow down and be more accepting.

HIGHBOY corresponds to efficiency; a tendency to avoid wasting time on unnecessary steps.

HIGHBROW indicates intelligence.

HIGH CHAIR represents an immaturity.

HIGH COUNTRY illustrates a path that presents deeper conceptual ideas for one to learn from.

HIGH COURT See Supreme Court.

HIGH-DENSITY stands for a "concentrated" aspect. This will be different for each dreamer as it relates to individualized associations.

HIGH FASHION See haute couture.

HIGH FINANCE doesn't necessarily refer to money; rather, it usually alludes to a difficult or complex situation in one's life that warrants careful consideration and planning.

HIGH GEAR portrays a phase of intense activity. This could relate to mental or emotional activity.

HIGH-HAT See top hat.

HIGH HEELS cautions against "raising self" above one's current level of development.

HIGH HOLY DAYS signify a time of great importance for the dreamer, usually spiritual.

HIGH HORSE reveals indignation; a continual complaining; advises acceptance.

HIGH JUMP means one is attempting to avoid or circumvent an issue or life problem.

HIGHLANDER characterizes an individual who has attained an advanced stage of personal development.

HIGH-LEVEL pertains to an elevated level of knowledge.

HIGH LIFE warns against misplaced priorities; advises a shift in what one places importance on.

HIGHLIGHTER (pen or marking) reveals the necessity of noting and remembering certain ideas that are important to the specific dreamer.

HIGH NOON emphasizes a specified time when a critical decision or situation will culminate.

HIGH-OCTANE indicates a "powerful" aspect in one's life. This could refer to a personal characteristic, relationship, or situation.

HIGH-PITCHED (tone) is a call to immediately increase awareness; a warning.

HIGH PRIESTESS characterizes one who has reached the attainment of knowledge coupled with wisdom.

HIGH PROFILE advises of high visibility. This is a cautionary symbol that reminds one that she or he is being observed by others.

HIGH RELIEF denotes an aspect in one's life that "stands out" and should be noticed or acted upon.

HIGH-RESOLUTION emphasizes clear, vivid dreams which may reveal an actual out-of-body experience.

HIGH-RISE connotes multilevel aspects to something in the dreamer's life. Surrounding dreamscape details will usually clarify this.

HIGHROAD portrays optimism; frequently warns against taking the easier path.

HIGH ROLLER characterizes an individual who has a tendency to take great risks.

HIGH SCHOOL typifies a symbol that represents a "step up" in one's level of learning.

HIGH SEAS constitute higher spiritual concepts; a place in one's path where she or he is ready to spiritually progress.

HIGH SIGN corresponds with good relationships.

HIGH-SPEED is most often an advisement to slow down or do things in a more attentive manner.

HIGH-STRUNG indicates a need for personal restraint. This symbol implies a person who flies off the handle without giving logic and reason to reactions.

HIGH TEA denotes an advisement for one to take time to "settle down" and contemplate or absorb that which has been experienced.

HIGH TECHNOLOGY denotes "advanced" knowledge or one's path progression.

HIGH-TENSION WIRE corresponds with intense power. This will directly relate to a certain aspect that is specific to each dreamer.

HIGH TIDE portrays a time of intense spiritual influx in one's life.

HIGH-TOPS allude to preparedness for one's walk through life.

HIGHWAY represents a life path taken by many others.

HIGHWAYMEN characterize individuals who attempt to gain by your life walk; an attempt to take something from your advancement.

HIGHWAY PATROL characterizes protective forces present along one's path.

HIGHWAY ROBBERY See highwaymen.

HIGH WIRE connotes a questionable leap in one's advancement; a fragile situation where one must maintain awareness.

HIJACK signifies a situation where one is being "robbed" of benefits personally acquired along his or her path.

HIKE connotes personal efforts applied to one's path advancement.

HILARITY typifies the importance of humor in one's life.

HILL stands for a time when extra efforts are needed.

HILLSIDE represents continued efforts.

HILLTOP corresponds with reaching a goal; place of accomplishment.

HINDQUARTER usually refers to concluding aspects; nearing an ending or closure.

HINGE alludes to probabilities.

HINT is almost always a "clue" for the dreamer. These should be recalled.

HIP (anatomy) may refer to relationships or it may be indicating an actual physical aspect.

HIP (rose) portrays the condition of one's physical health.

HIPPIE characterizes a diversion from "established" traditions or ideas.

HIPPOCRATES characterizes an individual who can discern the difference between truth and superstition.

HIPPOCRATIC OATH denotes a determined path; a pure intention.

HIPPOPOTAMUS typifies spiritual generosity; a continual giving nature.

HIRED GUN warns against having others settle your problems.

HIRED HAND represents one who is reimbursed for the help they give. This would mean there are those in your life from whom you elicit assistance and therefore who need to be paid in kind.

HIRING HALL See union hall.

HISTORIAN characterizes one who is interested in understanding how past experiences relate to the present.

HISTORICAL FIGURES hold a personal meaning for each dreamer. This meaning will usually be easily identified.

HISTORICAL NOVEL will have a karmic lesson to teach each dreamer.

HISTORICAL SITE usually has some type of personal connection to the dreamer and comes to reveal something important.

HIT (inhale) indicates a need for additional support; utilizing an assisting aspect.

HIT exposes unrestrained emotions; impulsiveness.

HIT-AND-RUN warns against running from responsibility; a refusal to answer for one's actions.

HITCH (snag) implies a temporary setback.

HITCH (tow connector) represents a life aspect that helps one progress along his or her path; that which provides the "start-up" action from a setback.

HITCHHIKER characterizes laziness; one who advances along the path by way of another's efforts.

HITCHING POST symbolizes the needed pauses taken during our path progression.

HITLER (Adolf) exemplifies the destructive effects of intensely negative forces; the result of manifested evil.

HIT LIST will usually reveal those who are detrimental in one's life. It can also refer to someone else's list which is an extremely informative piece of information for the dreamer.

HIT MAN See hired gun.

HITTER represents frustration; a lack of acceptance.

HIVE See beehive.

HIVES denote a lack of acceptance; a continued state of active irritation.

HOAGIE See submarine sandwich.

HOARDING warns against selfishness; may also indicate a need to "save up" something. Surrounding dream details will clarify this.

HOARFROST pertains to spiritual beauty.

HOARSENESS implies unclear communications.

HOAX reveals a deception present in one's life. The key is to recall what the hoax was and who generated it for what *reason*. This will not always represent a negative act.

HOBBIT characterizes a gentle and peaceful personality.

HOBBLE reveals perseverance.

HOBBY relates to manner of personal relaxation and interest.

Each hobby will have its own interpretation. See specific type.

HOBBYHORSE connotes an obsession.

HOBBY SHOP represents vast opportunities for constructive mental diversions in relation to satisfying one's need to rest from intensive researching and study.

HOBGOBLIN alludes to one's fears.

HOCK See pawn.

HOCKEY represents a spiritual game one plays.

HOCKEY STICK indicates a willful diversion employed to avoid spiritual responsibility.

HODGEPODGE may have positive or negative interpretations. The negative intent would be a warning against believing in completely unrelated ideas that comprise a concept, in other words, inconsistencies and contradictions. The positive meaning would be an underscoring of one's accurate conceptual belief comprised of divergent aspects that all interrelate.

HOE pertains to personal efforts applied to hard work and advancement.

HOEDOWN See square dance.

HOG cautions against a tendency to take on too much at once.

HOGAN signifies a natural way of living; simplicity of life.

HOGBACK indicates a need to do some backtracking to capture missed lessons or incomplete aspects.

HOIST symbolizes a life factor that has the capability of "uplifting" the dreamer.

HOLD (of ship) connotes one's capacity for goodness and the distribution of same among humanity.

HOLD BUTTON implies postponements; an opportunity to put something off for a time.

HOLDING PATTERN constitutes a temporary period of neutrality; a life phase that precludes advancement.

HOLDING TANK corresponds with spiritual beliefs one is currently deliberating; a time before a spiritual decision is made.

HOLDOUT characterizes one who is not in a position to change his or her mind on something.

HOLDUP defines a delay of some type.

HOLD-UP (with weapon) implies loss.

HOLE usually refers to an opening; an opportunity. Rarely will it represent a defect. Surrounding dreamscape details will clarify which interpretation was meant for the dreamer.

HOLIDAY denotes a rest time. This most often infers that one is working or concentrating too hard.

HOLISTIC may not be relating to health aspects. It usually refers to an advisement to stop "fragmenting" one's thoughts; a need to think in terms of "whole" concepts or ideas.

HOLLOW illustrates a lack of depth; a shallow attitude or concept.

HOLLY corresponds with a "fresh" spiritual idea or concept.

HOLLYHOCK implies cheerfulness; a bright outlook.

HOLLYWOOD typifies dream symbols that relate to superficiality.

HOLLYWOOD BED pertains to a lack of seriousness.

HOLOCAUST defines a monumental devastating event.

HOLOGRAM means a false perception of reality.

HOLSTER corresponds with a life aspect that has the capability of providing some type of personal protection.

HOLY COMMUNION reflects our connection to a Supreme Essence.

HOLY DAY See high holy days.

HOLY GRAIL connotes a need for spiritual proof.

HOLY WAR See crusades.

HOLY WATER exemplifies a need for spiritual affectations in order to feel power behind one's beliefs; a lack of faith.

HOMAGE warns against giving this to anyone but God Almighty.

HOME signifies one's place of comfort.

HOME BASE illustrates a personal operational base one works from.

HOMEBODY connotes contentedness; one who has few needs and even fewer wants.

HOMEBOUND stands for a nearly completed goal or path.

HOMEBRED portrays an individual who was raised with family values.

HOME-BREW denotes creativity and inventiveness; self-sufficiency.

HOME BUYER represents a desire to be settled; established roots.

HOMECOMING applies to a return to one's roots, beginnings.

HOMEGROWN suggests an ability to make one's own way in life.

HOMELAND indicates a sense of one's roots; a strong identity.

HOMELESS may not be the negative it appears on the surface. It may pertain to a journeyer; one who continually progresses along her or his life path.

HOMEMADE suggests resourcefulness.

HOMEOPATHY stresses solutions contained within the problem.

HOME PLATE represents a specific goal one has.

HOMEROOM portrays one's basic beliefs that are built on.

HOME RULE pertains to independence; a responsibility to self.

HOME RUN reveals an attainment of a goal.

HOMESICK emphasizes emotional sensitivity.

HOMESPUN denotes simplicity of character and self-reliance.

HOMESTEADER characterizes independence and confidence.

HOMESTRETCH advises of a nearly completed goal.

HOME STUDY illustrates high motivation and an independent search.

HOMICIDE See murder.

HOMING PIGEON pertains to a tendency to continually return to a specific belief or attitude.

HOMINOID represents "any" being that resembles the human form.

HOMOGENIZE relates to a lack of diversity.

HOMOPHOBIA warns against fearing diversity in others.

HOMO SAPIENS See hominoid.

HOMOSEXUALITY signifies a carryover spirit memory. When attraction to another or a sense of love is expressed on the spirit plane there are no genders to differentiate one spirit from another . . . love is love.

HONE implies a "sharpening" aspect in one's life; something that brings a factor into finer definition or proficiency.

HONEY represents "sweet" benefits generated from one's personal efforts.

HONEYCOMB illustrates bountiful benefits or rewards.

HONEYMOON indicates a harmonious and loyal relationship.

HONEYSUCKLE denotes earned graces.

HONKING (horn) defines a warning; a call to attention.

HONORABLE DISCHARGE comes as a commendation for accomplishments or efforts applied.

HONORABLE MENTION constitutes a commendation from one's Higher Self.

HONORARIUM warns against expecting recompense for gifts voluntarily shared with others.

HONOR SYSTEM reminds one to behave in an honest and trustworthy manner.

HOOCH See alcoholic beverage.

HOOD reveals high knowledge and wisdom.

HOOD See neighborhood.

HOODLUM characterizes an immature perspective; a self-centered nature; an inability to advance past primal instincts.

HOODWINKED reveals a deception.

HOOF implies a difficult situation or pathway.

HOOK alludes to certainty; security; a secure aspect.

HOOKAH refers to an attempt to cool a heated situation.

HOOKER See prostitute.

HOOKWORM warns of a potentially damaging factor that could easily be accepted into one's life.

HOOP denotes a completed aspect; coming full-circle.

HOOTENANNY represents spontaneous joy.

HOPE CHEST symbolizes one's dreams; aspirations.

HOPSCOTCH warns against a tendency to "jump" to only chosen points along one's path.

HORDE illustrates a great multitude. This could refer to many subjects; therefore, the dreamer will receive clarification through recalling the surrounding details.

HOREHOUND exemplifies that which is capable of clearing and sharpening one's communication skills.

HORIZON signifies one's individual perspective.

HORMONE corresponds with a life factor that directly affects one's mental or emotional responses.

HORN (animal) See antler.

HORN (sound) defines a warning.

HORNET/WASP indicates the "stinging" events in life.

HORNET'S NEST exposes a troublesome situation or relationship.

HOROSCOPE warns against a tendency to be led through life by what others say.

HORROR reveals our fears.

HORSE emphasizes a "wild" nature.

HORSEFLY refers to "biting" remarks.

HORSEHAIR signifies a coarse personality covered with a sleek veneer.

HORSE RACE alludes to a "controlled" speed; a fast-paced progression that is well-controlled.

HORSERADISH denotes "sharp" lessons learned; lessons well remembered.

HORSESHOE represents superstition; a belief in charms.

HORSE-TRADING implies clever negotiations.

HORTICULTURE (study of) stands for a high interest in cultivating people's natural talents.

HOSE (water) reveals a willful "direction" of one's spiritual expressions.

HOSPICE portrays empathy and compassion.

HOSPITAL comes as a rejuvenation advisement.

HOST suggests a receivership; means a beneficiary.

HOSTAGE represents a demand for security; a desire to obtain a goal without working for it.

HOSTELRY See hotel.

HOT most often refers to an intense condition or emotion.

HOT-BLOODED signifies a lack of self-control.

HOTCAKE See pancake.

HOT DOG refers to skill; having something "covered."

HOT-DOGGING warns of spiritual irresponsibility.

HOTEL symbolizes a transition stage; a temporary condition.

HOT FLASH pertains to a sudden flash of inspiration.

HOTFOOT advises of a need to slow down.

HOTHEADED applies to a quick temper.

HOTHOUSE reveals an oppressive condition or personality.

HOTLINE stands for an unbroken line of communication; the need to keep communication open.

HOT PLATE advises of a need to keep up efforts regarding a specific situation or relationship.

HOT POTATO relates to an extremely "touchy" aspect in one's life.

HOT ROD represents an individualized manner of speeding one's advancement.

HOT SEAT pertains to a situation where one is deeply involved in an undesirable position.

HOTSHOT characterizes an adept individual; an expert.

HOT SPOT portrays a place or situation that is intensely active.

HOT SPRING warns of an underlying anger.

HOT TODDY See alcoholic beverage.

HOT TUB signifies a need to ease tension.

HOT WATER denotes a position of great difficulty.

HOT-WATER BOTTLE advises of a need to "warm up" emotionally.

HOT-WIRE typifies an attempt to advance without having the prerequisite learning experience or knowledge (key).

HOUDINI (Harry) reveals an individual who impresses others through trickery; deception.

HOUNDS TOOTH CHECK (pattern) signifies delusions; perceptive illusions.

HOURGLASS reveals how much time is left to accomplish something.

HOUSE stands for the mind. See specific types for more information.

HOUSE ARREST indicates a need for one to remain in a neutral position.

HOUSEBOAT symbolizes a spiritual home atmosphere.

HOUSE BRAND connotes a tendency to stay with what one is accustomed to; a reluctance to expand one's experience or try new things.

HOUSE CALL pertains to an extension of one's generosity in regard to giving service to others.

HOUSECLEANING implies a need to get rid of extraneous aspects in life that clutter one's progress or perspective.

HOUSECOAT See bathrobe.

HOUSE DETECTIVE advises one to perform a mental self-examination regarding motives and performance.

HOUSEFLY reveals a negative aspect that has invaded one's home life.

HOUSEGUEST characterizes one whom you allow to get close to you.

HOUSEHOLD WORD connotes a commonly-held belief; easy recognition.

HOUSEKEEPER represents an individual who helps to keep one's perspectives in order.

HOUSELIGHTS portray one who has the attention of others.

HOUSE OF ILL REPUTE refers to a disregard for a negative element in one's life.

HOUSE PAINTER depicts a personal cover-up of some type being done.

HOUSE PHYSICIAN stands for yourself. You have the power to heal the negative attitudes and emotions of self.

HOUSEPLANT corresponds with one's openly displayed personality. See specific types for more information.

HOUSE SITTER alludes to someone you completely trust.

HOUSEWARMING denotes a desire to be liked.

HOVERCRAFT usually represents an out-of-body experience.

HOWITZER See cannon.

HOWLING relates to desolation; loneliness.

HUARACHE See sandal.

HUBCAP applies to the "center" of something to which the dreamer will relate.

HUCKSTER See peddler.

HUDDLED indicates a fear of self; lack of self-confidence and responsibility.

HUG connotes a desire to touch others; a desire to be close and convey same.

HULL (casing) represents a hard personality veneer.

HUM denotes a vibrational shift.

HUMAN signifies an "excuse" for mistakes or errors made.

HUMAN BEING See hominoid.

HUMANE SOCIETY See animal shelter.

HUMANITARIAN characterizes a compassionate and giving nature.

HUMAN RIGHTS imply an attempt to define and delineate inherent qualities.

HUMBLE PIE advises one to admit mistakes and take responsibility.

HUMID represents an atmosphere heavy with spiritual aspects.

HUMIDIFIER is an aspect that increases the level of spirituality.

HUMIDOR reveals a negative factor that depletes an individual or atmosphere of spiritual qualities.

HUMILIATION illustrates a feeling of dishonor or discredit.

HUMILITY usually advises one to give credit for accomplishments, even to self.

HUMMINGBIRD warns of frequent indecision; mental vacillation.

HUMP indicates a point in one's path where difficulties may arise and extra efforts will be required.

HUMPTY-DUMPTY characterizes a self-created (psychological) condition where one believes he or she cannot proceed without help.

HUMUS stands for a fertile condition or situation.

HUNCH portrays personal insights; psychic impressions. Recall what the hunch was because this will be an important message.

HUNCHBACK reveals one who is burdened with self-imposed psychological barriers and/or obstacles.

HUNGER constitutes an inner need; a personal requirement that needs fulfillment before one can proceed along the pathway.

HUNGER STRIKE implies personal activism; a sympathizer.

HUNG JURY relates to indecision, usually within self.

HUNTER may indicate a "killing of innocence" whereby one obliterates positive attitudes and spiritual truths or it may mean an individual who is "searching" for something important in life. Surrounding dreamscape details will clarify which meaning is intended.

HURDLE pertains to an upcoming difficulty the dreamer must experience.

HURRICANE warns of an emotional dysfunction caused by spiritual inundation. This means one has attempted to learn too many spiritual concepts without taking adequate time to properly absorb and comprehend each idea individually.

HURRICANE LAMP connotes preparedness for properly absorbing spiritual concepts.

HURT See injury.

HUSH MONEY See bribe.

HUSK denotes stripping away the extraneous aspects of an issue; getting down to basics.

HUSKY (dog breed) characterizes a strong friend or associate on whom one can depend.

HUTCH (furniture) implies that which we "display" publicly.

HUTCH (rabbit) warns against confining or hiding one's more innocent qualities for fear of ridicule.

HYACINTH symbolizes the "blossoming" of a new spiritual gift.

HYBRID portrays a blending of dissimilar aspects to create a new and fresh quality or effect. This symbol touches on the theory behind true Reality.

HYDRA (Greek mythology) characterizes a persistent problem that has many varying aspects connected with it.

HYDRANGEA connotes the utilization of one's spiritual talents in a generous manner.

HYDRANT See fire hydrant.

HYDRAULIC (system) constitutes an aspect in one's life that is capable of making advancement easier.

HYDROCEPHALUS pertains to an obsessive fascination with spiritual matters, especially the esoteric qualities.

HYDROELECTRIC PLANT symbolize spiritual energy and the regeneration of same.

HYDROGEN PEROXIDE is a symbol that contains duality, yet it most frequently refers to a "healing" aspect in one's life.

HYDROPHOBIA signifies a fear of anything spiritual.

HYDROPLANE See seaplane.

HYENA implies a lack of seriousness or a vicious nature. Surrounding dreamscape details will clarify which meaning is inferred.

HYGROMETER will reveal one's level of spirituality or spiritual comprehension. Recall what the instrument read.

HYMNAL denotes personal praise of God and our expressions of spiritual joy.

HYPE warns against excessive promotion of self or something one desires known.

HYPERACTIVITY cautions one to slow down; a need to conserve energy; a need to comprehend more.

HYPERSPACE pertains to a doorway to understanding the components of Reality.

HYPERVENTILATING advises of over-emotionalism; over-reacting; a need to gain acceptance.

HYPHEN indicates an aspect that serves as a connecting force.

HYPNOPHOBIA constitutes a fear of losing control of a situation; a fear of appearing helpless.

HYPNOTIST characterizes a manipulative personality; one who has the capability of easily swaying another.

HYPOCHONDRIA advises one to stop using psychological ploys to gain the sympathy of others.

HYPOCRITE warns against professing beliefs one does not honestly hold.

HYPODERMIC NEEDLE/SYRINGE reveals a serious need for one to regain inner balance. This may refer to any physical, mental, or emotional negative conditions currently present within self.

HYPOSENSITIVITY is a strong advisement to be more emotionally sensitive to others.

HYPOTHERMIA indicates a "cold" personality; insensitivity. This is closely related to the symbol of hyposensitivity.

HYPOTHESIS will usually come in dreams as a message that may bring solutions to specific problems.

HYSTERECTOMY represents the "removal" of problems that have caused difficulties in getting started on a new path.

HYSTERIA warns against losing control of logic and reason.

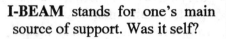

I

I-BEAM stands for one's main source of support. Was it self?

IBEX See goat.

IBIS denotes esoteric aspects to spirituality.

ICARUS (Greek mythology) implies unawareness and the hazards it creates.

ICBM (missile) pertains to a destructive force in one's life.

ICE signifies "frozen" spiritual truths, frequently voluntarily frozen by self.

ICE AGE represents an extensive span in one's life when spiritual matters are ignored or not held as a priority.

ICE AX connotes an attempt to "chip away," regaining one's formerly ignored spirituality.

ICE BAG See ice pack.

ICEBERG applies to spiritual aspects "looming" on the horizon of one's life. This is an attention-getting message.

ICEBOX See refrigerator.

ICEBREAKER (ship) is a warning message that tells one that she or he had better "break up" the spiritual aspects that have been frozen before further path progression can be accomplished.

ICE BUCKET portrays a "frequency" of denying one's spiritual aspects.

ICECAP relates to a hard spiritual "shell" one has created; a spiritual hardness that prevents the open gifting of one's gifts or talents.

ICE CREAM indicates the intake of spiritual aspects yet one doesn't externalize them.

ICE CREAM CONE implies spiritual aspects "carried around" but not shared with others.

ICE CREAM MAKER illustrates one's personal ability to generate spiritual growth yet rarely externalizes it.

ICE CREAM PARLOR applies to opportunities to share one's spirituality.

ICE CREAM SANDWICH connotes spirituality that is hidden by physical or material aspects.

ICE CREAM SODA implies an "effervescence" to one's spirituality but is not demonstrated to others.

ICE FLOE represents intermittent periods of spiritual frigidity; selective spiritual expressiveness.

ICEHOUSE corresponds with personality frigidity stemming from within the subconscious. These need to be thawed.

ICEMAKER symbolizes a "frozen" spiritual belief that there is but one way to God.

ICE MILK exemplifies a refusal to gain spiritual nourishment; a reluctance to admit to that which one involuntarily gains.

ICE PACK alludes to efforts applied to gaining spirituality yet there remains a small measure of doubt.

ICE PICK corresponds to personal energy put into "chipping away" at one's spiritual aspects that have been voluntarily hidden from view.

ICE SHOW demonstrates the beauty of bringing out one's spiritual aspects and utilizing them for the benefit of others.

ICE SCULPTURE illustrates the futility of trying to keep one's spiritual aspects frozen (hidden) in an unexpressive manner.

ICE SKATE connotes "skating" over one's frozen spiritual aspects. This is a clear message to unthaw these and begin utilizing them.

ICE STORM represents an inundation of spiritual concepts that one is not yet ready to comprehend.

ICE WATER suggests the intake of spiritual concepts that are a blend of those that are understood and those that need contemplating.

I CHING depicts a high interest in outcomes and the future; therefore, it also represents a lack of acceptance for *what is*.

ICICLE relates to a state of growing spiritual frigidity that has the capability of becoming so heavy it could "fall" back on one and cause personally devastating effects.

ICING See frosting.

ICON warns of misplaced adoration.

ICONOCLAST characterizes a spiritually destructive individual.

ICONOGRAPHY exemplifies a call for extensive contemplation.

IDEALIST stands for one who has high hopes yet lacks a clear perspective of reality.

IDENTICAL TWIN represents one's alter ego.

IDENTIFICATION CARD (ID) portrays that which one presents as his or her "exterior" self. Frequently this dream symbol will alter one's identity to reveal the "real" self.

IDENTITY CRISIS may come in dreams to correspond with crossover past life personalities that are beginning to break through the consciousness.

IDIOT usually reveals this characteristic as a message that advises how one is responding to a specific given issue or situation.

IDIOT BOX refers to that which wastes intellectual potential.

IDIOT LIGHT will usually reveal some type of guidance for the dreamer.

IDOL corresponds with whom or what one overly admires or is fascinated with. This gives a clear look into one's priorities and level of advancement, for no human or material object should be idolized.

IDYLLIC (scene or situation) represents one's hopes.

IGLOO constitutes a "cold" home life; emotionally unexpressive.

IGNITION KEY pertains to that which is capable of supplying one with proper nutrients that energize.

IGNORANCE is most often a warning to stop refusing to learn new things; a self-induced fear of knowledge.

IGUANA See lizard.

ILLEGAL is a warning of wrongdoing or of plans that are not in spiritual alignment.

ILLEGIBLE (writing) denotes mental confusion; perceptual dysfunction.

ILLEGITIMACY alludes to an attitude in error.

ILL-FITTING (clothing) connotes a free spirit or one who is restricting thoughts and/or expressiveness.

ILLITERACY warns of a condition of self-induced ignorance.

ILLOGICAL (aspects) indicate confusion or illogical thought present in the waking state.

ILLUMINATI reveal individuals in one's life who are, in reality, unenlightened. Nobody should claim absolute enlightenment.

ILLUMINATION reveals some important factor to which the dreamer should pay particular attention. This is a message.

ILLUSION will usually reveal a falsehood believed by the dreamer in her or his waking state.

ILLUSIONIST characterizes those who manipulate others or attempt to dazzle with their trickery.

ILLUSTRATION connotes a visual message specific to each dreamer. Recall what was illustrated.

IMITATING cautions one to be true to self; advises against emulating others or following in their footsteps.

IMITATION (objects) such as leather and fur convey a "preferred" aspect for one to utilize; however, if the object is something like food or original art pieces then the message is to "avoid" these.

IMMACULATE (condition) usually denotes an exact perspective with nothing out of place or focus.

IMMACULATE CONCEPTION will most often attempt to reveal

the accurate reality of this issue; "immaculate" in the sense of it being an in vitro fertilization.

IMMATURITY portrays an individual who is not yet ready for the next level of advancement. This could caution one against attempting to gain knowledge she or he is not properly prepared to absorb.

IMMERSION indicates a totality; a saturation; complete belief.

IMMIGRANT depicts one's voluntary choice to change something in his or her life. Surrounding details will clarify what this is.

IMMOBILIZED See paralysis.

IMMORALITY corresponds with one's spirit, the eternal life of it.

IMMUNITY connotes one's level and strength of personal methods of protection against negative aspects.

IMMUNIZATION advises one of a possible negative aspect invading her or his life; extra awareness and protective measures are needed.

IMP characterizes a recurring irritation. This indicates a need to address the problem for proper closure.

IMPACTED (tooth) indicates a serious need to "extract" some negative type of speech. This could refer to the verbalization of a specific attitude or belief that is causing harm to self or others.

IMPALA See antelope.

IMPASSABLE reveals a need to retrace one's steps. This will refer to a specific situation in the dreamer's life that she or he will readily identify.

IMPASSIVE stresses a need to express one's feelings; communicate.

IMPATIENCE calls for one to accept the proper timing of events in life.

IMPATIENS signify the frequent moments of joy that come into our lives.

IMPERFECTION may remind us that nothing is absolutely perfect in this world or it could reveal an error in one's behavior, situation, or perspective. Recall surrounding dream details for clarification.

IMPERSONATOR reveals one who is dissatisfied with self.

IMPETIGO emphasizes the need for balancing, most often a physical condition.

IMPLANT (medical) signifies a need to "replace" a negative in one's life. This may refer to a physical, mental, emotional, or spiritual aspect.

IMPLOSION reveals an inner fragmentation beginning. This is an important warning that indicates a self-destructive course is being set and will be devastating if the withheld negatives are not externalized by facing or openly expressing them.

IMPORT pertains to new ideas.

IMPORT SHOP portrays a multitude of opportunities to take advantage of valuable foreign ideas; being open to new experiences.

IMPOSTOR characterizes a deceiver.

IMPOTENCY means ineffectiveness.

IMPOVERISHED usually doesn't infer a financial meaning, but rather addresses one's emotional or mental aspects.

IMPREGNATE rarely pertains to sexual intercourse. This symbol will allude to one's success at "getting through" to another for the purpose of helping him or her in some manner.

IMPRESSION See imprint.

IMPRESSIONIST (entertainer) characterizes an individual who has the capability of "mirroring" others so they can see themselves as they really are. This would indicate a need to "see" self clearly.

IMPRIMATUR warns against censorship; a barrier to one's freedom to choose for self.

IMPRINT connotes that which has gone before; a sign of one's passing.

IMPROVISATION relates to an ability to cope; a quick wit.

IMPULSE BUYING denotes a lack of self-control.

INANIMATE OBJECT See specific type.

INARTICULATE corresponds to difficulty expressing self.

INAUGURATION underscores one's official "beginning" of something.

INCANTATION typifies one's need for spiritual trappings.

INCENDIARY (device) pertains to an "explosive" or fiery aspect in one's life.

INCENSE may represent a "calmative" or it can indicate spiritual embellishments. Surrounding dreamscape details will clarify which meaning was intended.

INCEST dramatizes the seriousness of a dangerously negative relationship.

INCH implies a small measurement that is usually related to one's amount of progress.

INCHWORM denotes a slow and steady progression or advancement.

INCINERATOR indicates the complete "disposal" of selective negatives in one's life.

INCISION symbolizes a need to "release" a negative attitude or emotion.

INCISOR (tooth) alludes to "cutting" remarks.

INCLINE See slope.

INCOGNITO reveals a disguised individual. Was this the dreamer?

INCOME rarely corresponds with finances; rather, it pertains to the "return benefits" generated from the spiritual talents shared with others.

INCOME TAX exemplifies required payments or dues. This usually connotes a karmic aspect.

INCOMPATIBILITY doesn't necessarily refer to a relationship; in fact, it most often will advise of a person's specific belief in something that is not vibrationally aligned with the individual.

INCOMPETENCY cautions against attempting to understand or take on higher concepts for which one isn't ready.

INCOMPREHENSIBLE indicates a concept or situation one isn't prepared enough to tackle.

INCONSISTENCY marks some type of discrepancy in one's life. Surrounding dreamscape details will help clarify what this is.

INCONSOLABLE defines a great need to feel loved. Regardless of why someone is consumed with deep grief, being held by another becomes the greatest healing comfort one can give.

INCONSPICUOUS refers to those "subtle" aspects in life that we often miss taking note of because of unawareness of our surroundings.

INCONTINENCE will not signify a physical condition in one's waking state, but rather it will caution of a need to use more restraint in life.

INCORRIGIBILITY illustrates a strong character; a refusal to be confined or controlled by another.

INCUBATOR denotes special nurturing care one gives to newborn concepts or paths.

INCUBUS warns against transferring aberrant psychological mechanisms to self-created (imagined) manifestations.

INDECENCY connotes a rebellion; a psychological need to shock others.

INDEFINABLE pertains to higher aspects of reality that we have no established terms to correspond with. Sometimes this symbol can refer to that which overwhelms one.

INDELIBLE (ink) symbolizes that which cannot be altered, reversed, or undone.

INDENTURE suggests a need to perform a "return" service for another.

INDEPENDENCE DAY See Fourth of July.

INDESTRUCTIBLE advises of something in one's life that cannot be undone or gotten rid of; enduring strength.

INDEX CARD indicates a need for organization.

INDEX FINGER usually implies an accusation of some type; also can indicate something to which the dreamer needs to give attention; or notice—a pointing finger.

INDIA INK stands for a need to get something better defined. This would indicate some type of "grey" area in one's life.

INDIAN See Native American.

INDIAN AGENT refers to a self-serving agenda.

INDIAN CORN connotes survivability; life-giving seed.

INDIAN GIVER portrays an ulterior motive.

INDIAN PAINTBRUSH relates to vibrant spiritual energy.

INDIAN SUMMER denotes a time of peaceful respite.

INDIAN WRESTLING See arm wrestling.

INDIGESTION indicates a situation or other aspect that one finds hard to "stomach" and represents a lack of acceptance.

INDIGO (color) signifies high spirituality.

INDISPENSABLE will define that which one "believes" is essential in life.

INDOOR-OUTDOOR (carpeting) represents a need to balance or bring uniformity to personal aspects that one holds privately (within self) and displays publicly (without).

INDOORS applies to the inner self; that which is private and rarely shown or expressed.

INDUCEMENT alludes to some type of personal motivation entering one's life.

INDUSTRIAL ARTS (study of) denotes a high interest in learning how to utilize spiritual tools (energy) to help others.

INDUSTRIALIST characterizes one who provides opportunities for others.

INDUSTRIAL PARK exemplifies a location where many energies are combining to generate specific outcomes.

INDUSTRIAL REVOLUTION pertains to a lack of self-reliance; a move that increases quantity and lessens quality.

INEDIBLE warns of something that shouldn't be intellectually ingested; a concept or idea that is negative.

INELIGIBILITY advises of one's lack of readiness.

INESCAPABLE reminds one to face reality.

INEXPENSIVE See cheap.

INEXPERIENCE underscores one's current level of advancement or personal development. This usually comes to a dreamer when she or he is planning on attempting to undertake research or an experience that is beyond adequate comprehension.

IN EXTREMIS reveals a short measure of time left to make amends, get affairs in order, or change ways.

INFALLIBLE comes as an advisement message. This underscores a validation for the dreamer who will quickly associate the symbol to some important aspect in her or his life.

INFAMOUS reveals a dangerous individual.

INFANT See baby.

INFANTICIDE pertains to actions that lead to the "killing" of a new path, direction, or concept.

INFECTION represents a harmful aspect in one's life; a negative factor that has the capability of being destructive.

INFERENCE implies forthcoming innuendos; possible new insight.

INFERIORITY COMPLEX represents a serious lack of acceptance in one's life; a failure to feel the loving essence of God within self.

INFERTILITY doesn't usually refer to the physical reproductive system, but rather it indicates a lack of spiritual fruitfulness; an absence of spiritual giving.

INFESTATION (insect) connotes a destructive force that has invaded an aspect of one's life.

Insects in air relate to one's mental or emotional state.

Insects in garden pertain to the utilization of one's gifts or skills.

Insects in house refer to the home life.

Insects in water apply to one's spiritual life.

INFIELD connotes "within" self; internal aspects; thought and psychological processes.

INFILTRATION warns of a negative aspect that has entered one's life.

INFINITESIMAL is a symbol that comes to remind us that everything, no matter how small, has importance in life.

INFINITY (sign) constitutes a neverending state; spirit immortality.

INFIRMARY See hospital.

INFLATE emphasizes something "blown" out of proportion.

INFORM comes as a guiding message and suggests that the dreamer communicate with a particular person.

INFORMAL refers to the state of a relationship or situation; congenial.

INFORMANT portrays an individual who possesses information or specific knowledge.

INFORMATION SUPER-HIGHWAY See Internet.

INGOT signifies materialism as being one's priority in life.

INGROWN (nail) warns of self-imposed pain.

INHABITANT infers viability of a situation.

INHALATOR See respirator.

INHALER corresponds with an aspect in one's life that has the capability of easing tension or problems.

INHERITANCE defines that which is "handed down" to another; what another has left behind for us to benefit from.

INHERITANCE TAX denotes strings attached to a benefit or gift.

INHIBITION corresponds with one's fears.

INITIALS are messages unique to each dreamer.

INITIATION marks a beginning of something the dreamer will recognize.

INJECTION applies to "new" aspects entering one's life. Recall what substance was injected to determine if this is a positive or negative message.

INJURY reveals some type of

harm done to one. Surrounding dream details will clarify this.

INJUSTICE defines a wrong conclusion or judgment made in one's life.

INK pertains to "recording" or marking so as to solidify or verify.

INKBLOT usually comes as a sign that something in one's life is amiss or not balanced.

INKBLOT TEST See Rorschach test.

INKWELL is a symbol for "writing" something down; a hint that points to a need for additional communication.

INLET portrays a spiritual pathway; a spiritual byway that can be explored.

INN connotes a resting place beside one's life path.

INNING reveals one's position on his or her path. Recall what inning it was.

INNKEEPER characterizes an individual who is capable of providing rest and comfort to another.

INOCULATION See immunization.

INQUEST advises of a need to fully investigate some aspect in one's life. There is something yet unrevealed.

INQUISITION pertains to an invasion of one's privacy. Usually this will be a validating symbol for the dreamer.

INSANITY implies a total loss of reality.

INSATIABILITY advises of an inner void that needs to be filled.

INSCRIPTION comes as a warning message. Recall what was inscribed.

INSECT See specific type.

INSIDE See indoors.

INSIDE INFORMATION most often refers to thoughts and insights that come as inspiration.

INSIDE TRACK underscores one's advantageous placement in life; a choice position on his or her path.

INSOMNIAC characterizes one who fights acceptance.

INSPECTOR stands for one's own Higher Self who acts as an advisor and guide.

INSTALLMENT (payment) connotes the gradual "balancing" of one's karmic debts.

INSTANT REPLAY advises of the wisdom of looking at something again, more closely. This indicates something was overlooked.

INSTRUCTOR See teacher.

INSTRUMENT (musical) See specific type.

INSTRUMENT PANEL portrays the "controls" one has in life.

INSULATION relates to one's personal quality and level of self protection.

INSULIN is a substitute for a vital aspect one needs in life. Surrounding details will clarify this.

INSURANCE implies protective measures.

INSURANCE AGENT characterizes one who has a predatory nature and takes advantage of others.

INTAGLIO is a sign that validates humankind's kinship with all intelligent life.

INTEGRATION rarely refers to ethnicity, but rather comes as an advisement to "combine" diverse aspects. This indicates that the dreamer was missing something, not including all possible factors associated with an issue or concept.

INTELLECTUAL characterizes one who has knowledge, yet may not have the wisdom to go with it.

INTELLIGENCE AGENT denotes an invasion of one's privacy. This is an advisement to be discerning when opening up to associates or friends.

INTELLIGENCE REPORT offers the dreamer valuable information she or he has been needing.

INTELLIGENCE TEST See aptitude test.

INTENSIVE CARE UNIT (ICU) is a warning to seek immediate help. This may refer to mental, emotional, or physical aspects.

INTERCEPTION connotes an interference in one's life. Surrounding dream details will clarify this if the dreamer isn't aware of such an event happening.

INTERCHANGE represents a decision regarding an upcoming change of course.

INTERCOM symbolizes inner communication between one's conscious and Higher Self.

INTEREST (bank) signifies added benefits gained through the sharing of one's talents.

INTERGALACTIC implies a beginning phase of understanding Reality.

INTERIOR DECORATOR characterizes an individual who continually attempts to change others. This could mean personality, opinions, perceptions, or beliefs.

INTERMEDIARY See mediator.

INTERMISSION advises of a need for a break from one's work or study.

INTERMITTENT CURRENT suggests indecision; vacillating.

INTERN characterizes an individual who has knowledge and is in the process of gaining experience.

INTERNET denotes information that's easily accessed.

INTERPRETER signifies a need for better understanding.

INTERSECTION See interchange.

INTERVIEW advises in-depth communication that will reveal more information.

INTIMATE emphasizes a close relationship; a companion; confidante.

INTOXICATED warns against losing one's total awareness.

INTRAUTERINE DEVICE (IUD) See birth control methods.

INTRAVENOUS (IV) comes to warn of a serious lack in one's life. Most often the dreamer will automatically know what this is.

INTRODUCTION advises of a need for new relationships or concepts in one's life.

INTROVERT pertains to quiet acceptance.

INTRUDER connotes an individual who disrupts specific aspects of one's life.

INTUITION corresponds with one's insights or feelings. This symbol comes as a message of validation for the dreamer.

INVALID calls for courage to continue on one's path regardless of adversities.

INVASION warns of a multitude of invasive aspects entering one's life.

INVENTOR characterizes intellectual exploration and creativity.

INVENTORY comes as an advisement to "take stock" of one's life.

INVERTED suggests a misinterpretation or misunderstanding; one has something backwards or upside down.

INVESTING doesn't usually refer to finances, but rather what one is "accepting" as truth and into which one is placing all his or her energy.

INVESTIGATOR advises to do more in-depth research.

INVISIBLE INK stands for hypocrisy; deception.

INVITATION means a request from another. Recall what the invitation was for. Who was it from?

IODINE indicates that which will soothe and heal. Surrounding dreamscape details will clarify this for the dreamer.

IPECAC is a severe warning that a highly destructive aspect has entered one's life.

IRIDESCENT comes as an attention-getting message. Recall "what" was iridescent.

IRIS connotes hope.

IRISH COFFEE exemplifies a life aspect that has the capability of providing balance.

IRON AGE represents strength.

IRON (appliance) advises of a need to "straighten" out a relationship, perception, or situation in one's life.

IRON HAND depicts an unyielding personality.

IRON LUNG is an advisement to be more independent; think for self; make your own decisions.

IRONWORKER characterizes a strong personality. Depending on the surrounding dream details, this may or may not be a positive sign.

IRRADIATION signifies an "altered" aspect.

IRRIGATION suggests a need to utilize more spiritual aspects in one's life.

IRRITATE denotes a lack of acceptance; inability to release negative attitudes.

IRS AGENT characterizes one who gains from the efforts of others.

ISIS (Egyptian mythology) emphasizes a bountiful aspect in one's life.

ISLAND represents a time to pause during one's spiritual search.

ISOLATION usually connotes a self-induced condition.

ISOMETRICS imply a conflict within self.

ISTHMUS See land bridge.

ITALICS is shown for the purpose of drawing your attention to something important you should be aware of; places emphasis on something.

ITCHING means a restlessness; calls for acceptance.

ITINERARY implies a "planned" course.

IVORY corresponds to the "value" of one's relationships. Recall what the ivory was shaped as.

IVORY TOWER stands for needed solitude; contemplative time. Rarely does this symbol refer to material riches.

IVY exemplifies bountiful knowledge; prolific creativity.

IVY LEAGUE denotes intellectual arrogance.

J

JABOT represents speech affectations; embellishments.

JACK (tool) denotes a life aspect that has the capability of easing one's burdens; lifting some of the weight.

JACKAL illustrates a predatory nature.

JACKBOOT See boot.

JACKET (book) will usually give a special message relating to the true perspective of something the dreamer is currently reading.

JACKET See coat.

JACK FROST characterizes one who could put a damper on spirituality.

JACKHAMMER symbolizes an individual's hard shell; a need to break open the hardened barrier behind which one has hidden for too long.

JACK-IN-THE-BOX implies insensitivity; an inability to recognize the more serious aspects of life.

JACK-IN-THE-PULPIT connotes spiritual expressiveness.

JACKKNIFE indicates impatience.

JACK-OF-ALL-TRADES relates to versatility.

JACK-O'-LANTERN reveals one's perspective on life. Recall how it was carved. Sad? Angry? Fearful? Scary?

JACK PINE See pine.

JACKPOT emphasizes benefits and rewards received throughout life.

JACKRABBIT See rabbit.

JACKS (game) pertain to the "pressure" under which one lives; this usually is a self-generated situation.

JACKSON (Andrew) epitomizes racism; genocide; greed.

JACQUARD (pattern) illustrates a complex situation or idea.

JACUZZI refers to comforting spiritual beliefs that soothe.

JADE (gem) alludes to healing qualities or talents; protective aspects.

JADED connotes weariness; worn down.

JAGGED (edge) implies a situation left with loose ends.

JAGUAR represents changeability; an altering personality.

JAIL reveals a state of self-confinement.

JAILBREAK defines an "escape" from a confining aspect in one's life.

JALAPENO alludes to a spirited personality.

JALOPY indicates a free thinker.

JAM (food) connotes a troubling situation.

JAMB indicates a situation where one feels closed in.

JAMES (Jesse) portrays an individual who gains from the efforts of others; a lack of personal responsibility.

JAMES (William) corresponds with deep thought.

JAMESTOWN (Virginia) illustrates perseverance.

JAM SESSION advises of a need to talk things out.

JANE DOE signifies a repressed personality; one who doesn't express emotions or opinions.

JANITOR constitutes a need to "clean up" one's act.

JANUARY pertains to a time of contemplation.

JAR often represents that which we "contain" within self.

JARGON indicates concepts or ideas that are beyond one's understanding.

JASMINE alludes to a mysterious quality to one's personality.

JASPER denotes a life aspect that has the capability of drawing negativity from the body.

JAUNDICE warns of waning strength.

JAVELIN See spear.

JAW pertains to the level of one's inner strength. Was the jaw strong? Thin?

JAWBREAKER represents that which depletes one's strength in reference to expending too much energy on "whole" concepts. This suggests a need to "break down" these concepts into their various aspects so they can be understood one at a time.

JAWS OF LIFE will correspond with a life aspect that can "extricate" one from a serious problem or situation.

JAY See bluebird.

JAYWALKING implies a tendency to cut corners; not always go by the book.

JAZZ applies to perseverance.

JEANS connote a nonconformist; a "relaxed" personality.

JEEP See four-wheel drive.

JEFFERSON (Thomas) characterizes striving for knowledge.

JEKYLL AND HYDE emphasizes a changeable personality; hypocrisy.

JELL-O implies anxiety; nervousness.

JELLY See jam.

JELLYBEANS refer to the small blessings we frequently overlook.

JELLYFISH warns of a lack of firm convictions; using one's "stinging" defense mechanisms to maintain an air of "free-floating" irresponsibility.

JELLYROLL connotes a frivolous, impassive personality.

JERRYBUILD alludes to a lack of integrity.

JERRY CAN relates to one's level of preparedness for life. Recall what the can contained; or was it empty?

JESTER characterizes a lackadaisical attitude; rarely attending to anything serious.

JESUS symbolizes a high spiritual messenger.

JESUS FREAK signifies spiritual fanaticism; an intolerance of another's belief system.

JET (color/gem) alludes to a deep mystery; high concepts.

JET (high-velocity) applies to a strong force; highly motivated; quick action.

JETLINER corresponds with spiritual advancement, the speed of same.

JETSAM exemplifies the extraneous aspects one needs to get rid of in life.

JET SET characterizes misplaced priorities.

JET SKI warns against "racing" over or through new spiritual concepts, thereby skimming rather than comprehending the depth of them.

JET STREAM defines popular beliefs or ideas; generally accepted and followed beliefs.

JETTY See pier.

JEWEL See gemstone.

JEWELER characterizes one who places a high priority on material aspects in life; or may symbolize one interested in fine detail.

JEWELRY (excessive) implies an attention-demanding personality; one who aggrandizes self.

JEWELRY BOX denotes one's collection of riches. Recall if they were more silver (spiritual aspects) or gold (material aspects).

JEWELRY STORE portrays exterior values that one may not necessarily hold within self.

JEZEBEL refers to one who tempts another into wrongdoing.

JIG (dance) signifies a moment of elation.

JIG (lure) connotes an unfair advantage.

JIGGER (measurement) depicts a small portion. The key here is to recall "what" was in the jigger. Sometimes a small amount of a volatile substance will be too much.

JIGGLE suggests an unstable condition.

JIGSAW denotes a need to cut corners.

JIGSAW PUZZLE indicates a problem in one's life and this dreamscape fragment may actually show the dreamer how to put the pieces together.

JILTED indicates a sudden termination of something in one's life.

JIMMY See crowbar.

JIMSONWEED emphasizes the duality or polarity of something in one's life; possessing positive and negative aspects, depending on how it's used.

JINGLING (sound) usually is a call to pay attention to something that's presently being ignored. Surrounding dream details will clarify this.

JINX constitutes an excuse. This implies a situation where one refuses to admit responsibility; using a scapegoat.

JITTERBUG (dance) represents a lack of direction.

JOAN OF ARC characterizes what can be accomplished by acting on one's visions (inspirations).

JOB (employment) reveals the dreamer's opinion of his or her work.

JOB-HOPPING cautions against instability; undependability.

JOB-HUNTING implies motivation; a desire to be productive.

JOBLESS may indicate a push toward being more productive or it may suggest a need to rest a while. The dream's surrounding details will clarify which interpretation is meant.

JOCKEY (any type) pertains to one who is skilled in maneuvering various aspects into their best position.

JOCK ITCH alludes to problems of a sexual nature, usually these are not physical, but rather tend to indicate a psychological source.

JOCKSTRAP connotes a need for psychological counseling (support) in respect to one's sexually-related attitudes.

JODHPURS symbolize selective arrogance. A high attitude regarding a specific subject.

JOGGING represents a steadily paced progression.

JOHN See bathroom.

JOHN (male customer) stands for the "source" of a negativity in one's life.

JOHN DOE See Jane Doe.

JOHNNY APPLESEED portrays one who spreads ideas; plants the "seeds" of specific concepts.

JOHN THE BAPTIST emphasizes a forerunner; a messenger.

JOINT (smoke) signifies a personal manner of calming self.

JOINT (union) alludes to some type of bond or link.

J

JOINT CHIEFS OF STAFF symbolize one's personal Advisor together with one's Higher Self.

JOINT VENTURE suggests a move to join efforts with another for a specific purpose.

JOKE will usually reveal something important for the dreamer, frequently about self.

JOKER (card) portrays humiliation.

JOLLY ROGER (flag) warns of a dangerous aspect in one's life. This could relate to a situation, relationship, or even self.

JOLT denotes a call to attention and sharper awareness. The dreamer is missing something important in life.

JONQUIL refers to peacefulness.

JOSS STICK See incense.

JOURNAL may indicate a need to keep a journal or it may reveal aspects happening in one's life that are being overlooked or not given enough attention.

JOURNALIST characterizes one who keeps track of events in one's life; could refer to one's Higher Self or those who "watch" us.

JOURNEY forewarns of an upcoming time of discovery or search.

JOUSTING applies to a personal combative state, frequently within self.

JOWLS relate to many difficulties overcome throughout life.

JOY RIDE warns of carelessness; a lack of personal responsibility.

JOYSTICK indicates "controlling" factors.

JUDAS (Iscariot) reveals misplaced trust.

JUDGE signifies decisions; one who can knowledgeably make a determination.

JUDGMENT DAY reminds us that all our life actions and thoughts will be one day reviewed and judged.

JUDO See martial arts.

JUG connotes common sense.

JUGGLER characterizes efficiency; organization.

JUGULAR (vein) connotes a vital aspect in one's life; that to which one is most vulnerable.

JUICE represents an "easing" factor in life.

JUICE HEAD See alcoholic.

JUICER refers to a life aspect that has the capability of producing a calming or easing effect.

JUJITSU See martial arts.

JUJU warns of a psychological aberration, particularly regarding the effects others have on you. This suggests a need to believe in self.

JUKE BOX alludes to that to which one chooses to listen. This usually comes as a warning to stop being so closed-minded.

JULY denotes a time for self examination; meditation.

JUMBLED denotes mental or emotional confusion.

JUMPER (dress) refers to simplicity.

JUMPER CABLE See booster cable.

JUMPING implies impatience with one's path progression or advancement.

JUMPING BEAN typifies restlessness.

JUMPING JACK signifies a lack of individualized thought; acting on the direction or thoughts of those around you.

JUMPING-OFF PLACE marks a "beginning" point.

JUMP ROPE pertains to being directed by others.

JUMP SEAT warns of gullibility.

JUMP-START symbolizes a renewed beginning generated through the motivational efforts of another.

JUMP SUIT represents one's preparedness to "jump in" and begin something new.

JUNCTION means a joining of forces.

JUNCTION BOX corresponds with one's mental analytical and reasoning ability.

JUNE denotes a time to review one's relationships.

JUNG (Carl Gustav) characterizes mental "reaching" to transcend current limitations.

JUNGLE warns of a confused spiritual state; schizophrenic.

JUNGLE FEVER pertains to a continued state of mental and emotional confusion.

JUNGLE GYM warns of a self-generated state of confusion and twisted perspectives.

JUNIPER signifies the "refreshing" aspects of spirituality and the living of same.

JUNK corresponds to the relativity of value.

JUNK ART denotes an altered perspective.

JUNK BOND warns of a high risk.

JUNK COLLECTOR refers to hidden values.

JUNKET signifies a self-serving act; selfishly gaining from ulterior motives of others.

JUNK FOOD warns against putting energy into learning unimportant concepts as they will not be fulfilling.

JUNK MAIL illustrates insignificance.

JUNKYARD symbolizes unexpected opportunities.

JUPITER (planet) refers to the Provider in us; caring for self and those around us.

JURY pertains to one's Higher Self.

JURY-RIG suggests improvisation.

JUSTICE OF THE PEACE stands for rash decisions; impulsiveness.

JUTE means a "rough" type of inner strength.

JUVENILE COURT portrays the "law" as it applies to a searching beginner; basic or novitiate philosophical concepts.

JUVENILE DELINQUENT characterizes one who rebukes philosophical and spiritual concepts during his or her beginning stage of discovery.

JUXTAPOSITION advises of a need to compare different aspects. The surrounding dreamscape details will clarify what the dreamer needs to analyze in life.

KABBALA symbolizes the higher esoteric facets of spiritual truths.

KABUKI (dancer) calls for a more frequent expression of one's emotions, especially by men.

KACHINA corresponds to our ancestral teachers; Starborn ones.

KADDISH reminds us to remember our dead.

KALE represents a personal need of some type. The dreamer will usually know what need she or he has.

KALEIDOSCOPE warns of distorted perceptions; vacillating attitudes.

KAMIKAZE characterizes a self-destructive personality.

KANGAROO cautions against overprotectiveness.

KANGAROO COURT constitutes one who is too quick to judge another.

KANGAROO RAT signifies long endurance.

KANT (Immanuel) illustrates one's ability to reason.

KAPOK denotes that which one uses to "soften" life difficulties.

KARATE See martial arts.

KARLOFF (Boris) indicates an individual the dreamer is uncomfortable with and somewhat fearful or skeptical of.

KARMA stands for making retribution.

KATYDID See grasshopper.

KAVA represents duality, positive and negative aspects of one thing.

KAYAK connotes a highly personal spiritual path.

KAZOO indicates immaturity.

KEA See parrot.

KEEL signifies the foundational and motivational strength of one's personal spiritual search.

KEELBOAT warns against the carrying of excess spiritual baggage.

KEEP See tower.

KEEPSAKE applies to respect and honor for one's memories.

KEG See barrel.

KELLY (Grace Patricia) represents hopes and dreams.

KELP corresponds to spiritual health. Recall the kelp's condition.

KENNEDY (Jacqueline) signifies inner strength.

KENNEDY (John F.) portrays leadership and wisdom.

KENNEDY (Robert F.) exemplifies tenacity.

KENNEL implies a "confining" relationship.

KENO applies to the taking of slim chances; taking risks.

KEOGH PLAN See retirement.

KERATIN depicts inner strength; that which generates strength.

KERATOSIS advises one to be more emotionally sensitive to others.

KERCHIEF See handkerchief.

KERNEL pertains to one's inner talents or abilities.

KEROSENE denotes one's ability to energize or motivate others.

KESTREL See falcon.

KETCHUP applies to elaborations; a need to "spice" something up.

KETTLE advises of something "brewing" in one's life.

KETTLEDRUM stands for a call to attention. There is something important in the dreamer's life that she or he is not noticing.

KEWPIE DOLL represents unrealistic expectations.

KEY denotes problematic solutions.

KEY (land) See reef.

KEYBOARD pertains to the freedom to "play" one's own song; indicates a suggestion to follow one's own path.

KEYCARD illustrates one's "right" to do something; having authority or permission.

KEY CLUB implies separatism; a specific chosen group.

KEYHOLE suggests an opportunity in life.

KEYNOTE (speaker) signifies one who is supposed to be experienced or have higher knowledge regarding a specific issue.

KEYSTONE defines an aspect in one's life that pulls things together and brings understanding.

KEYWORD See password.

KHAKI implies a regimented personality.

KIBBUTZ connotes community involvement.

KICKBACK warns against expecting recompense or monetary benefit from service given or efforts expended for another.

KICKING calls for acceptance; denotes impatience or lack of control.

KICKOFF marks a beginning.

KICKSTAND connotes the "stopping" and pausing points along one's path.

KID See children; goat.

KIDDIE RIDE alludes to immature aspects.

KID GLOVE exemplifies gentle treatment or interaction.

KIDNAP cautions against a thought or desire to possess another.

KIDNEY represents a "cleansing" factor, usually refers to mental or emotional aspects.

KIDNEY BEAN pertains to an "intake" of something that has the capability of cleansing or balancing self.

KIDNEY STONE advises of a "blocking" factor in one's life.

KIELBASA See sausage.

KILLER (anything) warns of a fatally negative facet in one's life. The dreamer will usually know what this is.

KILLER BEE infers a new danger from a foreign source.

KILLER T CELL means an avenger; something that eradicates a negative facet of one's life.

KILN denotes personal energy applied to one's advancement.

KILT implies pride in one's ancestral heritage.

KIMONO suggests servitude; inequality; suppression of opinion.

KIN See relative.

KINDERGARTEN denotes a beginning stage of learning or discovery.

KINDLING relates to aspects that exacerbate a condition or situation; something that will make matters more intense.

KINETIC ART alludes to the beauty of moving along one's path; making progress.

KING See royalty.

KING (Martin Luther, Jr.) characterizes courage to speak out against adversity and/or injustice.

KING COBRA warns of a major negative existing in one's life; an individual or situation that could be "venomous."

KINGDOM pertains to egotism and associated material desires; a personal realm where one proclaims self as king.

KING KONG characterizes an overbearing personality; seemingly unsurmountable problems.

KINGPIN corresponds to a major player in a relationship or specific situation; the one in absolute control.

KING-SIZE denotes a revealed measurement or quantity of something in the dreamer's life. Surrounding dreamscape details will clarify this.

KING SOLOMON suggests great wealth. This may not refer to material riches, but rather spiritual or moral wealth.

KINK implies a problem or setback.

KINNIKINNICK symbolizes bountiful and prolific gifts and talents.

KIOSK will reveal important information to the dreamer. This will be specific for each dreamer.

KIRK See church.

KIRK (Captain James) characterizes one who has the courage to explore the far reaches of reality ... "go where no one has gone before."

KIRLIAN PHOTOGRAPHY illustrates one's field of energy. Was it bright and strong? Weak? Flaring?

KIRMAN RUG (Persian) emphasizes wisdom and a high interest in knowledge.

KISMET means destiny; fate.

KISS pertains to a show of intention.

KISS OF DEATH connotes a fatal or destructive outcome.

KIT exemplifies the "parts" comprising a whole.

KITCHEN refers to the method of food preparation. Recall the kitchen's overall condition. Color. Style. Cleanliness.

KITE represents the effort one expends on reaching for inner understanding of his or her mental and emotional impulses.

KITTEN suggests an innocence of character; may indicate one who is helpless or at another's mercy. Surrounding dream details will clarify which meaning is meant.

KIVA illustrates one's personal manner of meditating. Recall the kiva's condition and occupancy to see if this is a good message or not.

KLEPTOMANIAC characterizes uncontrolled impulses.

KLIEG LIGHT is an attention-getting message that advises of a need to get some "light" on an issue or situation in one's life.

KNACK refers to a talent or skill.

KNACKWURST See sausage.

KNAPSACK connotes flexibility; free spirited.

KNEADING indicates time and effort given to something in one's life.

KNEE corresponds with adaptability; resiliency.

KNEE BENDS portray continual efforts applied to staying resilient.

KNEECAP See patella.

KNEE-DEEP stands for a situation of being heavily involved.

KNEEHOLE (space) denotes an accommodating situation or relationship.

KNEE-JERK (reaction) symbolizes a first impression or un-controlled responses.

KNEELING suggests a state of subjugation.

KNEEPAD indicates planning; good preparations done; foresight.

KNEE SOCK exemplifies protective qualities of self.

KNICKERS relate to immaturity.

KNIFE reveals a "cutting" off from some specific element in one's life.

KNIGHT characterizes an advocate; a champion of a cause or another individual; one who stands up for another.

KNITTING connotes planning.

KNITTING NEEDLE warns of manipulation.

KNOB illustrates a means of controlling something; self-motivation.

KNOCKDOWN refers to a destructive event or action.

KNOCKING usually is an attention-getting message for the dreamer. This means one needs to give more notice or serious attention to something in life that has previously been ignored.

KNOCK-KNEED pertains to a specific difficulty walking one's path. This unique problem will be recognized by the dreamer.

KNOCKOUT means impressive.

KNOCKOUT DROPS connote something that takes one by surprise; completely unexpected.

KNOLL indicates high ground and would suggest an upcoming need for more personal efforts to be expended in one's life.

KNOT represents a problem one needs to untangle.

KNOTHOLE constitutes a "natural" aspect; one that isn't covered or made perfect; the beauty of certain unique imperfections.

KNOTTY PINE connotes the attractiveness of simplicity.

KNOW-IT-ALL displays a lack of wisdom.

KNOWLEDGE is a message in itself. It comes to reveal specific information for each dreamer.

KNOW-NOTHING may know more than the Know-It-All. Those who admit they know nothing usually know more than we think.

KNUCKLE may refer to a conflict, frequently within self, or it may be relating to a need to apply self in a more serious manner.

KNUCKLE SANDWICH typifies repercussions forthcoming.

KOALA See bear.

KOAN symbolizes a need for contemplation; deeper analyzation; the exercising of one's thought processes.

KOHL See eyeliner.

KOHLRABI implies something in the dreamer's life that's difficult to sort out or understand.

KOKOPELLI characterizes an individual who easily compels others; one to whom others are drawn.

KOSHER pertains to the "proper" manner or process.

KOWTOWING can represent respect or it may indicate a state of subjugation.

KRAKEN (Norwegian legend) portrays spiritual fears.

KREMLIN signifies unstable authority; fragile power.

KRISS KRINGLE See Santa Claus.

KUDZU symbolizes a suffocating aspect in one's life.

KU KLUX KLAN denotes an attitude of superiority; separatism.

KUMQUAT applies to "small" needs that are as important as seemingly greater ones.

KUNDALINI illustrates spiritual energy.

KUNG FU See martial arts.

L

LABEL comes as a unique warning message for each dreamer. Recall what the label said.

LABELMAKER cautions against a need to "label" everything and everyone. Some concepts cannot be defined by a single term or cubbyholed.

LABOR (birth) See hard labor.

LABORATORY indicates a need for analyzation; self-discovery.

LABOR DAY celebrates one's personal efforts.

LABORSAVING (device) won't necessarily mean laziness; it may suggest a more efficient method of doing something. Surrounding dreamscape details will clarify this for the dreamer.

LABOR UNION represents justice in the work place.

LABYRINTH calls for patience and acceptance while one walks a complex path for a while.

LACE (fabric) may denote an aloof or extremely particular personality or it may allude to a sensitive and delicate nature. Recall other dream details for clarification.

LACERATION signifies a temporary setback; a slight injury to one's ego.

LACES/LACING represents a "secure" closure of something in one's life.

LACEWING symbolizes a method of getting rid of one's life irritations.

LACKEY characterizes a subservient individual.

LACKLUSTER See dull.

LACQUER symbolizes the manner in which something has attempted to be finalized. The key is the quality of the finish. Was it cracked? Shiny? Dull? Rough? Was there a specific color added?

LACTOSE INTOLERANCE indicates emotional sensitivity.

LADDER denotes upward progression being made.

LADDER-BACK (chair) indicates the need for a rest period before advancing further.

LADLE signifies generosity; one who is always ready to "pour" out his or her talents or abilities for others.

LADY depicts real femininity and quiet reserve.

LADYBUG connotes a positive aspect that negates the negative and irritating facets of one's life.

LADYFINGER (sweets) refer to a delicate or fragile situation.

LADY IN WAITING characterizes a supportive associate or friend.

LADY-KILLER implies male arrogance.

LADY'S MAN advises of a manipulative personality.

LADY'S SLIPPER (flower) portrays a possession of fragile natural talents. Those that must be nurtured.

LAGER See alcoholic beverage.

LAGGARD defines an irresponsible personality; a procrastinator.

LAGOON represents spiritual tranquility.

LAID-BACK usually will indicate a state of acceptance.

LAIR connotes the special place one goes to rest and recuperate from the stress and commotion of daily life.

LAKE suggests spiritual aspects in one's life.

LAKEBED indicates spiritual foundations; basic concepts.

LAKE EFFECT corresponds with the effect spiritual aspects have on one's life.

LAKEFRONT (land) emphasizes a need to be close to one's spiritual beliefs, taking daily comfort in them.

LAMAZE (training) symbolizes good intentions.

LAMB refers to God.

LAMB'S WOOL See fleece.

LAME defines ineffectiveness.

LAMÉ (fabric) typifies dream symbols pertaining to a "flashy" personality; a need to be noticed; a love of attention.

LAME DUCK characterizes inconsequential actions; ineffective.

LAMINATION implies a need to preserve something important; protection.

LAMP connotes "light" required on an aspect of one's life. This could refer to a relationship, an event, a situation, or even self.

LAMPLIGHTER characterizes those who light the way; bring understanding.

LAMPSHADE emphasizes a need to tone down the light on something in one's life; control the light's direction; soften the brightness so it's not so harsh and perhaps blinding.

LANCE See spear.

LANCET See scalpel.

LANDAU See carriage.

LAND BRIDGE signifies a path traveled with spirituality being to one's right and left; one who wants one's spiritual beliefs to guide the way.

LAND DEVELOPER implies the destruction of spiritual talents.

LANDFALL represents the end of one's spiritual searching and the beginning of his or her practical application.

LANDFILL reveals one's "covered up" negative aspects.

LAND GRANT exemplifies an open opportunity capable of fulfilling one's multiple goals.

LANDING GEAR signifies a "grounding" source. Recall if the gear was down or up. Broken? One wheel down and one stuck?

LANDING STRIP marks one's intended destination; an immediate goal or next stop along one's life path.

LANDLOCKED denotes a self-generated condition preventing one from access to higher concepts or advanced knowledge.

LANDMARK comes as a personal message for each dreamer. Recall what the landmark was. What state? Did it represent a specific historical site or time period? Did it pertain to a specific historical individual? In what condition was it?

LAND MINE reminds us to be always aware of the presence of pitfalls and setbacks that are hidden along our life path or spiritual search.

LANDSCAPE in dreams is a major symbol in itself. It sets the scene and often the mood too. Always recall what the landscape was.

LANDSCAPE GARDENER See gardener.

LANDSLIDE advises of a "backsliding" condition.

LANE connotes a pleasant phase of one's life journey.

LANGUAGE in dreams will add another dimension to the overall symbology. Foreign accents, biblical verbiage, obscenity, specialized terms, etc. all reveal clues to correct interpretation along with the "tone" of voice or mood.

LANGUAGE LABORATORY constitutes a personal effort to understand and fully comprehend higher knowledge.

LANKY usually defines efficiency; sticking to basics without adding anything extraneous.

LANOLIN advises of a need to "smooth" out some type of roughness or hardness in one's life.

LANTERN denotes more light is required on an issue or situation in one's life.

LAP (lick up) pertains to an eagerness to obtain something.

LAP (thighs) refers to a closeness; keeping something close to one.

LAP (track) connotes progression. What was the number of the last lap completed?

LAPBOARD corresponds with efficient work habits; keeping the process convenient.

LAP DOG is a friend or close associate who is overly eager to give assistance.

LAPEL will reveal one's quantitative ego.

   Clownish lapel portrays immaturity.

   Designer lapel signifies arrogance.

   Narrow lapel shows one who rarely thinks of self.

   No lapel denotes an absence of any egotistical aspects.

   Wide lapel indicates a large ego.

LAPIDARY (study of) represents a desire for precision; exactness.

LAPIS LAZULI connotes deep interest or research into high spiritual concepts.

LAP ROBE illustrates a desire to keep good relationships.

LAPSED refers to a voluntary omission of something from one's life.

LAPTOP (computer) reveals a desire to have information access at all times.

LARCENY See burglar.

LARCH illustrates a state of fragile balance one has caused her or his inner talents to be in.

LARD indicates a heavy coating; cover up or embellishment.

LARDER See pantry.

LARIAT signifies an attempt to "rope" something in; get a handle on it; secure it.

LARKSPUR implies spiritual talents that are generously shared.

LARVA reveals the beginning stage (gestation) of a negative aspect in one's life, possibly within self.

LARYNGITIS pertains to an inability to express oneself adequately, perhaps self-induced for psychological reasons.

LARYNX portrays one's expressiveness; whether or not inner emotions or attitudes are verbalized. Recall the condition of the larynx.

LASAGNA represents a multi-level relationship or situation; could also refer to some type of concept or idea one is absorbing.

LASER denotes consolidation or the condensing of multiple aspects into a single form.

LASER GUN advises of the wisdom to accurately target one's goal.

LASER SURGERY constitutes a step up from primitive thought or methods.

LASER PRINTER portrays a clear and sharp communication.

LASSO See lariat.

LAST (enduring) implies a perpetual state; will remain unchanged.

LAST (position) denotes an end to something.

LAST (say) connotes a concluding thought or statement.

LAST JUDGMENT comes as a strong warning message that implies one has little time left to balance his or her life.

LAST LAUGH signifies one's opinion had been proven out.

LAST MINUTE denotes a state of urgency.

LAST RITES rarely is a forewarning of death; it usually enters dreams as a strong warning to make reconciliations.

LAST STRAW advises one to become involved; take responsible action or intervention.

LAST SUPPER reveals forthcoming tribulations to overcome.

LAST WORD denotes a final opportunity to have one's way.

LAS VEGAS portrays indulgences; excesses.

LATCH See lock.

LATE implies a time expectation that is not met.

LATECOMER characterizes one who is slow to make realizations.

LATENT symbolizes the "hidden" aspects of self; those emotions or attitudes that are not openly expressed to others.

LATHE relates to a life aspect that has the capability of accurately "shaping" or defining one's self-expression or goals.

LATHER applies to confusion; possible frustration or anger.

LATITUDE usually represents some type of freedom; no limitations.

LATRINE See bathroom.

LATTICEWORK stands for one's defenses that are not perceived by others.

LAUDANUM See opium.

LAUGHING GAS See nitrous oxide.

LAUGHTER denotes a humorous situation or happiness. Recall who was doing the laughing. What was laughed at?

LAUGH TRACK reveals false happiness; an exterior presentation that differs from one's inner self.

LAUNCH PAD connotes a need to get something off the ground; put something into action.

LAUNDROMAT emphasizes some type of cleansing is required. Surrounding dreamscape details will usually clarify what this is.

LAUNDRY alludes to a specific item in one's life that needs cleaning up. Refer to specific clothing items for further clarification.

LAUNDRY LIST comes as a reminder of things to accomplish and not forget.

LAUREL (evergreen) exemplifies honor and praise.

LAVA warns of a personal state of inner turmoil. This symbol calls for a release of these withheld emotions or attitudes.

LAVATORY See bathroom.

LAVENDER portrays a gentle, comforting spiritual belief; spiritual wisdom and the peace it bestows.

LAW (study of) represents a high interest in societal perimeters. Frequently this symbol will refer to spiritual or moral issues.

LAWLESSNESS warns of a disregard for authority.

LAWN See grass.

LAWN (fabric) connotes aloofness.

LAWN EDGER implies a perfectionist; a tendency to attend to every loose end.

LAWN MOWER characterizes one who fears personal growth.

LAWSUIT pertains to a demand for retribution; forcing justice.

LAWYER See attorney.

LAXATIVE advises of a need to rid self of some type of negative aspect.

LAYAWAY signifies impatience.

LAYERED (clothing) doesn't refer to a homeless person; it indicates a preparedness for any eventuality.

LAYERED (haircut) implies one who keeps his or her thoughts "trimmed" thereby preventing an accumulation of extraneous, inconsequential factors; sticking to the basics.

LAYOFF connotes a "forced" termination of one's current work or path efforts; involuntary path setback.

LAYOUT (visual arrangement) most often enters a dream as a personal message for each dreamer. It will reveal a specific plan, solution, or condition relating to the dreamer. Was the layout confusing? Was it sharp and vivid?

LAYOVER implies a temporary setback; a delay in one's plans; a need to readjust one's timing.

LAZARUS (biblical) exemplifies the technical capabilities of interdimensionality comprising true Reality.

LAZY SUSAN depicts convenience.

LEACH implies a dilution or breaking down of something; suggests that one is too fanatical or zealous and needs tempering.

LEA See meadow.

LEAD (graphite) See pencil.

LEAD (guide) refers to someone who is capable of showing the way; guidance.

LEAD (lure) warns of being deceived; manipulated.

LEAD (metal) illustrates a potential negative aspect in one's life that could cause harmful effects.

LEAD (precede) usually signifies a messenger.

LEAD (primary) will designate a paramount concept, individual, or event.

LEAD (tether) See leash.

LEAD POISONING pertains to the harmful effects of a negative aspect in one's life.

LEAD-TIME suggests a need for more preparation; denotes a time extension required.

LEAF symbolizes natural abilities; natural talents.

LEAF MOLD represents the creation of a fertile or fruitful condition.

LEAGUE (association) pertains to a specific tie to another; having like interests.

LEAGUE (class) reveals a stage one is at. What level league was indicated?

LEAGUE (measurement) will correspond with one's level of spiritual attainment. A deeper depth denotes a higher advancement level.

LEAGUE OF NATIONS advises of an ineffective or meaningless title or representation.

LEAK may allude to a lack of one's protection effectiveness or it may advise of a loss of privacy or confidence.

LEAKPROOF connotes a secure condition or status.

LEAN (meat) refers to an absence of extraneous aspects. This may pertain to one's lifestyle or belief system.

LEANING (angled stance) reveals a "slanted" perspective.

LEANING (dependency) represents a need for some type of support system.

LEANING (propensity) indicates a strong opinion.

LEAN-TO See shed.

LEAPFROG illustrates competition.

LEAPING implies rapid progression; making great strides in advancement. It may also suggest a need to slow down in order to stop "missing" important aspects that require notice or attention.

LEAP SECOND advises one to accept the timing of events unfolding along one's path; don't attempt to speed things up or hold them back.

LEAP YEAR indicates an adjustment to one's personal timing needs to be made. This suggests that one is going too fast or too slow.

LEARNING will validate one's inner questioning as to whether or not she or he is progressing or acquiring additional knowledge. This symbol denotes an affirmative answer. You are learning.

LEARNING DISABILITY advises of a learning capability level. It counsels one to cease being frustrated or angry at not being able to understand certain concepts. It emphasizes the importance of operating within one's individual and unique framework.

LEASE represents an extension of time. Recall what the specific time was.

LEASH stands for self-imposed limitations. Even if someone else is holding the leash and attempting to control you, you alone have the power to break free. Are you "allowing" self to be controlled or limited?

LEATHER reveals one's manner of interaction with others. The key is whether this dream leather was soft and supple or hard an stiff.

LEATHER BACK symbolizes eternal spiritual truths.

LEATHERETTE connotes an ability to forge ahead in the face of setbacks or problematical situations; being able to utilize substitutes; creativity.

LEATHER WORK exemplifies one's individualized, uniquely personal manner of relating to others.

LEAVEN See yeast.

LEAVE OF ABSENCE alludes to a personal need for rest or diversity.

LECHERY reveals an individual who is not spiritually aware or advanced.

LECTERN implies a need to communicate.

LECTURE will be an individualized symbol unique to each dreamer. Recall what the lecture was about. This will have personal meaning.

LEDERHOSEN relates to perseverance.

LEDGE signifies a precarious situation or relationship.

LEDGER displays one's life debits and assets; a behavioral balance sheet.

LEECH signifies a freeloader; one who lacks self-respect and personal responsibility.

LEEK represents a counter force to negativity.

LEERING reveals an ulterior motive.

LEERY means distrust.

LEFT (directional position) characterizes diversification; a shift away from rigid, established perceptions or traditions.

LEFT-BRAIN pertains to a control or dominance over the establishment; a convincing power.

LEFT FIELD connotes new ideas; difficult to accept concepts.

LEFT-HANDED means ambiguous; perplexing statements or situations; tactless or cryptic.

LEFTOVERS advise one to utilize his or her total potential.

LEFT WING See left.

LEG denotes a supportive aspect in one's life. In what condition was this dream symbol? Was it strong or weak?

LEGACY constitutes that which we leave behind for others to benefit from or that which has been left for us by others.

LEGAL AID implies everyone's inherent right to justice.

LEGAL HOLIDAY See holiday.

LEGAL PAD indicates a need to make notes regarding a negative situation in one's life; note the chain of events.

LEGEND relates to basic facts or truths; referencing an actual event.

LEGGINGS refer to self-protective measures one utilizes while walking his or her path.

LEGION portrays a multitude.

LEGIONNAIRE connotes an individual who belongs to a large group; someone who has a strong backing.

LEGIONNAIRES' DISEASE indicates the presence of a potentially harmful negative aspect in one's life.

LEGISLATOR pertains to one who places restrictions on others.

LEGITIMIZE illustrates an act that rectifies wrongdoings; something brought into balance once again.

LEGROOM stands for a need for space; alludes to a "pressure" or stressed state.

LEGUME See pea.

LEG WARMERS emphasize a personal concern and efforts taken to insure one's progression isn't hampered.

LEGWORK corresponds with research; a need for gathering more information.

LEISTER See spear.

LEISURE (time) usually exemplifies the importance of taking mental and physical rest time from one's work or path advancement.

LEISUREWEAR connotes an informal situation or relationship.

LEMMING warns against a tendency to always be the follower of another rather than traveling one's personal path; a lack of individuality and/or personal thought.

L

LEMON constitutes bitterness or indicates a state of perpetual troubles.

LEMONADE suggests acceptance.

LEMON LAW connotes a life aspect that has the capability of breaking one's stream of consistent troubles.

LEMUR illustrates enigmatic aspects; difficult to understand situations or concepts; indistinct, ghostly facets in one's life.

LEMURIA (Mu) See Atlantis.

LEND represents assistance or helpfulness given to another.

LENGTHEN connotes an extension of some type being done or required.

LENIENT exemplifies forgiveness; making allowances.

LENS signifies personal perception. The key is to recall the condition of the dream lens. Was it cracked? Clean or dirty? Was there a coloration to it? If so, what color?

LENS COVER advises of a state of blindness; perceptual aberrations.

LENT warns against setting aside an "official" or traditionally designated time for self-examination. This should be a *daily* exercise.

LENTILS allude to time-tested aspects that emotionally or spiritually nourish.

LEOPARD symbolizes a resistance to change.

LEOTARD connotes perseverance; inner strength; a second skin.

LEPER pertains to strength of character; tenacity in spite of adversities.

LEPRECHAUN typifies hidden facets of spiritual development; wisdom.

LESION pertains to a life irritation that one has allowed to get under his or her skin; a lack of acceptance.

LESSONS come as a specific message for each dreamer. Recall what the lesson was on.

LETDOWN signifies a disappointment; advises against expectations.

LETHAL denotes a highly dangerous aspect in one's life.

LETHARGY most often reveals a depressive state; lack of motivation or faith.

LETTER implies correspondence needed. Frequently this will serve as a personal message for the dreamer. Recall what was in the letter.

LETTER (varsity) pertains to an individual accomplishment.

LETTER BOMB exemplifies a devastating communication or revelation.

LETTERBOX See mailbox.

LETTER CARRIER refers to an individual who conveys a message; a messenger.

LETTERHEAD connotes a message that points out importance. What did the dreamscape letterhead say? Was the lettering a specific color? Style of type?

LETTER OF CREDIT reveals one's level of responsibility. Was the letter a good or bad report?

LETTER OF INTENT signifies an insured or sealed promise; guaranteeing one's intention or an agreement.

LETTUCE represents the need to clear up a misunderstanding in one's life.

LEVEE connotes the purposeful directing of one's spiritual path.

LEVEL (ground) corresponds with a time frame when one's life path is relatively smooth.

LEVEL (tool) denotes stability and balance; a desire for same.

LEVER corresponds with an advantage.

LEVIATHAN relates to a great size or amount. Surrounding dreamscape details will clarify what this refers to.

LEVITATION implies personal efforts applied to one's advancement or development.

LEWDNESS reveals a lack of spiritual development; a preoccupation with the physical world.

LEWIS (Meriwether) characterizes fortitude.

LEY LINE portrays a field or course of flowing energy.

LHASA pertains to high spiritual aspects; acquired deep spiritual wisdom.

LIAISON indicates a "connecting" aspect. Surrounding dreamscape details will clarify this for the dreamer.

LIBERAL characterizes a freethinker; not confined by limitations or tradition.

LIBERAL ARTS symbolizes extensive general knowledge.

LIBERATION defines a state of freedom; release from limitations. Often one needs to liberate self.

LIBIDO as a dream symbol usually denotes personal motivation; one's mental and emotional strength.

LIBRARIAN corresponds with an individual who has the capability of guiding one's direction for gaining deeper knowledge.

LIBRARY relates to a multitude of opportunities to extend one's knowledge.

LICE reveal an unhealthy state of being.

Lice in hair indicates mental or emotional negativity.

LICENSE (any type) emphasizes one's credentials; permission; entitlement.

LICHEN refers to a fertile atmosphere; a bountiful condition.

LICORICE connotes mobility; a motivational factor.

LID (cover) applies to a limit marker; a cap on quantity.

LID (quantity) implies something that's within legal bounds.

LIE (untruth) reveals hidden facets of an individual; a concealed aspect of self.

LIE DETECTOR See polygraph.

LIEN represents a spiritual debt to be paid before further advancement can be accomplished.

LIFEBLOOD refers to one's driving force.

LIFEBOAT stands for something that spiritually rescues or saves one.

LIFEGUARD characterizes a savior-type individual in one's life.

LIFE INSURANCE advises of a state of fear; a lack of faith.

LIFE JACKET See life preserver.

LIFELESS portrays a lack of spirit; motivation; loss of energy or will.

LIFELINE signifies a life aspect that keeps one grounded; a facet that gives hope or acceptance.

LIFE PRESERVER corresponds with a second chance.

LIFE RAFT implies a spiritual belief that keeps one afloat.

LIFESAVER (candy) will literally make an implication of something needed to save a situation or reputation. It will denote a lifesaving aspect for the dreamer. Note the color.

LIFE-SUPPORT SYSTEM emphasizes an "essential" factor in one's life.

LIFTOFF denotes an activated beginning.

LIGAMENT defines an essential "bond" or connection in one's life.

LIGHT refers to good perception; added information; understanding.

LIGHT (weight) implies simplicity; general knowledge; easily understood or learned.

LIGHT BULB stands for a new thought; inspiration; sudden awareness.

LIGHTER pertains to illuminating factors in one's life; motivators.

LIGHT-FOOTED indicates a cautious progression; a reluctance to interfere in another's life; awareness.

LIGHTHEADED can refer to a state of being overwhelmed or it may indicate a frivolous personality who has no handle on reality.

LIGHTHEARTED reveals a state of acceptance in one's heart.

LIGHTHOUSE connotes spiritual guidance through wisdom.

LIGHT METER See exposure meter.

LIGHTNING signifies a connection with spiritual forces.

LIGHTNING ROD implies a desire to connect with spiritual forces; an active attempt to open communication with God.

LIGHT PROOF warns of a self-imposed state of ignorance.

LIGHTSHIP emphasizes a life aspect that serves to warn one away from destructive or grossly misleading spiritual ideas.

LIGHT SHOW sheds light of that which one should give attention to or something one should avoid. This is a call to attention or a warning, depending on other clarifying dream details.

LIGHTWEIGHT (person) characterizes one who is ineffective or of lesser importance.

LIGHT-YEAR defines a great distance removed from something; a long, long time away; sometime in the far, distant future.

LIKENESS applies to false appearance; something that appears like another.

LILAC represents spiritual purity.

LILITH (Hebrew folklore) characterizes a dangerous individual; a negative, pessimistic personality; one who cannot relate to others.

LILLIPUTIAN pertains to something of little consequence; trivial; may also reveal an inferiority complex.

LILY stands for innocence and purity; a new birth.

LILY OF THE VALLEY connotes naiveté; a lack of worldly experience.

LILY PADS indicate the fruits of spiritual work and expression.

LIMBER emphasizes tenacity; resourcefulness; acceptance.

LIMBO connotes a state of inactivity; ineffectiveness; inaction. It may also pertain to a phase when one remains in neutral until opinions or perceptions are well formed.

LIME (fruit) illustrates a negative emotion; bitterness.

LIME (mineral) See quicklime.

LIMELIGHT may reveal one's attitude of superiority or it may point out someone to whom one should listen. Surrounding dream details will clarify which meaning this symbol has.

LIMERICK (verse) although often frivolous, will usually bring a personal message to each dreamer.

LIMESTONE corresponds with a "foundation" type of belief or attitude.

LIMIT implies boundaries or restrictions.

LIMITED EDITION typifies something of higher value.

LIMITLESS relates to total freedom; permission to go or reach as far as possible.

LIMOUSINE alludes to an obsession with appearances; a preoccupation with self.

LIMP (flimsy) reveals a lack of inner strength; a defeatist.

LIMP (hobble) denotes perseverance.

LIMPET refers to one who gets his or her inner strength and nourishment from spiritual aspects.

LINCOLN (Abraham) represents integrity.

LINCOLN (Memorial) symbolizes all that one can be proud of in a people and nation.

LINEAGE denotes connecting aspects.

LINEAR stands for an alignment of some type. Surrounding dreamscape details will clarify this for the dreamer.

LINEAR PERSPECTIVE reveals a false perspective of time and distance. This indicates that the dreamer has a fear that a goal will take a long time to accomplish.

LINEBACKER pertains to one's "backup" or secondary defenses.

LINEMAN characterizes an individual in one's life who has the capability of restoring another's strength or reconnecting a line of communication.

LINE OF CREDIT See credit line.

LINE OF SCRIMMAGE marks a conflict demarcation between differing perspectives, attitudes, or opinions.

LINER See lining.

LINEUP connotes those associated with one another in some way.

LINGER may refer to a delay or it may indicate a persistent nature.

LINGERIE See underwear.

LINIMENT portrays that which soothes life's more difficult times.

LINING signifies an insulating or protective shield.

LINK corresponds with a "connective" factor in one's life. This will directly refer to a specific aspect in the dreamer's life.

LINOLEUM suggests a "hardness" to one's current life. The dreamer will know what this refers to.

LINSEED OIL alludes to "protective" characteristics one utilizes.

LINT advises one to get actively involved in ridding self of stagnating extraneous life aspects.

LINTEL reveals the strength or "rightness" of one's new direction. Was the dreamscape lintel sturdy or thin and weak appearing?

LION relates to a braggart. May imply strength of character.

LIONHEARTED exemplifies a courageous individual or action.

LIP See mouth.

LIPOSUCTION reveals the fact that one requires assistance in getting rid of the extraneous aspects in his or her life.

LIP READING typifies hidden meanings in what others say.

LIP SERVICE denotes false intentions.

LIPSTICK will denote inner personality traits. Was it a deep, dark color or a light one? Tend toward brown?

LIP-SYNCHING signifies a tendency to imitate the words or perspectives of others. A lack of individualized thought.

LIQUEFACTION (of soil) warns one is not on firm ground.

LIQUEUR See alcoholic beverage.

LIQUID See specific type.

LIQUIDATE suggests a need to unload superficial aspects in one's life. This may refer to emotional, mental, spiritual, or materialistic factors.

LIQUOR See alcoholic beverage.

LISP reveals an inability to verbalize one's thoughts accurately.

LIST advises of a need to remember details; infers forgetfulness.

LIST (ship movement) denotes spiritual imbalance.

LISTLESS may denote a lack of motivation or it may indicate a state of apathy.

LIST PRICE represents an opinion of worth.

LITANY suggests remembrance; may warn against an unforgiving nature.

LITERATURE will reveal an important message for each dreamer. Recall what type of literature was represented.

LITHE connotes tenacity; endurance and perseverance.

LITHOGRAPH alludes to an ability to keep different aspects separate in life.

LITMUS PAPER will refer to a life aspect that has the capability of gauging honesty or the rightness of something.

LITMUS TEST indicates an act of verification; concluding proof.

LITTER (bed) implies laziness or a disinterest in physical comforts.

LITTER (offspring) portrays multiple new ideas.

LITTER (refuse) pertains to mental or emotional confusion.

LITTERBAG signifies orderly thought processes.

LITTERBUG reveals an individual who broadcasts meaningless ideas.

LITTLE (size) will denote a small amount of something, but usually will also indicate "greater" importance.

LITTLE DIPPER reminds us that small spiritual works should be a continual aspect of our lives.

LITTLE FINGER relates to the smaller aspects of self that help to create the whole character.

LITTLE RED RIDING HOOD characterizes misplaced trust.

LITTLE THEATER connotes experimental methods of manipulation.

LITTLE TOE pertains to a personal aspect that adds to one's stability or the creation of proper balance in one's life.

LITURGY cautions against spiritual formality.

LIVE-IN denotes a surface association with someone; may extend the meaning to also include a "personal" relationship.

LIVELIHOOD won't necessarily correspond to one's awake-

state career. This symbol will usually reveal a hidden aspect of one's character.

LIVER illustrates fortitude.

LIVER DISEASE warns against giving up, losing motivation or faith.

LIVER SPOT represents hard work.

LIVER TRANSPLANT pertains to renewed energy and motivation.

LIVERWURST denotes a life factor that serves to energize or motivate.

LIVESTOCK See specific type.

LIVE WIRE reveals erratic, uncontrolled energies.

LIVING ROOM depicts one's attitudes toward daily life.

LIVING WILL signifies an understanding of death.

LIZARD connotes a lack of scruples.

LLAMA will correspond to one who has the capability of easing another's burden.

LOADING ZONE signifies a point in one's life when extra responsibilities become a priority to attend to.

LOAF (lazy) pertains to disinterest.

LOAF (shape) usually implies a type of inner benefit or nourishment.

LOAFERS (shoes) represents a lack of direction.

LOAM depicts a fertile situation or condition; bountiful "ground" one is currently on.

LOAN applies to a temporary stopgap solution.

LOAN OFFICER characterizes one who is capable of helping with another's problem.

LOAN SHARK reveals self-gain through negative methods.

LOATHING defines a personal aversion. This may reveal another's inner attitude that is not externalized in a public manner.

LOBBY (persuade) is an attempt to sway one's opinion.

LOBBY (room) refers to neutral ground.

LOBELIA stands for an emotionally calming aspect.

LOBOTOMY warns of a psychological aberration.

LOBSTER advises of a tendency to "grab" at any new idea or concept. This symbol calls for discernment.

LOBSTER POT denotes a controlling factor that curbs one's tendency to accept fad ideologies.

LOCAL ANESTHETIC See anesthetic.

LOCAL COLOR adds important clues to each individual's dream. Recall all the facets that were represented.

LOCK emphasizes a "secure" aspect. Depending on surrounding dream details, this symbol may reveal a need to "unlock" something.

LOCK (of hair) stands for personally treasured aspects of another.

LOCK (water) signifies an adjustment to one's spiritual level.

LOCKER relates to one's private aspects.

LOCKET corresponds to cherished relationships.

LOCKJAW See tetanus.

LOCKSMITH characterizes one who can solve problems. This person should be you. Every problem contains its own solution key.

LOCOMOTIVE See train.

LOCOWEED exemplifies a life factor that generates mental or emotional confusion.

LOCUST warns against something in one's life that has the potential to destroy spiritual belief systems.

LODE symbolizes a bountiful aspect or supply.

LODESTAR defines a guiding force or light.

LODESTONE indicates a strong attraction; a compelling force or drive.

LODGE refers to a safe haven.

LODGED implies a temporarily immovable situation; a time of inaction or neutrality.

LODGEPOLE PINE connotes that which one can build on or with; aspects that serve as building blocks or forces.

LODGER See live-in.

LOFT denotes high-minded attitudes.

LOG See journal. See logbook.

LOG (wood) suggests potential opportunity.

LOGANBERRY See blackberry.

LOGBOOK advises of a need to keep a record of events.

LOGGER See lumberjack.

LOGISTICS indicate a need to give attention to planning detail.

LOGJAM reveals mental or emotional confusion in association with spiritual beliefs.

LOGO will be a sign having diverse interpretations for each dreamer.

LOGOS denotes God's Word.

LOINCLOTH represents a basic need.

LOITERING implies a lack of purpose.

LOLLIPOP See sucker.

LONELY usually indicates a self-generated condition.

LONE RANGER applies to a desire to work individually.

LONE WOLF characterizes one who works best alone; one who walks a uniquely individualized path.

LONG (length) connotes a great measure of time or distance in association with an aspect in one's life.

LONGBOW pertains to directness; honesty.

LONG DISTANCE (call) advises of a need to "reconnect" with someone the dreamer has been out of touch with.

LONGEVITY reveals a "lasting" element in one's life.

LONG FACE signifies either sadness or disappointment.

LONG HAIR illustrates analytical thought; mental exploration; complex contemplation.

LONG HAUL relates to determination.

LONG HOUSE portrays an accommodating nature; acceptance of others.

LONGITUDE denotes a measure of acceptance or patience.

LONG JOHNS illustrate preparedness.

LONG JOHN SILVER characterizes manipulative arrogance.

LONG JUMP reveals an advancement; a great progression.

LONG-RANGE pertains to something that will cause extended or multiple resulting effects.

LONGSHOREMEN illustrate the utilization of one's spiritual aspects. Were goods being shipped out? Incoming? Busy dock? Empty?

LONG SHOT typifies the taking of a great chance; a small probability of success.

LONG SUIT corresponds with one's best quality; greatest talent.

LONG-TERM emphasizes a commitment.

LONG-WINDED stands for redundancy; repetitiveness; a tendency to prolong one's point.

LOOFA (sponge) indicates a need to perceive with greater depth.

LOOK-A-LIKE portrays one who imitates you; may reveal one's alter-ego.

LOOKING (behind you) reveals a sense of insecurity.

LOOKING GLASS See mirror.

LOOKING (down) implies defeat.

LOOKING (in) denotes in-depth thought or deeper curiosity.

LOOKING (out) refers to awareness.

LOOKING (over) exemplifies discernment.

LOOKING (past) indicates a far-reaching perspective.

LOOKING (under) symbolizes perceptual depth.

LOOKING (up) signifies acceptance and progression.

LOOKOUT represents watchfulness; a personal awareness.

LOOM connotes multiple elements that are woven into a whole issue or aspect.

LOON denotes mental or emotional confusion or convoluted thought processes.

LOOPHOLE implies a conniving nature.

LOOSE usually refers to extra "room" or leeway.

LOOSE CANNON illustrates unpredictability; irresponsibility; untrustworthy.

LOOSE CLOTHING signifies an open mind; open to new ideas.

LOOSE END corresponds to something that is left unfinished.

LOOT refers to a multitude of valuables. Recall surrounding dream details to determine whether or not this symbol is a positive one.

LOOTER indicates a lack of positive, individual resourcefulness; gaining from the efforts of others.

LOPE refers to a steady progression or advancement.

LOPSIDED typifies a dream symbol that means "slanted" opinions or perception.

LORE See folklore.

LORELEI (Germanic legend) symbolizes false spiritual lures.

LOSER alludes to a temporary setback; may refer to a lack of foresight or insight.

LOST alludes to a state of despondency; a time of self-doubt and insecurity.

LOST AND FOUND connotes opportunities and solutions.

LOT (land) represents one's chosen destiny. Recall surrounding dream details for further clarity.

LOTHARIO characterizes a manipulative personality; ulterior motives; a deceiver.

LOTION denotes a soothing aspect; a factor that smoothes out a rough situation or relationship.

LOTTERY connotes a tendency to take chances that have little potential for success.

LOTUS pertains to spiritual sacredness.

LOTUS-EATER (Greek mythology) reveals a spiritually unaware individual; an inability to perceive reality; lacking personal responsibility.

LOUD (sound) may be a call to attention or it may indicate unawareness.

LOUDMOUTH indicates one who must be the center of attention in order to feel any measure of self-worth.

LOUDSPEAKER emphasizes a message unique to each dreamer.

LOUNGE (room) relates to a designated time to pause or relax.

LOUNGE CHAIR usually indicates a lack of motivation.

LOUPE suggests a need for closer inspection; deeper analyzation.

LOURDES connotes misinterpretation; false perception; illusion.

LOUSE See lice.

LOUSEWORT reveals self-created problems.

LOUVER See shutter.

LOVE corresponds to feelings of great fondness; cherished.

LOVERS denote our loving nature. Recall what the lovers were doing for further clarification. Were they fighting? Loving? Strolling along a shoreline?

LOVE SEAT signifies a situation or condition directly associated with two specific individuals.

LOVESICK warns of a lack of emotional control; loss of awareness and focus.

LOW-BALL symbolizes an underestimation.

LOW BEAM (light) usually calls

for the need of more light on a subject; greater perspective is required for an accurate view.

LOWBORN denotes humility.

LOWBOY exemplifies a multitude of extenuating factors existing just out of one's current perceptual view.

LOW-DENSITY connotes conceptual simplicity.

LOWERCLASSMAN See underclassmen.

LOWER WORLD (mythology) See underworld.

LOW FREQUENCY indicates easily understood ideas.

LOW GEAR refers to a slow pace or progression.

LOW-KEY symbolizes a private individual; humility; one who tends to keep out of the public eye; a possible introvert.

LOWLAND denotes a relatively level path or phase of one's development.

LOW-LEVEL implies basics; beginning phase.

LOWLIFE reveals an unethical or immoral character.

LOW PRESSURE indicates a lack of emotional pressure.

LOW PROFILE See low-key.

LOW ROAD refers to deceitfulness.

LOW TIDE stands for a time for spiritual discoveries to be made.

LOZENGE calls for a need to correct one's manner of speech.

LUBRICANT indicates an irritated or rough situation or characteristic that requires smoothing.

LUCIFER See devil.

LUCITE connotes the preservation of integrity. This could refer to keeping one's beliefs unadulterated.

LUGGAGE stands for extraneous aspects one carries around.

LUG NUT alludes to extra strong protection or assurances.

LUKEWARM connotes a lack of enthusiasm.

LULLABY indicates something that tends to "lull" one into a sense of false security.

LUMBER pertains to any type of "tool" or "building" aspect that serves as a driving force for one's advancement or path progression.

LUMBERING (gait) won't necessarily refer to laziness or a lack of motivation; it usually commends perseverance and tenacity.

LUMBERJACK emphasizes a spiritually destructive force.

LUMBER MILL relates to the "shaping" of opportunities.

LUMBERYARD connotes the current existence of dormant talents and abilities in one's life. This is a call to "activate" them.

LUMINARIA represents spiritual celebration.

LUMP SUM suggests an abundance of something the dreamer will recognize.

LUMPINESS denotes multiple inconsistencies.

LUNACY may not indicate craziness; it may well reveal a mental state of Reality comprehension. Be careful to recall all surrounding dreamscape factors that have a bearing on this symbol.

LUNA MOTH alludes to spiritual insights.

LUNCHROOM implies a need to take time out from one's daily efforts to revitalize self.

LUNG connotes sustaining qualities; one's ability to "take in" and sort out the positive from the negative. Recall condition of lung.

LUNGWORT portrays perseverance.

LUPUS (disease) stands for repression.

LURE (fishing) warns of spiritual fads; misguided spiritual beliefs.

LURKING indicates a stealthy nature; underhandedness.

LUSHNESS denotes fertile ground to work from; multiple opportunities.

LUST constitutes a severe craving, not necessarily a sexual connotation.

LUSTER exemplifies a gentle inner beauty shining through, rather than a blinding brilliance.

LUTE portrays inner tranquility.

LUTHER (Martin) represents the separation of spiritual from materialistic aspects.

LUXURY doesn't necessarily refer to physical pleasure or material riches; it frequently relates to the inner feeling of comfort stemming from spiritual or moral fiber.

LYCRA See elastic.

LYE corresponds to that which has the potential to negate negative forces or efforts.

LYME DISEASE warns of internalizing personal irritations; a lack of acceptance.

LYMPH NODE represents personal defense mechanisms.

LYMPHOMA reveals an inability to defend self, usually self-generated by controlling psychological manipulations.

LYNCHING signifies guilt, usually self-guilt.

LYRE denotes harmony.

LYREBIRD emphasizes one's state of inner harmony; being at peace.

LYRICIST characterizes an individual who possesses strong emotions; an ability to express beautiful feelings.

$\mathcal{M}$

MACABRE relates to some personally unspeakable deed or situation; an appalling and abhorrent act or personality.

MACADAM See pavement.

MACADAMIA NUT alludes to quality inner nourishment.

MACARONI See pasta.

MACAW See parrot.

MACAROON denotes a beneficial outcome generated by a rough time.

MACBETH characterizes personal gain through serious misdeeds.

MACE (club) relates to aggressiveness.

MACE (spice) See nutmeg.

MACE (spray) signifies one's personal defenses against external negative forces or influences.

MACHETE denotes a forcing of one's advancement or enlightenment.

MACHIAVELLIAN exemplifies an attitude of using whatever means available to reach a goal or gain control; unethical and immoral methods of advancement.

MACHINE GUN reveals a continual state of anger.

MACHINERY refers to personally devised instrumentations that one utilizes to hasten or ease his or her path advancement.

MACHINE SHOP pertains to the creation of examples, models, or molds. Recall what condition the templates are in. What color? Shape? Are they defective in any way.

MACHINIST characterizes those who set the example and are looked to for guidance.

MACHOISM portrays arrogance and male superiority; an exaggerated sense of masculinity; an attitude of false power and ability.

MACHU PICCHU symbolizes ancient knowledge.

MACKEREL infers an unexpected event or development.

MACKINAW (coat) suggests personal security; confidence.

MACKINAW (blanket) suggests heavy protective measures.

MACKINAW (boat) pertains to a fresh spiritual search.

MACKINTOSH denotes personal methods of protecting self from spiritual fads; spiritual discrimination.

MACRAME represents twisted truths or convoluted ideas.

MACROBIOTICS cautions against extreme measures and advises one to temper the tendency to focus on one aspect; suggests wide diversification.

MACRO LENS signifies a need for closer inspection or research.

MACROCOSM implies the "entirety" of something. This will be associated with a specific facet of each dreamer's awake state consciousness.

MAD may not refer to craziness or anger, it often indicates a great difficulty or embroiled situation.

MADAM (brothel) connotes an individual who gains from the efforts of others.

MADAM (title) See lady.

MADCAP refers to one who appears recklessly adventurous; a reluctance to pay attention to warnings or possible dangers.

MADD (Mothers Against Drunk Driving) illustrates the powerful effects of working together for a strong purpose.

MADEIRA See wine.

MADE-TO-ORDER See custom-built.

MAD HATTER characterizes one who has confusing thoughts; disassociative ideas; impulsive behavior.

MADHOUSE denotes great confusion or intense activity; pressure and stress.

MADISON AVENUE applies to advertising; a need to share or broadcast one's ideas.

MAD MONEY corresponds with "extra" assets not designated for necessities.

MADRAS (pattern) portrays a casual attitude or personality; laid-back.

MADRIGAL denotes a "shared" opinion or idea.

MAELSTROM warns of mental or emotional confusion; an inability to focus thoughts or single out ideas.

MAESTRO characterizes one who is capable of leading groups. Recall if the sounds created were harmonious. Discordant?

MAFIA exemplifies manipulation for self-gain; strong-arm control methods.

MAGAZINE will connote a different message for each dreamer depending on the "type" of magazine presented in the dream. Recall if it was illumined or shadowed. What color was dominant?

MAGAZINE RACK indicates multiple opportunities for gaining information.

MAGENTA infers spiritual zeal.

MAGGOT reveals a self-serving personality who gains from the efforts of others.

MAGI apply to those who have

attained spiritual knowledge and wisdom.

MAGIC may refer to an illusion or it may stand for something in one's life that is difficult to figure out or understand.

MAGIC BULLET illustrates a solid solution.

MAGIC CARPET connotes a quick and secure method of enhancing or speeding the attainment of one's goal.

MAGICIAN characterizes false prophets and manipulative personalities who easily gain control and confidence of others.

MAGIC LANTERN denotes a need to examine something further; take a closer look at.

MAGIC SHOP advises of multiple methods of trickery and illusion available for unscrupulous people to utilize; methods of deceit.

MAGIC SQUARE verifies one's ideas or conclusions.

MAGISTRATE denotes an official authority.

MAGMA warns of internalized negative attitudes or emotions. These will need to be released.

MAGNA CARTA represents a guarantee of one's basic rights.

MAGNET reveals a compulsive nature; obsessive behavior.

MAGNETIC FIELD denotes a strong allure; an enticement or captivation.

MAGNETIC NORTH (MN) emphasizes the "greatest intensity" of something; strongest draw, force, or quality.

MAGNETIC RESONANCE IMAGING (MRI) relates to a need for close analyzation.

MAGNETIC STORM reveals a disruptive force or aspect in one's thought process; great mental and emotional confusion.

MAGNET SCHOOL pertains to an opportunity to gain from learning from an extensive source of higher knowledge; special focus on higher learning.

MAGNIFICAT reminds us to be aware and appreciative of our connection with God.

MAGNIFYING GLASS connotes closer inspection; deeper understanding.

MAGNITUDE (measurement) will indicate "intensity" or "extent" of something relevant to the dreamer. This could refer to a personal attribute, quality, knowledge, effectiveness, involvement, etc.

MAGNOLIA represents a fragile or delicate aspect in one's life.

MAGNUM (measurement) denotes a significant amount.

MAGNUM OPUS symbolizes greatness of creativity; a monumental work.

MAGPIE alludes to the absorption of insignificant or useless concepts.

MAGUS portrays one who has attained high wisdom.

MAHARANI suggests a dignified person; a lady.

MAHARISHI constitutes a spiritual teacher, usually someone associated with the dreamer.

MAHATMA defines a spiritually enlightened individual who lives her or his beliefs.

MAHJONG (game) implies a "right" combination is required. This will be a hint to a problem-solving resolution.

MAHOGANY (color) portrays an inner warmth of character.

MAHOGANY (wood) represents strength.

MAID See servant.

MAIDENHAIR FERN denotes delicate natural talents.

MAIDEN NAME will reveal something important about whoever one is dreaming about. There is much in a name.

MAID OF HONOR points out a placement position of a secondary importance.

MAIL (armor) illustrates the quality and strength of one's personal protective methods.

MAIL (postal) connotes communication forthcoming or needing to be sent.

MAILBOX refers to communication.

MAIL CALL advises of a forthcoming message or communication.

MAILER See envelope.

MAILLOT (fabric) implies honesty; no hidden aspects.

MAIL ORDER (M.O.) pertains to some type of "payment" made.

MAIL-ORDER CATALOG relates to multiple opportunities that are readily available and easy to take advantage of.

MAIL-ORDER HOUSE will denote an opportunity source.

MAIL PEOPLE See postal worker.

MAILROOM alludes to discernment in communicating ideas to the right people.

MAIMED denotes a temporary difficulty to overcome. The key here is "overcome."

MAIN DRAG warns against walking a road traveled by most everyone. This calls for individuality and personal decisions.

MAINFRAME emphasizes "the brain" aspect; the main source of knowledge or information; an intelligent leader or guide.

MAINLAND will usually represent a "grounded" state; one's home base.

MAINLINING won't always

infer hard drug use. This symbol will most often refer to a method or practice of absorbing conceptual information via the most efficient means; a tendency to recognize and accept the main truths of an issue or subject.

MAINSPRING relates to that which has the power; the energizing factor.

MAINSTAY symbolizes a main supporting facet; an anchoring idea or quality.

MAINSTREAM illustrates a widely accepted idea; beliefs held by the majority; commonality.

MAINTENANCE (work) advises of a need to "attend" to some aspect of one's life, perhaps an emotional or mental facet of self.

MAITRE D' connotes a person in charge; the head person.

MAIZE See corn.

MAIZE (color) pertains to a light-hearted disposition; optimism.

MAJOR-DOMO signifies a "preferred" assistant.

MAJORETTE See drum majorette.

MAJORITY illustrates the "greater" amount.

MAJORITY RULE applies to control held by those comprising the highest percentage of common belief or attitude.

MAJOR LEAGUE suggests a higher position acquired through greater experience and knowledge.

MAKE-BELIEVE may refer to innocent daydreaming or it may indicate a psychological condition of living false illusions; attempting to personally alter the truth to a fact or existing reality.

MAKE OVER pertains to an attempt to change self. This may be a positive or negative message, depending on the dream's surrounding details.

MAKESHIFT reveals clever innovativeness; self-reliance.

MAKEUP (cosmetics) may expose a false front one creates or it may indicate a need to address opportunities to enhance one's self-image.

MALACHITE typifies "healing" qualities or forces.

MALAISE indicates an uneasiness or sense of disturbance in one's life; a disquieting sense; often forewarns of an impending disruption.

MALAMUTE (dog breed) alludes to a friend or associate who has the capability to ease one's burden or quicken progression along a life path.

MALARIA warns against internalizing negativity; a lack of acceptance.

MALE CHAUVINIST See chauvinist.

MALEVOLENCE reveals the existence of multiple negative qualities or forces.

MALFUNCTIONS denote faulty functioning. This could refer to one's emotional, mental, spiritual, or physical aspects.

MALICE stands for a desire for revenge; intent to harm.

MALIGNANCY reveals a harmful negative existing in one's life or "within" self.

MALL (shopping) pertains to multiple opportunities available to one.

MALLARD applies to strong spiritual beginnings.

MALLEABLE symbolizes resiliency; a flexible personality.

MALLET signifies a life aspect utilized for the purpose of getting something started; an instigating agent.

MALLOW stands for broadscope natural talents.

MALPRACTICE refers to impropriety or negligence.

MALT (ale) See alcoholic beverage.

MALTED MILK implies a needed nourishing aspect that has to be enhanced to make it palatable.

MALTESE (dog breed) represents close companionship.

MALTESE CROSS indicates a specialized spiritual belief based on an ancient sect.

MAMMAL See specific type.

MAMMOGRAM advises of a need to examine one's recent expressions of compassion or emotional sensitivity. This also may refer to a physiological condition.

MAMMOTH (animal) corresponds with an overbearing individual in one's life.

MAMMOTH (size) reveals a true proportion of a situation or action; emphasizes totality.

MANACLE portrays limitations or restrictions; most often these are self-generated.

MANAGER characterizes one who organizes; an overseer.

MANATEE connotes spiritual largess; being generous with one's talents.

MANCHESTER TERRIER (dog breed) constitutes a friend or associate who protects one from negative personalities.

MANDALA is a spiritual sign that is meant to inspire or remind one of the beauty of spiritual expression.

MANDARIN COLLAR denotes personal restrictions; chosen limitations.

MANDARIN DUCK represents brilliant spiritual insights.

MANDARIN ORANGE See tangerine.

MANDATE symbolizes a command or action that must be followed, usually ordered by self as a means of insuring he or she stays on track.

MANDOLIN See lute.

MANDRAKE indicates a negative aspect in one's life.

MANE relates to cleverness.

MANGE alludes to the harmful irritations affecting a friend or associate.

MANGER (feed trough) See corncrib.

MANGLE (machine) denotes a need to "iron" out something in one's life.

MANGLED See mutilated.

MANGO pertains to a hardened exterior personality covering an inner sensitivity.

MANGROVE illustrates spiritual bounties.

MANGY (appearance) indicates a rough life that has been endured.

MANHATTAN PROJECT warns of a misuse of intelligence.

MANHOLE symbolizes self-generated setbacks and pitfalls.

MANHUNT suggests that there is someone you need to find; a need to seek out and locate someone special in your life.

MANIAC denotes a loss of reason and logic; a psychologically dysfunctional individual.

MANIC-DEPRESSIVE (illness) pertains to a vacillation between extremes.

MANICOTTI See pasta.

MANICURIST will indicate an individual who has the capability of "cleaning up" the reputation of others.

MANIFEST DESTINY constitutes an attitude of racial superiority.

MANIFOLD suggests the existence of multiple outlets or solutions.

MANILA PAPER depicts strong, firm communications.

MANIPULATION reveals a desire to control situations or others; frequently one allows self to be manipulated in order to avoid personal responsibility.

MANITOU represents a positive spiritual force.

MANNA exemplifies spiritual nourishment.

MANNEQUIN warns against apathy, unconcern whether or not one is being controlled or manipulated.

MANOR/MANSION emphasizes a pretentious personality.

MANSLAUGHTER warns against a tendency to be unaware; a devastating effect of being unaware.

MANTA RAY characterizes attractive spiritual aspects that may prove to be dangerous.

MANTEL pinpoints one's priorities in life. Mantels are a place of distinction in the home and usually display items of pride or personal interest.

MANTILLA connotes emotional sensitivity.

MANTIS See praying mantis.

MANTLE typifies a subconscious attempt to "cloak" one's inner feelings.

MANTRA portrays one's personal method of spiritual or psychological reinforcement.

MANUAL serves as a "reference" one relies on to double check his or her path progression; analyzation of one's direction.

MANUFACTURED HOME See mobile home.

MANURE (stable) represents a fertile situation or condition; an aspect "ready" for development.

MANUSCRIPT will most often connote an individual's private thoughts or detailed future plans. Recall who wrote the dream manuscript and what it was about. This can be an extremely revealing symbol about you or someone you know.

MANZANITA denotes a life factor that is capable of "cleansing." This dream symbol will signify the need for some type of cleansing to be done in the dreamer's life.

MAP comes as a personal "directional" message that will serve to guide one's path or supply other information pertinent to the dreamer's personal questioning.

MAPLE (tree) portrays current benefits or gifts that one hasn't yet recognized or acknowledged.

MAPLE SYRUP is a reminder to be appreciative of our needs that have been provided for in life.

MAPMAKER See cartographer.

MARABOU relates to personality affectations displayed for the benefit of others.

MARACAS are likened to the meaning of ceremonial rattles; they constitute a "clearing out" effort; a recognition of negative forces and the resulting act of attempting to repel or dispel them.

MARANTA illustrates nourishing "provisions" that exist for the dreamer to currently take advantage of.

MARASCHINO CHERRY defines a desired goal; an attainment; the perfect effect or result of something strived for.

MARATHON implies great efforts expended on an achievement.

MARAUDING See raid.

MARBLE (stone) refers to a "lasting" effort or aspect; enduring.

315

MARBLE CAKE pertains to an achieved goal that will hold its strength and form for a long time.

MARBLES (game) applies to immature competitiveness.

MARCH (month) signifies a time to begin activating initial steps toward one's desired goal.

MARCHING alludes to strength of one's belief. Recall who was doing the marching and the manner of marching. Proud? Weary?

MARCHING ORDERS stands for a time for one to leave something in his or her life behind; an end.

MARCO POLO characterizes adventuresome discovery time; a period when one should strike out and experience his or her unique path.

MARDI GRAS suggests it's time for one to openly express happiness or experience lighthearted freedom.

MARGARINE implies an effective substitute is available for the dreamer to utilize. This type of symbol will be personally recognized by each dreamer.

MARGARITA See alcoholic beverage.

MARGIN stands for limitations; staying within specified perimeters.

MARGINAL denotes a "questionable" factor in one's life.

MARIACHI (music) connotes carefree joy.

MARIE (Antoinette) characterizes insensitivity; arrogance; indulgent in excesses.

MARIGOLD comes as a sign of encouragement.

MARIJUANA is an indication to cut down on stressful situations; a need for emotional balance.

MARINA relates to spiritual associates or friends; spiritual camaraderie.

MARINARA (sauce) implies a "spicy" aspect to a situation; the addition of an interesting facet.

MARINATE symbolizes a need to let something "rest" for a time; a need to "absorb" all details or aspects of something.

MARINE LIFE See specific types.

MARINER characterizes one who is on a spiritual search or quest.

MARIONETTE is likened to a person who lacks personal responsibility or thought; no expression of individuality; lacking self-confidence.

MARIPOSA LILY represents hope.

MARJORAM alludes to a "delicate" aspect; a fragile situation.

MARKDOWN (price) indicates that something one needs in life is just as valuable but now is more accessible.

MARKER (pen) denotes a need to note or emphasize something. Recall what was being written or singled out with the marker. Who was using the marker?

MARKER (sign) will usually designate a personal message for each dreamer.

MARKER (token) represents an asset owned.

MARKET (sell) refers to an attempt to convince others of something's benefit or value.

MARKET (shop) relates to available opportunities; choices.

MARKET RESEARCH calls for a comparison; a hard look at priorities.

MARKET VALUE in dreams will usually reveal what something is "really" worth; will rarely indicate an inflated value.

MARKSWOMAN characterizes an individual who has the skill of "being on target" most of the time.

MARKUP emphasizes an inflated value of something.

MARLIN corresponds with spiritual focus; centered spiritual attention.

MARMALADE See preserves.

MARMOSET See monkey.

MARMOT signifies insecurities; a lack of self-confidence.

MAROON (color) relates to having spiritual depth; insights.

MAROONED reveals a self-imposed state of remoteness; willful distance from others.

MARQUEE almost always brings an important message for the dreamer. Recall what the marquee said.

MARQUETRY denotes intricate details; an attention to fine and complex concepts or situations.

MARQUISE (shape) connotes duality; perhaps even a Catch-22 situation.

MARQUISETTE (fabric) typifies a "transparent" personality or situation.

MARRIAGE See wedding.

MARRIAGE LICENSE suggests one's plans to commit to something in the near future.

MARROW See bone marrow.

MARS (planet) refers to the warrior within; inner strength; fortitude.

MARSEILLE (fabric) pertains to an emphasis needed. Recall what the raised area of the fabric was shaped like.

MARSH constitutes spiritually saturated ground one is walking on.

MARSHAL characterizes authority, usually one's Higher Self; one's conscience.

MARSH ELDER alludes to gifts of the spirit; spiritual talents.

MARSH GAS connotes heavy spiritual contemplation; fermenting ideas.

MARSHMALLOW relates to an abundance of spiritual gifts.

MARSH MARIGOLD brings spiritual encouragement.

MARTIAL ARTS represent multiple opportunities and methods of defending oneself.

MARTIAL LAW emphasizes the importance of "order" in one's life.

MARTIAN brings a subconscious subject or fear to the forefront.

MARTIN See swallow.

MARTINI See alcoholic beverage.

MARTYR characterizes one's psychological belief of being persecuted; paranoia.

MARY JANE See marijuana.

MARY MAGDALENE symbolizes spiritual companionship; unconditional love.

MARZIPAN denotes an unrecognized benefit or reward; a positive aspect in disguise.

MASCARA applies to an "emphasis" expressed or required.

MASCOT portrays a supporter; one who provides encouragement.

MASH (pulpy mixture) represents an incomprehensible concept or situation.

MASHED exemplifies a destroyed factor in one's life; something that is not capable of being reconstituted.

MASHER (man) characterizes a lack of respect for women.

MASK connotes hypocrisy; may reveal one's true character that is kept hidden.

MASKING TAPE pertains to an attention to detail; an ability to keep differing aspects separate.

MASOCHISM reveals a self-abusive individual.

MASON indicates a person with strong foundational beliefs.

MASON-DIXON LINE denotes a firm difference of opinion; a strong line one won't cross.

MASON JAR relates a message to "preserve" something important in one's life.

MASONRY reflects solid work; strong foundations.

MASQUERADE illustrates deceit. Recall who you or someone you recognized was dressed as. This is a very revealing message.

MASSACRE represents a grave misdeed done or forthcoming.

MASSAGE suggests a need to "work out" an internalized problem or negative.

MASSAGE PARLOR may warn of ulterior motives or healthful benefits depending on the other dreamscape aspects.

MASSEUSE depicts one who is capable of easing one's withheld stress.

MASS-MARKET implies something that is widely known or available.

MASS PRODUCTION pertains to a great quantity.

MAST See pole.

MASTABA advises of the wisdom of preserving and protecting truths.

MASTECTOMY reveals a fear of heart pain.

MASTER connotes proficiency or one who holds control.

MASTER KEY See passkey.

MASTERMIND refers to a highly intelligent person; one capable of complex analyzation or planning.

MASTER OF CEREMONIES will point to the person who directs operations or ensures efficiency.

MASTERPIECE pertains to excellence; near perfection.

MASTER'S DEGREE emphasizes higher learning; greater efforts applied to gaining knowledge.

MASTHEAD will reveal a name

or purpose. This constitutes a personal message for each dreamer.

MASTIFF (dog breed) refers to gentleness; a tame personality or situation.

MASTODON signifies an "overwhelming" situation or idea.

MASTURBATION reveals a subconscious desire to rid self of repressed emotions, attitudes, or other types of psychologically damaging factors.

MAT (pad) denotes an insulating quality or a means of protection.

MAT (tangle) signifies confusion.

MATADOR connotes a tempting of fate; seeking admiration through foolhardy means; false bravery.

MATCH (contest) implies competitiveness.

MATCH (lighter) will indicate a potentially explosive aspect in one's life.

MATCH (pair) suggests compatibility; equality.

MATCHLESS constitutes a lack of energy or motivation; an inability to incite interest.

MATCHMAKER pertains to a person who is capable of organization, bringing things together.

MATCH POINT symbolizes a "winning" effort or move.

MATCH UP represents comparable, nearly equal skills or level of development.

MATERIALISM reveals misplaced priorities.

MATERNITY WARD exemplifies a prime time to begin a new direction or new belief; fertile ground for nurturing new ideas.

MATHEMATICIAN will indicate a person in one's life who can offer solutions; one who can figure things out.

MATHEMATICS (study of) illustrates a high interest in analyzation, discovering interconnectedness.

MATINEE indicates a suggestion to take time out from one's workday to alleviate stressful situations.

MATRIARCH signifies a woman of wisdom who is chosen to lead others.

MATRICULATE connotes one who is accepted.

MATRIX portrays an identified "pattern" to something in one's life.

MATRON characterizes an experienced female elder.

MATTE (finish) suggests subtlety; refinement; avoidance of flashiness.

MATTE (frame) portrays individual traits or preferences; will reveal clues into one's hidden qualities.

MATTRESS will reveal one's manner and quality of rest. Recall the condition and color of the dream mattress. Hard or soft? Lumpy?

MATTRESS PAD represents a personal interest in the quality of one's rest; rejuvenation is important.

MAUL (overcome) defines an "overwhelming" aspect in one's life.

MAUL (tool) denotes the utilization of strength-producing aspects; intelligent use of available assistance.

MAUSOLEUM typifies buried memories or thoughts; hurtful memories locked away in the mind's dark vault.

MAUVE (color) implies a spiritual lightheartedness.

MAVERICK characterizes an open nonconformist; one who takes joy in living life "her" way.

MAXIMALIST symbolizes a person who advocates taking an issue to its full extension; a tendency to maximize opportunities or talents.

MAY (month) relates to the time to experience spiritual joy; rejoice in one's beliefs.

MAYANS warn of the devastating effects of a people being spiritually influenced by a dark, negative force; the dark side of spiritual power.

M

MAY DAY suggests a time of New Birth celebration; rejoice in Grandmother Earth's blossoming gifts to humankind.

MAYDAY (signal) connotes a severe "warning" message for the dreamer. Surrounding dreamscape details will pinpoint this warning.

MAYFLOWER (ship) stands for opportunities and "how" one takes advantage of them. This symbol is a type of advisement to utilize opportunities in positive ways. Opportunities can soon turn against you if they are used in any kind of negative manner.

MAYONNAISE relates to the utilization of positive aspects to aid in attaining a nourishing aspect or goal in life.

MAYOR usually represents one's Higher Self or conscience.

MAZE may illustrate a type of mental or emotional confusion, but it most often corresponds with the unnecessarily "complex" manner one is going about his or her life path.

MAZURKA connotes the outward expression of great joy.

MEAD See alcoholic beverage.

MEAD (Margaret) pertains to knowledge gained through observation.

MEADOW represents inner tranquility.

MEAL (grain) applies to "coarse" lessons that provide nourishment.

MEAL TICKET reveals a dependency on others to provide for self.

MEALWORM warns of a dangerously negative factor that has infiltrated that from which one is taking nourishment.

MEANDER (stream) means an aimless spiritual path.

MEASLES warn of the act of internalizing negative feelings.

MEAT refers to solid basics; highly nourishing elements.

MEAT AND POTATOES connote a preference for the "basics" or prime factors of an issue.

MEATBALLS indicate irrationality; times one loses sight of reason.

MEAT CLEAVER See cleaver.

MEAT HOOK denotes an aggressive nature; intrusiveness.

MEAT LOAF represents the "combining" of basic ideas.

MEATPACKING HOUSE illustrates the "quality" of foundational concepts of basic ideas one ingests. Recall the condition of the place. Was it clean? Were there rodents or bugs?

MEAT TENDERIZER alludes to one's special need to "soften" the hard facts one wants to believe; make them more palatable.

MECCA signifies a greatly desired goal or attainment.

MECHANIC characterizes one who is capable of "repairing" a dysfunction or negative in another's life.

MECHANICAL pertains to a lack of thought or personal input.

MEDAL is a sign of encouragement or commendation from one's Higher Self or conscience.

MEDALLION stands for a self-confirming sign; verification.

MEDAL OF HONOR pertains to personal benefits; inner joy as a result of ethical or spiritual deeds done.

MEDDLESOME applies to an interference by another; perhaps it was by the dreamer.

MEDEVAC advises of an immediate need for emotional or psychological help.

MEDIA EVENT defines a gravely important situation or issue needing one's attention.

MEDIAN STRIP represents a guideline along one's path; a protective measure that lets one know when he or she is making a reversal or backsliding.

MEDIATOR signifies an urgent need for assistance with a personal relationship.

MEDIC characterizes an individual in one's life who has the knowledge and skill to "repair" a

negative aspect within another.

MEDICAL BUILDING emphasizes a need for some type of personal care or healing.

MEDICAL EXAMINER (ME) characterizes one who is capable of pinpointing the source or cause of a problem.

MEDICARE applies to a dependence on others to protect you against future negative aspects.

MEDICATION connotes "external" solutions rather than working from within.

MEDICINE BALL denotes efforts given to strengthening one's inner self.

MEDICINE BUNDLE corresponds to one's personal inner power.

MEDICINE CHEST will reveal what one needs to cure an ill or it will display an excess that one is taking. Recall surrounding dream details for clarification.

MEDICINE PIPE emphasizes a sealed bond and good intentions.

MEDICINE SHOW reveals false cures or solutions.

MEDICINE WOMAN characterizes one who has the knowledge and skill to heal.

MEDIEVAL usually denotes a lack of intellectual reasoning; however, it may also refer to a past life experience, depending on surrounding details.

MEDITATION will advise one to be passive. This comes when one has been too active in something.

MEDIUM (amount) implies average; middle-of-the-road; neutral.

MEDIUM (art) alludes to quality or manner of self-expression. See specific type such as ink, oil, paint, etc.

MEDIUM (psychic) connotes the "connective link" between the conscious mind and one's Higher Self.

MEDLEY signifies a harmonic blend of ideas.

MEDUSA (Greek mythology) comes as a strong warning to straighten up one's thoughts before they become dangerous.

MEERSCHAUM (pipe) illustrates an analytical mind; reason and wisdom.

MEETING suggests a need for open communication.

MEETINGHOUSE represents shared ideas.

MEGALITH pertains to ancient truths that remain valid today.

MEGALOMANIA warns of misplaced priorities; a lack of enlightenment.

MEGAPHONE can be an advisement that one is not being heard or it can indicate a message unique to each dreamer depending on "who" is using the object.

ME GENERATION will warn against arrogance and selfishness.

MELANCHOLIA denotes a lack of acceptance; self pity.

MELANOMA See malignancy.

MELBA TOAST implies a strong character.

MELD See merger.

MELLOW relates to a state of acceptance.

MELODRAMA represents gross exaggerations; emotional manipulation.

MELODY may bring a message via a recognized "title" of the tune or it could connote a harmonic aspect in one's life. Surrounding dream details will distinguish which interpretation is intended.

MELON symbolizes inner nourishment obtained through personal efforts.

MELTDOWN reveals an absolute failure or collapse of something in one's life.

MELTING may refer to a need for some type of "softening" to be done or it may indicate a loss of definition (uniqueness or purity). Surrounding dream factors will clarify which meaning was intended.

MELTING POT will usually advise of the negative situation caused by "blurring" or confusing concepts or issues.

MEMENTO reminds us what should be kept as important aspects in life.

MEMOIR comes as a prompting to record one's life events and remember same. By doing this, one usually has some type of revelation.

MEMORABILIA will define a specific interest; may refer to a past life.

MEMORANDUM is a call to "remember" something important; may be a new revelation for the dreamer.

MEMORIAL brings a special message for each dreamer. Who or what was the memorial for?

MEMORIAL DAY may pinpoint a specific time for the dreamer or it may signify a need to give personal attention to courage.

MEMORIZING stands for a need to learn or remember something important.

MENACE reveals a harmful aspect in one's life. Recall who or what the menace was. Was it yourself?

MENAGERIE denotes a great assortment of something. Usually this refers to benefits gained from a "wide" search; utilizing multiple sources.

MENDICANT implies efforts expended for others.

MENDING (sewing) typifies an interest in repairing torn or broken relationships.

MENHIR See megalith.

MENIAL (work) symbolizes acceptance and humility.

MENOPAUSE defines a life or path change.

MENORAH reminds us of our beginnings; eternal spirits temporarily borrowing humanoid forms.

MENSWEAR See specific type.

MENTAL BREAKDOWN denotes a lack of acceptance; an inability to cope with reality.

MENTAL HOSPITAL See psychiatric hospital.

MENTALIST reveals deception.

MENTAL TELEPATHY See telepathy.

MENTHOL connotes a "fresh" or refreshing aspect.

MENTOR usually identifies someone in your life who has the knowledge and wisdom of guiding you.

MENU emphasizes one's multiple opportunities to gain inner nourishment.

MERCENARY portrays one who would do anything for personal gain or adventure.

MERCHANDISE suggests choices available to one. The type of merchandise will bring a different message to each dreamer.

MERCHANT will denote a person who can offer choices to another.

MERCURY (element) implies a fluctuating situation; vacillation.

MERCURY (planet) depicts an impossibility.

MERCURY (Roman mythology) characterizes a messenger in one's life.

MERCURY-VAPOR LAMP calls for "special" illumination required on a subject. The dreamer will make this association.

MERCY comes as a message to utilize same.

MERCY KILLING See euthanasia.

MERGANSER See duck.

MERGER denotes a blending; a bringing together.

MERINGUE reveals a deceptive surface appearance or cover; a "fluffy" presentation or representation of a more serious issue.

MERIT PAY exemplifies the earning of additional karmic assets.

MERLIN (bird) See falcon.

MERLIN (legend) characterizes the active manifestation of one's spiritual talents and the utilization of same for the benefit of others.

MERLOT See wine.

MERMAID reveals a state of spiritual confusion; indecision as to what is truth; may also represent a denial of Reality.

MERRY-GO-ROUND illustrates a lack of forward progress; no intellectual or searching advancement made.

MESA connotes high spiritual truths.

MESCAL BUTTON See peyote.

MESH suggests a need to be more congenial, compatible.

MESMER (Franz) characterizes a person in one's life who has an ability to convince others of his or her viewpoint.

MESMERIZED warns of a lack of awareness; usually a conscious move to avoid personal responsibility for one's beliefs or path.

MESQUITE defines the possession of extremely potent spiritual power; exceptional strength of spiritual knowledge and wisdom.

MESS (condition) alludes to a state of near-total confusion. This usually refers to mental and emotional factors.

MESSAGE brings a revelation of some type for the dreamer.

MESSENGER will reveal a person in one's life who will provide a solution, answer, or important clue.

MESSIAH corresponds with someone in the dreamer's life who will prevent his or her personal failure or loss of direction.

MESS KIT symbolizes the "tools" we use in life to gain inner nourishment, gain knowledge, or attain a measure of forward progression.

METAL See specific type.

METALLIC (finish) denotes a "lustrous" appearance that may or may not reflect that which is beneath.

METALLURGY (study of) represents a high interest in learning the various benefits and faults of utilizing differing "tools" to accomplish life goals.

METAMORPHOSIS suggests a complete change. This could refer to a situation, relationship, belief, or an aspect within self.

METAPHYSICIAN will indicate a person in one's life who is skilled in the knowledge and/or practice of spiritual gifts and the extensive workings of Reality.

METASTASIS means something has spread, widened in scope.

METATE suggests a more basic, simpler way of accomplishing something.

METEOR represents an influx of enlightenment or inner awareness.

METEOROLOGIST characterizes one who is highly interested in understanding converging factors that can affect conditions or situations.

METEOR SHOWER will warn of an inundation of spiritual ideas. This is a caution to be discerning.

METER (gauge) denotes the level of one's progress.

Electric meter will indicate knowledge. A low reading will advise more in-depth study or research.

Gas meter alludes to one's energy level.

Water meter implies spiritual aspects.

METHAMPHETAMINE connotes a need to either slow down or re-energize self.

METHANE See marsh gas.

METHODICAL connotes efficiency; organizational skills.

METHUSELAH applies to a great age; a time-tested aspect.

METRONOME calls for a need to "pace" self.

METROPLEX implies a high concentration of societal involvement; may be indicating an advisement to give more attention to spiritual matters.

MEZUZAH symbolizes an external sign of one's spiritual beliefs.

MEZZANINE stands for a mid-level position.

MIA corresponds to one who has lost his or her way while walking a spiritual path.

MIASMA warns of a dangerously negative atmosphere.

MICA relates to the "shiny" bits and pieces of joyful moments we experience while making our life journey.

MICE See mouse.

MICKEY MOUSE connotes acceptance of life's little irritations; an ability to utilize humor as a means of dealing with small problems.

MICRO will indicate a very small measurement. Surrounding dream details will clarify what this symbol is associated with.

MICROBE will correspond with something that has entered one's life unnoticed. Other dream factors will clarify whether or not this is a positive facet.

MICROBIOLOGY (study of) pertains to one who is highly analytical and interested in "knowing one's enemies."

MICRO BURST warns of an unexpected surge of knowledge or incoming information; an inundation.

MICROCOSM signifies a "small" example or replica of a larger comparable.

MICROFICHE represents a method of consolidating information.

MICROFILM illustrates the mind; memory.

MICROORGANISM See microbe.

MICROPHONE suggests a need for one to be heard.

MICROSCOPE calls for an advisement for one to look at something closer; more analyzation needed.

MICROSURGERY implies a delicate maneuver; a fragile move; great care required in order to avoid a wrong move.

MICROWAVE OVEN emphasizes an efficient and quick conclusion is needed.

MIDAIR pertains to an unfinished aspect; something "hanging" in limbo.

MIDAS TOUCH alludes to a record of success; an ability to conclude efforts in a positive manner.

MIDDAY (time) See noon.

MIDDLE (position) points out neutrality; may imply a lack of opinion or decision-making ability.

MIDDLE-AGED will exemplify a considerable level of experience but not enough to have gained deep wisdom.

MIDDLE AGES represent a time when one will begin to become more aware.

MIDDLE CLASS denotes "average."

MIDDLE FINGER indicates

centeredness; a balancing element.

MIDDLEMAN characterizes someone who is acting as a "go-between" in one's life. This may be an advisement to communicate directly instead of through another.

MIDDLE-OF-THE-ROAD applies to indecision; fear of taking a stand.

MIDDLE SCHOOL represents a stage or level of one's current advancement.

MIDDLEWEIGHT refers to one's level of effectiveness or influence. This symbol connotes an average amount of both.

MIDDY BLOUSE suggests a beginning spiritual search; a novice stage of spiritual knowledge.

MIDFIELD signifies an advancement position that places one halfway to one's goals.

MIDGET emphasizes a caution to never correlate power or knowledge with size. Larger never means more or greater.

MIDLIFE CRISIS indicates a lack of acceptance; an inability to recognize the God Force within self.

MIDNIGHT refers to intense spiritual energy.

MIDNIGHT SUN portrays the brilliance of spiritual forces or influences that are not always evi-

dent during one's darker times.

MIDSTREAM cautions not to stop efforts before something has been concluded or accomplished.

MIDSUMMER EVE suggests a time for celebration or the expression of joy. There are times in life when positive events come unrecognized and we need to be more aware and appreciative of these small blessings.

MIDTERMS call for a time to stop and analyze self; double-checking to make sure we've retained and learned from lessons we've experienced along our path so far.

MIDWAY (carnival) denotes misplaced priorities; an inability to have a mature perspective of Reality.

MIDWAY (position) represents a halfway marker.

MIDWIFE characterizes an individual in your life who has the knowledge and skill to assist in bringing about a new path or rebirth.

MIDWINTER See winter solstice.

MIGHTY MOUSE cautions against misjudgments; applies to an admonishment against forming solid opinions from first impressions or exterior appearances.

MIGRAINE indicates a state of pressure; great stress usually caused by self through lack of acceptance.

MIGRANT WORKER represents resourcefulness; efforts applied to advancement or path progression.

MIGRATION (birds) may suggest an actual, physical relocation or it may caution against mental vacillation.

MIKE See microphone.

MILD (quality) connotes amiability; easily accepted; something that lacks extreme aspects.

MILDEW illustrates inattention; a lack of awareness; letting something go for too long without giving it proper attention.

MILEPOST reveals one's current location along his or her life path.

MILESTONE signifies an event that marks a great accomplishment or turning point in one's life.

MILITANT won't necessarily denote aggression in dreams; it may indicate "activism" related to righteousness.

MILITARY alludes to "controlling" factors in one's life.

MILITARY CAP represents regimentation; an inability to think for self.

MILITARY INTELLIGENCE connotes ulterior motives for gaining information.

MILITARY OFFICER stands for arrogance; a love of power.

MILITARY POLICE (MP) pertains to an active and correct conscience; the "policing" of self.

MILITARY POST indicates a domineering personality or situation.

MILITIA refers to self-defense; one's personal, inner protective methods.

MILK connotes immaturity; or it may apply to some type of essential nourishment. Recall dream details for more clarity.

MILK GLASS alludes to an immature perspective; an inability to see things clearly.

MILKING pertains to taking fullest advantage of something. This may or may not be a positive symbol if one is taking advantage of others.

MILK OF MAGNESIA indicates a stressful situation or condition; advises more acceptance in life.

MILK RUN indicates multiple aspects to give attention to.

MILK SHAKE implies willful immaturity and the enjoyment of same.

MILK TOOTH symbolizes "first" experiences; beginning lessons in life.

MILK TRUCK connotes dairy products. This will advise a decrease or increase in one's dairy requirement. A truck driving "away" indicates a "reduction" in dairy foods.

MILKWEED See silkweed.

MILL corresponds with a need to "grind" or break down something into more manageable or visible parts. This symbol advises one to look more closely at the "parts" that comprise a large whole (situation).

MILLBOARD See hardcover.

MILLENNIUM is a time marker that comes to dispel fear and anxiety.

MILLET typifies a "filler" aspect; unimportant aspects or issues on which one expends efforts and time.

MILLINER characterizes a person who easily influences others.

MILLINERY connotes a "source" for diversity of ideas.

MILLING portrays an effort to reshape or redefine something.

MILLIPEDE relates to acceptance; an ability to overcome small setbacks.

MILLPOND defines spiritual benefits; an abundance of spiritual gifts.

MILLSTONE connotes a great burden.

MILLSTREAM defines a motivating factor; a source of energy.

MILL WHEEL represents one's continuing efforts to spiritually advance.

MILLWRIGHT characterizes an ability to put things in motion; having knowledge, skill, and motivation.

MILT implies an "active" aspect; a factor that's capable of joining with another to create a new idea or issue.

MIME represents honesty; visible attitudes and character.

MIMEOGRAPH applies to imitation; the utilization of a master image to duplicate its characteristics. This is usually not a positive symbol.

MIMIC is a caution to return to one's own individuality.

MIMOSA denotes a delicate innocence of character; a fragile yet strong nature.

MINARET depicts a method of gaining another's attention.

MINCE signifies a "halting" manner or progression.

MINCEMEAT alludes to the destruction of something in one's life.

MIND connotes one's thought process.

MIND-BOGGLING implies a lack of comprehension; an inability to understand.

MIND-EXPANDING relates to

an experience or learning event that results in greater understanding or new revelations.

MINDLESS signifies an inability to think for self or comprehend information.

MIND READING See telepathy.

MIND-SET reveals a "set" opinion, perception, or attitude that one refuses to alter.

MIND'S EYE defines mental visual insights; mental images.

MINE (earth) represents truths and natural talents that exist for one's self-discovery.

MINE (explosive) reveals negative aspects waiting along one's path.

MINE DETECTOR signifies one's inner sense or awareness to perceive upcoming troubles.

MINEFIELD symbolizes a "setup" or condition of entrapment existing in one's path.

MINER characterizes a spiritual searcher.

MINERAL See specific type.

MINERAL BLOCK implies essential life aspects; necessary basics.

MINERALOGY (study of) pertains to an interest in natural talents and their practical application in the world.

MINERAL OIL connotes a soothing aspect; a factor that eases rough phases in life.

MINERAL WATER illustrates "essentials" in life; that which is basic and without extraneous facets.

MINER'S HAT typifies "light" shed on ideas, concepts, or perceptions.

MINESHAFT represents "in-depth" research; digging down further and further for the more hidden aspects of something.

MINESTRONE corresponds with diverse information or conglomerate issues.

MINESWEEPER stands for heightened awareness; an inner knowing.

MINGLING suggests a need to experience diversity; a caution against being an ideological separatist.

MINIATURE will usually refer to compact knowledge; a great amount of information or power located within an unexpected source.

MINIATURE GOLF suggests a trial run; a practice experience before the real thing is attempted.

MINIMUM-SECURITY denotes a situation or path that holds few restrictions or operating limitations.

MINIMUM WAGE won't necessarily indicate a negative aspect; it most often underscores a "benefit" (though small) to an effort one expends.

MINISERIES connotes sequential "stages" to one's current experience, search, or path progression.

MINISTER See religious figure.

MINIVAN denotes a moderate amount of personal effort needs to be expended to accomplish something satisfactorily.

MINI-WHITES See amphetamine.

MINK pertains to cleverness.

MINKOIL emphasizes a "softening" aspect in one's life; a factor that is capable of easing experiences that are tough to get through.

MINNOW reveals spiritual insecurity.

MINOR (youth) indicates a more immature aspect or perspective.

MINORITY will imply an unpopular attitude or perspective; an idea or concept that veers from commonality or general acceptance.

MINOR LEAGUE defines a "secondary" factor; one that isn't perceived as a priority level issue.

MINOTAUR (Greek mythology) constitutes a "demanding" personality or situation.

MINSTREL signifies a person who tends to bring a measure of joy or lightheartedness into another's life.

MINT (money) denotes a high value on something.

MINT (plant) See specific type such as horehound, catnip, lavender, etc.

MINT JULEP See alcoholic beverage.

MINTMARK refers to an "originating" source.

MINUET pertains to a fragile relationship or situation; one where people need to carefully watch their step, their every move.

MINUTE represents a small measure of time. Recall surrounding dream aspects for further clarification and associative factors.

MINUTE HAND signifies the passing of time; will advise of the importance of mere minutes.

MINUTEMAN characterizes an individual who can be depended on for support.

MIRACLE corresponds to the "normal" workings of true Reality.

MIRACLE DRUG will stand for a solid solution.

MIRACLE WORKER portrays a person who provides solutions to difficult problems; one capable of making things happen.

MIRAGE connotes misperceptions; illusions; delusional behavior.

MIRED pertains to the condition of being overwhelmed; bogged down.

MIRROR stands for self-perception; a call for self-examination.

Clouded mirror implies a lack of clear perception of self.

Colored mirror denotes a "colored" perception. Refer to the specific color for further clarification.

Cracked mirror typifies a faulty self-image.

Magnifying mirror represents an egotistical view of self.

Pitted mirror relates to irregularities with one's self-image.

Slanted mirror suggests a biased viewpoint.

Warped mirror implies an unbalanced perspective.

MIRROR IMAGE usually personifies an alter-ego; one's hidden self.

MISCARRIAGE denotes the shedding of an erroneous spiritual belief.

MISCHIEF-MAKER spells trouble; reveals a problematical individual in one's life.

MISCOMMUNICATION reveals the need to recommunicate with someone.

MISCONCEPTION advises of an idea or attitude held in error. This is a wonderful message symbol that keeps you on track.

MISDEAL alludes to deceit.

MISDEMEANOR will warn of an offense one did. This type of symbol is in direct relation to one's conscience.

MISDIAGNOSES advises of a wrong cause or source attributed to an event in one's life.

MISDIAL depicts a situation where one communicates information to the wrong party.

MISER represents deep insecurities; may indicate selfishness.

MISERY implies a lack of acceptance; could reveal self-induced state.

MISFILED connotes a need for heightened awareness; concentrated attention required.

MISFIRE usually advises of a blessing that kept one from making a mistake or serious error in judgment.

MISFIT won't necessarily indicate a negative connotation. This symbol will usually denote individual expressiveness; following one's own drumming.

MISMATCHED reveals incompatibility; unsuitability.

MISPLACED alludes to a "reason" for temporarily being without something.

MISPRINT may indicate unawareness or it might pertain to a message for the dreamer, depending on how the misprint was done.

MISQUOTE warns of a lack of

concern for accuracy; cautions against claiming false knowledge.

MISSAL See prayer book.

MISSILE reveals a harmful negative aimed at one's experience. This could even be generated by self to another.

MISSING LINK illustrates a hidden factor that brings sense to a puzzling issue.

MISSION (church) will pertain to a specific work one needs to do; may point one in the right direction for his or her life purpose.

MISSIONARY corresponds to a person with a purpose. We are all missionaries in life. This symbol just underscores it for the dreamer as a reminder.

MISSION CONTROL will represent one's Higher Self.

MIST constitutes a spiritual atmosphere; may reveal a highly spiritual aura around someone. Recall if there was a color to the mist.

MISTAKE will almost always indicate the presence of an error one has made in life.

MISTLETOE represents good intentions.

MISTRIAL implies faulty procedure followed or a failure to agree on something. Surrounding dream details will point to which

meaning your dream had.

MISTY-EYED connotes an effort to control one's emotions.

MITE suggests a very small measure of something; an insignificant aspect.

MITER BOX corresponds with a need for precision; exactness.

MITTEN symbolizes a restrictive factor; a limiting condition.

MIXED DRINK See alcoholic beverage.

MIXED MARRIAGE portrays higher advancement; nondiscriminatory attitudes.

MIXER See blender.

MIX-UP reveals a lack of adequate communication.

MOANING indicates a regretful realization of transgressions; regret; may also infer sorrow or a lack of acceptance.

MOAT constitutes spiritual distance; the utilization of spiritual beliefs as protective or defensive measures.

MOB signifies a group of people with like attitudes or intentions; may not infer a negative connotation.

MOBILE HOME represents a temporary position on one's life path; good chance of relocation or moving forward.

MOBILE TELEPHONE See cellular telephone.

MOBSTER See mafia.

MOCCASIN illustrates a high level of awareness while cautiously progressing along one's life path.

MOCHA suggests a high quality; a richness.

MOCKERY indicates a feeling of humiliation; may indicate personal embarrassment.

MOCKINGBIRD denotes a lack of individualized expression.

MOCK ORANGE connotes contentedness.

MOCKUP See model.

MODEL (example) portrays an intended plan; a prototype.

MODEM relates to an opportunity to choose a variety of communication methods for a situation.

MODERN refers to a "current" time frame or method.

MODERN DANCE pertains to an ability to freely express self.

MODERNIZED implies an "updated" aspect; made current.

MODESTY stands for awareness; a considerate, respectful, and refined personality.

MODIFICATIONS exemplify an effort expended on improving something.

MOGUL characterizes a powerful and influential person.

MOHAIR (fabric) emphasizes an irritating or "heated" situation.

MOHAWK (hairstyle) reveals a person with a single train of thought; an inability to refocus or redirect an attitude or perspective.

MOIRE (fabric) depicts a rough exterior personality; a lack of expressive sensitivity.

MOISTURIZER portrays a need to express more compassion and overall sensitivity.

MOLAR indicates an ability to process ideas. Recall the condition of the molar for further clarification of this intended meaning.

MOLASSES defines a factor in one's life capable of providing needed energy or motivation.

MOLD See fungus.

MOLD See model.

MOLE (rodent) indicates a lack of communication; fearing reality.

MOLECULE denotes the smallest aspect of something. This refers to the importance of looking at every factor making up an issue or situation as being important.

MOLEHILL pertains to a lack of acceptance; a tendency to exaggerate a situation that would be better left alone.

MOLESKIN (fabric) alludes to a gentle personality.

MOLL See gun moll.

MOLLUSK warns against hiding from problems; withdrawal.

MOLOTOV COCKTAIL stands for a potentially explosive situation or attitude building.

MOLTEN implies an "embroiled" emotion or situation; one that needs cooling.

MOLTING signifies the shedding of negatives or excesses; letting go of the past.

MOM-AND-POP (store) represents a homelike atmosphere with associative attitudes of understanding and acceptance.

MOMENT OF TRUTH will relate to a revelation or it may indicate a need for introspection or open communication.

MOMENTUM is an advisement to keep up your pace of progression.

MONARCH (butterfly) connotes perseverance; going the distance.

MONARCH (ruler) won't necessarily depict the meaning of "ruler" but will usually indicate one's inner power and strength.

MONASTERY pertains to privacy in respect to one's spiritual beliefs.

MONASTICISM applies to a desire to lead a purely spiritual life and forsake societal involvement and material trappings.

MONDAY suggests the time to review one's motivations and strengthen them.

MONDAY MORNING QUARTERBACK cautions against claiming false wisdom.

MONEY stands for riches.

Gold signifies "physical" wealth.

Paper money stands for "opportunities" to share wealth.

Silver denotes "spiritual" wealth.

MONEYBAG symbolizes wealth.

Empty bag connotes poverty.

Full bag portrays an abundance.

MONEYCHANGER represents a "conversion" of one's assets; altering form such as turning it into a gift or shared talent.

MONEYLENDER characterizes a person who shares wealth for self-serving reasons.

MONEY ORDER connotes guaranteed payment; an assurance that an asset or benefit is a positive one.

MONEYROLL indicates an abundance of personal assets; these may refer to monetary, mental, or emotional wealth. A moneyroll will not signify a spiritual factor.

MONEY TREE pertains to riches gifted to another.

MONGOOSE represents a quick

wit and sharp awareness in respect to perceiving deception.

MONGREL will define a compound aspect of a situation. This means that something has manifested through diverse means and factors.

MONITOR relates to observation and usually comes in dreams to advise of a need for closer attention or observation to be done.

MONK represents spiritual reclusiveness. This may indicate a need or an advisement to be more open with one's spiritual talents or knowledge. Recall surrounding dream details for further clarification.

MONKEY indicates immaturity or a lack of individuality.

MONKEY BARS relate to the "contorted" maneuvers a person goes through to emulate others.

MONKEY FLOWER illustrates a carefree attitude.

MONKEYSHINES pertain to mischievous behavior. This behavior may be negative or acceptable depending on surrounding dream details.

MONKEY WRENCH usually warns of a disruptive aspect in one's life, perhaps even one's own behavior.

MONKSHOOD See wolfsbane.

MONOCHROMATIC (one color throughout dream) indicates an overall perspective or personality aspect that "colors" one's life. Recall what color washed the dreamscape then refer to the specific color.

MONOCLE denotes a singular mental focus; an inability to open self to a broader scope, greater availability to new ideas.

MONOGAMY may not refer to a marriage, but most often will correspond with one's belief system or center of attention.

MONOGRAM represents important initials that will have a specific meaning for each dreamer. Many times a monogram will turn out to be an acronym. Recall what the letters were.

MONOLITH connotes a particular facet of one's life that is perceived as being a great goal or burden.

MONOLOGUE will usually symbolize a "discussion" one needs to have with another or even with self; something needs to be talked out or analyzed.

MONOMANIA indicates a destructive fanaticism.

MONOPHOBIA pertains to a serious lack of self confidence.

MONOPLANE refers to assurance and fortitude.

MONOPLEGIA reveals a self-generated mental or emotional handicap.

MONOPOLY (game) alludes to misplaced priorities.

MONORAIL applies to one-mindedness; an inability or refusal to veer from one's course. This is usually a negative symbol, for there are many times we need to take a sidetracking detour to learn an important lesson in life.

MONOTHEISM points the Way.

MONOTONE signifies inexpressiveness; it calls for more outward expression.

MONOTONY suggests an expansion of one's horizons or goals.

MONROE (Marilyn) implies a draw toward physical aspects. This will usually indicate an "over-interest" in the physical facets of life that will result in an imbalanced character.

MONSOON reveals an inundation of spiritual information; one is attempting to seek out and assimilate a wide diversity of spiritual concepts too fast.

MONSTER will always symbolize a fear one has.

MONSTRANCE depicts that which one reveres. This is a revealing symbol that will point out whether or not what we revere is spiritually correct.

MONTAGE indicates a state of thought.

Related visuals denote a wholeness to one's perspective.

Unrelated visuals will warn of a disconnective or disassociative thought process.

MONTANE See mountain.

MONTESSORI METHOD pertains to a freedom to explore self and one's leanings; an expression of abilities.

MONTEZUMA II represents an advisement to "preserve" one's higher ideals, ethnicity, or best qualities.

MONTH denotes a time frame and will usually have a specific meaning for each dreamer.

MONUMENT alludes to individual loyalties.

Beautiful monument is a correct placement of one's loyalty.

Decrepit monument reveals misplaced loyalty.

MOODINESS cautions one to accept more in life; an inability to reconcile events.

MOON corresponds with spiritual gifts and their application.

MOONBEAM comes to shed a revealing or awakening light on one's spiritual talent. This will usually be a call for more active utilization.

MOON-FACED connotes an emotional openness.

MOONFLOWER VINE exemplifies the bountiful spreading of a singular spiritual deed.

MOONLIGHT signifies the "light" of spiritual gift utilization.

MOON LUTE See samisen.

MOONRISE reveals a "rising" spiritual talent within one; a developing gift.

MOONSHINE See alcoholic beverage.

MOONSTONE empowers one's spiritual talents; strengthens abilities.

MOONSTRUCK will caution against a tendency to be over zealous to the point of negating one's spiritual efforts.

MOOR See anchor.

MOOR means a stage in one's life path where one allows self to become "bogged" down by spiritual concepts that are too "heavy" or deep to currently comprehend.

MOOSE implies a spiritual burden.

MOP suggests a cleanup is required in one's life. This will refer to a uniquely individualized factor in each dreamer's life.

MOPED denotes the utilization of energizing thoughts; positive thinking.

MORAINE relates to a stage in one's life when a seemingly excess of burdens are presented.

MORALIST may be a positive or negative symbol, depending on the dream moralist's behavior.

This will be a revealing symbol for self or regarding someone with whom the dreamer is associated.

MORASS relates to an overwhelming aspect in one's life.

MORAY EEL warns against spiritual over-exuberance; spiritual aggressiveness.

MOREL See mushroom.

MORGUE will connote futility; a dead-end or an unproductive aspect.

MORNING (time) illustrates a new beginning; a fresh start.

MORNING GLORY calls for spiritual expression.

MORNING SICKNESS implies an inner anxiety to make a new beginning.

MORNING STAR defines encouragement. Mornings can be extremely difficult emotional times of day; the star shines to give support.

MOROCCO (leather) signifies a gentle emotional expressiveness.

MOROSE See melancholia.

MORPHINE See narcotic.

MORSE CODE suggests communication misunderstanding or a lack of comprehension.

MORSEL indicates a small amount. This may appear to be a negative symbol, yet a morsel is still something that may be just a beginning.

MORTALITY (rate) emphasizes a measure of viability. Recall surrounding dream detail to determine what this symbol referred to.

MORTGAGE pertains to a life debt; a karmic responsibility.

MORTICIAN See funeral director.

MORTUARY See funeral home.

MOSAIC symbolizes the many beautiful aspects that create a whole. This will have uniquely revealing meanings for some dreamers.

MOSES (biblical) characterizes a messenger; one who has the capability of overcoming adversity through perseverance.

MOSQUITO refers to mild setbacks or temporary irritations that can be disruptive forces.

MOSQUITO NET represents an awareness that offsets or deflects the minor irritations that can disrupt one's focused attention on his or her path.

MOSS denotes vitality.

MOSS ROCK portrays determination.

MOTE (size) corresponds to the presence or existence of something in one's life. This usually refers to an idea, emotion, or belief that is still alive.

MOTEL will allude to some type of transition phase in one's life.

MOTH constitutes a destructive belief; one that will appear to lead into the "light" yet will result in eventual harm.

MOTHBALL connotes a preventive measure applied to protecting one's direction from false trails.

MOTHER characterizes a nurturing aspect; may represent personal associations.

MOTHER GOOSE pertains to immaturity.

MOTHER HEN suggests interference; overly protective; may also indicate pessimism.

MOTHER-IN-LAW depicts added responsibility in one's life.

MOTHER LODE connotes a bountiful source.

MOTHER-OF-PEARL symbolizes the best aspect of something.

MOTHER'S DAY pertains to honor and respect.

MOTHER SUPERIOR (nun) See religious figure.

MOTHER TERESA characterizes a selfless personality; compassion.

MOTHER TONGUE represents an advisement to return to one's own level of understanding. This would denote an attempt to learn that which is too complex.

MOTHPROOF applies to the individualized protective measures

M

one utilizes to safeguard against misdirection.

MOTIF will reveal a dominating ideology, usually the one prevalent in one's life.

MOTION SENSOR stands for one's awareness level. Recall if the sensor was operating or in disrepair.

MOTION SICKNESS reveals psychological restrictions placed on self to prevent development or path advancement; a fear of advancing; lacking self-confidence or reliance.

MOTIVATIONAL SEMINAR may indicate low motivation.

MOTOR refers to a life aspect that can provide additional energy or motivation; an impelling force.

MOTORCADE denotes emphasis. The surrounding dream details will reveal the precise meaning for each dreamer.

MOTOR COURT See motel.

MOTORCYCLE applies to the freedom to follow one's unique path and the activation of same.

MOTOR HOME reveals a transitional sense of illness or lack of direction.

MOTOR MOUTH points to one who talks a lot yet has little to say.

MOTOR POOL indicates a "sharing" of that which is learned along one's life journey.

MOTTLED (pattern) denotes thought vacillation; indecision.

MOTTO will sometimes reveal one's basic attitude, yet it most often will come as a message that defines what one's perspective "should" be.

MOUND (earth) exemplifies hidden aspects that one hasn't perceived.

MOUND BUILDER characterizes one who cherishes truth and strives to protect and preserve it.

MOUNTAIN refers to a major obstacle to overcome in life.

MOUNTAIN BLUEBIRD typifies encouragement as one struggles to overcome life's burdens or obstacles.

MOUNTAIN CLIMBING stresses personal efforts expended toward reaching one's goal.

MOUNTAIN GOAT connotes a determined effort to persevere.

MOUNTAIN LION See cougar.

MOUNTAIN RANGE relates to a major "block" one needs to overcome and conquer, this usually being a self-generated restriction.

MOUNTAIN SICKNESS See altitude sickness.

MOUNTAINSIDE pertains to an insight into what one must encounter and overcome in his or her immediate future.

MOUNTAINTOP See summit.

MOUNT EVEREST represents a challenge in one's life.

MOUNTIE characterizes precautions one gives to attend to his or her direction.

MOUNT RUSHMORE represents spiritual desecration; spiritual apathy.

MOURNING See grief.

MOURNING DOVE calls for a greater expression of compassion or sympathetic attitudes.

MOUSE (computer) corresponds to precise control and the need for same in one's life.

MOUSE (rodent) connotes a negative aspect that has infiltrated one's life.

MOUSER (cat/dog/snake) portrays a deterrent to negative influences.

MOUSETRAP defines an attempt to rid one's life of destructive aspects.

MOUSSE (food) applies to superficial factors in one's life.

MOUSSE (hair dressing) warns against a lack of mental focus on important aspects.

MOUSTACHE illustrates a tendency to ineffectively express one's thoughts.

MOUSY (appearance) pertains to a timid or introverted personality.

MOUTH represents the manner in which one speaks or communicates.

MOUTHFUL calls for a need for the mind to be focused when communicating with others. Saying a "mouthful" can be hazardous to one's health.

MOUTH ORGAN See harmonica.

MOUTHPIECE suggests the advisement to speak for self.

MOUTHWASH comes to warn against harmful or abusive language.

MOUTH-WATERING alludes to a desire to be satisfied.

MOUTON reveals a deception.

MOVIE indicates a personal message for the dreamer. Recall what the movie was about. Was it fiction? Real?

MOVIE PRODUCER characterizes one who has the capability of bringing clarity to a situation through vivid visuals. This, in essence, will indicate any false perspectives one may have had.

MOVIE STAR may indicate hypocrisy or it might represent a glamorized or unreal perspective of life.

MOVIE THEATER connotes a possible unrealistic perspective and an attempt to clarify it.

MOVING See relocation.

MOVING SIDEWALK symbolizes an effortless phase of one's life journey.

MOVING VAN suggests a change of perspective or surrounding.

MOWING warns against "cutting" one's abilities or talents.

MOZZARELLA denotes an abundance of nourishing factors in one's life.

MUCILAGE See adhesive.

MUCK signifies a confused mind or situation.

MUCKRAKER characterizes an individual who is focused on the negatives in another's life.

MUCUS implies a "protective" agent in one's life.

MUD may represent perceptual distortion or it may indicate a "healing" factor in one's life. Recall surrounding dream details for further clarity.

MUD DAUBER See mud wasp.

MUDDLE-HEADED corresponds to mental confusion; an inability to do things right.

MUD FLAT denotes alternating phases of clarity and mental confusion.

MUDFLOW pertains to an inundation of confusing aspects in one's life.

MUDGUARD See splash guard.

MUD PUPPY See salamander.

MUDROOM alludes to negative attitudes brought into the home.

MUDSLIDE See mudflow.

MUDSLINGING warns against defiling another's reputation or character.

MUD TURTLE reveals a state of near-constant confusion that is self-generated.

MUD WASP pertains to an individual in one's life who has a tendency to interfere and confuse issues.

MUEZZIN suggests a "call to prayer."

MUFF connotes a tendency to avoid involvement.

MUFFIN represents small security factors in one's life.

MUFFLER stands for an advisement to use more communicative discretion.

MUG corresponds with a strong character. Recall if the mug had any words on it. This will give further interpretation to the symbol.

MUGGER characterizes one who gains through the efforts of others.

MUGGY See humid.

MUG SHOT will reveal something important to each dreamer. Who was the photograph of? What was it in reference to? Was it yourself?

MULBERRY represents joy.

MULCH defines a fertile atmosphere; the right timing.

MULE may symbolize stubbornness, yet it usually indicates independence; a reluctance to be influenced.

MULE DEER See deer.

MULESKINNER characterizes an extremely influential personality.

MULL (spice) implies a maturity is needed; more development.

MULL (think) See contemplation.

MULLEIN symbolizes a healing aspect in one's life.

MULLION (window) defines multiple perspectives to an issue.

MULTIDIMENSIONAL (visuals) will denote multi-layered factors to whatever is being presented. This is a valuable insight.

MULTIMILLIONAIRE illustrates an individual who is capable of providing a "wealth" of benefits to others. These benefits will most often refer to emotional or spiritual aspects.

MULTIPLE-CHOICE refers to the many opportunities available in life.

MULTIPLE PERSONALITY will reveal inner thoughts or attitudes.

MULTIPLICATION SIGN applies to the possibility of increasing something; opportunity to develop or advance.

MULTIVITAMIN will most often reveal a specific requirement in one's life.

MUM See chrysanthemum.

MUMBLE denotes a fear of expressing one's opinion or emotion.

MUMBO JUMBO pertains to illogical and irrational thought.

MUMMY exemplifies an unyielding personality; a lack of tenacity or open-mindedness.

MUMPS represent an inability to express emotional responses.

MUNCHING indicates an advisement to "chew" information; mentally process information better.

MUNCHKIN characterizes an "animated" personality; one who has an exuberance for life.

MUNDANE points out the balancing factors in life; a necessary counter to high spiritual levels.

MUNG BEAN See bean sprouts.

MUNITION See ammunition.

MURAL will reveal a specialized message for each dreamer. Recall what the mural depicted.

MURDER will usually represent a symbolic death.

MURKY denotes a lack of clarity; a confused issue or situation.

MURMUR (low sound) suggests a call to attention; the dreamer needs to "listen" better and give more attention to something in life.

MURPHY BED illustrates an efficient method; ingenuity.

MURPHY'S LAW implies a pessimistic outlook.

MUSCATEL See alcoholic beverage.

MUSCLE signifies effort applied. This symbol will reveal the quality of effort by displaying the condition of the muscle.

MUSCLE-BOUND warns against arrogance; self-love.

MUSCULAR DYSTROPHY pertains to an inability to motivate self.

MUSE See contemplation.

MUSE (Greek mythology) characterizes a source of one's inspiration.

MUSEUM relates to antiquated concepts.

MUSH See porridge.

MUSH (consistency) connotes unclear thoughts; confusion.

MUSHROOM represents a benefit resulting from a seemingly negative factor.

MUSIC will indicate a harmonic or discordant state depending on the type of music presented.

MUSICAL CHAIRS (game) defines a stagnant phase of one's path; a lack of forward movement; going in circles.

MUSIC BOX suggests melancholia.

MUSIC HALL denotes an interest and appreciation for harmony in one's life.

MUSICIAN indicates spiritual harmony within self.

MUSIC OF THE SPHERES defines spiritual balance and inner peace.

MUSIC SHOP reveals the state of one's spiritual awareness. Recall what type of music was being perused. Who was doing the looking? What kind of music did the shop specialize in?

MUSIC VIDEO will connote how one applies his or her harmonious inner aspects to life. What type of video was presented? Was it wild or gentle?

MUSK (scent) connotes a down-to-earth personality; one close to the earth; possessing primal (basic) spiritual beliefs without superficiality.

MUSKEG See bog.

MUSKETEER exemplifies a guarding aspect in one's life; a protective characteristic.

MUSKRAT signifies a repulsive attitude; an aversion.

MUSLIN (fabric) indicates simplicity.

MUSSEL refers to spiritual protectiveness, perhaps bordering on reclusiveness.

MUSTACHE See moustache.

MUSTANG reveals a wild type of individual freedom verging on recklessness.

MUSTARD signifies a desire to enhance life events; exaggerations.

MUSTARD GAS warns against a highly dangerous aspect in one's life; a factor that could suffocate freedoms or beliefs.

MUSTARD PLASTER denotes a need to address negative factors in life that repress freedoms; a need for breathing room; fresh air required.

MUSTARD SEED will most often indicate a new idea and the "planting" of same.

MUSTY indicates a need for fresh air (getting away from stale ideas).

MUTANT will indicate an "altered" perspective or character.

MUTE may call for silence.

MUTILATED refers to something destroyed beyond recognition; the destruction of integrity.

MUTINEER illustrates rebellion or the need for same. Surrounding dreamscape details will clarify which meaning this has for the dreamer.

MUTT (dog) represents a friend who will remain loyal.

MUTTER indicates insecurity; a lack of acceptance.

MUTTON See lamb.

MUTTONCHOPS imply spiritual verbosity.

MUTUAL FUNDS denote speculation.

MUUMUU relates to a carefree attitude.

MUZAK alludes to subliminal communicative methods.

MUZZLE (snout) suggests sensory insights.

MUZZLE (device) connotes a restraint on communication or insights.

MUZZLE (gun barrel) pertains to aggressive communication.

MUZZLE LOADER applies to antiquated communication methods.

MYNA (bird) depicts congeniality.

MYOPIA (nearsightedness) emphasizes a lack of long-range perspective.

MYRRH defines spiritual insights and wisdom.

MYRTLE refers to gentleness.

MYSTERY will correspond to a puzzlement in one's waking life and will usually contain demystifying factors.

M

MYSTIC (person) points to an over-emphasis on the paranormal facets of spirituality and Reality.

MYTHICAL CHARACTER will constitute a wide variety of interpretations. Refer to specific character.

N

NACHO connotes a wide range of personal expression.

NADIR represents a "beneath" or "under" position. This could refer to a less advanced or developed aspect.

NAG (bother) may correspond with one's conscience. Recall surrounding dream details for clarification.

NAG (horse) pertains to weariness.

NAIAD (Greek mythology) characterizes a spiritual force in one's life.

NAIL (finger/toe) See fingernail.

NAIL (metal) represents a need for attachments; connections.

NAIL BED will reveal one's state of health; may also refer to emotional health.

NAILBRUSH alludes to a need to change one's ways; "clean up" dirty methods and tactics.

NAIL FILE comes as an advisement to smooth out one's rough edges in reference to dealing with others.

NAIL HEAD will pertain to the basic aspect of an issue.

NAIL POLISH can reveal one's underlying personality or character. Recall depth of color and condition of polish.

NAIL SCISSORS illustrate an advisement to "cut down" and temper one's aggressive behavioral tendencies.

NAIVETÉ characterizes an innocent or uninformed person.

NAKEDNESS connotes an "open" heart; nothing to hide; no agendas or ulterior motives.

NAME will have special meanings for each dreamer. The dream name may not correspond to an individual's awake-state name.

NAME BRAND usually indicates a "preferred" choice for the dreamer. It may also signify a brand to avoid, depending on how it's presented.

NAME-CALLING can portray an individual's true attitude toward another.

NAME-DROPPING is a suggestion for the dreamer. This will indicate someone or something to connect with or avoid. Recall surrounding dream details for this clarification.

NAMELESS connotes a lack of ego.

NAMEPLATE pertains to an identity, a desire for same; implies a desire to be recognized.

NAMESAKE will indicate a respected or admired individual.

NANA See grandparent.

NANNY See babysitter.

NAP (fabric) can suggest a directional move. Recall if the nap was straight up or slanted to the right or left.

NAP (sleep) indicates a need for rejuvenating respite.

NAPALM denotes an explosive aspect in one's life.

NAPHTHA connotes a versatile factor.

NAPKIN applies to one's personal level and quality of preparedness in life. Recall color, fabric, and condition to gain deeper meaning.

NARC characterizes a person who exposes others.

NARCISSUS (flower) illustrates the dangers of egotism. The Narcissus has narcotic properties.

NARCISSUS (Greek mythology) warns against self-centeredness.

NARCOSIS warns against a self-induced state of apathy.

NARCOTIC defines an escape from reality associated with a lack of acceptance and personal responsibility.

NARRATIVE most often infers a dream as a message. Recall what the narrative was about and who was giving it.

NARROW (width) denotes a course or aspect with little room for error.

NARROW GAUGE (railway) represents a "straight and narrow" path. This isn't necessarily a positive dreamscape fragment to manifest, for few true paths follow such a set course as a railway.

NARROW-MINDEDNESS cautions one to expand intellectual explorations and inner perceptions.

NASDAQ relates to a "source" of specific information that may be valuable to the dreamer.

NASTURTIUM portrays natural talents, when utilized for the benefit of others, nourish self.

NATIONAL DEBT corresponds with a major obligation or responsibility in one's life.

NATIONAL GUARD pertains to a massive upheaval forthcoming in life.

NATIONAL MONUMENT will most often bring an important message specific to the dreamer. Check for personal associations with the presented monument.

NATIVE (indigenous) will symbolize one's "right" to something in his or her life that may currently be denied.

NATIVE AMERICAN exemplifies the inherent human bond with nature and all of true Reality.

NATURAL CHILDBIRTH (un-

planned emergency) signifies a premature manifestation of a goal or new life.

NATURAL FOOD (no additives) indicates a pure aspect; one having no affecting factors, such as a basic idea or attitude.

NATURAL GAS alludes to potentially explosive factors in one's life.

NATURAL HISTORY (study of) denotes a high interest in the human bond with all living things.

NATURALIST will most often reveal a spiritually enlightened individual.

NATURAL RESOURCES represent inherent characteristics and talents.

NATURAL SCIENCE (study of) denotes a high interest in discovering the extent of true Reality; an extended and reaching search.

NATURAL SELECTION alludes to the power of inner strength.

NATURE (aspects) symbolizes the base foundation of a dreamscape. In all its splendid diversity, nature plays an integral role in the accurate interpretation of a dream. Refer to specific aspects such as mountain, valley, geode, etc.

NATURE TRAIL connotes a life path chosen for the value of its multiple lessons.

NATUROPATHY symbolizes synergic solutions; the application or utilization of inherent healing qualities within self or nature.

NAUGAHYDE See leatherette.

NAUSEA warns of an inability to accept or "absorb" a disagreeable facet of one's life. This symbol will sometimes advise one of the wisdom to overlook more in life.

NAUTILUS (shell) defines the multidimensional interconnectedness of spiritual aspects and true Reality.

NAVAL BASE connotes spiritual protective methods.

NAVEL relates to a strong "bond" with another.

NAVIGATOR characterizes one who has planned out a set course in life.

NAVY YARD illustrates spiritual "repair" work that one needs to do.

NAYSAYER reveals a pessimistic attitude.

NAZI exemplifies one who desires to have control over others.

NEANDERTHAL will not necessarily mean "primitive" but usually refers to a willful state of ignorance.

NEAR BEER indicates a factor in one's life that "verges" on being negative; getting close to being a potentially destructive facet.

NEAR MISS denotes an off-center or unfocused direction; a path that will lead one off-course.

NEARSIGHTED See myopia.

NEBULA pertains to an obscure idea.

NECK reveals a person's inquisitiveness; intellectual curiosity.

NECK ACHE stands for a self-generated block to one's desire to gain further knowledge on a specific subject.

NECK AND NECK connotes competitive equality.

NECKERCHIEF alludes to perseverance; extended personal efforts.

NECKLACE emphasizes a type of personal interest or attraction; may reveal inner traits.

NECK OF THE WOODS See neighborhood.

NECKTIE warns against willfully choking off or smothering intellectual pursuits.

NECROMANCY signifies interdimensional communication; ease of multilevel communication.

NECROPHILIA comes as a message to focus on aspects of one's life rather than on the past.

NECROPHOBIA reveals a serious lack of acceptance and understanding of true Reality; a misunderstanding of the essence of self.

NECTAR corresponds with that which is sweetest in life; attained goals; fruitful relationships or concluding situations.

NECTARINE relates to a "fresh" idea or perspective.

NEEDLE (medical) See hypodermic needle.

NEEDLE (sewing) pertains to an aspect in life that has the potential to be utilized as a "repair" or connective method.

NEEDLECRAFT denotes a cleverness for finding solutions.

NEEDLE-NOSE (pliers) suggest a device (method) of attending to a delicate situation in life.

NEEDLEPOINT illustrates fortitude. Recall what type of needlepoint was presented. Who was doing it?

NEEDY emphasizes opportunities.

NE'ER-DO-WELL implies unrecognized direction and associative lack of any motivation.

NEGATIVISM signifies a pessimistic outlook; a cynic.

NEGLIGEE See nightgown.

NEGOTIATIONS indicate a desire for compromise.

NEIGHBOR will pinpoint someone who exists within close proximity to another, not necessarily an associate.

NEIGHBORHOOD represents a

cultural or economic indicator that will have a revealing affect on additional dream aspects. A neighborhood can expose one's inner attitudes or opinions, desires or fears.

NEMESIS (Greek mythology) corresponds with guilt; karmic justice forthcoming for misdeeds done.

NEON (fish) will pertain to a spiritual "light" for one to pay attention to.

NEON (light) will be an attention-getting sign. What was presented in neon lights?

NEOPHYTE See novice.

NEOPRENE defines a willful avoidance of spiritual aspects in one's life.

NEPOTISM warns against preferential treatment or behavior.

NEPTUNE (planet) refers to one's inherent natural abilities; spiritual gifts.

NEPTUNE (Roman mythology) See Poseidon.

NERVE will correspond with a specific type of emotional sensitivity. Recall surrounding dreamscape details for further clarity.

NERVE BLOCK usually refers to a self-generated, psychological "blocking."

NERVE DAMAGE suggests a self-generated disability caused by not reconciliating a past event.

NERVE GAS connotes a desire to control others. Recall "who" possessed the gas or where it came from.

NERVE-RACKING indicates an inability to overlook life irritations; a need for acceptance to generate inner tranquility.

NERVOUS BREAKDOWN signifies a need for inner strength and acceptance.

NEST denotes a security factor and will imply "insecurity."

NEST EGG symbolizes preparedness; efficient planning.

NESTING refers to foresight; insights that hint at needed preparations.

NESTLE exemplifies a comfortable situation; a feeling of security.

NESTLING See fledgling.

NET alludes to entrapments; method of "catching" another or not allowing anything to get by you.

NETTING (mosquito) constitutes some type of protective measure; an insurance-type of aspect.

NETTLE (plant) suggests some type of major annoyance in one's life.

NETWORKING signifies a chain of information-sharing; reveals a situation that is no longer private.

NEUROLOGIST characterizes one who has a high interest in determining causal psychological factors that prevent others from utilizing their full potential.

NEUROLOGY (study of) depicts a desire to understand the self-generated restraints utilized by others.

NEUROSIS defines a lack of acceptance resulting in a loss of inner peace.

NEUROTIC characterizes multiple inner fears; lack of trust and acceptance.

NEUTRAL (gear) typifies a situation that lacks any developmental aspects; a stage of non-movement; no opinion or desire to express same.

NEUTRAL GROUND defines a phase, situation, or condition that is without opposing factors; a time or place that allows for peace regardless of differing attitudes.

NEUTER denotes a cause or source affecting ineffectiveness.

NEUTRALIZED signifies a negation of power.

NEVER-NEVER LAND represents a fear of growing up; an inability to face the world and attending responsibilities of maturity.

NEW BLOOD (people) indicates a need for new and fresh ideas and perspectives.

NEWBORN will correspond with a new life, path, belief, or some type of personal discovery.

NEWEL (post) constitutes a main supportive aspect in one's life. This could refer to an emotional, mental, or spiritual issue.

NEWLYWED relates to a new relationship that has been forged.

NEW MOON alludes to hidden spiritual concepts that will be revealed.

NEWSCAST will almost always bring important information to light that is relevant to the dreamer.

NEWS CONFERENCE See press conference.

NEWSLETTER comes as a message specific to each dreamer. Its purpose is to keep one up to date on an aspect in his or her life.

NEWSPAPER represents an awareness within self.

NEWSPRINT (paper type) implies widespread information.

NEWS RELEASE pertains to a special announcement message the dreamer should note.

NEWSSTAND indicates the opportunity for readily-available information. This would usually refer to someone (possibly the dreamer) who believes he or she has little access to new ideas or information.

NEWT See salamander.

NEWTON (Isaac) pertains to the simplicity of true Reality.

NEW YEAR'S EVE connotes an opportunity for a fresh start.

NEW YEAR'S RESOLUTION sets one up for disappointment and self-deprecating situations. This symbol in a dream will come to infer that a "general" plan is wise, but a solid resolution is not reasonable nor, in the end, a productive promise to self.

NIAGARA FALLS connotes a spiritual renewal.

NIBBLE signifies a manner of taking in new information through discretion (nibbling).

NICHE will symbolize a "designated" proper place for something. This may refer to a deed, verbal expression of an emotion or opinion, or one's life purpose.

NICK alludes to a small setback or disappointment.

NICKEL (coin) connotes the presence of a "means" that has the capability of gaining power to accomplish a goal in one's life.

NICKEL (metal) implies a "replacement" method or means to utilize in place of a formerly planned approach.

NICKELS-AND-DIMES denote an insignificant amount that is capable of growing into an impressive volume.

NICKNAME will reveal an important characteristic or hidden aspect of someone.

NIGHT corresponds to the preferred time to explore hidden aspects of self or spiritual matters.

NIGHT BLINDNESS warns of a self-induced ignorance.

NIGHTCAP (drink) infers the existence of unresolved problems.

NIGHTCLUB pertains to missed opportunities for gaining deeper understanding.

NIGHT COURT represents the time for self-analyzation.

NIGHT CRAWLER typifies a personal incentive to actively delve into spiritual concepts that are generally considered "high" intellectual aspects.

NIGHTGOWN denotes a preparedness for one's planned activity.

NIGHTHAWK connotes extreme high awareness.

NIGHTINGALE (bird) relates to one's outward expression of spiritual joy.

NIGHTINGALE (Florence) exemplifies the power of determination and its resulting manifestations.

NIGHT-LIGHT represents a small measure of anxiety; a subconscious lack of self-confidence.

NIGHTMARE emphasizes one's inner fears.

NIGHT OWL characterizes a natural "knowing" of the most effectively powerful timing to engage in self-discovery or intellectual contemplation.

NIGHTRIDER warns of underhandedness; hidden aggression.

NIGHT SCHOOL advises of a need for immediate learning. There is something in the dreamer's life that he or she must quickly learn.

NIGHT SHIFT denotes a suggestion for one to apply self during the quiet night hours. This comes as a message for those who claim they have no time for advancing or developing through learning or study. This may even refer to a proper meditative time for the dreamer.

NIGHTSPOT See nightclub.

NIGHTSTAND/TABLE comes to visually display an important item (aspect) one needs to further his or her development or further understanding.

NIGHT TERROR relates to vulnerability; a deeply subconscious susceptibility to awake-state subliminal suggestive impressions.

NIGHT WATCHMAN connotes one's personal defenses; protective measures.

NIKE (Greek mythology) symbolizes great inner strength and strong determination to carry something through to a successful conclusion.

NILE (River) pertains to spiritual life.

NILE CROCODILE represents a potentially destructive spiritual force.

NIMBLENESS stands for tenacity; an ability to bounce back after a setback or disappointment.

NINE implies a productive path.

NINON (fabric) portrays a delicate aspect to one's personality; a specifically fragile sensitivity.

NIRVANA signifies a mental/emotional state of euphoria. This is not a positive dreamscape fragment, for it infers that the dreamer is living in a fantasy world and not within acceptance of reality. This usually indicates one living in his or her own world.

NITPICKING frequently comes from one's conscience.

NITROGLYCERIN emphasizes the existence of a highly explosive personality, situation, relationship, or belief system.

NITROUS OXIDE corresponds with a mechanism one utilizes to ease the pains and disappointments in life.

NOAH characterizes strong faith.

NOBEL PRIZE pertains to recognition by higher forces for one's efforts expended toward others.

NOBILITY implies a tendency to make class distinctions; an arrogance.

NOCTURNE alludes to a tranquil state of inner peace.

NOD suggests recognition or agreement.

NODULE represents an irregularity. Recall surrounding dreamscape details for further clarity.

NO-FAULT comes as a message to discount blame or judgment.

NO-HITTER underscores a successful endeavor that carried no setbacks or problems with it.

NOISEMAKER represents an "issue" made of something. This may infer that one needs to bring an issue to another's attention or it may warn to leave something alone instead of making an issue of it. This meaning will be clear after surrounding dream details are applied.

NOISE POLLUTION advises of a need for one to sort through information or communications for the purpose of getting to the basic idea.

NOMAD connotes the freedom to follow one's own chosen path in life.

NOM DE PLUME See pseudonym.

NOMINATION will reveal the best qualified person; the person of choice.

NONCHALANCE may not necessarily mean apathy or indifference; it may indicate an attitude or opinion that's "reserved" until further knowledge has been obtained.

NONCONFORMIST applies to a free-thinker; one expressing individualism.

NONFICTION will most often reveal the truth to a matter.

NONSENSE may not be nonsense in a dream; it frequently represents something the dreamer has not sorted out yet and has the potential to reveal solutions.

NONSTICK (surface) will symbolize an aspect in one's life that has the capability of "easing" one's way.

NOODLE See pasta.

NOON will pinpoint a preferred time designation associated with something one is planning. Each dreamer will associate various events with this symbol.

NOOSE forewarns of harmful or disastrous outcomes if a current path is followed.

NORTH denotes a direction that may need to be taken. North indicates an "above" or "higher" position.

NORTHERN LIGHTS See aurora borealis.

NORTH POLE comes as a directional advisement to obtain balance. North will indicate "higher" conceptual aspects to focus on.

NORTHWEST PASSAGE signifies guidance for one's spiritual search. The surrounding dreamscape details will make this more clear for the dreamer.

NOSE corresponds to a person's sense of direction; instincts; ability to recognize insights.

NOSEBLEED implies an interfering nature.

NOSE CONE pertains to a planned path that is efficiently austere; a direct methodology.

NOSEDIVE depicts a "headlong" immersion into something. This may be a positive or negative symbol, depending on surrounding dreamscape aspects that will clarify the intended meaning.

NOSEGAY connotes a small yet extremely meaningful act that serves to encourage or comfort another.

NOSEPIECE relates to protective measures one utilizes as he or she advances along a chosen path.

NO-SHOW emphasizes a reluctance to participate. Recall associative dream details to pinpoint what this refers to.

NOSTALGIA corresponds with one's memories. These always come as a message to either "remember" something in one's past or to "accept and go on" in life.

NOSTRADAMAS (Michel) advises of the wisdom of sharing that which one knows; stands for strength of one's convictions in spite of opposition or humiliation.

NOSINESS comes to caution against interfering in another's life.

NOTARY PUBLIC constitutes a personal "verification" of one's chosen direction in life; a nod of approval.

NOTATIONS pinpoint a matter of importance that one needs to give attention to or make note of.

NOTCH usually indicates taking note of or "marking" one's advancing steps in life.

NOTE will come as a personal message for each dreamer.

NOTEBOOK suggests a need to recall details.

NOTICE is an attention-getting symbol. Recall what the notice was about. This will be important.

NOTORIOUS will reveal an individual's hidden negative aspects.

NOUGAT alludes to a positive aspect or event that presents a measure of complexity to work through.

NOUVEAU RICHE warns against an attitude of arrogance regarding one's possessions, material wealth, or talent gifts.

NOVEL illustrates personal, sometimes hidden, interests one uses as an escape mechanism. Recall what type of novel it was. Mystery? Romance? War story? Gory or pornographic?

NOVELTY indicates a passing fancy; a temporary fad that usually pertains to a new and fascinating idea that proves to bare little substance when thoroughly analyzed.

NOVEMBER is a time to count one's blessings; appreciate the positive elements of one's life.

NOVICE reveals a lack of experiential or knowledgeable background; a beginner.

NOVOCAIN warns of a state of self-induced apathy; a purposeful avoidance of selective life aspects.

NOZZLE pertains to one's personal mode of "delivery." How one interacts with others. Recall the condition of the nozzle and if it was working. What was coming out of it? Was this substance hazardous? Clear? A color?

NUANCE connotes a subtle suggestion; a fear of openly expressing an opinion or personal attitude.

NUCLEAR FAMILY characterizes those closest to the dreamer.

NUCLEAR-FREE ZONE represents a personal desire for harmony and peaceful conditions in one's life.

NUCLEAR REACTOR defines a potentially contaminating negative facet in one's life.

NUCLEAR WINTER illustrates the devastating outcome of one's current behavior or path; a destruction of one's current condition and relationships.

NUCLEUS comes as a strong advisement to "get to the core" of an issue or concept. This would indicate a wasteful involvement with superficial facets instead of focusing on the basic premise.

NUDE See model.

NUDE See nakedness.

NUDGE symbolizes a "push" from one's Higher Self.

NUDIST COLONY portrays honesty among one's associates.

NUGGET applies to a small "treasure" found in one's life; an extremely valuable piece of information.

NUISANCE may exemplify one's own conscience; one's Higher Self.

NULLIFIED will pinpoint an unproductive aspect, thereby saving the dreamer time and effort expended on a path or purpose that is superficial and unproductive to his or her goal.

NUMBERS are extremely meaningful dream symbols and have a multitude of diverse meanings. See specific number.

Numbers on a house indicate a special association between the person residing there and the dreamer. It may also reveal a numerical interpretation for your own dwelling.

Numbers on a telephone denote a current or future relationship. A telephone symbolizes a forthcoming communication so try actually dialing the dream number to determine if there is a significance to it.

Numbers (dates) on a tombstone point to a death date. This date may refer to a physical death or a termination of something personally valuable to the dreamer. Usually the surrounding dream details will clarify this intention.

Numbers on a license plate usually warn of an upcoming vehicular accident involving the dreamer (or someone close to the dreamer) *and* the vehicle presented in the dream.

Numbers out of sequence on a timepiece imply that your life is out of order, your timing is off.

Numbers all the same on a timepiece call for a need to slow down. It's vitally important to recall the number that appeared on the timepiece. This will clarify the meaning further.

Numbers in an airport terminal come as strong warnings.

These may be attempting to warn you "away" from a specific flight number or they could be advising you to "take" the represented flight number. The dream details will clarify which meaning is intended.

Numbers circled on a calendar will define an important day having special significance for the dreamer.

Numbers in the sky connote a spiritual communication forthcoming.

Numbers in or on the water refer to the dreamer's spirituality.

Numbers on medication advise of a need to increase, decrease, or stop taking the medication altogether.

Numbers on grocery items come as a suggestion to increase or decrease the ingestion of the food presented. Diet dreams should never be ignored.

Numbers on foreheads of people reveal one's true mental or spiritual state of being.

Numbers over people's hearts emphasize their true emotional state or attitude.

Numbers on a lottery ticket usually suggest a forthcoming change in financial status. This is not necessarily a positive dream. Recall the condition and color of the dream ticket.

Numbers on a bankbook reveal a forthcoming change in the dreamer's status of wealth. Wealth does not specifically refer to money, but also to natural talents and spiritual gifts. Recall the state of the bankbook's condition and color.

Numbers surrounded in black will be a forewarning symbol often referring to a death of some type.

Numbers on billboards will be directly associated with whatever the sign is representing.

Numbers on playing cards will indicate the manner in which one lives life (plays the hand dealt).

Numbers on a book can reveal if the information provided within its pages is productive to one's knowledge base.

Numbers on mile marker can reveal how far one still has to go to attain a goal.

Numbers on a wall emphasize a fact that "should" be obvious to the dreamer; what one's course will manifest in the end.

Numbers on an infant will signify her or his purpose in life.

NUMBERS GAME signifies a slim chance one has taken or is thinking of taking in life.

NUMBNESS warns of a self-induced state of emotional or mental selectivity; a willful ignorance or insensitivity.

NUMEROLOGY cautions against basing one's overall opinions or perceptions on a singular set of narrow guidelines.

NUN characterizes the incorporation of spiritual facets throughout the fabric of one's daily life.

NURSE indicates a compassionate and selfless personality.

NURSE CAP indicates one whose thought process is tightly woven with compassion and deep caring.

NURSERY (botanical) represents the concentrated nurturing of one's natural talents and spiritual gifts.

NURSERY (infant) pertains to the special care given to one's new beginnings.

NURSERY RHYME can reveal an important message specific to the dreamer.

NURSERY SCHOOL pertains to the learning stages of a novice or beginning seeker.

NURSE'S AIDE will denote a person willing to help another.

NURSE SHOES reveal one who willingly gives assistance to others while walking her or his personal life path.

NURSING HOME represents one's perspective toward those who are more experienced and

N

have more knowledge. Recall the condition of the home. Who was residing there?

NUT (food & tool) both indicate a lack of logic and reason. In essence, someone who is a literal nut case.

NUTCRACKER will exemplify a need for resolutions and/or solutions.

NUTHATCH (bird) portrays an ability to discover solutions.

NUTMEG connotes an inherent, natural essence of self; an inborn ability.

NUTRITIONIST alludes to one who has the capability of advising others of what their life is lacking; providing what is needed for advancement.

NUTS AND BOLTS signify the "basics" of an issue.

NUTSHELL relates to self-devised "shells" one utilizes for self-protection. This symbol may also indicate a need to "consolidate" one's beliefs or perspectives into a basic, simple form. Recall surrounding dream details to determine which interpretation your dream intended.

NUZZLE corresponds to emotional expressions of love and companionship.

NYLON (fabric) implies some type of disassociative personality trait; a personal desire to distance self from others or certain situations.

NYMPH (Greek mythology) symbolizes a person who takes great inner joy from being close to nature; one possessing multiple natural (nature) qualities.

O

OAK denotes an unyielding personality; a lack of sensitivity.

OAR represents great personal efforts and suffering endured while on one's spiritual path.

OASIS pertains to rejuvenating respite phases in one's life.

OAT See grain.

OATH relates to promises that must be kept, even those to self.

OATMEAL signifies a life aspect that personally comforts and nourishes.

OBELISK denotes an important factor for the dreamer. Dreamscape shapes such as obelisks refer to spiritual conceptual truths.

OBESITY represents an overindulgence of some type.

OBI connotes personal encumbrances; superficial or extraneous beliefs, attitudes, or perspectives we carry around.

OBITUARY comes as a warning of a forthcoming death that may be emotional in respect to a relationship rather than an actual physical event. Recall surrounding dreamscape details for clarity. Was there a specific name presented? A date? Cause of death?

OBJECTIONS will reveal an individual's true opinion. An objection in a dream can also be a message from one's Higher Self.

OBJET D'ART will usually represent a personal message unique to each dreamer. This piece of art will symbolize something important in one's life.

OBLIVION means a state of mind that is devoid of emotion, purpose or humanitarian aspects.

OBLONG (shape) alludes to the act of "stretching" out one's efforts unnecessarily; extraneous work one believes is part of his or her path.

OBSCENITY won't necessarily denote a negative sign; it may present itself as a means of emphasis or revelation of an individual's hidden attitudes.

OBSERVATORY implies deeper knowledge and higher awareness needed.

OBSESSION will stress an overemphasis applied to a specific issue. This is a warning symbol.

OBSIDIAN expresses the beauty of the more esoteric spiritual concepts and gifts.

OBSTACLE COURSE indicates a life path containing difficult situations to overcome. This course *could* be self-generated and not necessarily an imperative factor of reality.

O

OBSTETRICIAN characterizes a person who has the knowledge and ability to bring forth a new life or spiritual awakening in others.

OBSTRUCTION is most often a problem one creates through psychological means.

OCCULT means "hidden" or little understood aspects; therefore, this symbol will refer to something in one's life that needs to be looked at harder and given deeper contemplative time to.

OCCUPATIONAL DISEASE indicates a suggestion to alter one's life course or change a harmful situation.

OCCUPATIONAL THERAPY implies a need to discover, learn, and apply enhanced methods and skills directed toward one's life path and/or manner of communication.

OCEAN alludes to spiritual facets in one's life.

OCEANFRONT See lakefront.

OCEANOGRAPHY relates to a high interest in diverse spiritual concepts.

OCTOBER represents a "uniting" time; sealing relationships; reaffirming personal bonds.

OCTOPUS warns of spiritual flailing; a situation where one is randomly reaching out in all directions for whatever spiritual idea he or she can grab onto.

ODD JOBS can bring significant learning experiences for the dreamer and usually come in dreams to represent this message.

ODDS will reveal probabilities for something the dreamer is anticipating doing or is concerned about.

ODDS AND ENDS symbolize remnant aspects that need to be attended to.

ODOMETER displays the amount of progression or advancement one has made in life.

High mileage indicates a great deal of ground has been covered.

Low mileage will suggest a need to get going.

ODORS provide important pieces of information that can reveal a negative or positive quality to something.

Floral scent will relate to the specific flower.

Food smell refers to the meaning of that specific food item.

Fresh scent alludes to a "fresh" idea.

Repulsive odor indicates an aversion to the dreamer.

Sea scent will relate to a spiritual aspect.

Sewer odor implies an extremely negative connotation.

Other olfactory sensations

such as gas fumes, exhaust etc. can be discerned by referring to the specific type in this dictionary.

ODYSSEY will represent a life path full of self-discovery.

OFF (position) defines a condition or state of affairs. This symbol may indicate a need to "turn something ON."

OFFAL pertains to "waste" aspects on which one shouldn't be expending personal efforts or attention.

OFF AND ON connotes a vacillation; an intermittent effort or attention.

OFFERING represents good intentions.

OFFICE always pertains to work or personal efforts applied.

OFFICE MANAGER characterizes one who has the capability to guide another through a more efficient manner of work or effort.

OFFICE SUPPLY STORE implies the need for additional tools to accomplish one's goals.

OFF-KEY illustrates a lack of harmony, perhaps even within self; being OFF regarding course or perspective.

OFF-LIMITS comes as a severe warning; one is trespassing where he or she shouldn't be.

OFF-BROADWAY represents an "experimental" attempt or move.

OFF-PEAK See off-season.

OFF-ROAD VEHICLE See four-wheel drive.

OFF-SEASON signifies a time when a certain activity is not generally carried out, yet this symbol may suggest that the Off-Season is the preferred time to accomplish something the dreamer is contemplating.

OFFSHOOT exemplifies a "resulting" manifestation generated by something one has said or done.

OFFSHORE directs one toward a spiritual aspect.

OFFSPRING represent aspects of ourselves or those qualitative elements that we leave behind.

OFF-THE-CUFF refers to spontaneity; instinctual reactions; impulsiveness.

OFF-THE-RACK alludes to something that is easily accessible.

OFF-THE-RECORD signifies a secret or information that is not for general dissemination.

OFF-THE-WALL represents shocking behavior; totally unexpected and irrational.

OFF-TRACK BETTING constitutes a chance taken without being aware of all the associative factors involved.

OFF-WHITE will indicate an "affecting" factor to something; not quite pure.

OGLE applies to a lack of respect and acceptable behavior.

OGRE stands for an inability to accept life; a poor self-image.

OIL indicates a lack of abrasiveness or friction; that which soothes and eases.

OIL CAN represents a means to lessen life irritations and rough relationships.

OILCLOTH denotes a need for more healthful eating habits, not "what" one eats, but the "manner" of eating.

OIL COLOR See oil paint.

OIL FIELD indicates a poor choice of opportunities, one that carries multiple negative side effects.

OIL PAINT signifies an inherent gift of creativity.

OIL PAN corresponds to efficiency; an ability to cover all aspects of an issue.

OIL REFINERY comes as a message to "refine" one's crude qualities; indicates a need to soften or control insensitive expressiveness.

OIL WELL corresponds to a great opportunity that must be carefully planned out in order to optimize its potential for good.

OINTMENT signifies a healing element in one's life.

OKTOBERFEST represents a reason to rejoice; a time to celebrate. This is a revealing symbol that usually points out a positive aspect in one's life that may not be recognized for the benefits it brings.

OLD-BOY NETWORK symbolizes the adage: "It's not what you know, it's who you know." This will have a specific meaning for the dreamer.

OLD COUNTRY pertains to long-held traditions.

OLD FAITHFUL denotes trust and dependability.

OLD-FASHIONED HATS represent antiquated ideas or attitudes.

OLD-FASHIONED SHOES warn of an out-dated way of accomplishing a goal; a path traveled via antiquated methods.

OLD FOLKS See elder.

OLD GROWTH indicates ideas that have endured and passed the test of time.

OLD GUARD suggests a reluctance to alter attitudes or opinions.

OLD HAND characterizes experience.

OLD HAT connotes an old-fashioned idea; something that's been around for a long time and well known.

OLD MAID (card game) implies an anxiety or fear of age; may refer to a fear of having to care for an elder relative.

OLD MONEY portrays "inherent" wealth of inner talents; qualities and abilities at which one is naturally skilled.

OLD SCHOOL alludes to strong, traditional perspectives that are not necessarily applicable at the current time.

OLD TESTAMENT comes as an advisement to readjust one's thinking on something. The dreamer will have a knowing of what this issue is.

OLD WIVES' TALE will reveal a piece of "truth" the dreamer will recognize.

OLEANDER reminds us that appearances can be deceiving; an appearance of something in one's life that "seems" to be good or a blessing may ultimately prove harmful.

OLEO See margarine.

OLIVE applies to a positive, beneficial element in one's life.

OLIVE BRANCH stands for one's intention to reconcile; a desire for peace.

OLIVE OIL symbolizes a quelling element.

OLYMPIC GAMES indicate a desire to be recognized as being the ultimate best at something.

OMBUDSPERSON characterizes an individual who has the ability to act as an intermediary; one who can investigate a complaint or suspicion.

OMEGA (Greek letter) will emphasize the "end" element of something in the dreamer's experience.

OMELET connotes multiple aspects connected to something with which the dreamer is associated.

OMEN comes as a sign. Recall surrounding dreamscape details to determine whether or not this is a positive or negative indication.

OMISSION will reveal an important message for the dreamer. It will pinpoint an aspect that has been left out of one's perspective or conclusion.

OMNIVORE characterizes a need to "take in" all elements available to one's intellectual search.

ON (position) represents a current state of affairs regarding one's personal life. This symbol may indicate a "right ON" perspective or it may warn of a need to turn an attitude or emotion OFF. Surrounding dream details will clarify this intention.

ONE symbolizes God or a High spiritual force.

ONE-ARMED BANDIT See slot machine.

ONE-HANDED refers to the success of one's personal efforts.

ONE-NIGHT STAND signifies a one-time event or experience.

ONE-SHOT underscores an opportunity that won't be repeated; the need to be successful the first time an attempt is made.

ONE-SIDED illustrates a biased presentation or attitude.

ONE-SIZE-FITS-ALL stands for an element open to everyone; a lack of preferential treatment or availability.

ONE-WAY (sign) comes as a reminder that there is no "turning back" or reversing direction once begun.

ONE-WOMAN SHOW applies to an action one must accomplish alone. Often this type of dream symbol will underscore the need for the dreamer to stop depending on others to help him or her along. This signifies a call to be independent in deed or thought.

ONION portrays a "healing" factor in one's life.

ONIONSKIN (paper type) relates to "fragile" truths; healing elements.

ONLOOKER may exemplify Those-Who-Watch. This may even refer to one's Higher Self or conscience. Someone is always watching us.

ONTOLOGY (study of) reveals a high interest in gaining an understanding of the connectedness between true Reality and self.

ONYX defines an attraction to high wisdom.

OOZE (exude) will indicate an element one can on longer contain or hide.

OOZE (mudlike) portrays a complex element, situation, or perspective caused by multiple psychological aspects.

OPAL symbolizes Truths-From-Many-Sources.

OPAQUE warns of negativity; an inability to see the light; dark ideas or nature.

OP ART connotes a simplistic manner of expression.

OPEC corresponds to a controlling power; an element or individual possessing the control.

OPEN (position) denotes a state of affairs. This may indicate a need to "close" something, such as one's mouth, heart, or wallet. It may also refer to an informational fact that allows the dreamer to see how "open" something is. This meaning will be different for each dreamer.

OPEN-AND-SHUT refers to a simple or basic aspect that has no complexities associated with it.

OPEN DOOR signifies accessibility; ease of attainment.

OPEN-END connotes a life aspect that has no limits or restrictions for the dreamer.

OPENER (device) points out an

element in one's life that is capable of serving as an access tool; used to accomplish a goal or desire.

OPEN-FACED (sandwich) suggests a concentrated effort of awareness for information gained.

OPEN-HEART SURGERY comes as a strong advisement to correct damaging emotions generated by psychological dysfunctions.

OPEN HOUSE represents a forthright personality; straightforwardness.

OPEN MARRIAGE is a strong warning against acting deceptively; an inability to exercise loyalty and respect.

OPEN-MINDED indicates an intellectual perception; one primed for gaining wisdom through attained knowledge.

OPEN-MOUTHED infers a mind-state of expectation or narrow attitudes.

OPEN SEASON implies a time of accessibility, not necessarily for positive purposes.

OPEN SESAME will denote a "key" one has been looking for; a solution or means to accomplish something.

OPEN WINDOW indicates a "clear view" of something. This will be understood by the individual dreamer.

OPERA connotes a mature perspective.

OPERA GLASSES relate to attentiveness; an interest in understanding situational events.

OPERA HOUSE typifies a "replay" of events, indicating a need to better understand a recent situation. May also refer to a counterproductive element in one's life.

OPERATING ROOM (O.R.) stands for the "tools" and "conditions" that are right for correcting a negative within self or another.

OPERATION (medical) advises of a need to "correct" a dysfunctional element or negative factor within self.

OPERATOR (any type) will represent one who has "operational" capability and knowledge of a specific element or ability.

OPHTHALMOLOGIST characterizes a person who has the insight and ability to straighten out another's altered perspective.

OPIUM corresponds to that which one voluntarily allows to dull one's senses, intelligence, reasoning, or perspective.

OPOSSUM denotes backward or inverted views; a caution to stop "turning things around" to suit self.

OPPONENT represents an adversary or competitor.

OPPORTUNIST may not infer a negative connotation; it may well indicate a need to begin taking advantage of opportunities presented along the dreamer's path.

OPTICAL ILLUSION points out an element in life that is not perceived with accuracy; a false view.

OPTIMIST characterizes one who has a tendency to look on the bright side of things; having a great measure of hope. This may or may not be a positive symbol. Recall surrounding dreamscape details for clarity.

OPTION presents itself as a dream symbol to reveal opportunities or alternate choices one has in life.

ORACLE usually reveals a forthcoming event in one's life. Yet this same symbol can also warn against being obsessed with the future.

ORAL TRADITION reminds us of the importance of preserving truths.

ORANGE (color) represents our physical and mental energies.

ORANGE (fruit) portrays the nourishing benefits of utilizing our inner energies for the benefit of others.

ORANGE STICK comes as a warning to "clean up" one's behavior and/or manner of interacting with others; utilize more honest methods.

ORANGUTAN See ape.

ORATION will reveal an important aspect for the dreamer; will emphasize something the dreamer has been wanting to know.

ORB See sphere.

ORBIT advises of an unproductive course, one that's going around and around without advancing toward a concluding goal or destination.

ORCA See whale.

ORCHARD almost always symbolizes an individual's inherent talents. For further clarification, recall what condition the orchard was in. Was it fruitful? Diseased? Infested with insects or drought? Flooded?

ORCHESTRA refers to group harmony.

ORCHID signifies a "fragile" talent or benefit that must be carefully maintained.

ORDINANCE will most often underscore a proper manner of behavior.

ORDNANCE defines the "tools" or means one has available to defend or protect self in life.

OREGANO alludes to an "added" emphasis placed on an issue; an enhancement.

ORGAN (musical) pertains to a complex aspect associated with an issue.

ORGAN (physiological) See specific type.

ORGANDY (fabric) portrays a "stiff" personality; insensitivity.

ORGAN GRINDER suggests a need for contemplation.

ORGANZA (fabric) reveals a "hardened" underlying personality.

ORGY warns of an inability to control self. This won't necessarily have a sexual connotation. The dreamer will make the correct association.

ORIEL See bay window.

ORIGAMI symbolizes a tendency to "reconfigure" events; a warning against altering facts or rearranging them to suit self.

ORIOLE relates to a "helpful" element in one's life, yet possesses a potential to generate a negative effect if utilized incorrectly.

ORNAMENT will indicate the presence of an embellishment or extraneous aspect in one's life.

ORNITHOLOGY (study of) refers to a high interest in learning the various psychological mechanisms associates utilize.

ORPHAN symbolizes individual thought; unique beliefs or perspectives; innovative thinking.

ORRISROOT will suggest a "stabilizing" element in one's life.

ORTHODONTIST signifies a person who has the ability and knowledge to help another communicate more effectively.

ORTHODOX connotes an adherence to strict basic beliefs; firm dogma.

ORTHOPEDIST exemplifies an individual who can redirect another's path toward a "straight" course.

OSCILLATING denotes instability; a continual variation.

OSIRIS (Egyptian mythology) characterizes renewal; a rebirth.

OSMOSIS emphasizes understanding.

OSPREY See hawk.

OSTEOPOROSIS indicates a failing of one's inner strength; waning motivation or sense of purpose.

OSTRICH connotes subconscious denials; an inability or refusal to face responsibilities and/or reality.

OTOSCOPE represents a need to analyze the cause of one's imbalanced perspectives.

OTTER implies the recognition of inner joy generated by spirituality.

OTTOMAN See footstool.

OUIJA BOARD comes as a severe warning to "look within" for answers instead of turning to a dependency on others.

OUTBOARD MOTOR relates to spiritual motivational factors.

OUTCAST pertains to an individual who doesn't follow the crowd; one who thinks for self. In rare instances, this symbol may indicate a "guilt" complex for being different.

OUTCROPPING is an attention-getting symbol. This attempts to draw the dreamer's attention to something important in life.

OUTDATED may not be a negative symbol, for it may apply to a long-held truth that few currently believe. Recall surrounding dream details for clarification.

OUTDOORSWOMAN characterizes a recognition of one's inherent bond with natural forces.

OUTER SPACE represents deeper knowledge; a "reach" for greater understanding of true Reality.

OUTGROWTH alludes to a resulting effect or manifestation.

OUTGUNNED connotes a failed attempt to "better" another. This may pertain to aspects of skill, intelligence, or accomplishment.

OUTHOUSE illustrates a need to rid self of wasteful elements in one's life.

OUTLANDER characterizes a person who stands out as being clearly different from those around her or him. This usually reveals a free-thinker, one unafraid to openly express unique and individualistic perspectives or ideas.

OUTLAW will indicate one who behaves in an unlawful manner; the "lawful" aspect can refer to ethical, moral, or spiritual elements.

OUTLET exemplifies an opportunity to "release" negative or retained aspects that restrict one's freedom or health.

OUTLET (electrical) provides one with an available source of energy or empowerment.

OUTLINE signifies a need for planning; suggests deep thought be applied before action is taken.

OUTNUMBERED implies that your plan, idea, or behavior is not shared by the majority. This is not necessarily a negative symbol. It may denote innovativeness.

OUT-OF-BODY presented in a dreamscape usually corresponds with a true experiential event. It also may reveal a need to look at something from a different perspective.

OUT-OF-BOUNDS stands for exceeding a limitation or restrictive barrier and may commend one for doing so.

OUT-OF-POCKET portrays determined personal effort; utilizing one's own resources to accomplish something.

OUTPATIENT illustrates a negative condition within self that can be healed only by self.

OUTPOST connotes resting points along one's right path. This assures the dreamer that, although her or his path may be far distant from others, there have been those who've gone before and the dreamer is not alone.

OUTRAGE comes as a message to gain a greater measure of acceptance and intellectual reasoning.

OUTRANKED will usually underscore one's "rightness" that has externally been overridden by another who is perceived as being more knowledgeable or experienced. This comes as a personal verification message.

OUTSIDE signifies an "external" position or source.

OUTSIDE CHANCE indicates the existence of a slim probability for something to manifest.

OUTSMARTED implies one didn't consider all aspects of an issue or situation. This is actually an experiential learning symbol.

OUTSPOKEN marks a candid, uninhibited communication; basic honesty.

OUT TAKE usually illustrates one's mistakes made. This can be a personally revealing dream symbol.

OUTWARD BOUND suggests a time or condition ripe for self-discovery.

OVAL (shape) See oblong.

OVATION comes as a personal commendation or sign of recognition from one's Higher Self.

OVEN signals a method to gain completion or accomplishment. Recall the condition of the oven. Was it ON?

OVEN CLEANER will denote an attempt or desire to insure one's methods are untainted.

OVENPROOF relates to precautions taken while applying methods of manifesting one's goals.

OVER (direction) pertains to a need to pass or climb over a difficult element blocking one's path. This will call for determination.

OVERALLS denote personal efforts; prepared for challenges; an attitude that has no fear of hard work.

OVERBALANCED connotes overcompensation.

OVERBITE represents the withholding of select thoughts.

OVERBLOWN alludes to an exaggeration.

OVERBOARD warns of spiritual impulsiveness.

OVER BOOKED symbolizes a lack of foresight, planning.

OVERCAST (sky) suggests mental or emotional cloudiness; a lack of perceptual clarity.

OVERCHARGED is a symbol that converts a karmic overpay-

O

ment from a "balance" status to an "asset" position.

OVERCOAT exemplifies a personal state of self-protection.

OVERDOSE pertains to an "excess." This will help the dreamer determine the proper amount of something she or he requires in life.

OVERDRAFT corresponds to impatience; one is too anxious and jumping ahead of self.

OVERDRIVE advises one to slow his or her pace. Going too fast and expending too much energy causes a loss of valuable lessons that are not noted.

OVEREXPOSURE signifies redundancy; overkill; beating an issue to death.

OVERFILLED (glass/bowl) reveals one's inability to comprehend all that is taken in; much will be missed. This symbol is likened to the message of "biting off more than one can chew."

OVERFLOW emphasizes a state of abundance. Recall "what" is overflowing. Did it have color? Consistency? From what was it flowing?

OVERGROWTH will apply to a lack of interest or care given to a personal talent or inherent ability.

OVERHAUL portrays an interest in caring for and maintaining optimum condition of an element in one's life. This could refer to

one's physical, mental, emotional, or spiritual aspects.

OVERHEATED warns of a need to pull back and analyze something in a rational manner.

OVERINDULGENCE connotes an excessiveness.

OVERKILL alludes to an exaggeration; an excessive amount of attention or effort applied to something in one's life.

OVERLAY may reveal an ulterior motive or it could represent a protective layer. Recall surrounding dream details for clarification.

OVERLOADED warns against taking on too much.

OVERLOOKS (scenic) indicate a need for a wider view of an issue. Something is literally being "overlooked."

OVERPASS reveals a directional solution to a problematical path obstacle.

OVERQUALIFIED will denote a person's inflated opinion of self. Every type of work supplies valuable learning experiences.

OVERRATED pertains to an attempt to greatly enhance something.

OVERRULED will come as a guiding message from one's Higher Self or even one's own conscience.

OVERSEER usually denotes one's Higher Self or conscience.

OVERSOLD suggests a promise that can't be kept; exaggerating one's abilities.

OVERSHADOWED may be an implication that one is vying for competition or a suffocating and demeaning situation is manifesting. Recall dream details for clarification on this intention.

OVER SHIRT alludes to an altered mood; a sense of preserving the essence of self from others.

OVERSHOES suggest an attempt to disassociate one's emotional responses from sensitive issues encountered along one's life path; a lack of bonding sensitivity with the earth.

OVERSIGHT comes to pinpoint an element the dreamer has overlooked in life.

OVERSIZED reveals some kind of aspect in the dreamer's life that is "too big" for him or her at the present time; connotes an issue or concept that one has not grown into yet.

OVERSLEPT is a serious warning to "wake up!" Be AWARE!

OVERSPENDING represents an over-extension of self.

OVER STAFFED indicates an excessive effort applied to an element in one's life.

OVERSTEPPING will symbolize an attempt to step over the line or cross limits. This is a message from one's Higher Self or conscience.

OVERSTUFFED indicates a lack of acceptance; an inability to take one moment at a time.

OVERTHROWN implies a missed goal; reaching too far.

OVERTIME suggests extra personal efforts are needed to accomplish one's goal.

OVERTURNED may indicate a need to reverse a decision or choice or it could suggest that one give closer inspection to something—leave nothing unturned.

OVERWEIGHT will not infer obesity, yet it means that one is carrying excessive burdens and responsibilities; a need to rid self of superficial or hampering aspects. This is most often in reference to emotional psychological self-generated mechanisms.

OVERWHELMED may refer to a lack of acceptance or a "forcing" of knowledge one isn't ready to comprehend.

OVERWORKED comes to emphasize that one can control the level and extent of personal efforts applied to a situation. This symbol will attempt to underscore WHO has the control over this.

OWL characterizes heightened observational skills and developed awareness coupled with sharpened perceptive abilities; wisdom resulting from high spiritual enlightenment.

OWLET will signify one on the correct spiritual path.

OXBLOOD (color) refers to earthy emotions and personality traits.

OXBOW (stream configuration) indicates a meandering spiritual path that is destined to bring enlightenment.

OXEN connotes overwork; suggests a psychological cause.

OXFORD (shoes) pertain to an immaturity; a desire to stay youthful and not be subjected to the responsibilities of adulthood.

OXYGEN MASK exemplifies a sense of suffocation; an inability to accept new ideas and the psychological panic they cause within self.

OYSTER represents inner fears of anything new or of having to interact with others.

OZARKS pertain to "basic" necessities in life; a personality or lifestyle lacking extraneous elements; understanding the value of simple basics.

OZ connotes a willful reluctance to face or accept reality.

OZONE LAYER portrays rarely-perceived protective elements in one's life and the ignorant unawareness of same; corresponds with the protective manifestations created by God, such as our own Spirit Essence of the Higher Self, Guiding Angels, etc.

𝒫

PABLUM is a soft baby food; therefore, it connotes simplistic ideas and easy methods; a fear of difficult situations or tasks; a tendency to keep things as easy as possible for self.

PACE CAR will usually guide the dreamer into a proper rate of progression. Depending on the speed of the dream pace car, it will indicate an acceleration or slowing down.

PACING interprets into anxiety or worry. This symbol comes to underscore the futileness of such mental exertion. One needs more acceptance in life.

PACEMAKER pertains to a need to regulate one's emotional displays and will most often signify a need to calm excitability.

PACHYDERM See specific type.

PACIFIER indicates an easier path chosen.

PACIFISM represents a fear of conflict and a tendency to take the most peaceful and less troublesome path.

PACK (of animals) portrays a multiple of whatever animal is pre-sented in the pack. This will indicate an "increase" or abundance.

PACKAGE applies to those material goods one perceives as being important in life. What was in the package? Was it gift wrapped?

PACKING (material) illustrates a need for "protection." This implies that something in one's life needs to be handled in a delicate manner.

PACKING (up) suggests a forthcoming move. This may not refer to an actual physical relocation, but may relate to an employment move or a situational one.

PACKINGHOUSE See meatpacking house.

PACK RAT warns of a tendency to collect insignificant or superficial aspects; advises of a return to the important basics.

PACK TRAIN signifies the presence of unnecessary elements in one's life.

PAD See cushion.

PAD (of paper) See notebook.

PADDING corresponds to the effect of "softening" or "easing" something in life. It may also indicate an exaggeration depending on surrounding dreamscape details.

PADDLE (re: boat) See oar.

PADDLE (discipline) See spanking.

P

PADDLE BOAT (paddle wheel) exemplifies an element that serves as a spiritual impetus.

PADDOCK See corral.

PADDY WAGON implies "being caught" for a misdeed. This will remind one that, in the end, one pays for wrongdoings.

PADLOCK represents hidden elements; aspects we keep hidden.

PADRE See religious figure.

PAGAN will usually symbolize the existence of a spiritual belief that differs from the dreamer's. This is not necessarily a negative connotation. Recall surrounding dreamscape details for further clarification.

PAGE (attendant) characterizes a helper; assistant.

PAGE (book) comes to point out something the dreamer should be aware of. Recall what was on the page. What type of book was it in? Color?

PAGER See beeper.

PAGODA signifies spiritual misconceptions associated with the Truths as related to the precepts of the Law of One.

PAIL signifies the amount of spirituality one utilizes in life. What was the pail made of? Was it full or empty? What quality was the content?

PAIN always represents a personally harmful element in one's life. This could be caused by an external source or it may be generated by self.

PAIN IN THE NECK will not be an actual physical indication, but rather will refer to a personal irritation usually caused by another individual for whom the dreamer has no tolerance. This suggests a need for greater acceptance.

PAINKILLER See analgesic.

PAINT represents a coverup of some type being done.

PAINT (artist's) denotes personal tools for self-expression.

PAINTBRUSH pertains to a desire to alter something in one's life.

PAINTING (picture) will usually contain an important element to which the dreamer needs to give attention.

PAIR may suggest duality or it may infer a "close connection" between two elements in one's life.

PAISLEY (pattern) signifies an element of true Reality.

PAJAMA See nightgown.

PALACE See castle.

PALATE corresponds to one's sense of "taste" in reference to behavior, choices, interaction, perceptual, etc.

PALAZZO See castle.

PALE (complexion) connotes a dispirited state.

PALEONTOLOGY (study of) represents an inherent curiosity regarding humankind's beginnings.

PALETTE indicates multiple opportunities to express one's thoughts.

PALETTE KNIFE applies to an available tool for "combining" and harmoniously blending ideas and concepts.

PALL See coffin.

PALL (dull) relates to a waning interest; boring.

PALLADIUM constitutes a personal safeguard; an element of personal protection.

PALLBEARER represents the "releasing" of personal pain.

PALLET See bed.

PALM (hand) emphasizes revealing qualities of one's character. Recall if the dream palm was soft or calloused. Did it hold something? Was it in a giving or taking position.

PALM (tree) will usually have a spiritual connotation. Recall surrounding dreamscape elements for further clarification.

PALMISTRY typifies irrationality; a lack of acceptance.

PALM SUNDAY defines an attitude of spiritual reverence.

PALOMINO illustrates a gentle freedom; a quiet appreciation for one's unique individuality.

PALPATE symbolizes the act of giving deeper inspection or attention to an issue.

PALSY will suggest a personally-generated impairment of some type. Review personal attitudes or fears.

PALTRY may seem to suggest "insignificance" but it usually indicates a personally-held perspective of grandeur that is not being realized. This is a caution to lower one's self-image, for it is inflated.

PAMPAS GRASS implies a fragile situation or personality, depending on surrounding dreamscape details.

PAMPERED pertains to actions that retard one's growth.

PAMPHLET denotes information specific to the dreamer. Recall what type of pamphlet was presented. What did it say? What design, if any, was on it? Color? Condition?

PAN (cook) represents a "tool" available to bring something to fruition or completion in life.

PAN (Greek mythology) characterizes a call to return to nature and the appreciation of same.

PANATELLA See cigar.

PANCAKE implies a "flat" quality. This will refer to a personal element in one's life, usually related to self-expression.

P

PANCREAS connotes a vital aspect in one's life that maintains a balanced perspective.

PANCREATITIS warns of a perception that is in error.

PANDA (bear) will reveal a friend with ulterior motives.

PANDEMIC suggests a "widespread" attitude or condition.

PANDEMONIUM emphasizes a state of confusion which usually constitutes an internal mental or emotional state.

PANDER advises one to stop giving in to weaknesses.

PANDORA (Greek mythology) characterizes a person who will eventually cause harm or bring negative elements into one's life.

PANDORA'S BOX (Greek mythology) defines a harmful situation that should be avoided; may also refer to an individual or issue.

PANE (glass) applies to a separation of self from a life element.

PANELING signifies an "enhancement" of some type; an attempt to improve conditions.

PANEL TRUCK portrays that which is carried over into the workplace, usually personal attitudes or needed "tools." Recall associative dream details for deeper meaning.

PANHANDLE (beg) stands for a state of desperation. Depending on the surrounding elements of the dream, this symbol may warn of laziness.

PANIC BUTTON represents high anxiety or an extreme state of confusion.

PANNIER See basket.

PANORAMA (view) implies a need to obtain a wider perspective of something in one's life.

PANPIPE exemplifies lightheartedness; a cheerful mood.

PANSY exemplifies a fearful personality; fear of ridicule or reprisal.

PANTHER suggests caution.

PANTING symbolizes overexertion or anxiety regarding high expectation; indicates a need for acceptance.

PANTOMIME See mime.

PANTRY stands for a reserve of inner strength. The key here is to recall if the pantry was full or empty. What did it contain?

PANTYHOSE will apply to some type of feminine aspect. Surrounding dream details will make a clarifying association.

PANTY RAID warns of sexual immaturity.

PAPAYA connotes a need to calm emotions or anxiety.

PAPER most often refers to some type of communication, yet can also have other interpretations depending on the specific type.

379

PAPERBACK (book) will have a personal meaning for each dreamer. Recall what the book's title was. Did this hold a special meaning for you? What was the book's condition? Where was it found?

PAPERBOY symbolizes "delivered" information. This may be advising one to seek his or her own information instead of receiving only that which someone else deems you should know.

PAPER CLIP suggests a need for attachments.

PAPER CUT indicates a careless use of information.

PAPER CUTTER pertains to a need to "trim" superficial or extraneous elements from a piece of information.

PAPERHANGER characterizes a person who attempts to cover up something; one who conceals or attempts to present a better image; may indicate deception.

PAPER MILL relates to the manner one processes information. Recall the type of paper being made. Was the mill's operation efficient? Did it require many workers or just a few?

PAPER MONEY See money.

PAPER PLANT See papyrus.

PAPER-THIN refers to weak; having little substance.

PAPER TIGER signifies false power; lacking authority or strength.

PAPER TRAIL exemplifies "evidence" one leaves behind.

PAPER WASP See hornet.

PAPERWEIGHT stands for a need to retain important information.

PAPERWORK may indicate unnecessary work associated with an element in one's life.

PAPETERIE represents mental organization; an efficient thought process.

PAPIER-MACHE portrays what is done with information one receives. Recall what was formed from the paper, this will be the revealing element.

PAPRIKA See red pepper.

PAPYRUS corresponds with "delicate" information that requires careful discernment.

PARABLE emphasizes valuable lessons that need to be learned or recalled.

PARACHUTE reveals psychological rationalizations. Recall the condition and color of the dream parachute. How did it work?

PARADE symbolizes a desire to be recognized; may indicate arrogance.

PARADIGM See example.

PARADISE relates to one's personal perspective of the perfect scenario, condition, or ultimate goal.

PARADOX reveals a situation or concept that "appears" contradictory.

PARAFFIN signifies a need to preserve or seal something. The dreamer will make the associative connection.

PARAGON characterizes one who has made an ultimate achievement at something; a person who has attained a prime position or status in respect to personal accomplishment.

PARAKEET represents a lack of analytical spiritual thinking.

PARALEGAL characterizes a person who understands the basics of an issue.

PARALLEL BARS signify an "equal" grip on something in one's life; a firm and balanced grasp of a situation or concept.

PARALYSIS reveals a psychological state of denial; a tendency to be emotionally numb or remain in an immobilized state.

PARAMEDIC defines an individual who is capable of an immediate, knowledgeable response.

PARAMOUR pertains to an intimacy, not necessarily a sexual one.

PARANOIA portrays inner fears.

PARANORMAL (events/abili-ties) reveals inherent talents or elements of true Reality.

PARAPHERNALIA connotes personal possessions that are unique or important to an individual.

PARAPLEGIA emphasizes the true "essence" of an individual; underscores the "mind" as being one's beingness.

PARAPSYCHOLOGY (study of) denotes a high interest in humankind's interconnectedness with true Reality.

PARASAILING implies a spiritually disassociative state; being close to spiritual matters yet not wanting to immerse self in them.

PARASITE alludes to a "draining" aspect in one's life. This could refer to a physical, mental, emotional, or spiritual element.

PARASOL connotes a frivolous spiritual attitude or belief system.

PARATROOPER usually relates to emotional disturbances.

PARCEL See package.

PARCHED signifies a great inner need. The surrounding dreamscape details will clarify this.

PARCHMENT (paper) illustrates an authoritative message or source. Recall if the paper had writing on it or if it was associated with related aspects of the dream.

PARDON typifies an exoneration; forgiveness intended to negate personal guilt.

PAREGORIC suggests a need for greater acceptance.

PARENT will represent a person to respect and honor. This symbol may have different meanings for each dreamer, depending on individual personal experiences.

PARENTHESIS will usually contain a word that is intended to further explain something.

PARFAIT applies to a variety of spiritual concepts that are combined in a confusing manner.

PARFLECHE portrays "basics." This alludes to an individual who sticks with basic necessities or bottom-line concepts.

PARIAH may not indicate a negative aspect. Depending on surrounding dreamscape factors, this symbol may refer to an individual who follows her or his own path.

PARING KNIFE will suggest a need to "pare down" something in one's life. Associative dream aspects will usually pinpoint this issue.

PARK (grounds) constitutes a place or time of respite.

PARKA connotes responsible reactions.

PARK AVENUE illustrates an egotistical personality.

PARKING signifies the defining and securing of a stable state or position, usually "temporarily" for the purpose of gaining needed information.

PARKING METER will always reveal a "specified" span of time allotted for one to give time or attention to a selective issue.

PARKS (Rosa) represents the recognition and practicing of one's inherent rights and freedoms regardless of possible repercussions.

PARKWAY connotes a phase of one's path that produces an accelerated, trouble-free advancement.

PARLAYED portrays an attempt to increase one's benefits, assets, or talents.

PARLEYED defines an attempt to negotiate a peaceful resolution.

PARLOR alludes to out-dated ideas or characteristics; old-fashioned.

PARODY See sarcasm.

PAROLE represents a time of testing one's integrity.

PAROLEE characterizes a person who needs to carefully watch his or her behavior. This Parolee will not necessarily indicate a "bad" individual but the associative concept that's important for the dreamer is the "extreme necessity of watching your P's and Q's for a time."

PARQUETRY (flooring) defines a personality rich in succinct wisdom.

PARQUETRY (woodcraft) reveals an attention to fine detail and associative thought.

PARROT typifies verbosity.

PARRY relates to a defensive position or action taken.

PARSLEY represents unrecognized benefits and nourishing elements in life.

PARSNIP signifies neglected opportunities.

PARSON See religious figure.

PARTICLE BOARD portrays multiple aspects of an issue.

PARTING SHOT implies a "last word" or the expressing of one's final say on something.

PARTITION exemplifies a separating or disassociative attitude.

PARTNER relates to someone closely associated with the dreamer.

PARTRIDGE See quail.

PARTY will represent a celebration for a specific reason. Recall what was being celebrated for further clarification.

PARTY LINE (telephone) comes as a warning to reveal a lack or loss of privacy unbeknownst to the dreamer.

PAS DE DEUX corresponds to a collaboration between two individuals. This may be a revealing event for the dreamer.

PASQUEFLOWER stands for spiritual inspirations.

PASS (mountain) relates to a "way through" a difficulty.

PASS (move past) may suggest something "missed" in life or it may indicate an element that doesn't require attention. Recall surrounding dream details for further clarification.

PASS (sanction) will reveal an acceptance or agreement of something one is planning.

PASS (succeed) indicates a stage or goal that has been accomplished.

PASS (vehicular) comes as a advisement to "go around" an element in one's way.

PASSAGEWAY will reveal a "way through" a difficult situation or confusing concept.

PASSBOOK See bankbook.

PASSE will infer that something is out-of-date, yet, depending on surrounding dream elements, this may reveal a person's personal opinion rather than actual fact.

PASSENGER portrays movement; actively applying efforts to advance along one's path.

PASSENGER PIGEON connotes "beauty destroyed by greed."

PASSION will not explicitly infer a sexual implication, but rather a nearly consuming emotion.

PASSION FLOWER alludes to the beauty of possessing a positive passion such as empathy, compassion, etc.

PASSION PLAY reveals a person's display of emotional dramatics; an exaggeration for the purpose of attention.

PASSIVE RESISTANCE will advise a peaceful way to resist or express opposition.

PASSIVE RESTRAINT connotes an automatic, usually concealed, method of restraint.

PASSIVISM suggests a peaceful personality, yet may come as an important advisement to start "expending" efforts toward a goal.

PASSKEY pertains to advancement opportunities; elements that provide key solutions or inspirations.

PASSOVER signifies the protective elements of innocence or being guiltless.

PASSPORT illustrates one's rite of passage; a readiness for advancement.

PASSWORD denotes aspects in one's life that serve as "keys" or "gateways" to prime opportunities.

PAST will sometimes serve as a "past" example or it will indicate something one should leave behind where it belongs.

PASTA constitutes a "substantial" or "basic" element in one's life.

PASTE suggests a need for temporary cohesiveness. This would infer the need to quickly make attempts at resolving a current problem or negative situation in one's life.

PASTEL (chalk) suggests a person's *intent* to soften a specific personality trait. Refer to the specific color in this dictionary for further interpretation.

PASTEL (hue) implies a gentleness or soft quality associated with the specific color's individual interpretation. Refer to specific color.

PASTE-UP See layout.

PASTEUR (Louis) characterizes a person who is interested in the basic, "pure" facts of an issue.

PASTEURIZATION signifies the intent to discount superficial or extraneous elements from an issue or concept.

PASTOR See religious figure.

PASTORAL (setting) portrays a tranquil atmosphere; a harmonic and restful condition.

PASTRAMI exemplifies a condition, concept, or other element that elicits an emotional response.

PASTRY relates a "perception" of high value, something

"sweet." This would be associated with an individual's unique personal perspective and not necessarily be a true indication. Recall what the pastry was and what condition it was in. Was it dripping with honey? Was it stale? Underbaked? Coated with sugar? Refer to other types of pastry listed in this dictionary.

PASTURE represents one's voluntary usefulness in life. Was someone out in the pasture? Who was in the dream pasture? What were they doing? What condition was the pasture in? Was it full of flowers or weeds? Was it completely barren?

PAT (on back) denotes a sign of encouragement.

PAT (on head) implies a patronizing response.

PATCH (repair) symbolizes a "temporary" solution.

PATCHOULI indicates an intense personality.

PATCH TEST connotes an attempt to discover and neutralize one's psychological responses.

PATCHWORK (pattern) comes to underscore the importance of variety in one's life; pertains to multiple perceptive qualities.

PATELLA reflects a vulnerable phase in one's life path.

PATENT signifies recognition or the protection of one's innovative ideas.

PATENT LEATHER depicts a personal need for attention.

PATENT OFFICE stands for authoritative recognition.

PATERNITY TEST warns against attempting to circumvent personal responsibility.

PATH will most often signify a person's individual road or direction in life.

PATHFINDER characterizes an individual who leads others to their life path. This is a direct warning, for nobody should tell another which path to take in life. This must be a personal decision.

PATHOLOGY (study of) indicates a need to analyze a negative situation that currently exists in one's life.

PATIENCE usually comes as an advisory message.

PATIENT (infirm) implies the need for care or healing. Recall the surrounding dreamscape details for further clarity.

PATINA denotes an overall sensation or impression; a general look to one's appearance and demeanor caused by acquired age or wisdom.

PATIO implies open-mindedness.

PATRIARCH connotes a person who acts as a figurehead.

PATRICIAN See nobility.

PATRICIDE illustrates a denial of an aspect of self.

PATRIOT represents loyalty.

PATROL pertains to watchfulness; an acute awareness.

PATROL CAR See squad car.

PATRON characterizes a supportive individual.

PATRON SAINT pertains to a guiding or protective ideal or motivational force.

PATTERNS indicate multiple characteristics, quality, and methods through which behavior is expressed. Refer to specific pattern types in this dictionary for individual interpretation.

PATTY SHELL (edible) symbolizes an unexpected and initially unrecognized benefit in one's life.

PAUL BUNYAN signifies the extent of one's potential.

PAUNCH connotes waning awareness and motivation.

PAUPER reveals a person who doesn't recognize the value of personal abilities or worth.

PAVEMENT implies a separation from one's natural bond with earth and inherent natural abilities.

PAVING relates to a desire for an easy life.

PAVLOV (Ivan) exemplifies a conditioned response. This sym- bol comes to remind one that this type of reaction can be altered through understanding.

PAW (pet's) portrays encouragement and loyalty of a friend.

PAWN (chess) applies to one who is "used" by another; may also indicate an opinion of self.

PAWN (hock) connotes a problematical solution or outlet.

PAWNBROKER will signify one who can provide temporary help for another.

PAWNSHOP represents sacrifices made.

PAWN TICKET stands for a "way out" of a problem; a solution.

PAYCHECK usually represents the value of one's deeds, beliefs, or relationships. Recall what amount the paycheck was for. Was it minimum wage? Was overtime on it?

PAYDIRT denotes a new element in one's life that has the capability of bringing multiple benefits.

PAY LOADER suggests a need for major "digging" to be done; an advisement to do research or some type of background inspection.

PAYMASTER characterizes spiritual law; those who know and understand the real value of deeds done.

PAYOLA connotes misdeeds and misplaced priorities; indicates one who would do anything for money; bribery.

PAYROLL usually reveals the value of associates. Recall who was doing the payroll. What were the check amounts?

PEA most often symbolizes a small amount of something. Recall what the pea was associated with in the dream.

PEACE CORPS symbolizes an opportunity to help others.

PEACEKEEPER portrays an individual who attempts to find a peaceful way of resolving conflict. A dream Peacekeeper may symbolize one's own Higher Self.

PEACE OFFERING connotes an attempt at reconciliation; an apology.

PEACE PIPE indicates harmonious intentions.

PEACE SIGN represents a friendly, peaceful greeting.

PEACH constitutes satisfaction; a desired element.

PEACOCK emphasizes arrogance.

PEACOCK BLUE (color) connotes a healing spiritual energy.

PEA JACKET symbolizes efforts applied to spiritual aspects in life.

PEAL (bells) indicates a call to attention; a need for increased awareness.

PEALE (Norman Vincent) reminds us to help ourselves; stresses our own inner power.

PEANUT will refer to the minor aspects of our life.

PEANUT BRITTLE pertains to a temporarily difficult situation.

PEANUT BUTTER corresponds to a source of energy or motivation.

PEANUT OIL refers to a rich source of nourishment which can imply mental, emotional, physical, or spiritual aspects. Recall surrounding dreamscape details for further clarification.

PEANUT SHELLS signify the utilization of all opportunities presented in one's life; a full experiential awareness.

PEAR represents duality.

PEARL applies to perseverance; spiritually-based fortitude.

PEARL DIVER typifies one who gleans spiritual "pearls" from his or her searching efforts.

PEARL HARBOR reminds us to remain aware in life.

PEARL OYSTER indicates a life aspect that will contain valuable spiritual elements.

PEASANT connotes simplicity and the value of same.

PEA-SHOOTER represents a negative aspect (tool) that could cause harm to others. The surrounding dream details will clarify this meaning for the dreamer.

PEA SOUP pertains to a cloudy view; unclear perspective.

PEAT suggests a life factor that has the capability of enriching something.

PEAT BOG See bog.

PEAT MOSS portrays a protective element; a supportive aspect that serves to retain and prolong the effects of multiple nourishing factors.

PEBBLE implies diversity.

PECCARY See boar.

PECK (pick at) relates to a lack of acceptance; irritable responses.

PECKING ORDER will attempt to remind one of his or her place. This symbol usually clarifies the cause of an irritating life situation.

PECTIN depicts a desire to "solidify" some aspect in one's life; a factor that has the capability of manifesting a goal or plan.

PECTORAL (necklace) suggests a representation of one's personal protective energy or force.

PEDAL (device) applies to an opportunity to advance or increase motivation.

PEDAL PUSHERS portray a personal preparation for work.

PEDDLER can reveal unexpected opportunities.

PEDESTAL comes as a warning against placing anything or anyone in a highly elevated position.

PEDESTRIANS allude to those around us who are "walking" their own paths in life, trying to learn through their own experiences.

PEDIATRICIAN characterizes one who has the capability and knowledge to heal or correct beginning problems with one's growth.

PEDICAB represents servitude or arrogance, depending on "who" was pulling the cab and who was sitting in it.

PEDICURE marks an attendance to one's manner of path progression.

PEDIGREE (certificate) refers to a "certification" of some type. Recall the surrounding dreamscape aspects for clarity here. Usually this symbol will be recognized by the dreamer.

PEEKABOO (game) warns of "game-playing" in life; sends a message to stop vacillating or creating personal agendas.

PEEL See paring knife.

PEEL See rind.

PEELER (utensil) denotes a need to "peel away" the surface layer of an aspect in one's life that is lacking clarity or definition.

PEEPHOLE indicates a hint associated with something the dreamer needs to know; a clue; insight.

PEEPING TOM See voyeur.

PEEP SHOW warns against wasting one's time and energy on superficial life elements; comes as a message to attend to the aspects of one's purpose.

PEERS may relate to personal associates, acquaintances, or friends and reveal an indication of associated characteristics; quality and type of one's circle.

PEG represents a marker; indicator; may denote a natural "connective" element.

PEGASUS (Greek mythology) emphasizes possibilities that are rarely considered.

PEGBOARD represents a method of organization; an opportunity to sort things out.

PEG LEG denotes the existence of an alternative.

PEKINESE (dog breed) portrays a self-absorbed friend or associate.

PELICAN pertains to a spiritual gluttony; possessiveness.

PELLET alludes to an element in one's life that contains multiple aspects.

PELLET STOVE defines an "inefficient" method of accomplishing something.

PELT (animal skin) will represent an "essence" bond with the presented animal. See specific animal type in this dictionary.

PELTED stands for an inundation of something in one's life; an overwhelming element.

PELVIS relates to the "center" or beginning point of one's inner strength.

PEMMICAN signifies an extremely high "concentration" of one's personal energy or high wisdom.

PEN (enclosure) illustrates confinement, usually self-generated.

PEN (writing) exemplifies the "recording" of something. Surrounding dreamscape details will indicate whether or not something "needs" to be written down.

PENAL CODE will always refer to spiritual law according to the Precepts of the Law of One . . . not to any confining earthly "religious" dogma.

PENALTY corresponds with a "balancing" element; a corrective justification.

PENALTY BOX signifies a "payment" made for a misdeed. Recall "who" was in the penalty box. What was the infraction?

PENCHANT See predilection.

PENCIL represents an "intention" that may or may not manifest.

PENDANT will always signify something important. Recall if it contained a gemstone. If so, what was the color and clarity? Was the Pendant in a specific shape? Form? Silver or gold?

PENDULUM stands for the swinging momentum of life; the ups and downs that can be expected.

PENETRATION (any type) connotes a successful effort.

PENGUIN suggests spiritual duality.

PENHOLDER implies a need for recording or noting something.

PENICILLIN calls for protective measures to be applied. Surrounding dreamscape details will clarify this; if not, the dreamer will usually make the right association.

PENITENTIARY denotes an ultimate result or conclusion. This is a dream symbol that stems from one's Higher Self or conscience.

PENKNIFE See pocketknife.

PENLIGHT represents a personally responsible state of awareness.

PEN NAME See pseudonym.

PENNANT applies to identity or loyalties. Recall what the pennant represented. What was the color? The condition?

PENNILESS will not refer to monetary aspects, but rather emphasize the value of humanitarian or spiritual riches.

PENNY See money.

PENNY-PINCHING indicates a frugal mind-set. Recall surrounding dream details to determine if this was a caution or advisement.

PENNYROYAL will symbolize an element in one's life that eases the effects of irritations; acceptance.

PEN PAL represents companionable relationships that are kept at a distance.

PENSION signifies benefits earned from long-suffering and perseverance.

PENTAGON characterizes secretive dealings; ulterior motives.

PENTHOUSE relates to an attitude of being above others.

PEON indicates a low class. This will represent a personal attitude toward self or another.

PEONY denotes sensitivity.

PEOPLE portray the more complex human components of dreams. They are more diverse in meaning than any other image; therefore, the dreamer needs to recall multiple elements about the people presented in order to accurately analyze these human facets. Who was the person? What was the age? Was an occupation presented? What was the person wearing? Any jewelry? Did this person speak? If so, what was said? Refer to specific occupations for further detail.

PEOPLE MOVER symbolizes a helpful element that will speed one's path when it is going in a general direction for a time.

PEPPER typifies a symbol that indicates a "response" is needed.

PEPPERCORN illustrates a necessary communication forthcoming.

PEPPER MILL calls for "finer" perceptions or levels of awareness to be utilized.

PEPPERMINT indicates a "cleansing" or freshening of one's choice of words; softer manner of communication.

PEPPERONI refers to an "interesting" or personally provocative idea.

PEP PILL See amphetamine.

PEP TALK connotes a motivational impetus; a need to boost morale.

PERAMBULATOR See baby carriage.

PERCALE (fabric) alludes to a "preferred" element.

PERCENT (sign) will reveal a specialized meaning for each dreamer who will make an individualized association.

PERCH See roost.

PERCH (fish) denotes spiritual neutrality; a lack of spiritual direction.

PERCHERON (horse breed) pertains to great personal efforts applied to one's chosen path.

PERCOLATOR indicates a state of "brewing." Recall surrounding situational presentation. Who was doing the brewing? Did the aroma have a disagreeable or pleasant scent?

PEREGRINE FALCON See falcon.

PERENNIAL (plant) will define a "lasting" element in one's life.

PERFORATED will reveal an aspect in one's life that is not complete or is lacking continuity; may indicate a deception of some type.

PERFUME refers to an effort to conceal; a cover-up.

PERIDOT (color/gemstone) denotes a sunny disposition that serves as an uplifting and healing force for others.

PERIL will warn of a forthcoming harmful event.

PERIOD (mark) implies an "end" or conclusion to something in one's life.

PERIODIC TABLE will usually have a specific element emphasized. This will have a personal indication for the dreamer. Perhaps one needs more iron in his or her system. Gold or silver may have specific meaning. Is lead a concern?

PERIPHERY comes as a symbol

to draw the dreamer's attention to some aspect that is positioned on the outer fringe of one's immediate circle and needs his or her greater attention.

PERISCOPE advises one to give more attention to daily life rather than keeping self immersed in spiritual matters. Spirituality needs to be interwoven in daily affairs, not kept separate.

PERISHABLES will signify a situation or issue that needs immediate attention before it is no longer viable.

PERIWINKLE (flower) represents a fragile talent or inherent ability.

PERIWINKLE (shell) marks a spiritually significant element.

PERIWINKLE (snail) exemplifies spiritual fortitude.

PERJURY pertains to a falsehood.

PERMAFROST connotes a "frigid" personality; one with a cold and unsupportive exterior.

PERMANENT (hair treatment) symbolizes mental stability; thoughts that are "set" because of verifiable research done.

PERMISSION usually comes from one's Higher Self or other authoritative sources to provide an encouraging or motivational element.

PERMIT reveals the "rightness" of a planned move or deed. Recall if the permit was being given or revoked. What was it for? Did it have a specific color?

PERMUTATION See transmutation.

PERNICIOUS always warns of an all-consuming element in one's life; an aspect that can have a fatal effect.

PEROXIDE indicates a need to cleanse or heal. This may also refer to a "whitewashing" or bleaching being done. Recall the surrounding dream details for a distinction here.

PERPETUAL MOTION (device) applies to high energy or some element that has been put into motion and will be difficult to stop.

PERSECUTION most often reveals a personal attitude toward self; a paranoid or neurotic thought process.

PERSEPHONE (Greek mythology) reminds us to "balance" our spiritual and physical life.

PERSIAN LAMB emphasizes an enduring bond.

PERSONAL COMPUTER (PC) See computer.

PERSONAL FOUL reminds one of his or her willful misdeed or unfair act.

PERSONALITY TEST calls for self-analyzation; introspection.

P

This symbol may reveal one's trouble areas in respect to getting along with others.

PERSONNEL (office) may portray a manager or specific records. This will be a revealing dream fragment for the dreamer.

PERSPECTIVE (artistic) denotes either how one currently views something or *should* view it. Recall dreamscape details for further clarity.

PERSPIRING alludes to great energy and effort expended.

PERTUSSIS See whooping cough.

PERUSE See reading.

PERVERSION applies to misdirection or misplaced priorities; an advisement to seek professional direction.

PESSIMISM connotes a lack of acceptance and may also indicate a person who uses this attitude as an escape mechanism to avoid personal responsibility.

PEST (any type) will be a call to stop being annoyed and take action to resolve the situation.

PESTILENCE will most often correspond with a negative element one brings upon self.

PESTLE connotes a life aspect that one has the opportunity to utilize for the purpose of clarifying or understanding a current puzzlement.

PET See specific type.

PETAL (of blossom) will denote a magnified emphasis of the presented flower. Refer to specific flower.

PETER PAN pertains to the power of belief and faith.

PETITE (size) reminds us that "size" cannot be a comparable when evaluating potential or power.

PETIT FOURS represent the small aspects in life that serve as benefits or "treats."

PETITION stands for a personal request. The key here is to recall who was petitioning whom and why.

PET NAME will reveal a little-known aspect of an individual.

PET PEEVE advises of a need to gain acceptance in life.

PETRI DISH calls for a need to "develop" or expand an aspect of one's life.

PETRIFIED See fossil.

PETRIFIED See scared.

PETRIFIED FOREST will correspond with one's inherent natural talents that have enduring qualities yet are not utilized.

PETROLEUM relates to an element in one's life that has multiple aspects and diverse uses. The dreamer will usually make this association.

PETROLEUM JELLY signifies a life element that has the capability of soothing or easing a rough or difficult situation.

PETTICOAT See underwear.

PETTING ZOO advises of a return to more basic perspectives and appreciations.

PETTY CASH depicts one's current supply of available resources; usually refers to personal talents or abilities.

PETTY OFFICER characterizes a person who possesses a higher-than-average level of intelligence, experience, and authority.

PETUNIA exemplifies a talent or other personal ability that will proliferate if cared for.

PEW won't necessarily constitute a church or have a religious connotation; it will usually symbolize a concept many "sit and listen to" or a "place" where same is done.

PEWTER signifies a simple form of basic spiritual value; a warm and personal embracing quality.

PEYOTE connotes the sacred aspects of personal spiritual attainment.

PHAETON See carriage.

PHANTOM may represent one's fears or it may present a spiritual message. Recall surrounding dreamscape details for clarity.

PHANTOM LIMB PAIN under-scores the reality of one's whole essence.

PHARAOH characterizes spiritual domination. Recall who the dream pharaoh was.

PHARISEE represents a spiritual hypocrite.

PHARMACIST will correspond with an individual in the dreamer's life who has the capability and knowledge to provide a healing element. This element may relate to spiritual, physical, mental, or emotional ills.

PHARMACY will suggest some type of medication or healing element.

PHASEOUT connotes a waning situation or condition; some element in one's life that should be let go of; may advise greater acceptance.

PHEASANT connotes a spiritual seeking.

PHILADELPHIA EXPERIMENT emphasizes elements of true Reality that are currently doubted or issues generating skepticism.

PHILANTHROPIST characterizes a generous nature; may indicate opportunities to be selfless.

PHILHARMONIC See symphony.

PHILOSOPHER alludes to one who engages in higher enlightenment through deeper thought and contemplation.

PHILOSOPHERS' STONE pertains to a magic potion or "miracle" one hopes to enter one's life in respect to bringing enlightenment or power.

PHLEBOTOMIST relates to a "draining" personality; one who uses others.

PHLEGM indicates a "congested" condition, usually within one's mind.

PHLOX denotes cheerfulness.

PHOBIA corresponds with one's fears and elements of anxiety.

PHOENIX (Egyptian mythology) stands for the quintessential example of a characteristic, ability, or attainment; may also emphasize a powerfully determined personality who bounces back and refuses to be defeated or blocked.

PHONE See telephone.

PHONE BOOK See telephone book.

PHONE BOOTH See telephone booth.

PHONICS signifies a "general idea" of something; an overall understanding without specific knowledge of the individual associated elements.

PHONOGRAPH refers to old information; a need to be updated.

PHONY naturally means a false element; an imitation or deception.

PHOSPHORESCENCE connotes an "illuminating" (enlightening) element in one's life.

PHOTO See photograph.

PHOTOCOPIER portrays repetitiveness. Recall the condition and color of the dreamscape machine to determine whether or not something actually needs repeating or if this is a warning to *stop* repeating or copying something or someone. Frequently this symbol infers that an individual is *repeating* past mistakes. Who was using the photocopier?

PHOTOELECTRIC CELL (electric eye) illustrates natural or reflex responses. This may be an advisement to "think" before acting.

PHOTO FINISH exemplifies a nearly equal level of ability, knowledge, or development.

PHOTOFINISHING represents the "development" of one's past efforts of associated elements; a "growth" through understanding.

PHOTOGRAPH will reveal a message of importance. Recall what or who was in the photo.

PHOTOGRAPHER advises of the wisdom of "grasping the moment" instead of living for the future or what might be.

PHOTOJOURNALISM illustrates the act of learning from one's experiential elements in life.

PHOTO OPPORTUNITY suggests opportunities that shouldn't be missed; a need to maintain constant awareness of unexpected experiences in life that carry valuable lessons or insights with them.

PHOTOPHOBIA connotes a personal fear or intolerance of knowledge or aspects of enlightenment.

PHOTORECEPTOR symbolizes a strong personal desire to expand one's knowledge; a thirst for truth.

PHOTOSENSITIVITY depicts a psychologically based negative response to spiritually-related truths or higher knowledge.

PHOTOSYNTHESIS portrays an inherent attraction and personal need for knowledge.

PHOTOTHERAPY denotes a personal recognition of and appreciation for the rich healing value of knowledge.

PHOTOVOLTAIC connotes the mental and emotional energy and motivation one gains from seeking and attaining knowledge.

PHRASE BOOK represents a desire to communicate better and the efforts applied to same.

PHRENOLOGY (study of head shape) comes as a warning that research or learning efforts are focused on a false premise.

PHYLACTERY pertains to a reminder of specific spiritual tenets. The dreamer will make individualized association here.

PHYSIATRIST See physical therapist.

PHYSICAL EDUCATION comes in dreams to stress the importance of exercise and hygiene. Recall which aspect was emphasized in the dream to gain specifics for yourself.

PHYSICAL EXAMINATION portrays a need to either have an actual physical exam by a physician or seriously engage in introspection.

PHYSICAL SCIENCE (study of) See specific science type.

PHYSICAL THERAPIST signifies someone in the dreamer's life who has the capability of helping him or her get back on track.

PHYSICAL THERAPY corresponds to a need to restore normal function of some element of self. Recall what was being manipulated or exercised, as this will pinpoint one's area of impairment.

PHYSICIAN represents a person who has the knowledge and capability of helping another overcome a life disability or ill. Recall what specialty the doctor had.

PHYSICIST will characterize someone who attempts to understand nature and reality; a high interest in the interrelatedness of all things.

PHYSIQUE (of people) stands for a multitude of symbolic characteristics and personality traits. Refer to a specific trait.

PIANIST signifies one who desires harmony.

PIANO denotes an opportunity to experience or create a harmonic situation or atmosphere, perhaps even within self.

PIAZZA See public square. See veranda.

PICADOR warns against an action that will serve to hamper or disable a situation, relationship or another individual.

PICANTE denotes a highly interesting (spicy) idea or event.

PICASSO (Pablo) suggests a distorted perspective and/or confused thoughts (a collage).

PICCOLO refers to a "higher" level; deeper knowledge; more advanced element.

PICK (tool) corresponds to an aspect that allows one to "get at" something.

Dental pick relates to self-analyzation for negatives such as ulterior motives, jealousy, etc.

Guitar pick indicates a need to choose one's words carefully.

Hair pick alludes to straightening out tangled thoughts or confusion.

Ice pick denotes an attempt to discover lost spiritual beliefs.

Lock pick implies a desire to "unlock" something. Was the lock yours?

Nut pick connotes efforts applied to absorbing nourishing life elements.

Tooth pick implies a concern over having correct language—good communication skills.

PICK (choose) corresponds with a specific choice one made or is contemplating.

PICK (gather) See gathering.

PICKAX indicates a determination to understand something; a desire to get to the bottom of an issue.

PICKEREL represents spiritual greed or arrogance.

PICKET See protest.

PICKET FENCE represents efficiency; tending to live and process information in an orderly manner.

PICKLE alludes to a difficulty that must be faced, accepted or resolved.

PICKLED See preserves.

PICK-ME-UP will relate to any life aspect that provides additional energy or motivation for the dreamer. This will, of course, be different for everyone.

PICKPOCKET pertains to a lack of positive resourcefulness or motivation; having no personal responsibility or self-respect.

PICKUP See truck.

PICKY indicates a firm sense of self. This may not connote any type of negative attitude, but will usually mean "knowing one's mind."

PICNIC corresponds to an enjoyable respite taken in life.

PICTOGRAPH will display a message unique to the dreamer.

PICTORIAL portrays a set of corresponding photographs that will be associated with the dreamer in some way. They may send a clear message or convey a story line to which the dreamer will relate.

PICTURE See photograph or painting.

PICTURE PUZZLE See jigsaw puzzle.

PICTURE WINDOW presents a wider view. This symbol advises the dreamer to look at something with a wider perspective.

PIE represents a benefit; the sweet "fruit" of an effort.

PIE (shape) reveals "three" sides to an issue.

PIEBALD (pattern) See spotted.

PIECEMEAL suggests a little at a time, rather than attempting to accomplish something all at once.

PIE CHART See chart.

PIED PIPER characterizes a person who has a strong magnetic personality and can convince others of almost anything; the "following" or susceptibility to these types.

PIE-EYED indicates an intoxicated condition. This usually refers to a sober mental or emotional state rather than a drunken one.

PIER denotes spiritual interest.

PIERCE is differentiated from "Perforate" in that "Pierce" implies a "breaking-through" type of event; an advancement or discovery.

PIETA symbolizes an internalized spirituality; deep emotional responses to one's spiritual beliefs.

PIETY reveals a person's spiritual state. The surrounding dream details will disclose whether or not this is a sincere state.

PIG See hog.

PIGEON connotes gullibility.

PIGEONHOLE implies a tendency to classify others rather than viewing them as individuals.

PIGEON-TOED defines an introverted manner of walking one's path; additional difficulties due to personalizing various external elements.

PIGGYBACK reveals personal irresponsibility. Recall "who" was *riding* piggyback and who was *carrying* another.

PIGGY BANK indicates immature goals.

PIGHEADED denotes an obstinate personality.

PIG LATIN refers to a backward way of communicating with others; an inability to express self.

PIGMENT See specific color.

PIG-OUT emphasizes avarice; gluttony; greed.

PIGPEN connotes disorder.

PIGSKIN alludes to a "tough" attitude, situation, or perspective.

PIGSTY reveals a lack of self-respect.

PIGTAIL See braid.

PIKA applies to quick thinking; mental maneuverability.

PIKE See tollbooth.

PIKE (fish) represents spiritual nourishment.

PILAF (rice) denotes an essential or basic element in one's life.

PILATE (Pontius) exemplifies fear of being bested and/or not liked; a fear of making own decisions; concern about what others think of one.

PILE (heap) illustrates a great amount. Depending on what this dreamscape pile contained, it may infer a backup of work to *attend to* or it may signify *unnecessary* efforts in one's life.

PILE (post) will constitute a "supportive" aspect.

PILE DRIVER indicates a need to express, impress, or make assurances. Something in your life needs reinforcement.

PILEUP (vehicular) alludes to a path journey that follows another too closely; inattention to where one is going and the manner of same.

PILGRIM indicates a "searching" or the need to discover something important.

PILGRIMAGE symbolizes a necessary journey to gain a significant aspect associated with one's personal search.

PILL will represent an agent of personal healing or correction. This may refer to an emotional, mental, spiritual, or physical aspect of self.

PILLAGE reveals a lack of overall respect. One doesn't respect self or others. This symbol indicates a total disregard for authority and order.

PILLAR (exemplary) illustrates a model example of a specific character. This may also warn against revering another.

PILLAR (post) See pile.

PILLBOX advises one to carry one's personal inner healing abilities with him or her. This symbol implies that one's talents are not always utilized at every opportunity.

PILLORY denotes guilt and self-reproach. This symbol suggests you not be so hard on yourself.

PILLOW pertains to an individual's true temperament, state of mind, or level of reasoning. The key here is to recall what the pillow was made of, what color it was. The condition? Did it have any design on it?

PILLOWCASE represents hidden elements of self. The Pillowcase itself will reveal *how* one covers up these aspects. Recall the color and design of the Case.

PILLOW TALK signifies the revealing of secrets; verbal intimacy.

PILLSBURY DOUGHBOY characterizes personal contentedness; a satisfaction with self and one's position.

PILOT connotes one who had the capability to control his or her path direction. The key here is to recall the dream Pilot's condition and ability.

PILOT FISH warns against a spiritual path that imitates another's.

PILOTHOUSE See wheelhouse.

PILOT LIGHT stands for one's living spirit; one's true essence.

PILOT WHALE See dolphin.

PIMP denotes a "user" type of personality.

PIN (bowling) represents a target; something one shoots for; a goal.

PIN (fastener) implies a need for temporary restorative or corrective measures to be taken.

PINA COLADA See alcoholic beverage.

PINA COLADA (scent) suggests a fresh beginning.

PINAFORE represents honesty and simplicity of character.

PINBALL portrays a striving to better self; improve one's success rate.

PINCERS indicate a "tight" aspect in one's life. This may refer to another individual, relationship, business deal, personal situation, or belief. Recall *who* was using the pincers? *What* was being pinched?

PINCH will usually represent an attention-getting sign.

PINCH-HITTER pertains to someone who can take over for another at a critical point in time or stage.

PIN CURL indicates restricted ideas; an unyielding thought process.

PINCUSHION illustrates one's ability to make allowances and/or devise alternatives.

PINE (scent) denotes a "refreshening" of one's interconnectedness with nature.

PINE (tree) pertains to "natural"

abilities; one's bonded relationship to nature.

PINEAL EYE constitutes one's inherent knowledge; insights.

PINEAPPLE connotes a "fresh" aspect of an element in one's life.

PINECONE refers to the "seeds" of one's natural talents.

PINE NUT portrays the "fruits" of a person's inherent, natural abilities.

PINE TAR applies to the "healing" elements of natural talents and gifts.

PING-PONG implies irresponsibility.

PINHEAD connotes ignorance; using a minuscule measure of one's intelligence or reason.

PINHOLE relates to an element without cohesive substance.

PINING alludes to a refusal to accept something in one's life; a great personal loss.

PINK reveals some type of weakness that can refer to one's mental or emotional state, physical aspect, or spiritual condition.

PINKEYE represents a personal perspective that is "infected" with some type of negative or distortion.

PINKIE See little finger.

PINKIE RING stands for an attempt to emphasize one's less obvious qualities; rounding out self.

PINKING SHEARS signify an attempt to keep something in one's life from falling apart, unraveling.

PINK LADY See alcoholic beverage.

PINK SLIP connotes an end to one's project or effort. This may be a message from one's Higher Self that indicates futility if he or she continues expending efforts on a specific phase or aspect.

PINNACLE stands for high points in one's life or spiritual journey.

PINOCHLE depicts a method of playing out one's life situations through the manner of maneuverability and cleverness.

PINPOINT will define the current "existence" of something in one's life that he or she may not have recognized. This is usually a good symbol that gives hope.

PINPRICK represents an attention-getting message. The surrounding dreamscape elements will usually clarify this for the dreamer.

PINS AND NEEDLES most often correspond with a high state of anticipation. This is synonymous with Expectation which is in direct opposition to Acceptance. This is an advisement to gain acceptance in one's life.

PINSTRIPE (pattern) typifies a thought process that finely vacillates between narrowly defined concepts.

PINTO (horse) marks the exercising of multiple experiential freedoms while following one's personal life path.

PINTO BEAN connotes an "essential" element in one's life.

PINUP won't necessarily indicate a sexual connotation, but usually represents that which one admires or is attracted to in life.

PINWHEEL relates to personal tenacity and flexibility to "go with the flow" and accept whatever comes.

PIONEER characterizes an individual who fearlessly forges ahead through unknown territory. This symbol usually pertains to one's life path.

PIOUS See piety.

PIPE (conduit) corresponds with "connecting" aspects; element that has the ability to relate one aspect to another.

PIPE (smoking) indicates an individual's quality of perception. Refer to Corncob, Peace pipe, Meerschaum, etc.

PIPE BOMB See bomb.

PIPE CARRIER symbolizes highly peaceful individuals; those who keep the sacredness of spirituality.

PIPE CLEANER pertains to a desire to keep one's perceptual thought processes clear of distorting elements and impurities.

PIPE CUTTER correlates to a precise move that results in a precision cut (severance). This is for the purpose of preparing self for a new aligned "connection."

PIPE DOPE signifies a double-checking thought process that insures certain ideas "hold" and are firm.

PIPE DREAM won't have to denote a fantasy or impossible goal; it usually defines a "high" aspiration that has a high probability of attainment if one's path is traveled accordingly.

PIPEFITTER characterizes an individual who has a knack for putting the connecting pieces of a concept or issue together without misinterpretation or error.

PIPELINE symbolizes the connective link that runs from the past through the present to the future.

PIPE ORGAN See organ.

PIPER See flutist.

PIPESTONE emphasizes the sacred manner in which a spiritual aspect is held within self or performed.

PIPE THREADER represents an attempt to make a precise connection.

PIPE WRENCH illustrates the "effort" expended to maintain information integrity.

PIPING (on fabric) applies to an emphasis placed on a specific aspect of one's character. Recall surrounding dreamscape elements to determine which aspect this refers to.

PIPSISSEWA refers to naturally-occurring opportunities that need to be noted.

PIRANHA reveals a spiritual narrow-mindedness; a vicious possessiveness of one's specific beliefs to the point of striking out at those who believe otherwise.

PIRATE characterizes unethical personalities who gain by stealing valuable aspects from others; spiritual greed.

PIROGUE See canoe.

PIROUETTE represents inner joy.

PISTACHIO alludes to cheerful generosity; a mildly healing element.

PISTOL See gun.

PIT See kernel.

PIT (casino area) applies to a situation or atmosphere that holds questionable elements; a call to caution when proceeding.

PIT (deep hole) constitutes a deeply troubling or difficult situation.

PIT (refueling area) connotes a need to re-energize self; a break in one's work is suggested.

PIT BOSS characterizes a person who oversees the actions of others; may refer to one's own Higher Self.

PIT BULL (dog breed) suggests aggressiveness.

PITCHER (baseball) portrays an individual in one's life who may attempt to foil another's advancement or success.

PITCHER (container) illustrates that which one views as a source that quenches a thirst or desire. The key is to recall *what* the dream pitcher held. Was it full or empty? Was another person holding it or pouring? What flowed from it? Color?

PITCHFORK typifies a "tool" that aids in accomplishing a goal.

PITCH PIPE represents a life element that will help to keep one on the right track.

PITFALL stands for a major setback or dangerous course leading to great difficulty.

PITH stands for the elemental essence of something.

PITH HELMET implies a tendency or desire to protect one's primal or elementary beliefs.

PIT STOP suggests a time for renewal; respite.

PITTANCE denotes the "existence" of some aspect in one's life that he or she thought gone or nonexistent. This won't necessarily have any reference to finances or a monetary connotation.

PITTED (surface) connotes inner strength; tenacity; experienced.

PIT VIPER See snake.

PITY usually refers to "self-generated" feelings; a method of eliciting sympathy from others; a self-defeating attitude.

PIXIE reveals the possibilities of true Reality.

PIZZA indicates multiple opportunities forthcoming.

PLACARD will usually come as a specific message for each dreamer. Recall what the placard said. Did it have colors or design?

PLACATE denotes an effort to soothe or ease a troublesome situation or mood.

PLACEBO exemplifies an aspect that serves as a temporary replacement in one's life. These will be those elements that are phoney or false. Frequently these refer to one's mental or psychological excuses for not following one's inner guidance.

PLACE MAT implies a mind for details.

PLACENTA corresponds to an essential element in one's life.

PLACER represents a life aspect that has a "trace" amount of value.

PLACE SETTING connotes an "expected" response or aspect.

PLAGIARISM portrays an idea that isn't one's own as claimed.

PLAGUE pertains to a serious negative element in one's life that has the potential to be emotionally, mentally, or spiritually fatal.

PLAID (pattern) relates to knowledge stemming from multiple sources.

PLAINS See prairie.

PLAINTIFF reveals the individual who brings a problem to attention.

PLAIT See braid.

PLAN denotes an intention or method of proceedings.

PLANARIAN correlates to an ability to rebound.

PLANCHETTE represents a tool for the subconscious.

PLANE pertains to quality and depth of thoughts. Recall condition of Plane—color, speed, etc.

PLANE (tool) illustrates a leveling out or smoothing intent.

PLANET refers to an influential element in one's life. See specific name.

PLANETARIUM denotes a need to expand one's perceptual scope.

PLANK See lumber.

PLANKTON alludes to foundational facts or "the basics" of something.

PLANT (botanical) connotes a

natural talent. Refer to various specific Plants.

PLANT (industrial) refers to one's "work" efforts. This symbol may not imply one's awake state place of employment, but rather apply to some other type of work the dreamer is involved in.

PLANT (sow) illustrates an attempt to establish or begin some element in one's life; an act of promoting or fostering.

PLANTATION signifies the quality and quantity of one's talents. Recall who was working the Plantation? What was planted? What was the condition of the growing vegetation?

PLANTER (container) will relate to a specific quality or personal characteristic of the individual associated with it. What was its color? Was there a special design on it?

PLANT FOOD See fertilizer.

PLAQUE (decorative) will reveal an important element about someone; will portray a little-known quality or characteristic.

PLAQUE (dental) represents a careless attitude regarding the manner of one's speech; unguarded communications.

PLASMA will represent an essential element to one's existence. This may not refer to a physical aspect, but usually indicates an emotional or mental factor.

PLASTER indicates a life aspect that has the capability of smoothing out or covering one's mistakes in life.

PLASTERBOARD connotes an attempt or chance for renewal.

PLASTER CAST represents a supportive factor that carries one through a healing period.

PLASTER OF PARIS represents a method of imitation or the recreation of something.

PLASTIC illustrates changeability; lacking high quality.

PLASTIC EXPLOSIVE See bomb.

PLASTIC SURGERY See cosmetic surgery.

PLASTIQUE See bomb.

PLAT MAP signifies a detailed perspective of something.

PLATE (dinner) connotes quality of nourishment in respect to one's personal attitude. This symbol refers to the specific "manner" or attention one gives to the absorption of mental, emotional, or spiritual nourishment. Recall what type of plate was presented. Was it made of china or paper?

PLATEAU will mark a time to pause and level off during one's journey through life.

PLATE TECTONICS emphasize the fact that an action will cause a reaction; the importance of routinely attending to one's stress level.

PLATFORM See stage.

PLATFORM SHOES suggest a desire to appear taller in the eyes of others; a low self-esteem.

PLATING (metal) constitutes a presentation of higher value that conceals an element of lesser value beneath it.

PLATINUM (metal) represents a life aspect that possesses multiple opportunities.

PLATINUM BLOND pertains to a shallow thought process.

PLATITUDE illustrates a lack of original thought; superficial responses.

PLATONIC (philosophy) denotes an intellectual focus on spiritual concepts rather than on the physical elements of life.

PLATOON represents a group of people with a like intent or purpose.

PLATTER (serving) connotes something easily obtained or attained.

PLATYPUS signifies an ability to incorporate spiritual elements such as beliefs and talents into one's daily life.

PLAY (drama) will usually correlate to something going on in one's awake state. This symbol comes to emphasize or clarify a situation.

PLAYBACK connotes something one needs to listen to again; "hear" what one said or "how" it was said.

PLAYBILL portrays a visual (poster) that serves as an attention-getting message. This symbol will attempt to draw one's attention to something he or she is missing in life.

PLAY BOOK See script.

PLAY BOOK (sports) correlates to the different "moves" one has available to him or her in life.

PLAYBOY connotes misplaced priorities; immaturity.

PLAY-BY-PLAY indicates a need to review one's actions in detail.

PLAYER characterizes a person who participates in a specified activity.

PLAYER PIANO denotes a lack of individuality or reasoning. This symbol infers that an individual depends upon others to be original. This represents an individual who "plays another's tune" instead of devising one's own.

PLAYGROUND relates to a lack of seriousness.

PLAYHOUSE pertains to an immature domestic life.

PLAYING (children) applies to a carefree and imaginative nature.

PLAYING CARD will represent an element associated to something one is currently doing. The

P

key here is to recall which card was displayed. Was it the ace? Joker?

PLAYING FIELD portrays the current "ground" on which one is operating. Recall the condition of the field. Were your associates present on the field? Was it muddy?

PLAYOFF constitutes a "final" chance at something in one's life.

PLAYPEN refers to a "babyish" manner of behavior.

PLAZA connotes a "wide" area. This symbol tells the dreamer that he or she currently has a lot of room to accomplish something.

PLEA See petition.

PLEA-BARGAIN indicates a desire to escape blame or responsibility.

PLEAT portrays "rigid" and sharply defined attitudes.

PLEBEIAN will refer to commonality; the general public in regard to an attitude or segment of people.

PLEDGE indicates a promise. Recall what was promised. To whom was the promise made? Self?

PLEURISY results from an "intake" of a negative idea or concept.

PLEURISY ROOT relates to a life aspect that has the ability to negate negative ideas or attitudes. This will refer to something that

causes a "turnaround" in respect to a harmful idea.

PLEXIGLAS connotes a strong substitute.

PLIABLE may allude to acceptance or an easily manipulative personality. Recall surrounding dreamscape details for clarification.

PLIERS refer to a situation where one attempts to pry something out before it's ready to come naturally. This is a clear warning not to "force" things in life.

PLODDING usually denotes perseverance.

PLOT (cemetery) will most often come as a mortality reminder. This reminder is most often necessitated by an awake-state life of misdeeds or lost course.

PLOT (land) See lot.

PLOT (plan out) pertains to "thought" given to one's future direction.

PLOT (scheme) corresponds to a devious nature.

PLOT (story line) signifies a synopsis of what is transpiring in one's awake-state life. It gives a vivid look at one's attitudes or lifestyle.

PLOW stands for a determination and perseverance to "plow" through difficulties encountered in life.

PLOWBOY implies a down-to-earth personality who clearly perceives the right directions to take.

PLUCKING symbolizes resourcefulness.

PLUG applies to voluntary "holds" or stoppages.

PLUM denotes an element of high quality as perceived by the dreamer. This may not necessarily be a true perspective.

PLUMAGE corresponds to the quality or health of an idea. Recall the condition of the bird's plumage. What kind of bird was it? Refer to the specific type in this dictionary.

PLUMB (weight) represents a "balancing" or equalizing element.

PLUMBER characterizes the presence of a negative situation; may indicate a physical dysfunction or disease.

PLUMBER'S SNAKE alludes to that which is capable of removing problematical elements.

PLUMB LINE connotes an attempt to keep an element in one's life straight and true.

PLUM PUDDING signifies satisfaction, usually resulting from a success or accomplishment.

PLUNDER See pillage.

PLUNGER represents a need to "unclog" something in one's life. Most often the dreamer will make this association.

PLURAL MARRIAGE See polygamy.

PLUS (sign) See addition symbol.

PLUSH (fabric) represents a pleasing or emotionally fulfilling element.

PLUTO (planet) indicates a healing element in one's life.

PLUTONIUM refers to a life element with a highly dangerous potential.

PLYWOOD connotes an aspect in one's life that has multiple uses and resulting benefits. Each dreamer will make this association.

PNEUMONIA represents a negative element in one's life that is causing a suffocating effect; a lack of breathing room.

POACHED (cook) pertains to bringing something to fruition through gentle methods.

POACHED (stolen) applies to something obtained through ill-gotten methods.

POACHER corresponds to stealth and dishonesty.

POCAHONTAS symbolizes intercession.

POCKET (billiards) signifies "steps" along one's path; advancement increments.

POCKET (clothing) relates to something one prefers to keep close or handy. This will be different for each dreamer.

POCKET (position) represents a

"closed-in" or blocked position; may indicate a Catch-22 situation.

POCKETBOOK See purse.

POCKETBOOK (book) See paperback.

POCKET CALCULATOR exemplifies efficiency; preparedness.

POCKETKNIFE pertains to experience and the lessons gained from same.

POCKET MONEY indicates a state of readiness; a tendency to maintain provisional elements in one's life.

POCKMARK (skin) typifies a life fraught with difficulties or negative aspects.

POD (group) symbolizes spiritual life.

POD (seed) refers to sources of knowledge or opportunities for same.

PODIUM pertains to a life factor that aids in communicating with others.

POE (Edgar Allen) characterizes a melancholy to morbid range of ideas that stem from deep thought.

POEM will usually serve as a message for the dreamer who will make the necessary association.

POET relates to the lyrical aspect of self which expresses inner thoughts and emotional elements associated with one's life.

POETIC LICENSE portrays conceptual development or expansion.

POGO STICK warns against attempting to advance along one's life path in an emotionally detached manner.

POINSETTIA illustrates spiritual celebration; an externalized spiritual expression of self.

POINT (advice) symbolizes suggestions from one's Higher Self.

POINT (bottom line/crux) reveals the essential idea or basic premise.

POINT (finger) will indicate an accusation or serve as a directional motion to draw one's attention to something. Recall surrounding dream details to determine which meaning was intended.

POINT (land) represents an "extension" into spiritual aspects.

POINT (phase) emphasizes attention or focus on a particular phase of one's life or path.

POINT (purpose) connotes a need to focus on the "reason" for something.

POINT (sharp end) suggests clarity.

POINT (verge) corresponds to a need to make an important decision.

POINT-BLANK emphasizes an "in-your-face," immediate, and direct element one needs to deal with.

POINTE (ballet) calls for a need to increase awareness and "keep on your toes" advisement.

POINTER (any type) will call one's attention to something important in his or her life.

POINT MAN will represent a forerunner; a messenger; one who checks out conditions before another follows behind.

POINT OF NO RETURN clearly signifies a point in one's life where there is no turning back; no chance to alter events or correct same.

POINT OF VIEW See perspective.

POISON will warn of an element in one's life that has the potential to cause great harm or a fatal effect.

POISON IVY will denote a hazardous path or direction.

POISON-PEN LETTER See hate mail.

POKE (jab) will either come as an attention-getting symbol or it will signify a "testing" type of inquisitiveness.

POKE (sack) See bag.

POKER (card game) implies ulterior motives.

POKER (tool) See andiron.

POKER FACE indicates a strong business sense; an ability to keep plans or secrets confidential; closed-mouthed.

POKEWEED refers to a plan possessing a negative premise.

POKEY See jail.

POKY (slow) may not imply procrastination, but rather this symbol usually alludes to an extremely careful and cautious manner of approach or progression.

POLAR BEAR relates to spiritual aloofness.

POLAR CAP alludes to spiritual frigidity; no interest in spiritual matters.

POLARITY pertains to a personality that exhibits extremes.

POLAROID (camera/photo) represents a need to immediately focus one's attention or memory on something that will be depicted in the photograph or scene.

POLAR REGIONS portray a cold and frozen spiritual attitude; one that isn't exercised or shared.

POLE (any type) pertains to a helpful aspect in one's life. The dreamer will make this personal association.

POLECAT See skunk for a like interpretation.

POLE VAULT warns against leaping over important elements in one's life that need to be experienced.

POLICE come in dreams as an advisement to self-analyze one's actions or plans; needed introspection.

POLICE DOG indicates a watchful and guiding friend.

POLICE STATE is an advisement to be more aware of that which is transpiring around self.

POLICE STATION refers to restraints; will suggest that someone is always watching you. Were you in the station? What were you doing? Were you the captain? In jail? Reporting a crime or being arrested?

POLIOMYELITIS illustrates a negative aspect that has hampered one's ability to develop or advance as planned; calls for an alternate plan.

POLISH defines a final finish applied to something. The dreamer will identify what this is.

POLITICIAN signifies a self-serving and hypocritical personality.

POLKA portrays a lively and cheerful attitude.

POLKA DOTS (pattern) corresponds to indecision.

POLL See survey.

POLLEN indicates elements in one's life that enhance the positive aspects.

POLLIWOG See tadpole.

POLLUTION characterizes the negative elements that adversely affect one's quality of life or advancement. The key here is to recall if there was a specific individual causing such affectations. Was it someone you know? Was it yourself? Do you need to change some of your ways? Pollution can also be verbally disseminated.

POLLYANNA implies blind optimism; an inability to accurately perceive reality.

POLO constitutes haughtiness; a presumptive personality.

POLO (Marco) emphasizes an adventurous and inquisitive personality.

POLO SHIRT suggests self-importance.

POLTERGEIST represents misunderstood spiritual concepts and their resulting self-generated fears.

POLYCHROMATIC (multiple colors) corresponds to a bohemian or eccentric personality; the freedom to openly express self.

POLYDACTYL (extra toes/fingers) stands for a heightened ability to efficiently accomplish goals.

POLYESTER (fabric) suggests a lack of originality; rarely expressed individualism.

POLYGAMY applies to arrogance and lack of respect for others.

POLYGRAPH will naturally indicate that a question of honesty is present. The key here is to recall who was hooked up to the machine.

POLYP (marine) See coral.

POLYP (medical) denotes the "growth" or "extension" of a specific aspect of self. Recall if it was a positive or negative growth.

POLYURETHANE illustrates an attempt or desire to preserve a successful conclusion or "finish" to an accomplishment.

POMADE (on hair) represents a fear of one's thoughts being affected or changed by others.

POMANDER reflects a tendency to surround self with positive elements and personally uplifting or beneficial aspects. If the dream Pomander was being gifted to another, this then represents a desire for others to be surrounded by same.

POMEGRANATE refers to justice; wisdom; rectifying mistakes.

POMERANIAN (dog breed) signifies heightened awareness required.

POMPADOUR (hairstyle) indicates an opinionated personality.

POMPON (decoration) connotes a cheerful personality.

POMPON (flower) See boutonniere.

PONCE DE LEON (Juan) characterizes a dysfunctional perception of reality and the folly that results from same.

PONCHO See serape.

POND symbolizes a spiritual source. Recall the Pond's condition and health to determine if this "source" is a positive or negative one.

PONTIFF See pope.

PONTOON suggest a lackadaisical spiritual attitude.

PONTOON BRIDGE portrays a "bridging" or "way over" troubling spiritual issues.

PONY See horse.

PONY EXPRESS typifies a mode of communication that travels from person to person; a word-of-mouth dissemination.

PONYTAIL reflects an accepting attitude; an ability to rebound.

POODLE (dog breed) indicates a dependable friend.

POOH-BAH signifies an ineffective person who believes he or she carries great authority.

POOL relates to one's quality and quantity of goodness; level of humanitarian interaction with others.

POOL (game) suggests cleverness combined with the skill to accomplish a goal.

POOLROOM corresponds with

a scheming atmosphere; plotting and planning occurring. The key here is to recall the condition of the room and those within it. Who was there? Do these elements lead to a determination of "dirty" dealings?

POOL TABLE represents the "issue" or "subject" of one's plans.

POOPER-SCOOPER portrays respectful assistance given to a friend; "picking up" after a friend's mistakes.

POOR usually refers to a condition of a specific element in one's life rather than denoting a monetary aspect.

POORBOX suggests being generous with our humanitarian acts.

POOR FARM/HOUSE portrays an inability to externalize one's inner wealth; withholding one's humanitarianism.

POP (soda) See soft drink.

POP ART depicts a clear visual that's intended as a personal message for the dreamer. Recall what was displayed.

POPCORN relates to a specific aspect of an idea; "developed" and "full-blown" elements.

POPCORN BALLS signify a concept containing all its associative aspects.

POPE characterizes religious domination.

POPEYE (The Sailor Man) stands for belief in one's strength.

POP-EYED symbolizes an astonishment; or fear.

POPLAR (tree) relates to a personal talent that has blossomed in an accelerated manner.

POPLIN (fabric) suggests a domineering personality.

POPPER (appetizer) represents a taste for interesting ideas; a draw to adventurous experiences and opportunities.

POPPER (popcorn) applies to a life element capable of "developing" ideas.

POPPER (uppers) See stimulant.

POPPY (flower) pertains to a natural talent having the duality of positive and negative elements, depending on utilization.

POPSICLE portrays personally altered spiritual perspectives that have been adjusted to one's specific "taste."

PORCELAIN applies to an extremely delicate situation, relationship, or other aspect such as mental state.

PORCH signifies the extent of one's personally-held distance from other people or life aspects.

Enclosed porches suggest a desire to maintain maximum distance.

Open porches denote a forthright and welcoming attitude.

Screened-in porches stand for a hesitant or cautious attitude.

PORCUPINE characterizes one's tendency to utilize subconscious defense mechanisms to obtain personal desires and goals. This is usually a strong warning to stop manipulating others. The symbol also means an instinctive responsiveness to "bristle and hide" from new ideas, relationships, or situations.

PORCUPINE FISH pertains to spiritual defensiveness.

PORCUPINE QUILL illustrates personal defenses.

PORE (minute opening) alludes to the existence of an "opening" or "exit" point or opportunity.

PORE (study) depicts intensive research or analyzation.

PORK corresponds with one's efforts at his or her work.

PORNOGRAPHY reflects a misplaced priority; wasting valuable time and energy that should be expended on one's purpose.

POROUS (surface) correlates to gullibility; easily manipulated.

PORPOISE stands for spiritual guidance; a humanitarian nature.

PORRIDGE signifies an enduring and nourishing life aspect. The surrounding dreamscape details will clarify this association for the dreamer.

PORRINGER See soup bowl.

PORT See seaport.

PORT (drink) See wine.

PORTABLE implies efficiency or convenience.

PORTAGE defines a burden of some type. The dreamer will recognize what this is.

PORTAL pertains to an "opening" or opportunity.

PORTENT will be a clear sign that forewarns of the potential for danger or a disruptive element of one's life course.

PORTER characterizes a helper of some type.

PORTFOLIO suggests a need to organize an aspect of one's life, perhaps thoughts or perspectives.

PORTHOLE correlates to a spiritual perception, usually a narrow view. Recall if the dream Portal was clear or cloudy.

PORTICO relates to an elaborate presentation or show of appearances.

PORTMANTEAU See luggage.

PORT OF CALL advises of a need to re-examine one's spiritual beliefs or humanitarian efforts.

PORT OF ENTRY defines a "right" move in life; underscores the right direction.

PORTRAIT signifies a true revelation of a person. Recall what type of Portrait it was. What was represented? Was it a beautiful painting? Grotesque? A caricature? A cartoon?

PORTUGUESE MAN-OF-WAR See jellyfish.

POSE can reflect various meanings depending on the type of posturing that was presented in the dream. An obvious character revelation will be defined by an exaggerated position.

POSEIDON (Greek mythology) most often signifies a spiritual application regarding one's life course, yet Poseidon may also represent earthly elements that are in turmoil.

POSH (atmosphere) will denote extravagance and/or arrogance.

POSITION See pose.

POSSE suggests one's assumptions and prejudgments.

POSSET See alcoholic beverage.

POSSUM See opossum.

POSTAGE STAMP refers to the "value" of communications. Recall what the stamp was on. What was its denomination? To whom was it addressed? Was the Stamp from a foreign country?

POSTAL ORDER See money order.

POSTAL WORKER reflects those who tend to be efficient and orderly to the extent of being detrimental.

POST CARD connotes a brief message or communication.

POSTER will represent a message of some type; may reveal a personal interest or attraction.

POSTGRADUATE stands for advanced research or searching.

POSTHOLE pertains to preliminary preparations being done to apply "supportive" efforts toward something.

POSTHOLE DIGGER illustrates one's "intention" to support something.

POSTHUMOUS implies that which we leave behind after we're gone; may not necessarily indicate death.

POSTHYPNOTIC SUGGESTION warns of a vulnerable state.

POSTMARK will pinpoint a specific date that will be important to the dreamer.

POSTMORTEM See autopsy.

POSTMISTRESS exemplifies a person who insures communications are carried out; this symbol may even refer to one's conscience.

POST OFFICE emphasizes a need to communicate with another; may refer to verbal or emotional expression.

POSTPAID indicates a well-planned communication.

POSTPONE may advise the

dreamer to temporarily set something aside or the symbol may indicate a need to STOP procrastinating.

POSTSCRIPT signifies an afterthought and the need to express same.

POST-SEASON corresponds to recent experiential events.

POST TIME reveals a phase in one's life when it's not advisable to take chances.

POSTTRAUMATIC STRESS DISORDER exemplifies extremely severe effects remaining from a highly stressful or emotionally impressionable experience.

POSTULANT relates to determined intentions. This symbol may not necessarily refer to a spiritual element.

POSTURE represents a multitude of interpretations. Recall if one was slouching, standing straight (too straight?), bent over, etc. These will depict obvious states of mind, character, or attitude.

POSTWAR reflects a phase in one's life that directly follows a difficult time or period of trial and stress.

POSY See flower.

POT (any type) will correlate with a "container" and the dreamer should refer to the specific type of pot presented in his or her dream.

POT See marijuana.

POTABLE relates to an "acceptable" element in one's life which could refer to an idea, concept, action, plan, or direction.

POTATO symbolizes an "essential" or "basic" element in one's life.

POTATO CHIP portrays "alternative" forms of a basic need; various methods and manners of obtaining essential aspects in one's life.

POTATO SKIN relates to the most potent element of an issue or aspect.

POTBELLY alludes to an absence of motivation and/or energy.

POTBELLY STOVE denotes a companionable atmosphere; a time for reflection and introspection.

POTHERB See herbs.

POTHOLDER suggests a controlled awareness in the face of heated issues or situations.

POTHOLE constitutes a negative element in one's life course that usually can be avoided; a temporary irritation.

POTION will pertain to a positive or negative element that one has to accept in life. Recall the surrounding dreamscape details to determine if this was a good or bad aspect that had to be accepted.

POTLATCH indicates an unconditional sharing of one's personal talents or gifts.

POTLUCK suggests the ability to make do; acceptance; appreciation of what one has.

POTPIE connotes multiple benefits; various sources of nourishing elements.

POTPOURRI defines a harmonious blend of elements; a pleasing mix.

POT ROAST signifies a "complete" aspect; the whole concept or issue that has a nourishing potential.

POTSHERD corresponds to a fact that provides partial validity to a specific concept, idea, or perspective.

POTTER characterizes creativity and talents that express one's individuality.

POTTER'S FIELD advises of the wisdom to make a difference in life. This is not implying that one should make a "name" for self, but to leave behind something valuable for others to benefit from.

POTTER'S WHEEL points out a "vehicle" for one to express his or her creativity and individuality.

POTTERY emphasizes the unique character of individuals. Recall who the Pottery belonged to. Where there designs on it?

Color? What was it made of? China? Ironstone?

POTTING SHED represents a close bond with nature; an appreciation for one's natural gifts or talents.

POTTY-CHAIR implies a need to "retrain" some negative aspect of self. Each dreamer will recognize what this refers to.

POUCH See pocket.

POULTICE will reveal a healing aspect specific to the dreamer.

POUNCE warns of an unexpected aspect; a surprise revelation.

POUND (animal) See animal shelter.

POUND (pommel) stands for "emphasis" or the insuring of one's extent of emotional depth or attitude is effectively conveyed.

POUND (weight) will illustrate a quantity of some quality of character or personal deed. This symbol emphasizes the "weight" something carries.

POUND CAKE reflects a positive element that possesses a concentration of multiple benefits.

POURING (liquid) typifies an act of disseminating information. Recall what the liquid was. Who was pouring it? Did it have color? Odor?

POURING (rain) signifies an inundation of fresh spiritual concepts.

POUT depicts selfishness; an absence of acceptance.

POVERTY will usually represent some type of character quality that is lacking.

POWDER (consistency) indicates a "fine" aspect; a "sifted" element.

POWDERED SUGAR symbolizes a "light" and uplifting benefit that has come one's way.

POWDER HORN portrays a questionable attitude of being ready to enter an altercation.

POWDER KEG reveals a potentially explosive situation, relationship, or attitude.

POWDER PUFF typifies a fragile nature or sensitive personality; may also refer to a prime or ideal situation or condition.

POWDER ROOM See bathroom.

POWERHOUSE correlates with a person who possesses the energy and ability to accomplish goals; one who successfully and expediently carries through with plans.

POWER MOWER See lawn mower.

POWER OF ATTORNEY pertains to a shift of responsibility.

POWER PLANT connotes one's inner drive and resulting energy output. The key with this symbol is to recall what condition the Power Plant was in. Was it operating at optimum level? Shut down?

POWER PLAY stands for taking opportunity of advantage.

POWER STEERING exemplifies utilizing elements in one's life that make advancement easier; progressing by a less strenuous method. However, this method may not always be the most dependable.

POW WOW signifies a need to communicate; a get-together is required.

POX portrays a phase of misfortune; continual bad luck.

PRACTICAL JOKE applies to a stress-releasing event. Recall whether or not this Joke was harmful. Who was the instigator? Who was the victim? What was the response?

PRACTICAL NURSE relates to a minor personal dysfunction of some type. The surrounding dreamscape elements will clarify what this means.

PRACTICING advises of a need to gain more experience and skill.

PRAIRIE reflects a "clear" path ahead.

PRAIRIE DOG portrays a communal watchfulness; awareness and attention given to friends and associates within one's circle.

PRAIRIE SCHOONER See covered wagon.

PRAISE correlates with recognition of personal efforts applied to one's life path by a person's Higher Self or spiritual forces.

PRALINE corresponds to a benefit that one perceives as being "sweet" and nourishing.

PRAM See baby carriage.

PRANCING illustrates a light-hearted mood; true acceptance.

PRANK See practical joke.

PRATTLE reveals mental confusion or an obsession with superficial or insubstantial life aspects.

PRAWN See shrimp.

PRAYER depicts a specific need in one's life. Recall what the prayer's subject was. Who was hearing this prayer? Who was saying it or showing the words?

PRAYER BOOK represents a tendency to have spiritual expectations; a dependency on higher forces to accomplish one's goals.

PRAYER MEETING advises of a state of spiritual weakness; a condition whereby one depends on the spiritual motivation and support of others.

PRAYER SHAWL reflects spiritual humility and respect.

PRAYER WHEEL warns of spiritual inattention or lack of attention; a tendency to place one's responsibility on God rather than recognizing and accepting one's own.

PRAYING MANTIS portrays spiritual hypocrisy; lip-service.

PREACHER See religious figure.

PREAMBLE will define an introductory element that precedes an event or situation; a forewarning.

PREBUILT suggests partially-completed elements; a course of action that already has several aspects in place.

PRECANCEROUS (condition) warns of a highly dangerous situation that has the potential of developing into a hopeless or fatal conclusion.

PRECAUTIONS reflect heightened awareness; an attention given to probabilities; preparedness.

PRECEPT usually indicates a spiritual, ethical, or moral law.

PRECIOUS STONE See gemstone.

PRECIPICE reveals a decision-making moment.

PRECOCIOUSNESS is a dream aspect that comes to advise one of a need to "control" one's mental energies; too much information or elements are being missed due to a racetrack mind.

PRECOGNITION usually underscores an awake-state natural ability.

PRECOOKED refers to having a situation, idea, or other element well prepared before presenting it to others.

PRECUT portrays an efficient manner of accomplishing a goal.

PREDATOR most often reveals a harmful individual in one's life.

PREDAWN (light) represents "beginning" insights that are yet to be clearly defined or wholly solidified; the recognition of a yet obscure theory or concept.

PREDECESSOR characterizes a person who attempted to present the same attitude, idea, or plan before you did; one who followed the same course.

PREDICAMENT will suggest a dilemma or entanglement. This dream may present a potential solution.

PREDICTION may, in fact, come as a actual event. Usually it reveals an outcome associated with the dreamer's current course in life.

PREDILECTION will reveal one's preference or tendency. Recall what this referred to. Was it a positive or negative element?

PREEMIE See premature.

PREEMPTED denotes a temporary interruption of an activity or plan.

PREENING may not infer an arrogant or self-absorbing nature; it usually refers to a "cleansing" or the attention to personal aspects.

PREFABRICATED indicates that certain elements of an issue or situation have been assembled in preparation for the composite completion.

PREFACE will pertain to an introductory communication; an ice-breaking element.

PREFECT indicates a person of moderate authority in one's life.

PREFERENTIAL (treatment) refers to partiality. The key here is to determine "who" gave this treatment and "why" it was given.

PREFERRED STOCK will indicate a priority.

PREGNANCY signifies an embryonic stage of a specific type of awareness or enlightenment.

PREHEAT (oven) alludes to preparations made.

PREHISTORIC (setting/element) constitutes a long-standing aspect.

PREJUDICE applies to a biased opinion or perspective.

PRELATE See religious figure.

PRELIMINARY suggests initial research is required.

PRELUDE portrays an event or situation that precedes the main element.

PREMATURE represents something that is not developed enough to attempt or give greater attention to; the "timing" isn't right yet.

PREMEDITATED correlates to a life aspect that has been well thought out.

PREMENSTRUAL SYNDROME (PMS) crosses the gender line to reflect a life element that personally affects someone.

PREMIER characterizes the prime individual in a situation.

PREMIERE correlates to a "debut" of some type.

PREMISE pertains to a theory or idea one has.

PREMIUM illustrates a specific type of "benefit" one gains from participating in a specialized activity.

PREMIX alludes to having all the necessary elements (ingredients) to develop or accomplish a goal.

PREMONITION signifies heightened awareness; an insightful impression.

PRENATAL typifies the phase or time before the actual beginning of a new course or research.

PREOCCUPIED (mental state) connotes an inability to focus one's attention.

PREPARATORY SCHOOL represents initial research or study.

PREPPY (appearance) implies a specific personal characteristic, usually studious and efficient.

PREREQUISITE indicates a necessary element one needs to obtain before proceeding.

PREROGATIVE depicts a "right" or personally sanctioned authority to engage in an activity or follow a specific course.

PRESAGE relates to a strong personal insight.

PRESCHOOL applies to basic information; learning essential elements.

PRESCRIPTION (medical) will come as an advisement indicating what one needs to maintain mental, emotional, or physical health. This symbol may also reveal the best course of action.

PRESEASON depicts a time for preparation.

PRESENT (gift) represents a benefit or offering. The key to correct interpretation is to recall what the Present was and who gave it.

PRESENTATION relates to the exposure or disclosure of something. The dreamer will make the right association as related to his or her life.

PRESERVATIVE will clearly indicate a need to maintain an awareness or memory of a specific aspect in one's life. The surrounding dream factors will clarify what this element is.

PRESERVES reflect a tendency to maintain fundamental elements of an aspect.

PRESHRUNK alludes to a time-tested element.

PRESIDENT (of a country) characterizes an individual who has the authority and power to lead many. This symbol may not, in actuality, refer to a specific Presidential individual.

PRESOAK illustrates a need to give added attention to an issue.

PRESS See cider press.

PRESS See iron.

PRESS See printing press.

PRESS See reporter.

PRESS AGENT characterizes an individual who speaks for another.

PRESS CONFERENCE signifies a revealing meeting; providing an explanation.

PRESS KIT indicates the dissemination of background information.

PRESS RELEASE will refer to an announcement of some type.

PRESS RUN (book) usually reflects the "extent" a piece of information has been disseminated.

PRESSURE See stress.

PRESSURE CHAMBER symbolizes the voluntary and involuntary pressures brought to bear on one's spiritual journey.

PRESSURE COOKER corresponds to an extremely stressful situation, relationship or element in one's life; may also apply to an advisement to retain more of the nutrients of the food eaten.

PRESSURE GAUGE comes as an advisement to monitor and keep aware of how you handle stressful situations.

PRESSURE POINT (physiological) will correlate to one's specific area of contention; one's "buttons" others can push.

PRESSURE SUIT implies the application of a compensating or equalizing aspect.

PRESTIGE pertains to personal distinction or stature among one's peers. This symbol may reveal a perceptual level the dreamer was unaware of or it may indicate a caution to stop inflating one's self-impression.

PRETENDER usually denotes a hidden activity or behavior. Recall "who" the dream presented as the Pretender.

PRETEST suggests attention given to one's qualifications or knowledge.

PRETEXT means an ulterior motive; a hidden agenda.

PRETRIAL exemplifies a clarification.

PRETTY corresponds with a pleasing element.

PRETZEL refers to a "twisted" perception or thought process.

This symbol may signify one's emotional or mental state and relate to a relationship, life situation, or even a specific belief system.

PREVAILING (wind) warns against indecision; mental or emotional vacillation depending on the opinion of others.

PREVIEW defines a "sampling" of something before a decision is made.

PREWASHED stands for a desire to maintain a state unaffected by impurities or foreign elements.

PREY will reveal a negative situation whereby an individual is the subject of another's negative intent or otherwise a victim. Recall "who" or what the prey was. More importantly, "who" was after him or her.

PRICE (of something) will usually denote true value. Sometimes this symbol will reveal an exaggerated inflated value or indicate a worth that isn't recognized by presenting it as ridiculously inexpensive.

PRICE-CUTTING suggests too high a value placed on a life aspect; an inflated perspective of worth.

PRICE-FIXING constitutes a misrepresentation of value and worth.

PRICE TAG portrays a "cost" for a benefit accepted or received. (Also see price.)

PRICE WAR characterizes a state of competition so strong that the participants may actually lose in the end.

PRICKLY HEAT See heat rash.

PRICKLY PEAR See cactus.

PRIDEFUL means arrogance; a self-absorbed individual.

PRIEST See religious figure.

PRIM represents a rigidly formal or puritanical personality.

PRIMA DONNA stands for an egotistical individual; placing self above others.

PRIMAL THERAPY indicates a need to rid self of withheld and internalized stress and negative emotions such as anger, frustration, and resentment.

PRIMARY CARE applies to routine maintenance and attention given to one's mental, emotional, and physical condition.

PRIMARY COLOR corresponds to a "basic" or elemental aspect. This will correlate to the specific color presented in the dream. Refer to that color in this dictionary.

PRIMARY ELECTION suggests a process of elimination is required. The individual dreamer will recognize what this is associated with in his or her life.

PRIMARY TOOTH See milk tooth.

PRIMAVERA (food) pertains to multiple benefits.

PRIMAVERA (tree) See white mahogany.

PRIME MERIDIAN symbolizes a starting point or point of reference.

PRIME MOVER indicates a motivational force; an element seen as the source of one's motivation.

PRIMER (explosive) will reveal an element in one's life that has the potential to be the main source of an "explosive" situation.

PRIMER (paint) portrays a "protective" or "sealing" element.

PRIMER (text) denotes a need to return to the beginning or foundational aspects of an issue or situation.

PRIME RATE will constitute the best option or a "preferred" course.

PRIME RIB represents a "choice" element in one's life.

PRIME TIME illustrates the most "productive" time or phase to provide optimum effectiveness.

PRIMEVAL reflects a "beginning" or original element or idea.

PRIMO implies a most desired aspect; excellent condition or situation.

PRIMORDIAL symbolizes the "first" stage of a development or progression.

PRIMROSE depicts an idea of perfection.

PRIMROSE PATH portrays a life of ease where all desires and goals are successfully attained; an over-idealistic goal and course that has a high potential for ending in disaster.

PRINCE See royalty.

PRINCE CHARMING pertains to an idealistic perception and overly optimistic goal; unrealistic plans.

PRINCESS See royalty.

PRINCIPAL relates to a main person or element.

PRINCIPLE portrays a guideline or rule; moral, ethical, or spiritual laws.

PRINTER suggests a finality; one's words imprinted on the fabric of reality.

PRINTING PRESS represents an ability to disseminate information.

PRINTOUT indicates a need for "hard" copies. This symbolizes "proof" or verification of something.

PRINT WHEEL alludes to the "type" of communication one should attempt for a specific purpose. Recall if the Wheel had a "bold" or fine type.

PRIORESS See religious figure.

PRIORY See monastery.

PRISM refers to a individual advisement to view an element from all angles.

PRISON symbolizes self-imposed restrictions. The key element here is to recall what your role was, if any. Were you the prisoner or guard?

PRISONER most often reflects a self-imposed confinement or restriction.

PRIVATE (military) characterizes a lesser ranking; less authority.

PRIVATE DETECTIVE correlates to a need for each person to do his or her own thinking and searching.

PRIVATE ENTERPRISE defines personal resourcefulness; ingenuity.

PRIVATE EYE See private detective.

PRIVATE SCHOOL denotes individualized thought processes.

PRIVATION See deprivation.

PRIVET (shrub) See hedge.

PRIZE represents specific goals or attainment as personally perceived.

PRIZEFIGHT warns against engaging in altercations for self-serving purposes.

PRIZEWINNER portrays an unexpected benefit.

PROBABILITY signifies the presence of an alternative element or course.

PROBABLE CAUSE illustrates the existence of a specific motive for doing something.

PROBATE COURT pertains to an authoritative validation.

PROBATION implies a "cautionary" phase or time; a time to watch one's behavior.

PROBATION OFFICER characterizes those individuals in one's life who serve to guide and advise. Use discretion with this, for someone presented as a Probation Officer may not be right for the dreamer. Recall what he or she wore. Their actions. Colors that were associated with the dream person.

PROBE means exploration; investigation; research.

PROBLEM will relate to just that—a problem in one's life, yet a dream problem will frequently define the difficulty more clearly and also may offer a solution.

PROCEDURE most often reveals an efficient course or direction.

PROCESSION symbolizes a chosen life path that follows many others.

PRO-CHOICE represents s decision that is not hindered by another's personal opinion; the personal freedom to make personal choices.

PROCLAMATION connotes a disclosure.

PROCRASTINATION implies an inability to motivate self or it may infer the existence of inner fears.

PROCTOLOGIST will constitute an individual in your life who has the knowledge and ability to help you face problems and gain acceptance.

PROD (device) illustrates a life element that has the potential to serve as a motivational or energy-building impetus.

PRODIGY (child) stands for inherent talents, memories, or knowledge "inherited" from one's total experiential existences.

PRODUCE (edibles) denote nourishing life elements. See specific type.

PRODUCER (film) typifies an individual who has the opportunity and ability to enlighten others.

PRODUCTION LINE See assembly line.

PROFANITY See obscenity.

PROFESSION signifies multiple interpretations. Refer to specific type.

PROFESSIONAL portrays quality behavior; ethical and/or moral.

PROFESSOR See teacher.

PROFICIENCY represents applied efficiency coupled with skill.

PROFILE (physical) See silhouette.

PROFILE (workup) defines one's personality characteristics.

PROFIT signifies benefits from expending one's efforts in a productive manner.

PROFITEER characterizes an individual who takes advantage of others or sees self-serving opportunities through negative means.

PROFIT SHARING denotes a synergistic relationship.

PROGENY See offspring or children.

PROGNOSIS will reveal a probable outcome.

PROGRAM (any type/source) signifies an individualized message for each dreamer. This dream Program will depict one's actions or clarify a situation or course of action.

PROGRAMMED refers to conditioned responses; brain-washed; manipulated and influenced.

PROGRAMMER exemplifies an individual who has the knowledge and ability to manipulate and/or strongly influence others.

PROGRESS will come as a message of encouragement if the dream depicts an advancement being made; otherwise, this symbol may reveal one's level or measure of progression along his or her life path.

PROGRESS REPORT See report card.

PROHIBITION represents restrictions placed by others; suppression.

PROJECT (venture) will usually symbolize or actually depict a preferred course of action for the dreamer; illustrates what one should be working on.

PROJECT (buildings) imply a lack of resources and/or motivation.

PROJECT See propeller.

PROJECT See protrusion.

PROJECTILE portrays the entry of an unexpected element. Recall what was going through the air for further clarity.

PROJECTION BOOTH symbolizes the "source" of specific information.

PROJECTOR (film) advises of a need to "project" an idea or attitude to another; a need to externalize and express emotions.

PROLETARIAT signifies the "blue collar" workers.

PRO-LIFE alludes to a respect for life, but not necessarily for rights.

PROLIFIC correlates with continual productivity.

PROLOGUE reflects an explanatory beginning; an introductory phase of a communication.

PROMENADE pertains to a stage in one's path where a leisure attitude will serve best; a time for acceptance through neutrality.

PROMENADE DECK indicates a time for spiritual pauses during one's search.

PROMISCUITY warns against apathy in regard to self; a loss of self-respect.

PROMISE illustrates a personal responsibility to carry something through.

PROMISED LAND most often applies to one's goals or the attainment of one's life purpose.

PROMISSORY NOTE defines one's firm intentions of balancing a debt.

PROMONTORY applies to a testing, inquisitive probe into spiritual concepts.

PROMOTER characterizes an individual who supports and promotes another individual or idea. See agent.

PROMOTION denotes advancement; progression along one's life path.

PROMPTER stands for a fear of forgetting important information or other life elements; that which aids one's memory.

PRONOUNCEMENT See proclamation.

PROOF-OF-PURCHASE stands for verification of an action taken.

PROOFREAD comes as a clear warning to be discerning of what is accepted as truth in respect to all forms of literature.

PROP may indicate a "supportive" factor or a type of personal "crutch." Recall surrounding dreamscape details for clarification.

PROPAGANDA signifies an attempt to indoctrinate others with one's personal beliefs; may indicate falsehoods.

PROPANE exemplifies a life aspect that contains the positive-negative duality element. Depending on how the Propane was presented in the dream, surrounding factors will clarify its meaning.

PROPANE TRUCK represents a need to eliminate excessive gases from one's system. This doesn't necessarily refer to intestinal gases, but usually indicates other gases within the system. Are you often a braggart? Thinking egotistically? Full of hot air?

PROPELLER signifies forces that have the ability to "propel" you along your intended path and bring you into a higher level of advancement.

PROPERTY See specific type.

PROPERTY TAX implies a "price" attached; "dues" for that which one has. These "dues" will not refer to a monetary aspect.

PROPHECY stands for a fore-thought; inspiration; foreknowledge.

PROPHESY relates to the act of disseminating one's foreknowledge.

PROPHET characterizes an astute and wise individual.

PROPORTION comes as a symbol taking multiple forms and usually will reveal proper life priorities.

PROPOSITION denotes probabilities or opportunities. Not all of these will necessarily represent a benefit to the dreamer and this is why this dreamscape fragment is so important. Recall what type of Proposition it was. Who did it come from? What colors surrounded it?

PROPRIETRESS emphasizes the rightful owner or originator of something. Surrounding dreamscape details will clarify this.

PROPRIETY stands for respectability; appropriate behavior.

PRORATED pertains to equality; balance.

PROSCIUTTO refers to an involvement in a personally interesting issue.

PROSECUTOR (legal) characterizes higher judgments from spiritual forces.

PROSPECTING represents a search of some type.

PROSPECTOR characterizes one who is "searching" for something in life. Recall what was being prospected for. Gold denotes financial gain, while silver will indicate a spiritual element.

PROSPECTUS indicates a need to research an issue thoroughly before accepting it.

PROSTHESIS denotes a substitute or alternative.

PROSTITUTE applies to ill-gotten gains.

PROSTRATION may refer to a reverential attitude or it may infer a submission.

PROTAGONIST implies a leader or advocate.

PROTECTOR portrays a guarding or method of self-protection one has in place.

PROTÉGÉE is one who has a personal mentor or special teacher.

PROTEIN will symbolize a necessary element in one's life.

PROTEST signifies an objection.

PROTOCOL defines the right way to accomplish something; a correct process or method of going about an action.

PROTOTYPE illustrates an initial sample of something that will follow; a model example.

PROTRACTOR comes as an advisement to look at all angles.

PROTRUSION exemplifies a "loose end" that needs to be handled.

PROVERB typifies an advisement or counsel.

PROVIDENTIAL alludes to a fortuitous event or element in one's life.

PROVIDER depicts a patron, care-giver or contributor.

PROVINCIAL infers an unsophisticated aspect or individual.

PROVING GROUND pertains to one's life; earthly existence.

PROVISO connotes ulterior motives or special provisions.

PROVOCATION emphasizes a need to gain greater acceptance.

PROW suggests spiritual priorities.

PROWLER stands for stealth. Recall who the Prowler was.

PROWL CAR See squad car.

PROXY pertains to a loss of input; a state of waning participation.

PRUNE refers to a distasteful or unappealing element.

PRUNING SHEARS relate to a need to "cut back" on something in life; trim down excesses.

PSALM reflects inner spiritual contentedness.

PSEUDONYM may infer a need to protect self or it may indicate an alter-ego, depending on the surrounding dreamscape factors.

PSYCHE (Greek mythology) characterizes one's soul.

PSYCHEDELIC signifies an altered perspective.

PSYCHIATRIC HOSPITAL may not have a negative connotation; it may represent a need for introspection; self analyzation.

PSYCHIATRIST illustrates a need to give deeper thought to one's behavior motivations or belief systems.

PSYCHIC corresponds to one's inherent natural abilities as they relate to the yet-undiscovered elements of true Reality.

PSYCHOANALYSIS See psychiatrist.

PSYCHOGENIC reveals a mental or emotional source.

PSYCHOKINESIS stands for repressed emotional energy.

PSYCHOMETRY suggests a heightened receptivity to others.

PSYCHOPATH characterizes an imbalanced perspective.

PSYCHOTHERAPY exemplifies a need to communicate in a more open manner and analyze one's motives.

PSYLLIUM portrays a tendency to take the easy path; suggests a more difficult course.

PTERODACTYL denotes antiquated thoughts; extinct attitudes.

PUBLIC-ADDRESS SYSTEM See microphone.

PUBLIC ASSISTANCE See welfare.

PUBLIC DEFENDER implies unbiased justice.

PUBLIC DOMAIN applies to an aspect that is open to all; not privately owned.

PUBLIC EYE refers to open exposure.

PUBLIC HOUSING See welfare.

PUBLIC INTEREST symbolizes an issue or element that is of general interest.

PUBLICITY See advertisement.

PUBLIC LIBRARY See library.

PUBLIC OPINION represents the attitude of the majority.

PUBLIC RELATIONS (PR) constitutes the dissemination of supportive and positive information associated with an individual, group, or situation.

PUBLIC SERVICE alludes to efforts given to help others.

PUBLIC SQUARE represents neutral ground.

PUBLIC TELEVISION symbolizes personal efforts expended toward a goal.

PUBLIC WORKS pertains to general life benefits.

PUBLISHER characterizes one who disseminates information.

Recall what type of material was being published.

PUCK (English literature) relates to a mischievous personality.

PUCKERED denotes a "snag" or problem associated with an element in one's life.

PUDDING indicates an "easy" aspect.

PUDDLE signifies something that has been left unfinished.

PUDGY infers a need to shed some type of excess.

PUEBLO relates to a synergistic relationship.

PUFF See powder puff.

PUFF (of smoke) alludes to "the first sign of trouble" with an aspect that surrounding dream elements will pinpoint.

PUFFBALL (plant) symbolizes a healing aspect in one's life.

PUFFER (fish) warns of a potentially dangerous spiritual element that one should defend self against.

PUFFIN represents spiritual arrogance.

PUG (dog breed) alludes to a disagreeable friend; one who rarely shares an opinion.

PUG NOSE portrays a lack of acceptance; a disagreeable nature.

PULITZER PRIZE reveals a prime accomplishment.

PULLEY indicates energy reserves; a supportive or assisting element.

PULLMAN (rail car) pertains to revealing dreams; ability to learn and advance during one's sleep state.

PULLOVER suggests a deception; something "pulled over" one's eyes.

PULL-TAB depicts an element that has the capability of making it easy to begin or "open" something.

PULP alludes to waste elements; that which is left over and of little use.

PULP FICTION reflects idle intellect; filling one's mind with useless information.

PULPIT signifies preaching; telling others what to do and how to live.

PULSAR connotes inspiration.

PULSATION exemplifies steadiness; dependability; continuum.

PULSE (heart) applies to emotional stability. Recall if the dream inferred a rate.

PULVERIZE See grinder.

PUMA See cougar.

PUMICE STONE suggests that something in one's life needs to be smoothed out.

PUMP implies motivation; that which serves as an impetus.

PUMPERNICKEL See rye.

PUMPKIN represents playfulness; a wide range of expressions.

PUMPKINSEED stands for an opportunity to express self.

PUN pertains to innuendos.

PUNCH alludes to an unexpected response.

PUNCH (drink) portrays a surprise element.

PUNCH AND JUDY characterize a love-hate relationship.

PUNCH BOWL denotes an aspect that has the potential to contain an unexpected element; a surprise factor.

PUNCHING BAG advises to release pent-up stress or emotions.

PUNCH LINE will reveal a solution or crux of a matter.

PUNCH-OUTS (paper) See cutouts.

PUNCH PRESS defines a need to make a strong impression or statement.

PUNCTUATION MARK See specific type.

PUNCTURE may advise one to make a breakthrough of some kind or it may denote an inconsistency or defect associated with an element of one's life.

PUNGENT symbolizes effective-ness; strong impression.

PUNISHMENT correlates to recompense; may infer personal guilt.

PUNITIVE DAMAGES suggest repayment; a karmic-balancing event.

PUNK ROCKER implies immaturity.

PUNT (boat) corresponds with a gentle yet cautious spiritual journey.

PUNT (football) signifies a lost opportunity.

PUNY applies to an inconsequential factor; insignificance.

PUPA reflects a state of transformation.

PUPIL (eye) portrays one's perceptual qualities. Recall this symbol's associative details.

PUPIL See student.

PUPPET reveals an easily manipulated individual.

PUPPETEER characterizes a manipulator.

PUPPY will denote a new friendship.

PUPPY LOVE may refer to a budding affection or an immature emotion.

PURCHASING POWER will reveal the quantity of one's personal assets. These will not be monetary, but rather humanitarian elements.

PUREE See strainer.

PURGATORY reflects reparations; self-analyzation and serious introspection followed by deeds that balance one's negative actions.

PURIST comes as an advisement to attain greater acceptance; one who is overly critical of others.

PURITAN characterizes a rigid personality.

PURPLE constitutes attained spiritual wisdom and enlightenment.

PURPLE HEART denotes recognition for one's service to others.

PURRING signifies contentedness; satisfaction.

PURSE illustrates an opportunity to utilize one's talents.

PURSER correlates to an individual who controls or manages financial aspects.

PURSE STRINGS symbolize one's assets. These don't need to refer to monetary assets, but could represent humanitarian or personal talents.

PURSLANE depicts an opportunity to gain inner nourishment; a source of emotional strength.

PURSUIT usually represents a personal quest of some type. If it depicts an actual chasing pursuit, the surrounding details need to be associated with it. Who was pursuing whom or what? Were their weapons involved?

PURULENT See infection.

PURVEYOR characterizes one who has the knowledge and ability to make "provision" or "supply" the necessary elements.

PUSHING warns of a "forcing" action in one's life. This indicates a need to gain more acceptance and stop attempting to push things before their time.

PUSHOVER signifies a weak personality; easily manipulated or controlled.

PUSHY represents a nagging or demanding nature.

PUSSYFOOT portrays a timid personality; may also denote a cautious manner of advancement.

PUSSY WILLOW corresponds to bountiful personal talents or gifts.

PUSTULE See infection.

PUTDOWN stands for a taunting attitude that may be generating from self; usually reveals a self-deprecating attitude.

PUTOFF can pertain to disgust, yet it most often "symbolizes" the act of putting something off; procrastination.

PUT-ON typifies an exaggeration; a teasing.

PUTREFY See decay.

PUTT depicts a cautious move.

PUTTER characterizes an individual who idles time; expending mental efforts on insignificant elements.

PUTTY relates to a "corrective" aspect in one's life. Depending on associated aspects, Putty can also indicate an easily controlled individual.

PUTTY KNIFE illustrates a method or opportunity to correct a fault or negative element in one's life.

PUZZLE signifies a tendency to complicate matters by reading into an issue things that aren't there.

PUZZLE PIECE denotes a part of a solution; one facet of a whole.

PYGMY constitutes unrecognized strength.

PYLON corresponds with a "supportive" factor in one's life.

PYORRHEA reveals falsehoods.

PYRAMID pertains to higher wisdom and knowledge.

PYRE (funeral) reveals the misdeeds and negative emotions that one "piles up" to create one's ultimate downfall.

PYRITE (iron) See fool's gold.

PYROMANIAC characterizes an individual who enjoys making trouble for others; may indicate a person who likes digging up skeletons in the closets of others and exposing them; one who enjoys an "explosive and fiery" event.

PYROTECHNICS See fireworks.

PYTHON will warn of a suffocating personality or situation.

Q-TIP See cotton swab.

QUACK (sound) represents a swindler; fraudulence.

QUACK GRASS refers to uncharacteristic attitudes; undesirable qualities.

QUADAPHONIC denotes high awareness.

QUADRUPLET (birth) constitutes a new life or new beginning that has four opportunities or benefits to it.

QUAGMIRE symbolizes a dilemma; a mired situation.

QUAIL stands for fearful thoughts; anxiety; lacking self-reliance.

QUAINT will not mean old-fashioned, but rather a "refreshing" type of element.

QUAKE See earthquake.

QUALIFICATIONS reveal the qualities or skills necessary to accomplish a task or goal.

QUALIFY indicates a need to prove one's skill or knowledge.

QUALITY CONTROLLER characterizes efficiency and a high standard of behavior or productivity.

QUALMS mean doubts; apprehension.

QUANTUM LEAP defines a major advancement regarding one's path progression or conceptual knowledge.

QUANTUM THEORY represents a beginning step toward understanding true Reality.

QUARANTINE advises of a need to separate self from a negative, harmful situation or relationship.

QUARREL means a disagreement. Sometimes the dreamer will be shown to have an internal conflict (quarreling with self).

QUARRY symbolizes a mother lode of knowledge or information; a rich source.

QUARRY See prey.

QUARTER (coin) See money.

QUARTER (football) See inning.

QUARTERBACK usually represents an individual who "calls the signals" or shots in one's life. Was this you or someone else?

QUARTER HORSE alludes to a "preferred" choice.

QUARTERLY will apply to a specific proportion of time related to an aspect of the dreamer's life.

QUARTERMASTER characterizes personal responsibility.

QUARTET will pertain to a harmonic relationship between four individuals.

QUARTZ correlates to spiritual purity of truths. Recall if the dream Quartz had color, then incorporate that symbol into the complete meaning.

QUARTZ LAMP See mercury-vapor lamp.

QUASAR constitutes a revelation; spiritual insight.

QUATRAIN See poem.

QUEASY will reveal guilt or a conscience-stricken mood.

QUEEN characterizes a domineering personality.

QUEEN ANNE'S LACE will represent an element possessing the duality of positive and negative aspects; may indicate a potentially harmful situation that, initially, looks inviting.

QUEEN-FOR-A-DAY connotes a recognition of one's efforts and perseverance.

QUEEN MOTHER will indicate an individual who can exert influence on a leader or other person of authority.

QUEEN REGNANT See queen.

QUENCH relates to information obtained or a goal attained.

QUEST illustrates a major goal in life.

QUESTION comes in a dream to pose a self-discovery element; points to an issue or element that one hasn't considered.

QUESTION MARK will suggest doubt or skepticism.

QUESTIONNAIRE corresponds to a need for the dreamer to spend valuable introspective time; self-analysis is required.

QUETZALCOATL means a spiritual rebirth.

QUEUE implies that one is not alone; there are many others in the same situation.

QUIBBLE portrays a nitpicking attitude; splitting hairs.

QUICHE connotes an unproductive effort; an insignificant aspect.

QUICK BREAD infers a "quick fix" to a problem that won't necessarily hold or suffice.

QUICKLIME refers to a highly destructive element in one's life.

QUICKSAND signifies a declining situation from which one needs to extract self.

QUICKSILVER See mercury.

QUICK STUDY refers to intellectual astuteness; absorption of information or knowledge.

QUICK WIT means swift responses. A lightning intellect.

QUILL stands for protective methods; self-preservation means.

QUILLWORK portrays an attitude of openness in reference to one's inner power.

QUILT pertains to a personal manner of acceptance and inner comfort. The revealing factor here will be to recall if there was design and color on the quilt presented in the dream.

QUINCE denotes an element in one's life that is effective only when brought into completion.

QUININE signifies that which serves as a healing agent in one's life.

QUINTET will imply an association with five individuals who create a harmonic group.

QUINTUPLET represents a new birth or beginning that will contain five separate aspects.

QUIP usually comes as a smart remark that reveals an important element that one has overlooked or voluntarily refused to acknowledge.

QUIRK exemplifies an unexpected flaw or problem.

QUIRT symbolizes a motivational factor.

QUIT may come in dreams as an advisement to quit something or it may reveal one who is behaving like a "quitter."

QUITCLAIM DEED exonerates one from further responsibility.

QUIVER See tremble.

QUIVER (arrow case) pertains to an intention to be well prepared to be focused on one's goals.

QUIZ will center on questions the dreamer needs to ask self.

QUIZ SHOW usually presents itself in order for the dreamer to gain a proper perspective of his or her knowledge regarding a specific issue.

QUONSET (hut) reflects a temporary situation.

QUORUM corresponds to an issue in one's life that requires the cooperation or agreement of others.

QUOTA warns against attempting to "force" quantity rather than focusing on quality.

QUOTATION will most often come as a message or some type of revelation, perhaps the solution to a life problem.

QUOTATION MARKS emphasize the words spoken or written in dreams and serve to make them stand out so the dreamer will recall them.

R

RABBI See religious figure.

RABBIT represents an obsessive preoccupation with mental and/or physical sexual activities. This is a warning. Sexual obsession is spiritual suicide. This symbol may also symbolize a quiet endurance of one's personal pain. Recall surrounding dreamscape details for clarification.

RABBIT EARS relate to awareness, one's personal antenna.

RABBIT FOOD See salad.

RABBIT'S FOOT denotes a belief in luck rather than oneself.

RABBLE-ROUSER characterizes a person who incites high emotional responses. This is usually a negative element in one's dream, yet it can indicate a motivating force in one's life.

RABIES portray a potentially fatal negative element in one's life.

RACCOON illustrates an industrious personality.

RACE (speed/fast pace) refers to a warning to slow down. This symbol may indicate competitiveness that is blinding, self-serving. A race may suggest that one isn't absorbing all one needs in life because he or she is going too fast to focus on the important issues.

RACECAR symbolizes a stressful and hectic work environment.

RACECOURSE exemplifies a "designated" course that one travels over and over again. This is an advisement to set one's own course and take it at a steady pace.

RACEHORSE illustrates competitiveness; a desire to be better and faster than one's peers; to get ahead of the rest.

RACE RIOT signifies repressed anger and the violent methods of releasing same; a lack of self-responsibility.

RACETRACK usually alludes to the "fast track."

RACE WALKING is an attempt to cover up the fact that one is rushing through life without absorbing important aspects or focusing on the minor, yet revealing, elements.

RACK See antler.

RACK See shelf.

RACKET See scam.

RACKET (sport) connotes where the responsibility lies. Was the dreamer hitting the ball back into another's area? Was someone else giving the ball to the dreamer? What was the Racket's color and condition?

RACKETEER See mafia.

RACONTEUR See storyteller.

RACQUETBALL (sport) corresponds with contemplation; personally accepting an issue to be placed back in one's own hands for further analyzation.

RADAR portrays an acute awareness; intuition; heightened perception.

RADAR DETECTOR represents a perception of another's thoughts, moods or attitudes; insight.

RADIAL SYMMETRY signifies an outward radiation from a single source, usually an individual; refers to the importance of giving, sharing one's inherent skills or talents.

RADIATION basically infers a dispersement. Recall surrounding dream elements to determine if this symbol indicates a positive or negative meaning.

RADIATION SUIT illustrates a protective measure against potentially dangerous situations or negative elements that could prove to be toxic to one's mental, emotional, or physical well-being.

RADIATOR (vehicle) corresponds with one's internal temperature in respect to "overheated" emotions. Recall what the condition of the Radiator was. Was it overheating?

RADIO exemplifies a need to "tune into self" for the purpose of understanding one's motives and responses.

RADIOACTIVITY warns of a potentially dangerous situational atmosphere.

RADIOGRAPH reveals a person's hidden character.

RADISH signifies an emotionally volatile situation.

RADIUM THERAPY pertains to an attempt to correct or heal a condition through potentially destructive methods.

RADON correlates with forces or elements in daily life that are hidden destroyers.

RAFFIA will suggest a life aspect that has the potential to bring multiple uses or solutions.

RAFFLE See lottery.

RAFFLE TICKET exemplifies a chance taken when an opportunity manifests.

RAFT represents spiritual ingenuity as associated with one's path of developed or attained enlightenment.

RAFTER (construction) denotes a "supporting" element in one's life.

RAG (cloth) relates to a remnant (leftover) factor in one's life that requires attention.

RAGAMUFFIN (child) most often will imply an adventurous

or precocious character or attitude.

RAGBAG portrays multiple "fragments" of some life aspect that need to be taken care of, finished.

RAGE warns of an inability to direct one's energies in a productive manner; emotional immaturity.

RAGGED EDGE stands for something left unfinished in life.

RAGOUT See stew.

RAG PICKER characterizes a person who attempts to utilize leftover aspects; may indicate a resourceful individual who efficiently recycles multiple aspects.

RAGWEED typifies a life element that has the potential to cause a strong reaction in someone.

RAID portrays the possibility of being discovered or "caught" at something.

RAIL FENCE reflects self-devised perimeters one sets.

RAILING See handrail.

RAILROAD constitutes a plan or decision that has been forced into an expedited state without time given to adequate thought.

RAIMENT See clothing.

RAIN symbolizes a methodical and consistent search for truth.

RAINBOW comes as an ac-

knowledgment of one's personal accomplishments or efforts.

RAINBOW TROUT represents a beautiful spiritual path.

RAIN CHECK connotes postponements; promises to fulfill at a later date; perhaps procrastination.

RAINCOAT denotes a personal desire to insulate oneself from spiritual aspects in life.

RAINDROP reflects a singular spiritual element.

RAIN FOREST constitutes spiritual bounties.

RAIN GAUGE will reveal one's level of spirituality; may specifically refer to depth of "wisdom" rather than knowledge.

RAINMAKER characterizes an individual who has a good record of getting results; high rate of success with attempted endeavors.

RAINSPOUT marks an attempt to channel one's spiritual aspects into a specific issue or method. This is usually an advisement to utilize one's spiritual aspects in a "broad-scope" manner that take advantage of "every" opportunity.

RAISIN pertains to a nourishing benefit that manifested from an aspect of another life element.

RAKE (tool) implies a need to "rake" through a current situation or concept; to carefully inspect something.

RALLY defines a supportive attitude.

RAM refers to an argumentative nature or it may be advising one to stop "beating one's head" against the wall, stop trying to force results.

RAMBLING represents a shiftless nature; a lack of direction or motivation.

RAMBO characterizes a desire or tendency to force solutions or closures through aggressive means.

RAMBUNCTIOUSNESS reveals a lack of acceptance; anxiety and impatience.

RAMP portrays a life aspect that has the capability of easing one's way.

RAMPAGE See rage.

RAMPART pertains to a means of defense or self-protection.

RAMROD signifies a forcing action.

RAMSHACKLE illustrates something that's been poorly constructed, devised, or executed.

RANCH signifies a domineering personality.

RANCID emphasizes that some element in one's life has gone sour; turned out bad; a spoiled result.

RANGE See prairie.

RANGE FINDER symbolizes one's personal priority to follow his or her path.

RANGER (forest) characterizes a person who recognizes and respects his or her natural talents.

RANGER STATION signifies watchfulness; self-restraint.

RANKLE implies an irritation; perhaps an intended aggravated act.

RANSACK corresponds with a thorough search. This may not indicate a negative reference.

RANSOM represents the "price of attainment." This comes as a severe warning; enlightenment should never have a price.

RANT portrays a lack of self-control and acceptance.

RAPE reflects a low self-image; a need to continually manipulate others in order to raise self up to a position of power.

RAPIER See sword.

RAP MUSIC infers a failed method of getting one's message across.

RAP SHEET will illustrate one's offenses in life; a record of misdeeds.

RAPTURE (emotion) suggests an enthralled sensation or attitude; overcome with captivation.

RAPTURE (event) constitutes a belief that one will be "saved" from something.

RARE (uncooked) symbolizes an unfinished aspect; something not complete.

RARE (unique) portrays an uncommon element in one's life.

RASCAL characterizes a mischievous nature.

RASH (skin) indicates emotional irritations or psychological difficulties generated by a lack of acceptance.

RASHER See bacon.

RASP (file) indicates a need to smooth out something in one's life.

RASP (sound) exemplifies an inability to accept something; an aspect that "grates" on one's nerves or sensibilities.

RASPBERRY depicts a distasteful or disagreeable element.

RASPUTIN (Grigori Efimovich) characterizes a manipulative personality; one who uses the impression of attained knowledge to control others and elevate self.

RAT pertains to a "diseased" element in one's life.

RATCHET signifies an opportunity to make an adjustment in one's life.

RATE OF EXCHANGE suggests the fact that people perceive differing values on things.

RATIO will illustrate priorities. Recall this symbol as accurately as possible, for it may suggest the proper Ratio or it may have portrayed your current set of priorities.

RATION comes in dreams to advise of a need to monitor one's use of a specific element; suggests over-extension or a need for moderation.

RATIONALE infers a precise reason or excuse for one's behavior. Recall the surrounding dreamscape elements for further clarification.

RAT RACE is a clear message that refers to the act of going nowhere fast.

RATTAN depicts a multi-use talent or ability.

RATTLE (ceremonial) represents an aid to getting in touch with one's inner strength and inherent abilities.

RATTLE (toy) will pertain to something one amuses self with and usually indicates insignificance.

RATTLESNAKE See snake.

RATTLETRAP stands for a person's physiological system and its worn or ill state.

RATTRAP represents a dangerous or unhealthy homelife.

RAVE constitutes a state of extremely high emotion. Recall dream details to determine if this was a positive or negative symbol.

RAVEN symbolizes watchfulness for and recognition of spiritual falsehoods.

RAVENOUS denotes a seemingly insatiable interest in or desire for something in life.

RAVISHING will represent a highly attractive situation, idea, or individual.

RAW usually stands for a basic, unaltered aspect in one's life.

RAWHIDE may allude to one's inner strength or it may infer a lack of emotional sensitivity.

RAY (of light) comes as a commendation or moment of inspiration.

RAY GUN most often portrays one's own quality of self-protective measures. It may also denote one's spiritual effectiveness with others.

RAYON (fabric) applies to imitation; a "synthetic" aspect that has no originality.

RAZOR stands for a delicate excising; careful removal of an unwanted element from one's life.

RAZOR BLADE emphasizes the "cutting edge" of something; symbolizes life's multiple dualities.

REACTION TIME will reveal one's level of awareness and resulting responses.

READING correlates to the attainment of information. The key here is to recall "what" was being read.

READY-MADE may suggest a time-saving aspect or it might advise of a need to devise something through one's own ideas or planning.

READY-MIX See premix.

REAL ESTATE pertains to possibilities; opportunities.

REAL ESTATE AGENT characterizes the potential for losing one's freedom or right to look at all options.

REAL ESTATE OFFICE refers to a fragmentation of one's talents.

REALIST is a person who refuses to consider alternative concepts or optional ideas.

REAM (of paper) exemplifies a measure of work. Recall if the paper was filled with print or blank.

REAM (tool) constitutes a need to clear out or broaden an aspect in one's life.

REAP See harvest.

REAR (position) brings a placement mark to some aspect in one's life. Each dreamer will make this specific association.

REAR-ENDED indicates an unexpected event; one wasn't being aware.

443

REAR GUARD advises one to "watch his or her back" and not leave self exposed.

REAR-VIEW MIRROR typifies symbols that advise one to be aware of what's coming up from behind or what's transpiring behind one's back.

REASSIGNED will constitute a new direction or purpose.

REASSURANCE comes as a verification or message of encouragement.

REBATE signifies benefits gained through efforts applied.

REBEL characterizes an individual who follows his or her own path; may also denote a continually disagreeable personality.

REBELLION marks resistance.

REBIRTH (spiritual) will not infer a spiritual connotation, yet it signifies a "renewal" of some type; new inspiration.

REBOUND denotes a "return" or backlash effect.

REBUILDING corresponds to applying one's efforts to new beginnings.

REBUTTAL refers to a defense of one's personal opinion or attitude.

RECALL usually doesn't imply one's memory, but rather it denotes a need to revive a forgotten element in one's life.

RECANT means a denial.

RECAPITULATE suggests a need to redefine or explain something in basic, simple terms.

RECEDING alludes to a "lessening" or waning of something in one's life. If this was associated with "water," the intent was associated with one's spirituality.

RECEDING (hairline) indicates a superficial and apathetic thought process; resting on false assumptions.

RECEIPT stands for "evidence" or proof.

RECEIVING BLANKET corresponds to one's quality of preparedness for accepting a new direction. The key here is to recall the Blanket's condition and color.

RECEIVING DOCK correlates to anticipation or expectation. Recall what was expected to arrive.

RECEIVING LINE will reveal those who claim alliance with another. The key here is "claim" and may not indicate a true attitude or position. Recall who was the "subject" of the greeting line.

RECEPTACLE See container.

RECEPTION (electronic) relates to the quality of one's comprehension.

RECEPTION (social) See receiving line.

RECEPTIONIST characterizes an initial contact.

RECESS denotes a period of rest that is being advised.

RECESSION implies a time of losing ground; slipping backwards.

RECIPE won't necessarily relate to the preparation of food, but rather will refer to the proper steps and right elements associated with accomplishing a goal.

RECIPIENT will reveal the beneficiary of something that may pertain to an object, benefit, reprimand, praise, or other life aspect. The surrounding dream elements will clarify this.

RECIPROCATION may refer to retaliation or compensation, depending on associated dream elements.

RECITAL connotes the act of taking a close look at what you know and the related skills.

RECKLESS exemplifies immaturity; a lack of responsibility.

RECKONING advises of the wisdom to "balance" one's behavior or character; to appraise one's past deeds and attitudes.

RECLAMATION most often signifies a need to take back one's self-control and/or individuality; to "reclaim" self and one's inherent rights to choose or make personal decisions.

RECLINER portrays acceptance; may represent indifference. Recall the symbol's surrounding dream details for clarity.

RECLUSE characterizes a remote and/or distant personality; may indicate a "need" to withdraw for a time in order to focus on one's purpose or path.

RECOIL portrays a fear response; a reluctance to face reality.

RECOLLECT See remembering.

RECOMMENDATION stands for a suggestion. In order to discover if this is a positive or negative symbol, recall "what" was recommended. For whom?

RECOMPENSE means a compensation or reimbursement.

RECONCILIATION denotes an arrangement to settle a disagreement.

RECONDITION suggests a repair or renovation of an element in one's life. Implies a current state of usefulness or viability.

RECONNAISSANCE warns of a need to thoroughly look something over and be aware of all aspects of it before proceeding.

RECONSTITUTE signifies a rejuvenation or reimplementation of an element in one's life.

RECONSTRUCTION denotes the analyzation of a situation.

RECORD (music) will reveal a message or mood, sometimes even one's character.

RECORD (written) pertains to evidence or historical process.

RECORDER (musical) See flute.

RECORDER (tape) underscores the need to correctly recall another's words.

RECORDING STUDIO symbolizes the opportunity to preserve one's words or history.

RECOVERY ROOM reflects a state of "recovery" from an emotional or damaging situational event.

RECREATIONAL VEHICLE (RV) will usually indicate a "time out" from one's work; a needed pause for relaxing activities.

RECRUIT characterizes an individual who recently changed his or her way of thinking; one who has begun a new effort.

RECRUITER relates to a person who easily coerces others; a manipulative personality.

RECTANGLE (configuration) represents firm attitudes; set in one's ways.

RECTOR See religious figure.

RECTORY denotes spiritual arrogance; spiritually elevating self.

RECUPERATION illustrates a span of time one should devote to regaining mental or emotional strength following a draining event.

RECYCLING applies to a life aspect's multiple uses; personal resourcefulness.

RED may refer to anger or danger, depending on the symbol's surrounding dream aspects.

RED-BLOODED refers to strength; highly-spirited; adventurous.

REDCAP See porter.

RED CARPET implies superiority or inferiority, depending on the dream's associated factors.

RED CLOVER represents a "cleansing" element in one's life. The dreamer will understand this meaning.

RED CROSS emphasizes assistance of some type.

REDECORATING portrays a desire to start over; make a new beginning.

REDEMPTION CENTER (savings stamps/coupons) constitutes an opportunity to restore one's inner peace; balancing out karmic aspects.

REDEYE comes as a strong warning the dreamer will understand.

RED-FACED reflects embarrassment; possible guilt.

RED HAND stands for "being caught" at something.

RED-HEADED alludes to a temperamental nature; easily incited.

RED HERRING reveals a superficial diversion; an aspect that diverts one's focused attention on his or her path or purpose.

RED INK represents a failing endeavor; an unsuccessful attempt.

RED LETTER will mark a special event, individual, or idea.

RED LIGHT appears as a strong warning to STOP something. The dreamer will make the correct association.

RED-LIGHT DISTRICT symbolizes a self-serving intention.

REDLINE exemplifies a refusal; rejection.

RED MEAT in dreams will not refer to food, but rather a highly beneficial element; an aspect providing basic factors.

REDNECK infers a bigoted personality; highly opinionated.

RED PENCIL signifies censorship.

RED PEPPER signifies an issue warming up with the potential of becoming hot.

RED RIBBON actually represents a Second Place position, so as a dream symbol it indicates high accomplishment.

RED TAPE reveals self-generated complications.

RED TIDE warns of a dangerous spiritual situation or concept.

REDUCTIONIST characterizes an individual who has the ability to simplify and clarify matters or concepts.

REDUNDANCY reveals ignorance; an attempt to impress with one's knowledge.

REDWOOD FOREST stands for inner strength; fortitude.

REED symbolizes resiliency.

REEF illustrates spiritual opportunities to attain inner balance.

REEFER See marijuana.

REEL (film) pertains to an opportunity to preserve an important element of one's life.

REEL (fishing) connotes a life factor that has the capability of providing spiritual discoveries.

REFECTORY corresponds to intellectual nourishment.

REFEREE characterizes life's duality; elements that contain positive and negative aspects, depending on utilization.

REFERENCE BOOK will come as an important message for the dreamer to research an issue more thoroughly.

REFERRAL signifies personal assistance and being directed to its source.

REFERRED PAIN reflects a refusal to acknowledge the specific source of a harmful element in one's life; the creation of a scapegoat.

REFINERY advises of the wisdom of accepting only pure truths rather than cluttering and confusing issues with inconsequential aspects.

REFINISHING exemplifies a desire to improve something; efforts applied to make something better.

REFLECTION comes in a dream to suggest one "reflects" on an important factor in his or her life.

REFLECTOR will be a guiding indicator.

REFLEXOLOGY (study of) symbolizes a high interest in understanding the responses of others.

REFORESTATION portrays a renewal of one's natural talents.

REFORM SCHOOL warns of a serious need to change one's behavior or alter slanted perspectives.

REFRESHER COURSE implies a need to keep abreast of new information. The dreamer will understand this intent.

REFRESHMENTS come as an advisement to "refresh" self; a rejuvenation or time to take a breather.

REFRIED BEANS portray a suggestion to re-analyze something; look at it again.

REFRIGERATOR refers to a "calming" state; advises one to "cool off."

REFUEL naturally means waning energy or motivation and the need to re-energize self.

REFUGE represents a protective force or situation.

REFUGEE characterizes a person who has experiential knowledge of a negative life element.

REFUND pertains to a "return" benefit.

REFURBISH See refinishing.

REGALIA illustrates pretension.

REGATTA warns against participating in spiritual competition.

REGENERATED See reconstitute.

REGISTER (enroll) symbolizes the "signing-up" or voluntary participation in a new venture.

REGISTER (machine) See cash register.

REGISTERED MAIL denotes a solid communication of some type. Recall who sent the mailed article. To whom was it addressed? What was it? Did it have a specific color?

REGISTRAR characterizes one who keeps the records. This will refer to the "one who knows" personal aspects of another's life.

REGISTRY (bridal) signifies a clear and definitive idea of what one wants in life; may reveal a specific character element.

REGRESSION indicates a backward direction. Recall the dream's surrounding details for more clarity.

REGRETFULNESS usually implies personal guilt.

REGULATIONS connote rules and limitations; may relate to personal guidelines one sets for self.

REGULATOR (device) represents a specific management setting one attempts to maintain for daily behavior; an intent to establish an even synchronization based on spiritual goals.

REGURGITATE won't correlate with a physiological act of getting sick, but rather will correspond to something one needs to "bring up" or get out of one's system.

REHABILITATION CENTER defines an advisement to change one's ways or it may represent a personal intent to do so.

REHEARSAL denotes the "practicing" of one's belief; walking one's talk.

REIMBURSEMENT See refund.

REINCARNATION comes in a dream to remind one of a "new beginning" and an opportunity to advance self.

REINDEER connotes a tendency to be easily led or controlled.

REINFORCEMENT applies to extra support, strength, or endurance needed.

REINS represent a caution to remember that choices made about one's life can be made only by self. Nobody else should be holding the reins of your life.

REINSTATED stands for an acceptance of something that was previously discounted.

REISSUE will usually relate to a popular idea or life aspect.

REJECTION SLIP portrays disapproval; a disaffirmation; a state of disfavor.

REJUVENATION will either symbolize a current state of renewal or it will indicate a need for same, depending on the associated aspects.

REKINDLE exemplifies new life brought into an aspect of one's life.

RELAPSE won't always indicate a negative element in a dream, for it may come to remind one that, sometimes, progression is accomplished only by taking a step or two backwards.

RELATIVE (genetic) pertains to those in one's awake state who have some type of elemental association with the dreamer. This "Relative" may not correspond with one's awake state actual relation.

RELATIVE HUMIDITY alludes to the depth and "quality" of spiritual aspects each of us absorbs individually.

RELATIVITY (theory) attempts to emphasize the fact that each individual perceives life elements in a diverse manner.

RELAXANT refers to a need for one to "relax" his or her focused mental or emotional energy. This specific dream symbol warns of a current state of overly-centered efforts or concentration that is hampering one's broadscope comprehension.

RELAY (race) cautions one to not depend on others for his or her personal progression or advancement.

RELAY (switch) corresponds to one's inner mechanism that maintains behavioral controls; the application of logic and reason instead of emotional outbursts or knee-jerk responses.

RELIC warns against having misplaced spiritual priorities.

RELIEF MAP connotes a need to gain a sharper perspective of one's position in relation to their purpose.

RELIEF PITCHER characterizes an individual who has the knowledge and capability to "stand in" for another; a temporary replacement.

RELIGION (any denomination) symbolizes altered truths or the perspective and application of same; spiritual truths distorted by human ideology and intervention.

RELIGIOUS FIGURE will usually come to draw attention to "spiritual" matters in one's life, not specific "religion" dogma.

RELINQUISHED portrays a life element one is advised to give up.

RELISH (condiment) will define something savored.

RELOCATION most often foretells of an actual change of one's location.

REMARKS that come from people within dreams will usually reveal their hidden opinions or perspectives.

REMATCH may advise of a need to recommunicate with someone or attempt a second effort.

REMEDIAL (study) depicts a desire to better understand an issue or situation.

REMEDY (any type) reflects a corrective or healing source.

REMEMBERING illustrates a need to recall a specific event or conversation in order to gain further clarity.

REMINISCING pertains to a state of nostalgia; the pleasure derived from retrospection.

REMISSION signifies an abatement of something in one's life; a diminishing or subsiding element. Depending on what this symbol is associated with, this could be a negative or positive sign.

REMNANT usually denotes an unnecessary element associated with one's path or purpose, yet it could also refer to a "loose end" to which one needs to attend.

REMORSE implies personal guilt that one refuses to acknowledge.

REMOTE (location) advises one to engage in deep contemplation.

REMOTE CONTROL (device) reveals a state of manipulation. Recall "who" had possession of the control.

RENAISSANCE (setting) illustrates a fertile atmosphere for renewal and opportunities for enlightenment.

REND (tear) may infer that something in one's life has been split apart or this symbol may reflect a defective element such as a belief system, idea, situation, or relationship.

RENDEZVOUS symbolizes a meeting of some type.

RENEGADE characterizes individual thought and behavior.

RENEGING warns against ignoring promises made.

RENOUNCE constitutes a denial; a rejection.

RENOVATION is an attempt to "save" or preserve some element in one's life.

RENT (payment) implies an access to an opportunity to accomplish something.

RENTAL (car) exemplifies an opportunity to attain a "progression."

RENTAL (dwelling) reflects "temporary" situations.

RENT STRIKE represents personal power and/or effectiveness.

REORGANIZING denotes an adjustment in priorities.

REPAIR See fix.

REPAIRPERSON characterizes a person in one's life who is capable of solving another's problems.

REPARTEE will reveal an individual's true or hidden thoughts.

REPEAL represents the act of voiding an action; revoking something.

REPEAT OFFENDER will come as a strong advisement to learn from mistakes.

REPELLENT (chemical) refers to the use of negative behavior for the purpose of maintaining social distance.

REPENTANT corresponds to self-reproach.

REPERCUSSION warns of an impending consequence or backlash.

REPERTOIRE correlates to the quality and quantity of one's natural talents.

REPERTORY See repository.

REPETITION may indicate the act of "repeating one's mistakes" or it may stand for a need to repeat things until the right lessons are learned.

REPLENISHING pertains to a current bountiful state; a desire to maintain full potential or level of energy.

REPLICA See copy; imitating.

REPORT CARD is a revealing dream symbol that illustrates the quality and rating of one's current behavior.

REPORTER (news) characterizes an individual who makes the activity of others their priority; exemplifies sensationalism and exaggerations.

REPOSITORY will correlate with a specific type of "source" within self; a personal store of strength, compassion, patience, etc.

REPOSSESSED portrays the resulting effect of irresponsibility.

REPRESENTATIVE characterizes a person with the authority to speak and act for others.

REPRESSION connotes a self-generated state of limiting controls.

REPRIEVE signifies a temporary suspension of a problematical or distressful situation.

REPRIMAND usually comes from one's own subconscious level of conscience to reflect a misdeed or other negative act.

REPRISAL warns against vindictiveness and revenge.

REPTILE See specific type.

REPUDIATION indicates some type of denial or condemnation.

REPULSIVE corresponds with a life aspect that is personally offensive. This may refer to a situation, event, statement, idea, etc.

REPUTATION usually comes as a revelation associated with a specific individual.

REQUIEM forewarns of a dying or quickly declining situation, relationship, or other element in one's life.

REQUIREMENT defines a necessary quality, skill, or perspective one must possess in order to accomplish a selective goal.

REQUISITION pertains to a personal request, often a prayer, for the necessary elements to accomplish a goal or purpose.

RERUN (program) indicates a need to learn something that was initially missed.

RESALE VALUE represents the extended "long-term" value of an action or communication.

RESCHEDULE advises of a more effective time to execute an effort or attempt some type of activity.

RESCIND See repeal.

RESCUE will come to emphasize the "saving" effect of one's efforts. Recall who was rescued. Who was the rescuer?

RESEARCH signifies a need to obtain greater knowledge or information on a specific issue.

RESERVATION (Native American) represents an advisement to "relate" or make associative connections between true Reality and spiritual aspects.

RESERVE (animal) symbolizes the preservation of natural inherent talents.

RESERVIST (military) characterizes personal preparedness; a "reserve" of inner strength.

RESERVOIR connotes the quality of one's spiritual aspects, specifically natural talents.

RESHUFFLE suggests a rearrangement of one's priorities or elements of a goal-reaching plan.

RESIDENT See inhabitant.

RESIDENTIAL (setting) depicts a specific "background" character to one's lifestyle or homelife.

RESIDUE alludes to that which is "left behind;" aftermaths; may refer to something left to attend to.

RESIGNATION stands for a new direction ahead.

RESILIENT defines one who has attained acceptance and manages problematical events with less difficulty and more grace than others.

RESIN constitutes a beneficial result.

RESISTANCE (underground) symbolizes courage; a refusal to be forced into something one doesn't believe in.

RESOLUTION pertains to determination.

RESONANCE denotes lasting strength.

RESORT typifies a strong advisement to obtain needed rest.

RESOURCE indicates an asset one has to utilize. This is oftentimes not recognized.

RESPIRATOR connotes an element in one's life that serves as a life-saving factor.

REST AREA will naturally imply a much needed rest from one's work or a stressful situation.

RESTAURANT reveals one's quality of diet. This diet may not refer to eating, but rather what one fills his or her life with as far as beliefs, behavior, type of associates, etc.

REST HOME See nursing home.

RESTITUTION illustrates compensation; reparation.

RESTLESSNESS warns of a lack of acceptance.

RESTORATION See renovation.

RESTRAINTS define hindrances, usually self-generated.

RESTRICTED AREA may represent some life element that one should avoid until further knowledge, wisdom, or skill has been attained. This symbol may also indicate that from which one voluntarily restricts self.

RESTROOM See bathroom.

REST STOP See rest area.

RESUMÉ stands for a need to honestly review one's accomplishments and goals.

RESURFACE (float up) exemplifies a spiritual concept or element at which one needs to take a closer look.

RESURFACE See paving.

RESURRECT portrays a renewed interest in something.

RESUSCITATOR defines a life aspect that serves to restore one's motivation, energy or interest.

RETAIL (store) applies to an opportunity. Recall the type for further clarification.

RETAINER (dental) stands for an attempt to maintain one's quality of speech or communication.

RETAINER (monetary) represents intention.

RETAINING WALL correlates with a "supportive" aspect that serves to "hold up" or hold back something.

RETALIATION denotes vindictiveness; reprisal.

RETARDANT See restraints.

RETARDATION alludes to a comprehension inability, most often self-imposed.

RETCH pertains to an attempt to rid self of a disagreeable situation or other life element; may reveal a lack of acceptance or evidence psychological escapism.

RETICENCE denotes a desire to avoid communication; diffidence.

RETINUE infers a belief that one requires a support group.

RETIREMENT illustrates a finalization; a life stage completion.

RETOOL implies a time to utilize a new set of plans and associated aids. This may even refer to one's behavior or perspective.

RETOUCHED pertains to final details and the attention given to same.

RETRACE advises one to look at something again, closer this time; may infer a need to "retrace" one's steps.

RETRACTION won't necessarily refer to one's "words;" it usually suggests a need to "pull back" or pull something "in," such as an unproductive behavioral aspect like being too forward, being tactless, giving incorrect advice, interference, etc.

R

RETREAD (tire) may denote fortitude or, depending on associated dream elements, it might apply to a need to "tread over" one's former path; backtrack.

RETREAT (military) constitutes an unproductive time to go forward.

RETREAT (respite) stands for a suggested rest; contemplation is called for.

RETRIBUTION corresponds to atonement; may also indicate retaliation, depending on the dream's surrounding aspects.

RETRIEVER (dog breed) characterizes an analytical friend; one who possesses the skill and wisdom to "bring back" or "show" you the true psychological motivations for your unproductive behavior.

RETROACTIVE exemplifies an aspect in one's life that is currently affected by his or her past.

RETROFIT suggests a need to revise one's perceptions by including new experiential or evidenced elements.

RETROGRADE reflects a move downward and backward. This symbol usually "advises" one to go back to a former issue and perceive an element from a lower, closer angle.

RETROGRESSION reveals lost ground in respect to one's attained level of behavior, knowledge, or progression.

RETROROCKET stands for a need to slow one's rate of advancement; too much is being missed.

REUNION indicates a suggestion to reconnect with a former associate.

REVELATION brings an insight; sudden understanding.

REVELRY points the dreamer to the "cause" of the revelry which will reveal an important element.

REVENANT characterizes a "return" of someone long absent from one's life.

REVENGE is a clear sign that an individual lacks spiritual enlightenment and has attained no acceptance in life.

REVENUE STAMP serves as a verification that one performed his or her obligation or responsibility.

REVERBERATION connotes dissemination.

REVERE cautions against excessive admiration or worship of anyone but God.

REVEREND See religious figure.

REVERIE suggests an advisement to deeply contemplate an element in the dreamer's life. This element will be recognized by the dreamer.

REVERSE (gear/direction) may suggest that one needs to "go back" to learn something or it could connote a retrogressive path or behavior.

REVERSED (clothing or other elements) comes as a severe warning and you need to refer to the specific piece of clothing or element that was reversed in the dream. Such an obvious reversal will indicate a serious dysfunctional aspect in one's life.

REVERSIBLE (clothing/object) usually signifies duality; something has a two-fold purpose or effect.

REVIEW is an advisement to become more familiar with a situation, idea, or individual.

REVIEWER (professional) characterizes an individual in one's life who can provide background information or a general overview.

REVISION represents an advisement to reassess one's life, goals, or path direction.

REVIVAL comes as a warning to revitalize an element in one's life; a need to be reinspired, re-energized, or motivated.

REVOKED is a suggestion to "rescind" or correct something in one's life.

REVOLUTION may not infer a violent military event, but rather stand for a "new way" or concept.

REVOLVER (weapon) See gun.

REVOLVING DOOR reveals an unproductive course.

REWARD signifies personal benefits derived from positive behavior and good deeds.

REWIND (audio/video tape) applies to "going back to the beginning."

REWIRE is a strong advisement to examine one's psychological processes and make correct connections.

RHEOSTAT pertains to the personal control of one's emotional responses.

RHESUS MONKEY vicariously indicates inhumane behavior; arrogance and a lack of compassion.

RHETORICAL QUESTION poses possibilities and impels self-analyzation.

RHEUMATISM See arthritis for comparable interpretation.

RHINESTONE reflects an effective alternative to a more "costly" method or course.

RHINOCEROS denotes controlled emotions; the utilization of intellect instead of emotionally instinctual reactions; may denote "thick-skinned" personality.

RHIZOME stands for deeply-rooted attitudes that affect perspectives.

RHODODENDRON represents a "source" of bountiful natural elements.

RHUBARB denotes a life aspect that contains dual elements.

RHYME may indicate a juvenile perspective, yet this symbol usually comes in dreams to relay a message.

RHYTHM will emphasize the "pace" at which one is currently progressing. This may also "suggest" a proper pace.

RHYTHM AND BLUES (R & B) represent path progression in spite of difficulties.

RHYTHM METHOD See birth control.

RIB (all types) stand for supportive aspects.

RIBALD pertains to uncouth behavior that reveals a lack of spiritual attainment.

RIBBON symbolizes a positive element in one's life. Recall the fabric and color for more in-depth interpretation.

RIB CAGE infers a protective element in one's life.

RICE See grain.

RICE PAPER connotes a fragile facet in one's life. The surrounding dreamscape details will clarify what this association is.

RICH (food) relates to bountiful benefits that carry multiple effects.

RICH (wealth) See money.

RICHTER SCALE will illustrate the resulting quantitative effect of an action or event and its level of intensity.

RICKETS reveal a lack of positive reinforcement; a poor self-image.

RICKETY (condition) warns of an unstable and/or precarious situation.

RICOCHET denotes an event that will produce multiple effects.

RICOTTA (cheese) portrays a nourishing life aspect that creates recurring benefits.

RIDDLE constitutes a self-devised complexity.

RIDGE relates to a major decision; a potential turning point.

RIDGEPOLE applies to an individual's personal shield or means of protection.

RIDICULE indicates a serious lack of understanding; reveals an unenlightened personality.

RIDING HABIT suggests an attitude of exaggerated self-worth when making a comparison between self and one's peers who are traveling the same path.

RIFFRAFF may represent those who most need one's help.

RIFLE (search through) may not infer a negative connotation, but rather this symbol usually comes as an advisement to "search" through one's own possessions, meaning motives and behavioral responses.

RIFLE (weapon) See gun.

RIFLESCOPE See scope.

RIFT (fissure) relates to a split or "fracture" present in a relationship, situation, belief system, or the manner of one's perception.

RIGGING typifies supporting elements for a specific aspect in one's life. This symbol will be clarified by the dream's surrounding facets.

RIGHT (direction/position) represents a supportive role.

RIGHT FIELD indicates a tendency to follow generally accepted norms.

RIGHT OF WAY is self-explanatory. The key here is to recall "who" had the Right of Way sign. Did you have to yield?

RIGHT WING means following a conservative perspective; fearful of attempting new endeavors or exploring innovative concepts.

RIGID implies an opinionated thought process; not open to alternative ideas.

RIGOR MORTIS symbolizes a dead state; an individual who maintains "stiff" thinking or conceptual reasoning.

RIME (coating) exemplifies a cold or hidden veneer.

RIND denotes that which harbors fruitful or bountiful aspects. This dreamscape fragment refers to the "tough" path or exterior that serves as the outlying regions of one's direction of fulfillment.

RING See circus.

RING (crime) See gang.

RING (jewelry) will reveal how one perceives self. Was the ring gold or silver.

RING (residue) pertains to a need for routine or consistent cleansing through self-analyzation.

RING FINGER alludes to how an individual chooses to present self; outward affectations of character.

RINGLEADER points out the instigator or initiator of a plan or idea.

RINGLET refers to an idea or thought process that turns back on itself; mental confusion.

RINGMASTER characterizes a person who directs the actions of others; possibly a manipulator; may indicate one who interferes into the lives of others.

RINGSIDE (seats) denote an "onlooker" position or perspective; one who prefers watching and waiting instead of participating.

RINGWORM advises one to be more aware of where he or she walks; going headlong into things without giving adequate investigation or planning.

RINK (skating) correlates to going around in circles; a lack of advancement.

RINKY-DINK corresponds to something that can't be trusted or depended upon; insubstantial; inconsequential.

RINSE (hair coloring) may relate to an intent to change one's thoughts or way of thinking or it may reveal hidden perspectives and attitudes.

RINSE (water) advises of a need to clarify something; indicates a misunderstanding or misconception.

RIOT signifies deep-seated discontent; demonstrative activism.

RIOT ACT defines a severe warning of some type. The dreamer will make the correct association.

RIP will reflect a dysfunction or some type of negative element associated with a life issue. Recall surrounding dreamscape details for clarity. This is usually a quickly recognized symbol for the dreamer to understand.

RIPCORD constitutes a life-saving aspect in one's life.

RIPE will point out a matured situation, process, or other element that is "ripe" for development.

RIPPLE (in water) stands for a continuing spiritual effect.

RIP TIDE warns of a dangerous spiritual belief or path.

RISER signifies a "step" above; rising oneself to a higher level.

RISK FACTOR reveals a life factor that has the potential of being a dangerous or harmful aspect in one's life.

RISQUÉ implies an impropriety; offensive behavior; reveals an unenlightened individual.

RITE corresponds with a self-devised process; a fascination with ceremony.

RITE OF PASSAGE portrays a transitional stage in one's life.

RITUAL pertains to superfluous elements one believes are necessary.

RITZY (setting) may signify sophistication or pretension. Recall the people and action within this dream setting.

RIVAL may not indicate an enemy, but rather someone perceived as an opponent or competitor in the dreamer's eyes.

RIVER corresponds with the spiritual elements running through one's life. Recall its flow, quality, and color.

RIVERBANK symbolizes a close proximity to a spiritual search or awakening.

RIVERBED See lakebed.

RIVERBOAT denotes indecision regarding one's direction or leaning in respect to spirituality versus materialism.

RIVERFRONT See lakefront.

RIVER ROCKS signify a spiritual "roundedness" to one's life.

RIVET exemplifies a "secured" aspect in one's life.

RIVULET portrays a new spiritual idea or insight.

ROACH (hairstyle) represents one-mindedness; rigidly focused ideas.

ROACH (insect) See cockroach.

ROACH See marijuana.

ROACH CLIP illustrates resourcefulness; a tendency to utilize every element of something.

ROAD will correspond with one's life path either currently or one that is being advised. Recall surrounding dreamscape details for further clarification.

ROADBED depicts the soundness of one's current path. Of what was the road constructed? Did it have a specific color? Was it solid?

ROADBLOCK comes as a warning advisement that one has yet to attain the experiential depth and knowledge to continue progression along the current course. This symbol may also indicate a self-generated "block" due to inner fears.

ROAD GRADER connotes a life aspect that has the potential of smoothing one's way.

ROAD HOG characterizes an individual who isn't focused on his or her path.

ROADHOUSE See motel.

ROAD MAP points out the multiple options available to reach a goal.

ROADRUNNER denotes impetuosity; advises one to give more thought before rushing forward.

ROAD SHOW refers to points of interest or observation placed along one's path; possible opportunities for expanded learning.

ROADSIDE may indicate a need to "pull over" and rest while traveling one's path or it may refer to something that should be noticed.

ROAD TEST symbolizes one's level of current knowledge and preparedness to continue his or her life course.

ROADWORK signifies that personal work and added effort need to be applied to one's chosen life path.

ROAMING won't necessarily indicate a loss of direction, but rather a seeking for what feels right.

ROAST (banter) portrays companionable respect.

ROAST (cook) represents a developing plan or idea.

ROAST (meat cut) relates to an issue or idea that one intends to develop.

ROASTING PAN refers to a method or opportunity to accomplish something.

ROBBERY indicates the utilization of negative methods to obtain a goal.

ROBE (bath) See bathrobe.

ROBE (ceremonial) relates to a desire to present self in an aggrandized manner; a need to exaggerate self-importance.

ROBIN emphasizes a rebirth of some kind.

ROBIN HOOD characterizes the courage to actively correct a wrong one observes; one who goes out on a limb to make a difference.

ROBOT warns one to begin thinking for self.

ROCK refers to the "hard," difficult elements or phases in life.

ROCK BOTTOM emphasizes a time to pick self up and go forward by looking to the sun.

ROCK CANDY signifies an issue requiring deep contemplation or thorough analyzation.

ROCKER See rocking chair.

ROCKET stands for high motivation.

ROCKET ENGINE symbolizes that which serves as a personal impetus.

ROCK GARDEN corresponds to the acceptance of life's difficulties and the blossoming of personal talents.

ROCK HOUND characterizes a person who recognizes the beauty of opportunities presented by life's difficulties and takes advantage of them.

ROCKING CHAIR pertains to a well-deserved rest period.

ROCKING HORSE may indicate unproductive efforts or deep thought. The dreamer will be given the associated elements to determine which meaning was intended.

ROCK SALT implies a personal effort to break through certain spiritual concepts or searches.

ROCK SHOP correlates with natural talents and how they're utilized for humankind's benefit.

ROCKSLIDE applies to an inundation of temporary difficulties.

ROCKWELL (Norman) characterizes the beauty of simplicity.

ROCOCO (ornate style) illustrates self-aggrandizement; low self-esteem evidenced by giving off an aura of power or knowledge.

RODENT See specific type.

RODEO portrays an exhibition of one's power or control over others; competing for control.

RODEO CLOWN stands for the taking of risks to save others or divert hazardous elements away from others.

ROGUE characterizes an unprincipled individual.

ROLE-PLAYING illustrates an attempt to understand another's perspective.

ROLL BAR refers to a specific protective measure; a safeguard.

ROLL CALL will reveal important names associated with the dreamer. Recall whose names were included. For what purpose was the roll called? What did the list represent to the dreamer? Did the dreamer's name belong to the list? Was it deleted?

ROLLER COASTER denotes an unstable path or personality; up and down emotions or vacillating attitudes.

ROLLER SKATE pertains to a desire to "skate" through life without having to take the responsibility of dealing with distasteful or difficult issues.

ROLLING PIN represents a need to "unroll" concepts or ideas that one has "balled up" in his or her head.

ROLLOVER (vehicle) may foretell of the possibility of an upcoming vehicular accident, but most often this type of dream event indicates a physiological dysfunction or "turn-around" with one's health.

ROLL-TOP DESK connotes a need to keep the specific aspects of one's life, work, or plans less public.

ROLODEX implies communication. The key here is to recall if there was a specific name presented.

ROMAINE (lettuce) refers to a lighthearted, perhaps humorous, misunderstanding.

ROMAN CANDLE See fireworks.

ROMANESQUE (style) represents fortification; over-emphasis placed on one's personal protection.

ROMANTICISM (style) relates to empathy; emotional expressiveness.

ROMANTICIZING reveals an inability to perceive reality without attributing overly optimistic or emotionally sensitive qualities to it.

ROMEO AND JULIET forewarn of an unproductive or doomed relationship.

ROOF pertains to one's priorities; highest "capping" thoughts.

ROOF GARDEN illustrates beautiful, bountiful thoughts.

ROOFING MATERIAL See shingles.

ROOK (chess piece) portrays a deception in one's life.

ROOKIE characterizes a beginner; one who lacks experience and knowledge.

ROOM See specific type.

ROOM AND BOARD corresponds to the two major necessities in life. Recall the dream's details for further information on this symbol.

ROOMING HOUSE relates to an opportunity for self-expression.

ROOMMATE implies companionship; may also allude to suppressed individuality.

ROOM TEMPERATURE would normally represent a "comfortable" attitude or atmosphere, yet the dreamer needs to recall if the room was cold or too warm to gain the intent here.

ROOST refers to a temporary rest period.

ROOSTER constitutes an awakening of some type.

ROOT (botanical) signifies the existence of a hidden personal talent.

ROOT (hair) depicts an unrealized perception, attitude, or plan.

ROOT BEER See soft drink.

ROOT CANAL symbolizes an urgency to "clean out and medicate" an infectiously harmful manner of speaking.

ROOT CELLAR exemplifies the opportunity to preserve one's inner talents and bountiful gifts.

ROOTSTALK See rhizome.

ROOT FEEDER stands for the nurturing care one gives to budding talents or humanitarian aspects.

ROPE alludes to a helpful element in one's life; an aid.

ROPE LADDER See ladder.

ROPE TOW See ski lift.

RORSCHACH TEST comes as an advisement to analyze one's perspectives.

ROSARY recommends a time to pray, more specifically, "turn" to God.

ROSE portrays strong admiration.

ROSÉ See wine.

ROSEBUD pertains to a beginning or "budding" attraction; beginning feelings of admiration.

ROSEHIP signifies the healing elements of love.

ROSEMARY is a sign of remembrance; comes as an advisement to not forget whatever it was associated with in the dream.

ROSE QUARTZ represents recognized and cherished spiritual gifts; may refer to new inspirations.

ROSETTA STONE portrays a "key" to understanding a specific personal situation or issue.

ROSETTE (configuration) pertains to the "solution within the problem."

ROSE WATER indicates an "altered" element.

ROSE WINDOW connotes a perspective derived from multiple associated aspects.

ROSEWOOD symbolizes an enduring natural talent or ability.

ROSIN warns against "slipping" off one's course; backsliding.

ROSS (Betsy Griscom) emphasizes the importance of symbolism; stands for honorable service.

ROSTER Refer to roll call for a like interpretation.

ROSTRUM See podium.

ROT is a symbol possessing duality. This symbol could refer to a humus type of aspect that infers a fertile ground or element, or it could pertain to a "rotten," decaying situation, attitude, or other aspect.

ROTATION PLANTING applies to wise planning; the prevention of a depleted condition.

ROTISSERIE connotes a method of developing a plan or goal that insures all aspects are given equal consideration.

ROTOR (device) relates to a balanced perspective.

ROTOTILLER stands for a "cultivation" of one's natural talents.

ROTUNDA symbolizes an atmosphere rich in opportunity.

ROUGE suggests an intention to present a healthy state of well-being.

ROUGH (language) indicates a vulgar individual.

ROUGH (physical appearance) may indicate a difficult life or a coarse personality.

ROUGH (sound) denotes a lack of harmony or serenity.

ROUGH (texture) portrays an unfinished state; needs refinement.

ROUGH (waters) stand for a turbulent spiritual path.

ROUGHCAST illustrates a "trial" or experimental endeavor.

ROUGH-CUT pertains to a lack of finesse; crude.

ROUGH-HEWN reflects major efforts by one's own hands; self-forged.

ROUGHHOUSING typifies an advisement to release pent-up emotions and/or stress.

ROUGHNECK represents a crude or coarse manner of behavior.

ROUGHSHOD signifies harsh control of others.

ROULETTE (Russian) warns of chances taken that have the potential of causing great harm or having severely adverse effects.

ROULETTE (table) stands for questionable chances taken.

ROUND (configuration) most often denotes a completedness; wholeness.

ROUND (boxing) See inning.

ROUNDHOUSE suggests a change in one's life course.

ROUNDTABLE indicates an upcoming conference, the need for same.

ROUND-THE-CLOCK typifies a necessary span of time to fulfill an activity one is planning.

ROUNDTRIP implies a "return" to the beginning or starting point in order to facilitate a closure or completion.

ROUNDUP advises one to "gather up" personal beliefs instead of allowing them to stray far afield or lie fallow.

ROUSTABOUT characterizes a person possessing multiple talents; diversity.

ROUTE See map.

ROUTER (tool) reveals a "way" through a current troublesome problem or difficulty.

ROVE See roaming.

ROW (line) connotes the act of setting priorities and getting affairs or elements of an issue "in line."

ROWBOAT applies to a "vehicle" or outlet for one to begin spiritual self-discovery through.

ROWING depicts a personal spiritual effort made.

ROWING MACHINE symbolizes efforts to improve or maintain a current situation.

ROYALTY represents egocentric authority.

RUBBER (material) alludes to an attitude, perspective, or other life aspect in one's life that creates a cushioning or buffering effect.

RUBBER BAND emphasizes the extension or "stretched" limit of an issue or perspective.

RUBBER BULLET refers to a method of controlling others.

RUBBER CEMENT See adhesive.

RUBBER CHECK illustrates a groundless or empty factor in one's life.

RUBBERNECK applies to the act of exhibiting unrestrained interest or curiosity.

RUBBER STAMP comes as a personal message that warns, advises, or commends. Recall what the stamp said for further clarity.

RUBBING (skin) will have several meanings depending on the dream's associated elements. Rubbing the skin may indicate an act of soothing, being bothered by an irritation, or ridding self of a distasteful or negative factor by attempting to debride it.

RUBBISH See trash.

RUBBLE refers to the remnants of something. Frequently these leftovers can be put to beneficial use depending on their condition.

RUBDOWN See massage.

RUBY refers to life force; motivational energy and fortitude.

RUCKSACK See knapsack.

RUDDER represents the direction and quality of one's spiritual course.

RUDDERLESS warns of a lack of spiritual direction.

RUDDY (complexion) reveals an individual who routinely expends personal efforts toward his or her goal or assisting others.

RUDENESS portrays a disrespect for others and implies a lack of advancement.

RUDIMENTARY correlates to elemental aspects; the beginning stage or basic idea.

RUFF (collar) signifies an opinionated personality.

RUFFIAN See hoodlum.

RUFFLE (fabric) depicts multiple aspects to an attitude or perspective.

RUG pertains to how one "covers" something. This will be a revealing dream element that relates to one's character, inner traits, or attitude.

RUG CLEANER applies to an attempt to keep one's personal "groundwork" or foundational perspectives clear of negatively affecting elements.

RUGGED (terrain) represents a life path that contains difficulties to either accept or overcome.

RUINS may literally infer a "ruination" of some type or it may indicate a personal revelation, depending on surrounding dreamscape elements. Ruins frequently denote deep wisdom or inspiration.

RULER (measurement) can signify an advisement to attend to a precise "rule" or personal belief or it can indicate a call to monitor one's utilization of a specific element such as manipulative speech, controlling behavior, gossip, etc.

RULER (person) characterizes an authoritative figure who may imply oneself, that is, one's conscience.

RUMBLE SEAT suggests a dissatisfaction with self for not taking control of one's life.

RUMMAGE SALE indicates an opportunity to obtain useful factors in one's life; opportunities.

RUMMY (card game) connotes a suggestion to "gather" one's facts.

RUMOR makes one responsible for information and the accuracy of same.

RUMPLED (appearance) may not represent a slovenly personality, but rather this symbol's most frequent interpretation is that of a persevering individual who is a little worse for wear but maintains his or her motivation and effort.

RUN See running.

RUN See campaign.

RUN (in fabric) represents a flawed perspective or presentation of self.

RUNAROUND represents an inability to attain a focused or centered perspective or position.

RUNAWAY stands for an element in one's life that has escaped his or her grasp.

RUNDOWN (condition) can mean various things, but the bottom line for most of them, is "neglect."

RUNE symbolizes a personal revelation; a key or solution.

RUNG (any type) depicts a "connective" aspect.

RUNNER See messenger.

RUNNING reveals an attempt to escape or catch up, depending on the dream's details.

RUNNING BOARD relates to a convenience; a life aspect that serves to assist one along his or her way or make progression easier.

RUNNING LIGHT indicates a state of preparedness; anticipatory attitude.

RUNNING MATE represents a companion; an individual who shares one's perspectives or plans.

RUNNING SHOE denotes a need to "get going" with some aspect in life. This may reveal a state of procrastination that needs to end.

RUNNING START illustrates a position of advantage.

RUNNING TRACK warns of unproductive efforts; going fast and getting nowhere.

RUNOFF represents ramifications.

RUN-THROUGH suggests a "trial" effort or a need to review all angles of a plan.

RUNWAY indicates a pathway leading to one's purpose.

RUPTURE denotes a flaw in a plan or one's thinking.

RURAL refers to a more "open" perspective; less affected.

RUSE applies to a cleverly devised scheme; perhaps an ulterior motive.

RUSH HOUR symbolizes a time to act.

RUSHMORE (Mount) warns against the invasion of another's sacredness; a disrespect for another's spiritual belief.

RUSSET (color) illustrates a rich, earthy perspective; an alignment with reality.

RUST will advise of a condition of spiritual atrophy.

RUSTIC exemplifies one's down-to-earth perspective and overall reasoning.

RUSTPROOF indicates personal efforts applied to protecting and maintaining one's spiritual state.

RUT pertains to a self-generated state of neutrality; lacking progression or advancement due to one's own inability to perceive opportunities.

RUTABAGA See turnip.

RUTHLESSNESS signifies a void of sensitivity; lacking moral fiber.

RUTTING (season) implies a time to plan.

RYE represents rejuvenation.

S

SABBATH See high holy day.

SABBATICAL represents periods of additional learning that are needed. This usually refers to those who consider themselves to be a teacher or leader of some type.

SABER See sword.

SABER RATTLING signifies a threatening intent.

SABLE (color/fur) portrays negativity; a dark mood.

SABOTEUR characterizes a two-faced personality.

SACAJAWEA symbolizes one who possesses the knowledge and capability of providing directional assistance to others.

SACCHARIN implies a tendency to be content with imitations.

SACHEM relates to a person with experiential knowledge and the attained wisdom that accompanies it.

SACHET connotes a coverup being done; a replacement "scent" or aspect being utilized.

SACK See bag.

SACKCLOTH relates to self-imposed guilt; unnecessary punishments.

SACRAMENT will pertain to any act that serves to earn grace.

SACRED COW applies to misplaced priorities.

SACRIFICE may indicate actual awake-state sacrifices one makes for the attainment of his or her spiritual goals or it may have a negative connotation that warns of a potentially dangerous direction or intent.

SACRISTY corresponds with the sacred place within self.

SACRUM correlates to the "root" of emotion.

SAD See melancholia.

SADDLE defines personal control of one's journey through life.

SADDLEBAGS denote that which we carry with us on our life journey. Recall the bag's color and condition. Was it full? With what?

SADDLE BLANKET typifies a symbol that gives an indication of what one's attitude is toward her or his path.

SADDLER characterizes a person who has the skill to enhance one's journey.

SADDLERY represents aids available to assist one's life journey.

SADDLE SHOE marks a path walked conservatively.

SADDLE SOAP exemplifies "care" given to one's path; personal monitoring and maintenance of its quality.

SADDLE SORE reveals a "forced" path progression; advises of a need to ease back on one's efforts that have become overly concentrated.

SADISM exposes an underlying obsession with self.

SAFARI represents a life path that follows that of another in which innocent victims are harmed along the way.

SAFARI JACKET denotes a predatory nature.

SAFARI TROPHY pertains to someone who has been victimized.

SAFE alludes to an element in one's life that provides personal security.

SAFECRACKER characterizes an individual who has the skill to break through the defenses of others.

SAFE-DEPOSIT BOX connotes aspects one perceives as his or her priorities.

SAFE HOUSE clearly symbolizes a "safe" or secure place, situation, direction, or perspective.

SAFETY BELT indicates an opportunity to protect oneself from a possible danger or harmful situation.

SAFETY CIRCUIT relates to personal attention and awareness given to one's thought process; maintaining mental and emotional control; discernment.

SAFETY FILM will pinpoint a potentially hazardous situation in one's life.

SAFETY GLASS signifies a right perspective; a protected one.

SAFETY MATCH illustrates a safeguard that prevents the utilization of potentially hazardous elements for the wrong purposes.

SAFETY NET suggests insecurity; a lack of self-confidence.

SAFETY PIN refers to a "secure" manner of providing a temporary stop-gap action.

SAFETY RAZOR See razor.

SAFETY VALVE exemplifies a personal control over one's emotions.

SAFFRON (color/plant) See orange.

SAGA portrays extensive details.

SAGE (person) characterizes an individual possessing high wisdom gained through enlightenment.

SAGE (plant) constitutes renewing elements in one's life.

SAGE BUNDLE indicates an expression of honor and respect.

SAGGING reveals some type of weakness or weakened condition.

SAGUARO represents a protected spiritual aspect of an individual.

SAIL alludes to an attitude of acceptance.

SAILBOAT relates to a spiritual direction led by destiny.

SAILCLOTH (fabric) correlates to endurance; a strong constitution.

SAILFISH typifies a symbol relating to spiritual destiny.

SAILOR characterizes a spiritual seeker.

SAINT will usually reveal a desired quality, but may also warn against a perspective that one believes self to be a saint.

SAINT BERNARD (dog breed) represents a helpful friend.

SAINT ELMO'S FIRE denotes inspiration.

SAINT JOHN'S EVE See Midsummer Eve.

SAINT PATRICK'S DAY is a call to turn one's attention to the spirit; stands for a return to spiritual matters.

SAINT VALENTINE'S DAY reminds us that love for others should be one's priority in life.

SALAD indicates diversity. Recall what the salad's condition was. What type of foods comprised it?

SALAD BAR alludes to choices in life. Recall what was offered. What was taken?

SALAD DRESSING/OIL pertains to the personal manner in which one "dresses up" or enhances opportunities.

SALAMANDER suggests the blending of spirituality through daily life.

SALAMI depicts an "interesting" aspect to an issue.

SALARY symbolizes recompense for efforts expended.

SALE (reduced price) may represent a good deal or opportunity, yet it also may only "appear" to be so.

SALESPERSON See clerk.

SALES TAX pertains to a "hidden cost" to something obtained.

SALINE SOLUTION implies a need to replace a needed element in one's life.

SALIVA refers to softened speech; thoughtful communication.

SALMON warns against going against a spiritual current; a spiritual search that's in error.

SALMONELLA applies to seriously negative results from ingesting harmful ideas or influences.

SALOME (biblical) characterizes one with ulterior motives.

SALOON portrays a state of unawareness.

SALSA connotes high interest; an exciting element in one's life.

SALT exemplifies a gregarious nature.

SALT-AND-PEPPER signifies duality; positive and negative elements.

SALTBOX (architecture) reflects a tendency to impress others.

SALTINE See cracker.

SALT LICK constitutes an attempt to provide others with what they need.

SALT MARSH emphasizes an inundation of spiritual elements; may infer a frequency of overwhelming spiritual aspects.

SALTSHAKER relates to an opportunity to cause an enhancement.

SALTWATER represents elemental spiritual truths.

SALTWATER AQUARIUM denotes a personal grasp of the elemental spiritual truths and the cherishing of same.

SALUTE defines an acknowledgment of another; respect; recognition.

SALVAGE (operation) connotes an attempt to save and restore something that would otherwise be lost.

SALVE See ointment.

SALVER See serving tray.

SALVO symbolizes a bombardment of some type that could indicate either a positive or negative response.

SAMISEN alludes to a vibratory alignment; balance within.

SAMPLE pertains to foreknowledge; knowing what one is getting into.

SAMPLER (stitchery) will imply variety or relay a specific message for the dreamer.

SAMURAI signifies inner strength.

SANATORIUM illustrates a life element that is capable of providing a return to physical, emotional, or mental health.

SANCTIMONIOUS (attitude) reveals a false piety.

SANCTUARY emphasizes respite; a place of peace. This symbol can refer to emotional, spiritual, or mental peace.

SAND suggests a "shifting" perspective or attitude.

SANDAL relates to a desire to walk close to the earth, yet the goal hasn't quite been attained yet.

SANDALWOOD (color/scent) implies an unaffected personality.

SANDBAG warns of a spiritual withdrawal.

SANDBAR represents a spiritual concept that requires contemplation.

SANDBLASTING pertains to an effort to get down to basics; discover the basic, foundational facts or issues.

SANDBOX indicates immaturity of thought and reason.

SANDCASTLE correlates to unrealistic plans; insubstantial ideas; lacking viability.

SAND DOLLAR portrays spiritual riches.

SANDER (tool) applies to a life element that has the capability of smoothing over a rough aspect.

SAND FLEA typifies irritations in life, most often one's juvenile relationships.

SANDMAN characterizes a need to rest one's mind.

SAND PAINTING illustrates spiritual healing knowledge.

SANDPAPER See sander.

SANDPIPER connotes spiritual ideas; giving spiritual aspects to one's thought process.

SANDPIT exposes a stage or place along one's life path where indecision will need to be overcome.

SANDSTONE corresponds with a weak foundation; lacking strong basics.

SANDSTORM stands for mental confusion.

SAND TRAP exemplifies problems in life; aspects that are intended to test one's inner strength.

SANDWICH constitutes a "boxed in" feeling; a situation, relationship, or belief that creates a confining effect.

SANDWICH BOARD will reveal a personal message for the dreamer.

SANGUINE See ruddy.

SANITATION WORKER See garbage collector.

SANITIZE represents an effort to remove negative aspects from some type of element in one's life.

SANTA CLAUS characterizes an overly optimistic personality; unrealistic expectations.

SANTA'S ELVES symbolize those who would encourage unrealistic expectations or promote false hopes.

SAP represents the life force of nature; inner strength.

SAPLING pertains to the tenuous but persevering nature of newly attained beliefs.

SAPPHIRE (gem/color) depicts a fragile spiritual nature.

SAPSUCKER See woodpecker.

SARCASM may be a positive or negative dreamscape element depending on who said what to whom. Recall the details for clarity.

SARCOPHAGUS See coffin.

SARDINE advises one to remove self from a suffocating situation or belief system; may even refer to a self-generated psychological perspective that is suffocating one.

SARI represents an unaffected personality.

SARONG denotes simplicity.

SARSAPARILLA symbolizes innocence.

SASH See belt.

SASHAY signifies a carefree attitude.

SASQUATCH See bigfoot.

SASSAFRAS implies well-being.

SATAN See devil.

SATCHEL portrays that which we consider important enough to always carry with us, usually relating to basic ethics and beliefs.

SATEEN (fabric) implies a "slick" personality; cleverness.

SATELLITE (man-made) reflects an "orbiting" of the truth instead of reaching and stretching self beyond the safe and charted confines of tradition.

SATELLITE (planet) denotes peripheral elements on which one places importance.

SATELLITE DISH suggests a need to be more receptive to others; implies a personal lack of awareness.

SATIN (fabric) reveals an overly optimistic perspective.

SATIRE See sarcasm.

SATURATED emphasizes a "fullness" or a level that has reached capacity. Recall what was saturated. What was the liquid? Water? Blood? Oil?

SATURDAY suggests a time to give personal attention to self. This symbol may refer to a wide variety of aspects such as physical, mental, or emotional rest.

SATURDAY NIGHT SPECIAL warns of highly volatile emotions.

SATURN (planet) implies wisdom and the attainment of same.

SATYR (Greek mythology) characterizes a lack of self control.

SAUCE signifies personal perspectives or character traits that alter basic elements.

SAUCEPAN indicates a desire to affect surrounding elements in a personal manner.

SAUCER relates to protective measures; means of containment.

SAUERBRATEN See pot roast.

SAUERKRAUT See cabbage.

SAUNA reveals a need for inner cleansing to rid self of negative attitudes and emotional impurities that serve as toxins.

SAUSAGE denotes a concise concept; a situation or plan that has been given every conceivable consideration.

SAUTÉ implies a need for contemplation; deep thought.

SAVANNA represents an "exposure" to personally sensitive concepts or ideas.

SAVANT exposes past-life knowledge.

SAVINGS ACCOUNT See bankbook.

SAVINGS BOND portrays foresight; an opportunity.

SAVORY signifies an appealing element in one's life.

SAVVY applies to being well-informed; knowledgeable.

SAW represents the capability of "cutting through" a problematical aspect in life.

SAWDUST denotes that which is "left over" or "left behind" after a problem has been resolved.

SAW GRASS illustrates a particularly troublesome phase in one's life.

SAWHORSE refers to a life aspect that has the capability of aiding efforts to resolve problems.

SAWMILL constitutes the act of personally identifying the basic factors of a problem.

SAW-TOOTHED implies an aggressive approach.

SAWYER (Tom) characterizes one who doesn't give logic and reason to the thought process.

SAXOPHONE alludes to melancholia.

SCAB (worker) advises of an improper substitution or replacement; a wrong alternative.

SCAB (wound) indicates a healing aspect or force.

SCABBARD signifies the "control" of one's emotions.

SCABIES stand for a "parasite" (negative) aspect that one has allowed to invade self.

SCAFFOLD correlates to the "safeguards" we personally create to protect us from hurtful emotional events.

SCALD most often identifies a "spiritual" burn of some type that results from accepting false concepts.

SCALE See climbing.

SCALE (fish) refers to spiritual caution.

SCALE (weight) illustrates "balance" of some type. Recall the "kind" of scale to determine this symbol's precise meaning.

SCALLOP portrays the ingestion of harmful spiritual elements.

SCALLOP (pattern) applies to being "grounded." This symbol refers to the tendency to "return" to one's center for the purpose of staying balanced and focused.

SCALP exemplifies one's sensitivity. Recall its condition.

SCALPEL infers a need to excise a negative element from self or another.

SCALP LOCK (hair style) represents narrow-mindedness.

SCAM reveals insincerity; ulterior motives.

SCAMPI See shrimp.

SCAN represents a "going over" or the need to review something.

SCANDAL connotes reprisals.

SCANDAL SHEET correlates to gossip; comes as an advisement to focus on the important elements in life.

SCANNER (police) signifies greater awareness.

SCAPEGOAT means an innocent individual; warns of a tendency to place blame on others; lacking personal responsibility.

SCAPULAR (religious) reminds one to maintain personal protection; alludes to the wisdom of watching one's back.

SCAR denotes a former wound.

SCARAB reflects one's inner self; the soul.

SCARECROW relates to a reinforcement of one's personal protection.

SCARED exposes one's inner fears.

SCARF defines an open attitude toward new ideas.

SCARLET See red.

SCARLET FEVER represents the harmful results of accepting a negative idea.

SCAR TISSUE See scar.

SCATTER pertains to a loss of essential elements.

SCATTER-BRAINED stands for a loss of emotional or mental focus.

SCATTERGUN See shotgun.

SCAVENGER usually exemplifies resourcefulness, yet whether this symbol is meant to infer a positive or negative message will depend on the surrounding dreamscape details.

SCENERY plays a major role in dream interpretation, for the scene of the dreamscape will always reveal important elements that are essential.

SCENT has a specific purpose in dreams. Refer to specific scent.

SCEPTER indicates false authority, usually spiritually related.

SCHEDULE signifies regimentation.

SCHEMATIC exemplifies the necessity of detailed planning.

SCHEME naturally indicates a "plan," but one needs to recall the details to determine if it was for productive and positive purposes.

SCHIZOPHRENIA marks an individual who is not true to self.

SCHNAPPS See alcoholic beverage.

SCHNAUZER (dog breed) portrays a friend who watches out for you.

SCHOLAR characterizes a person who possesses knowledge, usually for a specific subject.

SCHOLARSHIP stands for an opportunity to attain greater information or knowledge; a chance to learn something.

SCHOOL may indicate "learning" or it may refer to the negative aspect of being indoctrinated.

SCHOOLBOOK will reveal the area in which a dreamer is lacking adequate knowledge.

SCHOOL BUS corresponds to the "vehicle" or "way" a person can attain additional knowledge.

SCHOOL DISTRICT suggests an "environment" for learning.

SCHOOLHOUSE emphasizes "general" information.

SCHOOLTEACHER characterizes someone in the dreamer's life who is capable of "teaching" something important. This will be a specific element unique to the dreamer.

SCHOOLWORK reminds us that we have to apply ourselves if we want to learn.

SCHOOLYARD suggests a "paced" method of study.

SCIATICA exposes a displaced attitude or perspective.

SCIENCE constitutes expanded knowledge regarding a specific subject. Recall what the subject was.

SCIENCE FICTION denotes unrealistic attitudes or beliefs; an inability to understand true Reality.

SCIENTIST characterizes an individual who is highly interested in expanding our knowledge and understanding, yet is caught within self-imposed bounds.

SCIMITAR See sword.

SCISSORS denote a permanent separation. Recall what color they were.

SCOFF represents the expression of an opposing opinion.

SCOLD illustrates a reprimand. Recall the dream's surrounding details. Who was scolding? Who was being scolded?

SCOLIOSIS portrays an inability to stand up straight for self.

SCONCE will symbolize a life aspect that has the ability to "light" one's way. Recall if it had a lit candle. Was it empty?

SCONE portrays an essential piece of information.

SCOOP (utensil) See ladle.

SCOOP (information) exposes hidden elements to an issue.

SCOOTER implies an immature method of gaining information or reaching one's goal.

SCOPE reflects an indepth look; closer attention given.

SCORCH stands for too much pressure or "heat" brought to bare.

SCOREBOARD/CARD connotes an individual's personal spiritual balance sheet. Recall what it revealed. What color was it?

SCOREKEEPER represents oneself; responsibility to maintain balance.

SCORPION will stand for retaliation.

SCOTTISH TERRIER (dog breed) characterizes a loyal friend who is prepared to defend your honor.

SCOUR depicts deep cleaning. Recall what was being scoured. Who was doing the cleaning?

SCOUT indicates advanced research and exploration needed in one's life before further progression can be accomplished.

SCOUT LEADER pertains to a person who can serve as a guide along one's life path.

SCRABBLE (game) warns against the tendency to play "word games" and not communicate in a direct and clear manner.

SCRABBLE (grope) reflects an uncontrolled progression; lack of planning.

SCRAMBLED EGGS represent a mix of new ideas; a confused beginning.

SCRAMBLER (device) emphasizes a need to be discerning throughout our communications with others.

SCRAP will correspond with a single element in one's life that may or may not be currently relevant.

SCRAPBOOK signifies a personal need to remember accomplishments or events of one's past. Was the scrapbook for a specific event or time in your past?

SCRAPER reveals a need to "clear away" extraneous elements that cloud or cover basic aspects.

SCRAPHEAP represents that which is of no value. Recall what was in the dreamscape heap.

SCRATCHING implies a personal irritation in one's life.

SCRATCH PAD See notebook.

SCRATCH-PROOF portrays an aspect in one's life that is resistant to outside influence.

SCRATCH TEST is an attempt to define the source of one's life irritations.

SCRAWL indicates a communication made in haste.

SCREAM (silent) denotes repressed emotions or calls for help.

SCREE refers to a difficult path.

SCREEN (computer) See monitor.

SCREEN (mesh) exemplifies protected freedom.

SCREEN TEST relates to one's desire to perform a specific task or role and the appropriateness of same.

SCREW refers to an injustice.

SCREWDRIVER signifies pressures in life. These may be referring to self-induced pressures or problems. Recall who was holding the tool. Was it being used to *un*screw something? This would mean a *lessening* of pressure.

SCRIBBLE symbolizes a lack of mental focus.

SCRIBE characterizes the recording of communications.

SCRIM reflects an unclear perspective.

SCRIMMAGE corresponds to some type of struggle.

SCRIMP indicates extreme frugality. Recall surrounding dreamscape details to determine if this is a positive or negative message.

SCRIMSHAW See carve.

SCRIPT suggests a need to "play by the rules." This infers that an individual is not holding to his or her pre-chosen life path or purpose.

SCRIPTURE See bible.

SCRIPTWRITER will represent the one who has control of his or her direction.

SCROLL See scan.

SCROLL (ancient) emphasizes solid truths.

SCROLLWORK indicates an attention given to detail.

SCROOGE (Ebenezer) reminds us that it's never too late to change for the better.

SCRUB (brush) connotes a cleansing is needed.

SCRUB (terrain) alludes to an inactive stage of one's life path.

SCRUBBY (appearance) may signify a weary soul or it may stand for apathy, depending on the dream's surrounding details.

SCRUPULOUS will reveal a conscionable individual.

SCUBA DIVER depicts the attainment of spiritual gifts. Recall the working condition of the diver's apparatus. What was the diver looking at or collecting? Was the water clear or cloudy?

SCUBA GEAR represents aspects that allow one to attain spiritual goals.

SCUDDING connotes a forced progression.

SCUFFED defines wear; perseverance and fortitude.

SCUFFLE refers to an altercation of some type; may even be within self.

SCULLERY implies a need for cleaning. The dreamer will make the specific correlation here.

SCULPTING relates to the act of creating and formulating in a personal manner.

SCULPTURE will reveal an important element that the dreamer should give attention to.

SCUM portrays that which lacks value; extraneous elements.

SCURVY defines a lack of inner strength.

SCUTTLE See ashcan.

SCUTWORK reminds us that even menial tasks can have beneficial effects.

SCYTHE pertains to "cutting through" life's excesses or unnecessary aspects.

SEA correlates to life's spiritual aspects.

SEA BISCUIT See hardtack.

SEA BREEZE represents a spiritual "sense" to something; a "hint" of spiritual elements.

SEA CHEST portrays that which we carry with us on our spiritual search.

SEA FAN connotes spiritual vacillation.

SEAFOOD most often represents spiritual knowledge. Recall the condition of the food. What type was it?

SEAGULL pertains to spiritual thoughts.

SEA HORSE relates to an illogical spiritual search or belief and may indicate spiritual beliefs that are more fantasy than reality.

SEAL (animal) portrays the utilization of spirituality in one's daily life.

SEAL (closure) refers to a need to conclude or "seal" an aspect in one's life.

SEAL (emblem) will reveal a specific meaning to each dreamer.

SEA-LANE stands for a well-used spiritual path. This is usually a warning against following another's belief system rather than sensing one's own.

SEA LEGS suggests spiritual comfort; feeling at home with one's personal spiritual beliefs.

SEA LEVEL pertains to spiritual basic truths.

SEALING WAX defines privacy; confidentiality. Recall who was using the wax. What color was it? Was it impressed with a symbol or initial?

SEAM (any type) denotes a joining element.

SEAMLESS indicates unbroken; a complete element.

SEA MONSTER represents a spiritual danger.

SEAMSTRESS characterizes an individual who is capable of bringing various elements together.

SÉANCE exposes misplaced spiritual priorities.

SEAPLANE symbolizes spiritual thoughts.

SEAPORT corresponds to a spiritual transition.

SEAQUAKE warns of spiritually shaky ground.

SEAR See burn.

SEARCHING relates to a desire or need for specific information.

SEARCHLIGHT See flashlight.

SEARCH WARRANT portrays an invasion of privacy. Important elements associated with this symbol are the answers to such questions as "who" was serving the warrant on whom? For what reason?

SEASCAPE will reveal the quality of one's personal spiritual search or transition. Was the scene a rough cliff? A tropical and sandy shore? Was it rocky?

SEA SERPENT See sea monster.

SEASHELL defines spiritual gifts and talents. Recall the quantity and quality of the shells. Were they whole? Beautiful or full of barnacles?

SEASICKNESS stands for an individual's state of spiritual confusion; spiritual "dizziness" or nausea from taking in too much too fast.

SEA SLUG warns of spiritual laziness, or entrapment.

SEA SNAIL denotes a slow and methodical spiritual pace based on one's level of comprehension.

SEASON See specific type.

SEASONING will indicate personal characteristics. Refer to specific type.

SEASON TICKET represents planning ahead for the purpose of not missing elements of personal interest.

SEA STAR See starfish.

SEA SPRAY applies to spiritual gifts and the opportunity to accept same.

SEAT BELT connotes a protective measure.

SEA TURTLE typifies a cautious spiritual search or path.

SEA WALL refers to self-generated spiritual bounds.

SEAWEED pertains to spiritual indecision; spiritual vacillation.

SEA WORLD suggests a sampling of spiritual concepts.

SEAWORTHY illustrates one's personal preparedness to begin a spiritual quest or search.

SECLUDED most often is an advisement to engage in serious contemplation.

SECOND CLASS exemplifies an alternative.

SECONDHAND defines a "useable" element or idea.

SECOND MORTGAGE may be symbolized by the visual of "two" mortgage papers on a table or in one's hand. This dream fragment will identify a good prospect or solid plan.

SECOND SIGHT See clairvoyance.

SECOND WIND implies a re-energized state of being.

SECRET may indicate a revelation to the dreamer.

SECRETARY characterizes an individual who is capable of providing support and assistance.

SECRET AGENT exposes an individual who has ulterior motives.

SECRET BALLOT connotes a personal decision; inner thoughts.

SECRET POLICE comes as a strong advisement to be more aware of those around you.

SECRET SERVICE signifies a loss of privacy.

SECRET SOCIETY represents hidden activities.

SECTION EIGHT warns of undesirable character traits.

SECULARISM indicates spiritual indifference.

SECURITIES AND EXCHANGE COMMISSION stands for integrity.

SECURITY BLANKET denotes that which comforts or gives one a sense of security.

SECURITY GUARD characterizes an individual who is capable of providing protection.

SECURITY SYSTEM See alarm system.

SEDATIVE pertains to a calming element in one's life.

SEDENTARY is an advisement to expend greater efforts.

SEDIMENT represents that which remains or is left over; nonessential elements.

SEDUCTION warns of a situation that may lure one astray.

SEED See kernel.

SEEDLING stands for the birthing of new understandings. Recall what type of botanical the seedling was. What was its overall condition?

SEED PEARL symbolizes small imperfections.

SEEING EYE DOG characterizes a friend who has the ability to clarify confusing matters.

SEEPAGE exposes an insecure situation or piece of information.

SEERESS indicates an individual who has clear foresight.

SEERSUCKER (fabric) alludes to a lighthearted mood.

SEESAW relates to the unpredictability of life; the ups and downs.

SEETHE warns of a need to release one's pent-up emotions.

SEE-THROUGH See transparent.

SEGMENTED denotes a multifaceted element in one's life.

SEGREGATION may not infer a racial matter, but rather is a symbol that usually advises us to keep diverse issues separate. This dream symbol would imply that the dreamer has been mixing concepts.

SEISMOGRAPH constitutes watchfulness; cautions one to be more keenly aware of "undercurrents" in relationships, business, or personal situations in life.

SEISMOLOGIST emphasizes one's inner sensitivity to be aware when he or she is approaching unstable ground.

SEIZE won't usually be a negative symbol, for it most often is an advisement to grasp an opportunity while one can.

SEIZURE warns of a serious adverse reaction; some type of negative aspect that causes an instantaneous response.

SELECTIVE SERVICE emphasizes a "forced" effort.

SELF-ABSORBED warns against placing self as one's priority in life; completely devoted to satisfying oneself.

SELF-ADHESIVE relates to a cohesive aspect.

SELF-ANALYSIS reminds us to recheck our motives and perspectives for personal affectations.

SELF-APPOINTED cautions against making oneself an authority.

SELF-BASTING denotes an inner awareness for the purpose of maintaining smooth relationships.

SELF-CENTEREDNESS warns against thinking only of self; a love of one's ego.

SELF-CLEANING portrays a continual monitoring of one's motives and perspectives.

SELF-CONSCIOUSNESS signifies a tendency to feel inferior to one's peers.

SELF-CONTROL reflects a focused individual who has mastered emotional responses.

SELF-DEFEATING reveals unproductive plans, ideas, or acts.

SELF-DEFENSE CLASS suggests a way to protect self. This may not only refer to physical defenses, but may also represent emotional or spiritual aspects.

SELF-DOUBT implies one's personal lack of confidence in self.

SELF-EMPLOYED character-izes resourcefulness; self-suffi-ciency.

SELF-HELP (resources) consti-tutes a desire to improve oneself. Recall what *type* of self-help books, tapes, or seminars were utilized.

SELF-IMAGE See mirror.

SELF-INFLICTED exposes the fact that one's troubles were caused by self.

SELF-LIMITING stands for some type of inner fear that pre-vents one from reaching for fur-ther discovery or progressing quicker.

SELF-PORTRAIT will define how one sees self. This is a very important and revealing dream symbol.

SELF-PROCLAIMED corre-lates to how one wishes to be known.

SELF-PROPELLED indicates great stores of inner power (en-ergy).

SELF-RISING FLOUR sug-gests a resourceful individual; having knowledge and the asso-ciated wisdom.

SELF-SACRIFICE stands for placing others before self.

SELF-SERVICE represents a call to "help" self instead of de-pending on others for same.

SELF-SUFFICIENCY refers to a self-reliant personality; creativ-ity and resourcefulness.

SELLER'S MARKET symbol-izes a lack of opportunities; few choices.

SELLING POINT connotes a convincing aspect; an attractive element.

SELLOUT may indicate a popu-lar issue or concept, or it may represent some type of betrayal.

SELTZER See soda water.

SELVAGE (of fabric) relates to something that will remain intact; will not come apart or undone.

SEMICIRCLE See crescent.

SEMICONSCIOUS exposes a state of half awareness; advises one to be more aware.

SEMIFINAL indicates the stage of progression that has brought one close to the attainment of a goal.

SEMIGLOSS denotes a "finished" veneer to one's character. This re-fers to a refined appearance rather than a glossy, glitzy one.

SEMINAR connotes expanded education; more in-depth infor-mation.

SEMINARY pertains to deeper spiritual knowledge.

SEMISWEET symbolizes a dual nature; being slightly bitter along with a sense of sweetness.

SEMITRAILER exposes a physical overload; physical stress from overburdening oneself.

SENATE See Capitol Hill.

SENATOR characterizes an individual who is in a position to listen to the problems, complaints, and wishes of others.

SENDOFF reflects an expression of encouragement.

SENILITY See Alzheimer's Disease.

SENIOR CITIZEN represents experiential knowledge.

SENIOR CENTER corresponds with an opportunity to learn from those who have gained experience.

SENIORITY denotes a higher position; may refer to attained knowledge, experience, or spiritual advancement.

SENSATIONALISM cautions one to readjust priorities.

SENSITIVITY TRAINING comes as an advisement to be more emotionally responsive to others.

SENSORY DEPRIVATION is usually a warning to stop depriving self of emotional expression or interaction.

SENTENCING stands for a manner of retribution; a need to balance out a wrongdoing.

SENTIMENTALITY denotes an open heart; compassion and understanding.

SENTINEL characterizes height-ened awareness; watchfulness.

SENTRY See guard.

SEPARATIST will not necessarily depict a negative meaning; it may caution one to keep diverse concepts separate instead of combining them erroneously, or this symbol could come as a personal advisement to stay out of other people's business.

SEPIA (color/photograph) pertains to innocent ignorance; an undeveloped concept or perspective.

SEPTEMBER represents a waning period; a winding down.

SEPTIC TANK/SYSTEM illustrates the complete disposal of the extraneous mental/emotional waste of one's life; ridding self of the extra burdens we shouldn't be carrying.

SEPULCHER See mausoleum.

SEQUEL represents a continuation; not the end of something.

SEQUENTIAL signifies a need to take one thing at a time.

SEQUIN portrays a "flash" to one's personality or character which may directly refer to her or his "lights" of spiritual attainment.

SEQUOIA See redwood forest.

SERAPE symbolizes personal freedom; a unique life path.

SERENADE stands for an expression of affection.

SERENDIPITY pertains to a phase of fortunate events.

SERENITY indicates inner harmony.

SERF see servant.

SERGE (fabric) indicates an unyielding personality.

SERIAL KILLER will usually suggest a self-generated condition whereby one routinely performs in a self-defeating manner; the methodical "killing" of one's opportunities.

SERIAL NUMBER comes as a numerical message. Recall the sequence then add them together to determine the final number of the message.

SERIES CIRCUIT advises one to deduce in a logical and methodical manner.

SERMON usually brings a personal message for each dreamer.

SERPENT See snake.

SERPENTINE (configuration) denotes a "winding" life path.

SERRATED See saw-toothed.

SERVANT will caution one against being taken advantage of.

SERVICE CHARGE represents an encumberment connected to a decision or idea.

SERVICE MARK is an attempt to define one's purpose.

SERVICE ROAD signifies an alternate route.

SERVICE STATION See gas station.

SERVING TRAY reflects order; efficiency.

SESAME SEED/OIL alludes to a beneficial element in one's life.

SETBACK will usually indicate a need to "go back" and discover a missed aspect.

SETTEE See bench.

SETTLEMENT See colony.

SETTLEMENT (agreement) stands for a need to negotiate and reconcile.

SEVEN signifies a high spiritual attainment.

SEVEN DWARFS stand for the six main energy forces within the body in association with one's activating spiritual development.

SEVEN SEALS represent the stages of spiritual enlightenment.

SEVENTH AVENUE portrays one's outward affectations.

SEVENTH HEAVEN depicts a state of extreme happiness.

SEVENTH-INNING STRETCH advises of a need to take time out from over-expending one's efforts.

SEVER refers to a "cutting off" or cutting out of some type of aspect in one's life.

SEVERANCE PAY exemplifies a benefit or reward for efforts expended.

SEWAGE signifies life's basest elements.

SEWER will denote a condition, place, or situation that contains highly negative aspects.

SEWING applies to a bringing together; a desire to reconnect; coalesce. This symbol comes when one has severed self from a relationship, belief, or situation with which she or he now needs to reconnect.

SEWING MACHINE represents a tool and/or opportunity that can be utilized to correct a severed situation or relationship that has fallen apart.

SEX is a symbol that correlates with one's manner of communication with others; quality of relationships. Recall what type of sexual presentation was made. Gentle? Violent? Possessive?

SEX APPEAL won't necessarily relate to a temptress, for this symbol most often refers to one's personal magnetism; a type of personality that attracts others.

SEX CHANGE reflects an inability to accept and relate to the specific elements one has chosen to utilize for his or her current path progression. This symbol reveals a strong recognition with one's prime spirit identity which cannot be overcome by the current life status.

SEXTANT portrays a desire to understand one's personal relationship with spiritual elements.

SEXUAL ASSAULT denotes an irresistible desire for control.

SEXUAL DISEASE exposes the result of indiscriminate behavior; lack of responsible discernment.

SEXUAL HARASSMENT reveals a lack of respect; more importantly, it reveals a lack of spiritual advancement.

SHABBY (appearance) will usually denote weariness.

SHACK (dwelling) exemplifies disinterest in material possessions.

SHACKLES most often refer to self-imposed restrictions.

SHADE See ghost.

SHADE (window) pertains to privacy.

SHADE TREE applies to respite.

SHADOW may pertain to dark forces or it may represent self, depending on the dream's surrounding details.

SHADOW BOX (shelf) displays accumulated affectations and/or specific interests unique to the individual.

SHADOWBOXING reveals a conflict within self.

SHAFT See mineshaft.

SHAGGY (fabric) represents a disorderly thought process.

SHAKESPEARE (William) reminds us of moral and ethical obligations.

SHALE pertains to loose footing; a current state of instability.

SHALLOT See onion.

SHALLOW signifies "surface" aspects; a lack of depth.

SHAM (pillow) denotes an "empty" element; a "cover" story.

SHAMAN characterizes the higher spiritual abilities and the associated sacredness.

SHAMBLES symbolize ruination; the destruction of something in one's life.

SHAME typifies guilt.

SHAMPOO applies to the act of cleansing one's thoughts.

SHAMROCK symbolizes the three Aspects of God—Spirit, Female, and Male.

SHANTUNG (fabric) denotes roughly disguised finesse.

SHANTY See shack.

SHARD exemplifies a hint, clue, or beginning insight; a "fragment" of an idea.

SHARE (stock) refers to a personal interest in something; a stake.

SHARECROPPER characterizes the expending of efforts for the good of the whole.

SHAREHOLDER indicates those who have contributed toward something and have invested their resources and confidence.

SHARING portrays selflessness.

SHARK corresponds to religious fanatics; those who try to convert others to their beliefs in a relentless manner.

SHARKSKIN (fabric) relates to a spiritually unethical personality.

SHARPEN See hone.

SHARPSHOOTER suggests a need for discernment and accurate judgments.

SHARP-TONGUED denotes an inability to temper one's words.

SHARP-WITTED signifies astuteness.

SHATTER refers to a totally destroyed element.

SHATTERPROOF GLASS See safety glass.

SHAVER See razor.

SHAVINGS (metal) represent the "harsher" aspects of self that have been shed.

SHAVINGS (wood) stands for the formation of a personal method of utilizing one's natural spiritual gifts.

SHAWL alludes to personal ideals, thoughts, and beliefs that are gently concealed.

SHEAR (shave) relates to a desire to clearly comprehend the basics of an idea or concept.

SHEARLING denotes warmth of character.

SHEARS See scissors.

SHEATH implies self-control.

SHED will typify resource reserves; stored energy or inner strength.

SHEEN implies an inner beauty.

SHEEP reveals a lack of individuality and/or assertiveness.

SHEEPHERDER characterizes God's messengers and true spiritual teachers.

SHEER (fabric) reveals a transparent personality.

SHEER (steep) emphasizes caution in respect to there being no room for error.

SHEET (bed) See bedding.

SHEET LIGHTNING represents a reflection of one's spiritual essence within self; a reminder of such a presence.

SHEET METAL signifies personal strength that is utilized in all aspects of life.

SHEET MUSIC alludes to the personally-composed inner music with which we progress through life; may bring a special message if the sheet music was titled.

SHELF illustrates "stored" elements that may need to be set aside for a time; may reveal valuable aspects that need to be preserved.

SHELF LIFE connotes a specified span of time for an element in one's life to be viable.

SHELF ROAD represents a precarious path currently being traveled.

SHELL (bombard) constitutes an inundation.

SHELL (bullet) See ammunition.

SHELL (casing) pertains to an inner emptiness.

SHELL (egg) See eggshell.

SHELL (husk) suggests a need to break through or get at the core of something in one's life.

SHELL (sea) See seashell.

SHELL (structure) signifies an incomplete homelife or inner aspects of self.

SHELLAC represents a "finished" issue; a finalization.

SHELLFISH relates to an attempt to absorb as many spiritual aspects as possible.

SHELL GAME applies to evasion; a possible swindle; unethical methods.

SHELLPROOF reflects a well-protected self; wise precautions set in place to prevent the entry of unwanted or negative elements; high awareness and discernment.

SHELL-SHOCKED exposes traumatic effects.

SHELTER See specific type.

SHELTIE See Shetland pony; Shetland sheep dog.

SHEPHERD signifies watchfulness; awareness; may indicate a guardian in one's life.

SHEPHERD'S PURSE (plant) corresponds to beneficial elements.

SHERBET (frozen) applies to a desire to have fewer responsibilities in life.

SHERIFF typifies an authority figure representing the "rules" or laws.

SHERRY See wine.

SHERWOOD FOREST alludes to a place of safety; respite.

SHETLAND PONY pertains to concealed personal power.

SHETLAND SHEEP DOG (dog breed) depicts protectiveness; watchfulness.

SHIATSU portrays a need for clearing mental and emotional blocks.

SHIELD connotes one's personal form of self-protection that may include mental, emotional, or spiritual elements.

SHIFT (action) signifies an altered perspective or attitude.

SHIFTLESS implies a lack of motivation or energy.

SHIM reflects a temporary solution; a stop-gap move.

SHIMMER will most often indicate a spiritual connotation.

SHIN denotes vulnerability.

SHINGLE (roof) symbolizes subconscious defense mechanisms.

SHINGLES reveal an emotional disruption within self.

SHIP signifies a method or "vehicle" that facilitates a spiritual search.

SHIPBUILDING stands for personal efforts applied to one's planned spiritual search.

SHIPMENT relates to a forthcoming aspect one is awaiting; may also refer to something one is planning on doing or sending out.

SHIPWRECK illustrates a spiritual failure or misdirection.

SHIRT represents a basic need; a necessary aspect in one's life.

SHIRTTAIL relates to personal methods utilized to help others.

SHISH KABOB alludes to multiple nourishing elements in one's life.

SHIVER (cold) signifies an effort to counter a negative element.

SHOAL exposes spiritual shallowness.

SHOCK ABSORBER emphasizes emotional and intellectual stability.

SHOCK WAVE applies to future repercussions expected from a deed done.

SHOE usually indicates how one's path is traveled. Refer to specific type.

SHOEBOX correlates to the multiple personal methods utilized during one's progression in life; the various types of "shoes" worn. Recall any wording on the box.

SHOEHORN implies a need to take larger steps toward one's path progression or life goal instead of always trying to "stuff" self into a confined path or manner of walking.

SHOELACE indicates the condition of one's manner of walking his or her life path. Was the lace untied? Dirty? Too tight?

SHOEMAKER characterizes an individual who has the capability of guiding the life paths of others.

SHOESHINE refers to a desire to impress others with one's method or manner of moving through life.

SHOESTRING denotes a lack of resources.

SHOJI typifies a "thin" veneer to one's inner self.

SHOOT (plant) See sprout.

SHOOTING GALLERY (drugs) warns of a situation or relationship where potentially dangerous negative elements are present.

SHOOTING GALLERY (guns) corresponds to an advisement to give greater attention to one's personal protective measures.

SHOOTING SCRIPT represents one's finalized plan or theory.

SHOOTING STAR indicates the loss or "failing" of an important spiritual belief; suggests that one has ignored, forgotten, or allowed major spiritual truths to die out.

SHOOTOUT pertains to the resolving of a conflict and won't necessarily infer that this is done in a negative manner.

SHOP constitutes "supply" or opportunity. The type of shop will be the important element here.

SHOPKEEPER characterizes an individual who provides a service or opportunity for others.

SHOPLIFT See steal.

SHOPPING emphasizes the act of "looking" for something; searching.

SHOPPING BAG infers expectation; an intent to obtain a need or desire.

SHOPPING CENTER See mall.

SHOP STEWARD characterizes a person who listens to your ideas, complaints, etc.

SHOPTALK represents a need to

attend to one's business at hand; refers to a return to one's life goal or plan.

SHORE (land) will allude to the boundaries of one's spiritual search or direction.

SHORE (support) pertains to a temporary supportive move.

SHORE LEAVE symbolizes a break from one's spiritual search which will provide contemplative time or a required period of respite.

SHORE PATROL reflects one's inner spiritual guidance; conscience.

SHORT connotes a concise element; may also indicate a need to expand some aspect in one's life.

SHORTBREAD implies a source of energy.

SHORTCHANGED correlates to a debt owed. Recall who was shortchanged.

SHORT CIRCUIT reveals severe misconceptions and/or mental confusion.

SHORTCUT portrays a more efficient method of accomplishing something.

SHORTENING connotes a required aspect of an element.

SHORTHAND signifies resourcefulness.

SHORT ORDER COOK characterizes multiple capabilities.

SHORTSIGHTED emphasizes an inability to perceive the full scope of an issue or plan.

SHORTSTOP characterizes a versatile individual.

SHORT STORY typifies a specialized message for the dreamer.

SHORT-TERM defines a qualified span of time. Recall what this time was related to.

SHOT See ammunition.

SHOT See injection.

SHOT (wounded) exposes an inability to protect oneself; refers to an event that emotionally, mentally, or spiritually injured self.

SHOTGUN connotes a life element that has the capability of causing multiple ramifications.

SHOTGUN WEDDING constitutes a "forced" relationship.

SHOT PUT pertains to an attempt to make the most out of one's applied efforts.

SHOULDER will denote the quality and quantity of one's inner strength.

SHOULDER (of road) suggests an emergency contingency.

SHOULDER HOLSTER portrays strong protective measures.

SHOULDER PADS allude to false strength.

SHOUTING will serve as an individual message for each

dreamer. Recall who was doing the shouting and what was said.

SHOVE will usually represent a motivational push of some type.

SHOVEL connotes an individual's tendency to overindulge; may refer to the intake or output aspects.

SHOW-AND-TELL comes as a private message for each dreamer. Recall what was shown and told about.

SHOWBOAT warns of spiritual arrogance; spiritual flaunting.

SHOWCASE depicts what a person values; one's priorities. What was in the dreamscape showcase? Was the glass clear, clouded, or colored? Was the glass cracked?

SHOWDOWN represents the time for confrontation.

SHOWER (bathing) indicates a need for some type of inner cleansing.

SHOWER (rain) implies a gentle touch of spiritual elements.

SHOWER CURTAIN will expose one's inner character. Recall if there were designs on this curtain. What color was it? Was it dirty? Torn?

SHOWERHEAD reflects an individual's strength of intention. Recall what type of showerhead it was. Was it a Shower Saver? Was it a massage type? Was it running? If so, was it a hard or gentle spray?

SHOWOFF exposes a personal need for attention.

SHOW PLACE symbolizes a presentation of perfection to others.

SHOW ROOM will display an array of opportunities for the dreamer.

SHOWSTOPPER reveals an outstanding performance; implies commendation.

SHOW TUNE corresponds with a specific message for the dreamer. Recall what the tune was.

SHRAPNEL denotes those aspects in one's life that leave permanent damage behind.

SHRED (any type) signifies a fragment of whatever was depicted; refers to remains.

SHREDDER represents an attempt to hide or get rid of some type of evidence; concealment.

SHREW connotes an individual who is never satisfied; a complaining person.

SHRILL signifies a "harsh" message or lesson.

SHRIMP symbolizes the absorption of the more refined spiritual aspects.

SHRIMPBOAT corresponds with a desire to search out and obtain spiritual understanding.

SHRIMP COCKTAIL denotes a

tendency to maintain spiritual connotations throughout one's daily interactions.

SHRINE cautions against focusing on singular spiritual elements.

SHRINKING pertains to a "waning" effect; a diminishing factor.

SHRINK-WRAP represents an attempt to preserve some aspect in one's life.

SHRIVELED denotes a loss of energy and vitality. This may be a positive sign, depending on the surrounding dream details.

SHROUD exemplifies concealment of one's darker aspects.

SHRUBBERY implies natural talents and the opportunities to utilize same.

SHRUG illustrates indecision.

SHUCK See husk.

SHUDDER suggests an inner fear and the recognition of same.

SHUFFLE (cards) connotes an altering of probabilities; changing the possible outcomes.

SHUFFLE (feet) applies to a defeated attitude; may infer weariness.

SHUFFLEBOARD exemplifies congenial competition; friendly contention.

SHUN represents a voluntary disregard for something. Depending on the associated elements of the dream, this may be a positive symbol.

SHUNT means an intentional diversion; a setting aside for a time.

SHUT-IN comes as an advisement to "go within" for the purpose of self-discovery.

SHUTOFF VALVE represents an opportunity to gain needed control.

SHUTTER (camera) corresponds to one's personal perspective and how well it's utilized; awareness; insights.

SHUTTER (window) symbolizes open-mindedness. Recall if the shutters were closed tight or opened wide. What color were they? What was their overall condition?

SHUTTER SPEED reveals one's level of astuteness.

SHUTTLE illustrates intermediate paths and/or directions in life.

SHUTTLE (weaving) pertains to a facilitating element in one's life.

SHYNESS may reveal innocence or a lack of self-esteem.

SHYLOCK characterizes a self-serving individual who takes ruthless advantage of others.

SHYSTER portrays an unscrupulous individual; unethical.

SIAMESE TWIN exposes an absolute, compatible individual.

SIBERIA stands for "remoteness" of some type; a distancing; may refer to being far off the mark.

SIBERIAN HUSKY (dog breed) See Husky.

SIBLING won't necessarily represent a close relationship, but rather will pertain to someone you are meant to interrelate with for a time.

SIBYL (ancient Greek/Roman culture) characterizes an individual possessing strong prophetic abilities.

SICKBAY exposes a spiritual sickness of some type that may be caused by external sources or may be self-generated.

SICKLE pertains to an opportunity to rid self of extraneous aspects in one's life; cutting down on the unnecessary elements.

SICK PEOPLE illustrate mental dysfunctions or physical diseases. Recall what the illness was.

SIDEARM (throw) represents exceptional inner strength.

SIDEARM (weapon) See gun.

SIDEBAR corresponds to additional information.

SIDEBOARD symbolizes psychological elements that affect attitudes and opinions.

SIDEBURNS connote a desire to appear intellectual.

SIDECAR relates to a "free ride" or an attempt to progress along one's path without applying personal effort.

SIDE DISH will represent aspects that enhance a main element.

SIDE EFFECTS exemplify multiple ramifications of an action taken.

SIDEKICK reveals a close companion; an individual who can be counted on.

SIDELINE will illustrate a position of observation; may also indicate an extra activity in association with one's main purpose.

SIDESHOW refers to those aspects in one's life that are ridiculous or outrageous in respect to one's serious path or purpose.

SIDESTEP correlates to a diversionary tactic.

SIDESWIPED stands for a "brush" with a negative element; a close call.

SIDETRACKED depicts a loss of one's focus on a life goal.

SIDEWALK relates to "directed" paths to follow; implies a need to make one's own course.

SIDEWAYS (movement) will usually connote a move to avoid something; an elusive tactic.

SIDEWINDER See snake.

SIDING (on dwelling) signifies an attempt to alter appearances.

SIEGE applies to an overwhelming inundation of some type in one's life.

SIENNA (color) pertains to an earthiness to one's inner nature.

SIESTA See nap.

SIEVE warns of an inability to manage personal containment; lacking self-control.

SIFT represents extensive research.

SIGH typifies disappointment or weariness.

SIGHTLESS See blind.

SIGHTSEEING cautions against superficiality, cursory knowledge.

SIGN will come as a personal message for each dreamer. Recall what the sign said. Was it a directional one? Was it a STOP or YIELD?

SIGNAL (light) is an advisement regarding one's pace through life.

SIGNATURE may indicate authority or provide a specialized message for the dreamer.

SIGNET RING stands for a personal endorsement.

SIGN LANGUAGE reminds us that there are multiple forms of communication that can be effectively utilized.

SIGN PAINTER will bring a personal message for each dreamer. Recall what was being painted. What colors were used?

SIGNPOST stands for path markers. These need to be heeded.

SILENCE is an attention-getting dream element that most often advises us to listen to one's conscience.

SILENCER (gun) represents the quiet, "silent" negative forces that can affect those who do not maintain high personal awareness.

SILENT PARTNER usually stands for one's own conscience; inner guidance.

SILENT TREATMENT won't necessarily be a negative symbol, but rather a method of making others think for themselves.

SILHOUETTE constitutes an "outline" form and cautions one against accepting same as an entirety or whole.

SILICONE represents a multi-faceted and versatile opportunity.

SILK (fabric) suggests an inner refinement; a delicate strength.

SILK FLOWERS exemplify "lasting" beauty. Refer to specific flower type for deeper meaning.

SILK HAT pertains to a desire to appear successful; extravagance.

SILK-SCREEN denotes replication; may bring a personal message for each dreamer.

SILKWEED will reveal a beneficial element in one's life.

SILKWORM connotes the source of great inner strength.

SILL (geologic) suggests an out-of-character response or it may indicate a need to diverge from one's normal course.

SILL (window) represents the lower confines of one's overall perspective.

SILLINESS doesn't need to infer immaturity, but it may indicate a need to be less serious for a time.

SILO connotes that which is stored and may refer to an individual's emotional, mental, intellectual, or spiritual aspects.

SILT relates to spiritual elements that are not germane to one's personal advancement or development.

SILVER stands for the spiritual elements that exist for everyone. The key here is to recall what form the dream silver took and what was being done with it by whom.

SILVER CERTIFICATE represents a highly valuable aspect in one's life; a rarity.

SILVER DOLLAR denotes honesty.

SILVER LINING reveals an unseen or unrecognized benefit.

SILVER PLATE suggests a veneer of spiritual elements or aspects.

SILVERSMITH characterizes a spiritually ethical individual.

SILVER SPOON symbolizes a lack of experiential learning opportunities.

SILVER-TONGUE implies an influential and persuasive personality.

SILVERWARE relates to utilitarian elements in one's life.

SILVERWARE CHEST corresponds to a recognition and appreciation for the often unnoticed aids one utilizes throughout life.

SIMMER exemplifies thoughtfulness; contemplation; time expended on logic and rationale.

SIMPLETON See fool.

SIMPLICITY pertains to a firm understanding of correct priorities.

SIMULATION will denote a "reproduction" or practice effort.

SIMULCAST depicts a multiple venue of communication.

SINCERITY reveals honesty; genuineness.

SINEW symbolizes a staunch character; having stamina.

SING-ALONG relates to shared sentiments.

SINGE See scorch.

SINGER connotes a communicator. Recall the dream's details to determine whether someone is telling what they know or merely gossiping.

SINGLE-HANDED signifies independence; resourcefulness; an ability to perform without the aid of others.

SINISTER usually stands for a sense of foreboding; ominous sense.

SINK (basin) portrays a life element capable of providing a cleansing opportunity.

SINKHOLE indicates the pitfalls and dangerous regions of one's life path.

SINKING refers to the beginnings of failure or sense of defeat.

SIPHON denotes an advisement to rid self of extraneous spiritual elements.

SIREN defines a strong warning. Recall the associated dreamscape elements for further clarity.

SITAR portrays one's expression of inner feelings.

SITCOM brings a specific meaning to each dreamer. What was the show about and who were the players?

SIT-DOWN expresses an active difference of opinion; a protest.

SITTING may indicate a lax attitude or it may come as an advisement to take time out.

SITTING DUCK pertains to the act of going out on a limb and placing oneself in a position of exposure.

SITTING ROOM See living room.

SITZ BATH indicates a call for emotional peace; an advisement

to remove self from stressful situations.

SIX represents mental, emotional, and spiritual strength.

SIZZLING stands for intense anger.

SKATEBOARD exemplifies an attempt to "dodge" life's burdens and difficult periods.

SKATING (ice) See ice skate.

SKATING (roller) suggests a desire to "skate" through life without encountering the tribulations that are meant to be dealt with and overcome.

SKEET (shooting) implies a tendency to "shoot down" ideas and concepts that are outside one's personal range of perceptual belief.

SKEIN portrays the "threads" of a theory or situation.

SKELETON may signify the "bare bones" of an issue or it may allude to personal hidden elements.

SKELETON KEY illustrates a life aspect that serves as a "key" opening multiple opportunities.

SKEPTIC characterizes an individual with a narrow perspective and a mind closed to new, expanded concepts.

SKETCH denotes an outline or formation of a new idea.

SKEWER symbolizes a very dangerous or negative element about to appear in one's life. Recall what was on the skewer? Who was holding it?

SKIDDING warns of a loss of control; an out-of-control situation.

SKID MARKS reveal a former loss of footing along one's path.

SKID ROW represents a situation or issue in which one has become derelict.

SKIFF See boat.

SKIING (snow) connotes spiritual indifference; ignoring one's spiritual beliefs or responsibilities as if they were frozen or non-existent.

SKI JUMP pertains to the avoidance of spiritual aspects in one's life.

SKI LIFT represents material aspects one allows to "lift" him or her over spiritual responsibilities.

SKILL emphasizes one's unique talents.

SKILLET See frying pan.

SKIM (read) See scan.

SKIM (remove) indicates the act of selective choosing.

SKI MASK relates to those with shallow thoughts and those who have a tendency to avoid deeper concepts.

SKIM MILK illustrates a nourishing aspect in life that could've been more beneficial.

SKIN (animal) See pelt.

SKIN (human) relates to one's inner strength and general stamina. The condition, texture and color are important elements to notice.

SKIN DISEASE will suggest a weakened state.

SKIN DIVING exemplifies a serious spiritual search.

SKIN GRAFT portrays an attempt to improve one's stamina.

SKINNY constitutes a frail and timid personality; denotes a lack of motivation and energized determination.

SKINNY-DIPPING represents an intent to immerse self in spiritual concepts; a joyful desire to gain spiritual knowledge.

SKIN TEST See scratch test.

SKIPPING cautions one to stop "missing" important elements in life from which one needs to learn.

SKI POLE alludes to personal aids one utilizes for the purpose of avoiding spiritual responsibility.

SKI RESORT signifies spiritual shallowness; the avoidance of higher concepts.

SKI RUN corresponds with a means to swiftly avoid spiritual issues.

SKIRMISH infers a minor conflict.

SKULL represents the encasement of one's thoughts; the embodiment of a person's overall thought patterns.

SKULL AND CROSSBONES are presented as a dire warning. Recall the surrounding dreamscape details for more in-depth interpretation.

SKULLCAP corresponds to thoughts grounded in spiritual beliefs.

SKUNK connotes a strong desire for justice to prevail in life.

SKY reflects the venue for thoughts. Different types of sky will represent specific thought patterns and tendencies.

SKYCAP See porter.

SKYDIVE corresponds to a "dive" into a specific thought or issue. This may also warn of "uncontrolled" thought patterns which could indicate mental instability.

SKYJACKING exposes the "stealing" of another's thoughts or ideas.

SKYLIGHT applies to open-mindedness; a willingness to "let the light in." Recall if the skylight was a specific color. What condition was the glass in?

SKYLINE See horizon.

SKYSCRAPER denotes higher thought utilized throughout one's daily life.

SKYWALK implies the utilization of one's higher intellect in business dealings.

SKYWRITING comes as a personal message from one's inner self or higher awareness. Be sure to recall what was written. Was the writing done in a color?

SLACK represents a waning of energy or motivation.

SLALOM relates to a personally-devised course set to evade spiritual issues.

SLAM portrays emphasis; force.

SLAM-DUNK indicates assuredness; confidence.

SLANDER pertains to vindictiveness; falsehoods.

SLANG will reveal an aspect of an individual's character.

SLANTED illustrates an adulterated aspect; something that has been altered in some manner.

SLATE (rock) implies a "hardness" to one's personality.

SLAUGHTERHOUSE See meatpacking house.

SLAVE denotes servitude. The key here is to recall who was the slave and what he or she was doing for whom.

SLAVE DRIVER characterizes a person who demands hard work from others or perhaps only from self, depending on the surrounding dreamscape details.

SLEAZY portrays extremely poor taste; may indicate a contemptible element.

SLED connotes a life aspect that allows one to skim through life. This is not a positive dream symbol.

SLED DOG represents a friend who encourages an easy life path.

SLEDGE may refer to a "sled" type of symbol or it may indicate a helpful aid in life.

SLEDGEHAMMER depicts forcefulness; a severe personality.

SLEEKNESS suggests refinement.

SLEEPING correlates with unawareness, possibly by choice.

SLEEPING DOG signifies an unaware friend.

SLEEPING PILL exemplifies a willful psychological escape mechanism.

SLEEPWALKING may stand for walking through life without awareness or it may indicate a true "other state" awareness during the sleep state.

SLEET refers to unrecognized spiritual elements that come one's way.

SLEIGH indicates a means of traveling along one's path without exerting personal effort.

SLEIGHT OF HAND reveals deception.

SLEUTH See detective.

SLICE will symbolize a "fragment" of a greater element in one's life; a sample or piece.

SLICK See slippery.

SLICKER See raincoat.

SLIDE (lab) advises of the wisdom to look deeper into some aspect of one's life; a need for analyzation.

SLIDE (playground) warns against a tendency to "slide" through life without giving attention or awareness to important aspects.

SLIDE RULE alludes to the need to apply reason and logic.

SLIDING SCALE indicates the consideration of all associated aspects of an issue.

SLIME denotes an undesirable element with which one must deal.

SLING pertains to a state of being temporarily handicapped.

SLINGSHOT suggests inadequate measures of self-protection.

SLIPPER denotes a restful stage of one's path.

SLIPPERY cautions one to watch his or her step; be careful of one's footing.

SLIPSHOD signifies poor quality; carelessness.

SLIVER illustrates a fragment (negative element) which has the potential to "pierce" and become an irritant.

SLOBBERING exemplifies an inability to communicate one's ideas.

SLOE GIN See alcoholic beverage.

SLOGAN will present a personal message for each dreamer. Recall the exact words of the dream slogan.

SLOOP See sailboat.

SLOPE may represent a slightly more difficult path forthcoming or it may stand for a "slanted" perspective or path, depending on the associated details of the dream.

SLOPPY can be one of those "relative" symbols that will signify different meanings for each dreamer. The surrounding details will be your clarifying factor.

SLOSHING pertains to carelessness; a lack of control or efficient behavior.

SLOTH warns against procrastination.

SLOT MACHINE represents the chances taken in life; the shortcuts attempted.

SLOUCHING may indicate weariness or laziness, depending on the surrounding details.

SLOUCH HAT denotes a lazy mind; an unwillingness to apply mental energy.

SLOW-MOTION comes as an attention-getting device. This symbol advises one to pay closer attention to whatever action or event that has been slowed. This will be a personal message for each dreamer.

SLUDGE refers to waste in one's life; may depict elements that are extraneous or useless.

SLUG See bullet.

SLUG See snail.

SLUICE pertains to the directing of spiritual aspects through one's daily life.

SLUM See skid row.

SLUMBER PARTY represents a group of people who are not seeing an issue with clarity.

SLUMLORD characterizes a person who takes unconscionable advantage of others.

SLURPING refers to the intake of information in an indiscriminate manner.

SLURRING (words) connotes an inability to communicate accurately.

SLUSH applies to spiritual fallacies and extraneous, frivolous aspects of same.

SLUSH FUND portrays reserve resources.

SMALL merely connotes size and, depending on the associated dreamscape details, may indicate a positive or negative message.

SMALL CHANGE signifies insignificance.

SMALL POTATOES correspond to ineffectiveness or inconsequential aspects.

SMALLPOX pertains to a negative element that has infiltrated a person's life.

SMALL PRINT See fine print.

SMALL TALK implies an insignificant communication.

SMALLTIME applies to a minor aspect; of little importance.

SMASHED stands for a destroyed element.

SMEAR (spot) relates to an undefined aspect.

SMEAR CAMPAIGN denotes ruthlessness; slanderous activity.

SMELL applies to the act of testing; discernment.

SMELLING SALTS illustrate a warning to "wake up."

SMELT (fish) depict small spiritual insights.

SMELTER signifies an attempt to maintain a purity and separation of individual ideas and concepts.

SMIDGEN stands for an amount of something, a very small amount; a trace.

SMILE may suggest friendliness, yet the precise interpretation will depend on the surrounding dreamscape details. This smile may be a disguised or sarcastic one.

SMITHSONIAN INSTITUTE represents knowledge and the preservation of same.

SMITHY See blacksmith.

SMOCK infers intentions to work; prepared to expend personal efforts.

SMOG relates to distortion; an unclear perception.

SMOKE constitutes a sign that something is amiss.

SMOKE BOMB warns of deceit.

SMOKE DETECTOR corresponds with a person's inner awareness or insights that alert and warn of approaching trouble.

SMOKEHOUSE typifies preservation.

SMOKEJUMPER characterizes an individual who is capable of diverting or halting dangerous aspects in the lives of others.

SMOKE SCREEN relates to defenses or deceptions. Recall the surrounding dream details.

SMOKE SIGNAL connotes a hidden message; a private means of communication.

SMOKESTACK warns of a dangerous or highly negative aspect in a person's life.

SMOKING represents denied or suppressed emotions.

SMOKING GUN stands for evidence; verification; a cause for suspicion.

SMOKY QUARTZ indicates a clouded perception.

SMOKEY THE BEAR symbolizes watchfulness.

SMOLDERING warns of a volatile situation; an explosive element ready to blow.

SMORGASBORD will portray a variety of opportunities.

SMOTHER See suffocate.

SMUDGE (spot) refers to a marred or contaminated element.

SMUDGE (to clear) signifies an attempt to maintain clarity and rid self or others of negativity.

SMUDGE POT/STICK reflects preservation.

SMUGGLER characterizes deception.

SNACK implies rejuvenation or the reenergizing of self.

SNACK BAR typifies choices.

SNAG exposes an unexpected problem with an issue.

SNAIL stands for a cautious attitude.

SNAKE (nonpoisonous) exemplifies cleverness; proceeding with discernment.

SNAKE (venomous) pertains to swift retaliations or attacks.

SNAKEBITE emphasizes a lack of awareness; caught off guard.

SNAKE CHARMER characterizes a persuasive personality; may indicate manipulation.

SNAKE EYES (dice) advise that one is easily persuaded.

SNAKE OIL pertains to a lack of value; useless.

SNAKE OIL SALESMAN reveals a deceiver.

SNAKE PIT exemplifies a highly dangerous situation, relationship, or belief.

SNAKESKIN implies a swindler; a shiftless personality.

SNAP (fastener) represents a "quick" closure to an event or problem.

SNAPDRAGON illustrates secretiveness; an ability to hold one's tongue; integrity.

SNAPPING TURTLE refers to retaliations.

SNAPSHOT See photograph.

SNARE portrays some type of set-up; a trap.

SNARL warns of an unfriendly attitude; may indicate some type of entanglement.

SNEAKER See tennis shoe.

SNEAK PREVIEW will usually represent personal insights; foresight.

SNEEZE alludes to an adverse reaction to something.

SNICKER suggests concealed amusement.

SNIFF See smell.

SNIFTER implies an intention to ignore or divert one's awareness from responsibility or reality.

SNIPER characterizes a person who has a tendency to conceal true intentions or responses.

SNOB connotes arrogance.

SNOOPY cautions against prying into the affairs of others.

SNOOZE See nap.

SNOOZE ALARM reveals the need for a small amount of additional rest.

SNORING advises that one isn't getting solid rest; indicates a need to improve the quality of respite periods; may warn of an inner restlessness.

SNORKELING pertains to a "surface" spiritual search or interest.

SNOW connotes a strong comprehension and grasp of spiritual truths.

SNOWBALL infers a major spiritual concept. Recall who was throwing the snowball at whom.

SNOW BLINDNESS exposes spiritual blindness, usually self-imposed.

SNOW BLOWER pertains to an effort to rid self and one's surroundings of spiritual elements or influences.

SNOWBOARD See slalom.

SNOWCAP portrays a spiritual priority.

SNOWDRIFT relates to an accumulation of spiritual issues, usually refers to a confusing "buildup" regarding a specific aspect.

SNOW FENCE warns of an attempt to keep spiritual elements contained and out of one's way.

SNOWFLAKE stands for the multiple shimmering aspects of spiritual truths.

SNOW LINE illustrates a person's attempt to separate her or his spiritual aspects from daily secular elements. This may indicate the "hiding" of one's beliefs.

SNOWMAKING connotes the act of bringing one's personal spiritual beliefs into every aspect of life, which may be a negative act depending on this dream's surrounding details.

SNOWMAN emphasizes a state of spiritual arrogance; spirituality that is selective and temporary.

SNOWMOBILE relates to the ease that an individual moves through her or his utilization of spiritual beliefs.

SNOWPLOW denotes paths through spiritual difficulties. This refers to complex spiritual concepts that have been "plowed" through, thereby clearing the way for unobstructed comprehension.

SNOWSHOES represent spiritual respect; softly treading through spiritual elements.

SNOWSTORM warns of a condition of spiritual confusion; an inundation of spiritual issues, usually self-generated.

SNOWSUIT refers to an insulating effort to shield self from spiritual concepts or elements. May also connote a resistant attitude toward blending spirituality with daily life.

SNOW THROWER See snow blower.

SNOW TIRE suggests a desire to comprehend higher spiritual concepts; an attempt to "get through" the deeper elements of same.

SNOW WHITE characterizes an innocent personality; naiveté.

SNUFF (extinguish) portrays a desire to end something; a closure.

SNUFF (tobacco) See tobacco.

SNUFFBOX symbolizes a self-imposed need a for psychological aid.

SNUGGLING (alone under the covers or with your teddy bear) suggests insecurity.

SNUGGLING (with another) suggests warm companionship.

SOAK denotes a permeated condition.

SOAP advises of a cleansing of some type.

SOAPBOX pertains to a personal need to sway or convince others of one's own perspective or attitude.

SOAP OPERA relates to an over-dramatized situation or event.

SOAPSTONE connotes creativity.

SOARING correlates to personal elation; intellectual expansion.

SOBRIETY TEST is most often a call from a person's conscience to maintain awareness.

SOB STORY pertains to a desire or psychological need to obtain sympathy from others; an absorption with self.

SOCCER suggests clever moves; fancy footwork.

SOCIAL (event) alludes to interaction with others.

SOCIAL CLIMBER signifies a psychological need to be better or more successful than one's peers.

SOCIALITE stands for arrogance; a misplaced perspective of self.

SOCIAL REGISTER illustrates those who are self-absorbed.

SOCIAL SECURITY relates to questionable planning.

SOCIAL SERVICE reflects humanitarian intentions.

SOCIAL WORK defines a desire to help those less fortunate.

SOCIOLOGY (study of) indicates a personal interest in the behavior of one's peers.

SOCK See stocking.

SOCKET (electrical) See outlet.

SOCKET (eye) would infer that the socket is empty and therefore denotes a total lack of physical sight yet does not exclude perceptual sight or insights.

SOCKET SET/WRENCH symbolizes resourceful utilization of problem-solving abilities.

SOCRATES emphasizes the fact that solutions can be found within the problem, answers within the question.

SOD typifies an attempt to recover lost ground.

SODA (drink) See soft drink.

SODA CRACKER See cracker.

SODA FOUNTAIN applies to choices in life.

SODA WATER emphasizes spiritual elation.

SODDENED See soak.

SODIUM See salt.

SOFA See couch.

SOFA BED represents duality; multiple opportunities; utilitarian.

SOFT (tactile) signifies gentleness.

SOFT-CORE relates to a "tempered" approach.

SOFT DRINK refers to a "tasteful" and personally satisfying element.

SOFTHEADED denotes a compliant and commiserative personality.

SOFTHEARTED portrays a highly responsive and compassionate nature.

SOFT LANDING symbolizes a gentle closure to an issue.

SOFT-PEDAL pertains to a willful diminishing of something's value or importance; a somewhat deceptive maneuver.

SOFT SELL implies subtleness.

SOFT SHOULDER See shoulder.

SOFT SOAP warns of self-serving methods.

SOFT-SPOKEN usually denotes gentleness, yet may infer manipulation or deception.

SOFT SPOT exposes a specific sentimentality.

SOFT TOUCH cautions against being easily manipulated.

SOFTWARE represents multiple opportunities.

SOFT WATER constitutes groundwork having high potential.

SOGGY See soak.

SOIL corresponds with a person's foundation; ground to build on or progress along.

SOIL CONSERVATION typifies a desire to maintain firm and fertile foundations.

SOJOURN See journey.

SOLACE reflects some type of comfort that may come from others or be self-generated.

SOLAR See sun.

SOLAR BATTERY portrays inner strength.

SOLAR FLARE implies a disruption or intensification of personal strength and/or energy level.

SOLARIUM signifies the strong light that infuses a true spiritual belief system.

SOLAR PANEL connotes an individual's personal capacity for reenergizing oneself. Recall the condition of the solar panels. May also denote an opening of self to God's essence.

SOLAR PLEXUS stands for the center of one's sensitivity, susceptibility, and power.

SOLAR SYSTEM pertains to a fragment of true reality.

SOLAR WIND is a call to give heightened awareness to one's subtle insights.

SOLDER See adhesive for a similar interpretation.

SOLDIER characterizes a person who upholds the honor and safety of others.

SOLDIER OF FORTUNE pertains to a self-serving and nondiscriminatory individual.

SOLEMNITY may indicate high respect, sacredness, or gravity.

SOLICITOR relates to an individual who acts for or with another.

SOLIDARITY constitutes mutual interest or camaraderie.

SOLITAIRE stands for a state of aloneness; a singular element.

SOLITARY CONFINEMENT exposes a situation of absolute exclusion; may advise that one's state of aloneness has been self-induced.

SOLITUDE advises of a need to contemplate; a need for mental or emotional rest.

SOLO emphasizes the fact that one has acted alone or must proceed along his or her path alone.

SOLOMON'S SEAL (botanical) correlates to the strengthening of an individual's inner forces (energies).

SOLOMON'S SEAL (hexagram) constitutes one's inherent abilities; higher insights; strength of one's power.

SOLUBLE connotes the capability and possibility of being ended or concluded.

SOLUTION (liquid) will denote an answer stemming from multiple sources.

SOLUTION (resolution) will come as a key message and be specific to each dreamer.

SOMBRERO signifies withheld thoughts.

SOMERSAULT portrays complex maneuvers made to accomplish a goal or conclusion.

SOMNAMBULISM See sleepwalking.

SOMNOLENT See drowsy.

SONAR symbolizes an individual's inner perceptions; insights; heightened awareness.

SONG will pertain to a specific message according to what was sung.

SONG AND DANCE characterizes an elaborate excuse; complex explanation.

SONGBIRD reflects inner joy; personal happiness.

SONGWRITER characterizes an opportunity to compose and formulate one's own attitude or outlook.

SONIC BARRIER connotes the point at which a person surpasses goals or expectations.

SONIC BOOM signifies the "realization" that one has reached his or her goal.

SONNET See poem.

SONOGRAM portrays a visual impression; an insight; vision.

SOOT exemplifies negative elements that have the capacity to contaminate self or one's life.

SOOTHING will represent a stress-relieving element.

SOOTHSAYER See seeress.

SOPHIST characterizes a person with a tendency to come up with elaborate arguments.

SOPHISTICATE typifies worldly experience.

SOPRANO relates to excitability; an inability to control emotions.

SORBET See juice.

SORCERER warns against the negative utilization of inherent talents or spiritual gifts.

SORCERER'S APPRENTICE cautions against the desire to learn for misguided intentions.

SORORITY illustrates a group of like-minded individuals.

SORREL (color) symbolizes an earthiness; naturalness.

SORREL (botanical) suggests a life element that has the capability of providing inner nourishment.

SORROWFUL may denote melancholia or regret.

SORTIE refers to an attack that may be instigated by oneself depending on the dreamscape's associated details.

SOUFFLÉ reflects a delicate plan; fragile execution of same.

SOUL defines one's vital and prime essence.

SOUND will reveal multiple messages to dreams. Pay close attention to these.

SOUND BARRIER See sonic barrier.

SOUND EFFECTS connote self-generated methods of expressing emphasis.

SOUNDING corresponds to a probing attempt; a method of discovery.

SOUNDING BOARD symbolizes an advisement to share thoughts and emotions with others.

SOUND STAGE denotes a call to be aware of one's actions and words. Recall what type of set was presented. Who was there? Was it a historical period set? Was it lit up or in darkness?

SOUNDTRACK will expose a personal message for each dreamer. Recall what type of music was played. What were the words? Title?

SOUP represents a nourishing aspect generated from multiple elements.

SOUP BOWL means a desire to fulfill one's goals.

SOUP KITCHEN indicates an opportunity to nourish (help) others.

SOUPSPOON suggests an opportunity to "help oneself" to a beneficial resource.

SOUPY (atmosphere) illustrates an unclear or confusing situation.

SOUR indicates a distasteful situation to endure; a hard-to-take or hard-to-accept situation.

SOURBALL connotes a distasteful situation that one voluntarily accepts and plans to carry through to its conclusion.

SOURCE BOOK reveals multiple opportunities to take advantage of.

SOUR CREAM relates to the duality of having a "best case" situation yet possessing a somewhat problematical element.

SOURDOUGH implies unlimited benefits stemming from a singular aspect.

SOUR GRAPES allude to denial.

SOUTH (direction) connotes a "lower" level or a "going back to basics" message.

SOUTHPAW See left-handed.

SOUTH POLE pertains to "basic" elements of an issue or concept.

SOUVENIR symbolizes a reason to remember a specific event in one's life.

SOVEREIGNTY exemplifies preeminence; autonomy.

SOW See hog.

SOW See plant.

SOYBEAN symbolizes a highly nourishing belief.

S

SOYMILK represents the rich benefits of truth.

SPA See health club.

SPACE See cosmos.

SPACE AGE pertains to a minuscule step toward discovering the aspects of true Reality.

SPACE BAR (keyboard) applies to "intentional" spacing; a desire for more room; separation.

SPACE CADET reveals a lack of mental focus.

SPACECRAFT infers a means or opportunity to intellectually reach toward a beginning comprehension of the true Reality.

SPACED-OUT signifies a willful escape from reality and responsibility.

SPACE HEATER constitutes a desire for personal comfort in respect to one's immediate surround; a fear of being exposed to disagreeable situations.

SPACE PROBE represents an individual's choice or opportunity to extend his or her spiritual search to the farthest reaches.

SPACESHIP See spacecraft.

SPACE SHUTTLE reflects the existing freedom to self-discover the reaches of true Reality.

SPACE SUIT portrays a fear of venturing into the farthest reaches of true Reality; a sense one needs protection from discovering the truth.

SPACE WALK represents the tip of humankind's potential.

SPACIOUSNESS applies to unrecognized freedom to self-discover.

SPADE See shovel.

SPADE (card suit) denotes verification; assurances.

SPAGHETTI exemplifies an ability to absorb complexities.

SPANDEX See elastic.

SPANISH MOSS corresponds to little-understood aspects of true Reality; a frequently feared concept to delve into.

SPANKING most often comes as a message from one's conscience and suggests a wrongdoing for which one should make reparations.

SPARE PARTS connote preparedness; resourcefulness.

SPARERIBS typify a need to "get down to the bare bones" of an issue.

SPARE TIRE pertains to preparations made for possible eventualities encountered along one's life path.

SPARK may reflect inspiration or it may warn of a dangerous situation, depending on the surrounding dreamscape details.

SPARKLER emphasizes inner joy generated by spiritual insights.

SPARK PLUG represents an aspect in one's life that serves as an impetus toward action or advancement.

SPARROW corresponds to a gentle intellectual.

SPARSENESS correlates to frugalness; lacking materialism.

SPASM may not infer a shocking incident, but most often represents an "awakening" type of reaction.

SPATULA refers to a personal life element that serves as a beneficial aid.

SPEAKEASY defines shared secrecy.

SPEAKER (audio) indicates a need to hear more clearly; indicates a state of inattention, possibly self-generated.

SPEAKER (person) will usually constitute a message for the dreamer. Recall what was said and by whom.

SPEAKERPHONE indicates a personal ease in communicating with others or it may allude to a need to "share" a conversation.

SPEAKING IN TONGUES See glossolalia.

SPEAR refers to a method of obtaining a desired element or goal.

SPEAR GUN relates to a desire to "spear" specific spiritual truths for the purpose of clear comprehension.

SPEARMINT See mint.

SPECIAL DELIVERY connotes an important message.

SPECIAL EDUCATION stands for a need to gain additional basics.

SPECIAL EFFECTS symbolize emphasis; a need to dramatize for the purpose of greater understanding.

SPECIAL FORCES represent specialized, intensive efforts applied to the accomplishment of a goal.

SPECIAL INTEREST (group) will reveal an individual's concealed intention or attitude.

SPECIAL OLYMPICS stand for personal capabilities regardless of perceived handicaps.

SPECIFICATIONS pertain to the "details" of an issue, situation, or relationship.

SPECIMEN will relate to a sample; an example.

SPECKLED (pattern) denotes the existence of multiple elements.

SPECTATOR reminds us that "someone" is always watching, even if it's our own conscience.

SPECTER See ghost.

SPECTRUM will symbolize the full extent of something; the gamut or far reaches.

SPECULATION warns against making assumptions.

SPEECH portrays a specific message for each dreamer. Recall what was said to whom.

SPEECHLESS may indicate a dumbfounded reaction or it could infer wise discernment, depending on the surrounding dream elements.

SPEECH THERAPY indicates a need to convey thoughts with better clarity.

SPEECHWRITER is a caution to speak for self.

SPEED representations will greatly vary in dreams and will reveal multiple meanings, depending on associated elements.

SPEEDBOAT warns against "speeding" through a spiritual search.

SPEED BUMP exposes a need to slow down.

SPEED FREAK characterizes an individual who continually attempts to get the most out of life through over-expending energies.

SPEEDING reveals a cautionary advisement to slow one's pace for the purpose of recognizing realizations that have been formerly missed.

SPEED LIMIT defines one's suggested pace through life.

SPEEDOMETER will indicate the speed at which one is progressing through life or it will portray an "advisement" for one's proper pace.

SPEED-READING corresponds with a caution to "absorb" more of what one attempts to learn.

SPEED TRAP comes in dreamscapes to warn of the pitfalls of going too fast along one's life path.

SPELL (incantation) may not be a negative dream element, but usually comes as a behavioral advisement.

SPELLBOUND connotes a personal fascination of some type and warns against being in a state lacking logic and reason.

SPELLING BEE exposes specific words for emphasis. These words will come as a unique message for each dreamer.

SPELUNKER characterizes a person who delves far into the deeper elements of specific concepts and belief systems to self-discover any hidden aspects that could serve to broaden her or his understanding.

SPENDTHRIFT connotes efficiency; foresight.

SPHAGNUM See peat moss.

SPHERE implies completion.

SPHINX comes as an advisement that one is close to discovering the totality of true Reality.

SPICES represent personal qualities affecting aspects in one's life;

an individual's unique perspective and how it affects her or his behavior and experiences.

SPIDER may reveal a conniving individual or it may refer to a unique type of personal protective measure. Recall the dream's details for clarity of meaning.

SPIDERMAN represents the utilization of personal talents and insights.

SPIDER VEINS constitute fortitude; path progression in spite of burdens.

SPIEL denotes an effort to persuade.

SPIGOT See faucet.

SPIKE See stake.

SPIKED SHOE symbolizes resentment of one's life problems or burdens.

SPILLWAY represents spiritual excesses or that which is spiritually unnecessary.

SPINACH alludes to a nourishing life element; a beneficial aspect or opportunity.

SPINAL CORD signifies the strength of one's inner life force.

SPINDLE will denote an important part or aspect of another element.

SPINDRIFT See sea spray.

SPINE See backbone.

SPINELESS emphasizes a lack of courage or personal responsibility; may also indicate a lack of individuality.

SPINNING WHEEL corresponds with plans; mental maneuvers.

SPINOFF signifies a resulting product; a benefit or problem stemming from another source.

SPINSTER portrays self-reliance; confidence in self.

SPIRAL (configuration) pertains to the interrelated aspects in one's life.

SPIRE See steeple.

SPIRIT may refer to an entity associated with the dreamer or it may indicate the "power" and energy of one's own life force.

SPIRIT RAPPING connotes a desire to believe; self-deception.

SPITBALL refers to unethical practices.

SPIT CURL stands for an attempt to gain attention.

SPITTLE See saliva.

SPITTOON signifies a "proper place" for specific behavior.

SPLASH GUARD connotes defense mechanisms; methods of protecting self from negative elements.

SPLEEN reflects hidden emotions.

SPLICE signifies an attempt to join aspects; a bond or linkage.

S

SPLINT suggests a supportive measure; an attempt to maintain stability.

SPLINTER exemplifies the entry of a foreign element or belief; an aspect that doesn't belong; an invasion or defilement.

SPLIT represents a breach or fragmentation; a separation of some type.

SPLIT-LEVEL warns of an internal conflict.

SPLIT RAIL (fence) illustrates a self-devised personal perimeter; one's perceptual distance from others.

SPLIT SHIFT implies great personal efforts applied to one's purpose.

SPLURGING suggests self-indulgence; an attempt to comfort or satisfy self.

SPOILAGE relates to inattention given a specific issue or life element.

SPOKESPERSON characterizes a liaison.

SPONGE relates to absorption and most often pertains to a need to listen and/or comprehend better.

SPONGY (consistency) may infer resiliency or it could indicate a lack of firm strength. Recall the dream's details for clarity.

SPONSOR characterizes a person who takes responsibility for another.

SPOOK See ghost.

SPOOKED implies timidity; a fearful nature.

SPOOL See spindle.

SPOON typifies that which one "spoons" out to others or that which one "takes" in.

SPOOR alludes to evidence; proof of one's passing.

SPORE constitutes a small element capable of becoming a major aspect in one's life.

SPORTS symbolize a variety of meanings and need to be defined by the specific type of activity.

SPORTS CAR exemplifies a fast-paced lifestyle and manner of behavior.

SPORTSCAST suggests a personal interest and will reveal one's level of involvement in same.

SPORTS MASSAGE denotes a high interest in "staying in the game" and a determination for same.

SPORTS MEDICINE represents a high interest in healing those who sustain personal injuries while progressing along their life paths or are determined to accomplish their goals.

SPORTS STADIUM applies to a "sit and watch" attitude; procrastination.

SPOT may indicate a defect or

515

marred element in one's life or it can pertain to an attention-getting mark. Recall the dream's associated details.

SPOT CHECK connotes a desire to maintain a status quo condition; a monitoring and watchfulness.

SPOTLESS can denote a too-perfect condition or state.

SPOTLIGHT comes as a dreamscape fragment to point out and reveal important aspects for the dreamer to give attention to.

SPOTTED (pattern) portrays a hidden personality.

SPOTTED FEVER typifies the negativity (illness) brought on by allowing life irritations to "get under the skin" and infect one with resentment or blame.

SPOUSE will signify a bonded connection to another.

SPOUT exposes an inability to contain information.

SPRAIN corresponds with a temporary setback caused by a lack of awareness.

SPRAY (water) illustrates an exposure to new spiritual concepts.

SPREAD See bedspread.

SPREADER (seed) relates to a dissemination of new ideas.

SPREADSHEET constitutes an overall, "at a glance" perspective.

SPRING (metal) represents a tendency to bounce back after some

type of adversity or problem has been encountered; tenacity.

SPRING (season) defines a time for new beginnings.

SPRING (water) stands for a "well" of spirituality within self.

SPRINGBOARD denotes motivation; an impetus.

SPRING BREAK corresponds to a need to take time out from one's efforts applied to purpose or life path.

SPRING FEVER portrays inner joy and anticipation for the start of new beginnings.

SPRINGHOUSE pertains to the utilization of one's spiritual aspects to preserve and maintain the secular elements of life in peak condition and a positive state.

SPRINKLER signifies an attempt to inundate one's life with spiritual aspects; maintaining a spiritual priority with all things.

SPROCKET WHEEL represents a life element capable of maintaining one's forward progression.

SPROUT relates to the "birthing" of new ideas, especially spiritual concepts or the talents associated with same.

SPUN GLASS See fiberglass.

SPUN SUGAR See cotton candy.

SPUR (boot) reveals aggressiveness; the utilization of improper motivational methods.

SPUR TRACK cautions against allowing oneself to get sidetracked.

SPUTTERING implies incoherent communication; an inability to clearly communicate.

SPY indicates an untrustworthy individual.

SPYGLASSES See binoculars.

SQUAD refers to a group of people who have a like interest.

SQUAD CAR symbolizes the mobility (extent) of one's own conscience; an inability to escape one's conscience.

SQUALL represents a temporary state of emotional or mental confusion.

SQUALOR won't necessarily stand for a physical condition, but rather it usually pertains to one's state of mind or set of ethics.

SQUARE (configuration) denotes rigidness; narrow-mindedness.

SQUARE DANCE indicates integral interaction with others.

SQUARE KNOT denotes a firm hold.

SQUARE MEAL illustrates well-rounded nourishment; a fulfilling aspect.

SQUARE ONE connotes the beginning.

SQUARE SHOOTER exemplifies honesty; integrity.

SQUASH (crush) refers to the act of ending something.

SQUASH (fruit) implies a source of energy.

SQUASH (game) suggests a competitive situation, possibly even against self.

SQUASH BLOSSOM (jewelry) pertains to inner strength.

SQUEAKY relates to a stiff and rigid attitude or situation.

SQUEAMISHNESS alludes to a lack of courage.

SQUEEGEE connotes a need to gain clearer perceptions.

SQUEEZING signifies pressure.

SQUELCH stands for the act of silencing something.

SQUID represents a haphazard spiritual search.

SQUIGGLE (pattern) portrays a complexity.

SQUINT relates to an effort to see something better.

SQUIRM implies an uncomfortable situation.

SQUIRREL refers to the act of hoarding. Depending on the dreamscape's associated details, this symbol may indicate a "need" to reserve something or it may reflect a warning against retaining too much.

SQUIRT GUN alludes to unexpected "hits" such as responses from others that are un-characteristic; surprising events.

SQUISHY (consistency) depicts indecision; a lack of solid opinions.

STAB is a symbol containing duality. This could refer to an unexpected retaliation or injury from another, or it might signify an "attempt" at something.

STABILIZER BAR corresponds to a need to balance some aspect of one's life.

STABLE (barn) will reveal an individual's attitude toward her or his personal inherent abilities. Recall the stable's condition.

STACCATO defines an abruptness of personality.

STACK represents an amount of work to be done.

STADIUM denotes the act of observing; may represent a warning to become more involved.

STAFF (people) characterizes those who are ready and willing to assist another.

STAFF (stave) See walking stick.

STAG (deer) implies a self-reliant loner.

STAG (unaccompanied) exemplifies a personal choice to accomplish something by oneself.

STAGE connotes an opportunity or means of expressing self to a multitude of people.

STAGECOACH depicts a plod-ding manner of progression.

STAGE FRIGHT reveals a fear of expressing oneself.

STAGEHAND characterizes an individual who is capable of assisting another to express feelings or opinions.

STAGE-STRUCK portrays a fascination and great desire to perform before others; a need to be seen and heard by many.

STAGGER indicates a need for support; unsteadiness.

STAGNANT connotes a lack of vitality; something that has been allowed to go stale.

STAID portrays a quiet dignity.

STAIN will most often illustrate a negative element in one's life. Recall what was stained. What color was the stain?

STAINED GLASS represents multifaceted elements creating a singular aspect; may denote differential perceptions of various individuals.

STAINLESS STEEL stands for durability; resistant to decay.

STAIRS will pertain to one's ascent or descent in relation to one's life progression or advancement. Recall the type of stairs and the condition of same. Were they a specific color? Lit or dark?

STAKE (bet) indicates a personal interest in something.

STAKE (stick) will denote a "marker" or a "support" of some type.

STAKEOUT advises of a need to be acutely watchful of a particular aspect in one's life.

STALACTITE suggests a "growing" positive philosophy or deduction.

STALAGMITE symbolizes a growing negative element in one's life, most often from within self.

STALE denotes a worn-out issue or attitude; stands for a need to explore new concepts or veer onto a different path.

STALEMATE exposes a futile situation; no chance for an altered course or change to a specific issue.

STALKING warns of a silent pursuit, usually of another individual. Recall who was stalking whom for what purpose.

STALL (animal) See stable.

STALL (halt) indicates a temporary postponement of forward progression.

STALLED ENGINE signifies a waning of one's energy or motivation.

STALLION warns of an uncontrolled strength; a need to contain and direct one's energies.

STAMINA will represent perseverance; fortitude.

STAMMERING indicates an inability to express self clearly.

STAMP (foot) relates to emphasis; may denote impatience or anger.

STAMP (label) will reveal a personal message for each dreamer. Recall what was stamped on what object.

STAMP (postage) See postage stamp.

STAMP COLLECTION constitutes a recognition of a specific aspect's value.

STAMPEDE warns against losing self-control and personal direction; refers to the use of emotionalism rather than intellect.

STAMPING GROUND connotes a private and personal "comfort zone."

STAMP MILL represents intellectual deduction; extracting all informational elements from a singular aspect.

STANDARD (flag) correlates to what one stands for.

STANDBY relates to preparedness; readiness.

STAND-DOWN applies to a withdrawal; a relaxing of immediate plans.

STAND-IN indicates a capable replacement or alternative.

STANDING portrays an adherence to one's convictions.

STANDING ORDER defines a manner of behavior that is practiced until some element alters its effectiveness.

STANDING ROOM may portray a "popular" concept or attitude, or it may represent an advisement to pursue another issue.

STANDOFF See stalemate.

STANDOFFISH will usually portray a reserved individual.

STANDSTILL symbolizes a halt to progression or advancement.

STAPLE (basics) pertains to basic ethics, humanitarian elements, and spiritual foundational aspects.

STAPLE (fastener) typifies a "connective" aspect.

STAPLE GUN relates to a "quick fix."

STAR exemplifies truth and its ultimate search for same.

STAR BEING corresponds with the reality of all humankind; the totality of existing intelligence in all forms.

STARBURST (design) portrays illumination; intellectual enlightenment.

STARCH constitutes firmness. This symbol possesses duality and therefore may indicate a "need" to be more firm in one's relationships or it may reveal a method of behavior that is "too" firm.

STAR-CROSSED pertains to ill fortune; multiple difficulties.

STARDUST stands for moments of inspiration or illumined insights.

STARE suggests focused intensity and won't necessarily indicate any type of negative element.

STARFISH signifies spiritual truths.

STARGAZING represents spiritual speculation; intellectual reaching toward a grasp of the true Reality.

STARKNESS portrays the bare elements of an issue.

STARLIGHT connotes spiritual opportunity to accept the truth.

STARSHIP signifies the relatedness, the connective bond, between all intelligent species.

STARSTRUCK warns against allowing self to become fascinated with others.

STARTER (bread) See sourdough.

STARTER (engine) pertains to a first move; a beginning action that starts a plan or event; motivating factor.

STARTER (player) will indicate the individual who is meant to "begin" something; reveals who should make the first move.

STARTING GATE warns against life competition.

STARTING LINE reflects the beginning point.

STARTLED signifies an unexpected event.

STARVATION implies a serious lack of a nourishing element in one's life; the absence of mental, emotional, or spiritual nourishment.

STASH stands for hidden elements in one's life; that which one conceals.

STATEROOM cautions against the tendency to compartmentalize spiritual truths.

STATESWOMAN characterizes a respected person of authority.

STATIC (electricity) warns of a state of mental dysfunction.

STATIC (sound) connotes an interruption in communication that may be self-generated.

STATION (depot) See depot.

STATION (position) illustrates where one should be and what she or he should be doing.

STATION (transmitted) implies a frequency; a vibratory rate. Recall what was being said on the radio or TV station.

STATION BREAK refers to a temporary break in communication.

STATIONERY symbolizes a need to communicate with another.

STATISTICIAN characterizes a person who possesses verifying information.

STATUE presents a specific message for each dreamer. The type of statue will have a unique relation to the dreamer.

STATUE OF LIBERTY emphasizes the ideal of equality and freedom.

STATUESQUE pertains to a dignified personality.

STATUS SYMBOL reveals self-absorption; a desire to possess prime material goods. This dream symbol exposes a person who judges one's worth or success by what one owns.

STATUTE will signify a specific law that may relate to ethical, moral, or spiritual aspects.

STEAK connotes high energy; a motivational factor.

STEAL reveals an unwillingness to expend efforts toward goals; impatience.

STEALTHY implies dishonesty or secretiveness.

STEAM portrays spiritual activity.

STEAM BATH exemplifies being steeped in spiritual endeavors or elements.

STEAMBOAT represents a spiritual search generated by pure spiritual motivations.

STEAMER TRUNK stands for

the spiritual tools and elements we carry with us along our life path.

STEAM IRON relates to the utilization of spirituality to resolve problems.

STEAMROLLER will warn of negative control.

STEAM SHOVEL pertains to spiritual work.

STEEL relates to strength.

STEEL MILL connotes the many forms that strength can take in life.

STEEL TRAP illustrates astute intelligence; a quick wit.

STEEL WOOL symbolizes insensitivity.

STEEP (vertical) will most often stand for a great depth; rich in meaning or philosophical content. This symbol may also represent a difficult or exacting aspect.

STEEP (soak) exemplifies thoroughness.

STEEPLE suggests a "high point" to an issue or event.

STEEPLEJACK represents an individual who is not afraid to approach high concepts or reach for a comprehension to complexities.

STEER (guide) connotes directional control. Each individual needs to steer oneself along his or her life path.

STEINEM (Gloria) symbolizes the realization of one's self-worth and unlimited potential.

STELE signifies an "impression" of something important to the dreamer. This will be different for everyone.

STEM (stalk) represents the supporting factor of an element.

STENCH denotes the presence of a serious negative element.

STENCIL defines an example; a template to follow.

STENOGRAPHER characterizes an individual who remembers another's words; a record of communication.

STEP See stairs.

STEPLADDER signifies the careful taking of "one step at a time" for cautious life progression.

STEP STOOL represents an aid to progression.

STEREO (equipment) stands for the utilization of one's full potential.

STEREOTYPE pertains to a typecast personality or situation.

STERILE symbolizes a condition free of negative elements.

STERLING portrays the highest quality.

STETHOSCOPE defines emotional sensitivity.

STEVEDORE See longshore-men.

STEW stands for anxiety; worry; a confusing complexity.

STEWARDESS pertains to those aides around you while progressing along your life's path.

STICK signifies an opportunity for self-expression that may be a positive or negative element depending on the dreamscape's surrounding details.

STICKER (gummed) will present a personal message for each dreamer, depending on what the sticker symbolized or said.

STICKER (thorn) See thistle.

STICKER PRICE depicts an exaggerated worth

STICK FIGURE symbolizes the beginning formation of an idea or theory.

STICKINESS pertains to a precarious situation or relationship.

STIFF portrays rigidness; a hard personality.

STIFF-NECKED warns of an inability to view all angles; limited perceptual range.

STIFF UPPER LIP alludes to hidden emotions.

STIFLING cautions of a repressive element or situation.

STIGMA relates to a "sign" or mark revealing a specific quality or characteristic.

STILE applies to an aid to advancement.

STILETTO See dagger.

STILLBIRTH portrays an unproductive beginning; a bad start.

STILL LIFE (painting) will portray an important element for the dreamer to give awake-state attention to. This connotation will be different for each dreamer.

STIMULANT applies to a motivational factor.

STING represents an ulterior motive.

STINGER (insect) pertains to a negative rebound response.

STINGRAY exposes a false prophet.

STINGINESS warns against selfishness, greed, and being within a self-absorbed state.

STINK See stench.

STINK BOMB signifies retaliation; a serious rebounding action.

STINKBUG stands for natural talents utilized in a negative manner.

STIPEND connotes one's allowable limits.

STIPULATION reveals a "condition" associated with a specific element.

STIR usually implies that something in one's life is being "stirred up" and suggests watchfulness.

STIR-CRAZY denotes a lack of acceptance and/or patience.

STIR-FRY calls for a need to insure something is "cooked" thoroughly, as in fully completed.

STIRRUP portrays an advisement to get a firm foothold.

STITCH (pain) comes as a caution against going too fast or forcing an issue.

STITCH (sewn) indicates the act of pulling something together; an attempt to "connect" elements.

STOCK See cattle.

STOCK See stock certificate.

STOCK (soup) relates to a heartiness; rounded nourishment.

STOCK (supplies) represents preparedness; resourcefulness; forethought.

STOCKADE See corral.

STOCKBROKER characterizes one who takes risks with another's assets.

STOCK CAR See racecar.

STOCK CERTIFICATE relates to a personal interest (stake) in something.

STOCK EXCHANGE signifies great stress.

STOCKING pertains to "covering" one's footsteps.

STOCKING MASK refers to deception; an attempt to hide self.

STOCKPILE See storage. This symbol could advise one to *stop* hoarding and share with others. This depends on what was shown to be stockpiled.

STOCKROOM will reveal what one should be retaining and reserving.

STOCKYARD See corral.

STOKE implies a need to rekindle some aspect in one's life.

STOMACH alludes to fortitude.

STOMACHACHE reveals a lack of inner strength or may indicate heightened sensitivity.

STOMACH PUMP exposes an attempt to rid self of an undesirable life aspect.

STOMP typifies an adverse reaction; an inability to contain emotions.

STONE usually refers to life's smaller irritations.

STONE AGE connotes a backward or primitive idea, perspective, or manner of behavior.

STONECUTTER See jeweler.

STONE-FACED signifies a desire to conceal responses.

STONE-GROUND pertains to a "natural" method of accomplishing something.

STONEHENGE connotes lost aspects of true Reality.

STONEMASON See bricklayer.

STONEWALL implies delaying tactics.

STONEWARE symbolizes simplicity.

STONEWORK See masonry.

STOOGE characterizes one who is easily manipulated.

STOOL typifies an aid that assists one's advancement or progression.

STOOP See bent.

STOOP See stairs.

STOPCOCK See faucet.

STOPLIGHT portrays a temporary halt to one's advancement.

STOPOVER illustrates a need to experience a particular event or communion along one's life path.

STOP PAYMENT (order) constitutes a change in plans.

STOPPER correlates to containment; keeping something from getting away or escaping from one's control.

STOP SIGN represents an advisement to stop one's forward progression for a time. Frequently this will constitute a forewarning.

STOPWATCH cautions one to pace life according to "acceptance" rather than attempting to "force" matters, thereby making life more complex and difficult.

STORAGE connotes having reserves; preparedness.

STORE See shop.

STOREFRONT pertains to a perception of one's best opportunities that are currently available.

STOREKEEPER characterizes a person who is capable of providing various opportunities.

STORK typifies the approach of a new idea or perception; may denote a new direction.

STORM pertains to a troublesome time; emotional upheavals.

STORM CELLAR signifies one's personal methods of emotional defenses.

STORM DOOR relates to one's free will decision to open self to emotional involvement or to remain closed to same.

STORM DRAIN denotes an advisement to "release" one's emotional or psychological burdens and allow them to "flow" away from self.

STORM TROOPER characterizes a highly aggressive personality.

STORM WINDOW represents insulated (protected) perceptions; a desire to maintain personal distance.

STORYBOOK will reveal a personal message for each dreamer. Recall the storybook's title. What was the message of the story? Was someone reading it or handing it to you?

STORYTELLER characterizes

one who is interested in preserving the truth.

STOVE denotes an opportunity to complete an aspect in one's life; a means to "cook it" (bring to fruition).

STOVEPIPE connotes an "exit" route for negative elements in one's life.

STOVEPIPE HAT alludes to "tall" thoughts that are unexpressed or purposely suppressed; a need to release or express self.

STOWAWAY refers to personal unawareness.

STOWE (Harriet Beecher) represents human rights.

STRADDLE usually applies to indecision; may indicate a desire to remain neutral.

STRAGGLER won't necessarily indicate procrastination, but usually symbolizes one who is cautious and discerning when in a group situation.

STRAIGHT ARROW may portray an upright attitude or it may stand for a closed mind, depending on the associated dream details.

STRAIGHT FACE See stone-faced.

STRAIGHT RAZOR suggests a serious and focused personality.

STRAIGHT SHOOTER signifies honesty.

STRAINER implies the need to "sift" through something; cautions against "taking everything in" indiscriminately; discernment.

STRAITJACKET comes as a strong advisement to "straighten out" one's life, thoughts, emotions, perceptions, or belief systems.

STRAIT-LACED usually refers to an opinionated and unyielding nature.

STRANGER most often appears in dreams as a messenger. Recall how this stranger made you feel. How was she or he dressed? What was said or done?

STRANGLEHOLD connotes a state of being manipulated; forced or controlled.

STRANGULATION exposes a "choking" condition; a need to free self from a suffocating relationship or situation. Who was strangling whom?

STRAP portrays a means of carrying something through life; may indicate a support or burden depending, on the surrounding dreamscape details.

STRATEGIST characterizes an individual who is highly capable of thorough planning or analyzation.

STRAW represents an "insulating" quality.

STRAWBERRY constitutes a congenial, cheerful nature.

STRAWBERRY MARK See birthmark.

STRAW HAT represents confidence in one's perceptions and beliefs.

STRAW MAN See scarecrow.

STRAW VOTE denotes an interest in the opinions of others.

STREAK (mark) symbolizes a "touch" of a differing element contained in a specific aspect.

STREAK (run naked) pertains to an unexpected event or something presented for its shock value; may even mean a personal "wake-up" call.

STREAM applies to the changing course one's spiritual search takes.

STREAMBED connotes the opportunity to discover spiritual riches.

STREAMER correlates to an attention-getting message. It says, "Hey, look over here. Look at this!"

STREAMLINED typifies an element or life aspect, even a belief or perspective, that has been pared down to an efficient form consisting of its basic essence, rid of the extraneous, superfluous elements.

STREET will depict a byway; a course one has an option of traveling. Did the street have a name? Was it lit or dark? Was it deserted or crowded?

STREETCAR See cable car.

STREETLIGHT brightens one's path. Recall if the streetlight focused on a particular shop, dwelling, or individual. Did it light up a sign?

STREET SMARTS symbolize personal survival skills and pertain to how well one is prepared to handle difficulties encountered throughout life.

STREETWALKER See prostitute.

STREP THROAT exposes a state of negative communication; indicates a current stage of negativity toward another.

STREPTOMYCIN See antibiotic.

STRESS warns of a mental and emotional state in which the saving quality of "acceptance" is lacking.

STRESS TEST comes as a personal advisement to check self for how one is dealing with troublesome situations.

STRETCHER signifies a warning. Who was on the stretcher? This is a forewarning.

STRETCHING suggests "reaching" farther; expanding one's mind or perception of possibilities.

STRETCH MARK is a reminder that one has "stretched" his or her potential or perceptions in the past and can do it again.

STREUSEL signifies the "topping" (final touch) to something.

STRIKE (work halt) reveals a personal dissatisfaction with how one's life is progressing; a need for change.

STRIKEBREAKER represents a negative element that temporarily prevents one from changing his or her life course.

STRIKEOUT denotes unsuccessful attempts.

STRIKEOVER signifies an indifference toward one's mistakes; no attempt made to cover them.

STRING usually connotes an idea; the beginning formulation of a new concept or theory.

STRINGER (timber) alludes to a stabilizing factor in one's life.

STRINGER (writer) represents information from different sources.

STRIPE (pattern) indicates duality; multiple perceptions of one element; unpredictability.

STRIP MINE implies a negative aspect that distorts the quality or inherent integrity of something.

STRIPPED-DOWN relates to the existence of essential elements only.

STROBE LIGHT signifies an attempt to alter reality.

STROKE (brain) warns of a harmful negative idea or emotion existing within one.

STROKE (soothe) reflects sympathy; an effort to comfort self or another.

STROKE (sun) cautions against expending too much energy; calls for awareness and discernment.

STROLLER connotes a new birth or new course with which one is content; the feeling of ease a new attitude brings.

STROLLING signifies acceptance in one's life; the taking of each hour at a time; the understanding that one can't "force" certain things.

STRONG-ARM (tactics) warns of the harmful effects of attempting to "force" issues or results.

STRONGBOX suggests a recognition of life's valuable aspects.

STRONGHOLD portrays one's personally protected defenses.

STRONG SUIT reveals an individual's area of strength or talent.

STROP advises of a need to "sharpen" one's perception.

STRUGGLE usually defines an internal conflict; a lack of acceptance.

STRUMMING exemplifies a relaxed attitude; acceptance.

STRUNG-OUT warns of an inability to cope or deal with one life aspect at a time.

S

STRUT (brace) connotes a supportive element in one's life.

STRUT (stride) exposes arrogance.

STRYCHNINE See poison.

STUBBLE (bristly) represents roughness; incompleteness.

STUBBORN implies determination; strong sense of direction.

STUCCO refers to a lasting finish to something.

STUD (framing) applies to a supportive factor for an idea or plan.

STUD (pin/earring) indicates an altered perspective.

STUD (snowtires) portrays a desire to thoroughly grasp spiritual ideas.

STUDENT connotes one who requires further learning experiences.

STUDENT TEACHER signifies a future teacher who still needs more experience.

STUDENT UNION relates to the need for relaxation times interspersed with efforts applied to learning.

STUD FINDER illustrates a search for supportive elements in one's life.

STUDIO will pertain to one of the arts. Refer to photography, artist, etc.

STUDY See library.

STUDY HALL suggests serious efforts are required toward researching and discovering all facets of a particular issue or concept.

STUFFED SHIRT reveals a haughty personality.

STUFFING corresponds to a padding or filler element added to something; extraneous aspect; exaggerations.

STUMBLING depicts an attempt to find one's way; an unsure course.

STUMBLING BLOCK denotes a temporary setback.

STUMP (tree) portrays inherent talents or abilities that are denied.

STUN GUN may indicate the manifestation of an unexpected event that shocks one or it could signify a need to temporarily halt one's current efforts applied to a particular issue.

STUNT DOUBLE (acting) comes as a warning against letting others do your difficult tasks in life.

STUPOR implies a state of mental confusion or unawareness.

STUTTERING symbolizes an inability to communicate one's thoughts.

STY See pigpen.

STY (eye) applies to a negatively affected perception.

STYGIAN (atmosphere) denotes a heavy, negative atmosphere, often self-generated.

STYLUS pertains to precision.

STYPTIC STICK signifies an attempt to resolve a problematical element.

STYROFOAM represents an insulating quality to an aspect.

STYX RIVER (Greek mythology) comes as a warning to change one's ways or be on the watch for forthcoming dangers in one's life.

SUAVE stands for finesse; diplomacy.

SUBCONSCIOUS constitutes hidden issues and aspects of one's awake-state consciousness.

SUBCONTRACTOR characterizes an individual capable of assisting another or carrying a portion of another's burden.

SUBCULTURE suggests a differing perspective.

SUBDIVIDED implies a need to "break down" an idea for the purpose of clarification or analyzation.

SUBDIVISION (residential) denotes diverse perspectives; the existence of multiple ideas and issues.

SUBDUE refers to the act of overcoming something in one's life.

SUBFLOOR portrays an under-current; a secondary foundational factor.

SUBLET exemplifies the absorption or sharing of another's perspective.

SUBLIMINAL depicts an incomplete thought; hint; partial idea or unformed theory.

SUBMARINE comes as a warning against spiritual hypocrisy.

SUBMARINE SANDWICH reveals an unrecognized benefit in one's life.

SUBMERGED See immersion.

SUBMISSIVENESS refers to a tendency to be easily manipulated.

SUBORDINATE reveals one's position in relation to a specific life aspect.

SUBPOENA stands for a need to communicate important information.

SUBSCRIPTION will expose an individual's attitude, tendency, or personal interest; may even illustrate hidden perspectives or opinions.

SUBSERVIENCE denotes a tendency to defer to others.

SUBSIDY exemplifies some type of assistance given or obtained.

SUBSTANCE ABUSE connotes a lack of self-control; dependency; an inability to face reality and/or personal responsibility.

S

SUBSTANDARD exposes behavior or qualities that do not meet acceptable levels.

SUBSTANTIATE signifies some type of verification.

SUBSTITUTION denotes an alternative.

SUBTERFUGE indicates some type of deception.

SUBTITLE will constitute an explanation or give a clue to what something is about.

SUBTRACTION (symbol) refers to a need to lessen some element in one's life.

SUBURB connotes an intermediate placement or position; a middle of the road yet structured perspective.

SUBVERSION pertains to an attempt to undermine a plan or individual.

SUBWAY stands for an alternate course of action; clever evasiveness.

SUCCULENT (plant) connotes a highly desirable aspect or plan that will be successful.

SUCKER (candy) applies to an easily manipulated individual.

SUCKER (fish) reveals a state of spiritual gullibility.

SUCKLE depicts a dependence on another.

SUCTION PUMP represents a withdrawal; a pulling back movement.

SUEDE refers to a naturalness; no false affectations.

SUE See lawsuit.

SUET stands for multifaceted utilization.

SUFFERANCE suggests gentle acceptance; forbearance.

SUFFOCATE reflects a state of perceived smothering; usually reveals a self-generated condition.

SUFFUSED refers to a thoroughness; interspersed throughout.

SUGAR may exemplify an energizing element or it may allude to a highly desirable aspect in one's life.

SUGAR CANE FIELD suggests a "source" producing a desirable aspect.

SUGARCOATING warns of an attempt to deceive; trying to alter reality.

SUGAR DADDY characterizes an individual who retards one's inner growth.

SUGERHOUSE See maple syrup.

SUGGESTION BOX denotes one's ability to make improvements.

SUICIDE reveals a loss of inner strength and the perception of being a spiritual essence of God.

SUICIDE WATCH portrays a recognition and attentive monitoring given to an individual who has lost his or her course and strength to persevere.

SUIT pertains to a formality; formal behavior.

SUITE (rooms) implies a temporary state of comfort.

SUITOR relates to heightened attention given another.

SULFUR exemplifies a disagreeable element in one's life.

SULTANA pertains to an expectation of deference.

SULTRY portrays a tough or sticky situation.

SUMMARY will reveal a concise message that will mean something specific to the dreamer.

SUMMER (season) illustrates the fruitful time to give heightened attention and effort to life goals and spiritual journeys.

SUMMERHOUSE See gazebo.

SUMMER SCHOOL suggests a need for additional information or instruction.

SUMMIT stands for high points in one's life or spiritual journey.

SUMMIT CONFERENCE stands for a serious need for an important communication; an advisement to generate a major discussion.

SUMMONS exposes a serious warning for one to answer for erring ways.

SUMMONS SERVER indicates a conscious awareness of one's wrongdoings; an inability to hide from the truth.

SUMP PUMP signifies a need to rid self of negative or erroneous spiritual beliefs or perceptions.

SUN stands for God.

SUNBATHING applies to a desire to "absorb" spirituality within self.

SUNBEAM pertains to spiritual illumination.

SUN BLOCK denotes an attempt to keep a specified distance from spiritual matters.

SUNBURN forewarns of a state of being spiritually burned by a false concept or perception.

SUNBURST (design) symbolizes the simplicity of God's truths.

SUN DANCE represents inner strength.

SUNDAY connotes a time of reflection on one's behavior, perceptions, and life course.

SUNDAY SCHOOL signifies the deep insights gained from serious reflection and contemplation.

SUN DECK typifies a desire to remain connected with God's essence while on one's spiritual journey.

SUNDIAL comes as a message that advises of "now" being the time to reconnect with God.

S

SUNFISH refers to the joy taken in one's quiet comfort in personal spirituality.

SUNFLOWER specifically symbolizes spiritual joy.

SUNGLASSES expose an altered perspective that is colored by personal opinions or psychological elements. Recall the color of the lens.

SUNKEN represents a "lowering" direction which usually applies to an attempt to reach "basic" elements or get in touch with self by being grounded.

SUNKEN GARDEN signifies efforts to maintain one's inner integrity and remain grounded.

SUN LAMP reflects artificial spirituality.

SUNRISE pertains to an inner welling of spiritual joy.

SUNROOF stands for a desire to remain God-connected while traversing one's life path.

SUNROOM portrays a home life permeated with spirituality.

SUNSCREEN See sun block.

SUNSET constitutes the most spiritually intense or powerful time.

SUNSPOT connotes heightened spiritual activity.

SUNSTROKE represents a lack in personal spiritual discernment; an inability to control which concepts are accepted.

SUNTAN refers to a routine exposure to spiritual elements.

SUPERFICIAL reveals a fear of becoming involved; a hesitancy to delve into the deeper aspects of true Reality.

SUPERHUMAN (qualities) relate to inner strengths.

SUPERIMPOSED (image) exposes the existence of a dual nature or personality as evidenced by that which one presents to others and that which is kept hidden.

SUPERINTENDENT will usually signify who is in charge. Recall the surrounding dreamscape details to determine "what" this superintendent was in charge of.

SUPERMAN See superhuman.

SUPERMARKET See market.

SUPERNATURAL stands for perceptual and intellectual ignorance of the interrelating elements of true Reality.

SUPERNOVA marks the recognition of a major spiritual insight.

SUPERPOWER pertains to those with the most power and authority, but not necessarily possessing the proper ethics, morals, and spiritual qualities.

SUPERRICH identifies those with the greatest quantity of bountiful assets, thereby revealing those with the greatest spiritual responsibility to help others.

SUPERSONIC denotes a reach or

existence beyond popular, generally accepted concepts; into the realm of deeper thought.

SUPERSTAR represents great potential. The key here is to discern "how" this potential is utilized.

SUPERSTITION defines an ignorance of the interacting elements of true Reality.

SUPERSTORE portrays a chance to take advantage of a great range of opportunities.

SUPERSTRUCTURE refers to any idea, perception, plan, or belief developed beyond its basic elements.

SUPERTANKER warns against carrying excess burdens or extraneous elements while traversing one's spiritual course.

SUPERVISOR most often connotes self and one's conscience.

SUPINE (position) relates to a time of rest, neutrality, or acceptance.

SUPPER pertains to a need to re-energize and nourish self.

SUPPLENESS suggests personal tenacity; an ability to cope and manage almost any situation.

SUPPLEMENT infers the need for an additional element in one's life.

SUPPLICANT implies a lack of self-confidence and reliance.

SUPPORT HOSE means a personal recognition that one requires additional support as she or he travels through life.

SUPPOSITION will not denote an assumption, but rather one's deeper thoughts and exploratory reaches into deeper theories and concepts.

SUPPOSITORY suggests that something within self is lacking.

SUPREME BEING See God.

SUPREME COURT alludes to a need to give researched and contemplative time to a major decision or plan.

SURCHARGE exposes an overwhelming situation.

SURE-FOOTED relates to high confidence; self-reliance.

SURF illustrates spiritual movement; the living essence of same.

SURFBOARD pertains to the participation in a spiritual movement which can be within self rather than group-related.

SURGE connotes a sudden increase in activity, energy, or interest.

SURGEON relates to precision and skill.

SURGE PROTECTOR signifies a method of self-monitoring one's energy levels and guarding against "draining" elements or individuals.

SURGICAL SHOE COVERINGS represent a path walked in

fear of being touched by any negatives.

SURPLUS STORE represents multiple opportunities.

SURREALISM represents an altered perspective of reality.

SURRENDER usually represents an advisement to accept more rather than having expectations or attempting to force results.

SURREPTITIOUS portrays deception.

SURROGATE See substitution.

SURTAX denotes an additional element of payment or retribution attached to a specific life aspect.

SURVEILLANCE advises of a need to heighten one's awareness; watchfulness.

SURVEY (measure) cautions one to exercise precise planning.

SURVEY (poll) portrays an interest in the opinion of others.

SURVEYOR relates to an individual who is fragmenting his or her life course.

SURVIVALIST emphasizes self-reliance; resourcefulness.

SUSPECT marks a questionable individual, plan, or concept.

SUSPENDERS pertain to a "supportive" element that allows one to hold up under adversity.

SUSPENSE warns against anticipation; advises of the wisdom of maintaining acceptance.

SUSPENSION BRIDGE symbolizes an extended transition period.

SUTTEE exposes a negative self-sacrificing act.

SUTURE correlates to an initial aspect that serves to promote healing.

SVELTE connotes a tendency to keep to the essentials, basics.

SVENGALI reveals an individual who manipulates others for negative purposes.

SWAB pertains to a need to "go over" something; possibly recheck or review.

SWALLOW (bird) refers to shyness; timidness.

SWALLOW (consume) implies the ingestion of a specific aspect.

SWAMI See yogi.

SWAMP constitutes a weak or confused spiritual foundation.

SWAMP BOAT defines an effort to get through spiritual confusion.

SWAMP FEVER indicates the effects of becoming immersed in spiritual confusion.

SWAMP GAS refers to spiritual "gas" signifying conceptual "waste."

SWAN exemplifies an individual's beautiful and grace-filled spiritual nature; inherent spiritual essence and resulting gifts.

SWAN SONG stands for an end to a specific life stage of direction.

SWAP MEET represents the opportunities to share talents and abilities.

SWARM suggests an overwhelming element in one's life.

SWASHBUCKLER exposes a tendency to dramatize or flaunt self.

SWASTIKA (configuration) may not stand for a highly negative element, but rather for its original symbology, that of a religious sign of good luck or that one's fortune will be improving.

SWATCH (cloth) portrays a "sample" of one's hidden personality or inner character. Recall the type of cloth and color.

SWAYBACK reflects a burdensome phase of life.

SWAYING suggests a tendency to change one's mind; indecision.

SWEAR (cuss) implies an intent to express emphasis.

SWEAR (vow) signifies personal validation.

SWEAT indicates personal effort expended.

SWEATBAND represents an attempt to control one's efforts applied to a specific project or goal.

SWEATER suggests warmth of character. Recall the style, texture, and color for additional information.

SWEATSHOP warns against forcing efforts, especially the manipulating the efforts of others.

SWEEPING exemplifies a tendency to maintain a "clear" path in life.

SWEEPSTAKES See lottery.

SWEET most often reflects a desirable element in one's life.

SWEET-AND-SOUR marks an element containing the dual aspects of positive and negative factors; pleasing yet somewhat problematical.

SWEETENER indicates an attempt to make something more palatable or attractive.

SWEETHEART pertains to an individual for whom one has special affection.

SWEETGRASS BRAID implies thoughts of respect and honor.

SWEET PEA refers to a "clinging" idea; a solid grasp.

SWEET POTATO symbolizes an agreeable element in one's life; an essential aspect that is pleasing.

SWEET TALK See flattery.

SWEET TOOTH correlates to a strong desire for life to contain only desirable aspects; an inability to deal with reality without "sweetening" it with pleasure.

SWELLING See swollen.

SWELTERING represents an inability to deal well with pressure.

SWERVE comes as an advisement to heighten awareness; avoidance and the perceptual awareness to accomplish same.

SWIG suggests an ability to accept and deal with disagreeable elements.

SWIM FINS stands for impatience to gain spiritual development.

SWIMMING symbolizes a submersion in one's spiritual search.

SWIMMING POOL reflects a spiritual search going nowhere; spiritual concepts "treated" with artificial elements.

SWINDLER exposes an individual intent on deception and ulterior motives.

SWINE pertains to excesses indulged in.

SWING (child's) denotes perceptual innocence; an ability to be open to alternative views and broadscope concepts.

SWING SHIFT advises of a need to experience alternate phases and elements of a specific aspect.

SWIRL (pattern) relates to a convoluted idea, plan, or perspective.

SWITCH (any type) reminds us that we possess the power to make our own decisions; taking personal responsibility.

SWITCHBACK alludes to retaining past knowledge; infers that one isn't retaining that which has been learned and isn't applying experiential knowledge gained throughout life.

SWITCHBLADE exposes a tendency toward knee-jerk reactions.

SWITCHBOARD signifies an opportunity to make multiple contacts; a means of obtaining expanded information.

SWITCHMAN will signify an individual who is capable of altering one's course in life.

SWIVEL CHAIR represents convenience; a means of efficient methodology.

SWIVEL HOOK exemplifies a capability to analyze all angles.

SWIZZLE See alcoholic beverage.

SWIZZLE STICK pertains to a means of blending or coordinating various aspects.

SWOLLEN indicates an "expanded" element.

SWOON portrays an overwhelming response.

SWORD connotes a self-defensive element; means of protecting one's position.

SWORD DANCE corresponds to the feeling of confidence and self-reliance that one's protective measures provide.

SWORDFISH apply to spiritual defensiveness.

SYLPH characterizes spiritual grace.

SYLVAN See forest.

SYMBIOSIS exposes a personal need for another individual that may or may not be productive or mutually beneficial.

SYMMETRY portrays balance.

SYMPATHY may reveal a need to give compassion to another or it may warn against "using" same for self-gratification.

SYMPHONY pertains to coordinated efforts of multiple talents.

SYMPOSIUM illustrates the convergence of ideas.

SYNAGOGUE reflects spiritual associations and the living practice of one's beliefs.

SYNCHRONICITY represents destiny.

SYNDICATE connotes an affiliation of like-minded individual's with a common goal.

SYNDROME suggests a particular personality aspect generated from various causes; may denote a unique perspective derived from multiple experiential sources.

SYNOPSIS will symbolize a basic idea or elemental facts.

SYNTHESIZER stands for a means of combining various ideas or concepts.

SYNTHETIC applies to an artificial aspect; an alternate.

SYRINGE represents a means of interjection or application.

SYRUP portrays over-dramatization; flattery; false sincerity.

SYSTEMS ANALYST characterizes an individual who is capable of discovering the most efficient course of action or means of reaching a goal.

T

TABASCO represents a highly interesting subject; excitability.

TABERNACLE denotes sacredness or that which is perceived as being sacred. Recall what was in the tabernacle? Where was it? What color was it?

TABLE pertains to an element of support and convenience.

TABLEAU will illustrate an important message presented as a scene for the dreamer to view.

TABLECLOTH being fabric will reveal multiple aspects. Recall the condition, type of fabric, design, and color.

TABLE OF CONTENTS portrays the main or basic issues the dreamer currently needs to address in life.

TABLE SALT See salt.

TABLESPOON denotes a larger measure; in reference to some type of life aspect it would indicate an ingredient of considerable importance.

TABLET (ancient) suggests a true element of reality or a timeless truth.

TABLET (pill) See pill.

TABLE TALK connotes surface conversation; containing no deep or heavy material.

TABLEWARE See specific utensil.

TABLOID See newspaper.

TABOO exemplifies a subject or life aspect one fears or avoids.

TABULATE advises one to gather up all elements of an aspect and analyze it in a concise manner.

TACHOMETER indicates speed. Recall if the dreamer was being advised to slow up or increase rate of progression.

TACK (equipment) will relate to essential elements required for a specific purpose.

TACK (nail) pertains to a temporary attachment.

TACKLE (fishing) connotes spiritual accessories that are unnecessary for enlightenment or development.

TACKY implies a "sticky" situation.

TACTICS stand for plans.

TADPOLE correlates to spiritual immaturity; a novitiate seeker.

TAE KWON DO See martial arts.

TAFFETA (fabric) will indicate a "stiff" personality that appears to be amenable.

TAFFY symbolizes difficulties in

life; situations where one needs to "pull" self up and persevere.

TAG (game) warns against avoiding responsibility or a tendency to place same upon another's shoulders.

TAG See label.

TAGALONG portrays a lack of individual purpose or life course.

TAI CHI relates to self-control generated from spiritual inner peace.

TAIL (end) illustrates a position marking "last" or final element.

TAIL (follow) denotes a personal special interest in someone.

TAIL (pet) signifies a friend's attitude. Recall if the tail was wagging, hanging down, held up, etc.

TAILBONE See coccyx bone.

TAILGATING represents a lack of individuality; comes as a warning to stop "following another" so closely.

TAILLIGHT stands for an aspect (sign) that marks one's presence; making oneself visible or effective.

TAILOR See seamstress.

TAILOR-MADE See custom-built.

TAILPIPE portrays a means or outlet for negative emotions or attitudes.

TAILSPIN implies total confusion; chasing one's tail; going in circles.

TAIL WIND relates to an element that serves to increase the pace of one's life progression or enhances the time it takes to accomplish a goal.

TAKEOVER means overwhelmed; a loss of authority or personal responsibility.

TALCUM POWDER represents a personal means of self-control.

TALENTS correspond to inherent abilities unique to each individual.

TALENT SHOW defines the ability one perceives is his or her best talent.

TALISMAN connotes misplaced faith; possible superstition; lacking self-confidence.

TALKING STICK indicates who has the authority to speak.

TALK SHOW signifies an opportunity to express one's opinion or other type of previously withheld emotion, problem etc.

TALLY See scoreboard/card.

TALMUD connotes right living according to a specific belief system.

TALON represents control of one's potential aggressiveness.

TALUS constitutes fragmentation; a breakup into multiple elements.

TAMALE characterizes excitability; high emotions.

TAMBOURINE relates to a festive or joyful situation.

TAME portrays congeniality; neutrality or situational ease.

TAM-O'-SHANTER indicates perspectives affected by one's ethnicity.

TAMPERING warns of an alteration; intent to change the integrity of something.

TAN See suntan.

TAN (color) See beige.

TANDEM pertains to a partnership or dual aspects.

TANDEM BICYCLE refers to progression attained through the efforts of two individuals.

TANGERINE refers to a positive life element that nourishes and refreshes.

TANGLED represents a complexity; a problematical situation; a lack of order.

TANGLED HAIR signifies confused thoughts.

TANGO stands for the synchronized efforts of two people.

TANK (any type) symbolizes a means to store something.

TANK (military) warns of uncontrolled aggression; a lack of discernment while progressing through life.

TANKARD refers to a great need for personal support or strength.

TANNERY applies to a means of preservation.

TANTRUM illustrates a lack of self-control.

TAP-DANCE cautions against progressing through life by "tapping" the resources of others instead of one's own.

TAPE See adhesive tape.

TAPE MEASURE advises of a need to gauge limits, affects, responses, etc. before proceeding with a plan.

TAPESTRY will usually illustrate a visual symbolizing an important message for the dreamer. Try to recall the details of the tapestry if it was a scene; otherwise, this tapestry will signify *all* interacting elements of an aspect that need to be considered.

TAPEWORM warns of the existence of an internal negative consuming self; this will indicate a psychological aberration.

TAPIR pertains to the presence of a personal abnormality one should overcome.

TAR warns of an element or situation in one's life that has the potential of becoming permanent.

TARANTULA applies to a fearful perception.

TAR BABY characterizes a situation from which one cannot extract self.

TARDINESS cautions against procrastination; suggests the possibility that one's actions or response will be too late.

TARGET stands for a goal.

TARGET SHOOTING exemplifies practice; an attempt to sharpen one's skills.

TARIFF represents a "cost" attached to the exercising of one's skills or talents.

TARMAC See asphalt.

TARNISHED illustrates an inner or inherent ability left unused.

TAROT CARDS warn of a fascination with the sensationalist side of spiritual or inherent abilities.

TARPAPER portrays a method of one's personal spiritual protection.

TARPAULIN pertains to self-devised defense mechanisms.

TAR PIT forewarns of a "pitfall" situation about to enter one's life.

TART (pastry) See pie.

TART (taste) See sour.

TARTAN (pattern) See plaid.

TARTER SAUCE symbolizes a personal perspective applied to a specific spiritual belief for the purpose of adding a more tasteful element.

TARZAN characterizes an over-

blown perspective of self and one's abilities.

TASK FORCE represents a need to combine efforts in order to be effective.

TASSEL typifies extraneous elements that have been added to a basic aspect.

TASTE BUDS connote personal opinions and perspectives; a fact bearing on relativity.

TASTELESS refers to inappropriateness, uninteresting, or undesirable.

TATTERED relates to a worn out or well-used element; may indicate high value if it's well-used.

TATTERSALL (pattern) pertains to multiple elements forming a single aspect.

TATTING See lace.

TATTLETALE reveals an informant; an untrustworthy individual.

TATTOO signifies how one perceives self. Recall what the tattoo was. What color and size?

TAUNT See nag.

TAUT stands for a "tight" issue, situation, or aspect; well-covered; thoroughly considered.

TAVERN relates to a perceived place or source of respite where one may receive support.

TAX represents an additional responsibility or debt.

TAX COLLECTOR characterizes a freeloader.

TAX EVASION warns against attempting to avoid one's responsibilities.

TAX-EXEMPT stands for a release of a specific responsibility.

TAXI pertains to a means of assisting one's progress.

TAXIDERMIST suggests shallow beliefs or perspectives.

TAX RETURN represents one's finances; may portray one's assets.

TAX SHELTER indicates an attempt to avoid responsibility.

TEA alludes to healing strength.

TEACHER characterizes specific knowledge and the ability to transfer it.

TEACHER'S PET warns against favoritism displayed in life.

TEACHING HOSPITAL suggests a need to learn healing methods; may refer to self-healing.

TEACUP implies size; a small measure.

TEAKETTLE signifies a means to provide healing strength.

TEAR See rip.

TEARDROP indicates an emotional response that, depending on the dream's surrounding details, may connote sorrow, joy, or empathy.

TEAR GAS implies a means of controlling another.

TEAR SHEET corresponds to evidence; verification.

TEASPOON portrays a very small amount; a small measurement of something.

TECTONICS (study of) represents a high interest in understanding how certain life aspects are formulated and created; an interest in how things come about.

TEDDY BEAR illustrates a soothing and comforting aspect in one's life.

TEENAGER relates to a transitional phase in one's life.

TEETER-TOTTER See seesaw.

TEETH symbolize the manner of an individual's speech which reflects their inner personality.

TEETHING RING constitutes an attempt to ease one's pain.

TEETOTALER characterizes an individual who claims or believes he or she needs no support in life.

TEFLON stands for a protective shield; relates to self-defense mechanisms.

TELEGRAM will signify a personal message for each dreamer. Recall what the telegram said and who it was from.

TELEGRAPH OPERATOR symbolizes information or messages generated from one's inner perceptual senses.

TELEMARKETING denotes fast-talk; an attempt to "sell" through impersonal communication.

TELEPATHY signifies insights; a subtle knowing.

TELEPHONE refers to communication. Was the dream phone ringing? Was someone reaching for it as if to call another? Who was using it?

TELEPHONE BOOK pertains to a source of contacts.

TELEPHONE BOOTH exemplifies the "availability" of opportunities to communicate with others.

TELEPHONE OPERATOR characterizes a person capable of assisting one to communicate with others.

TELEPHONE TRUCK warns of a hearing impairment; one doesn't "listen" well.

TELEPHOTO LENS See zoom lens.

TELEPROMPTER implies assistance needed to clearly express one's thoughts.

TELESCOPE advises one to look beyond surface presentations.

TELEVISION (watching) See watching television.

TELLER reveals a person's utilization of personal assets such as wealth, natural abilities, or spiritual gifts. Recall if there was a deposit or withdrawal being made. Was someone in the vault?

TEMPER TANTRUM warns against being selfish; a lack of acceptance.

TEMPLATE See die.

TEMPLE (site) represents a spiritual element in one's life.

TEN corresponds to closure.

TENANT signifies a temporary situation or phase of one's life path.

TEN COMMANDMENTS come to remind one of the spiritual basics.

TENDERFOOT pertains to a lack of experiential knowledge; a beginner setting out to attain a goal.

TENDERIZER denotes an "easing" factor.

TENEMENT suggests an unsatisfactory situation.

TENNIS marks a constantly altering element.

TENNIS ELBOW advises of the negative effect of routinely attempting to hit the ball back into another's court.

TENNIS SHOE reflects a need to hold one's ground.

TENT reflects a temporary situation; may denote a fragile shelter.

TENTACLE warns of a "grasping" or "flailing" for support or firm footing regarding one's life course. Indicates a need to stabilize and ground oneself.

TEPEE corresponds to a pyramid configuration that centers and condenses one's inner strength.

TERMITE stands for underhandedness; undermining.

TERM PAPER reveals the extent of one's comprehension of a specific subject.

TERRACE See balcony.

TERRA COTTA See pottery.

TERRARIUM portrays a recognition and respect for one's natural abilities.

TERROR See fear.

TESLA (Nikola) characterizes a comprehension of a few elements comprising true Reality.

TEST symbolizes a verification of one's true motivation, knowledge, experiential skill, etc. Often these refer to a self-testing.

TEST CASE denotes a precedent-setting situation or element in one's life.

TEST DRIVE represents the testing of a new course or method of traveling that course.

TESTIMONIAL underscores or recommends a specific concept or perspective for the dreamer.

TEST PATTERN illustrates the current focus and sharpness of one's present perspective. Recall if the pattern was well defined or blurred.

TEST PILOT refers to self-confidence.

TEST TUBE signifies personal experiments.

TEST-TUBE BABY connotes a personally engineered plan for a new life or direction.

TETANUS reveals a lack of awareness; carelessness.

TEXTBOOK indicates a specific type of study needed.

TEXTURE will portray a multitude of meanings. Refer to specific type.

THANKSGIVING DAY reflects one's thankfulness or gratitude. Reminds us to count our daily blessings.

THANK YOU NOTE usually points out a blessing that has been overlooked.

THATCH pertains to natural defenses.

THAW indicates a softening attitude; beginning to express more emotions.

THEATER constitutes a need to "see" more of what transpires around self.

THEME applies to a specific perspective that will shed light on the dreamer's current puzzlement.

THEME PARK correlates to the manner in which one chooses to relax or find enjoyment.

THEME SONG connotes a particular relationship meaning; may represent some type of personal behavior or psychological element.

THEOLOGIAN denotes deeper spiritual study and a need for same.

THERAPIST characterizes an individual who is capable of routinely assisting another to a more balanced attainment.

THERMOMETER reflects temperament. Recall what degree was presented.

THERMOSTAT suggests personal control in being able to regulate the intensity of a relationship or situation.

THESAURUS indicates a need to choose more appropriate words when communicating with others.

THESIS pertains to thought extension; an advisement to carry one's thoughts further.

THICKET See bush.

THIEF See burglar.

THIMBLE implies a very small amount of something; may also refer to a need to protect self.

THINK TANK advises to spend time in deep contemplation or analyzation.

THIRD CLASS represents a commonality; less important.

THIRD DEGREE relates to great intensity.

THIRD EYE stands for insights.

THIRST signifies an inner need or void; exposes a drive or desire.

THISTLE see thorn.

THISTLEDOWN pertains to a dual nature. The soft side that frequently accompanies a problematical situation.

THOREAU (Henry David) reminds us to not lose sight of the beauty and examples of wisdom that nature freely displays.

THORN relates to the thorny elements in life.

THOROUGHBRED connotes a singular element unaffected by outside influences; a pure aspect.

THREAD may refer to a "connective" element or it may indicate a singular, thin idea or chance.

THREADBARE implies a "worn out" aspect.

THREAT exposes an opposing or interfering element.

THREE symbolizes inner energy and strength; fortitude.

THREE-LEGGED RACE suggests coordinated efforts.

THREE-RING CIRCUS exemplifies a ridiculous situation or a confusing chain of events.

THREE STOOGES expose a counterproductive relationship.

THRESHING MACHINE alludes to getting down to basics, essentials.

T

THRESHOLD stands for a beginning point; poised at the entrance.

THRIFT SHOP relates to resourcefulness; effective management.

THRILL-SEEKER characterizes an individual who has lost his or her appreciation of life; a desensitized perspective.

THROAT portrays the "inflections" in speech; how we often don't realize how we "sound" to others.

THROAT CULTURE reveals a need to listen to self and realize the need to alter the "tone" in which we speak.

THRONE symbolizes a high position requiring respect and honor. This dream fragment may reflect the true level of an individual or it may represent an arrogant perspective of self.

THROTTLE (control) pertains to a means to closure.

THUMB implies a "grasp" or guide.

THUMBTACK See tack.

THUNDER emphasizes an attention-getting spiritual warning related to a specific issue the dreamer will recognize in his or her life.

THUNDERBIRD applies to inner power.

THUNDERHEAD represents forthcoming trouble; a problem or altercation brewing.

THUNDERSTRUCK relates to a response to an unexpected event.

THURSDAY is the time to analyze situations and events; give deep thought to one's recent behavior.

TIARA See crown.

TIC (nervous) exposes a subconscious effect or response.

TICK (fabric) connotes a gentle and soft inner nature.

TICK (insect) exemplifies a negative life element that has the potential to fester beneath one's skin.

TICKER TAPE PARADE illustrates a major reason for celebration.

TICKET (admission) validates one's right of entry or preparedness.

TICKET (traffic) exposes negative methods of progression along one's life path.

TICKING (sound) emphasizes the passing of time; time may be running out.

TICK-TACK-TOE signifies alignment; implies a need to work at priorities.

TIDAL WAVE forewarns of a spiritually overwhelming state if the current course is not altered.

TIDDLYWINKS refer to a haphazard approach to accomplishing goals.

TIDE reflects spiritual vacillation.

TIDE POOL suggests opportunities to experience and appreciate the ever-changing aspects of spiritual beauty.

TIE (fasten) pertains to tying up loose ends.

TIE See necktie.

TIE (winners) signify equal skill, talent, or knowledge; may apply to a caution against competitiveness.

TIEBREAKER constitutes a need to prove excellence or superiority.

TIE CLASP/TACK will reveal a hidden aspect of character. Recall the style, color, design, or gemstone.

TIE-DYED reflects acceptance; implies nonchalance.

TIFFANY GLASS infers comfort within self; acceptance; centeredness.

TIGER implies an aggressive nature; emotionally volatile.

TIGER-EYE (stone) connotes awareness; acute perception.

TIGHT See taut.

TIGHT (clothing) exposes self-imposed constrictions; a tendency to restrict oneself and set narrow limits.

TIGHTFISTED warns of selfishness; ego-centered.

TIGHTLIPPED most often reflects a reserved personality rather than being standoffish.

TIGHTROPE signifies a precarious course one is walking.

TIGHTS exemplify an ability to freely express self.

TILE relates to versatility.

TILL (cash drawer) connotes reserves.

TILL (earth) stands for a "freshening" of one's natural talents or gifts; the "turning over" of abilities through utilization.

TIMBERLINE represents the demarcation point between being surrounded by opportunities and having to rely on one's own resources.

TIME BOMB warns of an explosive element in one's life.

TIME CAPSULE illustrates the main events and most important aspects of one's life. Recall what was placed within the capsule.

TIME CLOCK comes as an advisement to stop watching the clock.

TIMED-RELEASE proposes a need to spread out one's efforts and not expend them on one life element; may indicate an "overtime" expanse.

TIME MACHINE is an interesting dreamscape fragment, for it may specify a particular period in time the dreamer needs to give

T

attention to or it may indicate, through a broken mechanism, that one needs to stay focused on the present.

TIME-OUT expresses a "break" should be taken.

TIMER denotes a stressful situation that has been self-generated through one's obsession with deadlines.

TIME-SHARING implies a joint endeavor.

TIMETABLE pertains to schedules.

TIMEWORN most often stands for an outdated aspect.

TIME ZONE portrays the fact that time is perceived differently among people; time is relative, nonlinear.

TIN most often connotes an inferior element.

TIN CUP refers to a handout or request for same.

TINDER stands for a highly flammable aspect or situation; a volatile element.

TINFOIL See aluminum foil.

TINKER characterizes an individual who attempts repairs without having the skill.

TINKERER See watchmaker.

TINKERBELL emphasizes the importance of having faith in one's potential.

TINKERTOYS provide an opportunity for experimentation.

TINSEL illustrates glitter without substance.

TINSEL TOWN portrays a place containing little real value.

TINSMITH relates to a specialized skill.

TIN SNIPS signify a life aspect that is capable of making it easier to "cut through" difficulties.

TIPTOE suggests proceeding with caution.

TIRE pertains to one's condition as she or he progresses through life.

TIRE IRON See crowbar.

TIRE TREAD indicates a well prepared and energetic (new treads) outlook toward one's life journey, or a weary and unmotivated (worn) attitude.

TISSUE applies to a life element that has the potential to keep negative aspects from affecting oneself.

TITANIC (ship) emphasizes spiritual arrogance. Folks claimed it was the ship even God couldn't sink.

TITHE relates to spiritual support, never financial support.

TOAD See frog.

TOADSTOOL See mushroom.

TOAST (bread) alludes to a difficult yet nourishing life element.

TOAST (honor) comes as a personal message for each dreamer. Recall who was toasted by whom and what was said.

TOASTER implies a forthcoming disagreement or disagreeable situation.

TOBACCO (native) emphasizes respect and honor.

TOBACCO BRAID constitutes a gift representing honor.

TOBOGGAN See sled.

TODDLER implies one's beginning steps toward a new endeavor, direction or belief.

TOE refers to an aspect in one's life that contributes to a balanced course.

TOE SHOES caution against a tendency to flit through life without setting one's feet firmly on the ground and taking life seriously.

TOFFEE typifies a difficult aspect to accept.

TOFU alludes to a totally nourishing life element.

TOGA pertains to an incomplete idea.

TOGGLE BOLT stands for a strong issue; one that will "hold up" under scrutiny.

TOILET constitutes a need for eliminations. This means any type of negative element present in one's life.

TOKE suggests experimentation; a sampling.

TOKEN symbolizes a sign or indication.

TOLLBOOTH applies to a "payment" required for further advancement along one's chosen course.

TOMAHAWK See hatchet.

TOMATO implies an agreeable or attractive idea.

TOMBOY defines the expression of one's individuality; personal freedom.

TOMBSTONE See gravestone.

TOMCAT corresponds with indiscriminate behavior.

TOME reflects an extensive volume of information.

TOMMYKNOCKER infers a serious warning; a forewarning of a dangerous situation or element.

TOM-TOM See drum.

TONGS portray an aid in comprehension; something that provides greater understanding; a "grasp" on things.

TONGUE relates to the quality of one's manner of communication.

TONGUE DEPRESSOR advises silence; indicates gossip.

TONGUE-TIED pertains to a loss for words; inability to respond.

TONGUE TWISTER reflects a

difficult idea or concept that one may or may not be able to articulate through understanding.

TONIC stands for a helpful or healing element that could be difficult to accept.

TONSILLECTOMY relates to the removal of negative elements that have hampered one's ability to communicate or adequately express self.

TOOL symbolizes aids, opportunities, or methods for utilizing personal abilities.

TOOTH See teeth.

TOOTHACHE exposes hurtful speech.

TOOTHBRUSH suggests a need to clean up one's speech. This may indicate hurtful or thoughtless words.

TOOTH FAERIE exemplifies a lack of reality in one's life; a belief that flattering speech will serve self.

TOOTHPASTE refers to the attitude, belief, or perspective that will "clean up" one's manner of speech.

TOOTHPICK connotes the presence of a negative aspect "lodged" in one's routine communication style.

TOP (position) usually reflects an "above" or higher level.

TOP (toy) represents spinning, often out of control.

TOPAZ (gemstone) alludes to optimism.

TOP GUN portrays the perfection of a skill.

TOP HAT cautions against intellectual arrogance.

TOP-HEAVY reveals the presence of an imbalanced state.

TOPIARY warns against attempting to personally "shape" one's reality.

TOPOGRAPHER characterizes an individual who is capable of charting or directing another's course.

TOPPING represents the "frosting on the cake" kind of symbology, thereby indicating a final element for a specific event or issue.

TOP-SECRET connotes innermost thoughts and memories.

TOPSOIL refers to "surface" issues, emotions, or appearances.

TORAH signifies an individual's high spiritual belief system. Refer to the condition and color of the dreamscape Torah. Was it protected or left exposed

TORCH won't usually refer to a light; rather, it stands for that which we hold close within. This may pertain to negative feelings such as blame, hate, revenge, or it may apply to positive emotions such as special affection or admiration.

TORNADO/HURRICANE sym-bolizes great inner turmoil. The tor-nado connotes emotional or mental problems. The hurricane correlates to spiritual aspects.

TORPEDO pertains to spiritual warfare and will be associated with one's personal life relation-ships.

TORRENTIAL RAIN consti-tutes an inundation of spiritual elements in life.

TORRID emphasizes a scorching or passionate emotion and most often comes as a warning.

TORTOISE See turtle.

TOSSUP implies a questionable issue; indecision.

TOTAL ECLIPSE characterizes the darkness (ignorance) before the light (illumination).

TOTAL RECALL denotes in-sights into the subconscious's store of knowledge.

TOTE BOARD relates to infor-mation at a glance; an overall view.

TOTEM suggests an object of special importance to a person; a connective bone.

TOTEM ANIMAL symbolizes a unique bond shared between an individual and a particular animal which transfers into a comforting sense of good fortune or safety.

TOTEM POLE indicates a corre-lated spiritual belief system whereby one spiritual aspect is connected to another as though "stacked" in succession.

TOUCAN implies beautiful thoughts.

TOUCHDOWN alludes to being grounded; grasping a fact; gain-ing understanding.

TOUCHSTONE connotes excel-lence.

TOUCHUP relates to an im-provement; an effort to bring completion or wholeness.

TOUPEE reflects false thinking.

TOUR constitutes a desire to fa-miliarize self with something.

TOUR GUIDE characterizes an individual who is well-informed on a particular issue and is pre-pared to share that knowledge with others.

TOURIST suggests an effort to learn about a specific issue, con-cept, or subject.

TOURIST TRAP cautions a seeker to "be aware" and use dis-cernment when searching through chosen issues.

TOURMALINE (gemstone) in-fers a healing element in one's life.

TOURNAMENT See contest.

TOURNIQUET denotes an effort to staunch further progression of something.

TOW pertains to assistance needed or given.

T

TOWBOAT defines spiritual help; an uplifting or comforting concept.

TOWEL depicts a life aspect capable of absorption. This means an ability to lessen difficulties.

TOWER exemplifies the superconscious aspect of the mind where spiritual talents and gifts await to be awakened and utilized.

TOWER OF BABEL warns of spiritual confusion.

TOWLINE will represent a "saving" life aspect; assistance.

TOWN CRIER enters dreams as a messenger who brings a warning of some type. Recall what was cried out.

TOWN HALL alludes to a meeting place, more explicitly, a meeting that is needed.

TOWPATH connotes a helpful path or course.

TOXIC WASTE signifies residual effects that remail volatile.

TOXIN See poison.

TOY implies a lack of seriousness or perhaps a serious "toying" with something.

TOY SHOP portrays the child within. It often refers to childish behavior, perceptions, or fears. This symbol can also suggest methods adults utilize to "toy" with others.

TRACE (amount) indicates a "hint" of something; a subliminal presence.

TRACE (draw) cautions against attempting to copy another.

TRACER BULLET corresponds to an intent to leave evidence of the source which affected something.

TRACK (evidence) illustrates a sign of one's passing.

TRACK (follow) infers a search.

TRACK (sports) signifies a circling; lack of progression.

TRACK (train) warns against a rigid path with no capability for diversion or alteration.

TRACKER characterizes a person intent on following another; may denote an intensive search.

TRACKING NUMBER advises of the wisdom to follow a particular concept through various issues.

TRACKING STATION represents heightened awareness, particularly in respect to spiritual insights.

TRACK RECORD denotes experiential validation.

TRACTOR relates to a powerful help; highly effective assistance.

TRADE signifies one's interest; field of endeavor; where efforts are applied.

TRADEMARK illustrates a revelation; exposes true attitudes, beliefs, and intentions of others. Recall the symbols and colors of the trademark.

TRADER characterizes one who possesses a "give and take" attitude; open to options.

TRADE SCHOOL refers to specific instruction that will provide skill to progress along one's chosen life path.

TRADE SECRET correlates to a unique method or ingredient associated with successful operations or progression.

TRADE UNION See union.

TRADE WIND implies thoughts and ideas that follow a common route; a lack of individual thought.

TRADING CARD will usually depict a visual of an important message for the dreamer.

TRADING POST applies to a current need to be giving. This symbol comes when an individual isn't compromising.

TRAFFIC exemplifies traveling activity; stands for the state of one's chosen path. Was the road crowded? Hectic?

TRAFFIC JAM applies to a setback, a temporary one, appearing along one's path.

TRAFFIC LIGHT marks the rightness of one's path. Did the light show green . . . yellow (slow down)? Did it indicate a time to turn off onto another road?

TRAIL (drop back) may not be the negative symbol it initially appears to be, for frequently we need to drop back in order to get a better perspective of what's ahead.

TRAIL (extend) pertains to "extended" effects; lasting benefits.

TRAIL (path) indicates an individual's unique direction or course.

TRAILBLAZER connotes the courage of one who endeavors to self-discover a new course.

TRAILER (semi truck) typifies a long haul; an intention to see something through.

TRAIN (rail) warns against following closely behind another who is following a popular tried-and-true course.

TRAIN (teach) cautions against indoctrination; being "formed" into a particular mold.

TRAINEE connotes a follower.

TRAIN ENGINEER exemplifies an individual who leads others along a smooth and easy path.

TRAINING TABLE cautions against being "fed" concepts chosen by others.

TRAIN WHISTLE comes as a message that warns against separating self from others; reminds of humanitarian responsibility.

TRAITOR reveals a lack of loyalty; a betrayer.

TRAM See cable car.

TRAMP/HOBO characterizes a free-thinker; a nonconformist.

TRAMPOLINE relates to a tendency to gain insights then discount them.

TRANCE refers to a state of altered or shifted consciousness which opens one to high insights.

TRANQUILIZER will represent any life aspect on which an individual depends for soothing effects; a means for calming.

TRANQUILIZER GUN symbolizes a great need to calm a situation or individual.

TRANSCEIVER directly corresponds to one's open channel within the superconscious mind.

TRANSCRIPT denotes a review of a conversation or communication; verification of what was said.

TRANSFER (ticket) exemplifies a need to alter one's course in life.

TRANSFORMER comes as a strong suggestion to switch efforts to a different goal or issue.

TRANSFUSION connotes "bad blood" is present within; a need to repair bad relations.

TRANSLATOR characterizes an individual capable of bringing understanding or clarifying misunderstood communication.

TRANSLUCENT refers to a neb-

ulous idea, one that is beginning to formulate.

TRANSMISSION means pacing oneself.

TRANSMITTER portrays a need to send a message to another or express an important communication that is being withheld.

TRANSMUTATION depicts some type of transformation needed or currently happening.

TRANSPARENT indicates a lack of deception or ulterior motive; open and honest relationships; nothing hidden.

TRANSPLANT relates to "new ground" in which to develop; fresh beginning.

TRANSVESTITE exposes an identity crisis; an identification with a past life that is difficult overcome.

TRAP (catch) illustrates the pitfalls that entrap one in life such as arrogance, the ego, materialism, etc.

TRAP (drain) pertains to an opportunity to clean out the negatives in one's life or existing within self.

TRAPDOOR reflects unawareness.

TRAPEZE reveals an unproductive means of attempting to progress along a life path.

TRAPEZE ARTIST See aerialist.

TRAPPER indicates a conniving personality.

TRAPSHOOTING typifies a desire to maintain personal skills.

TRASH connotes the useless and extraneous elements in one's life.

TRASH CAN cautions one to throw out the life aspects that are useless.

TRAUMA TEAM will stand for a need to take care of the most obvious and harmful negative elements in one's life.

TRAVEL AGENCY denotes inadequacies.

TRAVEL ALARM defines an attempt to maintain a schedule.

TRAVELER'S CHECKS represent the personal assets on which one can draw while making life's journey.

TRAVELING SALESPERSON characterizes a person intent on spreading beliefs far and wide. This may indicate a fanatic.

TRAVELOGUE refers to research into different life courses.

TRAVERSE ROD denotes a means of keeping issues open or closed; the "choice" of doing same.

TRAVOIS suggests a journey is required for path advancement.

TRAWLER warns of a belief that "drags" on one's overall spirituality.

TREADLE applies to the energy applied to keep one's momentum going.

TREADMILL reveals an unproductive method; a lack of advancement; a neutral position.

TREASURE signifies a personally-perceived boon.

TREASURE CHEST represents the expected or awaited-for boon. The key with this symbol is to recall if the chest was full or empty.

TREASURE HUNT applies to expectation.

TREASURE ISLAND usually implies a dreamer; not willing to work for one's goals.

TREASURY DEPARTMENT exemplifies the source of one's assets, meaning inherent talents and qualities.

TREATY relates to agreements that cause a closure.

TREE symbolizes life force; living gifts; natural talents.

TREE FARM indicates the "cultivation" of natural talents and gifts; the increment of same.

TREE HOUSE relates to living one's spiritual beliefs through the utilization of inherent talents and gifts.

TREE-TRIMMERS characterize an individual who continually "trims" and cares for his or her inherent talents and gifts.

T

TRELLIS correlates with a "guiding" direction given to one's natural abilities.

TREMBLE reveals a loss of control; instability.

TREMBLOR See earthquake.

TRENCH denotes perseverance and personal faith in self.

TRENCH COAT refers to protective measures one devises to maintain personal strength and fortitude.

TRESTLE warns of a life path or course possessing no grounding factor, no foundation.

TRIAD most often symbolizes God and His Female and Male Aspect.

TRIAGE advises of a need to establish and maintain priorities.

TRIAL comes as a suggestion to honestly analyze one's motives and recent behavior.

TRIANGLE (shape) signifies the three Aspects of God.

TRIBESPEOPLE correspond to the universal "unit" of humankind.

TRIBUNAL pertains to self-judgment.

TRICKSTER typifies cleverness; a quick wit.

TRIDENT stands for the three Aspects of God.

TRIFOCALS emphasize multiple perspectives as utilized to gain a complete comprehension.

TRI-FOLD reveals three separate aspects to something.

TRIGGER (any type) indicates the singular element that has the capability of "setting off" multiple responses or ramifications.

TRILITHON pertains to a "doorway" or entrance.

TRILOBITE illustrates a time-tested spiritual concept; a solid truth.

TRILOGY signifies the existence of three aspects creating a whole.

TRIMMINGS (festive) denote expanded aspects.

TRINKET usually refers to personal value applied to a specific object or subject.

TRIP (fuse) cautions against expending too much energy or efforts on a specific issue.

TRIP (journey) connotes a forthcoming directional course that will prove productive in providing valuable lessons.

TRIP (stumble) relates to a temporary setback that may serve to provide a beneficial element to one's life.

TRIPLETS constitute three new beginnings or starts forthcoming. This doesn't mean a choice between them needs to be made. These three new aspects will usually be very different from each other and will exist simultaneously in one's life.

557

TRIPOD suggests a need to "steady" oneself; a need to get focused without any distortion.

TRIPWIRE warns of an attempt to foil another; a deception.

TRIVET symbolizes a protective measure insuring insulation; a means to avoid being burned.

TRIVIA denotes unimportant aspects to an element.

TROJAN HORSE reveals stealth; deception.

TROLL represents the skeptical, unbelievable concepts in one's life.

TROLLEY CAR See cable car.

TROLLING warns against accepting spiritual debris.

TROPHY (animal) exposes a lack of courage; false power.

TROPHY (award) comes as a sign of accomplishment and serves as encouragement.

TROPICS suggest stifling spiritual beliefs.

TROUBLESHOOTER characterizes a person capable of discovering the source of a problem and resolving it.

TROWEL connotes a personal tool used to smooth over rough times in life.

TRUANT OFFICER represents one's own conscience.

TRUCE constitutes a desire to resolve relationship difficulties.

TRUCK correlates to personal efforts and the energy expended for same.

TRUCKER relates to one who is conscientious regarding closures; one who wants to see things through.

TRUCK STOP portrays a necessary resting phase along one's life path.

TRUFFLE applies to a personal comfort.

TRUMP CARD will signify the "key" to a goal or successful conclusion.

TRUMPET reveals a forthcoming message for the dreamer.

TRUNDLE BED connotes the availability of accommodating a partner or assistant. This may infer a companion or some other type of associate.

TRUNK (baggage) denotes "heavy" burdens; excesses perceived as valuable.

TRUNK (tree) applies to inner strength.

TRUNK (vehicle) corresponds with the "hidden" aspects carried along one's path.

TRUNK LINE relates to the "main" line of communication.

TRUSTEE reveals a trusted individual.

TRUST FUND represents one's "intentions" for others.

TRUTH SERUM comes as a strong advisement for honesty.

TRYST refers to an intended meeting.

TSETSE FLY warns of the presence of an undetected element in one's life that has a great potential to cause harm.

T-SQUARE represents an effort to get something straight; understanding.

TSUNAMI connotes spiritual overkill or a state of being spiritually overwhelmed.

TUBER stands for a new life.

TUBERCULOSIS advises of a need for breathing room; something in one's life is suffocating the very breath out.

TUESDAY suggests a need to sharpen one's awareness; attend to sharper perceptions and discernment.

TUGBOAT See towboat.

TUITION corresponds to some type of payment due in exchange for the information one desires. Reveals unscrupulous behavior if tuition is demanded for *spiritual* information.

TUMBLEWEED portrays shallow aspects of oneself.

TUMOR warns of the presence of a negative attitude that has the capability of consuming self.

TUNA refers to spiritual generosity.

TUNDRA typifies spiritual aspects yet to be discovered.

TUNE-UP reflects a need to make internal adjustments and suggests a perception or attitude that's out of alignment or peak condition.

TUNIC See toga.

TUNING FORK suggests that something is not ringing true; a call to make an adjustment.

TUNNEL connotes an alternate route or a way to discovery.

TUNNEL VISION advises of the wisdom of widening one's perceptual scope.

TURBAN exposes twisted thoughts.

TURBINE exemplifies a source of power; strong motivation.

TUREEN suggests bounty.

TURNIP reflects a reversal; a changed attitude or decision.

TURNKEY indicates completeness; entirety.

TURNOVER (employment) a lack of stability; restlessness.

TURNOVER (pastry) implies a desirable benefit.

TURNPIKE See tollbooth.

TURN SIGNAL symbolizes one's intention to alter present course.

TURNSTILE cautions one to focus on a single aspect at a time; a method of slowing one's pace.

TURPENTINE illustrates a life aspect that is capable of eradicating residual elements.

TURTLE pertains to a fear of facing responsibility or reality.

TURTLENECK implies a reluctance to expose self; lacking self-confidence.

TURQUOISE (color/stone) defines spiritual health and well-being.

TURRET corresponds to hidden psychological elements.

TUSK pertains to natural defense mechanisms.

TUTANKHAMEN stands for the killing effects of jealousy and greed.

TUTOR points out an individual capable and willing to assist another.

TUXEDO signifies a desire to presents only one's best side.

TWEED (fabric) denotes quiet intelligence and wisdom.

TWEEZERS relate to a life element capable of extracting an irritating aspect from self or one's life.

TWELVE stands for spiritual or purpose completion.

TWILIGHT corresponds to the "magic" time, the "window," when one is most receptive to higher insights.

TWILIGHT ZONE reflects experiences one has difficulty accepting.

TWINS relate to the duality of life; the polarity.

TWINE portrays a means of attaching, connecting, or tying something together; closure.

TWIN-ENGINE represents balanced efforts. Recall if both were working.

TWINKLING refers to the "sparkle" that accompanies enlightened insights.

TWISTER See tornado/hurricane.

TWISTING ROAD reflects one's fortitude and perseverance while progressing a burdensome and difficult life path.

TWIST-TIE denotes a means of closure.

TWITCH See tic.

TWO represents weakness and vacillation.

TWO CENTS implies a worthless aspect; not worth one's time or energy.

TWO-EDGED connotes duality.

TWO FACES expose duplicity.

TWO FISTS signify great strength.

TWO-WAY STREET alludes to something being available to opposing parties to utilize or take advantage of.

TYCOON characterizes an individual capable of providing great benefits to others.

TYPECAST warns against pre-judgments or placing others in personally perceived categories.

TYPEWRITER symbolizes preserved ideas.

TYPHOID FEVER warns of the harmful effects of spiritual untruths.

TYPO pertains to an unintentional error or life mistake.

TYRANNOSAUR corresponds to an overwhelming situation or highly demanding, manipulative individual.

TYRANT stands for an arrogance for one's perceived power or authority.

U

U-BOAT warns of a negative spiritual element in one's life.

U-BOLT represents a strong support.

UDDER alludes to a nourishing factor in one's life.

UFO See unidentified flying object.

UGLY will usually denote a disagreeable aspect as perceived by the dreamer.

UGLY DUCKLING pertains to misconceptions associated with first impressions.

UKULELE exemplifies a carefree personality.

ULCER warns of stress that has been internalized and the need to alleviate same.

ULTIMATUM connotes a last resort choice.

ULTRALIGHT suggests gentle thoughts; kindness.

ULTRASONIC See supersonic.

ULTRASOUND portrays a need to "get inside" something; take a more thorough look at an issue, event, or other element in one's life.

ULTRAVIOLET LAMP symbolizes an aid to personal growth.

UMBER (color) relates to earthiness; being natural.

UMBILICAL CORD signifies vital connections; a strong bond.

UMBRELLA constitutes skepticism and a willful insulation from spiritual issues.

UMPIRE characterizes a person's conscience; maintaining behavior that is confined within the bounds or rules.

UNABRIDGED pertains to a "complete" rendition; leaving no elements out.

UNANIMOUS suggests total agreement; no dissention.

UNBALANCED warns of a lack of alignment or an unstable factor that's present in one's life.

UNBREAKABLE most often refers to inner strength, yet may relate to a relationship, agreement, or bond of some type.

UNBRIDLED (horse) constitutes an uncontrolled state, but could imply a "freedom" to express one's individuality.

UNBUTTONED won't infer sloppiness; it most often applies to a personal confidence or comfortable sense of self.

UNCHARTED (course) illustrates an unplanned direction which may, of itself, be specifically planned that way. This indicates someone who desires to let life guide him or her.

UNCIVILIZED suggests an absolute disregard for others.

UNCLE comes as an advisement to take personal responsibility and admit to mistakes made in life.

UNCLE SAM corresponds to the fact that no one is completely independent and free of those who make themselves a part of one's life.

UNCLOG typifies the act of ridding self of a confusing issue or relationship.

UNCONCERN speaks of apathy.

UNCONDITIONAL represents a lack of strings being attached; a true unrestricted element.

UNCONSCIOUS usually denotes ignorance or unawareness, yet may indicate complete insensitivity.

UNCTION See anointing.

UNCONTROLLED signifies a lack of direction or planning; may indicate an aspect that has gotten out of hand.

UNCONVENTIONAL frequently comes as personal advise to follow one's own path or ideas.

UNCOUTH implies rudeness.

UNCOVERED represents something that has been exposed, revealed.

UNDECIDED suggests a need to give more thought and analyzation to an issue.

UNDERAGE usually refers to being unprepared.

UNDERBRUSH stands for hidden problems.

UNDERCARRIAGE denotes a supportive or foundational element.

UNDERCLASSMEN characterize those who are less experienced and knowledgeable in one's life.

UNDERCOATING pertains to a protective measure; an intent to preserve.

UNDERCOVER connotes secretiveness.

UNDERCURRENT stands for a sense of a different attitude.

UNDERCUT reflects the act of undermining; attempting to better another.

UNDERDEVELOPED relates to a lack of full preparedness; needing further growth; immature.

UNDERDOG characterizes an individual "perceived" as weaker by the dreamer, yet this may come in a dream to advise differently.

UNDEREXPOSED (film) signifies an aspect in one's life that requires more time, needs more development.

UNDERFOOT represents those facets in life to which we need to attend.

UNDERGROUND symbolizes the need for an individual to keep certain elements of his or her life to self. This may also advise the dreamer to "get out in the open" and contribute one's talents. The surrounding dreamscape details will clarify this.

UNDERGROUND RAIL-ROAD pertains to a secretive endeavor.

UNDERGROWTH connotes developing aspects to an issue; yet-undetected activity.

UNDERHAND applies to unethical practices.

UNDERLINED illustrates emphasis. Recall what was underlined. This will be what the dreamer needs to give attention to.

UNDERPAID implies a lack of appreciation or recognition of one's experience, skill, or knowledge.

UNDERPASS portrays a "way under" something; an alternate course.

UNDERSCORE See underlined.

UNDERSHIRT See underwear.

UNDERSIDE suggests a need to look at all aspects (angles) of an issue.

UNDERSTUDY reflects a desire to emulate another. Recall who was studying with whom. What was being studied?

UNDERTAKER See funeral director.

UNDER-THE-COUNTER represents unethical or secretive dealings.

UNDERTONE See undercurrent.

UNDERTOW warns of negative spiritual beliefs that will eventually "pull one under."

UNDERWATER pertains to a state of being submerged in spiritual issues.

UNDERWEAR alludes to a covering up; a fear of exposure.

UNDERWORLD (criminal) stands for the hidden elements in one's life.

UNDERWRITER characterizes approval; an endorsement.

UNDRESSED represents honest intentions.

UNEARTH applies to the exposure of something; a new aspect come to light.

UNEARTHLY exemplifies a puzzlement; an inability to recognize or comprehend something.

UNEMPLOYED connotes an unproductive state. This may not infer a negative implication because it could suggest a "designated" phase when one needs to take a break.

UNEMPLOYMENT COMPENSATION signifies a "benefit" gained from a time period when one isn't applying self. This usually refers to the need for rest and a distancing from stressful elements.

UNFINISHED connotes a call to finish what was begun.

UNHINGED depicts a lack of control; loss of balance.

UNICORN reflects real possibilities; the reaches of reality.

UNICYCLE denotes self-reliance and resourcefulness; self-sufficiency.

UNIDENTIFIED FLYING OBJECT (UFO) represents the totality of intelligent life.

UNIDENTIFIED SKY OBJECT pertains to the endless possibilities of the scope of true Reality.

UNIFORM signifies a specific intention or attention to a focused effort. Recall what the uniform represented. Waitress? Police?

UNINHABITED defines self-discovery; an uncharted course or goal.

UNINSURED correlates to high confidence.

UNION portrays a sense of security.

UNION HALL corresponds with a desire to utilize one's talents and skills.

UNION LABEL denotes pride in one's work.

UNITED NATIONS stands for a peaceful relationship or association.

UNIVERSE See cosmos.

UNIVERSITY typifies higher knowledge; expanded learning.

UNLEAVENED infers fundamental aspects unaffected by extraneous elements.

UNLOAD comes as an advisement for self-analyzation; suggests a need to express self.

UNLUCKY pertains to a lack of self-confidence.

UNMASKING symbolizes a need to accurately perceive others; seeing with clarity; getting rid of that which one hides behind.

UNORGANIZED implies a need to be methodical, efficient; alludes to a disoriented thought process.

UNPACKING signifies the act of looking at different aspects; may indicate a need to "unload" or unburden self.

UNPLUGGED reveals a disconnection. This may refer to one's own rationale.

UNPREPARED suggests a lack of planning; no foresight.

UNQUALIFIED denotes an immature stage in life; needing more experience and knowledge.

UNQUENCHABLE See thirst.

UNRAVELED represents approaching solutions; one is in the process of reaching new understandings.

UNREADABLE relates to a personal lack of comprehension and may denote concepts or ideas for which one isn't yet ready.

UNRESPONSIVE won't necessarily denote a lack of emotion or communication; it may suggest deep thought.

UNSANITARY implies an unhealthy condition or situation.

UNSCREWING reflects a lessening of stress and pressure in one's life.

UNSTEADY exemplifies a lack of self-confidence; on shaky ground.

UNVEILING correlates to a discovery of some type.

UNWASHED comes as an advisement to remove the negative elements from some aspect in one's life.

UPDATE stands for the presence of new information of which one should be aware.

UPHOLSTERER relates to a new outlook or attitude.

UPPER CRUST typifies arrogance; placing self or others into a high-class position.

UPROOTED pertains to a disconnection or disassociation; may refer to personal relationships or a plan or it may connote an actual geographical relocation forthcoming.

UPSIDE DOWN exposes a misconception or idea that isn't perceived correctly.

URANIUM warns of a "contaminating" aspect in one's life.

URANUS (planet) suggests one attends to philosophical issues.

URBAN SPRAWL illustrates a loss of control; the ease by which something gets away from you.

URCHIN (child) pertains to a mischievous immaturity.

URCHIN (sea) portrays spiritual immaturity.

URINE relates to necessary waste; the idea that some elements in one's life are harmful if retained.

URN (warming) pertains to the need to keep some aspect in your life "warm" (current).

USHER characterizes an individual capable of guiding another; may represent a counselor, friend, or even oneself.

UTILITY COMPANY stands for work and the efforts applied to same.

UTOPIA corresponds to an unrealistic goal or perspective of life.

U-TURN advises of a need to "go back" or return to a former issue.

V

VACANCY (sign) represents availability.

VACATION signifies the need to get away; may also denote a warning against being on vacation too long.

VACCINE pertains to the awareness of having the foresight to protect self from negative elements in one's life

VACUUM (space) relates to an emptiness, usually a lack of emotion.

VACUUM CLEANER indicates that a "clean up" is needed. This may refer to a situation, relationship, or even some type of negative within self.

VAGABOND characterizes a person who follows her or his own course.

VAGRANT will reveal self-reliance; an independent person.

VALANCE connotes a superficial idea.

VALE See valley.

VALEDICTORIAN signifies a personal opinion.

VALENTINE implies affection.

VALERIAN suggests a calming, soothing aspect in one's life.

VALET represents servitude.

VALHALLA stands for heroic efforts.

VALLEY won't indicate a "low" point in life; rather, it symbolizes a place (or time) of respite.

VALLEY OF THE KINGS (Egypt) corresponds to undiscovered spiritual aspects of the true Reality.

VALVE portrays control and the regulation of same.

VAMPIRE characterizes an individual who "uses" others for self-serving purposes.

VAN alludes to great personal efforts expended.

VANDAL will pinpoint a destructive personality, possibly self-destructive.

VANE See weathervane.

VANGUARD represents a leader or the leading edge.

VANILLA (flavor/scent) indicates renewal.

VANISHING POINT exemplifies a perceived end or finalization, yet the horizon is endless. This reveals the fact that "what is seen" may not necessarily be fact.

VANITY CASE portrays enhanced appearances.

VANITY LICENSE PLATE reveals a personal attitude or idea.

VANITY TABLE correlates to self-absorption.

VAPOR See fumes.

VAPORIZER indicates a review of one's spiritual beliefs; a "refresher" endeavor.

VAPOR LOCK represents an obstructed flow of energy current through one's system; a psychological block causing multiple dysfunctions.

VAPOR TRAIL See contrail.

VARIABLE STAR warns against depending on the fluctuating opinions of others to control the unique individuality and brightness of self.

VARICOSE VEINS reflect a difficult path that has been traversed.

VARIETY SHOW connotes ideas derived from multiple sources.

VARIETY STORE stands for opportunities and the availability of same.

VARNISH relates to a desire to "finish" an issue. Recall the quality of the varnish work. Was it cracked? Beautiful and smooth?

VARSITY portrays the principal elements or individuals.

VASE reflects various personality characteristics that aren't always evident.

VASECTOMY represents ineffectiveness.

VAT symbolizes a "container" of great size, meaning a large issue to contain in one's life.

VATICAN exemplifies a specific "religious" belief rather than a pure spiritual one.

VAUDEVILLE alludes to an attempt to "try out" one's idea or plan.

VAULT (bank) signifies worth; that which one values.

VAULT (leap) relates to a desire to avoid an undesirable element or personal responsibility.

VEAL pertains to a highly nourishing aspect in one's life.

VECTOR corresponds to a "carrier" or possibly even a messenger, depending on the surrounding dreamscape details.

VEER may mean an attempt to avoid something or it may indicate a diversion from one's life course.

VEGETABLE OIL portrays a factor that contributes to the completion of something.

VEGETABLE STEAMER denotes the preserving of important elements.

VEGETARIAN represents a separate opinion or attitude.

VEHICLE correlates to the physiological system. Refer to specific types.

VEIL emphasizes "veiled" thoughts; concealment of one's emotions or attitudes.

VEIN (blood) relates to a life force element; an essential factor.

VEIN (mineral) reveals the presence of a beneficial aspect in one's life.

VELCRO infers an easy, quick attachment. This may refer to relationships or the acceptance of new ideas.

VELVET (fabric) denotes a soft and soothing situation, relationship, or state of mind; a very comfortable sense.

VENDETTA stands for family discord associated with revenge and blame.

VENEER signifies a false exterior; a self-designed presentation of self.

VENEREAL DISEASE applies to the negative effects of not being aware.

VENETIAN BLINDS relate to selective perception; seeing only what one wants to admit to.

VENISON portrays an unethical "source" from which nourishment is obtained.

VENOM See poison.

VENT represents an opportunity to get rid of negative factors in one's life that will ultimately cause harm. This usually refers to negative emotions or attitudes.

VENTILATION applies to an attempt to maintain fresh ideas; a method of preventing staleness.

VENTRILOQUIST pertains to a person who tends to speak for another, yet is not necessarily given the authority to do so.

VENTURE CAPITAL exemplifies one element in association with preparing for a goal or new course.

VENUS (Roman mythology) signifies deep affection.

VENUS (planet) alludes to dreams and their associated symbology; may refer to a personal dream or desire.

VERANDA represents an opportunity to obtain fresh ideas.

VERDICT pertains to a settled decision.

VERDIGRIS applies to evidence of spiritual affects.

VERMICULITE illustrates an uplifting and nurturing life factor.

VERMIN relates to severe negatives in one's life.

VERTIGO reflects dizziness, confusion; an inability to think straight.

VESPERS suggest the wisdom of evening reflection over one's day for the purpose of analyzing behavior and responses.

VEST indicates something that is "close to one's heart" and therefore protected.

VESTIBULE See foyer.

VESTMENTS stand for outward signs of one's position or belief.

VESTRY denotes a segregation of one's spiritual beliefs from daily life.

VETERAN will characterize an experienced individual.

VETERINARIAN indicates self-lessness; compassion.

VETO comes as a decision-making advisement.

VIBRATION signifies an insight or indication.

VICE SQUAD usually stands for one's own conscience.

VIDEO CAMERA See camcorder.

VIDEO GAME denotes unrealistic scenarios or plans.

VIEW FINDER symbolizes a need for clear perception.

VIGIL infers perseverance.

VILLAIN reveals a wrongdoer, yet may only represent whomever the dreamer "perceives" as being in the wrong.

VINE relates to "far-reaching" effects.

VINEGAR connotes a distasteful life aspect.

VINEYARD exemplifies the fruit of one's efforts. Recall the condition of the dreamscape vineyard.

VINYL denotes an imitation.

VIOLATION implies a message from one's conscience.

VIOLET (color/flower) alludes to a healing spiritual element.

VIOLIN represents emotional range of expression.

VIPER FISH applies to a spiritual skepticism.

VIRGA symbolizes a spiritual thirst or unfulfillment.

VIRTUAL REALITY constitutes an overactive imagination; an inability to discern clearly.

VIRTUOSO signifies one possessing a masterful talent and skill.

VIRUS will pertain to a dangerous negative element that is contaminating one's life.

VISA stands for one's right-of-passage, preparedness to proceed, yet only for a specified span of time.

VISCERA refers to the internal workings or hidden elements of an issue.

VISE (tool) illustrates an advisement to get a firm grip on something, may also indicate building pressure or stress.

VISIONARY characterizes one who has attained deep wisdom through experiential knowledge.

VISION QUEST applies to a desire to know self and one's direction.

VISITING NURSE will imply someone in the dreamer's life

who is capable of providing healing assistance or counsel.

VISOR CAP typifies impaired perception.

VISUAL AIDS will denote life aspects that bring clarity to one's perception or comprehension.

VITAL SIGNS are a direct message regarding an individual's state.

VITAMIN corresponds to a specific nutrient. Recall the particulars associated with this dream symbol, for this message could infer that the dreamer needs more of this vitamin or is perhaps ingesting too much.

VIXEN implies a playful cleverness.

VOCATIONAL SCHOOL comes as an advisement to gain greater skill or knowledge.

VOLCANO may forewarn of an actual event, yet this symbol most often indicates emotional explosions.

VOLTMETER suggests a need to monitor one's energy output. This indicates a vacillation due to selective discrimination.

VOLUNTEER denotes the selfless giving of self.

VOODOO reflects spiritual misunderstanding.

VORTEX exposes an "opening" of some type; an unconventional course.

VOTING MACHINE defines the right to freely choose or make a personal decision.

VOTIVE CANDLE connotes spiritual comfort.

VOUCHER pertains to validation; reasons behind behavior.

VOW stands for a promise; strong intention; a pledge, often to self.

VOYAGER characterizes an individual who is free to follow his or her own spiritual course.

VOYEUR exposes personal inadequacy and a poor self-image. This dream element usually has nothing to do with sexual implications, but rather comes to reveal personalities who are incompetent and dependent upon others.

VULTURE warns of greedy and aggressive individuals; a user.

W

WAD represents an amount or measurement implying a "considerable" quantity.

WADDLE signifies a personal burden; great weight carried.

WADERS (fishing) portray a curious interest in spiritual matters yet hesitant to get the feet wet.

WADING stands for "testing spiritual waters" and getting one's feet wet with new spiritual issues.

WAFER connotes an "acceptable" form or more utilitarian configuration of some life element with which one needs to be associated.

WAFFLE depicts indecision; vacillation; evasiveness.

WAFFLE IRON represents a firm sense of neutrality.

WAGE See salary.

WAGER connotes one's degree of self-confidence. Recall how much the wager was for. Who was it with? What was it for?

WAGON applies to a helpful aid that eases burdens.

WAGON TRAIN suggests a lack of personal direction or inability to gain confidence in a personal sense of purpose or course.

WAIF characterizes a victim of circumstance; those less fortunate.

WAINSCOTING exemplifies a half-truth; an attempt to cover or hide a portion of something.

WAITING LIST illustrates a popular or desirable aspect.

WAITING ROOM symbolizes expectations. Recall what type of room was presented. Was it a delivery room?

WAITPERSON indicates servitude.

WAIVER relates to a voluntary refusal; a decision to decline.

WAKE (death) See funeral.

WAKE (water) implies the effects left behind after one has performed a spiritual deed.

WALKER pertains to self-help methods serving one's progression.

WALKING connotes progression.

WALKING (on air) symbolizes the qualities of acceptance and centeredness that come with spiritual joy.

WALKING (on water) reveals spiritual arrogance.

WALKING PAPERS infer a dismissal; a sign that indicates the end of a particular issue.

WALKING STICK signifies a means of being independent.

WALKOUT applies to defending one's ethics; standing up for beliefs.

WALK-THROUGH stands for an attempt to familiarize oneself with a particular issue or element.

WALL may signify various connotations, depending on where the wall is and the surrounding details. Usually a plain wall symbolizes some type of barrier that needs to be dealt with.

WALLET See purse.

WALLFLOWER reveals a lack of self-confidence.

WALL HANGING will represent a multitude of meanings that will provide insight for the dreamer. Recall what the hanging was. What was it made of? What condition and color? Was it straight?

WALLOWING relates directly to self-pity.

WALLPAPER reflects personal characteristics. Recall the design and colors.

WALL PLUG See outlet.

WALL STREET indicates economic elements that may not be solid or dependable.

WALNUT refers to a utilitarian life element.

WALRUS suggests spiritual righteousness.

WALTZING typifies a lack of seriousness in life; one is waltzing through life.

WANDERLUST corresponds with one's inner promptings to "get going" and be on one's way.

WAR portrays an ongoing conflict.

WAR BONNET reveals an "intention" to instigate or become involved in an altercation.

WAR CHEST stands for a state of preparedness for conflict.

WAR CORRESPONDENT characterizes an interest in maintaining current information on an opponent.

WAR CRY signifies instigating acts and/or words.

WARDEN applies to imprisoning elements in life, often self-inflicted.

WARDROBE reveals particulars regarding an individual's character. Recall the types and colors of the clothing.

WAREHOUSE exemplifies storage; may infer one's memory.

WAREHOUSE WORKER connotes organizational skills.

WAR GAMES depict a desire to maintain optimum skill and strategy.

WAR HAWK characterizes an aggressive personality who favors the resolution of conflicts through warring means.

WARHEAD exposes a potentially explosive situation, relationship, or other type of life element.

WARLOCK stands for imagined power.

WARLORD pertains to a recognized aggressive personality.

WARM relates to a comfortable perspective of self through humanitarian and spiritual acts.

WARM FRONT applies to a forthcoming time of personal peace; a phase consisting of less stress and problematical situations.

WARMING PAN refers to a life aspect that soothes and comforts.

WARMONGER See war hawk.

WARNING will always denote just that, a warning. Recall the dream's surrounding details for specific information.

WAR PAINT illustrates the "intent" to engage in some type of conflict.

WAR PARTY portrays an impending or ultimate altercation.

WARPATH advises that one is proceeding along a course that has a strong probability of ending in an altercation.

WARPED warns of a distorted perspective, attitude, emotion, or belief.

WARP SPEED suggests an immediate need to hasten a closure or conclusion.

WARRANTY refers to validation.

WARREN (rabbit) most often symbolizes the quiet endurance of personal pain.

WARRIOR usually stands for perseverance; personal strength.

WARSHIP signifies a spiritual altercation; ready to defend one's beliefs.

WART pertains to a negative aspect (perhaps emotion or attitude) that one has allowed to "grow" under one's skin.

WASHBOARD alludes to a need to "scrub" or apply diligent efforts to rid a negative element from one's life.

WASHCLOTH represents a cleansing aspect.

WASHER (seal) connotes a "sealing" effort; an attempt to confine.

WASHING portrays a desire to be surrounded by positive aspects.

WASHING MACHINE pertains to an aid that is capable of cleansing negative elements from one's life.

WASHOUT See erosion.

WASHROOM See bathroom.

WASP See hornet.

WASSAIL implies festive attitudes; goodwill.

WASTEBASKET denotes that which is discarded. Recall what was in the dream's wastebasket. Did it really belong there?

WASTELAND signifies a barren or unproductive phase in one's life.

WASTEPAPER reveals unnecessary elements in one's life. It's important to determine what these pieces of paper were. Letters? Plans?

WATCH See clock.

WATCHBAND may reveal how time is personally perceived. Recall what material the band was made of. Gold? Gemstones? Leather or vinyl? What was the color or design?

WATCHDOG defines alertness; acute awareness.

WATCH FIRE comes as an attention-getting dream fragment. Recall the surrounding details for clarification.

WATCHING TELEVISION will reveal the current quality and state of one's perspectives. A cartoon would represent immaturity; news would represent keeping current with daily events, etc. The key is what one is watching.

WATCHMAKER constitutes precision.

WATCHMAN See guard.

WATCHTOWER See lookout.

WATCHWORD See password.

WATER always reflects spiritual aspects.

WATER BALLET portrays spiritual inner joy.

WATERBED reveals a state of "sleeping" spirituality and advises one to "wake up" his or her spiritual aspects and utilize same.

WATER BLISTER stands for a spiritual "burn" one has received.

WATER BUFFALO indicates a spiritual arrogance.

WATER CLOSET See bathroom.

WATERCOLOR will reveal a visual (painting) related to a spiritual aspect in one's life.

WATER COOLER portrays spiritual refreshment.

WATERCRESS suggests spiritual nourishment.

WATERED-DOWN reveals waning spiritual strength or interest.

WATERFALL represents a flow of spiritual energy.

WATER FAUCET See faucet.

WATER FILTER pertains to spiritual discernment.

WATERFOWL stands for spiritual thoughts.

WATERFRONT See lakefront.

WATER GAUGE will reveal one's level of spirituality and the utilization of same.

WATER GUN See squirt gun.

WATER HOLE infers a source of spiritual nourishment.

WATERING CAN symbolizes a personal effort to spiritually nourish or affect others.

WATER LILY reflects spiritual beauty.

WATER LINE signifies one's level of spirituality. Recall if the line was low or at peak level.

WATERLOGGED warns of spiritual drowning, an indication of a forced progression whereby spiritual aspects have not been absorbed (comprehended).

WATER MAIN will refer to an individual's spiritual foundation.

WATERMELON portrays spiritual nutrients.

WATER METER will reveal a person's "use" of spiritual talents and overall beliefs.

WATER MILL symbolizes the fact that spiritual aspects are the driving force in one's life.

WATER PIPE See hookah.

WATERPROOF pertains to spiritual apathy.

WATER-REPELLENT signifies a fear of being touched by spiritual aspects.

WATERSHED exemplifies a diverted spiritual course; the "source" of one's spiritual belief system.

WATER-SKIING suggests "skimming" over spiritual matters.

WATER SNAKE represents spiritual elements that may or may not need avoiding. Recall if the snake was poisonous or otherwise dangerous.

WATERSPOUT depicts a sudden spiritual insight.

WATER SPRITE portrays the often unrecognized elements of spiritual reality.

WATER TABLE implies a spiritual grounding.

WATERTIGHT denotes spiritual confinement. The key here is to recall if water (spiritual aspects) were kept out or retained.

WATER TOWER implies the presence of spiritual reserves.

WATER WHEEL See water mill.

WATER WINGS portray personal preventive measures taken to insure against becoming spiritually inundated.

WATER WITCH See dowsing rod.

WATERWORKS connote the amount of spiritual talents one utilizes.

WATTAGE relates to the quantity and extent of one's inner strength.

WAVE (greeting) pertains to an acknowledgment given another.

WAVE (water) represents the continually renewing effects of spirituality in one's life.

WAVER implies a hesitation; perhaps indecision.

WAVERING (atmosphere) pertains to an unstable or questionable situation.

WAX typifies a pliable personality or plan.

WAXED PAPER connotes an air-tight condition.

WAX MUSEUM depicts the "mask" that people present to others.

WAYLAID suggests a pause or temporary halt to one's life progression.

WAY STATION stands for a stopping point or meaningful situation one should experience.

WEAK-KNEED relates to a lack of courage or self-confidence.

WEAKNESS (physical) represents a lack of courage; fear of responsibility.

WEALTH usually relates to inherent, natural abilities; will denote monetary connotations if presented as gold.

WEANED portrays inner growth.

WEAPON won't necessarily indicate a negative meaning, but usually applies to a preparedness to protect self from negative elements in life.

WEASEL alludes to a cowardly act; may illustrate evasiveness depending on the surrounding dreamscape details.

WEATHER will bring a multitude of meanings into the overall dream interpretation. Refer to specific type.

WEATHER BALLOON emphasizes one's cautionary tendency to "test the air" of a situation or relationship.

WEATHER-BEATEN constitutes a difficult life and the fortitude that exists to continue on.

WEATHER BUREAU represents a personal effort to monitor one's own awareness of impending situational changes.

WEATHERED correlates with extensive experiential difficulties and the inner strength and power that has been gained.

WEATHER MAP comes as a "forecasting" of upcoming situational conditions.

WEATHERPROOF signifies the effectiveness of one's personal protective methods.

WEATHER STRIPPING symbolizes an attempt to maintain emotional calm; an avoidance of difficulties.

WEATHERVANE cautions against changing opinions or attitudes, depending on whatever way the wind blows.

WEATHERWORN See weather-beaten.

WEAVER signifies the totality of true Reality and the multidimensional elements that are woven into it.

WEB stands for the complexities that one weaves in life.

WEBBING exemplifies interrelated aspects to one element.

WEDDING usually won't relate to the "ceremonial" meaning with religious figure and two betrothed people, but rather it will signify a "joining" of some type which will be clarified by the surrounding dream details.

WEDDING RING comes in dreams to portray a "symbol" of one's bond or joining with another individual or element in life such as a concept or belief.

WEDGE stands for interference.

WEDNESDAY correlates to a suggested time for reenergizing self.

WEED depicts falsehoods; may apply to spiritual ideas that are extraneous and human-devised for the purpose of control.

WEED EATER connotes the routine monitoring of one's beliefs and the "clearing" out of unrelated concepts.

WEEPING naturally reflects sorrow. Recall the dream's surrounding details to determine what this sorrow is associated with.

WEEPING WILLOW symbolizes the beauty and sensitivity of nature.

WEEVIL pertains to negative elements that have the potential to destroy one's natural and inherent abilities, these negatives most often being jealousy, egotism, etc.

WEIGHTLESSNESS usually reveals a "freed spirit" experience.

WEIGHT LIFTER characterizes an individual's "perceived" strength.

WEIGHTS pertain to burdens, some wilfully taken on.

WELCOME WAGON implies one's state of acceptance by others.

WELDING connotes an attempt to make strong connections.

WELFARE applies to situations that *may* require the assistance or intervention of others.

WELFARE WORK See social service.

WELL (water) relates directly to a spiritual source; may refer to spiritual resources. Recall if the well was full or empty. Was it contaminated?

WELL-DONE (cooked) exemplifies a full conclusion or closure.

WELL DRILLING implies a search. If the driller was looking for *water* this meant a *spiritual* search. If the search was for *oil*, it meant a *financial* search.

W

WELLS FARGO TRUCK illustrates a source of bounties, both material and spiritual.

WELT (skin) exposes an injury other than a physical one, such as a business event, an emotional hurt, etc.

WEREWOLF pertains to a dysfunction that alternately varies behavior.

WEST (direction) connotes a near-completed goal.

WEST POINT infers a rigid routine; a need to be more flexible.

WET BLANKET suggests a lack of enthusiasm; emotionless.

WETLANDS stand for the richness of spiritual bounties or inherent natural gifts; a wealth of both.

WET SUIT portrays a willful distancing from spiritual aspects; an insulating measure.

WHALE corresponds to a person's spiritual generosity or magnanimity; a giving and compassionate individual.

WHALEBOAT symbolizes that which destroys goodness.

WHALEBONE alludes to spiritual strength.

WHALE OIL defines spiritual and humanitarian qualities that are continually utilized for the benefit of others.

WHALER See whaleboat.

WHARF See pier.

WHEAT signifies some type of nourishing element in one's life. This "nourishment" usually refers to mental or emotional.

WHEAT GERM suggests a highly potent nourishing aspect.

WHEEL represents completion; full-circle; closure.

WHEELBARROW stands for burdens shouldered. Recall what was in the dream wheelbarrow and who was pushing it.

WHEELCHAIR pertains to an inability to stand on one's own feet, yet won't be a negative connotation. This usually infers a temporary setback regarding one's path progression.

WHEELHOUSE stands for the singular control one has over his or her spiritual direction.

WHEELWRIGHT characterizes a person capable of helping another get back on track.

WHETSTONE reflects a life element that will "sharpen" one's skills or understanding.

WHIP relates to a motivational source.

WHIPLASH warns against allowing others to "push" or force progression.

WHIRLPOOL exposes a spiritual entanglement that could ultimately "pull one down."

WHIRLWIND reveals "twisted" thought; conclusions or assump-

579

tions that have been reached too quickly.

WHISKBROOM suggests a need to routinely pick up after oneself. This refers to one's behavior and the effects of same.

WHISKERS (animal) allude to awareness; acute sensitivity.

WHISKEY See alcoholic beverage.

WHISPERING represents a "quiet" communication which may have various sources such as another individual, one's inner guidance, or even from the conscience.

WHISTLE most often typifies an attention-getting sound. Recall the surrounding details of the dream for further clarification.

WHISTLE BLOWER exposes a betrayer; may portray an aspect of self which would then signify one's own conscience.

WHISTLE STOP emphasizes a message; a need to stop and pay attention to an existing situation.

WHITE applies to purity and goodness; the positive aspects in life.

WHITECAPS represent the positive effects of a highly active spiritual life.

WHITE ELEPHANT stands for a rarity in life.

WHITE FLAG connotes a desire for peace.

WHITE HOUSE signifies "perceived" authority; a tendency to heavily rely on others who act as decision-making advisors.

WHITE KNIGHT corresponds to someone perceived as one's rescuer; one who has the capability of saving the day.

WHITE KNUCKLES may indicate fear, anxiety, worry, anger, etc., yet the bottom line interpretation is a lack of acceptance.

WHITE MAGIC stands for one's inherent gifts utilized for the benefit of others.

WHITE MAHOGANY reveals a rare strength of character.

WHITEOUT See blizzard.

WHITE TIE alludes to a formality.

WHITEWASHING exposes a cover-up, deception.

WHITE WATER warns of highly dangerous spiritual paths that could bring harm to those not well prepared to travel them.

WHITMAN (Walt) characterizes a gentle nature.

WHITTLING relates to a calculated plan for one's life.

WHIZ KID characterizes intellectual attainment, yet may not indicate that this intelligence is accompanied by the "wisdom" that should go hand in hand with it.

WHOLESALE represents a deal; getting something for less cost to self.

WHOOPING COUGH reveals an inability to deal with reality, life.

WICK stands for that which generates some type of illumination; a source of revealing information; possibly high insights.

WICKER pertains to ingenuity; resourcefulness.

WIDE-ANGLE LENS connotes an advisement to broaden one's scope of perception.

WIDOW rarely relates to a death, but rather symbolizes a solitary state. This may refer to reclusiveness, a need to be alone for a time, an independence, or a remote path that has been chosen.

WIDOW'S PEAK (hair) reveals a strong characteristic to one's personality, most often some type of singular ideal.

WIDOW'S WALK defines perpetual awareness.

WIG may reveal "artificial" thoughts as in deception, or it could mean an attempt to alter one's thoughts or correct same.

WILD CARD pertains to a questionable element of an aspect.

WILD DOG exposes an unpredictable friend or close associate.

WILDERNESS connotes an unaffected element; untouched, thereby existing in a pure state.

WILD-EYED most often represents fear or great confusion.

WILDFIRE emphasizes a loss of control; something has gotten out of one's hands.

WILDFLOWER pertains to the beauty of making free choices in life.

WILD-GOOSE CHASE signifies an unproductive effort.

WILD WEST (scene) won't stand for *wild* as much as *free* to travel one's chosen life course without red tape, restrictions, or limiting confinements.

WILDWOODS See wilderness.

WILL-O'-THE WISP as opposed to a dictionary definition will mean quite the contrary in dream symbology. This little dream fragment stands for subliminal insights or enlightened ideas.

WILLOW pertains to tenacity.

WILTED See withered.

WINCH implies an uplifting element in one's life.

WIND corresponds to mental activity; the thought process; psychological functioning.

WINDBAG reveals meaningless talk; verbosity; much talk and little substance.

WINDBLOWN alludes to an inundation of ideas; overwhelming concepts.

WINDBREAK indicates a personally devised method of protecting self from being overwhelmed or inundated by useless information or gossip-type talk.

WINDBURN reveals the dangerous condition of being "burned" by allowing oneself to be exposed to negative or harmful ideas.

WIND-CHILL FACTOR warns of ideas that are more dangerous than they seem.

WIND CHIMES symbolize comforting thoughts; perhaps a gentle calling.

WINDFALL pertains to an unexpected benefit or bounty.

WINDMILL cautions against mental laziness; indicates a lack of individual thought.

WINDOW portrays the quality and quantity of personal perception.

WINDOW BOX suggests personal attention given to accurate perception.

WINDOW-DRESSING applies to "dressed" perceptions; perceptions that one alters according to individual attitudes or qualities.

WINDOW LEDGE may indicate a precarious viewpoint or it may refer to a perception "supported" by strengthening elements.

WINDOW PANE comes to reveal the accuracy of one's personal perception. Recall the condition, color, and glass type of the dream window. Was it dirty? Cracked? Shattered? Tinted? Rippled?

WINDOW SHADE warns of a "shaded" perspective.

WINDOW-SHOPPING implies a search for ideas.

WINDOW WASHER characterizes someone capable of clarifying another's perspective on an issue.

WIND SHEAR reveals a thought or idea that could "cut one down" if close awareness or monitoring is not maintained.

WINDSHIELD suggests the "eyes" through which perspectives are formed. Check the condition of the dream windshield. Was it tinted? Slanted? Shielded? Cracked? This symbol is very much like that of a window.

WINDSOCK cautions against a tendency to care about the opinions of others by watching which way the wind blows.

WINDSURFING warns against letting popular opinion direct your life path.

WIND TUNNEL exposes mental aberrations and psychological dysfunctions; perceptual inability.

WINE denotes fully-developed ideas a healthy element in one's life.

WINE CELLAR stands for a wealth of ideas.

WINEGLASS represents a specific new idea that has full potential.

WINEMAKER characterizes the "quality" of an idea; the formulated "potential" of same.

WINEPRESS stands for the "formulation" of good ideas.

WINGS emphasize personal freedoms.

WING CHAIR applies to intellectual reaches; high insights.

WINGMAN characterizes guided thoughts.

WING NUT pertains to intellectual leverage.

WINK illustrates an unspoken message.

WINTER (season) exemplifies a time to contemplate spiritual beliefs.

WINTERIZE applies to spiritual preparations.

WINTER SOLSTICE reflects a time to celebrate the comfort of inner peace.

WIRE (electric) alludes to the transmission and current of one's inner energy.

WIRE (metal) illustrates a strengthening or supportive factor.

WIRE (transmission) See telegram.

WIRE BRUSH exemplifies a heavy cleaning or the act of scraping away unwanted elements in one's life.

WIRE CUTTER cautions against severing a supportive element in one's life.

WIRETAP reminds us that someone is always listening, even our own conscience.

WISECRACK will usually reveal one's true attitude that was heretofore hidden.

WISHBONE implies hope.

WISTERIA reflects spiritual beauty and grace.

WITCH won't usually denote a negative connotation, for Wicca is a bonafide Nature Religion celebrating the seasons and the natural gifts inherent in everyone. A witch most often represents an individual who "recognizes" those natural abilities to help others.

WITCH DOCTOR represents the dual aspects of inherent abilities, whether they're used for negative or positive purposes.

WITCH HAZEL denotes a healing life aspect.

WITCH-HUNT exposes spiritual and moral immaturity and ignorance.

WITCH'S BREW applies to a blend of various effective elements.

WITHERED suggests a need for refreshing elements in one's life; a spiritual renewal or emotional uplift.

WITNESS reminds us that someone is always watching, even our own subconscious; may ultimately pertain to one's conscience.

WITNESS STAND connotes an "exposure" of a formerly hidden deed or thought.

WIZARD refers to arrogant intelligence, often an alleged intelligence.

WIZARD OF OZ reveals a deception.

WOLF signifies cleverness and evasiveness; will sometimes infer self-interest.

WOLFSBANE reflects a dangerous association.

WOLVERINE implies vicious aggressiveness.

WOOD BETONY See lousewort.

WOODCARVING typifies creativity through gentleness; acceptance of life.

WOOD CHIPPER (machine) portrays an intent to preserve and enrich one's inherent abilities or gifts.

WOODCHUCK See groundhog.

WOODPECKER relates to an effort to rid self of negative aspects.

WOODPILE represents preparedness; personal effort expended.

WOODSHED applies to thorough planning.

WOODSPLITTER connotes an aid for maintaining one's preparedness.

WOODSTOCK (event) suggests free expression.

WOODSY OWL comes to remind us of our responsibility to the earth.

WOODWORKING refers to utilizing one's inherent talents in creative ways.

WOOL See shearling.

WOOLGATHERING alludes to daydreaming which may or may not be productive thought, depending on the surrounding dream details.

WONDER WOMAN emphasizes one's inner power and its unlimited potential.

WORD PROCESSOR relates to the ease of communication that one may be fearing or denying.

WORKBENCH represents personal efforts needed to be expended.

WORKBOOK implies more study is required; "work" to learn more.

WORKERS' COMPENSATION portrays benefits or alternative aspects that enter one's life while one is temporarily unable to proceed along his or her chosen course.

WORKING PAPERS relate to a verification that one is pursuing the right course.

WORKOUT reveals the need to expend great personal effort toward a specific goal.

WORKROOM represents the quality and quantity of effort one puts into achieving goals.

WORLD SERIES pertains to competitive efforts applied to aspects unrelated to one's goal or life course.

WORLD'S FAIR attempts to broaden one's perspective and reveal the existence of unlimited opportunities.

WORM connotes an interference; a "forcing" of one's way into something.

WORMWOOD illustrates obstructed creativity; an inability to apply self due to distractions.

WOUND See welt for a like interpretation.

WOUNDED KNEE (event) reminds us of our "right" to stand up for our rights.

WRANGLER characterizes a confining thought process.

WREATH symbolizes various sentiments, depending on what it's made of and the color. Refer to the specific flower type and color.

WRECK (boat) corresponds to spiritual damage.

WRECK (vehicle) correlates to emotional or physiological damage.

WRECKAGE reveals a destructive end or conclusion.

WRECKING BALL refers to a destructive force or element in one's life.

WRENCH warns against using force to accomplish a goal or closure.

WRESTLER exposes an aggressively manipulative personality.

WRESTLING stands for an attempt to get one's way.

WRINGING implies an effort to get the most out of a life element.

WRINKLED (clothing) implies indifference to the opinion of others; self-confidence without having to "show" it.

WRINKLED (skin) exemplifies fortitude gained through expending great personal effort.

WRIST represents tenacity; ability to maneuver effectively.

WRITER pertains to a desire to express inner thoughts, ideas, or sensitivities.

WRITER'S BLOCK stands for a temporary absence of inspiration.

WROUGHT IRON pertains to strong ideas or concepts forged from personal creativity.

XANADU See Camelot.

XENOPHOBIA (fear of strangers) signifies paranoia; lacking self-confidence or faith in one's protective measures.

XMAS See Christmas.

X-RATED reveals some type of negative element.

X-RAY suggests a need to thoroughly analyze something; a look at what lies beneath the surface.

X-RAY TECHNICIAN characterizes an individual who has a tendency to analyze and thoroughly research an issue or concept.

XYLOPHONE represents opportunities for an individual to attain balance and personal alignment.

YACHT comes as a sign of spiritual arrogance; a tendency to "buy" one's spiritual attainment.

YACHT CLUB denotes a desire to associate with only those who are "perceived" as being as spiritually "elevated" as self.

YAK relates to a "wild" strength; lacking discernment regarding the utilization of inner strength.

YAM See sweet potato.

YANKEE DOODLE characterizes loyalty.

YARD (back) See backyard.

YARD (front) implies that which lies in one's future; may also suggest what one presents to the public.

YARDARM connotes a life element that allows one to be "blown" along by whatever spiritual wind is blowing.

YARD GOODS See fabric/sewing shop.

YARD SALE denotes multiple opportunities.

YARDSTICK indicates a gauge of one's path progression.

YARD WORK stands for personal efforts expended on improving one's surroundings.

YARMULKE See skullcap.

YARN pertains to falsehoods or that which could lead to complications.

YARROW alludes to a sign of independence.

YAWNING illustrates a lack of interest and suggests getting motivated toward learning and progression.

YEARBOOK alludes to a need to review or remember past relationships or experiences to facilitate learning from current life events.

YEARLING connotes immaturity; a need to grow and learn.

YEARNING See thirst for a like interpretation.

YEAST relates to a life element that will bring fulfillment or completion to a specific aspect or issue.

YELLOW stands for contentedness; inner peace.

YELLOW FEVER exposes a poor self-image; frequently signifies a huge ego that constantly needs stroking from all those surrounding self.

YELLOW JACKET See hornet/wasp.

YELLOW PAGES reflect a wide range of opportunities that are readily available.

YELLOWSTONE (Park) pertains to nature's beauty and bounty reflected inside each of us if we'd only look within.

YES MAN warns against agreeing with others for the purpose of wanting to be liked or accepted.

YIELD SIGN cautions against an effort to oppose an issue or person, perhaps even one's own conscience; suggests a need to "yield" to one's better judgment.

YIN-YANG reminds us of our duality; female and male aspects within self.

YODA characterizes the inner peace that true wisdom brings.

YODELING defines a braggart.

YOGA applies to self discipline; method of attaining inner peace.

YOGI usually implies spiritual showmanship.

YOGURT relates to some type of healthful element in one's life.

YOKE (crossbar) exemplifies a burden.

YOLK (egg) See egg yolk.

YORE (time frame) is presented in dreams for a specific purpose and brings a unique message to each dreamer.

YO-YO denotes an unstable emotional life or one's lack of decision-making capabilities; a tendency to vacillate or change course.

YUCCA relates to a "cleansing" element in one's life.

YULE LOG represents a tendency to uphold tradition; stand on ceremony.

YURT alludes to simplicity. This may refer to a lifestyle, perspective, or character.

ZEALOT correlates with fanaticism.

ZEBRA represents the good-evil, right-wrong polarity of various elements in one's life.

ZEN pertains to methods for attaining enlightenment, inner peace, and the activation of natural, inherent abilities.

ZENITH stands for the high point; fulfillment; reaching a goal.

ZEPHYR symbolizes gentle thoughts, insights.

ZERO reveals an unproductive idea or plan; emptiness; a lack.

ZEST illustrates high interest and motivation; excitement.

ZEUS (Greek mythology) corresponds to a Godhead; symbolizes God.

ZIGZAG (motion/pattern) defines a routinely altered course; may infer vacillating attitudes or perspectives.

ZINC portrays a "galvanized" issue; a protective measure.

ZINC OINTMENT relates to a healing element available in one's life.

ZINGER may reveal a hidden attitude exposed through a remark or it may turn out to be a revelation of some kind.

ZINNIA symbolizes multiple benefits or gifts in one's life that have not yet been recognized.

ZIP CODE will reveal a number message or point to a specific locale that holds particular importance for the dreamer.

ZIP GUN exemplifies ineffective protective methods.

ZIPPER warns against a tendency to control situations; pertains to an indiscriminate opening and closing of one's receptivity.

ZIRCON (natural) constitutes a grounded and centered individual.

ZITHER illustrates multiple opportunities to express self.

ZODIAC comes in dreams as commendations from the highest source.

ZOMBIE warns against the utilization of psychological manipulation for any reason.

ZONING COMMISSION applies to an attempt to control the activities of others.

ZONING OUT may indicate a wilful state of unawareness or it may refer to a much-needed break from mental exertion.

ZOO correlates to the beautiful elements of individuality that are being confined, perhaps even by self.

ZOOKEEPER characterizes a manipulative and repressive personality.

ZOOM LENS symbolizes an opportunity or need to get a closer look or analyze a specific aspect in one's life.

ZOOPHOBIA (fear of animals) stands for a fear of one's own inner self and/or inherent natural abilities.

ZUCCHINI signifies an unrealized benefit or positive element in one's life.

ZWIEBACK applies to an attitude of indifference to the difficulties one needs to face in life.

Afterword

. . . Excerpt from *Spirit Song*

"Are we still going to talk about dreams?"

"Summer think No-Eyes change mind?"

"No."

"Good! Now, Summer dream all nights. Many dreams Summer's spirit go out to future. Summer see changes on Earth Mother. Many dreams Summer's spirit go out to past. Summer see playmate, Egyptian king. Many dreams Summer's spirit tell what wrong in life, tell who no good in life."

. . . . .

"Peoples need know how to read dream stuff."

"That's another side of the coin."

"That what?"

"Sorry. That's a different matter."

"Summer tell peoples that stuff."

"It's not that simple, No-Eyes."

"It simple. Summer write book."

I laughed. Even though it wasn't really funny to me. "That definitely isn't easy."

"Summer writer. Summer write. That simple."

. . . . .

"I don't think so, No-Eyes. Why would they believe mine over another?"

"Summer's right! That why!"

"We seem to be back where we started. No-Eyes, they wouldn't know mine would be right."

"They know! They know here!" She pounded her chest.

— No-Eyes, 1982

Books by Mary Summer Rain

Since 1985, when **Spirit Song** *first appeared, uncounted thousands have discovered Mary Summer Rain and "No-Eyes," the wise old Native American woman who taught the young Mary Summer Rain many things. The following books have been written and published:*

Spirit Song: The Visionary Wisdom of No-Eyes (1985), relates how the two first met. Although totally blind from birth, No-Eyes lived on the land, identifying everything she needed by smell and touch. Using gentle discipline, humor, and insight, she guided Summer Rain through a remarkable series of experiences, giving her the accumulated knowledge of her own eight decades.

Phoenix Rising: No-Eyes' Vision of the Changes to Come (1987), used the analogy of the phoenix, the mythical bird that symbolizes rebirth and eternal life, to provide a powerful warning of the earth changes in store for us. This unforgettable prophecy has already begun to come true, as the daily newspaper and TV news broadcasts demonstrate.

Dreamwalker: The Path of Sacred Power (1988), is the story of No-Eyes' introduction of Mary to Brian Many Heart, who taught Mary the power of the Dreamwalker by bringing her to face some painful realities. In it, she deals with many unanswered questions about her own identity and her role in traveling the path of knowledge. One of the best spirit-walking books in print.

Phantoms Afoot: Journeys Into the Night (1989), is a fascinating description of the quiet work done by Mary and her husband Bill in liberating spirits lost between two worlds. You might call these ghost stories, but ghost stories told with concern for the welfare of the ghost! Like the previous three volumes, *Phantoms Afoot* is very much set in Colorado. All the wild beauty of the Colorado countryside enters into the story.

Earthway (1990), Mary Summer Rain's fifth book, is a presentation of the knowledge of the Native Americans. Interweaving the inspired teachings of No-Eyes with a wealth of practical knowledge of all kinds, she demonstrated a practical, gentle, *civilized* way of life. Divided into sections for body, mind and spirit, the book aimed at restoring wholeness. (Published by Pocket Books, but available from Hampton Roads.)

Daybreak: The Dawning Ember (1991), Mary's sixth book, is divided into two parts. "The Communion" consisted of extensive answers to questions she had received from readers over the years. Ranging from prophecy to Native American history, from metaphysics to just plain common sense, here were nearly 450 pages of wisdom, including an extensive section on dream interpretation.

The second section, called "The Phoenix Files," is a comprehensive collection of maps, charts, lists, and tables describing nuclear facilities, toxic-waste dumps, oil refineries, hurricane, tornado and flood-hazard zones, as well as a suggested pole-shift realignment configuration. Together, it made an indispensable resource manual.

Soul Sounds: Mourning the Tears of Truth (1992), is the book Mary's readers long waited for: her own story, in her own words, of the experiences that shaped her extraordinary life, from childhood to her most recent meetings with Starborn friends. This was her private journal, written for herself and for her children. She didn't want it published. But her advisors insisted, and finally she gave in. . .and the reader reaction has been nothing short of phenomenal.

Mountains, Meadows and Moonbeams: A Child's Spiritual Reader (1984, 1992), was originally privately printed by Mary and Bill. Only in 1992 was the first trade paperback edition made available by Hampton Roads Publishing Company. This simple, delightful, easy-to-read book is full of illustrations for coloring; it will help parents nurture the creativity and imagination of their children; and will help children to understand where we come from and who we as humans really are.

Whispered Wisdom (1993) is a collection of beautiful photographs taken by Mary Summer Rain which depict the four seasons of Colorado. It is a celebration of nature, accompanied by a collection of verse, prose, vignettes, and sayings taken from her woods-walking journal. Together the pictures and words weave a wonderful tapestry of the many faces of Mother Earth.

Ancient Echoes (1993) is a magical collection of chants, prayers, and songs of the Anasazi people, who lived in pueblos on the plateau area of the American Southwest from around 100 to 1300 A.D. Mary Summer Rain brings forth the beauty and sensitivity of the Anasazi heart by recreating many of the chants used by one Anasazi community called the Spirit Clan. The information came from "spiritual memory recall," whereby she received, in deep meditative states, both the words and the spirit of the words. These chants, prayers, and songs also have many practical uses, for healing, blessings, child sleep songs, for a broken heart. Illustrated with line drawings, it is a stunning and practical book.

The Seventh Mesa (1994) is Mary Summer Rain's first novel, though she pointedly asks the question for the reader to decide: is it *really* fiction? It's about a hidden pyramid buried beneath a Southwest mesa, and a guarded chamber that holds the sacred scrolls and tablets which reveal the answers to humanity's most puzzling mysteries through the ages. But is it time for us to discover those answers? Have we gained enough wisdom to know what to do with that information? Four interesting characters come together to take that fascinating and dangerous adventure.

Bittersweet (1995) is a continuation of the *Soul Sounds* journal, but in the format of a collection of stories, rather than a day-by-day diary. It deals with the outstanding events in Mary Summer Rain's life since 1992. Some of these events, including her interactions with her Starborn friend, are quite astounding in their implications. Illustrated with line drawings, and a twelve-page color photo section, *Bittersweet* will be one of the most informative, interesting, and controversial books for Mary Summer Rain's readers.

The Visitation: An Archangel's Prophecy (1997). In a vivid dream in June 1996, Mary Summer Rain had a visitation. "I was sitting in my reading chair, and the room began growing brighter and brighter until a radiant being appeared." He had shoulder-length blond hair and electric blue eyes, and she sensed that he was an archangel. He gave what amounts to an address on the "state of the human soul," the prophetic consequences of humanity's present course of action "as time marches on toward Armageddon." This discourse is our wake-up call, a plea to stop the precipitous slide toward disaster for ourselves, our planet, our children—before it's too late. The Visitation may be Mary Summer Rain's most powerful message to the world.

Star Babies (1997). Few children's books convey the message that we are not alone in the universe. Mary Summer Rain, who has had contact with the "Starborns" for many years, dedicates *Star Babies* ". . . to the new and enlightened generation of children who will foster the understanding that our true reality is a vast universe peopled with God's children, that we are all intelligent human beings sharing one Universe, one neighborhood, and that there is no such thing as an alien." It is Mary's hope that this generation of children will pave the way for first contact, but they must be shown that there is nothing to fear from our neighbors in the stars.

Millennium Memories (1997). This Millennium ends on the last day of the year 2000. The period from 1998 through 2000 is considered by prophets from Nostradamus to Edgar Cayce as one of the most important in human history. It's predicted to be a time of great change—physical, mental, and spiritual—for the Earth and all its inhabitants. Since mind is the builder, what we focus on is what we will create in the years ahead. Here Mary Summer Rain, who has been keeping a daily journal for years, shares the wisdom and the wonder of the journaling experience with her readers. She has created a day-by-day journal for this three-year period, filled with inspirational wisdom, encouraging people to keep a daily record of their lives. By focusing on the positive and maintaining a spiritual perspective, we can all see our way through the difficult times ahead to the birth of a new world.

Fireside (1998). In a series of fireside chats, in her isolated cabin deep in the mountains, Mary Summer Rain shares, for the first time, her own philosophical views about many subjects. Here she integrates the teachings from No-Eyes with the wisdom she has learned through life experiences, study, and deep contemplation. Some issues covered in her dialogue with her friend Sally are "quantum meditation" and "virtual meditation" (terms she herself has coined), the meaning of value, what real power is, the wisdom of silence, unconditional goodness, what children need to be taught, the eight qualities of wisdom, the nature of the web of consciousness, the enlightened physicists, and much more, including a few predictions for the future. There is even a close encounter of the "bear" kind. *Fireside* is one of the most fascinating and instructive books Mary Summer Rain has ever written.

Spirit Song's unique interaction between teacher and student provides the emotional power behind the profound teachings of the old woman. And this interaction, above all, is brought to life in this new and quite extraordinary audio recording.

Indeed, some strange and technically unexplainable events in the studio seemed to emphasize that No-Eyes was still playing a role in Mary's life: there were mysterious gaps in the tape at strangely significant places in Mary's reading (those had to be re-recorded) and occasional wind sounds *only* in the microphone used by Carole Bourdo (who played the role of "No-Eyes").

Those who love the book will love this compelling recording. It's read by Mary Summer Rain herself, with Carole Bourdo as "No-Eyes."

5 Tapes, 7 hours
Directed by Cliff Korradi
Music by Rick Burness, from his album *Dancing on Glass*
Recorded at Get Reel Productions, Colorado Springs, by Allan Blackwell